INITIA AMHARICA

INITIA AMHARICA

An Introduction to Spoken Amharic

BY

C. H. ARMBRUSTER, M. A.
Sudan Civil Service;
Late of H.M. Administration, British Central Africa;
sometime Minor Scholar of King's College, Cambridge

PART II
ENGLISH-AMHARIC VOCABULARY WITH PHRASES

GYAN

Published by

Gyan Publishing House
5, Ansari Road
Daryaganj, New Delhi-110002
Phone: 011-47034999, 9811692060
E-mail: books@gyanbooks.com

Distribution Network
gyanbooks.com
India, USA, Canada, UK, Australia, France

ISBN : 978-81-212-4433-6 (Set)
ISBN : 978-81-212-4864-8 (PB)
First Published, 1910

2nd Impression 2020

Printed at: Gyan Press, Delhi.

Initia Amharica
Author: C. H. Armbruster

INITIA AMHARICA

An introduction to spoken Amharic

BY

C. H. ARMBRUSTER, M.A.

Sudan Civil Service;
late of H.M. Administration, British Central Africa;
sometime Minor Scholar of King's College, Cambridge

Part II

ENGLISH-AMHARIC VOCABULARY WITH PHRASES

Cambridge:
at the University Press
1910

ἐμοὶ δὲ παρὰ πάντα τὸν λόγον ὑποκέεται ὅτι τὰ λεγόμενα ὑπ' ἑκάστων ἀκοῇ γράφω.

HEROD. II. 123.

To

Carleton Skarratt

PREFACE.

THE words and phrases in this work have been taken down from the mouth of natives[1]. As many as possible of the phrases are such as have been said spontaneously, i.e. are not the products of cross-examination. The Abyssinian, like other members of partially civilised peoples, or uneducated individuals of highly civilised races, does not always speak naturally when questioned by a stranger. If he has had no education of any kind he experiences the same difficulty in answering enquiries concerning the language he unreflectingly uses as would, in similar circumstances, an uncultured European. Those, on the other hand, who have any smattering of learning tend to supply one with 'fine language'[2], which may or may not be idiomatic, instead of the ordinary conversational expressions current among themselves. In any case it is of course incompatible with the position of the white man that natives should address him in the style in which they address one another. I have, therefore, paid more attention to what I have heard natives say to each other than to what they have said to me, and have not excluded

---

[1] While the language of all sorts and conditions of men has been noted, it is hardly necessary to say that care has been taken to avoid as informants individuals speaking Tĭgrĭñña, Agåuñña, Gallĭñña, Arabic, etc., and knowing Amharic only as an acquired tongue.

[2] cp. the so-called عربي عالي and نحوي.

words or modes of expression on account of their so-called vulgarity[1]: the object in view being to give some description not so much of what, in the opinion of learned Europeans and natives, Abyssinians ought to say as of what in point of fact they do say.

In dealing with a spoken language I have not hesitated to use colloquial English.

Those who wish to pursue their acquaintance with Amharic beyond this 'Introduction' I would refer to the writings of Guidi, my indebtedness to which I desire to acknowledge most gratefully. In his magnificent 'Vocabolario', a work indispensable to serious students of the language, there is a brief bibliography of Amharic and kindred subjects.

In the few cases where I have differed from Guidi in regard to the meaning of words[2] it has been with diffidence, and only after repeated verification. Differences as regards form are of more frequent occurrence, as I have concerned myself with the spoken rather than the written word.

The publication of this series has been rendered possible by the financial assistance of the Egyptian Government, as advised by Lord Cromer, and by the liberal attitude of the Syndics of the University Press, Cambridge.

---

[1] Quot homines, tot sententiae: e.g. Mondon-Vidailhet, Gram. p. 201 እንትን ፡ 'Cette façon de parler passe aujourd'hui pour vulgaire': yet I heard this useful word employed repeatedly by Däjjazmáč Gḁssḁ́sḁ, a man of great courtesy and refinement.

[2] In cases like እዚያ or እዝያ = there, Guidi's 'quello là' (Vocab. p. 487) may be the original meaning: I give the one I find in use.

I wish to express my cordial thanks, for valuable information supplied and for assistance rendered in many ways, to Lieut.-Gen. Sir F. Reginald Wingate, K.C.B. etc., Sirdar and Governor-General, A. F. Broun, Esq., Mrs H. M. Broun, A. L. Butler, Esq., J. B. Christopherson, Esq., M.D. etc., J. Grieve, Esq., H. H. King, Esq., Maj. W. S. R. May, Capt. R. C. R. Owen, C.M.G., F. M. Simpson, Esq., M.A. and Lt.-Col. E. B. Wilkinson, of the Sudan Government: to Lt.-Col. Lord Edward Cecil, D.S.O. and Capt. the Hon. C. James, of the Egyptian Government: to Capt. R. B. Black, Capt. C. Garvice, D.S.O. and El Yuzbashi Mustafa Effendi Izzeddin, of the Egyptian Army: to H. Farnall, Esq., C.B. etc., of the Caisse de la Dette, to Dr A. Forel, to W. B. Heard, Esq., late H.M. Vice-Consul at Addis Abeba, to Dr E. A. Wallis Budge, of the British Museum, and at Cambridge to Prof. F. C. Burkitt, Dr M. R. James, George Wherry, Esq., M.A. etc., R. T. Wright, Esq., M.A., A. R. Waller, Esq., M.A. and to J. Clay, Esq., M.A. and his staff, notably Mr W. J. Foreman: እንግዲህ፡ ለኢትዮጵያ፡ ሰዎች፡ በስራዬ፡ ለረዱኝ፡ ሁላቸው፡ አመሰግናቸዋለኍ።

Notices of errors and suggestions for improvements will be thankfully received, and should be addressed to me

c/o The Sudan Agent,
War Office,
Cairo.

C. H. ARMBRUSTER.

CAMBRIDGE,
August, 1910.

CONTENTS.

ABBREVIATIONS.

abbr. abbreviated, (-tion).
acc. accusative.
act. active.
adj. adjective, (-val, -vally).
adv. adverb(ial, -ially).
Ag. Ág̥a͡u (Áuṅi, Am. Ag̥á͡uñña).
Am. Amḣaric.
an. animate.
App. Appendix.
approx. approximate(ly).
Ar. Arabic.
art. article.
aux. auxiliary.
B. Bʸégämdi̥r.
card. cardinal.
caus. causative.
comp. compound.
compos. composition.
conj. conjunction, (-tive).
conjug. conjugation.
conn. connected.
constr. constructed, (-tion).
cont. contingent (mood).
cp. compare(s).
D. Dámbya.
dat. dative.
dem. demonstrative.
dist. distributive.
e.g. for instance.
eccl. ecclesiastic(al, -ally).
emph. emphasis, (-atic).
encl. enclitic.
Eng. English.
esp. especial(ly).
Eth. Ethiopic.
euphem. euphemism, (-istic, -istically).
Eur. European.
f. feminine.
fin. final.
Fr. French.
G. Gojjám.
Gall. Gallí̥ñña.
gen. general(ly).
Ger. German.
Gr. Greek.
i. intransitive.
i.e. that is.
ib. in the same place.
id. the same.
imp. imperative.
imperf. imperfect.
impers. impersonal(ly).
inan. inanimate.
ind. indicative.
indecl. indeclinable.
indef. indefinite.
inf. infinitive.
inter. interrogative.
interj. interjection.
iron. ironical(ly).
It. Italian.
juss. jussive.
l. line.
lit. literal(ly).
m. masculine.
med. medical.

mil. military.
neg. negative.
nom. nominative.
num. numeral.
obj. object.
onom. onomatopoetic.
ord. ordinal.
p. page, passive.
part. participle.
perf. perfect.
pers. person(al, -ally).
pl. plural.
plup. pluperfect.
pol. polite, the form for addressing superiors.
poss. possessive.
pref. prefix(ed).
pron. pronoun (-nominal).
prop. proper(ly).
prov. proverb.
prp. preposition.
q.v. which see (in vocabularies).
r. reflexive.
rad. radical(ly).
recip. reciprocal(ly).
s. substantive.
s.v. under the word (in vocabularies).
sc. namely; understand (something unexpressed).
sg. singular.
simp. simple.
sp. species.
subj. subject.
subst. substantive, (-val, -vally).
suff. suffix(ed).
Š. Šḁ͡ua (Shoa).
t. transitive.
Tē. Tị́grē (χá́sa).
Tña. Tịgrị́ñña.
us. usual(ly).
v. verb.
vet. veterinary.
vocab. vocabulary, (-ries).
1st, 2nd, 3rd: the respective persons.

√ root or stem.
– long.
⌣ *very* short.
–⌣ sometimes long, sometimes short.
′ stress accent; words marked with two accents usually have the first when final, the second before another word (§ 8).
† not in general use.
* theoretical form.
= amounts to, is equal to, the same as.
§ refers to the paragraphs of the Grammar (Part I.).
Names of plants also denote their flowers and fruits: e.g. በለስ bḁlḁs, s. fig (tree and fruit).

USE OF BRACKETS AND HYPHENS.

In English

(*a*) Inclusive:

dirt, s. (-ty, adj.) = dirt, s. and dirty, adj. (for which Amharic uses the same word).

He (it) is = he is; also: it is.

(*b*) Explanatory:

Disposition (character) = disposition in the sense of character.

In Amharic

i̥d(i̥)f = i̥di̥f and i̥df.

ti̥q(i̥š)šā = ti̥qi̥ššā and ti̥qšā.

[የ]ትም[ህ]ርት = የትምህርት, also ትምህርት, የትምርት and ትምርት.

sḁbábbḁrḁ (-yḁ-, -är-) = sḁbábbḁrḁ; also sḁyábbḁrḁ, sḁbábbärḁ and sḁyábbärḁ, (see § 7*d*).

In English the masculine is intended unless the feminine is specified, and 'you' and similar words are singular unless marked plural.

In the phrases the Eng. verbs in the 2nd pers. are sg.; pol., pl., after the translation of a phrase = the same phrase with the *subject* in the pol. or pl.

Pull it: ሳበው ። sáyḁu͡,

pl. -ቡት ። -yut = Pull (pl.) it: ሳቡት ። sáyut.

Has he been summoned? ተጠርቷል ። tḁṭártoa͡l?,

pol. & pl. -ተዋል ። -tḁu͡āl? = Has he (pol.) *or* have they been summoned? ተጠርተዋል ። tḁṭártḁu͡āl?

ABBREVIATIONS OF WORKS REFERRED TO.

Afevork, Gram. Grammatica della lingua amarica, di G. J. Afevork, Roma, 1905.

Blandford, Geol. & Zool. Observations on the Geology and Zoology of Abyssinia, by W. T. Blandford, London, 1870.

Broun, Cat. Catalogue of Sudan Flowering Plants, by A. F. Broun, Director of Woods and Forests, Sudan Government, Khartoum, 1906.

Chaine, Gram. Éth. Grammaire Éthiopienne, par le P. M. Chaine S. J., Beyrouth, 1907.

Cust, Lng. Afr. A Sketch of the Modern Languages of Africa, by R. N. Cust, London, 1883.

Guidi, Coniug. Sulle coniugazioni del verbo amarico. Di I. Guidi, in the Zeitschrift für Assyriologie, VIII.

Guidi, Gram. Grammatica elementare della lingua amariña, 2nd edition, Roma, 1892.

Guidi, Prov. Proverbi, strofe e racconti abissini, tradotti e pubblicati da Ignazio Guidi, Roma, 1894.

Guidi, Redupl. Sulla reduplicazione delle consonanti amariche, di I. Guidi, in the Supplementi Periodici all'Archivio Glottologico Italiano, Roma, 1895.

Guidi, Vocab. Vocabolario Amarico-Italiano, compilato da I. Guidi, Roma, 1901.

Isenberg, Gram. Grammar of the Amharic Language, by the Rev. C. W. Isenberg, London, 1842.

Lepsius, St. Alph. Standard Alphabet for reducing unwritten languages and foreign graphic systems to a uniform orthography in European letters, by C. R. Lepsius, 2nd edition, London, 1863.

Ludolf, Lex. Æth. I. Ludolfi Lexicon Æthiopico-Latinum, editio secunda, Francofurti ad Moenum, 1699.

Mondon-Vidailhet, Gram. Grammaire de la langue abyssine (amharique), par C. Mondon-Vidailhet, Paris, 1898.

Munzinger, Vocab. Vocabulaire de la langue tigré, par W. Munzinger, Leipsic, 1865.

Praetorius, Am. Spr. Die Amharische Sprache, von F. Praetorius, Halle, 1879.

Praetorius, Gram. Æth. Grammatica Æthiopica, scripsit Dr F. Praetorius, Carlsruhe, 1886.

Reinisch, Chamir. Die Chamirsprache in Abessinien, von Leo Reinisch, I. & II., Vienna, 1884.

Reinisch, Quara. Die Quarasprache in Abessinien, von Leo Reinisch, I. & II., Vienna, 1885, III. Vienna, 1887.

Reinisch, Wört. Beḍ. Wörterbuch der Beḍauye-Sprache, von Leo Reinisch, Vienna, 1895.

Vollers and Burkitt, Gram. A Grammar of the Modern Egyptian Dialect of Arabic, by K. Vollers and F. C. Burkitt, Cambridge, 1895.

NOTE ON PHONOLOGY.

(*The following paragraphs are quoted from Initia Amharica, Part I.*)

Phonetic Alphabet.

§ 3 In order to designate the pronunciation of Amharic as far as possible without ambiguity I employ the following phonetic alphabet. The principle held in view is that one letter should never represent more than one sound, and one sound should not be represented by more than one letter[1]. In regard to the consonants this is a feasible system; but the fluctuating character of some of the short vowels precludes a strict adherence to it, which would involve the use of an impracticably large number of letters to represent variations of no essential importance. The indications, then, by means of examples taken from European languages of the value of the sounds which occur are, especially in the case of the vowels, only approximately exact.

With the exception of the 'explosive[2]' sounds represented by p̣, q, ṭ, č̣, ṣ, and the guttural χ (frequently pronounced k by Abyssinians themselves) the pronunciation of Amharic presents little difficulty to an Englishman.

---

[1] Lepsius, St. Alph. pp. 31, 32, 38.

[2] See end of this §.

Vowels.

All vowels are pronounced short unless marked
¯ = long, ‿¯ = long or short, ˘ = *very* short.

a	a in It. fatto.
ā	the same lengthened.
ä	e in bet, but more open.
ǟ	the same lengthened.
ḁ	a in formula, e in Fr. le.
ḁ̄	the same lengthened.
e	e in bet, but less open.
ē	the same lengthened.
i	i in It. minuto.
ī	the same lengthened.
i̥	i in quick, but pronounced with the lips more closed.
ī̥	the same lengthened.
ü	u in Fr. absolument.
ω	a in was.
o	o in It. caro, but more open (not o aperto).
ō	the same lengthened.
u	u in full.
ū	u in It. luna.

ä ḁ and ω represent the same vowel in Amharic (g̥i̥z § 4). The above examples show, approximately, the commonest pronunciations of this variable vowel[1]. When ä ḁ ω are given as alternatives they represent a gradation of sounds from e in 'bet' through approx. u in 'but', eu in Fr. neuf, e in Fr. le, ö in Ger. Götter to a in 'was' (§ 7*d*).

---

[1] Guidi, Gram. § 4*b*, 'suono non ben determinato'; see Lepsius, St. Alph. p. 48, and cp. our varying pronunciations of e in 'offering', i in 'girl', u in 'occurrence.'

Diphthongs.

Diphthongs are merely their component vowels pronounced in rapid succession without any intervening hiatus. They are marked ͡. The following approximations are fairly close:

á͡i̥	i in bite.
ā́͡i̥	ai in Ger. Waise.
á͡u	au in Ger. aus.
ḁ́͡u	o in no.
ώ͡i̥	oy in boy.

Consonants.

χ	ch in Ger. noch.
h	h in he.
q	an explosive guttural pronounced a little further back than k[1]; the centre of the tongue is raised towards the palate.
k	k in kin.
g	g in go.
ṅ	ng in singing.
ṭ	tt in hottest, but pronounced with an explosion.
ṣ	sibilant ṭ, similar to ts in pots, but pronounced with an explosion.
ç̣	ch in church, but pronounced with an explosion.
č	ch in cheese.
š	sh in she.
ž	j in Fr. je.

[1] but not as far back as Syrian ق.

j	j in jam, but the tongue comes nearer the teeth.
y	y in you.
ñ	ñ in Spanish señor.
t	dental t, as in Fr. tu.
d	dental d, as in Fr. de.
s	s in so.
z	z in size.
l	l in let.
r	r in red.
n	n in no.
p	p in pot.
p̣	p pronounced with an explosion.
b	b in be.
f̣	bilabial f, (the teeth not touching the lips).
ṿ	bilabial v, b in Spanish arriba.
f	labio-dental, f in fan.
v	labio-dental, v in van.
w	w in wan, but the lips are more open: u in It. uomo.

[h], [y], [w], are h, y, w, pronounced very slightly, [y] and [w] almost merged into the adjacent vowel (§ 7*d*), and [h] final tending to disappear. y and w may be regarded as the consonantal forms of i̥ and u respectively; after a vowel they often pass into those vowels and form diphthongs (cp. y in layer, w in lower): a + ya = a͡i̥a, a + wa = a͡ua; similarly i̥ and u when doubled (§ 6) become yy, ww (uw).

q, p̣, ṭ, ṣ, č̣ are pronounced with emphasis, and appear to be separated from a following vowel by a slight explosion of breath. They are radically different from k, p, t, s, č.

The Amharic Characters.

§ 4*a* Amharic employs the Ethiopic syllabary, with additional signs representing sounds not occurring in Ethiopic. The characters are read from left to right. There are seven forms of each character, each representing the consonant followed by (and including) a different vowel. These seven classes are known by their Ethiopic names (of which the Amharic pronunciation is given).

I.	ግዕዝ	g͡ı̥ı̥z, original, representing the consonant followed by	ḁ (ä, ω)
II.	ካዕብ	k͡áı̥y, second, " " "	ũ
III.	ሣልስ	sálı̥s, third, " " "	ĩ
IV.	ራብዕ	rávı̥, fourth, " " "	ã
V.	ኃምስ	hámı̥s, fifth, " " "	^{y}ẽ
VI.	ሳድስ	sádı̥s, sixth, " " "	ı̥ or no vowel
VII.	ሳብዕ	sávı̥, seventh, " " "	^{w}õ

There is also a series of characters representing the consonant followed by w and a vowel; this w is often pronounced õ before ã.

g͡ı̥ı̥z	k͡áı̥y	sálı̥s	rávı̥	hámı̥s	sádı̥s	sávı̥
ሀ hã	ሁ hũ	ሂ hĩ	ሃ hã	ሄ h^{y}ẽ	ህ hı̥, h	ሆ h^{w}õ
ለ lḁ	ሉ lũ	ሊ lĩ	ላ lã	ሌ l^{y}ẽ	ል lı̥, l	ሎ l^{w}õ
ሐ hã	ሑ hũ	ሒ hĩ	ሓ hã	ሔ h^{y}ẽ	ሕ hı̥, h	ሖ h^{w}õ
መ mḁ	ሙ mũ	ሚ mĩ	ማ mã	ሜ m^{y}ẽ	ም mı̥, m	ሞ m^{w}õ
ሠ sḁ	ሡ sũ	ሢ sĩ	ሣ sã	ሤ s^{y}ẽ	ሥ sı̥, s	ሦ s^{w}õ
ረ rḁ	ሩ rũ	ሪ rĩ	ራ rã	ሬ r^{y}ẽ	ር rı̥, r	ሮ r^{w}õ
ሰ sḁ	ሱ sũ	ሲ sĩ	ሳ sã	ሴ s^{y}ẽ	ስ sı̥, s	ሶ s^{w}õ

gḭ̊iz		kḁ̂i̥y		sā́li̥s		rā́yi̥		hā́mi̥s		sā́di̥s		sā́yi̥	
ሸ	šḁ, šä	ሹ	šū̆	ሺ	šī̆	ሻ	šā̆	ሼ	šʸē̆	ሽ	ši̥, š	ሾ	šʷō̆
ቀ	qḁ	ቁ	qū̆	ቂ	qī̆	ቃ	qā̆	ቄ	qʸē̆	ቅ	qi̥, q	ቆ	qʷō̆
በ	bḁ	ቡ	bū̆	ቢ	bī̆	ባ	bā̆	ቤ	bʸē̆	ብ	bi̥, b	ቦ	bʷō̆
ተ	tḁ	ቱ	tū̆	ቲ	tī̆	ታ	tā̆	ቴ	tʸē̆	ት	ti̥, t	ቶ	tʷō̆
ቸ	čä	ቹ	čū̆	ቺ	čī̆	ቻ	čā̆	ቼ	čʸē̆	ች	či̥, č	ቾ	čʷō̆
ኀ	hā̆	ኁ	hū̆	ኂ	hī̆	ኃ	hā̆	ኄ	hʸē̆	ኅ	hi̥, h	ኆ	hʷō̆
ነ	nḁ	ኑ	nū̆	ኒ	nī̆	ና	nā̆	ኔ	nʸē̆	ን	ni̥, n	ኖ	nʷō̆
ኘ	ñä	ኙ	ñū̆	ኚ	ñī̆	ኛ	ñā̆	ኜ	ñē̆	ኝ	ñi̥, ñ	ኞ	ñō̆
አ	ā̆	ኡ	ū̆	ኢ	ī̆	ኣ	ā̆	ኤ	ʸē̆	እ	i̥	ኦ	ʷō̆
ከ	kḁ	ኩ	kū̆	ኪ	kī̆	ካ	kā̆	ኬ	kʸē̆	ክ	ki̥, k	ኮ	kʷō̆
ኸ	χḁ	ኹ	χū̆	ኺ	χī̆	ኻ	χā̆	ኼ	χʸē̆	ኽ	χi̥, χ	ኾ	χʷō̆
ወ	wḁ, wω	ዉ	wū̆	ዊ	wī̆	ዋ	wā̆	ዌ	wʸē̆	ው	wi̥, wŭ, u	ዎ	wō̆
ዐ	ā̆	ዑ	ū̆	ዒ	ī̆	ዓ	ā̆	ዔ	ʸē̆	ዕ	i̥	ዖ	ʷō̆
ዘ	zḁ	ዙ	zū̆	ዚ	zī̆	ዛ	zā̆	ዜ	zʸē̆	ዝ	zi̥, z	ዞ	zʷō̆
ዠ[1]	žḁ, žä	ዡ	žū̆	ዢ	žī̆	ዣ	žā̆	ዤ	žʸe	ዥ	ži̥, ž	ዦ	žʷō̆
የ	yä	ዩ	yū̆	ዪ	yī̆	ያ	yā̆	ዬ	yē̆	ይ	yi̥, i, i̥	ዮ	yō̆
ደ	dḁ	ዱ	dū̆	ዲ	dī̆	ዳ	dā̆	ዴ	dʸē̆	ድ	di̥, d	ዶ	dʷō̆
ጀ	jä	ጁ	jū̆	ጂ	jī̆	ጃ	jā̆	ጄ	jʸē̆	ጅ	ji̥, j	ጆ	jʷō̆
ገ	gḁ	ጉ	gū̆	ጊ	gī̆	ጋ	gā̆	ጌ	gʸē̆	ግ	gi̥, g	ጎ	gʷō̆
ጠ	ṭḁ	ጡ	ṭū̆	ጢ	ṭī̆	ጣ	ṭā̆	ጤ	ṭʸē̆	ጥ	ṭi̥, ṭ	ጦ	ṭʷō̆
ጨ	č̣ä	ጩ	č̣ū̆	ጪ	č̣ī̆	ጫ	č̣ā̆	ጬ	č̣ʸē̆	ጭ	č̣i̥, č̣	ጮ	č̣ʷō̆
ጰ	p̣ḁ	ጱ	p̣ū̆	ጲ	p̣ī̆	ጳ	p̣ā̆	ጴ	p̣ʸē̆	ጵ	p̣i̥, p̣	ጶ	p̣ʷō̆
ጸ	ṣḁ	ጹ	ṣū̆	ጺ	ṣī̆	ጻ	ṣā̆	ጼ	ṣʸē̆	ጽ	ṣi̥, ṣ	ጾ	ṣʷō̆
ፀ	ṣḁ	ፁ	ṣū̆	ፂ	ṣī̆	ፃ	ṣā̆	ፄ	ṣʸē̆	ፅ	ṣi̥, ṣ	ፆ	ṣʷō̆
ፈ	fḁ	ፉ	fū̆	ፊ	fī̆	ፋ	fā̆	ፌ	fʸē̆	ፍ	fi̥, f	ፎ	fʷō̆
ፐ	pḁ	ፑ	pū̆	ፒ	pī̆	ፓ	pā̆	ፔ	pʸē̆	ፕ	pi̥, p	ፖ	pʷō̆

[1] also ዠ žḁ, žä, ዡ žū̆, ዣ žā̆, ዤ žʸē̆, ዥ, ዥ ži̥, ž, ዦ žʷō̆.

ግዚ = ግ + ዚ gzī̆.

gʿi̥z	sā́li̥s	rā́ṿi̥	hā́mi̥s	sā́di̥s	rā́ṿi̥
		ሏ lwā̃, lŏ͡ā̃			ፙ myā̃[2]
		ሟ[1] mwā̃, mŏ͡ā̃			ፘ[3] ryā̃
		ሯ rwā̃, rŏ͡ā̃			
		ሷ swā̃, sŏ͡ā̃			
		ሿ šwā̃, šŏ͡ā̃			
ቈ qwω	ቊ qwī	ቋ qwā̃, qŏ͡ā̃	ቌ qwē̃	ቍ qwi̥, qwŭ	
		ቧ bwā̃, bŏ͡ā̃			
		ቷ twā̃, tŏ͡ā̃			
		ቿ čwā̃, čŏ͡ā̃			
ኈ hwḁ, hwω	ኊ hwī	ኋ hwā̃, hŏ͡ā̃	ኌ hwē̃	ኍ hwi̥, hwŭ	
		ኗ nwā̃, nŏ͡ā̃			
		ኟ ñwā̃, ñŏ͡ā̃			
ኰ kwω	ኲ kwī	ኳ kwā̃, kŏ͡ā̃	ኴ kwē̃	ኵ kwi̥, kwŭ	
ዀ χwω	ዂ χwī	ዃ χwā̃, χŏ͡ā̃		ዅ χwi̥, χwŭ	
		ዟ zwā̃, zŏ͡ā̃			
		ዧ žwā̃, žŏ͡ā̃			
		ዯ yu͡ā̃ yŏ͡ā̃			
		ዷ dwā̃, dŏ͡ā̃			
		ጇ jwā̃, jŏ͡ā̃			
ጐ gwω	ጒ gwī	ጓ gwā̃, gŏ͡ā̃	ጔ gwē̃	ጕ gwi̥, gwŭ	
		ጧ ṭwā̃, ṭŏ͡ā̃			
		ጯ č̣wā̃, č̣ŏ͡ā̃			
		ጿ ṣwā̃, ṣŏ͡ā̃			
		ፏ[4] fwā̃, fŏ͡ā̃			

[1] also ᎃ, ሟ.

[2] according to Chaine, Gram. Éth. p. 3, = mua.

[3] used for rwā̃, rŏ͡ā̃, by those who reject ሯ: native opinion on the point is divided; ryā̃ is also written ፘ.

[4] also ፚ.

Value of Characters.

In the traditional Ethiopic pronunciation the vowels of all the classes except gi͡iz and sádi̥s are considered long; but in spoken Amharic they are all constantly shortened (§ 7*d*). § 4*b*

The vowel of gi͡iz differs from that of rấḅi̥ not so much in quantity (rấḅi̥ often being short) as in quality, in which it varies (§ 3) in different words. But in ሀ ሐ ኀ አ ዐ[1] it is of the same quality[2] as rấḅi̥. The above are its commonest values after the various consonants; but ለ lä, lω, and ቸ čḁ, čω also occur. For this and other variations in pronunciation see § 7*d*.

Some characters which represented different sounds in Ethiopic are now pronounced the same and are interchangeable in writing:

ሀ = ሐ = ኀ ha
ሠ = ሰ sḁ
አ = ዐ a
ጸ = ፀ ṣḁ

ቋ is also written ቁዋ, ሟ = ምዋ etc., and ሯ = ርያ or ሪያ.

አ and ዐ (§ 2) contain no consonant, but are vowels and as such may be blended with an adjacent vowel (§ 7*a*)[3].

---

[1] gi͡iz in these 5 letters as in the rest is theoretically short, and is usually pronounced so unless the accent (§ 8) falls on it when it is often pronounced long.

[2] hḁ, hä occur as pronunciations of ከ ኸ; e.g. see App. B, § 7*d*.

[3] ያለ (for የ- + አለ § 7*a*) sometimes sounds yä͡álla, i.e. the crasis is not always complete; but no hiatus occurs between ä and á in any way comparable with ء.

Punctuation.

§ 4*c* ፡ marks the end of a word.
፤ corresponds to a semicolon.
። ,, ,, full stop.
፨ marks the end of a paragraph.

Doubling of Consonants.

§ 5 In English we pronounce doubled consonants as if they were single, only one f being heard in offer, stiffer, etc. In Amharic doubled consonants are pronounced double: ff as -ff f- in 'off fur' (pronounced without any hiatus between the words) or ff in Italian goffo; ṭṭ as -t t- in 'hot tea', etc.

The Amharic characters represent not only single but also double consonants with a following vowel: ለ = lḁ or llḁ.

Thus since ት = t, ti̥, tt or tti̥
ን = n, ni̥, nn or nni̥
ሽ = š, ši̥, šš or šši̥,

ትንሽ tí̥nni̥š, small, might be transliterated in 64 different ways.

There are no means of indicating by Amharic characters whether a consonant is doubled or not, or whether the consonant of a character in column VI of the syllabary (sắdi̥s) is followed by a vowel or not: and in both cases both alternatives are common:

አመመ á-mmḁ-mḁ, it ached.
እመም í̥-mḁ-m, pain.
ቅልጥም qí̥-l-ṭi̥-m, marrow.
ንግግር ni̥-gí̥-ggi̥-r, pronunciation.
ምድር ḿ-di̥-r, ground.

CORRIGENDA.

Page	line	for	read
9	7	mḁṭṭákk^{w}o	mḁṭṭákk^{w}ó
10	5, 6	(í̥)kk^{w}o [(ŭ́k-); usually enclitic	(i̥)kk^{w}ó (ŭk-; alone,
10	7	hi̥dí̥kk^{w}o hi̥dúkk^{w}o	hi̥dí̥kk^{w}ó hi̥dúkk^{w}ó
19	3, 25	addḁbába͡i̥ (-ḁṿáṿa͡i̥).	addḁbábā́͡i̥ (-ḁṿā́ṿā́͡i̥; § 8)
59	23	(í̥)kk^{w}o (ŭ́k-; often enclitic	(i̥)kk^{w}ó (ŭk-; alone,
59	27	ŭ́kk^{w}o	ŭkk^{w}ó
59	28	anṭā́kk^{w}o	anṭā́kk^{w}ó
84	21	ńkwān	ńkwā́n (§ 8)
88	17	iyyä-	īyyä-
90	2	áfḁr	ā́fḁr
93	30	ágḁr	ā́gḁr
96	29	iyyä-	īyyä-
107	2	ái̥ṭ-	á͡i̥ṭ-
114	23	should follow l. 26.	
123	26	addḁbába͡i̥ (-ḁṿáṿa͡i̥)	addḁbábā́͡i̥ (-ḁṿā́ṿā́͡i̥; § 8)
126	10	persons	animate objects
133	24	(i̥)rḁ́ddã	(ī̥)rḁ́ddã
139	18	hulḁ́tt	húlḁtt
148	4	ndi̥h	ndí̥h
155	2	onto	on to
157	24	gwŭlbḁt	gwŭ́lbḁt
161	8	nd^{y}i̥h	nd^{y}í̥h

Page	line	for	read
168	5	abstract	general
168	6	concrete	particular
182	2	ŭkkū́lḁ	ŭkkúlḁ
186	31	tḁ	tḁ-
187	22, 23	ndi̥t, nd^{y}ēt	ndí̥t, nd^{y}ḗt
195	9	atti̥ỵḁ́lu	attí̥ỵḁlu
201	11	yi̥ttázzḁzi̥lli̥hāl	yi̥ttazzḁzí̥lli̥hāl
202	27	addḁbā́ba͡i (-ḁỵā́ỵa͡i̥)	addḁbā́bā́͡i̥ (-ḁỵā́ỵā́͡i̥; § 8)
203	20	lá͡i̥	la͡i̥
206	15	past imperf. etc.	ተገባ tḁgḁ́bbā̃
206	16	should follow l. 30	
206	26	ndi̥h	ndí̥h
206	30	§ 24	§§ 24*b*, 33*a*, 63*b*
208	20	lá͡i̥	la͡i̥
232	17	ndi̥h	ndí̥h
236	7	yādḁ́rrḁgḁbbḁti̥n	yādḁrrḁgḁ́bbḁti̥n
236	11	ṭut	-ṭut
246	19	Emperor	King
266	1	(yä)ç̣á͡u	(yä)ç̣á͡u̥
266	12	tomorrow	to-morrow
279	6	20*b*	20*c*
281	12	§ 74*a*	§ 47*a*
287	21	20*b*	20*c*
301	3	onto	on to
332	27	20*b*	20*c*
339	29	20*b*	20*c*
364	9	20*b*	20*c*
378	31	di̥mt	di̥mṭ

ENGLISH-AMHARIC VOCABULARY

§ *refers to the paragraphs of the Grammar* (*Initia Amharica, Part I*).

A

a, indef. art., not translated:
  Horse: ፈረስ፡ fḁ́rḁs.
  A horse: ፈረስ፡ fḁ́rḁs.

abandon, v.t. ተወ tḁ́wḁ (tḁ́͡uḁ).
  ጣለ ṭḁ́lḁ.
  ለቀቀ lḁ́qqḁqḁ.

abandon (be abandoned § 68), cause or allow to, v.t. አስለቀቀ aslḁ́qqḁqḁ.

abandoned, be, v.p. ተተወ tḁtḁ́wḁ (-ḁ́͡uḁ).
  ተጣለ tḁṭálḁ.
  ተለቀቀ tḁlḁ́qqḁqḁ.

abate, v.i. ጐደለ gwώddḁlḁ.

abdomen, s. ሆድ h^{w}ŏd.
  (lower) በጀድ bắjäd.

able, be, v.i. (= can) ቻለ čắlḁ.
  ተቻለው tḁčắlḁ͡u (impers. § 43*a*).
  See § 63*c*.

Are you able to walk? ችለህ፡ ትሔዳለህ። čı̥läh tı̥hä-dálläh?, pol. ችለው፡ ይሔዳሉ። čı̥lḁ͡u yı̥hädállu?

abound, v.i. በዛ bḁ́zzā̃.

ተረፈ tḁ́rrḁfḁ (tắr-).

about, adv. (=approximately) ያህል yáhi̥l (yahl; s.v. አከለ).

About twenty: ሃያ፡ ያህል፡ hḁ͡ʸa yáhi̥l.

about, prp. (=around) በ-...፡ አጠገብ bḁ-... aṭḁ́gḁb (-ḁy; §47b).

Round about the house: በቤት፡ አጠገብ፡ bḁyʸét aṭḁ́gḁy.

about, prp. (=concerning) የ-...፡ ነገር yä-... nágḁr (-gär; §47b).

What is it about? የምን፡ ነገር፡ ነው። yämi̥n nḁgár (§8) nḁ͡u?

above, adv. ላይ lá͡i̥.

በላይ bḁ́lá͡i̥ (§8).

above, prp. (of position) በ- [ከ-, ተ-] ...፡ ላይ bḁ- (kḁ-, tḁ-)... la͡i̥ (§§8, 47b).

Above the house: በቤት፡ ላይ፡ bḁyʸét la͡i̥.

above, prp. (=exceeding) ከ-[ተ-]...፡ የሚበልጥ kḁ- (tḁ-)... yämmi̥bḁ́lṭ (እሚ- (i̥)mmi̥-, -i̥y-, -álṭ; §58c).

Or use other parts of በለጠ bḁ́llḁṭḁ, to exceed.

Above ten: ታሥር፡ እሚበልጥ፡ tássi̥r i̥mmi̥yálṭ.

They are above ten: ታሥር፡ ይበልጣሉ tássi̥r yi̥yäl-ṭállu.

abscess, s. እበጥ í̥bḁṭ (í̥y-, -äṭ).

እብጠት í̥bṭḁt (í̥yṭ-, -ṭät).

እበጭ í̥bbáč̣ (§8).

abscond, v.i. ጠፋ ṭḁffā̃.

absent, be, v.i. use neg. of ነበረ nḁ́bbḁrḁ and of አለ állä (§39).

He is absent: የለም። yálläm.

He was absent: አልነበረም። alnḁbbḁrḁm.

Who is absent? ማን፡ ነው፡ የሌለ። mán-nḁ͡u yälʸállä?

Why were you absent? ምን፡ ነው፡ አልነበርህም። mi̥n-nḁ͡u alnḁ́bbärhi̥m?

abstract, v.t. ወሰደ wḁ́ssḁdḁ (wώs-).

abstracted, be, v.p. ተወሰደ tḁwḁ́ssḁdḁ (tḁ͡uḁ́-, -ώs-).

abundance, s. ትርፍ ti̥rf.

abundant, adj. ብዙ bí̥zu.

abuse (abusive language), s. ስድብ sí̥dib (-i̥ỵ).

abuse (revile), v.t. ሰደበ sḁ́ddḁbḁ (-ḁỵḁ).

abuse one another, v.i. ተሰዳደቡ tḁsḁdā́ddḁbu (täsäd-, -ḁỵu).

abused, be, v.p. ተሰደበ tḁsḁ́ddḁbḁ (täs-, -ḁỵḁ).

Abyssinia, s. ሀበሻ hábḁšã (háỵ-, -äš-).

ኢትዮጵያ ityṓpỵã.

Abyssinian, adj. የሀበሻ yähábḁšã (-háỵ-, -äš-).

Abyssinian, s. የሀበሻ፡ ሰው yähabḁšá sḁ͡u (-haỵ-, -äš-; § 8).

ሀበሻ hábḁšã (háỵ-, -äš-).

Acacia Suma (*A. campylacantha*; Broun, Cat. 181), s. ግማርዳ gi̥mā́rdã.

accept, v.t. ተቀበለ tḁqḁ́bbḁlḁ.

I will not accept it (them § 61*b*): አልቀበልም። ali̥q-qḁ́bbḁli̥m.

accord, of one's own: እንዲያው (í̥)ndya͡u (§ 8).

እንደው (í̥)ndḁ͡u (§ 8).

Ger. (§ 35) of አሰበ ássḁbḁ (-ḁỵḁ).

He (it) did so of his (its) own accord: እንዲያው፡ አደረገ። ndyá͡u adḁ́rrḁgḁ.

They gave it me of their own accord: አስበው፡ ሰጡኝ። ássi̥ỵḁ͡u sḁ́ṭṭuñ.

according as, conj., and
according to, prp. (=in proportion as, to), እንደ-...፡ በተዋረድ፡ (i̥)ndḁ- (-dä-)... bḁtḁwárḁd (y̥ḁ-, -ḁuá-).
According as they work: እንደሚሰሩ፡ በተዋረድ፡ ndämmi̥sḁ́ru y̥ḁtḁuárḁd.
According as they have worked: እንደሰሩ፡ በተዋረድ፡ ndäsḁ́rru y̥ḁtḁuárḁd.
According to your (pl.) work: እንደስራችሁ፡ በተዋረድ፡ ndäsi̥ráččyuh y̥ḁtḁuárḁd.

account, s. (bill) እሳብ i̥sáb (-áy̥; § 8).
ቍጥር qwi̥ṭi̥r (qwŭṭ-).
This account is not correct: ይህ፡ እሳብ፡ ትክክልም፡ አይደል። yi̥h i̥sáy̥ ti̥kí̥kki̥li̥mm ái̥däl (§ 7d).
The account was closed: ደፍተር፡ ተፋቀ። dḁ́ftär tḁfáqḁ.
Don't do it on any account: ምንም፡ ቢሆን፡ አታድርግ። mí̥ni̥mm bi̥hʷón attádri̥g, pl. -ርጉ። -ri̥gu.

account-book, s. ደፍተር dḁ́ftḁr (-tär).
accusation, s. ክስ ki̥ss.
accuse, v.t. ከሰሰ kḁ́ssḁsḁ.
accused, be, v.p. ተከሰሰ tḁkḁ́ssḁsḁ.
accused (the), s. ተከሳሽ tḁkḁ́sáš (§ 8).
accuser, s. ከሳሽ kḁ́sáš (§ 8).
accustomed, be (become), v.i. ለመደ lḁ́mmḁdḁ.
ache, s. እመም i̥mḁm.
ache, v.i. አመመ ámınḁmḁ (impers. § 43*a*; § 63*d*, *e*).
My head aches: ራሴን፡ ያመኛል። rásʸēn (§ 56*c*) yámmḁññāl.

Acheta sp., s. ፌንጣ fʸénṭã.
acquaintance, s. (knowledge) እውቀት i̥w(ŭ)qḁt.
ልማድ li̥mád (§ 8).
acquainted with, be, v.t. አወቀ áuwḁqḁ (-wωq-).

acquit, v.t. ፈረደ፡ ለ- fḁ́rrḁdḁ lḁ- (§ 47*a*).

The Rās acquitted him: ራስ፡ ፈረዱለት። rās fḁ́rrḁdullḁt.

acquitted, be, v.p. ተፈረደለት tḁfḁ́rrḁdḁllḁt (impers. § 43*a*; § 47*a*).

across, bring (take), v.t. አሻገረ aššággḁrḁ (-gär-).

across, come (go), v.i. & t. ተሻገረ tḁšággḁrḁ (täš-, -gär-).

They came across the river: ወንዙን፡ ተሻገሩ። wǿnzun tḁšággḁru.

act, v.i. አደረገ adḁ́rrḁgḁ.

active, adj. ንቁ ní̥qu.

activity, s. ንቅነት ni̥qí̥nnḁt (-nät).

Adansonia digitata (Broun, Cat. 65), s. ፍርጣጣ fi̥rṭáṭã.

add, v.i. & t. (up), ጀመለ jḁ́mmḁlḁ.

- (to) ጨመረ č̣ḁ́mmḁrḁ (-mär-).

added, be, v.p. (up) ተጀመለ tḁjḁ́mmḁlḁ.

(to) ተጨመረ tḁč̣ḁ́mmḁrḁ (-mär-).

addition, s. (increase) ጭማሪ č̣i̥mmári.

additional, adj. ጭማሪ č̣i̥mmári (§ 57*b*).

address, s. (on letter) ምልክት mi̥lí̥kki̥t.

admirable, adj. ማለፊያ mālā́fyã.

መልካም mḁ́lkám, pl. also መልካካም mḁlkákám (§ 8).

admiration, interj. expressing: እጡብ í̥ṭúb! (-ū́y; § 8; hḁṭūū́y!).

admit, v.t. አስገባ asgḁ́bbã.

adore, v.t. ሰገደ sḁ́ggḁdḁ (ság-, -gäd-).

adorn, v.t. አስጌጠ asg^{y}éṭḁ.

adorned, adj. ሽልም ší̥lli̥m.

adornment, s. ጌጥ g^{y}ēṭ.

ሽልማት ši̥llí̥mát (§ 8).

adult, adj. ትልቅ tí̥lli̥q.

adult, s. ጐበዝ gʷṓbḁz (-ṓyḁ-).
adulterer, s. ውሽማ wŭši̥mmã (-šŭ́m-).
adultery, s. ውሽምነት wŭši̥mmi̥nnḁt (-šŭm-, -nät).
adultery, commit, v.i. (of the man) ወሸመ wḁ́ššamḁ (wώš-).
(of the woman) ውሽማ፡ ያዘች wŭ-ší̥mma yã́zäč (-čč § 6).
advice, s. ምክር mi̥ki̥r.
advise, v.t. መከረ mḁkkḁrḁ (-kär-).
affair, s. ጕዳይ gwi̥ddá͡i̥ (gwŭ́d-, gúd-; § 8).
ነገር nḁgḁr (-gär).
afraid, be, v. i. ሰጋ sḁggã.
ፈራ fḁrrã (fã́r-).
Don't be afraid: አትስጋ። atti̥sgã, pl. -ጉ። -gu.
(encouragingly): አይዞህ። á͡i̥zʷōh !, pol. አይዞዎት። á͡i̥zʷo͡ʷot !, f. አይዞሽ። á͡i̥zʷōš !, pl. አይዟችሁ። a͡i̥-zṓáččyuh ! (§ 7*d*).
after, prp. ከ- [ተ-]... ፡ በኋላ kḁ- (tḁ-)... bḁhwā́lã (yḁ-, -ḁ͡uhā́- § 7*d*; § 47*b*).
After tea: ከሻይ፡ በኋላ፡ kḁšá͡i̥ yḁ͡uhā́la.
after—may be rendered by ተከተለ tḁqḁ́ttalḁ, to follow:
I will go after you (him, her, it, them, § 61*b*): ተከትዬ፡ እሄዳለሁ። tḁkḁ́ttīyye i̥hädállḁu[h] (§ 7*d*).
afternoon, in the, (speaking beforehand) ተኩለቀን፡ ወዲያ tḁkkúlḁqḁn wώdyã́ (§ 8).
Good afternoon: (on meeting) እንዴት፡ ዋልህ። ndʸēt wālh?, pol. እንዴት፡ ዋሉ። ndʸēt wā́lu?, pl. እንዴት፡ ዋላችሁ። ndʸēt wāláččyuh? (§ 7*d*).
afterwards, adv. ኋላ hwā́lã.
በኋላ bḁhwā́lã (bḁ͡uhā́- § 7*d*).
again, adv. ደግሞ dḁgmʷo [(dã́g-), ደሞ dḁmmʷo (dã́m-)].
again, do, v.t. ደገመ dḁ́ggḁmḁ (dã́g-).
Do it again: ድገም። di̥gḁm, pl. -ሙ -mu.

age, s. እድሜ ịdmʸe.
(old) እርጅና ịrjịnnā.
What is your age? እድሜህ፡ ስንት፡ ነው። ịdmʸeh sịntị nau?
aged (elderly), adj. አሮጌ arʷőgʸe.
ሽማግሌ šịmāgịllʸe.
agent, s. ሁነኛ hunáññā (-náñ-).
ago, adv. የዛሬ yäzárʸe.
Use አደረገ adárraga (q.v.).
Ten days ago: የዛሬ፡ አሥር፡ ቀን፡ yäzárʸe assịr qan.
How many years ago is it? የዛሬ፡ ስንት፡ ዓመት፡ ነው። yäzárʸe sịnt āmát nau?
He came two months ago: የዛሬ፡ ሁለት፡ ወር፡ ነው፡ የመጣ። yäzárʸe húlatt wωr nau yämátṭa; or ሁለት፡ ወር፡ ሁኖታል፡ ከመጣ። húlatt wωr húnʷotāl kamátṭa (ተመጣ። tamátṭa).
I sent him (it) three days ago: ሶስት፡ ቀን፡ አድርጌ፡ ላከሁት። sʷōst qan ádrịggʸe lákhut.
A little time ago: ቀድም፡ qịddịm.
Long ago: አያሌ፡ ጊዜ፡ ayyálʸe gịzʸe.
agree, v.i. እሺ፡ አለ (ị)šši (-šị, -šʸ) ála (s.v. √በለ, § 44*a*).
ደስ፡ አለ dass (däss) ála.
ደስ፡ አለው dass (däss) álau (impers. § 43*a*).
If he agrees to this: በዚህ፡ እሺ፡ ቢል፡ bazzịh ịššị yịl.
Do you agree to this? በዚህ፡ ደስ፡ ይለሃል። bazzíh däss yịlähāl?
I agree (to a proposal, or grant a request): ምን፡ ከፋኝ። mịn káffañ?, or
ምን፡ ቸገረኝ። mịn čággaräñ?
agree together, v.i. ተሰማሙ tasamámmu (täsäm-).
ተጠቃቀሙ taṭaqáqqamu.
ተዋደዱ tawáddadu (tauá-).

agreeable (amiable), adj. ጠፍተኛ t̥affi̥tḁ́ññã (-tā́ñ-).
agreeable (amiable), be, v.i. ጠፍ፡ አለ t̥aff álḁ (s.v. √በለ, § 44*a*).
agreement, s. ቍርጥ qwŭrt̥.
ውል wŭl.
They made an agreement: ቍርጥ፡ አደረጉ። qwŭrt̥ adḁ́rrḁgu.
He broke the agreement: ቍርጥ፡ አፈረሰ። qwŭrt̥ afḁ́rrḁsḁ.
Until the agreement terminates: ውል፡ እስኪያልቅ፡ ድረስ፡ wŭl i̥skyálq di̥rḁs.
agriculture, s. አዝመራ azmḁ́rã (-mā́r-).
ahead, adv. በፊት bḁ́fīt (-fi̥t; § 8).
ወደፊት wωdḁ́fīt (-fi̥t; § 8).
He has gone on ahead: በፊት፡ ሒዷል። bḁfi̥t hi̥dŏ͡āl, or ወደፊት፡ ሔደ። wωdḁfít hā̆dä.
air, s. ነፋስ ni̥fás (§ 8).
alarm, s. (fear) ፍራት fi̥rát (§ 8).
(rousing) ቅስቀሳ qi̥sqḁ́sã.
alarm, v.t. (frighten) አስፈራ asfḁ́rrã (-fā́r-).
(rouse) ቀሰቀሰ qḁsḁ́qqḁsḁ.
alarm-clock, s. ባለደወል፡ ሰዓት bālḁdḁ́u͡ḁl sḁ͡ā(t).
alert, adj. ንቁ ni̥qu.
alight, be, v.i. (fire, lamp) ተበራ tḁbḁ́rrã (-ḁyḁ́-).
Is the lamp (candle, any light) alight? መብራት፡ ተበርቷል። mḁyrát tḁyḁ́rtŏ͡āl?
alive, adj. ተነነፍሱ tḁnnḁnḁ́fsu.
all, pron. ሁል- hull- with pers. suff. (§ 16, § 12*b*).
s.v. አከለ.
Not all of it: መች፡ ሁሉ፡ mḁč húllu.
Take it all away: ውሰደው፡ ሁሉ። wŭsḁdḁ͡u húllu.

Is that all? ይህ ፡ ሁሉ ፡ ነው ። yi̥he húllu nḁ͡u?

Let them all come: ሁላቸው ፡ ይምጡ ። hulláččḁ͡u yi̥mṭu.

All the men: ሰው ፡ ሁሉ ፡ sḁ́͡u húllu (cp. § 52*a*).

They are coming back, transport and all: ይመለሳሉ፡ ተንጓዛቸው ። yi̥mmḁllḁsállu tḁnnḁgwāzáččḁ͡u.

He has come after all! መጣኮ ። mḁṭṭákkʷo! (s.v. እኮ).

Where has all that money gone to? ያን ፡ ያህል ፡ ገንዘብ ፡ ዬት ፡ ሔደ ። yan yahl gḁ́nzḁv yēt hắdä? (§ 56*c*; s.v. እከለ).

all right! interj. እሺ (i̥)šši! (-ši̥).

በጀ bḁ́jjä! (bắj-).

ይሁን yi̥hun!

at all, adv. ምንም mi̥ni̥mmi̥n (§ 16), only with neg. verb (§ 38).

ከቶ kḁ́ttʷo (s.v. ከተተ).

It is of no use at all: ምንም ፡ አይረባም ። mi̥ni̥mmi̥n ḁ͡irḁ́yām.

allegory, s. ምሳሌ mi̥ssálʸe.

Allium cepa, s. ሹንኩርት šúńkwŭrt.

ቀይ ፡ ሹንኩርት qḁ́i̥ (qḁyy § 6) šúńkwŭrt.

Allium sativum, s. ነጭ ፡ ሹንኩርት näčč šúńkwŭrt.

allow, v.t. ተወ tḁ́wḁ (tḁ́͡uḁ).

Or use causative in አስ- as- (§ 22*a*); s.v. √በለ.

allowed, be, v.p. ተተወ tḁtḁ́wḁ (-ḁ́͡uḁ).

Is it allowed? ይተዋሉይ። yi̥ttḁ́͡uāllwi̥? (s.v. -ወይ).

It is not allowed: አይተውም። ḁ͡ittḁ͡um.

aloe (*A. abessinica*, Broun, Cat. 573), s. [እ]ሬት (i̥)rʸét (§ 8).

alone, adv. ብቻ bi̥ččā, with pers. suff. (§ 12*b*).

ለብቻ- lḁbi̥ččā- (-ḁyi̥-) „ „

It stands alone: ብቻ ፡ ነው ። bi̥ččá (§ 8) nḁ͡u.

Leave him alone: ለብቻው ፡ ተወው ። lḁyı̥́čča͡u tḁ́u͡ḁu, pl. .... ፡ ተዉት ። .... tḁ́ut.

I wish to be alone: ብቻየን ፡ ነው ፡ እምሆን ። bı̥čča͡ʸän (§ 56*d*) nḁ͡ummhʷon.

along, adv. (intensive) [እ]ኩ (ı̥)kkʷo [(ǘk-); usually enclitic and a suffix].

Go along! ሒድኩ ። hı̥dı̥́kkʷo!, pl. ሒዱኩ ። hı̥dúkkʷo!

along (-side of), prp. ከ-[ተ-]... ፡ ጥግ kḁ- (tḁ-)... ṭı̥gg (§ 8, § 47*a*).

Alongside of the wall: ከግድግዳ ፡ ጥግ ፡ kḁgı̥rgı̥ddá (§ 7*d*) ṭı̥gg.

alphabet, s. ፊደል fı̥́däl.

also, adv. ደግሞ dḁ́gmʷo (dǻg-).

ደሞ dḁ́mmʷo (dǻm-).

-ም -m (-mm § 6; § 48*b*).

እዛወዲያ (ı̥)z(z)áʷωdyǻ (-zǻd-; § 8).

altar, s. ታቦት tábʷót (-ǻẏó-; § 8).

alter, v.i. (be altered, v.p.) ተለወጠ tḁlḁ́͡uwḁṭḁ.

It must alter (be altered): ይለወጥ ። yı̥llḁ́͡uḁṭ.

alter, v.t. ለወጠ lḁ́͡uwḁṭḁ.

Don't alter it: አትለውጠው ። attı̥lḁ́͡uwŭṭḁ͡u.

alteration, s. ለውጥ lḁ́͡uṭ.

altogether, adv. ጭራሽ čı̥̣rrǻš (§ 8).

It was omitted altogether: ጭራሽ ፡ ቀረ ። čı̥̣rrǻš qḁ́rrḁ.

always, adv. ሁልጊዜ húllgı̥zʸe (-ለግ- -llḁgı̥-).

ዘወትር zḁ͡uώtı̥r.

amber, s. ዘይት zé͡ı̥t.

ambiguous, adj. ውልውል wŭlı̥́wwŭl.

አጓጕል agwǻgwŭl.

amble, v.i. ሠገረ sḁ́ggḁrḁ (-gär-).

ambush, v.t. (lie in ambush, v.i.) አደባ adḁ́bbẵ.

Amharic, adj. & s. አምኃርኛ amāri̥ññã.

What is this called in Amharic? ይህ ፡ ባምኃርኛ ፡ እንዴት ፡ ይባላል ። yi̥he ẏamāri̥ñña nd^{y}ēt yi̥bbálāl?

Do they understand Amharic? አምኃርኛ ፡ ይሰማሉ ። amāríi̥ñña yi̥sḁmállu?

amiability, s. ጠፍታ ṭḁ́ffi̥tã.

amiable, adj. ጠፍተኛ ṭḁffi̥tḁ́ññã (-tắñ-).

amiable, be, v.i. ጠፍ ፡ አለ ṭḁff ắlḁ (s.v. √ባለ, § 44a).

ammunition, s. [እ]ርሳስ (í̥)rsắs (§ 8).

ጥይት ṭíyyi̥t (ṭí̥y-; § 52a, δ).

amount to, v.t. ወጣ wώṭṭã.

ደረሰ dḁ́rrḁsḁ.

አከለ ákkḁlḁ.

What does it amount to? ስንት ፡ ይወጣል ። si̥nt yuώṭāl?

amuse, v.t. አጫወተ ač̣č̣á͡uwḁtḁ (-wωt-).

አሣቀ assắqḁ.

amused, be, v.i. ሣቀ sắqḁ (at በ- bḁ- § 47a).

amusement, s. ጨወታ č̣ḁ́wḁtã (č̣ḁ́͡u-, -ωt-).

amusing, adj. መሣቂያ mḁsắqyã.

and, conj. -ም -m (-mm § 6).

-ና -nnã.

(§ 48b, § 72).

The horse is a bad one and the mule is too dear: ፈረሱ ፡ ከፉ ፡ ነው ፡ በቅሎውም ፡ ውድ ፡ ነው ። fḁ́rḁsu kí̥fu nḁ͡u ẏḁ́ql^{w}oum wǘddi̥ nḁ͡u.

Bring some water and the medicine: ውኃና ፡ መድኃኒቱን ፡ ይዘህ ፡ ና ። wŭhánna mḁdhắn^{y}itun yi̥zắh (§ 8) na.

and, conj.—often not expressed (§ 74*c*):

He went and saw and returned : ሔደ ፡ አየ ፡ ተመለሰ ። hădä áyyä tḁmḁ́llḁsḁ.

There is bread, meat and water: ዳቦ ፡ ሥጋ ፡ ውሃ ፡ አለ ። dább^{w}o sí̥ga wŭ́ha állä.

Where English co-ordinates, Amharic subordinates one or more sentences, especially by the use of the gerund (§ 74*a*, *b*):

Come back and take it away: ተመልሰህ ፡ ውሰደው ። tḁmállisäh wúsḁdḁu.

He has taken and eaten the meat: ሥጋ ፡ ይዞ ፡ በልቷል ። sí̥ga yí̥z^{w}o yḁltōäl.

Go to the market and buy some grain and come back: ገበያ ፡ ሔደህ ፡ እህል ፡ ገዝተህ ፡ ና ። gḁ́yya hí̥däh í̥hi̥l gḁztáh na.

Fill it and hang it up: መልተህ ፡ ስቀለው ። mḁ́ltäh sí̥qḁlḁu.

and, conj. joining numerals over 99 and fractions (§ 20), ተ- tḁ-.

180: መቶ ፡ ተሰማንያ ፡ mḁ́t^{w}o tḁsḁmányã.

1 1/3: አንድ ፡ ተሶስትያ ፡ and tḁs^{w}ostíyya.

and, conj. (= in order to) እንድ- (i̥)nd(i̥)-, pref. to contingent (§ 45).

Come and see: ና ፡ እንድታይ ። nā ndi̥ttái̥.

anger, interj. expressing: አዬ a^{y}é! (a^{y}ē-é!).

anger, s. ኵርፍያ kwŭ́rfyã.

ቍጣ qwŭ́ṭṭã.

angry, be, v.i. (with, v.t.) ተቈጣ tḁqwóṭṭã (§ 63*d*, *e*).

I am not angry: አልተቈጣሁም ። altḁqwóṭṭahum.

I am angry with you: ተቈጥቼሃለሁ ። tḁqwoṭi̥čč^{y}e-hállḁu^{h}.

When I am angry do not come near me: ስቈጣ፡ ወደኔ፡ አትምጣ። si̥qqwǿṭṭā wωdḁnʸé attı̥mṭā.

animal, s. (wild) አርዌ áurʸe (§ 7*d*), pl. አራዊት arā́wı́t (§ 8).

(domestic) እንስሳ (i̥)nsḁsā (§ 7*d*).

(horses, cattle, etc.) ከብት kḁyt (kḁft § 7*d*).

ankle, s. ቍርጭምጭሚት qwŭrči̥mči̥mi̥t (-čı́mči̥mt, -ጭም ጭማት -či̥mčı́mā́t § 8; § 52*a*, γ).

I (have) sprained my ankle: ቍርጭምጭማት፡ ወለም፡ አለኝ። qwŭrči̥mči̥mā́t wḁlḁmm ā́läñ.

annoy, v.t. አስቈጣ asqwǿṭṭā.

annoyed, be, v.i. ተናደደ tḁnā́ddḁdḁ (at, with, በ- bḁ- § 47*a*).

I am annoyed with you: ተናደድሁብህ። tḁnáddadhubbi̥h.

Anogeissus leiocarpus (Broun, Cat. 188), s. ክርክራ ki̥rkı́rrā.

anoint, v.t. ቀባ qḁbbā.

anointed, be, v.p. ተቀባ tḁqḁbbā.

answer, s. ምላሽ mi̥llā́š (§ 8).

Is there an answer?—No. ምላሽ፡ አለ። የለም። mi̥llā́š állä?—yállām.

answer, v.i. & t. መለሰ mḁllasḁ (mā́l-).

What did he answer? ምን፡ መለሰው። mi̥n mā́llḁsḁu?

ant, s. (small black) ቊንጫጭ qú(n)čā́č (§ 8).

(large, black or red) ትንኳሽ tŭ́ṅkwā́š (§ 8).

(large black, harmless) ገብረ፡ ጕንዳን gḁbrḁ (-ḁyr-) gwŭ́ndā́n (§ 8).

(large black, biting) ግንዳ gi̥ndā.

(driver, biting) ጕንዳን gwŭ́ndā́n (§ 8).

(white, = termite) ምስጥ mi̥sṭ.

See § 52*a*, δ.

antelope, s. (small) የሜዳ፡ ፍየል yäm^{y}éda fíyyäl.
anthelmintic, s. ኮሶ k^{w}ós^{w}o.
ant-hill, s. አርባጫ arbáč̣č̣ã (-rỵá-).
anus, s. [እ]ሬብ (ĭ̥)r^{y}éb (-éỵ).
anvil, s. መዝፍ mḁzf (§ 7d).
any, indef. pron. ማናቸውም mānnáč(č)ḁ͡um (-mm § 6; §16).
　　እንዳች ándáčč (§ 8; § 16).
　　እንዳቸውም andáčččḁ͡um (-mm § 6; § 16).
I haven't seen any of them: ማናቸውንም፡ አላየሁ። mānnāččḁ́͡unni̥mm aláyyä͡u^{h} (§ 7d).
He may come any day: ድንገት፡ በማናቸውም፡ ቀን፡ ይመጣል። dí̥ngʼḁt ỵḁmānnāččḁ́͡um (§ 8) qḁn yi̥mḁ́-ṭāl.
Haven't you seen any? እንዳች፡ አላየህም። andáčč aláyyähi̥m?
Haven't you seen any of them? እንዳቸውንም፡ አላየህ። andāččḁ́͡unni̥mm aláyyäh?

any—often not expressed:
There isn't any water: ውሃ፡ የለም። wúhā yállām.
Is there any? አለ። állä? (§ 32d).
Are there any? አሉ። állu?
If there is any, bring it: እንዳለ፡ አምጣው። ndállä, ámṭa͡u, (ndallánṭa͡u § 7d).
Was there any? ነበረ። nḁ́bbḁrḁ? (§ 33d).

anybody (anyone), indef. pron. ማንም mánni̥m (-mm, § 6; § 16).
　　ሰው sḁ́͡u.
Do not let anyone come in: ማንም፡ አይግባ። mánni̥mm ḁ́͡igỵā.
Is there anybody there? ሰው፡ አለን። sḁ́͡u állän? (s.v. -ን).

anything, indef. pron. ምንም mı̥nı̥m (-mm, § 6; § 16).
  There isn't anything: ምንም ፡ የለ ። mı̥́nı̥mm yállä (§ 39).
apart, adv. ብቻ bı̥́ččã.
ape, s. ጦጣ ṭʷóṭã.
appear, v.i. (come into sight) ታየ táyyä.
  ዘለቀ zḁ́llḁqḁ (q.v.).
  (seem) መሰለ mḁ́ssḁlḁ.
appearance, s. (form, colour) መልክ mḁlk.
appoint, v.t. (fix) ቀጠረ qḁ́ṭṭḁrḁ (-ṭär-).
  (to an office) ሾመ šʷṓmḁ.
appointed, be, v.p. (fixed) ተቀጠረ tḁqḁ́ṭṭḁrḁ (-ṭär-).
  (to an office) ተሾመ tḁšʷṓmḁ (täš-).
appointment, s. (to meet) ቀጠሮ qḁ́ṭḁrʷo (-ṭär-).
approach, s. መምጫ mḁ́mčã.
approach, v.i. & t. ቀረበ qḁ́rrḁbḁ (-ḁyḁ) constr. with ወደ- wωdḁ-.
approximately, adv. ያህል yáhi̥l (yahl; s.v. አከለ).
April, s. see calendar.
Arab, s. አረብ árḁb (-ḁy).
Arabic, adj. አረብኛ arḁbı̥́ññã (-ḁyı̥́-).
  Is there anyone here who speaks Arabic? አለ ፡ እዚህ ፡ አረብኛ ፡ የሚናገር ። állä zzı̥́h arḁyı̥́ñña yämmi̥nnággḁr?
arbitrate, v.i. ዳኘ dáññä.
argue, v.i. ተከራከረ tḁkḁrä́kkḁrḁ (-kärä́kkär-).
argument, s. ክርክር ki̥rı̥́kki̥r.
ark, s. (eccl.) ታቦት tábʷót (-ä̃yʷó-; § 8).
arm, s. ጡንቻ ṭúnčã (prop. upper arm; § 52*a*, γ).
armed, adj. ባለመሳሪያ bālḁmḁssä́ryã.
arm-pit, s. ብብት bı̥́bbi̥t (§ 52*a*, γ).

arms, s. (weapons) መሳሪያ massárya̋ (cp. § 52*a*, δ).
ብረት bɨrat (-rät; „ „).
army, s. ሰራዊት saráuwit (sär-, -wit).
around, prp. በ-...፣ አጠገብ ba-... atágab (-av; § 47*b*).
arrange, v.t. ሰራ sárra̋ (sár-).
arranged, be, v.p. ተሰራ tasárra̋ (täsár-).
arrangement, s. ሥራት sɨrát (§ 8).
arrest, v.t. ያዘ yáza.
arrested, be, v.p. ተያዘ tayáza (taiá-).
arrested, have, (cause to be), v.t. አስያዘ asyáza (§ 68).
arrival, (time or place of), s. መምጫ mámča̋.
arrive, v.i. ደረሰ dárrasa.
ገባ gábba̋.
When he arrives: ሲደርስ፣ sidárs.
When they arrive: ሲደርሱ፣ sidársu.
arrive, cause or allow to, v.t. አደረሰ adárrasa.
arrow, s. ቀስት qast (q.v.).
artillery, s. መድፍ madf (marf § 7*d*).
artillery-man, s. መድፈኛ madfáñña̋ (marf-, -fáñ-).
artizan, s. ሰራተኛ sarra̋táñña̋ (sär-, -táñ-).
ባለጅ bálájj (§ 8).
as, conj. እንደ- (i)nda- (-dä-) pref. to simp. perf.
ስ- si- pref. to cont., past imperf., etc.
ስለ- sila-, pref. to simp. perf.
(since) ከ- [ተ-] ka- (ta-), pref. to simp. perf.
Or use the gerund.
Make another as you made this: ይህነን፣ እንደሰራሁ፣ ሌላ፣ ስራ። yihánnän indäsárrah léla sɨra.
As he was going, he stopped: ሲሄድ፣ ነበር፣ ቆመ። sihád nábbar, qʷóma.

As they have work to do, give them more forage: ስራ፡ ስላላቸው፡ ገፈራ፡ ጨምርላቸው። si̥ra si̥lalláč-čḁu, gḁ́fḁrā çḁmmi̥ri̥lláččḁu.

As they have no work, don't let them eat much: ስራ፡ ስለሌላቸው፡ ጥቂት፡ ጥቂት፡ ይብሉ። sí̥ra si̥-lḁlʸällḁ́ččḁu, ṭí̥qi̥t ṭí̥qi̥t yí̥ylu.

As he has come, let him stay: ተመጣ፡ ይቀመጥ። tḁmḁ́ṭṭa, yi̥qqḁ́mḁṭ.

As he was tired I left him on the road and came on: ደክሞት፡ ተመንገድ፡ ትቼው፡ መጣሁ። dḁ́ki̥mʷot tḁmḁ́ngḁd tí̥ččʸeu mḁ́ṭṭauʰ (§ 7*d*).

as far as, prp. እስከ- (i̥)skḁ- (§ 47*a*).

እስተ- (i̥)stḁ- („).

as for, prp. -ማ -mmā̃ (encl.).

As for that: ይህማ፡ yi̥hámma.

as long as, conj. ሳለ sállä (= ስ- + አለ § 32) after gerund.

As long as you are ill you must not go out: አሞህ፡ ሳለ፡ አትውጣ። ámmʷoh sállä attwúṭa.

As long as I am here: ተዚህ፡ እስታለሁ፡ tḁzzí̥h i̥s-tállä͡uʰ (§ 7*d*).

I will wait as long as I can: እንደምችል፡ እቈያለሁ። ndämmi̥či̥l i̥qwωyyállḁuʰ (§ 7*d*).

I waited as long as I could: የቻልሁትን፡ ያህል፡ ቈየሁ። yäčálhuti̥n (§ 56*c*) yahl qwώyyä͡uʰ (§ 7*d*).

ascend, v.i. ወጣ wώṭṭã.

v.t. በ-...፡ ላይ፡ ወጣ bḁ-... la͡i̥ (§ 8, § 47*b*) wώṭṭã.

ascent, s. (rising ground) አቀበት áqḁbḁt (-ḁyḁt).

(way up) ማውጫ má͡uçã.

ascertain, v.i. & t. አወቀ á͡uwḁqḁ (-wωq-).

(ask) ጠየቀ ṭḁ́yyḁqḁ (-yäq-).

Let him ascertain and tell me: ጠይቆ፡ ይንገረኝ። ṭḁ́yyi̥qʷo yí̥ngäräñ.

ascertained, be, v.p. ታወቀ táuwaqa (-wωq-).
ash (ashes), s. አመድ ámad.
ashamed, be, v.i. አፈረ áffara (-fär-).
I am ashamed to look (at it): አፍራለኍ ፤ ሳይ ። afrállauh (§ 7d) sái (§ 61b).
ask (for), v.i. & t. ጠየቀ táyyaqa (-yäq-).
Ask him: ጠይቀው ። táyyiqau, pol. ይጠይቁት ። yitáyyiqut, pl. ጠይቁት ። táyyiqut.
Ask them: ጠይቃቸው ። tayyiqáččau, pol. ይጠይ ቋቸው ። yitayyiqwáččau, pl. ጠይቋቸው ። tayyiqwáččau.
Did you ask him? ጠየቅሀው ። táyyäqhau?, pol. ጠየቁት ። táyyäqut?, pl. ጠየቃችሁት ። tayyäqáččihut?
Ask whether there is any: ጠይቅ ፤ እንዳለ ። táyyiq indállä.
Ask the headman for a house: ሹሙን ፤ ቤት ፤ ጠይቅ ። šúmun byēt táyyiq.
They (will) bring him whatever he asks for: እም ጡሉኝ ፤ የሚሉቸውን ፤ ያመጡለታል ። ántulliñ (§ 7d) yämmiláččaun yāmátullatāl, (s.v. √በለ, § 44a).
Ask the cook for it (them, some, § 61b): ስጠኝ ፤ በለው ፤ ወጥ ፤ ቤቱን ። sítäñ yálau wωt vyētun.
Ask me for it (etc.) to-morrow: ይስጡኝ ፤ በለኝ ፤ ነገ ። yístuñ yálañ nága.
asked (for), be, v.p. ተጠየቀ tatáyyaqa (-yäq-).
asleep, be, v.i. ተኛ táññā (táñ-, -ñä; § 63d, e).
He is asleep: ተኝቷል ። táññitōāl.
If I had been asleep it would all have been spoilt: ተኝቼ ፤ ቢሆን ፤ ሁሉ ፤ ይበላሽ ፤ ነበር ። táññiččye bihwón, húllu yibbalášš nábbär (§ 81d, μ).
ass, s. አህያ ahíy(y)ā.

assembly, s. ጉባኤ gubáʸe (-uẏá-).
  ሸንጎ šḁ́ṅgʷo.
assembly, place of, s. አደባባይ addḁbábai̯ (-ḁẏáẏai̯).
assist, v.i. & t. [እ]ረዳ (i̯)rḁddã.
  If you (pol.) will assist me: ቢረዱኝ፡ bi̥rḁ́duñ.
assistance, s. እርዳታ i̥rdátã.
astonished, be, v.i. ተገረመ tḁgḁ́rrḁmḁ.
  ገረመው gḁ́rrḁmḁu (impers. § 43*a*; § 63*d*, *e*).
  I am astonished: ገረመኝ። gḁ́rrḁmäñ.
at, prp. ከ- kḁ- [ተ- tḁ-] } (§ 47*a*).
  በ- bḁ-
  Is he at Addis Abeba? ታዲስ፡ አበባ፡ ነው። táddi̥s (§ 7*a*) aẏḁẏá nḁu? (§ 8).
  He was engaged at ten dollars: በሥር፡ ብር፡ ተቀጠረ። bássi̥r ẏi̥rr tḁqḁ́ṭṭḁrḁ.
Atbara, s. ጎንግ gŏáṅṅ.
attack, v.i. & t. ተናሣ tḁnḁ́ssã በ- bḁ- (§ 47*a*).
  Did they attack you? ተናሡብህ። tḁnḁ́ssubbi̥h?
  If they attack us: ቢናሡብን፡ bi̥nnḁ́ssubbi̥nnḁ.
attend, v.i. (pay attention) አስተዋለ astḁwálḁ (-ḁuá-).
attention, s. (heed) ልብ li̥bb.
  Your attention is over there: ልብህ፡ ከዚያ፡ ነው። lí̥bbi̥h käzzyá nḁu.
audience hall, s. አደባባይ addḁbábai̯ (-ḁẏáẏai̯).
auger, s. መውጊያ mḁúgyã.
  ወስፌ wósfʸe.
August, s. see calendar.
aunt, s. አክስት áki̥st (§ 8).
authority, s. ሹመት šúmḁt (-mät).
  ችሎት čí̥lʷot (§ 8).

avalanche, s. መርግ m̥arg (märg).
avarice, s. ንፍገት ní̥fgḁt.
avaricious, adj. ንፉግ ní̥fug.
avoid, v.t. ሸሸ šḁ́ššä (šắš-).
await, v.t. ቈየ qwώyyä.
await each other, v. recip. ተቈያዩ tḁqwω͡i̥áyyu.
awake, adj. ንቑ ní̥qu.
awake, be, v.i. ነቓ nḁ́qqã (§ 63*d*, *e*).
Is he awake? ነቕቷል። nḁ́qt͡ŏāl?, pol. ነቕተዋል። nḁ́qtḁ͡uāl?
I am awake: ነቕቻለኹ። nḁqi̥ččállḁ͡uʰ (§ 7*d*).
away, adv.
Is he away? የለሞይ yắllämmwi̥? (s.v. -ወይ; § 39).
away, go, v.i. ሔደ hä̃́dä (hḁ̃́-, hʸḗ-, -dḁ, § 7*d*).
ወገደ wώggḁdḁ.
Go away! ሒድ። hi̥d!, f. ሒጅ። hi̥j!, pl. ሒዱ። hí̥du!
(more forcibly) ወግድ። wώgi̥d!, f. ወግጅ። wώgi̥j!, pl. ወግዱ። wώgi̥du!
away, be put (taken), v.p. ተወሰደ tḁwḁ́ssḁdḁ (tḁ͡uḁ́-, -ώs-).
ተነሣ tḁnḁ́ssã.
away, move, v.t. ሳብ፡ አደረገ sãbb adḁ́rrḁgḁ.
Move him (it) away a little: ጥቂት፡ ሳብ፡ አድርገው። tí̥qi̥t sabb ádri̥gḁ͡u (ắrg- § 7*d*), pl. -ጉት። -gut.
away, put (take), v.t. ወሰደ wḁ́ssḁdḁ (wώs-):
አነሣ anḁ́ssã.
Take him (it) away: ውሰደው። wǘsḁdḁ͡u, pl. -ዱት። -dut.
awl, s. መሰፍቻ mḁssafi̥čã.
መውጊያ mḁ͡ugyã.
ወስፌ wώsfʸe.

axe, s. መጥረቢያ mḁṭrḁ́byã (-ḁ́ỵyã).
axilla, s. ብብት bí̥bbi̥t (§ 52*a*, *γ*).

B

§ refers to the paragraphs of the Grammar (Initia Amharica, Part I.)

baboon (*Cynocephalus sp.*), s. ዝንጀሮ zi̥njḁ́rʷo (-jώr-).
baby, s. አራስ ā́rā́s (§ 8). አራስ ፡ ልጅ arā́s li̥j.
ጨቅላ ç̣ā́qlã.
ሕጣን hí̥ṭā́n (§ 8).
back, s. (of body) ጀርባ jā́rbã (-rỵã, -rwã).
back (again), come (go), v.i. ተመለሰ tḁmḁ́llа̥sḁ (-mā́l-).
Come back (again): ተመለስ ። tḁmḁ́lḁs, pl. -ሱ ። -su.
back (again), send (bring), v.t. መለሰ mḁ́llḁsḁ (mā́l-).
Bring him (it) back (again): መልሰው ። mā́lli̥sḁu͡, pl. -ሱት ። -sut.
back(-wards), adv. ወደኋላ wωdḁhwā́lã (-dḁ͡uhā́- § 7*d*).
bad, adj. (morally) ክፉ kí̥fu (kū́fu, kŭ́fu § 7*d*).
(physically) ግም gi̥m.
bad, be (become), v.i. (morally) ከፋ kḁ́ffã.
(physically) ግም ፡ ሆነ gi̥m hʷṓnḁ.
bad-tempered, adj. ቍጡ qwū́ṭṭu.
ተናዳጅ tḁnā́dā́j (§ 8).
አሞታም amʷṓtā́m (§ 8).
badly, behave, v.i., (treat, v.t.) በደለ bḁ́ddḁlḁ (bā́d-).
bag, s. ከረጢት kḁrḁṭí̥t.
(wicker-work) አኮፋዳ akʷofā́dã.
baggage, s. እቃ í̥qã.
Baggage train (of troops): ጓዝ gwāz.
baggage-mule, s. አጋሰስ ፡ በቅሎ ፡ agā́ssi̥s bḁ́qlʷo (ỵḁ́-).

baggage-pony, s. መጋጃ mḁgájjā̃.
bake, v.t. ጣዳ ṭādḁ.
balance, s. (scales) ሚዛን mízān (§ 8).
(remainder) የቀረ yäqḁrrḁ (§ 62*b*, *c*).
ቅሬታ qi̥rrʸétā̃.
I received five dollars; you have the balance: አምስት፡ ብር፡ ተቀበልሁ፤ የቀረው፡ ታንተ፡ ነው። ámmi̥sti̥ yi̥rr tḁqḁ́bbḁlhu; yäqḁ́rrḁu tantá nḁu.
balance, v.t. መዘነ mḁ́zzḁnḁ.
Balanites ægyptiaca (Broun, Cat. 88), s. ኩድኩዳ kudkúddā̃.
ቁጣ qúṭ(ṭ)ā̃ (Ag.).
Š. ቃጮና qā́čʷonā̃.
bald, adj. በራ bḁrā̃.
ball, s. ኳስ kwās.
(እ)ሩር (i̥)rūr.
bamboo (*Oxytenanthera abessinica*, Broun, Cat. 677), s. ሽመል ši̥mḁl (-mäl).
banana (*Musa sapientium*, Broun, Cat. 559), s. ሙዝ muz.
bandage, s. ማሰሪያ māsḁryā̃ (-sár-, -yä).
Undo the bandage and let me see: ማሰሪያውን፡ ፍታ፤ ልይ። māsáryaun fi̥ta, lī.
bandolier, s. ዝናር zi̥nnār (§ 8).
bang, s. (report) ድምጥ di̥mṭ.
bang, v.i. ጓ፡ አለ gwā álḁ (s.v. √በለ, § 44*a*).
ግም፡ አለ gi̥mm álḁ „ „
banish, v.t. አወጣ awǿṭṭā̃ (auǿ-).
banjo, s. ክራር ki̥rār (§ 8).
bank, s. (of river, etc.) ዳር dār.
ድምበር di̥mbḁr (-bär).
This bank: ወዲህ፡ ማዶ፡ wǫdi̥h mádʷo.
The other bank: ማዶ፡ mádʷo.

On the bank of the river: ተወንዝ ፡ ዳር ፡ tạuẃnzị dār.

banquet, s. ድግስ dígg̣is.

ግብር gíb(ị)r (-íy-).

baobab (*Adansonia digitata,* Broun, Cat. 65), s. ፍርጣጣ fịrṭắṭã.

baptized, be, v.p. ተጠመቀ tạṭámmạqạ.

barber, s. ላጪ lắč̣(č̣)i.

bare, adj. (naked) ራቁት rắqut (§ 56*d*).

(arid) ደረቅ dárạq.

bark, s. (of dog) ጩኸት č̣úhạt (-hät).

(of tree) ልጥ lịṭ.

bark, v.i. ጮኸ č̣ʷóhạ.

ቡ ፡ አለ bu ắlạ (s.v. √ቡለ, § 44*a*).

barley, s. ገብስ gạbs (gạys, gạfs).

barn, s. ጎተራ gʷotạrã (-tắr-; § 8).

barracks, s. የወታደር ፡ ከተማ yäwωttáddạr kạtạ́mã.

barrel, s. (of gun) አፍ āf.

A double-barrelled gun: ሁለት ፡ አፍ ፡ ጠበንጃ ፡ húlạtt āf ṭạyạ́nja.

basin, s. መታጠቢያ mạttāṭạ́byã (-ạ́yyã).

(for washing the face) የፊት ፡ መታጠቢያ yäfịt mạttāṭạ́yyã.

basket, s. ቅርጫት qịrčắt (§ 8).

አገልግል agạ́lgịl (agắl-).

(small) ሙዳይ múdấị (§ 8).

(bag-shaped) አኮፋዳ akʷofắdã.

basket-work, s. ስፌት sịfʸẽt (§ 8).

bat, s. የሌት ፡ ዎፍ yälʸét wõf (ʷõf).

bath, s. (process) መታጠብ mạttāṭạb (-ạy).

(utensil) መታጠቢያ mạttāṭạ́byã (-ạ́yyã).

Or use ታጠበ:

He is in his bath: ይታጠባል ። yi̥ttáṭṭḁvāl.

I am in my bath: እታጠባለሁ ። i̥ttāṭṭḁvállа̥͡u^{h}.

I am going to have a bath: ሊታጠብ ፡ ነኝ ። li̥ttāṭ-ṭḁ́v̥ (§ 8) näñ.

bathe, v.i. ታጠበ tá̈ṭṭḁbḁ (-ḁv̥ḁ).

bathe, v.t. አጠበ áṭṭḁbḁ (-ḁv̥ḁ).

battalion, s. ጦር ṭ^{w}or.

battle, s. ውጊ wụ́ggi.

Bauhinia reticulata (Broun, Cat. 167), s. ዳብዲ dǟ́bdi (dǟ́v̥di).

be, v.i. ሆነ h^{w}ṓnḁ.

አለ állä (§ 32, § 39).

ነበረ nḁ́bbḁrḁ (-bär-, -በር -bbḁr, -bbär, § 33).

ኖረ n^{w}ṓrḁ.

ነው nḁ͡u (§ 13*b*, § 40).

Where have you been? ወዴት ፡ ሁነሃል ። wωd^{y}ét húnähāl?

When I was in Egypt: ተምስር ፡ ሳለሁ ። tḁmi̥ssi̥r sállä͡u^{h} (§ 7*d*).

Let it be as it was: እንደነበረ ፡ ይኑር ። ndänḁ́bbḁrḁ yi̥nur.

Give me what there is: ያለ ፡ ስጠኝ ። yállä si̥ṭḁñ.

There isn't any: የለም ። yállām (§ 39).

There are two: ሁለት ፡ አሉ ። húlätt állu.

They are two: ሁለት ፡ ናቸው ። húlätt náččḁ͡u.

They have not been here before: ተዚህ ፡ ቀደም ፡ አልመጡም ። tḁzzíh qḁ́ddḁm almḁ́ṭṭum.

He is to go: ይሒድ ። yi̥hi̥d.

Didn't you know you were to go? መሔድህ ፡ አላወቅህም ። mḁhádi̥h alá͡uwωqhi̥m?

bead, s. (small) ሻሜ šám^{y}e.
(large) ዶቃ d^{w}ǒqã̄.

beam, s. (of light) ጭላንጭል č̣i̥lánč̣i̥l.
(of wood) ጠርብ ṭḁrb (ṭär-, -rẏ).
እንጨት (i̥)nč̣ät.
እንጬት (i̥)nč̣^{y}et.

bean, s. (broad, *Vicia faba*, Broun, Cat. 141) ባቄላ bā-q^{y}élã̄.
(*Phaseolus sp.*) አደንጓሬ adḁṅgwắr^{y}e (-dωṅ-).

bear, v.t. (carry) አነሣ anḁ́ssã̄.
(endure) ቻለ čắlḁ.
(children) ወለደች wḁ́llḁdäč (wắl-, wώl-; -čč § 6).
I can't bear it: አልችልም። alčí̥li̥m (§ 61*b*).

beard, s. ሪዝ rīz.
Š. ሸንጎበት šḁṅg^{w}óbḁt (-óẏ-, -ät).

beast, s. (wild) አርዌ áur^{y}e (§ 7*d*), pl. አራዊት arắwít (§ 8).
(horse, cattle, etc.) ከብት kḁẏt (kḁft).

beastly, adj. (repulsive) ጸያፍ ṣḁ́yyắf (ጠ- ṭḁ́-; § 8).

beat, v.t. ገረፈ gḁ́rrḁfḁ (gắr-).
መታ mḁ́ttã̄.
(in a game, case, etc.) [እ]ረታ (i̥)rḁ́ttã̄.
Don't beat him (it): አትምታው። attí̥mtau.

beaten, be, v.p. ተገረፈ tḁgḁ́rrḁfḁ (-gắr-).
ተመታ tḁmḁ́ttã̄.
(in a game, etc.) ተረታ tḁrḁ́ttã̄ (tär-).

beating, s. ግርፋት gí̥rfắṭ (§ 8).

beautiful, adj. ውብ wŭb (wŭẏ).
መልካም mḁ́lkắm, pl. also መልካካም mḁl-kắkắm (§ 8).

beauty, s. ውበት wŭ́bḁt (wŭ́-, -ẏḁ-, -ät, § 7*d*).

because, conj. ስለ- si̥lḁ- with simp. perf. or rel. + cont. (§ 48*a*).

I drink because I am thirsty : እጠጣለሁ ፡ ስለጠማኝ ። i̥ṭḁṭṭállḁu^{h} si̥lḁṭámmāñ (§ 63*d*).

He won't come because he won't know : አይመጣም ፡ ስለማያውቅ ። ḁimḁ́ṭām si̥lḁmmai̥áuq.

because of, prp. ስለ- si̥lḁ- (§ 47*a*).

Because of the rain : ስለዝናብ ፡ si̥lḁzi̥nā́ṿ (§ 8).

beckon, v.i. ጠቀሰ ṭáqqḁsḁ.

become, v.i. ሆነ h^{w}ṓnḁ.

bed, s. (-clothes) ምንጣፍ mi̥nṭáf (§ 8).

(-stead) አልጋ álgã.

In bed : ታልጋ ፡ tálga.

bed-curtain, s. አጎበር ag^{w}óbḁr (-óṿ-, -är).

bed-room, s. የምኝታ ፡ ቤት yämi̥ññi̥táb^{y}ēt (-ā́ṿ^{y}ē- ; § 70*b*).

He (it) is in his (the) bed-room : ተምኝታ ፡ ቤት ፡ ነው ። tḁmi̥ññi̥tāṿ^{y}ét (§ 8) nḁu.

bee, s. ንብ ni̥b (ni̥ṿ).

beef, s. የበሬ ፡ ሥጋ yäbḁ́r^{y}e (yäṿḁ́-) si̥gã.

beer, s. ጠላ ṭḁllã.

beeswax, s. የማር ፡ ሰም yämár sḁm.

beetle, s. እንዝዝ (i̥)nzi̥z.

ትንዚዛ ti̥nzízã.

before, adv. ከዚህ ፡ ፊት kḁzzíh (hḁ-, ተ- tḁ-, -äz-, -zi̥h ; § 46) fĩt (fi̥t ; § 47*b*).

ከዚህ ፡ ቀደም kḁzzíh (hḁ-, ተ- tḁ-, -äz-, -zi̥h ; § 46) qḁ́ddḁm.

ዱሮ dúr^{w}o.

Have they been here before? ተዚህ ፡ ፊት ፡ መጡ ። tḁzzíh fi̥t mḁ́ṭṭu?

before, conj. ስ- s(i̥)- with (§ 7*a*) neg. imperf. (§ 38), which loses its -ም -m. If the tense is to be specified it is done by the addition of other words.

Yesterday, before he came: ትናንት ፡ ሳይመጣ ፡ ti̥nánt sa͡i̥mḁ́ṭa.

To-morrow, before he comes: ነገ ፡ ሳይመጣ ፡ nágḁ sa͡i̥mḁ́ṭa.

Before you start(ed): ሳትነሣ ፡ sāttịnnássa.

How long will it be before you come? እስከስንት ፡ ዘመን ፡ ትመጣለህ ። i̥skḁsi̥nt zḁ́mḁn ti̥mḁṭállăh?

before, prp. (of time and place) በ-... ፡ ፊት bḁ-... fīt (fi̥t; § 8, § 47*b*).

ከ- (ተ-)... ፡ በፊት kḁ-(tḁ-)... bḁ́fīt (vḁ́-, -fi̥t; § 8, § 47*b*).

Before Monday: ተሰኞ ፡ በፊት ፡ tḁsḁ́ñño vḁ́fi̥t.

beg, v.i. & t. ለመነ lḁ́mmḁnḁ.

He begged for this: ይህንን ፡ ለመነ ። yi̥hánnän lḁ́mmḁnḁ.

Don't beg: አትለምን ። āttịlḁ́mmi̥n, pl. -ኑ ። -nu.

beggar, s. ለማኝ lḁ́mmáñ (-ññ § 6; § 8).

begin, v.i. & t. ጀመረ jḁ́mmḁrḁ (-mär-).

Where shall I begin? ተዬት ፡ ልጀምር ። tḁyét li̥jḁ́mmi̥r?

beginning, s. መጀመሪያ mḁjḁmmḁ́ryā̃ (-már-).

begun, be, v.p. (begin, v.i.) ተጀመረ tḁjḁ́mmḁrḁ (-mär-).

Where does it begin? ተዬት ፡ ይጀመራል ። tḁyét yi̥jjḁ́mmäräl?

behave, v.i. አደረገ adḁ́rrḁgḁ.

Don't behave in this way: እንዲህ ፡ አታድርግ ። ndíh attádri̥g, pl. -ጉ ። -gu.

behind, adv. በኋላ bḁhwālā̃ (bḁ͡uhá- § 7*d*).

He is behind: በኋላ ፡ ነው ። bḁ͡uhālá (§ 8) na͡u.

He has stopped behind: ቀርቷል ። qḁ́rtōāl, (from ቀረ qḁ́rrḁ § 42*b*).

behind, prp. ከ- (ተ-)... ፡ በኋላ kḁ- (tḁ-)... bḁhwā́lā̃ (yḁ-, -ḁuhā́-, § 7*d*; § 47*b*).

Behind the house: ከቤት ፡ በኋላ ፡ kḁyʸét yḁuhā́la.

beisa (*Oryx beisa*), s. ሳላ sā́lā̃.

belief, s. እምነት ḭmnḁt (-nät).

believe, v.i. & t. አመነ ámmḁnḁ.

ታመነ tā̃́mmḁnḁ (ger. & part. type B, § 35).

መሰለው mḁ́ssḁlḁu (impers. § 43*a*).

I believe you: አምንሃለሁ ፡፡ amnḭhállа̥uʰ.

I do not believe you: አላምንህም ፡፡ alámnḭhḭm.

Do you believe he came? ይመስልሃል ፡ የመጣ ፡፡ yḭmḁ́slḭhāl yämḁ́ṭṭḁ?

Do you believe he will come? ይመስልሃል ፡ እሚመጣ፡፡ yḭmḁ́slḭhāll (§ 6) ḭmmḭmḁ́ṭa?

believed, be, v.p. ታመነ tā̃́mmḁnḁ (ger. & part. type A, § 34).

bell, s. (small) ቃጭል qā́čḭl.

(large) ደወል dḁ́uḁl (dḁ́uωl).

bellow, v.i. አገሣ agḁ́ssā̃.

belly, s. ሆድ hʷō̥d.

below, adv. & prp. s.v. beneath.

belt, s. መታጠቂያ mḁttāṭḁqyā̃ (-ṭā́q-).

ድግ dḭg.

bend, v.i. (be bent, v.p.) ጠመመ ṭḁ́mmḁmḁ.

ታጠፈ tā́ṭṭḁfḁ.

(incline) ተዘቀዘቀ tḁzḁqḁ́zzḁqḁ.

bend, v.t. አጠመመ aṭḁ́mmḁmḁ.

አጠፈ ḁ́ṭṭḁfḁ.

(incline) ዘቀዘቀ zḁqḁ́zzḁqḁ.

beneath, adv. በታች bḁ́tā́č (-čč § 6; § 8).

beneath, prp. በ-...፡ ታች bḁ-... tāč (-čč § 6; § 8; § 47*b*).
ከ-[ተ-]...፡ ሥር kḁ- (tḁ-)... si̥r („ „).

bent, adj. ጠማማ ṭḁmámã.

Berebera ferruginea (Guidi, Vocab. p. 322), s. ብርብሬ bi̥rbí̥rrã (-ryí̥-).

beside, prp. (around) በ-...፡ አጠገብ bḁ-... aṭḁ́gḁb (-ḁy; § 47*b*).
(near to) ከ-[ተ-]...፡ ጥግ kḁ- (tḁ-)... ṭi̥gg (§ 8, § 47*b*).

besides, adv. ደግሞ dḁ́gm^{w}o (dǻg-).
ደሞ dḁ́mm^{w}o (dǻm-).
እዛወዲያ (i̥)z(z)á^{w}ωdyǻ (-zǻd-; § 8).

besides, prp. ከ-...፡ በቀር kḁ- (ተ- tḁ-)... bḁ́qḁr (yḁ́-; § 47*b*).
There are four besides this one: ተዚሀ፡ በቀር፡ አራት፡ አሉ። tāzzi̥h yḁ́qḁr arǻtt állu.

best, adj. የተሻለ yätḁšálḁ (-täš-).
የሚሻል yämmi̥ššál (እሚ- (i̥)mmi̥-).
See § 14.
What is the best thing for me to do? ምን፡ ባደርግ፡ ይሻላል። mi̥n bādǻrg yi̥ššālāl?

bet, s. ውርርድ wŭrḯrri̥d.

bet, v.i. & t. ተወራረደ tḁwḁrǻrrḁdḁ (tḁuḁ-, -ωrǻ-) constr. with በ- bḁ- (§ 47*a*).
How much will you bet? በስንት፡ ትወራረዳለህ። bḁsí̥nt ti̥wwḁrarrḁdállāh?
I bet 100 dollars he will come: በመምጣቱ፡ በመቶ፡ ብር፡ እወራረዳለሁ። bḁmḁmṭǻtu yḁmaṭ^{w}ó yi̥rr i̥wwωrarrḁdállḁu^{h}.

betray, v.t. ጠቈመ ṭḁ́qqwωmḁ (ṭώq-).

better, adv. ይበልጥ yi̥bálṭ (-i̥y-, -ál-) } (§ 58*c*) constr. with
ይሻል yi̥ššál } ከ- kḁ- (ተ- tḁ-, § 47*a*).

Can't you do better than that? ተዚህ፡ ይበልጥ፡ አትችልም፡ ታደርግ። tḁzzi̥h yi̥vḁlṭ atti̥čči̥li̥m tādárg?

Warrata rides better than Gabru: ወረታ፡ ተገብሩ፡ ይሻል፡ ይቀመጣል። wḁ́rrḁta tḁgḁ́vru yi̥ššāl yi̥qqḁ́mmḁṭāl.

better (=preferably)—use the jussive:

He (it) had better remain here: ይቀመጥ፡ እዚህ። yi̥qqḁ́mḁṭ í̥zzi̥h.

better (after illness) በጎ bḁ́ggʷo.

Are you better? እግዚአብሔር፡ ይማርህ፡ በጎ፡ ነህ። i̥gzi̥avhʸér yi̥mári̥h, vḁggʷó (§ 8) näh?, pol. እግዚአብሔር፡ ይማረዎ፡ በጎ፡ ነዎ። i̥gzi̥avhʸér yi̥márḁ͡ʷo, vḁggʷó nḁ͡ʷo? (lit. God have mercy on you, are you better?).

Yes, thanks: እግዚአብሔር፡ ይመስገን፡ በጎ፡ ነኝ። i̥gzi̥avhʸér yi̥mmḁ́sgḁn, vḁggʷó näñ (lit. God be praised, I am better).

better, be, v.i. (surpass) ተሻለ tḁšālḁ (täš-), constr. with ከ- kḁ- (ተ- tḁ-, § 47*a*).

(after illness) ተሻለው tḁšālḁ͡u (täš-; impers. § 43*a*; § 63*d*, *e*).

This is better than that: ይህ፡ ተዛያ፡ ይሻላል። yí̥he tḁzzyá yi̥ššālāl.

I am better to-day: ዛሬ፡ ይሻለኛል። zárʸe yi̥ššálḁññāl.

Is he better? ተሻሎታል። tā́ši̥lʷotāl?

better, get, (recover from illness), v.i. ዳነ dā́nḁ.

You will get better: ትድናለህ። ti̥di̥nállāh, pol. ይድናሉ። yi̥di̥nállu.

He will get better: ይድናል። yi̥dí̥nāl.

Did they get better? ዳኑ። dā́nu?

between, adv. በማሀል bḁmáhal.

It lies between : በማሀል ፡ ነው ። bḁmahál (§ 8) nḁ͡u.

between, prp. በ-…-ና ፡ በ-… ፡ ማሀል bḁ-…-nnā bḁ- (yḁ-)… máhal (§ 47*b*).

Between the river and the hill: በወንዙና ፡ በተራራው ፡ ማሀል ። bḁ͡uώnzunnā yḁtḁrāra͡u máhal.

beware, v.i. ተጠነቀቀ tḁṭḁnáqqḁqḁ.

Beware ! ተጠንቀቅ ። tḁṭḁ́ṅqḁq !, pl. -ቀቁ ። -qḁqu !

Let him beware : ይጠንቀቅ ። yi̥ṭṭḁ́ṅqḁq, pl. -ቀቁ ። -qḁqu.

beyond, adv. ወድያ wώdyā́ (§ 8).

beyond, prp. ከ- (ተ-)… ፡ ወድያ kḁ- (tḁ-)… wώdyā́ (§ 8, § 47*b*).

Beyond this: ተዚህ ፡ ወድያ ፡ tḁzzi̥h wώdya.

biassed, be, v.i. አደላ adḁ́llā̃ (-dā́l-).

Bible, s. ቅዱስ ፡ መጣፍ qi̥ddús mḁ́ṭā́f (§ 8).

biceps, s. (of arm) አይጥ áyi̥ṭ (á͡i̥ṭ).

(of thigh) ሹልዳ šulli̥dā̃ (-lŭ́d- ; § 52*a*, γ).

bifurcation of a road, s. መንታ mḁ́ntā̃.

big, adj. ትልቅ tí̥lli̥q.

bile, s. አሞት ámʷṓt (§ 8).

bill, s. እሳብ i̥sā́b (-ā́y ; § 8).

ቊጥር qwí̥ṭi̥r (-wṹṭ-).

bill-hook, s. መቊረጫ mḁqwŭrḁ́čā̃ (-rā́č-).

bind, v.t. (tie) አሰረ ássḁrḁ (-sär-).

(a book) ሸፈነ šḁ́ffḁnḁ (šā́f-).

bind-weed (*Convolvulus sp.*), s. አረግ árḁg.

bird, s. ዎፍ wōf (ʷōf).

birthday, s. (his) የተወለደበት ፡ ቀን ፡ yätḁuállḁdḁbbḁt (§ 8) qḁn.

(your) የተወለድህበት ፡ ቀን ፡ yätḁuállḁdhi̥bbḁt qḁn.

(your, pol.) የተወለዱበት ፡ ቀን ፡ yätḁuállḁdub-bḁ́t qḁn.

bit, s. (piece) ቁራጭ qúrrắč̣ (§ 8).
(of bridle) ልጓም lı̥́gwám (lū́gám § 7*d*; § 8).

bitch, s. [ሴት ፡]ውሻ (sʸēt § 54*b*) wū́ššā̃ (ʷúš-).
እንስት ፡ ውሻ i̥nı̥́st wū́ššā̃ (ʷúš-).

bite, v.i. & t. ነከሰ nắkkḁsḁ.

bite (be in the habit of biting), v.i. ተናከሰ tḁnắkkḁsḁ.
Does it (do they § 52*a*, δ) bite? ይናከሳሉዊ ፡፡ yi̥nnák-kḁsāllwı̥́? (s.v. -ዊ).
Don't let it get into the habit of biting: አይናከስ ፡፡ a͡i̥nnákḁs.
Biting flies: የሚናከስ ፡ ትንኝ ፡ yämmi̥nnákkḁs tı̥́ni̥ñ (§ 52*a*, δ).

bitten, be, v.p. ተነከሰ tḁnắkkḁsḁ.

bitter, adj. መራራ mḁrắrā̃.

black, adj. ጥቁር ṭū́qur.

blackberry (*Rubus sp.*), s. እንጆሪ (i̥)njʷóri.

blacksmith, s. ብረት ፡ ሰሪ bı̥́rḁt (-rät) sắri (sắr-).
ብረተኛ bi̥rḁtắññā̃ (-rätắñ-).

bladder, s. ፊኛ fı́ññā̃.

blanket, s. ምንጣፍ mı̥́nṭắf (§ 8).
የብርድ ፡ ልብስ yäbı̥́rdi̥ li̥bs (yävı̥́-, li̥vs).

bleat, v.i. ጮኸ č̣ʷóhḁ.

bled, be, v.p. ታገመ tắggḁmḁ.

bleed, v.i. ደማ dắmmā̃ (dắm-).

bleed, v.t. አገመ ággḁmḁ.

bleed at the nose, v.i. ነሰረው nắssḁra͡u (-sär-; impers. § 43*a*; § 63*d*, *e*).
My nose is bleeding: ነሰረኝ ፡፡ nắssäräñ.
I am subject to nose-bleeding: ይነስረኛል ፡፡ yi̥nắs-räññāl.

blind, adj. እውር ı̥́wwūr.
ዓይነ ፡ ስዉር á͡i̥nä sı̥́wwur (syū́wur).

blistered, be (become), v.i. አጐረበ agwórrḁbḁ (-ḁvḁ).

block, s. (wooden) ግንድ gi̥nd.
blood, s. ደም däm.
bloom, v.i. አበበ ábbḁbḁ (-ḁv̥ḁ).
blossom, s. አበባ ábḁbã (áv̥ḁv̥ã).
blotting-paper, s. ማድረቂያ ፡ ወረቀት ፡ mādrā́qya wḁ́rḁ-
qḁt.
blow, s. ምታት mi̥tā́t (§ 8).
blow, v.i. ነፈሰ nḁ́ffḁsḁ.
When it blows hard: ብዙ ፡ ሲነፍስ ፡ bi̥zu si̥nḁ́fs.
blow (on), v.t. እፍ፡ አለ i̥ff(i̥) ā́lḁ (s.v. √በለ, § 44*a*).
(an instrument) ነፋ nḁ́ffã.
Blow it (away): እፍ ፡ በለው ። i̥ffi̥ v̥ḁ́lḁu.
Blow the fire: እሳቱን፡ እፍ ፡ በለው ። i̥sátun i̥ffi̥ v̥ḁ́lḁu.
blows, come to, v.i. ተማታ tḁmā́ttã.
blue, adj. ሰማዊ sḁmáwi.
board, s. ጠርብ ṭḁrb (ṭär-, -rv̥).
እንጨት (i̥)nč̣ät.
እንጬት (i̥)nč̣^{y}et.
boast, v.i. ፎከረ fḁ́kkḁrḁ (-kär-).
boast (-ing), s. ፍከራ fi̥kkḁ́rã (-kā́r-).
boat, s. ጀልባ jálbã (-lv̥ã).
bodkin, s. መስፊያ mḁ́sfyã.
መስፌ mḁ́sf^{y}e.
መሰፈቻ mḁssḁffḁ́čã (-fā́č-).
body, s. (human) ገላ gḁ́lã.
ሰውነት sḁ́unnḁt (-nät).
(dead) በድን bḁ́di̥n (bā́d-; -i̥nn § 6).
bog, s. ጨቀጨቅ č̣áqḁč̣äq.

boil, s. (small) ብግር bí̥gi̥r (bŭ́gŭr).
(large) ብጕንጅ bŭ́gi̥nj (§ 7*d*).
This boil is not mature: ይሀ፡ ብጕንጅ፡ አልበሰለም። yí̥he yŭ́gi̥nj alyḁ́ssḁlḁm.
boil, v.i. ፈላ fḁ́llā̃.
When it boils: ሲፈላ፡ sifḁ́lā̃.
boil, v.t. (a liquid) አፈላ afḁ́llā̃.
(in a liquid) ቀቀለ qḁ́qqḁlḁ.
Boil some water: ውሃ፡ አፍላ። wŭ́ha áfla.
Boil the potatoes: ድንቹን፡ ቀቅለው። dí̥nni̥čun (§ 52*a*, δ) qḁ́qqi̥lḁu.
Boil it (water) and let it cool: አፍላውና፡ ይብረድ። āfláunnā yí̥yrḁd.
boiled, be, v.p. (in a liquid) ተቀቀለ tḁqḁ́qqḁlḁ.
Boiled water: የፈላ፡ ውሃ፡ yäfḁ́lla wŭ́ha (-láuha).
boiling, adj. ፍል fi̥l.
Boiling water: ፍል፡ ውሃ፡ fi̥l wŭ́ha.
bold, adj. ደፋር dḁ́ffā́r (§ 8).
bolt, v.i. ደነበረ dḁnḁ́bbḁrḁ (-bär-).
The mule has (mules have § 52*a*) bolted: በቅሎ፡ ደንብሯል። bḁ́ql^{w}o dā́mbi̥rōal (§ 7*d*).
bone, s. አጥንት ā́ti̥nt (§ 8, § 52*a*, γ).
ቅልጥም qí̥lti̥m (§ 52*a*, γ).
book, s. መጽሐፍ mḁ́s(i̥)hā́f (§ 8).
መጣፍ mḁ́tā́f (§ 8).
boot, s. ጃዝማ jā́zmā̃ (§ 52*a*, δ).
ጫማ čā́mmā̃ („).
These boots will not stand the stones: ይሀ፡ ጃዝማ፡ ደንጊያ፡ አይችልም። yí̥he jā́zma dā́ngya ai̥či̥li̥m.
Those others will: ያ፡ ይችላል። yā yi̥či̥lāl.
boot-lace, s. የጃዝማ፡ ማሰሪያ yäjā́zma māsḁ́ryā̃ (-sā́r-, -yä).
Borassus flabellifer (Broun, Cat. 599), s. ሰሌን sḁ́l^{y}én (§ 8).

bore (through), v.i. & t. ሰረሰረ sḁrḁ́ssḁrḁ (sär-, -särḁ).
bore (weary), v.t. አደከመ adắkkḁmḁ.
bore into, v.t. ፈለፈለ fḁlḁ́ffḁlḁ.
bored (through), be, v.p. ተሰረሰረ tḁsḁrḁ́ssḁrḁ (täsär-, -särḁ).
bored (wearied), be, v.i. & p. ደከመ dắkkḁmḁ (§ 63*d*, *e*).
ደከመው dắkkḁmḁu (impers. § 43*a* ; § 63*d*, *e*).
bored into, be, v.p. ተፈለፈለ tḁfḁlḁ́ffḁlḁ.
boring into, instrument for, s. መፈልፈያ mḁfḁlfḁ́yā̃ (-fäl-, -ạ̊ịā̃).
born, be, v.i. ተወለደ tḁwḁ́llḁdḁ (tḁuḁ́-, -ắl-, -ώl-).
borne, be, v.p. ተነሣ tḁnḁ́ssā̃.
borrow, v.i. & t. ተበደረ tḁbḁ́ddḁrḁ (tḁy-, -ắddärḁ).
Bos caffer œquinoctialis, s. ጎሽ gʷošš.
bosom, s. (breast) ደረት dḁ́rḁt.
(fold of dress) ጕስጓስ gwűsgwás (§ 8).
both, pron. ሁለት húlḁtt (-lätt).
Bring them both: ሁለቱን ፡ አምጣው ። hulḁ́ttun ánṭau (§ 7*d* ; § 52*a*, δ).
both...and, conj. ...-ም ፡ ...-ም ...-m(m) ...-m(m), (§ 6).
Is it (a shirt) called both ç̣ärq and qḁ́mīs? ጨርቅም ፡ ቀሚስም ፡ ይባላል ። ç̣ắrqi̥m qḁmísi̥m yi̥bbálāl?
bottle, s. ጠርሙዝ ṭḁ́rműz (ṭắr- ; § 8).
(small) ብልቃጥ bi̥lqắṭ (§ 8).
(not G.) ቃሮራ qārʷórā̃.
bottom, s. መሠረት mḁsḁ́rḁt (-särät ; § 8).
At the bottom: በታች ፡ bḁ́táč (-čč § 6 ; § 8).
bought, be, v.p. ተገዛ tḁgḁ́zzā̃.
bounce, v.i. ነጠረ nḁ́ṭṭḁrḁ (-ṭär-).
bound, s. (leap) ዝልያ zí̥llyā̃.
bound, v.i. (leap) ዘለለ zḁ́llḁlḁ.

bound, be, v.p. (tied) ታሰረ tássarḁ (-sär-).
(of a book) ተሸፈነ tḁšáffḁnḁ (-šáf-).
bow, s. (weapon) ደጋን dágán (§ 8).
bow, v.i. እጅ ፡ ነሣ i̥jj nḁ́ssã (to, ለ- lḁ- § 47*a*).
bowel, s. አንጀት ánjät (§ 52*a*, γ).
bowels, s. ሆድ ፡ እቃ hʷődi̥qã.
Are your bowels free? በጤናህ ፡ እዳሪ ፡ ትወጣለህ ፡፡ bḁtʸénāh i̥ddári ti̥wωṭállāh?, pol. በጤናዎ ፡ እዳሪ ፡ ይወጣሉ ፡፡ bḁtʸénaʷo ddári yuωṭállu?
bowl, s. ቅል qi̥l.
ፋጋ fágã.
box, s. ሳጥን sáṭi̥n.
boy, s. ልጅ li̥j.
(big) አሽከር áškḁr (-kär).
(small) ማሞ mámmʷo.
ጋሜ gámmʸe.
bracelet, s. አምባር ámbár (§ 8).
braces (pair of), s. መያዣ mḁyážã (mḁi̥á-).
brag, v.i. ፈከረ fḁ́kkḁrḁ (-kär-).
brag(-ging), s. ፍከራ fi̥kkḁ́rã (-kár-).
brain, s. አንጎል áṅgʷol.
bramble (*Rubus sp.*), s. እንጆሪ (i̥)njʷóri.
branch, s. ጫፍ č̣āf.
brandish, v.t. አወዛወዘ aụwωzáụwωzḁ.
brass, s. ነሐስ nḁ́hás (§ 8).
brave, adj. ጀግና jḁ́gnā (jág-).
bray, v.i. ጮኸ č̣ʷóhḁ.
Brayera anthelminthica, s. ኮሶ kʷósʷo.
bread, s. (α, made in European fashion) ቂጣ qi̥ṭṭã.
(„ „ „ , wheaten) ዳቦ dábbʷo.
(β, native) እንጀራ (i̥)njʸérã (-ጀ- -já-).
New bread: ለምለም ፡ ዳቦ ፡ lḁ́mlḁm dábbʷo.

breadth, s. ወርድ wḁrd (wωrd).
ስፋት sı̥fát (§ 8).

break, v.i. (be broken, v.p.) ተሰበረ tḁsḁ́bbḁrḁ (täs-, -bär-).
Take care it doesn't break: እንዳይሰበር። ndai̯ssḁ́b-bär.

break, v.t. ሰበረ sḁ́bbḁrḁ (-bär-).
(an animal) ገራ gḁ́rrã.
Have you broken it? ሰበርሀው። sḁ́bbärhḁu?, pl. ሰበራችሁት። sḁbbḁráččı̥hut?

break down, v.i. ደከመ dákkḁmḁ (§ 63*d*, *e*).
ደከመው dákkḁmḁu (impers. § 43*a*; § 63*d*, *e*).

break one's word, v.i. አበለ ábbḁlḁ.

breakfast, s. የቡን፡ ቁርስ yäbúnn (-äyú-) qurs.
After breakfast: ተቡን፡ ቁርስ፡ በኋላ፡ tḁyúnn (§ 70*b*) qurs yḁuhála (§ 7*d*).

breast, s. (chest) ደረት dḁ́rḁt.
(mamma) ጡት ṭut (§ 52*a*, γ).

breath, s. ትንፋሽ tı̥nfáš (-ı̥mf-; § 8).
He is out of breath: ልቡ፡ ወልቋል። lı̥bbu wωlqŏāl.

breathe, v.i. ተነፈሰ tḁnḁ́ffḁsḁ.

breeches, s. (Eur.) አጭር፡ በንጠሎን áčči̥r bḁnṭḁlʷőn (yḁ-).
(native) ሱሪ súrri.

breeching, s. (of pack-saddle) ወዶላ wωddʸéllã (ወ- wŭ-).

bribe, s. ጉቦ gúbbʷo.

brick, s. ጡብ ṭub (ṭuy).
አፈር áfḁr (áfär).
Let them make bricks: አፈር፡ ያንጡ። áfḁr (§ 52*a*, δ) yánni̥ṭu.

bridge, s. ድልድይ dı̥ldíy (§ 8).
He built a bridge: ድልድይ፡ ሰራ። di̥ldíy sḁ́rrā, or ድልድይ፡ ደለደለ። di̥ldíy dḁlḁ́ddḁlḁ.

bridle, s. ልጓም lí̥gwám (lŭgám § 7*d*; § 8).
Let him put a bridle on the horse: ፈረሱን ፡ ይለጒም ። fḁ́rḁsun yi̥lḁ́ggwŭm.
If it has a bridle on: ቢለጐም ፡ bi̥llḁ́ggwωm.
bridle, v.t. (an animal) ለጐመ lḁ́ggwωmḁ.
bridled, be, v.p. (of an animal) ተለጐመ tḁlḁ́ggwωmḁ.
brigand, s. ወንበዴ wωmbḁ́d^{y}e (§ 7*d*).
brigandage, s. ወንበዴነት wωmbḁdí̥nnḁt (-nät, § 7*d*).
bright, adj. ብራ bí̥rrā̃ (§ 57*b*, used only of weather).
That bright one: ያ ፡ የሚያበራው ፡ yā yämmyāṿḁ́rau.
Bright weather: ብራ ፡ bí̥rrā̃.
bright, be, v.i. አበራ abḁ́rrā̃ (aṿḁ́-).
brim, s. (of vessel) ከንፈር kḁ́nfḁr (-ḁ́mf-, -fär § 7*d*).
አፍ āf.
(of hat) ጆሮ j^{w}ór^{w}o.
Don't fill it up to the brim: እስታፉ ፡ አትሙላው ። i̥stáfu attí̥mlau.
A wide-brimmed hat: ትልቅ ፡ ጆሮ ፡ ያለው ፡ ባርኔታ ። tí̥lli̥q j^{w}ór^{w}o yállḁu ṿarnéta.
bring, v.t. አመጣ amḁ́ṭṭā̃.
(conduct) አደረሰ adḁ́rrḁsḁ.
Bring it: አምጣው ። ánṭau (§ 7*d*), pl. አምጡት ። án-ṭut.
Don't bring it: አታምጣው ። attánṭau, pl. አታምጡት ። attánṭut.
Bring a chair: ወምበር ፡ ይዘህ ፡ ና ። wómbḁr yi̥záh na, (s.v. ያዘ).
bring back, v.t. መለሰ mḁ́llḁsḁ.
Bring it back: መልሰው ። mállı̥sḁu, pl. -ሱት ። -sut.
bring near (-er), v.t. አቀረበ aqḁ́rrḁbḁ (-ḁṿḁ).
Bring it near (-er): አቅርበው ። áqi̥rṿḁu, pl. -ቡት ። -ṿut.

bring out, v.t. አወጣ awώṭṭã (a͡uώ-).

Bring it out: አውጣው። á͡uṭa͡u, pl. -ጡት። -ṭut.

bring up, v.t. (children) አሳደገ asáddḁgḁ.

brink, s. አፋፍ ā́fāf (§ 8).

brisk, adj. ንቁ ní̥qu.

(quick) ቀልጣፋ qḁlṭā́ffã.

briskness, s. ንቅነት ni̥qí̥nnḁt (-nät).

brittle, be (become), v.i. ኰሽ፡ አለ kwωšš ā́lḁ (s.v. √ባለ, § 44*a*).

It is brittle: ኰሽ፡ ይላል። kwωšš yi̥lāl.

broad, adj. ሰፊ sḁ́ffi.

ወርዳም wḁ́rdā́m (wώr-; § 8).

broad, be, v.i. ሰፋ sḁ́ffã.

broad-chested, adj. ደረታም dḁ́rḁtā́m (§ 8).

broken, adj. ሰባራ sḁbā́rã (-ḁyā́-).

broken, be (get), v.p. ተሰበረ tḁsḁ́bbḁrḁ (täs-, -bär-).

(of an animal) ተገራ tḁgḁ́rrã.

Take care the glasses (spectacles) don't get broken: መነጥር፡ እንዳይሰበር። mḁnḁ́ṭṭi̥r i̥nda͡i̥ssḁ́bbär.

bronchocele, s. እንቅርት (i̥)n̄qi̥rt.

broom, s. መጥረጊያ mḁṭrḁ́gyã.

broth, s. መረቅ mḁ́rḁq.

brother, s. ወንድም wώndi̥m (-mm § 6), pl. also ወንድማሞች wωndi̥mā́mʷōč (-čč § 6).

His brother: ወንድሙ፡ wώndi̥mmu.

brother-in-law, s. አማች ḁ̄́māč (§ 8).

brought, be, v.p. መጣ mḁ́ṭṭã (§ 23*a*).

brought, have (cause or allow to be), v.t. አስመጣ asmḁ́ṭṭã.

Please have (pol.) him (it) brought: እስቲ፡ ያስመጡት። i̥sti yasmḁ́ṭṭut.

I will have him (it) brought: አስመጣዋለኍ። as-mḁṭṭa͡uálla͡u^{h}.

brought up, be, v.p. አደገ áddḁgḁ.

Where were you brought up? የት፡ ነው፡ ያደግህበት። yēt nḁ͡u yáddḁghi̥bbät? (s.v. √ነ-).

brown, adj. ዳማ dā́mã.

Light brown, adj. ወይባ wώi̥bã (-i̥ỵã).

ቡላ búllã.

brush, s. (clothes-) መጥረጊያ mḁtrḁgyã.

(hair-) ማበጠሪያ mābạ̥ṭṭḁryã (-āỵḁ-, -äṭṭár-).

(tooth-) መፋቂያ mḁfā́qyã.

brush, v.t. ጠረገ ṭḁ́rrḁgḁ.

(hair) አበጠረ abḁ́ṭṭḁrḁ (aỵḁ́-, -ā́ṭṭär-).

brushed, be, v.p. ተጠረገ tḁṭḁ́rrḁgḁ.

Bubalis tora, s. ቶራ t^{w}ṓrã.

bucket, s. ጀርዳል járdäl.

(metal) ቈርቈሮ qwωrqwώrr^{w}o.

(دلو) መቅጃ mḁ́qjã.

buckle, s. መቈለፊያ mḁqwωllḁ́fyã (-láf-).

ቍልፍ qwŭlf.

buckle, v.i. (be buckled, v.p.) ተቈለፈ tḁqwώllḁfḁ.

buckle, v.t. ቈለፈ qwώllḁfḁ.

Bucorax abessinicus, s. እርኩም i̥rkúm (§ 8).

bud, v.i. በቀለ bḁ́qqḁlḁ (bā́q-).

buffalo (*Bos caffer æquinoctialis*), s. ጐሽ g^{w}ošš.

buffoon, s. አሥቂኝ ássi̥qiñ (-qi̥ñ; -ññ § 6).

bug (*Cimex sp.*), s. ትኋን ti̥hwán (túhán § 7*d*; § 8).

bugle, s. መለከት mḁ́lḁkḁt (§ 8).

Sound the bugle: መለከት፡ ንፋ። mḁ́lḁkḁt ni̥fa.

bugler, s. መለከተኛ mḁlḁkḁtḁ́ññã (-táñ-).

build, v.i. & t. ሰራ s̥árrā̃ (sắr-).
bull, s. በሬ b̥áry̆e.
bull̥ace (*Prunus insititia*), s. እንኰይ (i̥)ṅkwḁi̥.
bullet, s. [እ]ርሳስ (i̥)rsás (§ 8).
bunch, s. ስብሳቢ si̥bsábi (si̥v̥s-, -ấv̥i).
bundle, s. እስር i̥si̥r.
ሸክም šák̥i̥m (šák-).
Buphaga erythrorhynchus (Guidi, Vocab. p. 441), s. አሪጭ ấräç̣.
burden, s. ሸክም šák̥i̥m (šák-).
buried, be̥, v.p. ተቀበረ tḁqáb̥barḁ (-bär-).
burn, v.i. (be burnt, v.p.) ተቃጠለ tḁqắṭṭḁlḁ.
ነደደ nád̥dad̥ḁ.
(be hot) ተኰሰ tákkwωsḁ (tώkkosḁ).
burn, v.t. አቃጠለ aq(q)ắṭṭḁlḁ.
(scorch, sting) ተኰሰ tákkwωsḁ (tώkkosḁ).
Burn it: አቃጥለው። aqqáṭlḁu, pl. -ሉት። -lut.
Burnt ground (i.e. of which the vegetation has been burnt, حريقه): ትኳሾ tŭkkwášʷo.
burst, v.i. (be burst, v.p.) ተሰነጠቀ tḁsḁnḁ́ṭṭḁqḁ (täsän-).
ፈነዳ fḁnáddā̃.
burst (cause to), v.t. ሰነጠቀ sḁnḁ́ṭṭḁqḁ.
አፈነዳ afḁnḁ́ddā̃.
bury, v.t. ቀበረ qáb̥barḁ (-bär-).
bush, s. (shrub) ቍጥቋጦ qwŭṭqwáṭʷo.
(jungle) በረሃ bárḁhā̃.
bushbuck (*Tragelaphus scriptus decula*), s. ዱኩላ dukkwŭlā̃.
bushel, s. ማድጋ mādi̥ggā̃.
bush-fire, s. ቋያ qwáyyā̃.

business, s. (affair) ጕዳይ gwi̥ddá͡i̥ (gwúd-, gúd-; § 8).
(trade) ንግድ ni̥gd.

busy, be, v.i. ሰራ sḁrrã (sár-).

I am busy: እሰራለኹ ። i̥särállḁ͡uʰ.

When I am busy: ስሰራ ፡ si̥sára.

If he is not busy let him come: ስራ ፡ እንደሌለው ፡ ይምጣ ። si̥ra ndḁlʸállḁ͡u yi̥mṭa.

but, conj. ግን gi̥n (may come second in its clause, § 75; § 8).

ነገር ፡ ግን nḁgár (-gár) gi̥n.

It is very nice, but it spoils my teeth: እጅግ ፡ ማለፊያ ፡ ነው ፡ ጥርሴን ፡ ግን ፡ ያበላሻል ። íjji̥g māläfyá nḁ͡u, ṭi̥rsʸén gi̥n yābbḁláššāl, or ...ነው ፡ ግን ፡ ጥርሴን ፡... nḁ͡u, gi̥n ṭi̥rsʸen etc.

When the second of two clauses is introduced by 'but,' the former may take -ስ -s, -ss:

There is hot water but no tea: ፍል ፡ ውሃስ ፡ አለ ፡ ሻይ ፡ የለም ። fi̥l wúhass állä, šá͡i̥ yálläm.

When 'but' is connective rather than adversative it is usually not rendered:

I told him, but he said nothing: ነገርሁት ፡ ዝም ፡ አለ ። nággärhut, zi̥mm álḁ.

butcher, s. ሥጋ ፡ ሻጭ si̥gáššáč̣ (§ 8), pl. ሥጋ ፡ ሻጮች si̥ga-šáč̣ʷōč (-čč § 6).

butler, s. አጋፋሪ aggafári.

butt, s. (of a gun) ሰደፍ sḁdḁf.

butt, v.i. ወጋ wóggã (ʷóg-).
(habitually) ተዋጋ tḁwággã (tḁ͡uá-).

butter, s. ቅቤ qi̥bʸe (qi̥ẏʸe).

buttercup (*Ranunculus sp.*), s. የውሃ ፡ በርበሬ yá͡uha bḁr-bḁ́rʸe (ẏärẏár-).

butterfly, s. ብራብሪት bi̥rrábi̥rit (-ā́yi̥-; gen. f.; § 52a, δ).

buttock, s. ቂጥ qi̥ṭ (§ 52a, γ).

button, s. ቍልፍ qwŭlf.

button, v.i. (be buttoned, v.p.) ተቈለፈ tḁqwώllḁfḁ.

button, v.t. ቈለፈ qwώllḁfḁ.

button-hole, s. የቍልፍ ፡ ቀዳዳ yäqwŭ́lf qḁdā́dã.

የቍልፍ ፡ ጒድጓድ yäqwŭ́lf gúdgwā́d (-úrgw- § 7d; § 8).

button-hook, s. መቈለፊያ mḁqwωllḁ́fyã (-lā́f-).

buy, v.i. & t. ገዛ gḁ́zzã.

All right, I will buy it (them § 61b): እሺ ፡ እገዛለኍ ። í̥šši̥, i̥gḁzállḁu͡ʰ.

Well, I shall not buy it (them): እንኳን ፡ አልገዛም ። ńkwān, algḁ́zām.

Don't buy it: አትግዛው ። attí̥gza͡u̥.

Buy it for me: ግዛልኝ ። gí̥zalli̥ñ.

If he had brought it I should have bought it: አምጥቶት ፡ ቢሆን ፡ ገዛሁ ፡ ነበር ። ámtị̥tʷot yị̥́hʷon, gḁ́zza͡uʰ (§ 7d) nḁ́bbḁr (cp. § 81d).

by, prp. በ- bḁ-.

It is sold by weight: በሚዛን ፡ ይሸጣል ። bḁmīzā́n yi̥ššā́ṭāl.

They (will) work by time: በጊዜ ፡ ይሰራሉ ። bḁgí̥zʸe yi̥sḁrállu.

Let him travel by night: ሌሊት ፡ ይሒድ ። lʸēlít yí̥hi̥d.

by, prp. (agent) በ- … ፡ እጅ bḁ-… i̥jj.

By whom was it built? በማን ፡ እጅ ፡ ተሰራ ። bḁmā́nn i̥jj tḁsḁ́rra?

C

§ *refers to the paragraphs of the Grammar* (*Initia Amharica, Part I.*)

cage, s. ማጥመጃ māṭmḁjã (-mḁ́j-).
ቤት bʸēt.

calculate, v.i. & t. ቈጠረ qwώṭṭḁrḁ (-ṭär-).

calculated, be, v.p. ተቈጠረ tḁqwώṭṭḁrḁ (-ṭär-).

calculation, s. ቍጥር qwí̥ṭi̥r (-wŭ́ṭ-).

calendar:—

The Abyssinian year has 12 months of 30 days and 1 of 5 days.

Sep. 11th—Oct. 10th መስከረም mḁskḁ́rḁm (-kắr-).
Oct. 11th—Nov. 9th ጥቅምት ṭí̥qi̥mt (§ 8).
Nov. 10th—Dec. 9th ሕዳር hí̥dắr (§ 8).
Dec. 10th—Jan. 8th ታኅሣሥ tḁ́sắs (tắs-, tí̥s-; § 8).
Jan. 9th—Feb. 7th ጥር ṭi̥rr (ṭḁrr § 7*d*).
Feb. 8th—Mar. 9th የካቲት yäk(k)átit.
Mar. 10th—Apr. 8th መጋቢት mḁggábit (-áỵi-, -ỵʸi̥t).
Apr. 9th—May 8th ማዝያ mázyã.
May 9th—June 7th ግንቦት gí̥nbʷŏ́t (gwí̥n-, gwŭ́n-, -nỵʷŏ́-, -ỵḁt; § 8).
June 8th—July 7th ሰኔ sḁ́nʸe (sắn-).
July 8th—Aug. 6th ሐምሌ hắmlʸe (ắm-).
Aug. 7th—Sep. 5th ነሐሴ nḁhắsʸe.
Sep. 6th—10th ቋግሜ qwágmʸe.

The year begins on 1st mḁskḁ́rḁm = Sep. 11th, and is then 7 years behind the European date; on and after 23rd tḁ́sās = Jan. 1st up till 5th qwágmʸe = Sep. 10th it is 8 years behind:

Dec. 31st, 1908 = 22nd tḁ́sās, 1901.
Jan. 1st, 1909 = 23rd tḁ́sās, 1901.
Feb. 28th, 1909 = 21st yäkkā́tit, 1901.
Mar. 1st, 1909 = 22nd yäkkā́tit, 1901.

As with us, every 4th year is leap-year, when qwā́gm^{y}e receives a 6th day.

This 6th qwā́gm^{y}e = Sep. 11th in the (European) year preceding our leap-year; and mḁskḁ́rḁm and its successors up to ṭḁrr then begin and end and yäkkā́tit begins a day later than the corresponding dates given above, till Feb. 29th = 21st yäkkā́tit, which restores the correspondence:

Dec. 31st, 1907 = 21st tḁ́sās, 1900.
Jan. 1st, 1908 = 22nd tḁ́sās, 1900.
Feb. 28th, 1908 = 20th yäkkā́tit, 1900.
Feb. 29th, 1908 = 21st yäkkā́tit, 1900.
Mar. 1st, 1908 = 22nd yäkkā́tit, 1900.

The omission of leap-year in 1900 was not made in the Abyssinian calendar: so that in translating a date in the last century the European dates given above must be put back a day, mḁskḁ́rḁm being Sep. 10th—Oct. 9th, etc.

calf, s. (very young) እምቦሳ (i̥)mb^{w}óssā̃.
(during first year) ጥጃ ṭí̥jjā̃.
(of leg) ባት bāt (§ 52*a*, γ).
ፈርስ fḁrs (färs; § 52*a*, γ).

calico, s. አቡ ፡ ጀዲድ ábu (áy̥u) jädíd.

call, v.i. & t. (summon) ጠራ ṭḁ́rrā̃.
See √በለ (§ 44*a*).
(wake) አስነሣ asnḁ́ssā̃.
(designate) አለ álḁ (√በለ).

Call him: ጥራው ። ṭí̥rau, or ና ፡ በለው ። nā yḁ́lḁu.

Call them: ጥሩቸው ። ṭi̥ráčča͡u, or ኑ ፡ በሏቸው ። nu ṿḁláčča͡u.

Call me early: ጧት ፡ አስነሣኝ ። ṭwāt asnḁ́ssāñ.

Don't call me: አታስነሣኝ ። attāsnḁ́ssāñ.

called, be, v.p. (summoned) ተጠራ tḁṭḁ́rrã.

(named) ተበለ tḁbálḁ (-ḁṿá-).

What is it called? ምን ፡ ይበላል ። mi̥n yi̥bbálāl?

callosity (hardened or thickened skin), s. ጉብር gúbbi̥r.

calm, adj. (of water and persons) [እ]ርጉ ri̥gu (i̥rgu).

(of persons) ዝግተኛ zi̥ggi̥tḁ́ññã (-táñ-).

calm, be (become), v.i. (of water and persons) [እ]ረጋ (i̥)rḁ́ggã.

(of persons) ዝግ ፡ አለ zi̥gg álḁ.

calmness, s. (of water and persons) [እ]ርጋት ri̥gát (i̥rg-; § 8).

(of persons) ዝግታ zi̥ggi̥tã (§ 8).

camel, s. ግመል gi̥mḁl (-mäl).

camp, s. ሰፈር sḁ́fḁr (-fär).

camp-bedstead, s. የመንገድ ፡ አልጋ yämḁ́ngḁd álgã.

camping-ground, s. መሳፈርያ mḁssāf(f)ḁ́ryã (-fár-).

መሰፋፈርያ mḁssḁfāf(f)ḁ́ryã (-fár-).

can, s. ታኒካ tánikã.

can, v.i. ቻለ čálḁ.

ተቻለው tḁčálḁ͡u (impers. § 43*a*).

Can they come? ችለው ፡ ይመጣሉ ። či̥lḁ͡u (ger.) yi̥mḁṭállu?

If I can: ብችል ፡ bi̥či̥l.

If you can: ብትችል ፡ bi̥tti̥či̥l, pol. ቢችሉ ፡ biči̥lu, pl. ብትችሉ ፡ bi̥tti̥či̥lu.

I can't open the door: መዝጊያውን ፡ መክፈት ፡ አይቻለኝም ። mázgya͡un mḁ́kfḁt a͡i̥ččáläññi̥m.

He (it) can't get out: መውጪ ፡ የለውም ። m̥ắuc̣a yắll̥aum.

One cannot make it reach (so far): አልደርስም ፡ አለ ። aldắrsịmm ā́l̥a (s.v. √በለ, § 44*a*).

cancel, v.t. አፈረሰ afắrr̥as̥ḁ.

cancelled, be, v.p. ፈረሰ fắrr̥as̥ḁ.

The agreement is cancelled: ውል ፡ ፈርሷል ። wŭl fắrsŏā̂l.

candle, s. ሰም s̥am.

ጧፍ ṭwāf.

(lighted) ማብሪያ mā́bryā̃ (-ā́ỵr-).

መብራት m̥ā́brā́t (-ḁ̄́ỵr- ; § 8).

Have you any candles? ሰም ፡ አለህ ። s̥am állāh?

Bring a candle: ማብሪያ ፡ አምጣ ። mā́ỵrya ánṭa (§ 7*d*).

cane, s. ሸምበቆ š̥ambḁ̄́qq^wo.

Canis simensis (Guidi, Vocab. p. 276), s. ቀበሮ qḁ̄́bar̥^wo (ቃ- qá-, -ỵḁ-, -är-).

canister, s. ታኒካ tā̃́nikā̃.

cannon, s. መድፍ m̥adf (m̥arf § 7*d*).

canopy, s. አጎበር ag^wóbar̥ (-óỵḁ-, -är).

canter, s. ደንገላሳ d̥aṅg̥alā́sā̃.

canter, v.i. ደንገላሳ ፡ ሔደ d̥aṅg̥alā́sa hā̆́dä.

canvas, s. ሸራ š̥ā́rā̃ (šā́rā̃).

cap, s. ቆብ q^wōb (q^wōỵ).

capital, adj. ድንቅ di̥ṅq.

capon, s. ሙክት ፡ [ዶሮ] múkki̥t (d^wór^wo).

Capparis tomentosa (Broun, Cat. 28), s. ገመሮ gḁ̄́mar̥^wo (-mär-).

Capra vali or *walie*, s. ዋልያ wā́lyā̃.

Capsicum annuum (Broun, Cat. 391), s. በርበሬ bar̥bḁ̄́r^ye (bär-, -rỵḁ̄́-, -ā́r^ye).

capture, v.t. ያዘ yázḁ.

(in war) ማረከ mā́rrḁkḁ.

captured, be, v.p. ተያዘ tḁyā́zḁ (tḁi̥á-).

(in war) ተማረከ tḁmā́rrḁkḁ.

Carduus sp. ያህያ ፡ ሾህ yahī́yya šʷoh.

caravan, s. ጓዝ gwāz.

caravan, start one's, v.i. ተጓዘ tḁgwā́zḁ.

care, s. አሳብ ás(s)ā́b (-ā́ỵ; § 8).

He has no cares: አሳብ ፡ የለውም ። assā́ỵ yállḁum.

care, take, v.i. አስተዋለ astḁwā́la (-ḁuá-).

(of, v.t.) ጠበቀ ṭḁ́bbḁqḁ.

(of oneself, v.r.) ተጠነቀቀ tḁṭḁnḁ́qqḁqḁ.

Take care! (Look out! Mind!): ተጠንቀቅ ። tḁṭḁ́n-qḁq! pl. -ቀቁ ። -qḁqu!

Take care of him (it): ጠብቀው ። ṭḁ́bbi̥qḁu.

'Take care' may be expressed by እንድ- (i̥)nd- and the neg. imperf. (§ 38):

Take care it doesn't fall: እንዳይወድቅ ። ndai̥wώdĭ̥q.

careful, adj. አስተዋይ astḁ́wā́i̥ (-tḁ́uā́i̥; -ā́yy § 6; § 8).

carefully, adv.—use ger. of አስተዋለ:

Carry (lift) him (it) carefully: አስተውለህ ፡ አንሣው ። astḁ́uläh ánsau.

caress, v.t. አቈላመጠ aqqwωlā́mmḁṭḁ.

Carissa edulis (Broun, Cat. 337), s. አጋም ágam.

carpenter, s. ጠራቢ ṭḁrā́bi (-ā́ṿi).

አናጢ an(n)ā́ṭi.

carpet, s. ሰጋጃ si̥gā́jjã.

carriage, s. ሠረገላ si̥rḁgḁ́llã (ሥ- sä-).

carried, be, v.p. ተነሣ tḁnḁ́ssã.

carried away, be, v.p. (removed) ተወሰደ tḁwḁ́ssḁdḁ (tḁuḁ́-, -ώs-).

carried off, be, v.p. (by force) ተቀማ tḁqḁ́mmā̃.
carrion, s. ጥምብ tḁimb.
carry, v.i. & t. አነሣ anḁ́ssā̃.
ቻለ čálḁ.
(on animals) ጫነ č̣ā́nḁ.
How much does this mule carry? ይህ፡ በቅሎ፡ ስንት፡ ይችላል፡፡ yḁ́he yḁ́qlʷo sḁint yḁičḁ́lāl?
This one can't carry anything: ይህ፡ አያነሣም፡፡ yḁ́he a͡iḁanḁ́sām (§ 63c).
What are you (pl.) carrying (on your animals)? ምን፡ ጭናችኋል፡፡ mḁin č̣ḁinā́ččyuhāl?
carry away, v.t. (remove) ወሰደ wḁ́ssḁdḁ (wώs-).
carry off, v.t. (by force) ቀማ qḁ́mmā̃.
cart, s. ሥረገላ sḁirḁgḁ́llā̃ (ሠ- sä-).
cartridge, s. ጥይት ṭíyyḁit (ṭḁ́y-).
carve, v.i. & t. (wood, etc.) ጠረበ ṭḁ́rrḁbḁ (-ḁyḁ).
አነጠ ánnḁṭḁ.
(meat) ቈረጠ qwώrrḁṭḁ.
case, s. (receptacle) ቤት bʸēt.
ሳጥን sā́ṭḁin.
(legal) ሙግት múggḁit.
cast-off, adj. ውራጅ wǘrrā́j (§ 8).
castor-oil plant (*Ricinus communis*, Broun, Cat. 528), s. ጒልቋ gwǘlqwā̃.
castrated, adj. (of calf, goat, ram, or cock) ሙኪት múkkḁit.
cat, s. ድመት dḁ́mmḁt (-mät).
cat, interj. to call a, ኡር urrr!
— to silence or drive it away, ክፍ kḁiff!
catch, v.t. ያዘ yā́zḁ (§ 44c).
Catch him (it): ያዘው፡፡ yā́zḁ͡u, pl. -ዙት፡፡ -zut.
caterpillar, s. የጕመን፡ ትል yägwώmmā́n (§ 8) tḁil.
የቅጠል፡ ትል yäqḁiṭḁ́l (-ṭā́l) tḁil.
(hirsute) አባ፡ ጨጓሬ ábba č̣ḁggwā́rʸe.

cattle, s. ከብት kḁỵt (kḁḟt § 7*d*).

cattle-plague, s. የከብት፡ በሽታ yäkḁ́ḟt ỵḁ́ši̥tã.

cause, s. ምክንያት mí̥knyát (§ 8).

Without cause: ያለምክንያት፡ yālḁmí̥knyāt.

cause, v.t.—use causatives in አ- a- and አስ- as- (§ 22*a*).

cautious, adj. አስተዋይ astḁ́wá͡i̥ (-ḁ́͡uá͡i̥; -áyy § 6; § 8).

cautious, be, v.i. አስተዋለ astḁwálḁ (-ḁ͡uá-).

cautiously, adv.—use ger. of አስተዋለ:

Let him go cautiously: አስተውሎ፡ ይሒድ። astḁ́͡ulʷo yí̥hi̥d, pl. -ለው፡ ይሒዱ። -lḁ͡u yí̥hi̥du.

cavalry, s. ፈረሰኛ fḁrḁsḁ́ññã (-sáñ-; § 52*a*, δ).

cave, s. ዋሻ wáššã.

centipede, s. አምሳግር amsági̥r.

central, adj. ማሀለኛ mahalḁ́ññã (-láñ-).

centre, s. ማሀል máhal.

Cephalophus abessinicus, s. ምዳቋ mi̥dáqqwã.

certainly! interj. እሺ í̥šši! (-ši̥).

በጀ bḁ́jjä! (báj-).

(=I agree) ምን፡ ከፋኝ። mi̥ṅ kḁ́ffañ?

ምን፡ ቸገረኝ። mi̥n čággḁräñ?

cerumen, s. ኩክ kukk.

Cervicapra bohor, s. ቦሀር bʷóhḁr (-hωr).

chain, s. ሰንሰለት sḁnsḁ́lḁt (-lät; § 8).

chain (up), v.t. (put in chains) አሰረ ássḁrḁ (-sär-).

The Rās put him in chains: ራስ፡ አሰሩት። rās ássḁrut.

chained (up), be, v.p. (chains, be in, v.i.) ታሰረ tássḁrḁ (-sär-; § 63*d, e*).

He is in chains: ታስሯል። tásrŏ͡āl.

chair, s. ወምበር wómbḁr (-bär).

Bring a chair: ወምበር፡ አምጣ። wómbḁr ánṭa (7*d*).

chamber, s. (room) ቤት bʸēt.

ቅርጥ qi̥rṭ.

እልፍኝ i̥lfi̥ñ (-ññ § 6; § 8).

chamber-pot, s. መሻኛ mḁšḁ́ñã (-šáñ-).

ባሬታ bārʸétã.

(euphem.) መክፈያ mḁkfḁ́yã (-fḁ́i̥ã).

change, s. (alteration) ለውጥ lḁ́uṭ.

(small money) ምንዛሬ mi̥nzárʸe.

መሐለቅ mḁhállḁq.

change, v.i. (be changed, v.p.) ተለወጠ tḁlḁ́uwḁṭḁ.

change, v.t. ለወጠ lḁ́uwḁṭḁ.

(money) መነዘረ mḁnḁ́zzḁrḁ (-zär-).

Go and change this gold: ሒድ፡ ይህን፡ ወርቅ፡ መንዝር። hi̥d, yi̥hán wωrq mḁ́nzi̥r.

changed, be, v.p. (money) ተመነዘረ tḁmḁnḁ́zzḁrḁ (-zär-).

channel for irrigation (جدول), s. መስኖ mḁ́snʷo.

ቦይ bʷói̥.

ፈሰስ fḁ́sḁs.

chapter, s. ምዕራፍ mi̥ráf (§ 8).

character, s. (nature) ባሕሪ báhri (bhári § 7*d*).

(statement of qualifications) ምስክር mi̥si̥k-ki̥r.

I have written you a good character: ምስጋና፡ ጣፍሁልህ። mi̥sgána ṭáfhulli̥h.

charcoal, s. ከሰል kḁ́sḁl.

charge, s. (accusation) ክስ ki̥ss.

(price) ዋጋ wágã.

(for hire) ኪራይ ki̥rái̥ (§ 8).

charge, v.t. (accuse) ከሰሰ kḁ́ssḁsḁ.
(a price) ፈለገ fḁ́llḁgḁ.
charged, be, v.p. (accused) ተከሰሰ tḁkḁ́ssḁsḁ.
(a price) ተፈለገ tḁfḁ́llḁgḁ.
charm, s. (talisman) ጠልሰም ṭḁ́lsḁm.
chat, s. ጨዋታ č̣ḁ͡uā́tā̃.
ወግ wωg.
chat, v.i. ተጫወተ tḁč̣á͡uwḁtḁ (-wωtḁ).
chat with, v.t. አጫወተ ač̣č̣á͡uwḁtḁ (-wωtḁ).
cheap, adj. (እ)ርክሽ rí̥kkắš (i̥rkkắš; § 8).
cheat, s. ቀጣፊ qḁṭáfi.
cheat, v.i. & t. ቀጠፈ qḁ́ṭṭḁfḁ.
አታለለ attā́llḁlḁ.
አሞኘ amʷóññä.
cheated, be, v.p. ተቀጠፈ tḁqḁ́ṭṭḁfḁ.
ተታለለ tḁtā́llḁlḁ.
cheating, s. ቅጥፈት qí̥ṭfḁt (-fät).
ቅጥፍና qi̥ṭfí̥nnā̃.
cheek, s. ጕንጭ gwŭnč̣ (§ 52*a*, γ).
cheese, s. [እ]ርጎ rí̥gʷo (i̥rg-).
አይብ á͡i̥b (á͡i̥y̥).
Chelonia sp., s. ኤሊ ʸéli.
chess, s. ሰንጠረጅ sḁnṭḁ́rḁj (-ṭắr-).
chest, s. (box) ሳጥን sā́ṭi̥n.
(thorax) ደረት dḁ́rḁt.
(of animals) ፍርንብያ fi̥rí̥mbā̃.
His (man's, horse's) chest is too narrow: ደረቱ ፡ ጠባብ ፡ ነው ። dḁ́rḁtu ṭḁbbắy̥ nḁ͡u.
chicken, s. (young) ጫጩት č̣ắč̣ŭt (-ắyŭ- § 7*d*).
(older) ቄብ ፡ ዶሮ qʸēb (qʸēy̥) dʷórʷo.

chick-pea (*Cicer arietinum,* Broun, Cat. 140), s. ሽምብራ ši̥mbí̥rā̃.

chief, s. አለቃ álḁqā̃.

ሹም šum, pl. also ሹማምት šumámi̥t.

ዓይነተኛ a͡i̥nḁtḁ́ññā̃ (-nät-, -táñ-).

(local, village) ጭቃ፡ ሹም či̥qá šum, often abbr. to ጭቃ čí̥qā̃.

(local, district) ምስለኔ mi̥slḁ́nʸe (-lán-).

Where is the chief's house? የሹሙ፡ ቤት፡ ዬት፡ ነው። yäšúmu yʸēt yēt nḁ͡u?

child, s. ልጅ li̥j.

ጉብል gúbi̥l (-úvi̥-).

(small) ጨቅላ čáqlā̃.

How many children has she? ስንት፡ ልጅ፡ አላት። si̥nt li̥j állāt?

How many children has she had? ስንት፡ ወለደች። si̥nt wállḁdāč?

childhood, s. ልጅነት li̥jí̥nnḁt (-nät).

childless, adj. መሃን mḁhán (§ 8).

children, interj. to silence, እሽ i̥šš!

chin, s. አገጭ ágḁč (-gäč).

ሸንጎበት šḁngʷóbḁt (-óv-, -ät).

chip, s. ፍላጭ fi̥lláč (§ 8).

chisel, s. መሮ mḁrʷo.

choose, v.i. & t. (select) መረጠ mḁ́rrḁṭḁ.

(prefer) ወደደ wóddadḁ.

Choose as you please: እንደፍቃድህ፡ ምረጥ። ndäfi̥qā́di̥h mí̥rḁṭ, (pol.) እንደፍቃደዎ፡ ይምረጡ። ndäfi̥qā́dḁ͡wo yí̥mrḁṭu.

chosen, be, v.p. ተመረጠ tḁmḁ́rrḁṭḁ.

Christian, s. ክርስቲያን krí̥styán (§ 8).

Christmas, s. ልደት lí̥dḁt (-dät).

church, s. ቤተ ፡ ክርስቲያን bʸētḁkrįstyán (bḁtḁ́skyā́n ; § 8).
ደብር dā́bi̥r, pl. also አድባር ádbā́r (-dy̥ā́- ; § 8) and አድባራት adbā́rā́t (-dy̥ā́- ; § 8).

Ciconia Abdimii (Guidi, Vocab. p. 205), s. ሸመላ ši̥mā́lā̃.

cigar, s. የተጠቀለለ ፡ ትምባኾ ፡ yätḁtḁqḁ́llalḁ ti̥mbḁ́uhā̃ (§ 7*d*, tŭm-, -bṓhā̃).

cigarette, s. በወረቀት ፡ የተጠቀለለ ፡ ትምባኾ ፡ bḁuḁ́rḁqḁt yätḁtḁqḁ́llalḁ ti̥mbḁ́uhā̃ (§ 7*d*, etc.).

circle, s. መክበብ mḁ́kbḁb (-ky̥ay̥).

circular, adj. ክብ ki̥bb.

circumcise, v.t. ገረዘ gḁ́rrḁzḁ.

circumcised, be, v.p. ተገረዘ tḁgḁ́rrḁzḁ.

circumference, s. ዙርያ zúryā̃.

What is its circumference? ዙርያው ፡ ስንት ፡ ነው ። zúryau sí̥nti̥ nḁu?

civet cat (*Viverra civetta*), s. ዝባድ zí̥bā́d (-í̥yā́- ; § 8).
ጥርኝ ṭi̥rí̥ñ (-ññ § 6 ; § 8).

civilised, be, v.i. ቀና qḁ́nnā̃.

clarified, be (become), v.i. ነጠረ nḁ́ṭṭḁrḁ (-ṭär-).

clarionet, s. እንቢልታ (i̥)mbí̥ltā̃ (§ 7*d*).

clatter, v.i. (of persons) አንኳኳ aṅkwā́kkwā̃.
(of things) ኳ ፡ አለ kwa ā́lḁ (s.v. √በለ, § 44*a*).

Don't let the things clatter: እቃ ፡ ኳ ፡ አይበል ። í̥qā kwa ḁ́iy̥ḁl.

claw, s. ጥፍር ṭí̥fi̥r (§ 52*a*, γ).

clean, adj. ንጡሕ ní̥ṭuh.

clean, v.t. ጠረገ ṭḁ́rrḁgḁ.
(by wiping) ወለወለ wḁlḁ́uwḁlḁ.
(purify) አጠራ aṭḁ́rrā̃.
(the teeth) ሟጨ mwā́č̣č̣ä.

Clean it: ጥረገው ። ṭí̥rḁgḁu, (ወልውለው ። wḁ́lwŭlḁu, አጥራው ። ā́ṭrau), pl. -ጉት ። -gut, (-ሉት ። -lut, -ሩት ። -rut).

clean, be, v.i. ጠራ ṭḁ́rrā̃.

Are the clothes clean? ልብስ፡ ጠርቷል። li̥ẏs (§ 52*a*, δ) ṭártōāl?

cleaned, be, v.p. ተጠረገ tḁṭḁ́rrḁgḁ.

(wiped) ተወለወለ tḁwḁlḁ́uwḁlḁ (tḁuḁ-).

(the teeth) ተሟጨ tḁmwā́čča̤.

Has it been cleaned? ተጠርጓል። tḁṭḁ́rgōāl?

Yes, I have cleaned it: አወን፡ ጠረግሁት። ā́wωn, ṭḁ́rrḁghut, or ጠርጌዋለሁ። ṭḁri̥ggʸewállḁuʰ.

When it has been cleaned, show it me: ሲጠረግ፡ አሳየኝ። si̥ṭṭḁ́rrḁg, asā́yyäñ.

clear, adj. (obvious) እውቅ i̥wuq (i̥ʷuq).

(of water, etc.) ጥሩ ṭi̥ru (ṭú̥ru).

(not confused) ብሩ bi̥ru.

He has a clear head: ልቡ፡ ብሩ፡ ነው። li̥bbu ẏi̥ru nḁu.

clear (be), v.i. ጠራ ṭḁ́rrā̃.

clear away, v.t. አነሣ anḁ́ssā̃.

Clear it away: አንሣው። ánsau.

Don't clear them away: አታንሣቸው። attansā́ččḁu.

Clear (pl.) it away: አንሡት። ánsut.

Don't (pl.) clear them away: አታንሧቸው። attan-swā́ččḁu.

clear off (out), v.i. ወገደ wώggḁdḁ.

Clear off! ወግድ። wώgi̥d!, f. ወግጅ። wώgi̥j!, pl. ወግዱ። wώgi̥du!

clear up, v.i. (of the weather) አበራ abḁ́rrā̃ (aẏḁ́-; said also at night).

When it clears up: ሲያበራ፡ syāẏára.

clerk, s. ጣፊ ṭā́fi.

clerk, chief, s. ጸሐፊ፡ ትዛዝ ṣḁhā́fʸe tí̥zā́z (§ 8).

clever, adj. ራሳም rásám (§ 8).
ብልሃተኛ bi̥lhātḁ́ññā̃ (-tấñ-).
ጥበበኛ ṭi̥bḁbḁ́ññā̃ (-i̥yḁy-, -ấñ-).
cliff, s. ገደል gḁ́dḁl (gấdäl).
climb, v.i. ወጣ wώṭṭā̃.
climb, v.t. ከ-...፡ ላይ፡ ወጣ kḁ-... la͡i̥ (§ 8, § 47*b*) wώṭṭā̃.
He climbed the hill: ከተራራ፡ ላይ፡ ወጣ። kḁtḁrārá (§ 59*a*) la͡i̥ wώṭṭa.
clip, v.t. ቀጠጠ qḁ́ṭṭḁṭḁ.
clipped, be, v.p. ተቀጠጠ tḁqḁ́ṭṭḁṭḁ.
clippers, s. መቅጠጫ mḁqṭḁ́č̣ā̃ (-ṭấč̣-).
clitoris, s. ቂንጠር qí̥nṭḁr (-ṭär).
cloak, s. በርኖስ bḁ́rn^{w}os.
ለምድ lḁmd.
ካባ kắbbā̃.
(woollen) ማቅ māq.
clock, s. ሰዓት sḁ͡ắ(t)—(s.v. time, watch).
It is eight o'clock: ስምንት፡ ሰዓት፡ ነው። sí̥mmi̥nt sḁ͡ất nḁ͡u.
At eight o'clock: በስምንት፡ ሰዓት፡ bḁsí̥mmi̥nt sḁ͡ất.
clod, s. ጕሊት gwúlīt (-li̥t).
close (near), adj. (close to, prp.) ቅርብ qi̥rb (qi̥ry).
close, v.i. (be closed, v.p.) ተዘጋ tḁzḁ́ggā̃.
The door won't close: ሳንቃው፡ አይዘጋም። sấṅqa͡u a͡i̥zzḁ́ggām (§ 63*c*).
The road has been closed to cattle: መንገዱ፡ ተጠበቀ፡ ከብት፡ እንዳያልፍ። mḁ́ṅgḁdu tḁṭḁ́bbḁqḁ kḁft i̥nda͡i̥álf.
close, v.t. ዘጋ zḁ́ggā̃.
(a lid) ከደነ kḁ́ddḁnḁ.

Close the door: መዝጊያውን፡ ዝጋው። mązgyau͡n zįgau͡.

Close the box: ሳጥኑን፡ ክደነው። sąṭįnun kįdąnąu͡.

close(r) together, be, v.i. ተቀራረቡ tąqąrắrrąbu (-ąyu).

They are to be close(r) together: ይቀራረቡ። yįqqąrắrąyu.

They are not to be so close together: አይቀራረቡ፡ እንደዚህ። a͡įqqąrárąyu ndắzzih.

close(r) together, put, v.t. አቀራረበ aqqąrắrrąbą (-ąyą).

cloth, s. (gen.) ጨርቅ č̣ärq.

(for wear) ልብስ lįbs (lįys).

(for wiping) መጥረጊያ mąṭrągyã.

(for wrapping) መጠቅለያ mąṭąqląyã (-ṭäq-, -ą͡įã).

Assortment of cloths: ጨርቃጨርቅ č̣ärqắč̣ärq (§ 8).

clothe, v.t. አለበሰ aląbbąsą.

clothed, be, v.i. ለበሰ ląbbąsą.

clothes, s. ልብስ lįbs (lįys).

Fine clothes: ጌጥ gʸëṭ.

cloud, s. ደመና dąmmąnã (§ 8).

clove, s. ቅርንፉል qįrúnful (qŭr-, -ŭmf-, -ፉድ -fud, § 7*d*).

clover (*Trifolium sp.*), s. ዋጅማ wắjmã.

G. ጕርጠብ gwωrṭąb (-ąy).

Š. ስዲሳ sįddísã.

club, s. (weapon) ዱላ dúllã.

coagulate, v.i. [እ]ረጋ (į)rąggã.

coal, s. ከሰል፡ ደንጊያ kąsąl dắngyã.

Live coal: ፍም fįm (§ 52*a*, δ).

coarse, adj. (scabrous) ኰስኳሳ kwωskwắssã.

(rude) ባለጌ bắlągʸe (-läg-).

coarse-grained, adj. ክክ kįkk (kükk § 7*d*).

coat, s. (Eur.) †ኮት kʷōt.

(of animal) ጠጕር ṭągwŭr.

Cobus defassa, s. ዲፋሳ d̥ifásā.

cobweb, s. የሸረሪት ፡ ቤት yäšḁrḁrít yʸēt.

cock, s. አውራ ፡ ዶሮ a͡urá dʷórʷo.

At cock-crow: አውራ ፡ ዶሮ ፡ ሲጮኽ ፡ a͡urá dʷórʷo si̥čʷóh.

cockroach, s. በረሮ bḁrḁrʷo.

coffee, s. ቡን bunn (plant, berry and drink).

Coffee and milk: ቡንና ፡ ወተት ። búnni̥nnā wώtḁt.

Coffee without milk: ቡን ፡ ያለወተት ። bunn yālḁ-wώtḁt (-ḁ͡uώ-).

Don't put sugar into the coffee: ሱክር ፡ ተቡን ፡ አታድርግበት ። súkkar tḁyúnn attádri̥gi̥bbḁt (-tárg-).

coil, v.i. (be coiled, v.p.) ተጠመጠመ tḁṭḁmḁ́ṭṭḁmḁ, round, በ- bḁ- (yḁ-; § 47*a*).

The snake coiled round me: እባብ ፡ ተጠመጠመብኝ ። i̥yáy tḁṭḁmḁ́ṭṭḁmḁbbi̥ñ.

coil, v.t. ጠመጠመ ṭḁmḁ́ṭṭḁmḁ.

coin, small, s. መሐለቅ mḁhállḁq (§ 52*a*, δ).

cold, adj. ቀዝቃዛ qḁzqázzā.

(of weather) ብርድ bi̥rd (§ 57*b*).

Cold water: ቀዝቃዛ ፡ ውሃ ፡ qḁzqázza wŭha (-zá͡uha).

Cold weather: ብርድ bi̥rd.

Very cold weather: ውርጭ wurč̣.

Is it cold there? ካዚያ ፡ ብርድ ፡ ነው ። kḁzzyá yi̥rdi̥ (§ 7*d*) nḁ͡u?

cold, s. (weather) ብርድ bi̥rd.

(in the head) ጉንፋን gúnfán (-úmf- § 7*d*; § 8).

I have caught a cold: ጉንፋን ፡ ያዘኝ ። gumfán yázäñ (lit. a cold has seized me).

cold, be (get), v.i. በረደ bárrḁdḁ.

ቀዘቀዘ qḁzḁ́qqḁzḁ.

If it is cold: ቢበርድ ፡ bi̥yárd.

Let it get cold: ይብረድ ። yí̥yrḁd.

Don't let it get cold: አይብረድ ። a͡i̥yrḁd.

cold, be (feel), v.i. በረደው bḁ́rrḁda͡u̥ (impers. § 43*a*; § 63*d*, *e*).

I feel cold: ብርዶኛል ። bḁ́rd^{w}oññāl.

Coleus tuberosus (Guidi, Vocab. p. 676), s. ድንች dí̥nni̥č (-čč § 6).

collect, v.i. (be collected, v.p.) ተሰበሰበ tḁsḁbḁ́ssḁbḁ (täs-, -ḁỵḁ́ssḁỵḁ).

collect, v.t. (bring together) ሰበሰበ sḁbḁ́ssḁbḁ (sḁỵḁ́ssḁỵḁ).

(pick up) ለቀመ lḁ́qqḁmḁ.

collected, be, v.p. (picked) ተለቀመ tḁlḁ́qqḁmḁ.

collection, s. (group) ስብሳቢ si̥bsábi (si̥ỵsáỵi).

colonel, s. (native) ባላምባራስ bālámbarās.

colour, s. መልክ mḁlk.

ቀለም qḁ́lḁm.

(of animals) ጠጕር ṭḁgwŭr.

comb, s. ሚዶ mī́d^{w}o (mí̥d^{w}o).

መንቀሻ mḁnqḁ́šā.

(of fowl) Š. ኮከን k^{w}ókḁn (-kän).

G. ጕቲያ gwŭttíyā.

comb, v.t. ነቀሰ nḁ́qqḁsḁ.

come, interj. (intensive) [እ]ኮ (í̥)kk^{w}o (ŭ́k-; often enclitic and suffix).

እንጂ (i̥)njí (encl.).

በል bḁl.

Come, bring it (them § 61*b*)! እኮ ፡ አምጣ ። ŭ́kk^{w}o ánṭa! (§ 7*d*), or አምጣኮ ። anṭákk^{w}o!

Come, put it down! አስቀምጠው ፡ እንጂ ። asqḁ́mmi̥ṭa͡u̥njí!

Come, give it me! ስጠኝ ፡ እንጂ ። sí̥ṭḁññi̥njí! (§ 6), or በል ፡ ስጠኝ ። bḁl sí̥ṭḁñ!

come, v.i. መጣ mḁ́ṭṭã, (imperative ና nã, pl. ኑ nu).

Come here! ና ፡ ወዲህ ። na wωdíh!

Come (here), please: ና ፡ እስቲ ። násti, pol. ይምጡ ፡ እስቲ ። yi̥mṭústi, pl. ኑ ፡ እስቲ ። nústi.

Tell him to come: ና ፡ በለው ። nā ỵḁ́lḁ͡u, pl. ና ፡ በሉት ። nā ỵḁ́lut.

Tell them to come: ኑ ፡ በላቸው ። nu ỵḁláččḁ͡u, pl. ኑ ፡ በሏቸው ። nu ỵḁlwáččḁ͡u.

Where does he (it) come from? ተወዴት ፡ ነው ፡ እሚመጣ ። tḁwωd^{y}ét nḁ͡u mmi̥mḁ́ṭḁ?

come and go, v.i. ተመላለሰ tḁmḁlállḁsḁ.

come, cause (or allow) to, v.t. አስመጣ asmḁ́ṭṭã.

come in, v.i. ገባ gḁ́bbã.

Come in! ግባ ። gí̥ỵa!, pol. ይግቡ ። yí̥gỵu!, pl. ግቡ ። gí̥ỵu!

come in, cause (or allow) to, v.t. አስገባ asgḁ́bbã.

come out, v.i. ወጣ wώṭṭã.

Come along out! ና ፡ ውጣ ። na wŭ́ṭā! (nḁ́͡uṭā!).

The stain has come out: እድፉ ፡ ለቀቀ ። í̥dfu lḁ́qqḁqḁ.

come out, cause (or allow) to, v.t. አስወጣ aswώṭṭã.

comfortable, adj. ደኅና dáhnã.

I am comfortable: ደኅና ፡ ነኝ ። dähná (§ 8) näñ.

I am not comfortable: ይቈረቍረኛል ። yi̥qwωrḁ́qqwŭräññāl.

Are you comfortable? ደኅና ፡ ነህ ። dähná näh?, pol. ደኅና ፡ ነዎ ። dähná nḁ͡^{w}o?, pl. ደኅና ፡ ናችሁ ። dähná náččyuh? (§ 7*d*).

He is in comfortable circumstances: ዓለመኛ ፡ ነው ። ālḁmäññá nḁ͡u.

command, s. (order) ትዛዝ ti̥záz (§ 8).

(authority) ሹመት šúmḁt (-mät).

command, v.i. & t. አዘዘ ázzḁzḁ.
commandant (commander), s. አለቃ álḁqā̃.
commerce, s. ንግድ ni̥gd.
commissariat officer, s. በጅሮንድ bäji̥rʷónd.
commode, s. መሻኛ mḁšḁñā̃ (-šā́ñ-).
ባሬታ bāryétā̃.
(euphem.) መክፈያ mḁkfḁyā̃ (-fḁi̥ā̃).
common (plentiful), be, v.i. መላ mḁllā̃ or ሞላ mʷóllā̃.
Is it common? ሞልቷላ። mʷóltŏāllá? (s.v. -አ, § 6).
communicate, v.i. (receive Holy Communion) ቈረበ qwǿrrḁbḁ (-ḁyḁ).
companion, s. ባልንጀራ bāli̥njárā̃.
company, s. (mercantile) ኩባኒያ kubbāníyyā̃.
He is good company: ጨዋተኛ፡ ነው። č̣ḁuatäññá (§ 8) nḁu, pol. -ተኛ፡ ናቸው። -tā́ñña náččḁu.
compensation, s. ካሳ kásā̃.
Compensation for homicide: የነፍስ፡ ዋጋ፡ yänḁvs (§ 7*d*) wága.
complain, v.i. ጮኸ č̣ʷóhḁ, of, በ- bḁ- (yḁ-; § 47*a*).
I complain of him (it): እጮኸበታለሁ። i̥č̣ʷohi̥bbḁtállḁuʰ.
I complain of the headman: በሹም፡ እጮኸበታለሁ። bḁšúm i̥č̣ʷohi̥bbḁtállḁuʰ.
Whom do you complain of? በማን፡ ትጮኻለህ። bḁmán ti̥č̣ʷohálläh?, pol. በማን፡ ይጮኻሉ። bḁmán yi̥č̣ʷohállu?
complainant, s. ከሳሽ kḁsā́š (§ 8).
complaint, s. (grievance) ጩኸት č̣úhḁt (-hät).
(ailment) see disease, pain.
I have a complaint: ጩኸት፡ አለኝ። č̣úhḁt álläñ.
What is your complaint? ጩኸትህ፡ ምንድር፡ ነው። č̣úhäti̥h mi̥ndi̥r nḁu?

complete, adj. ሙሉ mŭlu (ምሉ mi̥lu).
complete, v.t. ጨረሰ č̣ḁ́rrḁsḁ (č̣árräsḁ).
completed, be, v.p. ተጨረሰ tḁč̣ḁ́rrḁsḁ (täč̣árräsḁ).
completely, adv. ጭራሽ č̣i̥rrā́š (§ 8).
በውል bḁ́wŭ́l (bḁ́uŭ́l ; § 8).
compliments, s. ከንቱ ፡ ውዳሴ kḁ́ntu ʷuddásʸe.
compress, v.t. አጣበቀ aṭṭábbḁqḁ.
compressed, adj. ጥብቅ ṭi̥bq (ṭi̥vq).
compressed, be, v.p. ጠበቀ ṭḁ́bbḁqḁ.
compulsion, s. ግድ gi̥dd.
compulsory, adj. (-orily, adv.) በግድ bḁ́gí̥dd (§ 8).
comrade, s. ባልንጀራ bāli̥njárã.
concave, adj. ጐድጓዳ gwωdgwáddã (-ωrgw- § 7*d*).
conceal, v.t. ሰወረ sḁ́uwḁrḁ.
ሸሸገ šḁ́ššḁgḁ (šáššägḁ).
concealed, be, v.p. ተሰወረ tḁsḁ́uwḁrḁ (täs-).
ተሸሸገ tḁšḁ́ššḁgḁ (täšáššägḁ).
conceit, s. ኩራት kúrā́t (§ 8).
conceited, adj. ኩሩ kúru.
ተከባሪ tḁkḁbbā́ri.
concubine, s. የጭን ፡ ገረድ yäč̣í̥n (-í̥n) gḁ́rḁd.
condemn, v.t. ፈረደ ፡ በ- fḁ́rrḁdḁ bḁ- (vḁ- ; § 47*a*).
condemned, be, v.p. ተፈረደበት tḁfḁ́rrḁdḁbbḁt.
condition, s. (stipulation) ቍርጥ qwŭrṭ (§ 52*a*, δ).

These are the conditions on which you will work: በዚህ ፡ ቍርጥ ፡ ትሰራለህ ። bḁzzíh qwŭrṭ ti̥sḁráll̈ah.

condition (training), be (get) out of, v.i. ተጐዳ tḁgwώddã.
ከሳ kḁ́ssã.
See § 63*d*, *e*.

He (it) is out of condition: ተጐድቷል ። tḁgwώdi̥-tōāl (-ώrt- § 7*d*).

condition, lack of, s. ጕዳት gwŭ́dā́t (§ 8).

conduct, s. ስራ sı̥rã.
conduct, v.t. (guide) መራ mḁ́rrã.
(bring) አደረሰ adḁ́rrḁsḁ.
conducted, be, v.p. ተመራ tḁmḁ́rrã.
confidence, s. እምነት ı̥́mnḁt (-nät).
confine, v.t. አሰረ ássḁrḁ (-sär-).
confined, be, v.p. ታሰረ tássḁrḁ (-sär-).
confiscate, v.t. ወረሰ wώrrḁsḁ.
conflagration, s. ቋያ qwáyyã.
confound, v.t.
Confound you! ይይልሀ። yı́llı̥h! (s.v. አየ).
confuse, v.t. (mix) ደበለቀ dḁbḁ́llḁqḁ (-ḁyḁ́-).
(mentally) G. አሰሳተ assḁsátḁ.
Š. አሳሳተ assãsátḁ.
confused, be, v.i. & p. (mixed) ተደበለቀ tḁdḁbḁ́llḁqḁ (-ḁyḁ́-).
(mentally) G. ተሰሳተ tḁsḁsátḁ (täsäs-),
Š. ተሳሳተ tḁsãsátḁ (täs-).
congratulate, v.t. (on achieving):
I congratulate you: እንኳን፡ እግዚአብሔር፡ እረዳሀ። ṅkwán i̥gzi̥ayhʸér i̥rḁ́ddāh, pol. ... እረዳዎ። ... i̥rḁ́d-da͡ʷo.
consent, v.i. እሺ፡ አለ (ı̥)šši (-ši̥, -šʸ) álḁ (s.v. √በለ, § 44*a*).
በጄ፡ አለ bḁ́jjä (bǻj-) álḁ („ „).
I consent: እሺ። ı̥́šši̥, or ይሁን። yı̥́hun.
consequently, adv. እንግዲህ (i̥)ṅgdʸéh.
እዛወዲያ (i̥)z(z)áʷωdyá (-zád-; § 8).
consider, v.i. & t. አሰበ ássḁbḁ (-ḁyḁ).
consul, s. ቆንጽል qwúnsı̥l.
consult, v.t. ተማከረ tḁmákkḁrḁ (-kär-) ከ- kḁ- (ተ- tḁ-, § 47*a*).
Consult the head-man: ተሹሙ፡ ተማከር። tḁšúmu tḁmákär.

consume, v.t. በላ bḁ́llã.

consumed, be, v.p. ተበላ tḁbḁ́llã (tḁyḁ́-).

contagious, be, v.i. አለፈ állḁfḁ.

Is the disease contagious? በሽታ፡ ያልፋሉዋይ። bḁ́ši̥ta yálfāllwi̥? (s.v. -ዋይ, § 6).

contain, v.t. ያዘ yázḁ (§ 44*c*).

ቻለ čálḁ.

How much will it contain? ምን፡ ያህል፡ ይይዛል። mi̥n yahl yi̥yízāl?

What does it contain? ምን፡ አለበት። mi̥n álläbbḁt?

contempt, interj. expressing: አረግ ḁ́rḁg! (ḁrḁ̄ḁ́g! § 7*d*).

content, v.t. ደስ፡ አሰኘ dḁss (däss) assáññä.

content, be, v.i. ደስ፡ አለ dḁss (-ä-) álḁ (s.v. √በለ, § 44*a*).

ደስ፡ አለው dḁss (-ä-) álḁu (impers. § 43*a*). See § 63*d, e*.

Is he content? ደስ፡ ብሎታሉዋይ። däss yi̥lʷotāllwi̥? (s.v. -ዋይ, § 6).

contrary, on the, እንጂ (i̥)njí.

He is not to go: on the contrary, he is to stay: አይሒድ፡ ይቈይ፡ እንጂ። ái̥hi̥d, yi̥qwωyy i̥njí.

convent, s. ገዳም gḁ́dám (gád-; § 8).

conversation, s. መነጋገር mḁnnḁgágḁr (-gär).

ወግ wωg.

converse, v.i. ተነጋገረ tḁnḁgággarḁ (-gär-).

ተጫወተ tḁčáuwḁtḁ (-wωt-).

converse with, v.t. አጫወተ aččáuwḁtḁ (-wωt-).

convolvulus sp., s. አረግ árḁg.

cook, s. ወጥ፡ ቤት wώtbʸēt (-tʸy-).

ወጥ፡ ሰሪ wώtḁ sári (sári; § 9*d*).

cook, v.t. አበሰለ abḁ́ssḁlḁ (ayḁ́-).

Cook it: አብስለው። áyṣịḷau.

Can you cook? ወጥ፡ታውቃለህ። wωṭ tauqállāh?

cooking (cookery), s. ወጥ wωṭ.

cool, adj. ቀዝቃዛ qạzqázzā̃.

cooler, s. ማብረጃ mā̃brájā̃ (-ā̃yr-, -rā̃j-).

co-operate, v.i. ተጠቃቀሙ tạṭạqā̃qqạmu.

copied (out, in writing) be, v.p. ተገለበጠ tạgạlábbạṭạ.

ተቀዳ tạqáddā̃.

copper, s. ነሃስ náhā̃s (§ 8).

copulate, v.i. (inire) በዳ báddā̃ (bā̃d-).

(of the female) ተበዳች tạbáddā̃č (täbā̃d-, -äyā̃-; -ā̃čč § 6).

(euphem.) ተኛ tạññā̃ (tā̃ñ-, -ñä).

copulation, s. ብዳት bídā̃t (§ 8).

copy (out, in writing), v.t. ገለበጠ gạlábbạṭạ.

ቀዳ qáddā̃.

Cordia abessinica (Broun, Cat. 371), s. ዋንዛ wā̃nza.

coriander, s. ድምብላል dímbịlā̃l (§ 8).

corkscrew, s. የጠርሙዝ፡መፍቻ yäṭạrmū̃z (-ṭär-) máfčā̃.

corn, s. ስንዴ síndʸe.

What is the price of corn? ስንዴ፡ዋጋው፡በስንት፡ነው። síndʸe (§ 55*b*) wā̃gau yạsíntị nau?

corn, Indian (*Zea mays*), s. የባሕር፡ማሽላ yäbāhịr (-äyā̃-) mā̃šíllā̃.

corner, s. ማዘን mā̃zạn.

corpse, s. በድን bádịn (bā̃d-; -ịnn § 6).

correct, adj. (-ly, adv.) ደኅና dā̃hnā̃ (§ 8).

ትክክል tịkíkkịl.

ልክ lịkk (§ 57*b*).

በልክ bálíkk (§ 8).

ጠፍተኛ tạffịtáññā̃ (-tā̃ñ-).

correct, be, v.i. ተከከለ tḁkắkkḁlḁ.
ጠፍ፡አለ ṭḁff álḁ (s.v. √በለ, § 44*a*).

correct, (render), v.t. አስተከከለ astḁkắkkḁlḁ.
ጠፍ፡አደረገ ṭḁff adḁ́rrḁgḁ.

corrupt, v.t. (a person) አሳተ assắtḁ.

Corvus sp., s. ቁራ qúrã.

cost, s. ዋጋ wắgã.

cost, v.i. ተገዛ፡በ- tḁgḁ́zzã bḁ- (yḁ-; § 47*a*).
What did it cost? በስንት፡ተገዛ። bḁsı̥nt tḁgḁ́zza?
What does it cost? ዋጋው፡ምን፡ያህል፡ነው። wắga͡u mı̥n yahl nḁ͡u?

cotton, s. (-plant, -wool) ጥጥ ṭı̥ṭ.
(thread) ክር kı̥rr.

cotton soil (بادوب), s. ዋልካ wálkã.
መዛጋ mḁzḁ́gã (-zắg-).

cough, s. ሳል sāl.
Have you got a cough? ትስላለህ። tı̥sı̥lállăh?, pol. ይስላሉ። yı̥sı̥lállu?

cough, v.i. ሳለ sálḁ.
Does he cough? ይስላል። yı̥sı̥lāl?, pol. ይስላሉ። yı̥sı̥lállu?

count, v.i. & t. ቈጠረ qwώṭṭḁrḁ (-ṭär-).
Count it (them § 52*a*, δ): ቍጠሩው። qwŭ́ṭärḁ͡u.
Have you counted it (them)? ቈጠርሀው። qwώṭṭärhḁ͡u?

counted, be, v.p. ተቈጠረ tḁqwώṭṭḁrḁ (-ṭär-).

country, s. (gen. inhabited) አገር ắgḁr (-gär).
(opposed to town; uninhabited) በረሃ bḁ́rḁhã.
What is your country? አገርህ፡የት፡ነው። ắgärı̥h yēt nḁ͡u?

In your country: በገርህ፡ bắgäri̥h.

A man that knows the country: አገር፡የሚያውቅ፡ ሰው፡ ắgär yämmyá͡uq sḁ͡u.

countryman, s. (rustic) ባለጌ bắlḁgʸe (-läg-).
ባላገር bālắgḁr (-gär).
ገበሬ gắbḁrʸe (-ḁ̆́ỵḁ-, -är-).

courage, s. ልብ li̥bb.

course, of, interj. እንዴታ (i̥)ndʸétā.
እንኳን ńkwān.

Yes, of course bring it! እንዴታ፡አምጣው፡እንጂ። ndʸétā, ánṭa͡unjí! (§ 7*d*).

court, s. (of justice) የፍርድ፡ቤት፡ yäfi̥rdi̥ bʸēt (ỵʸ-).
ሰገነት sḁgḁnnät.

In court: በወምበር፡ፊት፡ bḁ͡uωmbḁ́r (§ 8) fi̥t.

cousin, s. ያጎት፡ልጅ yaggwώt (§ 8) li̥j (uncle's child).
ዘመድ zḁmḁd (relation).
ወንድም wώndi̥m (prop. brother), pl. also
ወንድማሞች wωndi̥mámʷōč (-čč § 6).

He is my cousin: ያጎቴ፡ልጅ፡ነው። yaggwώtʸe li̥j nḁ͡u.

cover, s. (lid) መክደኛ mḁkdḁ́ñã (-dáñ-).
ክዳን ki̥dán (§ 8).
(of cloth, etc.) ልብስ li̥bs (li̥ṿs).

cover, v.t. (clothe) አለበሰ alḁ́bbasḁ (§ 56*f*).
ሸፈነ šḁ́ffḁnḁ (šắf-).
(as a lid) ከደነ kḁ́ddḁnḁ.

Cover the sore: ቍስሉን፡አልብሰው። qwū́si̥lun álṿi̥sḁ͡u.

Cover the sore on his back: የጀርባውን፡ቍስል፡አልብሰው። yäjắrṿa͡un qwū́si̥l álṿi̥sḁ͡u.

Cover the sore on her back: የጀርባዋን፡ቍስል፡አልብሳት። yäjärṿá͡uān qwū́si̥l álṿi̥sāt.

covered, be, v.p. (cover oneself, v.r.) ተሸፈነ tḁšḁ́ffḁnḁ (täšä́f-).
coverlet, s. ምንጣፍ mi̥nṭä́f (§ 8).
cow, s. ላም lām.
coward, s. (-ly, adj.) ፈሪ fḁ́ri (fä́ri).
crack, s. (fissure) ንቕ ni̥q, pl. also ንቃቓት ni̥qä́qät (§ 8).
ስንጥቕ si̥nṭi̥q.
(in soil) ኮረኮራ k^{w}orḁk^{w}órã (-rωk-; § 52*a*, δ).
crack, v.i. (be cracked, v.p.) ነቃ nḁ́qqã.
ተተረተረ tḁtḁrḁ́ttḁrḁ (-tärḁ́ttärḁ).
ተሰነጠቀ tḁsḁnḁ́ṭṭḁqḁ (täsän-).
The jar will crack: እንስራው፡ይተረተራል። nsi̥rau yi̥ttärḁ́ttäräl.
crack, v.t. ተረተረ tḁrḁ́ttḁrḁ (tärḁ́ttärḁ).
ሰነጠቀ sḁnḁ́ṭṭḁqḁ.
It will crack the jar: እንስራውን፡ይተረትራል። nsi̥raun yi̥tärḁ́tti̥räl.
cracked, adj. ሰንጣቃ sḁnṭä́qqã.
Is the soil there cracked? ተዚያ፡መሬት፡ሰንጣቃ፡ ነው። tḁzzyá mḁr^{y}ét sḁnṭäqqá nḁu? (§ 8).
crackle, v.i. ተንኰሸኰሸ tḁṅkwωšákkwωšḁ.
crafty, adj. ብልጥ bi̥lṭ.
crash, v.i. ጓ፡አለ gwā álḁ (s.v. √ባለ, § 44*a*).
ግም፡አለ gi̥mm álḁ („ „).
creak, v.i. ተንኳኳ tḁṅkwákkwã.
crease, s. ማጠፊያ māṭḁfyã.
credit, s. እዳ i̥dã.
On credit: በዳ፡ bḁdã (§ 7*a*).
No credit given: በዳም፡አይዶል። bḁdámm ái̥däl (§ 7*d*).

creditor, s. ባለገንዘብ bālḁgḁ́nzḁb (-ḁy̥).
  አበዳሪ abḁddā́ri (ay̥ḁ-, -äd-).
crest, s. (of bird) ቁንጮ qúnč̣ʷo.
crevice, s. ንቅ ni̥q, pl. also ንቃቃት ni̥qā́qāt (§ 8).
cricket (*Gryllus sp., Acheta sp.*), s. ፌንጣ fʸénṭã (§ 52*a*, δ).
crime, s. ኃጢአት (h)ā́ṭyā́t (§ 8).
  በደል bḁ́däl (bā́d-).
croak, v.i. ጮኸ č̣ʷóhḁ.
croak (-ing), s. ጩኸት č̣úhḁt (-hät).
crocodile, s. አዞ ázzʷo.
crooked, adj. ጠማማ ṭḁmā́mã.
crop, s. (planted field) እርሻ i̥ršã (§ 52*a*, δ).
  (harvest) አዝመራ azmḁ́rã (-mā́r-).
  Are the crops good? አዝመራ፡ በጀ። azmḁ́ra y̥ā́jjä?
cross, s. መስቀል mḁsqḁl.
cross, v.i. & t. ቈረጠ qwώrrḁṭḁ.
  ተሻገረ tḁšā́ggḁrḁ (täš-, -gär-).
  Cross it and go straight on: ቈርጠህው፡ ፊት፡ ለፊት፡ ሒድ። qwώrṭäha͡u fi̥t lḁfi̥t hi̥d.
  To cross one's legs: እግሩን፡ ፈተለ፡ i̥grun (§ 52*a*, γ) fḁ́ttḁlḁ.
cross (in a bad temper), be (become), v.i. ተመረረ tḁmḁ́rrḁrḁ (-rärḁ; § 63*d*, *e*).
cross-roads, s. መንታ mḁntã.
  When you reach the cross-roads: መንታው፡ ስትደርስ፡ mḁntá͡u si̥tti̥dā́rs.
crouch, v.i. አደባ adḁ́bbã.
crow (*Corvus sp.*), s. ቁራ qúrã.
crow, v.i. ጮኸ č̣ʷóhḁ.
crowd, s. ሕዝብ hí̥zi̥b (-i̥y̥), pl. also አሕዛብ áhzā́b (-ā́y̥; § 8).
crown, s. ዘውድ zḁ́͡ud.
crucified, be, v.p. ተሰቀለ tḁsḁ́qqḁlḁ (täs-).

crucify, v.t. ሰቀለ sḁ́qqḁlḁ.
cruel, adj. ጨካኝ č̥ḁ́kkā́ñ (-ññ § 6 ; § 8).
crupper, s. ወዴሏ wωddʸéllā̃ (ው- wŭ-).
crush, v.t. ወቀጠ wώqqḁṭḁ.
crushed, be, v.p. ተወቀጠ tḁwώqqḁṭḁ (tḁ͡uώ-).
cry, s. ጩኸት č̣úhḁt (-hät).
cry, v.i. ጮኸ č̣ʷóhḁ.
(weep) አለቀሰ alḁ́qqḁsḁ.
cub, s. ግልገል gḭ́lgḁl.
Cucumis melo (Broun, Cat. 206), s. ዱባ dúbbā̃.
Cucurbita maxima (Broun, Cat. 209), s. ቅል qḭl.
cultivate, v.i. & t. (sow) ዘራ zḁ́rrā̃ (zā́r-).
(plant) ተከለ tḁ́kkḁlḁ.
cultivated, be, v.p. (sown) ተዘራ tḁzḁ́rrā̃ (täzā́r-).
(planted) ተተከለ tḁtḁ́kkḁlḁ.
cultivation, s. (cultivated land) እርሻ ḭ́ršā̃.
(practice) አዝመራ azmḁ́rā̃ (-mā́r-).
cultivator, s. ገበሬ gḁ́bḁrʸe (-ḁ́vḁ-, -är-).
cunning, adj. ብልጥ bḭlṭ.
cup, s. ፍንጃል fḭ́njál (§ 8).
ዋንጫ wā́nč̣ā̃.
ፋጋ fā́gā̃.
(of enamelled ware) ታኒካ tā́nikā̃.
cup, v.t. አገመ ággḁmḁ.
cupped, be, v.p. ታገመ tā́ggḁmḁ.
cupping-horn, s. ዋገምት wā́gḁmt.
curdle, v.i. [እ]ረጋ (ḭ)rḁ́ggā̃.
Curdled milk : አይብ á͡ḭb (á͡ḭv).
curds, s. [እ]ርጎ rḭ́gʷo (ḭ́rg-).
cure, v.t. ፈወሰ fḁ́͡uwḁsḁ.
cured, be, v.p. ተፈወሰ tḁfḁ́͡uwḁsḁ.

curse, s. [እ]ርግማን ri̥gí̥mán (i̥rg-; § 8).
curse, v.i. & t. ረገመ rḁ́ggḁmḁ.

Curse you! ምን፡አባትህ። mi̥n abbáti̥h?

curtain, s. መጋረጃ mḁggārā́jā̃.

አጐበር agʷóbḁr (-óy̥-, -är).

Let down the curtain: መጋረጃውን፡ጣለው። mḁg-gārā́ja͡un ṭálḁ͡u.

curve, v.i. አጐነበሰ agwωnḁ́bbḁsḁ.
cushion, s. መከዳ mḁk(k)ḁ́ddā̃.
custom, s. ሥራት si̥rát (§ 8).

እድር í̥ddi̥r.

ወግ wωg.

Is it an ancient custom? የቀድሞ፡እድር፡ነው። yä-qḁ́dmʷo i̥ddí̥r (§ 8) nḁ͡u? (-qärmʷód- § 7*d*).

custom-house, s. መቅረጫ mḁqrḁ́č̣ā̃ (-rā́č̣-).

በር bḁrr.

customs, s. ቀረጥ qḁ́rḁṭ.

How much are the customs? ቀረጡ፡ምን፡ያህል፡ነው። qḁ́rḁṭu mi̥n yahl nḁ͡u?

customs, collect, v.i. ቀረጠ qḁ́rrḁṭḁ, on, ከ-[ተ-] kḁ- (tḁ-, § 47*a*).
customs, pay, v.i. ተቀረጠ tḁqḁ́rrḁṭḁ.

Everything will have to pay customs: ሁሉ፡እቃ፡ይቀረጣል። húllu í̥qa yi̥qqḁ́rrḁṭāl.

I do (shall, will) not pay customs: አልቀረጥም። ali̥q-qḁ́rrḁṭi̥m.

customs official, s. ቀራጭ qḁ́rā́č̣ (§ 8).

በረኛ bḁrrḁ́ññā̃ (-rā́ñ-).

cut, v.i. & t. ቈረጠ qwώrrḁṭḁ.

(corn, grass) አጨደ áč̣č̣ḁdḁ (-č̣ädä).

Cut it: ቍረጠው። qwúrḁṭḁ͡u, pl. -ጡት። -ṭut.

Don't cut it: አትቍረጠው። atti̥qwűrḁṭḁ͡u, pl. -ጡት። -ṭut.

cut, be, v.p. ተቈረጠ tḁqwǿrrḁṭḁ.

cut-throat, s. ጋዱ gáddu.

Cynocephalus sp., s. ዝንጀሮ zi̥njḁ́rʷo (-jǿr-).

D

§ refers to the paragraphs of the Grammar (*Initia Amharica, Part I*).

dagger, s. ጩቤ ç̣űbʸe (-űỵʸe).

daily, adj. የሁለቀን yähullḁ́qḁn.

daily, adv. ሁለቀን hullḁ́qḁn.

daisy, s. ዝግባ zí̥gbã (-gỵã).

Dalbergia melanoxylon (Broun, Cat. 158), s. ዞቢ zʷóbbi.

dam, s. ግድብ gí̥ddi̥b (-i̥ỵ).

dam, v.t. ገደበ gḁ́ddḁbḁ (-ḁỵḁ).

damage, s. ጕዳት gwűdát (§ 8).

damage, v.t. ጐዳ gwǿddã.

damaged, be (get), v.p. ተጐዳ tḁgwǿddã (§ 63*d, e*).

See that it doesn't get damaged: እንዳይጐዳ። nda͡i̥g-gwǿdda, ...that they don't get... -ዱ። -ddu.

damp, adj. [እ]ርስ (i̥)rí̥ss.

ለዛዛ lḁzázã.

These clothes are damp: ይህ፡ልብስ፡እርስ፡ነው። yí̥he li̥ỵs (§ 52*a*, δ) i̥rí̥ssi̥ (§ 7*d*) nḁ͡u, or ይህ፡ልብስ፡ይርሳል። yí̥he li̥ỵs yi̥rí̥sāl.

damp, be, v.i. [እ]ረሰ (i̥)rásḁ.

dance, s. ዘፈን zḁ́fḁn (záf-).

dance, v.i. ዘፈነ zḁ́ffḁnḁ (záf-).

danger, s. ችጋር čí̥ggár (§ 8).

dare, v.i. & t.

I dare say: ይሆናል። yịhʷṓnāl.

dark, adj. (devoid of light) ጨለማ ç̣ällámā̃ (§ 8, § 57*b*).

(in colour) ጥቁር ṭṹqur.

(of complexion) ጠይም ṭạ́yyịm.

The room is (too) dark: ቤቱ፡ጨለማ፡ነው። bʸétu ç̣ällämá nạu.

dark, be, v.i. ጨለመ ç̣ấllämạ.

darkness, s. ጨለማ ç̣ällấmā̃ (§ 8).

date, s. (day) ቀን qạn (§ 8).

(fruit) ተምር tạ́mịr (§ 52*a*, δ).

date-palm (*Phoenix dactylifera*, Broun, Cat. 595), s. ሰሌን sạ́lʸén (§ 8).

Datura stramonium (Broun, Cat. 394), s. አስተናግር as-tạnágịr (-tän-).

daughter, s. ሴት፡ልጅ sʸét-lịj (§ 8).

dawn, s. ንጋት nị́gát (§ 8).

አጥቢያ ā̃ṭbyā̃ (-ṭy̥y-).

dawn, v.i. ጠባ ṭạ́bbā̃.

ነጋ nạ́ggā̃.

Before the day dawns: ምድር፡ሳይጠባ፡ mdịr saị-ṭạ́vạa.

day, s. ቀን qạn (§ 8).

[ዕ]ለት (ị)lạt (-lất).

See § 52*a*, δ.

Every day, adv. ሁለቀን hullạ́qạn.

በየቀኑ bạyyấqạnu.

እየቀኑ iyyấqạnu.

He works (will work) by the day: በቀን፡ይሰራል። bạqạ́n yịsạ́rāl.

We shall start in three days: በሶስት፡ቀን፡እንነሣለን። bạsʷṓst qạn ịnnịnnạssállän.

Ten days ago: አሥር፡ቀን፡አደረገ፡ assı̥́r qḁn adḁ́rrḁgḁ.

In how many days? በስንት፡ቀን፡ bḁsı̥́ntı̥ qḁn?

Half a day: እኩሌታ፡ቀን፡ ŭkkul^{y}ētá qḁn.

He (has) worked for half a day: ተኩሌታ፡ቀን፡ሰራ። tḁkkul^{y}ētá qḁn sḁ́rra.

day before yesterday, the, adv. ተትናንት፡ወድያ tḁtı̥nánt wώdyã́ (§ 8).

day-labourer, s. ባለሟያ bālḁmwáyã (-á͡ı̥ã).

deaf, adj. ደንቈሮ dḁṅqwώr^{w}o.

dear, adj. (beloved, and expensive) ውድ wŭdd.

This is too dear at five dollars: ይህ፡በምስት፡ብር፡ውድ፡ነው። yı̥he bammı̥́stı̥ yı̥rr wŭ́ddı̥ (§ 7*d*) nḁ͡u.

Oh dear! (surprise): አረ። ḁ́rḁ!

death, s. ሞት m^{w}ot.

death, put to, v.t. አስገደለ asgḁ́ddḁlḁ (-gád-).

debt, s. እዳ ı̥́dã.

ብድር bı̥́ddı̥r.

He is 100 dollars in debt: መቶ፡ብር፡እዳ፡አለበት። mḁt^{w}ó yı̥rr ı̥́da állābbḁt.

debtor, s. ባለዳ bálḁdã́ (§ 8).

ባለብድር bālḁbı̥́ddı̥r (-ḁyı̥́-).

decanter, s. ማብረጃ mãbrájã (-ãyr-).

deceit, s. ቅጥፈት qı̥ṭfḁt (-fät).

ቅጥፍና qı̥ṭfı̥́nnã.

እብለት ı̥́blḁt (ı̥́yl-, -lät).

deceive, v.t. ቀጠፈ qḁ́ṭṭḁfḁ.

አበለ ábbḁlḁ በ- bḁ- (yḁ-; § 47*a*).

አታለለ attállḁlḁ.

አሞኘ am^{w}óññä.

He deceived me: አበለብኝ። ábbḁlḁbbı̥ñ.

Mind he doesn't deceive you: እንዳያታልልህ። nda͡i̥at-tálli̥li̥h.

deceived, be, v.p. ተቀጠፈ tḁqḁ́ṭṭḁfḁ.

ተታለለ tḁtā́llḁlḁ.

deceiver, s. ቀጣፊ qḁṭā́fi.

December, s.v. calendar.

decide, v.i. (in a case) ፈረደ fḁ́rrḁdḁ.

decided, be, v.p. ተፈረደ tḁfḁ́rrḁdḁ.

decision, s. ፍርድ fi̥rd.

declare, v.t. አለ ā́lḁ (s.v. √በለ, § 44*a*, § 80).

(on oath) ማለ mā́lḁ (§ 80).

decorate, v.t. አስጌጠ asgʸéṭḁ.

decorated, adj. (gen. & mil.) ሽልም ši̥lli̥m.

decoration, s. (gen. & mil.) ሽልማት ši̥lli̥mā́t (§ 8).

decree, s. ሥራት si̥rā́t (§ 8).

ትዛዝ ti̥zā́z (§ 8).

decree, v.t. ሰሯ sḁ́rrã.

አዘዘ ázzḁzḁ.

decreed, be, v.p. ተሰሯ tḁsḁ́rrã (täsár-).

deep, adj. (of water) ጥልቅ ṭi̥lq (§ 57*b*).

ጠሊቅ ṭḁ́liq.

(of a cavity) አይቅ á͡i̥q.

It is deep: ጥልቅ፡ነው። ṭi̥lqĭ (§ 7*d*) nḁ͡u.

How deep is the water? ውሃ፡ጥልቁ፡ስንት፡ነው። wū́ha ṭi̥lqu si̥ntĭ nḁ͡u?

Is it too deep to ford? ሰው፡አያስኬድም። sḁ́͡u a͡i̥as-kā́di̥m? (a͡ʸas-).

deep, be, v.i. ጠለቀ ṭḁ́llḁqḁ.

It is too deep for him (it): ይጠልቀዋል። yi̥ṭā́lqḁ͡uāl.

defeat, v.t. ድል፡አደረገ di̥l adḁ́rrḁgḁ.

ድል፡መታ di̥l mḁ́ttã.

defeated, be, v.p. ድል፡ሆነ di̥l h^{w}ŏ́nḁ.
ድል፡ተመታ di̥l tḁmḁ́ttã.
defecate, v.i. እዳሪ፡ወጣ (i̥)ddári wώṭṭã.
ሜዳ፡ወጣ m^{y}éda wώṭṭã.
defend, v.t. ጠበቀ ṭḁ́bbḁqḁ.
defendant, s. ተከሳሽ tḁkḁ́sáš (§ 8).
defended, be, v.p. ተጠበቀ tḁṭḁ́bbḁqḁ.
deficient, adj. ጐደሎ gwώdḁl^{w}o.
define, v.t. ወሰነ wώssḁnḁ.
delay, v.i. ቈየ qwώyyä.
ቀረ qḁ́rrḁ (§ 42*b*).
Don't delay: አትቈይ። attí̥qwώi̥, pl. አትቈዩ። atti̥qwώyyu, or አትቅር። attí̥qi̥r, pl. አትቅሩ። attí̥qru.
delay, v.t. አቈየ aqwώyyä.
አስቀረ asqḁ́rrḁ.
deliberate, v.i. መከረ mḁ́kkḁrḁ (-kär-).
délu (دلو), s. መቅጃ mḁ́qjã.
demand, v.t. አለ álḁ (s.v. √በለ, § 44*a*) with imperative of ሰጠ sḁ́ṭṭḁ:
They demanded money: ገንዘብ፡ስጠን፡አሉ። gḁ́nzḁv si̥ṭänn álu (or …፡ ስጡኝ፡አሉ። … si̥ṭäññ álu).
demon, s. ዛር zār.
deny, v.t. አለ álḁ (s.v. √በለ, § 44*a*) with neg. conjug. (§ 38).
(disown) ካደ kádḁ.
He denies that he saw him (it): አላየሁትም፡ይላል። aláyyähuti̥m yi̥lāl.
He denied the debt (dishonestly): እዳውን፡ሸሸገ። i̥daun šḁ́ššagḁ.
depict, v.t. ሳለ sálḁ (conjug. like ሳለ to cough).
deposit, s. (on trust) አደራ ádḁ́rã (-dár-; § 8).
depth, s. እርዝመት i̥rzi̥mḁt (-mät).
(of water) ጥልቅ ṭi̥lq.

derived, be, v.p. ወጣ wώṭṭã.

Dervish, s. (of the Sudan) ደርቡሽ dárbuš (ዱ- dḭ́-, -rẏu-).

descend, v.i. ወረደ wώrrḁdḁ.

descending, adj. ደፋታ dḁfátã.

descent, s. (slope) ቍልቍለት qwŭlqwŭlḁt (-lät; § 8).

(way down) መውረጃ mḁu͡rájã.

describe, v.t. መሰለ mḁ́ssḁlḁ (type B § 35).

I will describe him (it): እመሰለዋለሁ። ḭmḁssḭlḁu͡ál-lḁu͡ʰ (§ 7d, § 12c).

Describe him (her, it, them § 61b) to me: መሰሊልኝ። mḁ́ssḭlḭllḭñ (§ 47a).

description, s. ምስል mḭ́sḭl.

ምሳሌ mḭssálʸe.

desert, s. በረሃ bḁ́rḁhã.

deserted, adj. ፍች fḭčč (§ 57b).

deserve, v.t. ተገባው tḁgḁ́bbau͡ (impers. § 43a).

He deserves praise: ምስጋና፡ይገባዋል። mḭsgána yḭg-gḁ́bbau͡āl.

desire, s. ምኞት mḭ́ññot.

desire, v.t. ፈለገ fḁ́llḁgḁ.

ተመኘ tḁmḁ́ññä.

despair, v.i. ተስፋ፡አጣ tḁ́sfa (tás-) áṭṭã.

desperado, s. ጋዱ gáddu.

destroy, v.t. ፈጀ fḁ́jjä (fáj-).

አፈረሰ afḁ́rrḁsḁ.

(consume) በላ bḁ́llã.

destroy utterly, v.t. ፈጃጀ fḁjǟjjä (fäj-).

destroyed, be, v.p. ፈረሰ fḁ́rrḁsḁ.

ተፈጀ tḁfḁ́jjä (-fáj-).

destruction, s. ፍርስ fḭrs.

detain, v.t. አቈየ aqwώyyä.

አስቀረ asqḁ́rrḁ.

determine, v.i. & t. (intend) ፈቀደ fḁ́qqḁdḁ.
(fix) ወሰነ wóssḁnḁ.

determined, adj. ጨካኝ č̣ḁ́kkãñ (-ññ § 6 ; § 8).

devastation, s. ጥፋት ṭi̥fát (§ 8).

devil, s. ሰይጣን sa͡i̥ṭán (§ 8).
ዲያብሎስ dʸáb(i̥)lʷós (dá-, -áy̥(i̥)l- ; § 8).

The devil take him (it)! ገደል፡ይግባ። gádäl yi̥gy̥a!

The devil take you! ምን፡አባትህ። mi̥n abbáti̥h?

devoid of, prp. ያለ- yálḁ- (§ 47*a*).
የሌለበት yälʸálläbbḁt (-bät ; §§ 39, 47*a*, 62*c*).

A place devoid of grass: ሣር፡የሌለበት፡ስፍራ፡ sār yälʸálläbbḁt si̥fra.

In a place devoid of grass: ሣር፡በሌለበት፡ስፍራ፡ sār y̥ḁlʸálläbbḁt si̥fra.

devour, v.t. ጐረሰ gwórrḁsḁ.

dew, s. ጤዛ ṭʸézã.

dewlap, s. ዳልጋ dálgã.

diamond, s. አልማስ álmás (§ 8).

diaphragm, s. እርግብግባት i̥rgi̥bgi̥bát (-i̥vgi̥vát ; § 8).

diarrhœa, s. ቅዘን qi̥zḁn.
ትቅማጥ ti̥qmáṭ (§ 8).

diarrhœa, have, v.i. ቀዘነ qḁ́zzḁnḁ.

diarrhœa, cause, v.i. (in, v.t.) አስቀዘነ asqḁ́zzḁnḁ.

die, v.i. ሞተ mʷṓtḁ.

What did he (it) die of? በምን፡ሞተ። bḁmi̥n mʷótḁ?

differ, v.i. ተለየ tḁlḁ́yyä.

difference, s. መለየት mḁllḁ́yät.

different, adj. ልዩ líyyu.
ሌላ lélã.

This is different from that: ይህ፡ልዩ፡ነው፡ያም፡ልዩ፡ነው። yi̥he líyyu na͡u yam líyyu na͡u.

difficult, adj. ጭንቅ či̥nq.
   ችጉር či̥ggur.
   This is difficult to climb: ይህ፡መውጣቱ፡ችጉር፡ነው። yi̥he (§ 55*b*) ma͡u̥ṭátu či̥ggúr (§ 8) na͡u̥.
   Amharic is difficult to learn: አማርኛ፡አይያገዝም። amārí̥ñña a͡i̥yyázi̥m (§ 63*c*).
difficulties, be in, v.i. ቸገረው čággara͡u̥ (-gär-; impers. § 43*a*).
difficulty, s. (distress) ችጋር čí̥ggár (§ 8).
dig (up), v.i. & t. ቈፈረ qwóffarḁ (-fär-).
   ኳተ kwátḁ.
dignified, adj. ከባድ kḁ́bbád (§ 8).
dik-dik (*Madoqua Saltiana* and *Nanotragus Hemprichianus*), s. ምዳቋ mi̥dáqqwã.
diligence, s. ትጋት tí̥gát (§ 8).
diligent, adj. ትጉ ti̥gu.
diligent, be, v.i. ተጋ tḁ́ggã.
dí̥lu (دلو), s. መቅጃ mḁ́qjã.
Dinder, s. አይማ á͡i̥mã.
dinner, s. እራት i̥rát.
   Is dinner ready? እራት፡ተሰናድቷል። i̥rát tḁsḁnádĭ̥tŏ͡āl? (-nárt- § 7*d*).
   Put it on the table and let it wait: ቀርቦ፡ይቈይ። qḁ́rỵ^{w}o yí̥qwω͡i̥ (-ỵ^{w}ó͡i̥q-).
direction, s. ወገን wḁ́gḁn (wóg-).
   He went in this direction: በዚህ፡ወገን፡ሔደ። bḁzzí̥h wógḁn hádä; or በዚህ፡በኩል፡ሔደ። bḁzzí̥h ỵák̥kul hádä, (s.v. አከለ).
dirt, s. (-y, adj. § 57*b*) እድፍ í̥d(i̥)f.
dirty, be, v.i. አደፈ áddafḁ (§ 63*d*, *e*).
   It is dirty: አደፈ። áddafḁ.
   It will get dirty: ያድፋል። yádfāl.

disappear, v.i. እልም፡አለ i̥lli̥mm álḁ (s.v. √በለ, § 44*a*).
  ዘለቀ zḁ́llḁqḁ (q.v.).
disappearance, s. ጥፋት ṭi̥fát (§ 8).
disbelief, interj. expressing, አረግ ḁ́rḁg! (ḁrḁ̄ḁ́g! § 7*d*).
disclose, v.t. ገለጠ gḁ́llḁṭḁ (gál-).
  Do not disclose it: አትግለጠው። attí̥glḁṭḁ͡u, pol. አይግለጡት። á͡i̥glḁṭut, pl. አትግለጡት። attí̥glḁṭut.
disclosed, be, v.p. ተገለጠ tḁgḁ́llḁṭḁ (-gál-).
discomfort, cause, v.i. ስቅቅ፡አለ sí̥qi̥qq álḁ (s.v. √በለ, § 44*a*).
  ቈረቈረ qwωrḁ́qqwωrḁ.
  He (it) causes us discomfort: ይቈረቍረናል። yi̥qwω-rḁ́qqwŭrḁnnāl.
discourteous, adj. በለጌ bálḁgʸe (-läg-).
discover, v.t. ገለጠ gḁ́llḁṭḁ (gál-).
discovered, be, v.p. ተገለጠ tḁgḁ́llḁṭḁ (-gál-).
disease, s. በሽታ bḁ́ši̥tā.
  ደዌ dḁ́wʸe (dḁ́͡uʸe).
  He (it) has a disease of the lungs: ሳምበውን፡ታሟል። sámba͡un (§ 52*a* γ, § 56*c*) támmŏāl.
disgrace, s. እፍረት i̥frḁt (-rät).
disgusting, adj. ጸያፍ ṣḁ́yyáf (ጠ- ṭḁ́-; § 8).
dish, s. ሰሐን sḁ́hán (§ 8).
dish-cloth, s. መጥረጊያ mḁṭrḁ́gyā.
dishonest, adj. ቀጣፊ qḁṭáfi.
dishonesty, s. ቅጥፈት qi̥ṭfḁt (-fät).
  ቅጥፍና qi̥ṭfí̥nnā.
  እብለት i̥blḁt (i̥yl-, -lät).
dislike, v.t. ጠላ ṭḁ́llā.
dislocated, be, v.i. ወለቀ wḁ́llḁqḁ (wώl-).
  My ankle is dislocated: እግሬ፡ወልቋል። i̥grʸe wώl-qŏāl.

dislocation, s. ውልቅ wŭlq.
dismiss, v.t. አሰናበተ assḁnā́bbḁtḁ (-bät-).
dismissal, s. ስንብት si̥ní̥bbi̥t.
dismissed, be, v.p. ተሰናበተ tḁsḁnā́bbḁtḁ (täsän-, -bät-).
disobedience, s. አመፅ ā́mḁṭ.
disobedient, adj. አመጠኛ ãmḁṭḁ́ññã (-ṭā́ñ-).
disobey, v.i. & t. አመጠ ámmḁṭḁ በ- bḁ- (vḁ-; § 47*a*).
  Are you going (do you mean) to disobey me? ልታምጥብኝ፡ነው። li̥ttāmmi̥ṭi̥bbí̥ñ nḁu?
  You are disobeying me: ታምጥብኛለህ። tāmmi̥ṭi̥bbi̥ññállăh.
disperse, v.i. (be dispersed, v.p.) ተበተነ tḁbḁ́ttḁnḁ (tḁvḁ́-, -ā́ttän-).
  The crowd (was) dispersed: ሕዝብ፡ተበተነ። hí̥zi̥v tḁvā́ttänḁ.
disperse, v.t. በተነ bḁ́ttḁnḁ (bā́ttän-).
disposition, s. (arrangement) ሥራት sí̥rā́t (§ 8).
  (character) ባሕሪ báhri (bhā́ri § 7*d*).
dispute, s. ክርክር ki̥rí̥kki̥r.
  ሙግት múggi̥t.
dispute, v.i. ተከራከረ tḁkḁrā́kkḁrḁ (-kärā́kkär-).
dissolve, v.i. (dissolved, be, v.p.) ሟሟ mwā́mmwã.
distance, s. [እ]ርቀት rí̥qḁt (í̥rq-).
  What is the distance? ርቀቱ፡ምን፡ያህል፡ነው። rí̥qḁtu mi̥n yahl nḁu?
distant, adj. [እ]ሩቅ (i̥)rúq.
distant, be, v.i. [እ]ራቀ (i̥)ráqḁ.
distinguish, v.t. ለየ lḁ́yyä.
distinguished, be, v.p. ተለየ tḁlḁ́yyä.
distress, s. (grief) አዘን ázḁn.
  (misfortune) ችጋር čí̥ggár (§ 8).

distress, be in, v.i. ቸገረው čággḁrḁu (-gär-; impers. § 43*a*; § 63*d*, *e*).

distressed, be, v.i. & p. አዘነ ázzḁnḁ.

distribute, v.t. አካፈለ akkā́ffḁlḁ.

distributed, be, v.p. ተከፈለ tḁkḁ́ffḁlḁ.

district, s. (gen.) አገር ā́gḁr (-gär).
(administrative) ግዛት gi̥zát (§ 8).

disturb, v.t. አናወጠ annā́uwḁṭḁ (-wωṭ-).

disturbance, s. ነውጥ nḁ́wŭṭ (nḁ́uṭ).
A disturbance occurred: ነውጥ ፡ ተነሣ ። nḁ́uṭ tḁnḁ́ssa.
He raised a disturbance: ነውጥ ፡ አደረገ ። nḁ́uṭ adḁ́rrḁgḁ.

disturbed, be, v.p. ተናወጠ tḁnā́uwḁṭḁ (-wωṭ-).

ditch, s. ቦይ b^{w}ói̥.
ጉድባ gúdbã (-dy̥ã).
መስኖ mḁ́sn^{w}o.
ፈሰስ fḁ́sḁs.

dive, v.i. ጠለቀ ṭḁ́llḁqḁ.

divide, v.i. (be divided, v.p.) ተከፈለ tḁkḁ́ffḁlḁ.

divide, v.t. ከፈለ kḁ́ffḁlḁ.
Divide it into three parts: ክፈለው ፡ በሶስት ። kí̥fḁlḁu y̥ḁ́s^{w}ōst.

division, s. (act of) መክፈል mḁ́kfḁl.
(part) ክፍል kí̥fi̥l.

divorce, s. ፍች fi̥čč.

divorce, v.t. ፈታ fḁ́ttã.

divorced, be, v.p. ተፈታች tḁfḁ́ttāč (-čč § 6).

do, v.t. አደረገ adḁ́rrḁgḁ.
What are you doing? ምን ፡ ታደርጋለህ ። mi̥n tādärgálläh?, pl. -ጋላችሁ ። -galláččyuh?

Don't do so: አታድርግ። attádri̥g, pl. -ርጉ። -ri̥gu.

Don't do anything to him (it): ምንም፡አታድርግለት። mi̥ni̥mm attádri̥gi̥llḁt, pl. -ርጉለት። -ri̥gullḁt.

That will do: ይበቃል። yi̥vḁ́qāl.

This is done with, isn't it? ይህ፡አልቆ፡አይዶል። yi̥h álqʷo (§ 65*b*) a͡i̥däl (§ 7*d*)?

It is done with: አብቅቷል። áv̥qi̥tǒāl, or አልቋል። álqǒāl.

(emphasizing a verb) [እ]ኮ (i̥)kkʷó (ŭk-), usually enclitic:

Do wait: ቈይኮ። qwω͡i̥kkʷó.

doctor, s. ሀኪም hấkim (-i̥m; hấkĩm § 8).

ባለመድኃኒት bālḁmḁdhánʸit (-dáhnit § 7*d*).

ወጌሳ wωgʸéssã (Gall.).

dog, s. ውሻ wŭššã (ʷúš-).

Wild dog (*Lycaon pictus*): ተኩላ tḁ́kwŭlã (§ 52*a*, δ).

dog, interj. to call a, ቡች፡ቡች búčči̥ yučč!

dollar, s. ብር bi̥rr (§ 8, § 52*a*, δ).

One dollar: አንድ፡ብር፡ ándi̥ vi̥rr.

Two dollars: ሁለት፡ብር፡ hulátti̥ vi̥rr.

Ten dollars: አሥር፡ብር፡ assír vi̥rr.

How many dollars? ስንት፡ብር፡ si̥nti̥ vi̥rr?

dōm (دوم, bifurcating palm), s. ጭፋር či̥fár (§ 8, § 52*a*, δ).

done, be, v.p. ተደረገ tḁdḁ́rrḁgḁ.

donkey, s. አህያ abíy(y)ã.

don't—rendered by substituting አት- att(i̥)- for the initial ይ- y(i̥)- of the jussive (§ 27):

Let him go: ይሒድ። yíhi̥d, pl. -ዱ። -du.

Don't go: አትሒድ። attíhi̥d, pl. -ዱ። -du.

Let him come: ይምጣ። yímṭa, pl. -ጡ። -ṭu.

Don't come: አትምጣ። attímṭa, pl. -ጡ። -ṭu.

Let him do it: ያድርገው። yádri̥gḁ͡u (yárgḁ͡u § 7*d*), pl. -ጉት። -gut.

Don't do it: አታድርገው። attádri̥gḁ͡u (attárgḁ͡u), pl. -ጉት። -gut.

door, s. መዝጊያ mḁ́zgyā̃ (mä́z-).

ሳንቃ sáṅqā̃.

ደጅ dḁjj (däjj).

Shut the door: ሳንቃውን፡ዝጋው። sáṅqa͡un zí̥ga͡u.

He is not to leave the door open: መዝጊያውን፡ ክፍት፡አይተው። mḁ́zgya͡un ki̥ft á͡i̥tḁ͡u.

Open the door for him: ክፈትለት። kí̥fḁti̥llḁt.

door-keeper, s. በረኛ bḁrrḁ́ññā̃ (-räñ-).

ከልካይ kḁ́lká͡i̥ (-áyy § 6; § 8).

doorway, s. ደጃፍ dájjáf (§ 8).

double, adj. ሁለት húlḁtt (-lätt).

(of consonant in pronunciation) ጥብቅ ṭi̥bq (ṭi̥vq).

doubt, v.i. & t. ጠረጠረ ṭḁrḁ́ṭṭḁrḁ (ṭärḁ́ṭṭärḁ).

doubted, be, v.p. ተጠረጠረ tḁṭḁrḁ́ṭṭḁrḁ (-ṭärḁ́ṭṭärḁ).

doubtful, adj. ውልውል wŭlí̥wwŭl.

doubtless (no doubt), adv. እንኳን ńkwān.

dough, s. ቡሆ búh^{w}o.

dove, s. (domestic) [እ]ርግብ rí̥gi̥b (i̥rg-, -i̥v).

(wild) ዋልያ wályā̃.

down, adv. (below) ታች tāč.

በታች bḁtáč (§ 8).

They are down there: ከዚያ፡በታች፡ናቸው። kḁzzyá y̥ḁtáč náčča͡u.

down, s. (rising ground) ጉራ g^{w}órā̃.

down, come (go), v.i. ወረደ wɔ́rrḁdḁ.

He has gone down: ወርዷል። wɔ́rd͡ōāl.

The price will come down: ዋጋ፡ይላላል። wága yi̥lállāl.

downhill, adv. ቍልቍለት qwŭlqwŭ́lḁt (-lät; § 8).

down-stream, adv. ፈረሰኛ fḁrḁsḁ́ññã (-sáñ-).

downwards, adv. ቍልቍል qwŭ́lqwŭl.

ወደታች wωdḁ́táč (§ 8).

doze, v.i. አንቀላፋ aṅqḁláffã.

draw, v.i. & t. (pull) ሳበ sábḁ (sáṿḁ).

(portray) ሳለ sálḁ (conjug. like ሳለ to cough).

መሰለ mḁ́ssḁlḁ (type B, § 35).

(water) ቀዳ qḁ́ddã.

drawer, s. (of table, desk, etc.) ሳጥን sáṭi̥n.

drawers, s. (garment) ሱሪ súrri.

(woman's) ልበልባ li̥bbálbã (-lṿã).

drawing, s. (picture) ስል si̥l.

drawn, be, v.p. (pulled) ተሳበ tḁsábḁ (täs-, -áṿḁ).

(of water) ተቀዳ tḁqḁ́ddã.

dream, s. ሕልም hi̥lm (እልም i̥lm).

drench, v.t. አበሰበሰ abḁsḁ́bbḁsḁ (aṿḁ-).

drenched, be (get), v.p. በሰበሰ bḁsḁ́bbḁsḁ.

dress, s. ልብስ li̥bs (li̥ṿs).

dress, v.t. አለበሰ alḁ́bbḁsḁ.

dress (another) well, v.t. አስጌጠ asg^{y}éṭḁ.

dress (oneself, be (get) dressed), v.i. ለበሰ lḁ́bbḁsḁ.

Wait till I'm dressed: ቈይ፡እስትለብስ። qwωyy i̥sti̥lḁ́ṿs.

dress (oneself) well, v.i. አጌጠ ag^{y}éṭḁ.

drill, s. (mil.) ሰልፍ sḁlf (sälf).

drill, v.i. (be drilled, v.p.) ተሰለፈ tḁsḁ́llḁfḁ (täsál-).

drill, v.t. አሰለፈ assḁ́llḁfḁ (-sál-).

drink, s. (something to) መጠጥ mḁ́ṭḁṭ (-ḁṭṭ § 6).

Are the drinks in the water-jar? መጠጦች ፡ ተንስራ ፡ አሉ ። mḁ́ṭḁṭṭʷōč tḁnsi̥ra állu?

drink, v.i. & t. ጠጣ ṭḁ́ṭṭã.

When did he (it) drink? መቼ ፡ ጠጣ ። mḁ́čʸe ṭḁ́ṭṭa?

drink, give to, v.t. አጠጣ aṭḁ́ṭṭã.

(infants) ጋተ gátḁ.

drinking-place, s. መጠጫ mḁṭḁ́č̣č̣ã.

drip, v.i. ነጠበ nḁ́ṭṭḁbḁ (nắṭ-, -ḁyḁ).

drive, v.i. & t. ነዳ nḁ́ddã.

Let him drive the mules: በቅሎች ፡ ይንዳ ። bḁ́qlʷōč yi̥nda.

drive away (out), v.t. አወጣ awώṭṭã (a͡uώ-).

driven, be, v.p. ተነዳ tḁnḁ́ddã.

drop, s. (liquid) ነጥብ náṭi̥b (-i̥y).

One drop is enough: አንድ ፡ ነጥብ ፡ ይበቃል ። and náṭi̥y yi̥yḁ́qāl.

drop, v.i. (be dropped, v.p.) ወደቀ wώddḁqḁ.

ተጣለ tḁṭálḁ.

drop, v.t. ጣለ ṭálḁ.

drop off (down), v.i. ዱብ ፡ አለ dubb álḁ (s.v. √ባለ, § 44*a*).

(of more than one person or object) ዱብ ፡ ዱብ ፡ አለ dubbi̥dúbb álḁ (s.v. √ባለ, § 44*a*).

drown, v.i. (be drowned, v.p.) በውሃ ፡ ሞተ bḁwű́ha (bḁ́͡uha) mʷṓtḁ.

ውሃ ፡ አጥልቆት ፡ ሞተ wű́ha ắ ṭi̥lqʷot mʷṓtḁ.

drown, v.t. አጠለቀ aṭḁ́llḁqḁ.

Drown it: አጥልቀው ። ắṭi̥lqa͡u.

drowsiness, s. እንቅልፍ (i̥)ṅqi̥lf (§ 7*d*, § 8).

drum, s. ከበሮ kḁ́bḁr^{w}o (kḁ́y-, -är-).
(big) ነጋሪት nḁgărit.
Beat the drum: ከበሮ፡ምታ። kḁ́yḁr^{w}o mí̥ta.
drunk, be, v.p. ተጠጣ tḁṭḁ́ṭṭã.
drunk (intoxicated), be, v.i. ሰከረ sḁ́kkḁrḁ (-kär-).
drunkard, s. ሰካር sḁ́kkăr (§ 8).
drunkenness, s. ስካር sí̥kăr (§ 8).
dry, adj. ደረቅ dḁ́rḁq.
(of climate) ድርቅ di̥rq (§ 57*b*).
(of weather) ብራ bí̥rrã („).
Dry season: በጋ bḁ́gã [Jan. Feb. & Mar.].
dry, v.i. ደረቀ dḁ́rrḁqḁ.
Let it dry: ይድረቅ። yí̥drḁq, pl. -ቁ። -qu.
dry, v.t. አደረቀ adḁ́rrḁqḁ.
Dry it: አድርቀው። ádri̥qḁ͡u, pl. -ቁት። -qut.
dry, spread out to, v.t. አሰጣ asḁ́ṭṭã.
Spread it out to dry: አስጣው። ásṭa͡u, pl. -ጡት። -ṭut.
dry up, v.i. (weather, ground after rain) ጠፈፍ፡አለ ṭḁ́fḁff álḁ (s.v. √ባለ, § 44*a*).
When it dries up: ጠፈፍ፡ሲል፡ ṭḁ́fḁffi̥ (§ 7*d*) sil.
dryness, s. ድርቅ di̥rq.
duck, s. Š. ዝዬ zí̥yye (§ 52*a*, δ).
G. ካይንት káyi̥nt (§ 52*a*, δ).
dug (up), be, v.p. ተቈፈረ tḁqwóffḁrḁ (-fär-).
ተኳተ tḁkwátḁ.
duiker (*Cephalophus abessinicus*), s. ምዳቋ mi̥dáqqwã.
dumb, adj. ዱዳ dúdã.
during, prp. በ- bḁ- (§ 47*a*).
ከ- kḁ- („).
ተ- tḁ- („).
የ- [በ-]...፡ጊዜ yä- (bḁ-)... gí̥z^{y}e (§ 47*b*).

During the rains: በክረምት፡ bḁ́kǐrḁ́mt (§ 8).
During the night: ተሌሊት፡ tḁl^{y}ēlít.
During breakfast: በቡን፡ቁርስ፡ጊዜ፡ bḁyúnn qurs gí̥z^{y}e.

dust, s. (raised by wind) አዋራ awắrrã.
(minute, accumulated) ትቢያ tí̥bbyã.

duster, s. መጥረጊያ mḁṭrḁ́gyã.

dwarf, s. ድንክ di̥ṅk.

dye, s. ቀለም qḁ́lḁm.
The dye will not come out: ቀለም፡አይለቅም። qḁ́lḁm a͡i̥lḁ́qqi̥m.

dye, v.t. ቀለመ qḁ́llḁmḁ.

dyed, be, v.p. ተቀለመ tḁqḁ́llḁmḁ.

E

§ refers to the paragraphs of the Grammar (Initia Amharica, Part I).

each, dist. pron. እየ- ...-u, iyyä- ... -u (§ 18); -u may be replaced by the pers. suff. (§ 12*b*), and after numerals is dropped.
አንዳንድ ándánd (§ 18, § 8).
See § 83*a*.

Give them a dollar each: አንዳንድ፡ብር፡ስጣቸው። andándi̥ (§ 7*d*) y̥irr si̥ṭắččḁ͡u.

Give a little to each of the horses: እየፈረሱ፡ጥቂት፡ስጠው። iyyäfḁ́rḁsu tí̥qi̥t sí̥ṭḁ͡u.

Put some in each box: በየሳጥኑ፡አድርግ። bḁyyä-sắṭi̥nu ārg (§ 7*d*).

Pay each man himself: ከፊላቸው፡ለየራሳቸው። ki̥fḁ-lắččḁ͡u lḁyyärāsắččḁ͡u.

They are (cost) half a dollar each: በኩል፡እኩል፡ብር፡ናቸው። bḁkkul ŭkkúl (§ 8) yi̥rr nắččḁu.

Ten at half a dollar each: አሥር፡በየኩል፡እኩል፡ብር፡ ássi̥r yḁyyắkkul ŭkkúl yi̥rr.

Ten at one dollar each: አሥር፡በያንዳንድ፡ብር፡ ássi̥r yḁyyandándi̥ yi̥rr.

Ten at two dollars each: አሥር፡በየሁለት፡ብር፡ ássi̥r yḁyyähulắtti̥ yi̥rr.

Two at ten dollars each: ሁለት፡በያሥር፡ብር፡ húlätt yḁyyassí̥r yi̥rr.

each other, reciprocal pron. እርስ፡በርስ- í̥rsḁ [እርስ፡ i̥rs] bḁrs- (yḁ-, -ärs-, § 19) with the plural pers. suff. (§ 12*b*).

They bite each other: እርስ፡በርሳቸው፡ይናከሳሉ። í̥rsḁ yärsắččḁu yi̥nnakkḁsállu.

eager, be, v.i. (for, v.t.) ተሻማ tḁšẫmmā (täš-).

eagle, s. አሞራ amʷṓrā.

ear, s. ጆሮ jʷórʷo (§ 52*a*, γ).

early, adv. ጧት ṭwắt.

ማለዳ mắlḁdā (§ 8).

በማለዳ bḁmắlḁdā (§ 8).

If we start early we shall reach it: ማለዳ፡ብንሔድ፡እንደርስበታለን። málḁda yi̥nni̥hắd, i̥nni̥därsi̥bbḁtállän.

early, rise (do anything), v.i. ማለደ mállḁdḁ.

Come early: ማልደህ፡ና። māldáh nā (§ 8).

I shall start early: ማልጄ፡እነሣለሁ። mắli̥jjʸe i̥nnḁssállḁuʰ (§ 7*d*).

He is to go early: ማልዶ፡ይሔድ። máldʷo yí̥hi̥d.

earn, v.t. አተረፈ atḁ́rrḁfḁ (-tár-).

earring, s. ጕትቻ gwŭtí̥ččā (§ 52*a*, δ).

earth, s. (soil) መሬት mḁ́r^{y}ẽt (§ 8).
(loose) አፈር áfḁr (-fär).
(world) ዓለም ā́lḁm.
What on earth is it? ምን፡መሳይ፡ነው። mi̥n mḁsā́͡i̥ nḁ͡u?
earthenware, s. ሸክላ šḁ́klã (šák-).
earthquake, s. መነቃነቅ mḁnnḁqā́nḁq.
An earthquake occurred: ምድር፡ተነቃነቀ። ḿdi̥r tḁnḁqánnḁqḁ.
ear-wax, s. ኩክ kukk.
ease, s. እርፈት i̥rfḁt (-fät).
east, s. ምሥራቅ mi̥sráq (§ 8).
Easter, s. ትንሣኤ ti̥nsá͡i̥.
ፋሲካ fásikã.
easy, adj. ምቹ mí̥čču.
ቅን qi̥n.
eat, v.i. & t. በላ bḁllã.
Something to eat: መብል፡ mḁvi̥l.
Give him (it) something to eat: አብላው። ā́vla͡u, pl. -ሉት። -lut.
eat greedily, v.t. ጎረሰ gwórrḁsḁ.
eaten, be, v.p. ተበላ tḁbḁ́llã (tḁvḁ́-).
ebony (*Dalbergia melanoxylon*, Broun, Cat. 158), s. ዞቢ z^{w}óbbi.
economise, v.i. ቈጠበ qwóṭṭḁbḁ (-ḁvḁ).
eddy, s. አዟሪ azwā́ri.
edge, s. ዳር dã̄r.
ድምበር di̥mbḁr (-bär).
ጫፍ ç̣ãf.
(of plateau, of precipice) አፋፍ ā́fã̄f (§ 8).
edible, adj. የሚበላ yämmi̥bbḁ́llã (§ 14, § 63*c*).
Is it edible? ለመብል፡ይረባል። lḁmḁ́vi̥l yi̥rḁ́vāl?

educate, v.t. አሳደገ asáddḁgḁ.

egg, s. እንቍላል (i̥)ṅqwŭ́lā́l (§ 8, § 52*a*, δ).

Boiled eggs: ቅቅል፡እንቍላል፡ qí̥qqi̥l i̥ṅqwŭ́lāl.

Fried eggs: ጥብስ፡እንቍላል፡ ṭi̥vs i̥ṅqwŭ́lāl.

Poached eggs: ያለቅርፍት፡የተቀቀለ፡እንቍላል። yālḁ-qí̥rfi̥t yätḁqḁ́qqḁlḁ ṅqwŭ́lāl.

eggshell, s. የንቍላል፡ቅርፍት yäṅqwŭlā́l qi̥rfi̥t.

Egypt, s. ምስር mí̥ssi̥r.

Egyptian, adj. የምስር yämí̥ssi̥r (s.v. የ-, § 47*a*, § 70).

Egyptian, s. የምስር፡ሰው yämi̥ssí̥r (§ 8) sa͡u̥.

eh? interj. (= what did you say?) ምን፡አልህ። mi̥n alh?
(after a phrase) -ወይ -wa͡i̥? (-wǒ͡i̥; -oይ -wi̥; § 6, § 8).
-አ -ā́? (§ 6, § 8).

This is finished (done with), eh? ይህ፡አልቆ፡ያለወይ። yi̥h álqʷo yálla͡äuwi̥?

He wants money, eh? ገንዘብ፡ይፈልጋሎይ። gḁ́nzḁv yi̥fḁ́lli̥gāllwi̥?

You'll tell me if you go, eh? ብትሔድ፡ትለኛለሃ። bi̥tthā́d ti̥läññállähá?

eight, card. num. ስምንት sí̥mmi̥nt.

eighteen, card. num. አሥራ፡ስምንት asrā́ sí̥mmi̥nt.

eighty, card. num. ሰማንያ sḁmā́nyā.

either ... or, conj. ወይ፡ ... ፡ወይ wa͡i̥... wa͡i̥ (wǒ͡i̥ ... wǒ͡i̥).
ወይም፡ ... ፡ወይም wa͡i̥m (-mm § 6) ... wa͡i̥m (-mm) [wǒ͡i̥m (-mm) .... wǒ͡i̥m (-mm)].

Either pay the money or return the goods: ወይ፡ገንዘቡን፡ክፈለው፡ወይ፡እቃውን፡መልስ። wǒ͡i̥ gḁ́nzḁyun kí̥fḁla͡u wǒ͡i̥ í̥qa͡un mā́lli̥s.

elastic, be (become), v.i. ጕትት፡አለ gwŭ́tḁtt álḁ (s.v. √በለ, § 44*a*).

Is it elastic? ጕትት፡ይላል። gwŭ́tḁtt yi̥lāl?

elbow, s. ክርን ki̥rn (§ 52*a*, γ).

elephant (*Elephas africanus*), s. ዝሆን zóhʷon (ዘ- zḁ́-).

Eleusine multiflora (Guidi, Vocab. p. 624), s. ዘንጋዳ zḁ́ṅgā́dã (§ 8).

Eleusine tocusso (ib. p. 691), s. ዳጉሳ dāgússã.

eleven, card. num. አሥራ፡ሐንድ asrãhánd.

ember, s. ፍም fi̥m.

embrace, v.t. አቀፈ áqqḁfḁ.

አቈላመጠ aqqwωlā́mmḁṭḁ.

embroider, v.t. ጠለፈ ṭállḁfḁ.

embroidered, adj. (-ery, s., cp. § 57*b*) ጥልፍ ṭi̥lf.

embroidered, be, v.p. ተጠለፈ tḁṭállḁfḁ.

emerge, v.i. ወጣ wώṭṭã, from, ከ- kḁ- (ተ- tḁ-; § 47*a*).

emperor, s. ንጉሠ፡ነገሥት ni̥gŭ́sḁ (§ 9*d*) nḁ́gḁ́st (§ 8); abbr. ንጉሥ ní̥gŭ́s (§ 8); spoken of and addressed as ጃንሆይ jánhʷó͡i̥ (§ 8; § 53*b*); also spoken of as አጤ ā́ṭʸe with his name.

The Emperor Menilek: አጤ፡ምኒልክ፡ ā́ṭʸe mi̥nili̥k.

A foreigner of high rank may address him thus by name: አጤ፡ምኒልክ። ā́ṭʸe mi̥nili̥k.

Present me to the Emperor (pol.): ተንጉሥ፡ ያገናኙኝ። tḁni̥gús yāggḁnáññuñ.

What does the Emperor say? ጃንሆይ፡ምን፡ይላሉ። jānhʷó͡i̥ mi̥n yi̥lállu?

employ, v.t. አሰሩ assḁrrã.

employment, s. ተግባር tḁ́gbā́r (-gyā́-; § 8).

Out of employment: ተግባረ፡ፈት፡ tḁgyā́rḁ (§ 9*d*) fḁtt.

empress, s. እቴጌ (i̥)tʸḗgʸe.

empty, adj. ባዶ bắd^{w}o.
enamelled ware, s. ታኒካ tắnikā̃.
encamp, v.i. ሰፈረ sḁ́ffḁrḁ (-fär-).
When we get out of the trees we will encamp: ተዛፍ፡ስንወጣ፡እንሰፍራለን። tḁzắf (§ 52*a*, δ) si̥nn-wώṭa i̥nnsḁfrállän.
encampment, s. ሰፈር sḁ́fḁr (-fär).
enceinte, adj. ርጉዝ rí̥gúz (§ 8).
እርጉዝ í̥rgúz (§ 8).
enclosure, s. (for cattle) በረት bḁ́rḁt (bắrät).
end, s. (completion) መጨረሻ mḁč̣ḁrrḁ́šā̃ (-č̣ar-).
(conclusion) ማለቂያ mālắqyā̃.
(extremity) ዳር dār.
end, v.i. አለቀ állḁqḁ.
end, v.t. ጨረሰ č̣ắrrḁsḁ (č̣ắr-).
endure, v.t. ቻለ čắlḁ.
enemy, s. (personal) ጠላት ṭḁ́lắt (§ 8).
(in war) ጠበኛ ṭḁbḁ́ññā̃ (ṭḁvắñ-; § 52*a*, δ).
engage, v.t. ቀጠረ qḁ́ṭṭḁrḁ (-ṭär-).
(for another) አቃጠረ aqqắṭṭḁrḁ (-ṭärḁ).
I (will) engage you: እቀጥርሃለሁ። i̥qḁṭrähállḁu^{h}.
Engage a servant for me: ሎሌ፡ቀጥረህ፡አግባልኝ። l^{w}ōl^{y}e qḁ́ṭräh ắgvalli̥ñ.
engaged, be, v.p. ተቀጠረ tḁqḁ́ṭṭḁrḁ (-ṭär-).
How much is he (can he be § 63*c*) engaged at? በስንት፡ይቀጠራል። bḁsí̥nt yi̥qqḁ́ṭṭäral?
How much are (were) you engaged at? በስንት፡ ተቀጥረሃል። bḁsí̥nt tḁqḁ́ṭrähāl?
engineer, s. መሀንድስ mḁhándi̥s.
England, s. የንግሊዝ፡አገር yäṅglíz ágḁr (-gär; s.v. የ-, § 70).
እንጊልጣራ (i̥)ṅgi̥lṭárrā̃.

It is made in England: ተንግሊዝ፡አገር፡ይበጃል። tḁṅglíz ágär yi̥bbájjāl.

English, adj. የንግሊዝ yáṅglíz (§ 8; s.v. የ-, § 47*a*, § 70).

Englishman, s. እንግሊዝ (i̥)ṅglíz (§ 8).

engrave, v.t. (portray) ሳለ sálḁ (conjug. like ሳለ to cough).

engraving, s. ስል si̥l.

enjoy, v.t. አማረው amárḁu (impers. § 43*a*; § 63*d*, *e*).

I (shall) enjoy eating this: ይህ፡መብል፡ያምረኛል። yi̥he mḁ́yi̥l yámräññāl.

enlarge, v.t. (increase) ጨመረ čḁ́mmḁrḁ (-mär-).
(widen) አሰፋ asḁ́ffā̃.

enlarged, be, v.p. (increased) ተጨመረ tḁčḁ́mmḁrḁ (-mär-).
(widened) ሰፋ sḁ́ffā̃.

enough, adj. & adv. የሚበቃ yämmi̥bḁ́qā̃ (እሚ- (i̥)mmi̥- § 14; -i̥yḁ́-).

enough, adv.—often omitted:

This (that) is not strong enough: ይህ፡ብርቱም፡አይደል። yi̥he yi̥rtŭmm ái̥däl.

enough, be, v.i. በቃ bḁ́qqā̃ (báq-).

That is enough: ይህ፡ይበቃል። yi̥he yi̥yḁ́qāl.

The fence is not high enough: አጥሩ፡እርዝመቱ፡አይበቃም። áṭi̥ru (§ 55*b*) i̥rzí̥mḁtu ai̥yḁ́qām.

Is it enough for you? ይበቃሃል። yi̥yḁ́qahāl?, pol. ይበቃዎአል። yi̥yḁ́qaʷoāl?, (... you, pl.) ይበቃችኋል። yi̥yḁqáččyuhāl? (§ 7*d*).

enough, have, v.i. (of food, etc.) ጠገበ ṭḁ́ggḁbḁ (-ḁyḁ).

I have had enough: ጠግብያለሁ። ṭḁgi̥bbyállḁuʰ.

enquire, v.i. & t. ጠየቀ ṭḁ́yyḁqḁ (-yäq-).

enter, v.i. & t. ገባ gḁ́bbā̃ ከ- [ተ-] kḁ- (tḁ-; § 47*a*).

enter, cause or allow to, v.t. አስገባ asgḁ́bbā̃.

entrails, s. ሆድ፡ እቃ hʷōdịqā̃.
ፈርስ fạrs (färs).
entrance, s. (way in) መግቢያ mágbyā̃ (-gyy-).
envelope, s. አምቦሎክ ambolʷōk.
envelope, v.t. ያዘ yáza (§ 44c).
ጠቀለለ ṭaqállala.
enveloped, be, v.p. ተያዘ tayáza (taiá-).
ተጠቀለለ taṭaqállala.
envious, adj. ቀናተኛ qannātáññā̃ (-táñ-).
environs, s. ዙርያ zúryā̃.
envoy, s. መላክተኛ malāktáññā̃ (-ልክ- -lịk-, -táñ-).
envy, s. ቅናት qịnát (§ 8).
epiglottis, s. አንቃር áṅqār (§ 8).
epilepsy, s. ትግሪዳ tịgrídā̃.
equal, adj. ትክክል tịkíkkịl.
equal, v.i. አከለ ákkala.
equal, be, v.i. ተካከለ takákkala.
equalize, v.t. አስተካከለ astakákkala.
equerry, s. ሊቀመኳስ liqamakwás (lịq-, -qum-, -kás).
Eragrostis abessinica (Schweinfurth), s. ጤፍ ṭʸēf.
err, v.i. ሳተ sáta.
error, s. ስተት sịtat (-tät).
Erythrina tomentosa (Broun, Cat. 147), s. ቋራ qwārā̃.
Š. ኮርች kʷorč.
D. ሆርች hʷorč.
escape, v.i. ጠፋ ṭáffā̃.
If a prisoner escapes you will be punished: አስረኛ፡ ቢጠፋ፡ ትቀጣለህ። asráñña yiṭáfa tịqqaṭṭálläh.
escape, allow to, v.t. አስወጣ aswṓṭṭā̃.
escape from, v.t. (a person) ነጠቀ náṭṭaqa (náṭ-).
(a place) ወጣ፡ ከ- wṓṭṭā̃ ka- (ተ- ta-; § 47a).

escort, s. ሸኝታ šḁññi̥ttã (šäñ-).
escort, v.t. ሸኘ šḁ́ññä (šä́ñ-).
escorted, be, v.p. ተሸኘ tḁšḁ́ññä (täšä́ñ-).
Ethiopic, adj. & s. ግዕዝ g̥i̥͡i̥z.
euphorbia (*E. abessinica*, Broun, Cat. 508), s. ቍልቋል qwŭ́lqwā́l (§ 8).
European, s. ፈረንጅ fḁ́rḁ́nj (fä́rä́nj; § 8).
even, adj. ትክክል ti̥ki̥kki̥l.
even, adv. ደግሞ dḁ́gm^{w}o (dä́g-).
ደሞ dḁ́mm^{w}o (dä́m-).
-ም -m (-mm § 6; §§ 48*b*, 37*e*).
Fly? Why, they can't even stand up! እንኳን፡ መብረር፡ አይነሡም። ṅkwā́n mḁ́yrḁr a͡i̥nnḁ́ssum!
even, be, v.i. ተካከለ tḁkā́kkḁlḁ.
even, make, v.t. አስተካከለ astḁkā́kkḁlḁ.
evening, s. ማታ mátã.
Towards evening: ወደማታ፡ wωdḁmáta.
Good evening! (on meeting) እንደ-ት፡ አመሸህ። nd^{y}ēt amḁ́ššäh?, pol. -ሹ። -šu?, pl. -ሻችሁ። -šä́ččyuh? (§ 7*d*); (on leaving, dismissing, etc., = good-night, s.v. night).
evening, become, v.i. መሸ mḁ́ššä.
evening, pass the, v.i. አመሸ amḁ́ššä.
ever, adv. (see always)— ከቶ kḁ́tt^{w}o (s.v. ከተተ) with neg.
ምንም፡ ቢሆን፡ mi̥ni̥mm bíh^{w}ón (bi̥-; § 8) with neg. verb (§ 38).
What ever is it? ምን፡ መሳይ፡ ነው። mi̥n mḁsa͡i̥ nḁ͡u?
every, adj. ሁሉ- hull- with pers. suff. (§ 12*b*, § 16).
እየ-...-u iyyä-... -u (§ 18); -u may be replaced by the pers. suff. (§ 12*b*), and after numerals is dropped.
s.v. all, each.

everything, pron. ሁሉም húllum (-mm § 6; § 16).
evidence, s. ምስክር mi̥si̥kki̥r.
If you have any evidence, give it: ምስክር፡እንዳለህ፡ ስጠው። mi̥si̥kki̥r i̥ndálläh, si̥ṭau.
evidence, give, v.i. መስከረ mḁsḁkkḁrḁ (-kär-), for, ለ- lḁ-, against, በ- bḁ-, (§ 47*a*).
evident, adj. እዉቅ i̥wuq (i̥ʷuq).
ትይዩ ti̥(y)íyyu.
evident, be, v.i. ታወቀ táuwḁqḁ (-wωq-).
ታየ tấyyä.
It is evident to us: ይታየናል። yi̥ttáyyännāl.
evil, adj. ክፉ ki̥fu (kúfu, kŭ́fu § 7*d*).
evil, s. ክፋት ki̥fát (kúf-, kŭ́f-; § 8).
ewe, s. በግ bḁg.
exact, adj. (-ly, adv.) በልክ bḁli̥kk (§ 8).
exalted, adj. ክቡር ki̥bur (-i̥yu-).
examine, v.t. አየ ấyyä.
መረመረ mḁrḁmmḁrḁ (märḁmmärḁ).
examined, be, v.p. ታየ tấyyä.
ተመረመረ tḁmḁrḁmmḁrḁ (-märḁmmärḁ).
excavate, v.t. ቈፈረ qwóffḁrḁ (-fär-).
ኳተ kwátḁ.
excavated, be, v.p. ተቈፈረ tḁqwóffḁrḁ (-fär-).
ተኳተ tḁkwátḁ.
exceed, v.t. በለጠ bḁllḁṭḁ ከ- kḁ- (ተ- tḁ-; § 47*a*).
excellent, adj. ምርጥ mi̥rṭ.
መልካም mḁlkám pl. also መልካካም mḁlkákấm (§ 8).
ጥሩ ṭŭ́ru.
ድንቅ di̥ṅq.
It is excellent: አይገኝም። ai̥ggḁññi̥m.

except, prp. ከ- ...፡ በቀር kḁ- (ተ- tḁ-)... bḁ́qḁr (ṿḁ́-; § 47*b*).
ሲቀር síqḁr (sı̥q-; s.v. ቀረ § 42*b*; follows its word).

All except so-and-so: ተገሌ፡በቀር፡ሁሉ፡ tḁgḁ́lʸe ṿḁ́qḁr húllu, or እገሌ፡ሲቀር፡ሁሉ፡ ı̥gḁ́lʸe sı̥qḁr húllu.

Take out all the furniture except the table: ከገበታው፡በቀር፡ሁሉን፡እቃ፡አውጣው። kḁgḁ́ṿḁta͡u ṿḁ́qḁr húllun ı̥qa á͡uṭa͡u.

Let them all go except one: አንድ፡ሰው፡ሲቀር፡ ሁሉ፡ይሒዱ። and sá͡u sı̥qḁr húllu yı̥hı̥du.

exchange, s. ለውጥ lá͡uṭ.

exchange, v.t. ለወጠ lá͡uwḁṭḁ, for, በ- bḁ- (ṿḁ-; § 47*a*).

Exchange it: ለውጠው። lá͡uwŭṭa͡u, pl. -ጡት። -ṭut.

Will he exchange the horse for a mule? ፈረሱን፡ በበቅሎ፡ይለውጣል። fḁ́rḁsun bḁṿḁ́qlʷo yı̥lá͡uwŭṭāl?

exchanged, be, v.p. ተለወጠ tḁlá͡uwḁṭḁ, for, በ- bḁ- (ṿḁ-; § 47*a*).

Can the mule be exchanged for a horse? በቅሎው፡ በፈረስ፡ይለወጣል። bḁ́qlʷo͡u ṿḁfḁ́rḁs yı̥llá͡uwḁṭāl? (§ 63*c*).

excommunicate, v.t. ገዘተ gḁ́zzḁtḁ.

excommunicated, be, v.p. ተገዘተ tḁgḁ́zzḁtḁ.

excommunication, s. ግዝት gı̥zzı̥t.

excrement, s. (animal) ፋንዲያ fandíyyā.
(human) አር ār.

excuse, s. (reason) ምክንያት mı̥knyát (§ 8).

excuse, v.t. ይቅር፡አለ፡ለ- yı̥qı̥r álḁ (s.v. √በለ, § 44*a*) lḁ- (§ 47*a*).

Excuse me: (pol.) ይቅር፡ይበሉልኝ። yı̥qı̥r yı̥ṿḁlullı̥ñ.

execute, v.t. (put to death) ደበደበ dḁbḁ́ddḁbḁ (dḁṿḁ́ddḁṿḁ, -ṿád-).

executed, be, v.p. ተደበደበ tḁdḁbḁ́ddḁbḁ (-ḁỵḁ́ddḁỵḁ, -ỵád-).

executed, cause or allow to be, v.t. አስደበደበ asdḁbḁ́d-dḁbḁ (-ḁỵḁ́ddḁỵḁ, -ỵád-).

executioner, s. ደብዳቢ dḁbdábi (dḁỵdáỵi).

exhaust, v.t. (tire) አደከመ adḁ́kkḁmḁ.

exist, v.i. አለ állä (§§ 32, 39).

ተገኘ tḁgḁ́ññä.

It exists: አለ። állä, pl. አሉ። állu.

It does not exist: የለም። ỵállām, pl. የሉም። ỵállum.

existence, s. (presence) መኖር mḁ́nʷōr (§ 8).

exit, s. (way out) ማውጫ máu͡ç̣ã.

expect, v.t. ጠበቀ ṭḁ́bbḁqḁ.

I expect so: ይሆናል። yi̥hʷōnāl.

expedition, s. (mil.) ዘመቻ zḁmḁ́čã.

expense, s. ዋጋ wágã.

They must do it at their own expense: በገንዘባቸው፡ ያደርጉት። bḁgḁnzḁỵáččḁu͡ ỵádri̥gut.

expensive, adj. ውድ wŭdd.

explain, v.i. & t. ፈታ fḁ́ttã.

Please explain this to me: ይህንን፡ ፍታልኝ። yi̥hán-nän fí̥talli̥ñ, pol. ይህንን፡ ይፍቱልኝ። yi̥hánnän ỵíf̥-tulli̥ñ.

explanation, s. ፍች fi̥čč.

explode, v.i. (be exploded, v.p.) ፈነዳ fḁnḁ́ddã.

Look (pl.) out, it is going to explode: ተጠንቀቁ፡ ሊፈነዳ፡ ነው። tḁṭḁ́nqḁqu, lifḁnḁddá nḁu͡ (§ 8).

explode (cause to), v.t. አፈነዳ afḁnḁ́ddã.

explore, v.i. & t. ሰለለ sḁ́llḁlḁ (sál-).

export, v.i. & t. አስወሰደ aswḁ́ssḁdḁ (-wǿs-).

extend, v.i. ደረሰ dḁ́rrḁsḁ, to, እስከ- i̥skḁ- (§ 47*a*).

extend, v.t. (stretch) ዘረጋ zḁrḁ́ggā (zär-).
(widen) አሰፋ asḁ́ffā.
exterior, adj. የውጭ yáwi̥ç̣ç̣ (§ 8).
exterior, s. ውጭ wi̥ç̣ç̣.
extinguish, v.t. አጠፋ aṭḁ́ffā.
Extinguish it: አጥፋው። áṭfa͡u, pl. -ፉት። -fut.
extinguished, be, v.p. ጠፋ ṭḁ́ffā.
extra, adj. ጭማሪ ç̣i̥mmári.
extract, v.t. አወጣ awώṭṭā (a͡uώ-).
eye, s. ዓይን á͡i̥n (§ 52a, γ).
Keep an eye on Jim or he'll steal something: ጅምን፡ተመልከተው፡እንዳይሰርቅ። ji̥mmi̥n tḁmálkḁ-tḁ͡u nda͡i̥sárq.
eyebrow, s. ቅንድብ qí̥ndi̥b (-i̥v; § 52a, γ).
eyelash, s. ሽለፈት šḁ́lḁfḁt (-fät; „).
ሽፋሽፍት ši̥fáši̥ft („).

F

§ *refers to the paragraphs of the Grammar* (*Initia Amharica, Part I*).

fable, s. ተረት tḁ́rḁt.
ምሳሌ mi̥ssál^{y}e.
face, s. ፊት fīt (fi̥t).
facetious, adj. ቧልተኛ bwāltḁ́ññā (-táñ-).
ዋዘኛ wāzḁ́ññā (-zāñ-).
fade, v.i. ደረቀ dḁ́rrḁqḁ.
faded, adj. ደረቅ dḁ́rḁq.
faint (feel), v.i. ደከመው dákkḁmḁ͡u (impers. § 43a; § 63d, e).
I feel faint owing to the heat: እኔ፡ደከሞኛል፡ ስለሙቀት። i̥n^{y}é (§ 55b) dáki̥m^{w}oññāl si̥lḁmúqḁt.

fair, adj. ውብ wŭb (wŭy̥).
(of weather) ብራ bi̥rrã.
faith, s. ሃይማኖት ha͡i̥mán^{w}ot.
fall, v.i. ወደቀ wώddḁqḁ.
Take care he (it) doesn't fall: እንዳይወድቅ። nda͡i̥-wώdi̥q, ...care they don't...: -ቁ። -qu.
fall off (down), v.i. ዱብ፡ አለ dubb álḁ (s.v. √ባለ, § 44*a*).
(of more than one person or object) ዱብ፡ዱብ፡አለ dubbi̥dúbb álḁ (s.v. √ባለ, § 44*a*).
false, adj. (of persons) ውሸታም wŭšátám (§ 8).
(of things) ውሸት wi̥šät (wŭ́š-; § 57*b*).
(coin) ግም gi̥m.
A false dollar: ግም፡ብር፡ gi̥m bi̥rr.
falsehood, s. ውሸት wi̥šät (wŭ́š-).
falsetto voice, have a, v.i. ጭጭ፡ አለ č̣i̥č̣č̣ (§ 6) álḁ (s.v. √ባለ, § 44*a*).
A man with a falsetto voice: ጭጭ፡የሚል፡ሰው፡ č̣i̥č̣ yämmi̥l (§ 8) sa͡u̥.
Famaka, s. አፈ፡መካ áfḁ mákkã (mák-).
family, s. ዘመድ zámḁd.
ሥጎች si̥g^{w}ōč (-čč § 6).
famine, s. [እ]ራብ (i̥)ráb (-áy̥).
fan, s. ማራገቢያ mārraggḁ́byã (-ḁ́y̥yã).
ማርገብገቢያ margḁbgḁ́byã (-ḁy̥gáy̥yã).
fan, v.t. (oneself, v.r.) አራገበ arrággḁbḁ (-ḁyḁ).
far, adv. [እ]ሩቅ (i̥)rúq.
Is it far? እሩቅ፡ነው። i̥rúq na͡u̥?
far (off), be, v.i. ራቀ ráqḁ.
How far is it to the river? ወንዙ፡ምን፡ያህል፡ይርቃል። wώnzu mi̥n yahl yi̥ŕi̥qāl?

To be rather far (off): ሳብ፡አለ፡ sãbb ála (s.v. √በለ, § 44*a*).

It is rather far (off): ሳብ፡ይላል። sabb yilāl.

fare, s. ኪራይ kirái (§ 8).

Let him travel at the fare they fixed: በውሰኑት፡ ኪራይ፡ይሒድ። bauássanut (§ 62*c*) kirái yihid.

farmer, s. ገበሬ gábar^{y}e (-áy-, -är-).

farther (one), the, dem. pron. [የ]ወድያኛው (yä)wωdyáñ-ñáu (§ 8, § 13*a*).

Shut the farther one: የወድያኛውን፡ዝጋው። yäwωd-yāññáun zígau.

fast, adj. (in action) ቀልጣፋ qaltáffã.

ፈጣኝ fátãñ (fát-; -ññ § 6; § 8).

Fast travelling: ግስገሳ፡ gisgásã.

fast, adv. ቶሎ t^{w}ólo.

Very fast: ቶሎ፡ቶሎ፡ t^{w}ólo t^{w}ólo.

Send him fast: አቀልጥፈህ፡ስድደው። aqáltifäh sí-dadau, pol. አቀልጥፈው፡ይስዱዱት። aqáltifau yís-dadut, pl. አቀልጥፉችሁ፡ስዱዱት። aqältifáččyuh (§ 7*d*) sídadut.

As fast as I gave him money he got rid of it: ገንዘቡ፡እየሰጠኁ፡እያጠፋ። gánzay īyyäsáttau^{h} (§ 7*d*) īyyatáffa (s.v. እየ-).

fast, s. ጦም t^{w}ōm.

fast, v.i. ጦመ t^{w}ōma.

fast, be (act), v.i. ቀለጠፈ qaláttafa.

ቶሎ፡አለ t^{w}ólo ála (s.v. √በለ, § 44*a*).

ፈጠነ fáttana (fáttäna).

The watch is fast: ሰዓቱ፡ቀድሟል። saátu qármωāl (§ 7*d*).

fast, cause to act, v.t. አቀለጠፈ aqaláttafa.

fast, cause to travel, v.t. አገሰገሰ ag(g)asággasa.

fast, travel, v.i. ገሰገሰ gasággasa.

Travel fast: ገስግስ። gásgis, pl. -ሱ። -su.

How many days will you take to get there travelling fast? በስንት፡ቀን፡ገስግሰህ፡ትደርሳለህ። basinti qan gásgisäh tidärsálläh?

fasten, v.i. (be fastened, v.p.) ታሰረ tássara (-sär-).

ተቈለፈ taqwǿllafa.

fasten, v.t. አሰረ ássara (-sär-).

ቈለፈ qwǿllafa.

Fasten it: እሰረው። ísarau, pl. -ሩት። -rut, or ቈልፈው። qwǿllifau, pl. -ፉት። -fut.

Fasten them: እሰራቸው። isaráččau, pl. -ሯቸው። -rwáččau, or ቈልፋቸው። qwǿllifáččau, pl. -ፏቸው። -fwáččau.

fat, adj. ጮማ čómã.

ወፍራም wǿfrám (§ 8), pl. also ወፋፍራም wǿfãffirám (§ 8).

Very fat: ገፋፋ gafáfã.

fat, s. ስብ sib (siv).

fat, be (become), v.i. ወፈረ wǿffara (-fär-).

father, s. አባት ábbát (§ 8).

Who is his father? አባቱ፡ማን፡ነው። abbátu mān nau?

What is his father? አባቱ፡ምን፡ይሰራል። abbátu min yisárāl?

The question አባቱ፡ምን፡ነው። abbátu min nau? *or* ምን፡አባቱ። min abbátu? *is a term of abuse.*

father-in-law, s. አማት ámát (§ 8).

fatigue, s. ድካም dikám (§ 8).

ልፋት lifát (§ 8).

favour, s. (kind action) ውለታ wŭlḁtã (-lắt-; § 8).
He (pol.) did me a favour: ውለታ፡አደረጉልኝ። wŭ-lätá adḁrrḁgullị̥ñ.
favour, v.t. አደላ adḁllã (-dắl-) ለ- lḁ- (§ 47a).
Does he favour him? ያደላለታል። yādḁlállḁtāl?
fear, s. ፍራት fị̥rắt (§ 8).
fear, v.i. & t. ፈራ fḁrrã (fắr-).
feast (banquet), s. ግብር gị̥b(ị̥)r (gị̥ṿ-).
(-day, eccl.) ባል bāl.
feather, s. ለቦባ lḁbʷṓbã (lḁṿʷṓṿã, § 52a, γ).
ላባ lábã (láṿã, § 52a, γ).
February, s.v. calendar.
feed, v.i. (be fed, v.p.) ተመገበ tḁmḁ́ggḁbḁ (-ḁṿḁ).
በላ bḁ́llã.
Has he (it) been fed? በልቷል። bḁ́ltŏ͡āl?
feed, v.t. መገበ mḁ́ggḁbḁ (-ḁṿḁ).
አበላ abḁ́llã (aṿḁ́-).
Feed him (it): አብላው። ắṿla͡u.
Feed them: አብላቸው። āṿláččḁ͡u.
feel (oneself), v.i., use ነው nḁ͡u (§ 13b).
Do you feel well? ጤናህ፡ነህወይ። ṭʸénah náhw͡ǿị̥?,
pol. ጤናዎ፡ነዎወይ። ṭʸénaʷo nḁ͡ʷowǿị̥? (s.v. -ወይ).
Do you feel all right? ደኅና፡ነህወይ። dáhnā náhw͡ǿị̥?,
pol. ደኅና፡ነዎወይ። dáhnā nḁ͡ʷow͡ǿị̥?
How do you feel? እንደምን፡ነህ። ndämị̥n nḁh?,
pol. እንደምን፡ነዎ። ndämị̥n nḁ͡ʷo?
I feel better: ተሻለኝ። täšálāñ (§ 63d).
feel, v.t. (handle) ዳሰሰ dắssḁsḁ.
(perceive) ሰማ sḁ́mmã (§ 63d, e).
ተሰማው tḁsḁ́mma͡u (täs-; impers. § 43a; § 63d, e).

I feel it: ይሰማኛል። yi̥ssḁ́mmaññāl.

I don't feel it: አይሰማኝም። a͡i̥ssḁ́mmaññi̥m.

Do you feel it prick you? የወጋህ፡ይሰማሃል። yäwǿggāh yi̥ssḁ́mmahāl?, pol. የወጋዎ፡ይሰማዎታል። yäwǿgga͡^{w}o yi̥ssḁ́mma͡^{w}otāl?

Let me feel it: ልዳሰው። li̥dássa͡u.

I feel the cold: ብርድ፡እሰማለሁ። bi̥rd i̥sḁmálla͡u^{h}.

Felis leo, s. አንበሳ anbḁ́ssā̃ (ambḁ́-, anỵḁ́-, § 7*d*).

Felis pardus, s. ነብር nḁ́bi̥r (nā́-, -ỵi̥r).

fell, v.t. ቈረጠ qwǿrrḁṭḁ.

felt, be, v.p. ተሰማ tḁsḁ́mmā̃ (§ 63*d*, *e*).

female, s. & adj. (of persons and animals) ሴት s^{y}ēt.
(of animals) እንስት i̥ni̥st (§ 8).

femur, s. ጭን č̣i̥n (§ 52*a*, γ).

fence, s. አጥር ā́ṭi̥r.
(strong) ገረገራ gḁrḁgḁ́rā̃.

The space within the fence is not broad (enough): ያጥሩ፡ግቢ፡ሰፊ፡አይደለም። yáṭi̥ru gi̥bbyi̥ sḁ́ffi a͡i̥dálläm (§ 7*d*).

ferment, v.i. ቦካ b^{w}ókkā̃.

fern, s. G. ጆራስፋ j^{w}orā́sfā̃.
G. ጆርስፌ j^{w}or^{w}ósfi.
Š. ስንስን si̥nsi̥n.
Š. የሴት፡ምላስ፡ yäs^{y}ét mi̥lā́s (§ 8).

ferocious, be, v.i. ተጣላ tḁṭállā̃.

Is it ferocious? ይጣላል። yi̥ṭṭállāl?

ferried over, be, v.p. ተሻገረ tḁšággа̥rḁ (täš-, -gär-).

ferry, s. መሻገሪያ mḁššāggḁ́ryā̃ (-gā́r-).

ferry over, v.t. አሻገረ aššággḁrḁ (-gär-).

festival, s. (eccl.) ባል bāl.

fetch, v.t. አመጣ amáṭṭã.

መጣ máṭṭã with ger. of ያዘ (§ 44c).

Fetch it: ይዘሀው፡ና። yizäháu na, f. ይዘሽው፡ነይ። yizäšyú nái, pl. ይዛችሁት፡ኑ። yizäččihút nu (§ 8).

Let him fetch it: ይዞት፡ይምጣ። yízʷot yímṭa, f. ይዘው፡ትምጣ። yízau tímṭa, pl. ይዘውት፡ይምጡ። yízaut yímṭu.

Go and fetch him (it): ሒድ፡አምጣው። hid ánṭau (§ 7d).

Fetch a pair of boots: ጫማ፡ይዘህ፡ና። čámma yizäh na.

What (price) did it fetch? ምን፡ያህል፡አወጣ። min yahl auώṭṭa?

fetch and carry, v.i. & t. አመላለሰ ammaláll asa.

fetch out, v.t. አወጣ awώṭṭã (auώ-).

fetlock, s. ግልገል፡ሸሆና gilgal šahʷónã (šωh-, -ኾ- -χʷó-, -ኮ- -kʷó-; §§ 8, 7d, 52a, γ).

fetlock-joint, s. የሸሆና፡ማጠፊያ yäšahʷoná māṭáfyã (§ 52a, γ).

የጠናግል፡ማጠፊያ yäṭanágil māṭáfyã (§ 52a, γ).

fever, s. ንዳድ nídād (§ 8).

few, adj. (a, pron.) ጥቂት tíqit.

እንዳንድ ándánd (§ 8; § 16).

A few will do: ጥቂት፡ይበቃል። tiqit yiváqāl.

A few mats: ጥቂት፡ደውጆች፡ tíqit dáujjʷōč.

There are a few: እንዳንድ፡አለ። andánd állä.

Ficus carica (Broun, Cat. 533), s. በለስ bálas (bálās).

Ficus sycomorus (Broun, Cat. 533), s. ባምበ bámbã.

field, s. (cultivated) እርሻ íršã.

(of grass) መስክ mask.

field-glasses, s. ትልቅ፡መነጥር ti̥lli̥q mḁnḁ́ṭṭi̥r.
field-mouse, s. አይጠ፡መጐጥ áyi̥ṭḁ mágwώṭ (ái̥ṭ-; § 9*d*; § 8).
fifteen, card. num. አሥራ፡አምስት asrámmi̥st.
fifty, card. num. አምሳ ámsã.
fig (*Ficus sp.*), s. (edible) በለስ bḁ́lḁs (bä́läs).
(wild) ባምባ bã́mbã.
ወርካ wḁ́rkã (wώr-, ዋ- wá-).
ሾላ šʷólã.
fight, s. ውጊ wṹggi.
fight, v.i. ተጋደለ tḁgã́ddalḁ.
ተዋጋ tḁwã́ggã (tḁu͡ã́-).
file, s. ሞረድ mʷórḁd.
file, v.t. ሞረደ mʷórrḁdḁ.
fill, v.i. & t. መላ mḁ́llã or ሞላ mʷóllã.
(a pipe) ሾመ šʷṓmḁ.
The river filled: ወንዝ፡መላ። wωnz mḁ́llã.
Fill it: ምላው። mí̥la͡u, pl. -ሉት። -lut.
Don't fill it: አትምላው። attí̥mla͡u, pl. -ሉት። -lut.
Fill it with water: ውሃ፡ሙላው። wúha mṹla͡u.
Fill the pipe and give it to me: መጠጫውን፡ሹመህ፡ ስጠኝ። mḁṭḁ́čča͡un šúmäh sí̥ṭäñ.
filled, be, v.p. መላ mḁ́llã or ሞላ mʷóllã (§ 63*d, e*).
(of a pipe) ተሾመ tḁšʷṓmḁ (täš-).
filter, s. ማጥፊያ mã́ṭfyã.
filth, s. (filthy, adj. § 57*b*) እድፍ i̥d(i̥)f.
filthy, adj. (loathsome) ጸያፍ ṣḁ́yyáf (ጠ- ṭḁ́-; § 8).
find, v.t. አገኘ agḁ́ññä (-gã́ñ-).
Have you found him (it)? አገኘሀው። agḁ́ññähḁ͡u?, pl. አገኛችሁት። agḁññáčči̥hut?
Find him (it): አግኘው። ági̥ññḁ͡u, pl. አግኙት። ági̥ñ-ñut.

find out, v.i. & t. አወቀ á͡uwḁqḁ (-wωq-).

Find out and let me know: አውቀህ፡አስታውቀኝ። á͡uŭqäh astá͡uŭqäñ.

fine, adj. (excellent) ምልካም mḁ́lkám, pl. also መልካካም mḁlkákám (§ 8).

(small) ትንሽ tí̥nni̥š, pl. also ትንንሽ ti̥ní̥nni̥š.

(of powder) ልዝብ lí̥zzi̥b (-i̥v̥).

(of weather) ብራ bí̥rrã.

It is very fine (excellent): አይገኝም። a͡i̥ggḁ́ññi̥m.

fine, s. አፈላማ afḁlámã.

ካሳ kásã.

You will have to pay a fine: አፈላማ፡ትከፍላለህ። afḁláma ti̥kḁflálläh.

fine, v.t. አስከፈለ askḁ́ffḁlḁ.

finger, s. ጣት ṭāt (§ 52α, γ).

finger-tip, s. ዘርፍ zḁrf (zärf; § 52α, γ).

finish, v.i. (finished, be, v.p.) አለቀ állḁqḁ.

ተጨረሰ tḁč̣ḁ́rrḁsḁ (täč̣ắrräsḁ).

The work is finished: ስራ፡አልቋል። sí̥rā álqo͡ãl.

finish, v.t. ጨረሰ č̣ḁ́rrḁsḁ (č̣ắrräsḁ).

Finish it: ጨርሰው። č̣ắrri̥sḁ͡u, pl. -ሱት። -sut.

I am going to finish it: እጨርሰዋለሁ። i̥č̣ärri̥sḁuál-lḁ͡u[h].

fire, s. እሳት i̥sát.

(conflagration) ቋያ qwáyyȁ.

Light the fire: እሳቱን፡አንድድ። i̥sátun ándi̥d.

Set fire to it: እሳት፡አንድድበት። i̥sát ándi̥di̥bbḁt.

fire, v.i. & t. (gun) ተኰሰ tḁ́kkwωsḁ (tώkkosḁ § 7d).

Fire: ተኵስ። tώkkwŭs, pl. -ሱ። -su.

Don't fire: አትተኵስ። atti̥tώkkwŭs, pl. -ሱ። -su.

firebrand, s. Š. ክፋይ ki̥ffái̥ (§ 8).
G. ትንታግ ti̥ntág (§ 8).
fired, be, v.p. (gun) ተተኰሰ tḁtḁ́kkwωsḁ (-tώkkosḁ § 7*d*).
fireplace, s. ማንደጃ mandájã.
firm, adj. ጠንካራ ṭḁṅkárrã.
first, ord. num. ፊተኛ fitḁ́ññã (fi̥t-, -tấñ-).
(initial) መጀመሪያ mḁjḁmmḁ́ryã (-mấr-).
On the first day of the month: የወሩ፡በመጀመሪያ፡ ቀን፡ yäwώru yḁmḁjḁmmḁryá qḁn (§ 8).
firstborn, adj. ታላቅ tállấq (§ 8).
fish, s. ዓሣ ấsã (§ 52*a*, δ).
Abounding in fish: ዓሣም፡ ấsấm (§ 8).
Are there fish in it? ዓሣ፡አለው፡፡ ấsa állḁu?
fish-hook, s. መቃጥን mḁqấṭi̥n.
fishing-net, s. መረብ márḁb (-ḁy).
fissure, s. ንቅ ni̥q, pl. ንቃቃት ni̥qấqất (§ 8).
ስንጥቅ si̥nṭi̥q.
fist, s. ቡጢ búṭṭi (§ 52*a*, γ).
fit, adj. ምቹ mi̥čču.
fit, v.i. & t. (be fit, v.i.) ተመቸ tḁmḁ́ččä (-mấč-) ለ- lḁ- (§ 47*a*).
five, card. num. አምስት ámmi̥st.
fix, v.t. (appoint) ቀጠረ qḁ́ṭṭḁrḁ (-ṭär-).
(settle) ወሰነ wώssḁnḁ.
I will fix a day: ቀን፡እቀጥራለሁ፡፡ qḁn i̥qḁṭrállḁu^{h}.
fixed, be, v.p. (appointed) ተቀጠረ tḁqḁ́ṭṭḁrḁ (-ṭär-).
As (it) was fixed: እንደተቀጠረ፡ ndätḁqḁ́ṭṭḁrḁ.
flag, s. ዓላማ alámã.
ባንዲራ band^{y}érã.
flag-staff, s. ሰንደቅ sḁ́ndḁq.
flame, s. ነበልባል nḁbḁ́lbāl (-ḁyḁ́lyā-).
ንብልባል ni̥bí̥lbāl (-i̥yí̥lyā-).

The flame of this lamp is not good: የዚህ፡መብራት፡ ንብልብል፡ዳገም፡አይዶል። yäzzịh mạyrắt nịyịlyāl dạ́ggịmm a͡ịdäl (§ 7d).

flash, v.i. አብለጨለጨ abläčállăčă (ayl-).

flask, s. ራዋት ra͡uwắt (ራውሃት ra͡uhắt; § 8).

flat, adj. ትክክል tịkịkkịl.

(of ground) ሜዳ myēdā.

ሰንጣ sạnṭā.

flat, be, v.i. ተካከለ tạkắkkạlạ.

flat-iron, s. መተኰሻ mạtạkkwώšā (-tωk-).

flat-nosed, adj. ደፍጣጣ dạfṭắṭṭā.

flatten, v.t. አስተካከለ astạkắkkạlạ.

flatter, v.i. & t. አቈላመጠ aqqwωlámmạṭạ.

ሸበሸበ šạbạ́ššạbạ (šạyạ́ššạyạ).

flea (*Pulex irritans*), s. ቍንጫ qwŭnịččā (§ 52a, δ).

flee, v.i. (from, v.t.) ሸሸ šạ́ššä (šắš-).

flexible, adj. ለስላሳ lạslássā.

flexible, be (become), v.i. ለሰለሰ lạsạ́llạsạ.

flexible, render, v.t. አለሰለሰ alạsạ́llạsạ.

flexor muscle of thigh, s. ሹልዳ šullịdā (-lŭd-; § 52a, γ).

flies, infested with, adj. ዝምባም zịmbắm (§ 8).

flint, s. ቡላድ búl(l)ád (§ 8).

flock, s. መንጋ mạ́ṅgā.

A flock of sheep: የበግ፡መንጋ፡ yäyạ́g mạ́ṅga.

flood, s. ጐርፍ gwωrf.

floor, s. መሬት mạ́ryēt (§ 8).

flour, s. ዱቄት dwŏqyēt (§ 8).

Is it fine or coarse? ክክ፡ነው፡ልዝብ። kúkkị nạ͡u lịzzịy?

flourish, v.t. (brandish) አወዛወዘ a͡uwωzá͡uwωzạ.

flow, v.i. ፈሰሰ hădä (hạ́-, hyē-, -dạ, § 7d).

flower, s. አበባ ábḁbã (áṿḁṿã; § 52*a*, δ).
flutter, v.i. ተርገበገበ tḁrgḁbḁ́ggḁbḁ (tär-, -ḁṿḁ́ggḁṿḁ).
flutter, v.t. አርገበገበ argḁbḁ́ggḁbḁ (-ḁṿḁ́ggḁṿḁ).
fly (*Musca domestica*), s. ዝምብ zi̥mb (§ 52*a*, δ).
fly, v.i. በረረ bḁ́rrḁrḁ (-rär-).
fly-whisk, s. ጭራ č̣i̥rã.
foal, s. ግልገል gi̥lgḁl.
foam, s. አረፋ arḁ́fã.
fog, s. ጉም gūm.
ጥጋግ ṭi̥gāg (§ 8).
fold (up), v.i. (be folded (up), v.p.) ታጠፈ tā́ṭṭḁfḁ.
fold (up), v.t. አጠፈ áṭṭḁfḁ.
Fold it (up): እጠፈው። i̥ṭḁfḁu, pl. -ፉት። -fut.
follow, v.i. & t. ተከተለ tḁkḁ́ttḁlḁ.
Follow him to his house: እስተቤቱ፡ተከተለው። i̥stḁṿʸétu tḁkḁ́ttḁlḁu, pl. -ሉት። -lut.
food, s. መብል mḁ́bi̥l (-ḁ́ṿi̥-).
እንጀራ (i̥)njʸérã (-ጀ- -jā́-).
ማድ mādd.
Is the food ready? እንጀራ፡ቀርቧል። njā́ra qā́rṿōāl?
Food and drink: ማድና፡መጠጥ፡ mā́ddi̥nna mḁ́ṭḁṭ.
fool, s., foolish, adj. ሞኝ mʷoññ.
He (has) made a fool of me: አሞኘኝ። amʷóññäñ.
fool, play the, v.i. ቀበጠ qḁ́bbḁṭḁ.
foolishness, s. ሞኝነት mʷoññi̥nnḁt (-nät).
foot, s. እግር i̥g(i̥)r.
ጫማ č̣ámmã.
(of hoofed animals) ሸሆና šḁhʷónã (šωh-, -ኾ- -χʷó-, -ኮ- -kʷó-, § 7*d*; § 8).
(of animals with claws) መዳፍ mḁdā́f (§ 8).
See § 52*a*, γ.

He is to go on foot: በግሩ፡ይሂድ። bágru yíhid, pl. በግራቸው፡ይሂዱ። bagráččau yíhidu.

Did you come on foot? በግርህ፡መጣህ። bágrih máttāh?, pl. በግራችሁ፡መጣችሁ። bagráččyuh (§ 7*d*) mattáččyuh?

At the foot of the hill: ከተራራ፡ጥግ፡ katarārá tigg (§ 8, § 47*b*).

foot-soldier, s. እግረኛ igráññā (-rāñ-, § 52*a*, δ).

for, prp. ለ- la-, ል- l(i)- (§ 47*a*).

It is for you: ላንተ፡ነው። lantá nau.

For me: ለኔ፡ lánʸé (lán-; § 8).

Whom is it for? ለማን፡ነው። lamán nau?

forage, s. ገፈራ gafárā (-fár-; § 8).

(grain) ጥሬ tírʸe.

Forage for the horse (-s, cp. § 52*a*): የፈረስ፡ገፈራ፡ yäfáras gafára.

forbid, v.t. ከለከለ kalákkala.

See √በለ (§ 44*a*).

The doctor has forbidden me to eat meat: ሀኪም፡ሥጋ፡አትብላ፡አሉኝ። hakím síga attíyla áluñ.

force, s. (strength) ኃይል háil.

ብርታት birtát (§ 8).

(body of troops) ጦር tʷor.

By (physical) force: በኃይል፡ bahá il (§ 8).

By force (compulsorily): በግድ፡ bágidd (§ 8).

Don't use any force: በኃይል፡አታድርግ። bahá il attádrig (-tárg § 7*d*), pl. -ጉ። -gu.

forced march, s. ግስገሳ gisgásā.

forced march(es), cause to make, v.t. አገሰገሰ ag(g)asággasa.

ford, s. መልካ málkā.

ford, v.t. ቈረጠ qwórrḁṭḁ.

We forded the river: ወንዙን፡ቈረጥነ። wónzun qwórrḁṭnḁ.

forearm, s. ክንድ kı̥nd.

(vet.) ማሀል፡አገዳ máhal (māl) ágḁdā̃.
See § 52*a*, γ.

forehead, s. ግምባር gı̥mbār (§ 8).

forenoon, s. ረፋድ rḁffād (§ 8).

In the forenoon: (speaking beforehand) ተኩለ፡ ቀን፡ወዲሀ፡ tḁkkúlḁ qḁn wódíh (-dı̥h; § 8).

forest, s. ውድማ wǘdmā̃.

ዱር dūr.

forget, v.i. & t. [እ]ረሳ (ı̥)rḁssā̃.

Don't forget it: አትርሳው። attı̥rsau.

I have forgotten: እረሳሁ። ı̥rḁssa^{h}u (-sau^h § 7*d*).

forgive, v.i. & t. ማረ márḁ.

forgiven, be, v.p. ተማረ tḁmārḁ.

forgotten, be, v.p. ተረሳ tḁrḁssā̃ (tär-).

fork, s. ሹካ šúkkā̃.

form, s. መልክ mḁlk.

It's bad form: ነውር፡ነው። nḁúr nḁu.

formerly, adv. በፊት bḁfít (-fı̥t; § 8).

ቀድሞ qḁ́dm^{w}o (qārm- § 7*d*).

ዱሮ dúr^{w}o.

fort, s. እርድ ı̥rd.

He (it) is in the fort: በርድ፡ውስጥ፡ነው። bḁrd (§ 7*a*) wǘsṭı̥ nḁu.

fortunate, adj. ሀብታም hábtám (-áṿt-, -áḟt- § 7*d*; § 8).

fortune, s. (good or bad) እድል ı̥ddı̥l.

(good) ሀብት habt (haṿt, haḟt).

forty, card. num. አርባ árbā̃ (-rṿā̃; § 20*a*).

forward, adv. ፊት fït (fi̥t).

ወደፊት wǝdḁ́fḯt (-fi̥t; § 8).

found, be, v.p. ተገኘ tḁgḁ́ññä (-gắñ-).

He (it) has not been found: አልተገኘም። altḁgḁ́ññäm.

Is it (to be) found? ይገኛል። yi̥ggḁ́ññāl?, pl. ይገኛሉ። yi̥ggḁññállu?

found out, be, v.p. ታወቀ tá͡uwḁqḁ (-wǝq-).

foundation, s. መሠረት mḁsḁ́rḁt (-sắrät; § 8).

four, card. num. አራት árắtt (§§ 8, 20*a*).

fourteen, card. num. አሥራ፡አራት asrárắtt (§§ 8, 20*a*).

fowl, s. ዶሮ dʷórʷo (§ 52*a*, δ).

Buy young fowls, not old ones: አሮጌ፡ዶሮ፡አትግዛ፡ ታናናሽ፡እንጂ። arʷṓgʸe dʷórʷo atti̥gzā, tanannā́š i̥njí.

France, s. ፍራንሳ fránsā.

francolin, s. ቆቅ qʷoq (§ 52*a*, δ).

fraud, s. ቅጥፈት qi̥tfḁt (-fät).

ቅጥፍና qi̥tfi̥nnā.

እብለት i̥blḁt (i̥vl-, -lät).

free, adj. (freed) አርነት፡የወጣ arri̥nnḁt (-nät) yäwǿṭṭā (§ 14).

free, v.t. ፈታ fḁttā.

He was a slave once, but now he is free: ፊት፡ባርያ፡ ነበር፡አሁን፡አርነት፡ወጣ። fi̥t ṿārya nḁ́bbḁr, áhun arri̥nnät wǿṭṭa.

freeborn, adj. ጨዋ č̣ḁ́u͡ā, pl. ጨዋዎች č̣ḁuā́wōč (č̣ḁu͡ā́uōč; -čč § 6).

freedom, s. አርነት arri̥nnḁt (-nät).

freeze, v.i. (become solid) [እ]ረጋ (i̥)rḁ́ggā.

French, adj. የፍራንሳ yäfránsā.

የፍራንሳዊ yäfransáwi.

S.v. የ-, §§ 47*a*, 70.

Frenchman, s. ፍራንሳዊ fransáwi, pl. -ዎች -wōč (-čč § 6).
fresh, adj. (new) አዲስ áddi̥s.
(other) ሌላ lélã.
(of bread) ለምለም lḁmlḁm.
(of water) ጥሩ ṭi̥ru (ṭǘru).
Is there no fresh news? አዲስ፡ወሬ፡የለም። áddi̥s wώr^{y}e yálläm?
Bring some fresh bread: ለምለም፡ዳቦ፡አምጣ። lḁm-lḁm dább^{w}o ámṭa (ánṭa § 7*d*).
Pour the water out of that and put in fresh: የሱን፡ውሃ፡አፍሰው፤ጥሩ፡ውሃ፡አድርግበት። yässún ẇǘha afi̥ssḁu͡, ṭǘru wǘha ádri̥gi̥bbḁt (ắrg- § 7*d*; s.v. and).
fresh air, s. ንፋስ ni̥fás (§ 8).
fresh air, get, v.i. ተናፈሰ tḁnắffḁsḁ.
Friday, s. አርብ arb (arẏ).
friend, s. ወዳጅ wώdáj (§ 8).
friendly, adj. (mil.) አማኝ ámắñ (-ññ § 6; -má͡i̥ § 7*d*; § 8).
friendship, s. ፍቅር fi̥qi̥r.
fright, s. ፍራት fi̥rát (§ 8).
(sudden) ድንጋጤ di̥ṅgáṭ^{y}e.
frighten, v.t. አስፈራ asfḁrrã (-fắr-).
Don't frighten him (it): አታስፈራው። attasfḁrrau͡, pl. -ሩት። -rrut.
frightened, be, v.i. & p. ፈራ fḁrrã (fắr-).
ሰጋ sḁggã.
(suddenly) ደነገጠ dḁnắggạtḁ.
fringe, s. ዘርፍ zḁrf (zärf).
frivolous, adj. ቧልተኛ bwāltắñña̅ (-tắñ-).
ዋዘኛ wāzắññã (-zắñ-).
frog, s. ጓጉንቸር gwãgúnčär (§ 52*a*, δ).
እንጓጉቸር (i̥)ṅgwãgúčär („).

from, prp. ከ- kḁ- (§ 47*a*).
  ተ- tḁ- („).
  Take it from him: ያዘው፡ ተጁ። yázḁu (pl. ያዙት፡ yázut) tā́jju, or ውሰድበት። wū́sḁdḭbbḁt, pl. -ዱበት። -dubbḁt.
  Where does he (it) come from? ተየት፡ ይመጣል። tḁyḗt yḭmā́ṭāl?
front, s. ፊት fīt (fḭt).
  In front, adv. በፊት bḁ́fīt (-fḭ́t; § 8).
front of, in, prp. በ-...፡ ፊት bḁ-... fīt (fḭt; § 8, § 47*b*).
  ከ- (ተ-)...፡ በፊት kḁ- (tḁ-)... bḁ́fīt (y̥ḁ́-, -fḭ́t; § 8, § 47*b*).
  In front of the house: ከቤት፡ በፊት፡ kḁy̥ʸét y̥ḁ́fḭt.
front, put in (send in), v.t. አስቀደመ asqḁ́ddḁmḁ.
frontier, s. ያገር፡ ዳርቻ yā́gḁr (s.v. የ-, §§ 7*a*, 47*a*, 70) dārḭččā.
  ድምበር dḭmbḁr (-bär).
  On the frontier: ታገር፡ ዳርቻ፡ tā́gḁr darḭčča.
frost, s. ውርጭ wurč̣.
full, adj. ሙሉ mū́lu (ምሉ mḭlu).
full, be, v.i. መላ mḁ́llā or ሞላ mʷóllā.
fundament, s. መቀመጫ mḁqqḁmḁ́č̣ā.
fungus, s. እንጉዳይ (ḭ)ṅgúdā́ḭ (§§ 8, 52*a*, δ).
funny, adj. (of persons) ቧልተኛ bwāltḁ́ññā (-táñ-).
  (of things) መሣቂያ mḁsā́qyā.
fur, s. ጠጕር ṭḁ́gwūr.
furniture, s. እቃ ḭqā.
  የቤት፡ መሣሪያ yäbʸét (-äy̥ʸé-; s.v. የ-, §§ 47*a*, 70) mḁssáryā (-yä).
furrow, s. ጉድባ gúdbā (-dy̥ā; § 52*a*, δ).

G

§ *refers to the paragraphs of the Grammar* (*Initia Amharica, Part I*).

gain, s. ትርፍ tirf.

gain, v.i. & t. አተረፈ atárrafa (-tár-).

What does he gain by this? በዚህ፡ምን፡ያተርፋል። bazzíh min yātárfāl?

The watch gains: ሰዓቱ፡ይቀድማል። saátu yiqádmāl.

gait, s. አካሔድ akkáhäd.

gaiter, s. ገምባሌ gambállä (§ 52a, δ).

, አጉምባሎ agumbállʷo (§ 52a, δ).

gale, s. አውሎ áulʷo.

gall, v.t. ጋጠ gáta.

See that the straps do not gall him (it): ጠፍር፡ እንዳይገጠው። táfir (§ 52a, δ) indaigítau.

Gallabat, s. መተማ matámmā̃ (mätám-).

gallop, s. ግልብያ gílbyā̃ (-lyyā̃).

gallop, v.i. & t. ጋለበ gállaba (-aya).

Let the horse gallop: ፈረሱ፡ይጋልብ። fárasu yígāly.

Don't gallop the horse: ፈረሱን፡አትጋልብ። fárasun attígāly.

game, s. (amusement) ጨወታ čáwatā̃ (čáua-, -ωt-).

(animals) አረዌ áurʸe (§ 7d), pl. አራዊት aráwít (§ 8).

Who won the game? ማን፡ነው፡የረታ። mān nau yärátta (§ 14)?

garden, s. አታክልት atákilt.

Gardenia Thunbergia (Broun, Cat. 237), s. ጋምብሎ gambíllʷo (ኋም- gwam- B.).

garlic (*Allium sativum*), s. ነጭ፡ሽንኩርት näč̣č̣ šúṅkwŭrt.

You must not come when you have been eating garlic: ነጭ፡ሽንኩርት፡ስትበላ፡አትምጣ። näč̣č̣ šúṅkwŭrt si̥ttyḁ́la atti̥mṭa.

gash, s. ቍስል qwŭ́si̥l.

Gash, s. (river) መረብ mḁ́rḁb (-ḁy).

gate, s. ደጅ dḁjj (däjj).

በር bḁrr.

gate-keeper, s. በረኛ bḁrrḁ́ññã (-rấñ-).

ከልካይ kḁ́lkái̥ (-áyy § 6; § 8).

gather, v.i. (gathered, be, v.p.) ተሰበሰበ tḁsḁbḁ́ssḁbḁ (täs-, -ḁyḁ́ssḁyḁ).

gather, v.t. (bring together) ሰበሰበ sḁbḁ́ssḁbḁ (sḁyḁ́ssḁyḁ).

(pick) ለቀመ lḁ́qqḁmḁ.

Gather them together: ሰብስባቸው። sḁysi̥yáččḁu, pl. -ቧቸው። -ywáččḁu.

gathered, be, v.p. (picked) ተለቀመ tḁlḁ́qqḁmḁ.

gathering, s. መሰብሰቢያ mḁsḁbsḁ́byã (-ḁysḁ́yyã).

gecko, s. ገበሎ gḁ́bḁl^{w}o (gḁ́yḁ-; § 8).

gelding, s. ሰንጋ፡ፈረስ sḁ́ṅga fḁ́rḁs.

general, s. (mil.) ደጃዝማች däjjázmáč (§ 8).

generosity, s. ቸርነት čäri̥nnḁt (-nät).

generous, adj. ቸር čär.

genitals, s. ብልት bi̥lli̥t.

gentle, adj. ገር gḁr (gär).

gently! interj. ቀስ qḁss!

gently, act (be gentle), v.i. ዝግ፡አለ zi̥gg álḁ (s.v. √በለ, § 44*a*).

German, adj. የነምሳ yänámsã.

የነምሳዊ yänḁmsáwi.

S.v. የ-, §§ 47*a*, 70.

German, s. ነምሳዊ nḁmsáwi, pl. -ዎች -wŏč (-čč § 6).

Germany, s. ነምሳ nạmsã.

It was made in Germany: ከነምሳ፡አገር፡ተበጀ። kạ-nạ́msa ágär tạyä́jjä.

gesture, s. ጥቅሻ tị́q(ị̌š)šã.

get, v.i. (arrive) ደረሰ dạ́rrạsạ.

He (it) will not get there in time: አይደርስም። a͡idársịm, pl. -ሱም። -sum.

get, v.i. (become) ሆነ hʷṓnạ.

How did he (it) get like this? እንዴት፡እንዲህ፡ሆነ። ndʸét ịndíh hʷónạ?, pl. -ኑ። -nu?

get, v.t. አገኘ agạ́ññä (-gä́ñ-).

Where did you get it from? ተዬት፡አገኘህው። tạyét agạ́ññähạ͡u?, pl. -ሁት። -hut?

Where can I get it? ዬት፡አገኘዋለሁ። yēt agạññä͡u-állạ͡uʰ?

Get me some: ፈልግልኝ። fạ́llịgịllịñ, pl. -ጉልኝ። -gullịñ.

I have got some: አለኝ። állän.

Have you got any? አለህ። álläh?, pol. አለዎ። állạʷ͡o?, pl. አላችሁ። allä́ččyuh? (§ 7*d*).

Have you got me any? አገኘህልኝ። agạ́ññähịllịñ?

Has he got any? አለው። állạ͡u?, pl. አላቸው። allä́č-čạ͡u?

Did he get any? አገኘ። agạ́ññä?, pl. -ኙ። -ññu?

ghost, s. ውቃቢ wŭqābʸe (-ä́yʸe).

gift, s. ስጦታ sịṭʷṓtã.

መተያያ mạttạyä́yã (-tạ͡iä͡iạ̃).

gimlet, s. መሰርሰሪያ mạsạrsạ́ryã (-särsár-).

gin, v.i. & t. (cotton) ዳመጠ dámmạṭạ.

ginger, s. ዝንጅብል zịnjị́bịl (ጅን- jịn-, -ị́vịl).

ginned, be, v.p. ተዳመጠ tạdámmạṭạ.

ginning-machine, s. መዳመጫ mạdāmạ́č̣ã (-mä́č̣-).

giraffe (*Giraffa camelopardalis*), s. ጅራተቀጭን ji̥rātạ-q̥áčči̥n (§ 9*d*).

girdle, s. መታጠቂያ mḁttāṭ̥áqyā̃ (-ṭ̥áq-).

መቀነት mḁqḁnnḁt (-nät).

girl, s. ቈንጆ qwónjʷo, pl. also ቈናጅቶች qwonáji̥tʷōč (-čč § 6), ቈነጃጅቶች qwonḁjáji̥tʷōč (-čč § 6).

ልጃገረድ li̥jāgárḁd.

(small) ማሚት mámmit (-mi̥t).

girth (saddle-, horse's, mule's, etc.), s. መቀነቻ mḁqḁn-nḁ́čā̃ (-náč-).

give, v.t. ሰጠ sḁ́ṭṭḁ (§ 61*a*).

Give me it (them): ስጠኝ። si̥ṭḁñ.

I (will) give it (them) to you: እሰጥሃለሁ። i̥sḁṭḁhál-lḁu͡h.

I gave it (them) to you: ሰጠሁህ። sḁ́ṭṭḁhuh.

Did you give it (them) to him? ሰጠሀው። sḁ́ṭṭḁhḁu͡?

The man you (pol.) gave us (has) disappeared: የሰጡነው፡ሰው፡ጠፋ። yäsḁṭṭunnḁ́u͡ (§ 8) sḁu͡ ṭḁ́ffa.

What did you give for it? በስንት፡ገዛሀው። bḁsi̥nti̥ gḁ́zzahḁu͡?

give each other, v.t. ተሰጣጡ tḁsḁṭáṭṭu (täsäṭ-).

give up, v.t. ለቀቀ lḁ́qqḁqḁ.

give up (be given up § 68), cause or allow to, v.t. አስለቀቀ aslḁ́qqḁqḁ.

given, be, v.p. ተሰጠ tḁsḁ́ṭṭḁ (täsáṭ-).

given up, be, v.p. ተለቀቀ tḁlḁ́qqḁqḁ.

glad, be, v.i. ደስ፡አለ dḁss (däss) álḁ (s.v. √በለ, § 44*a*).

ደስ፡አለው dḁss (-ä-) álḁu͡ (impers. § 43*a*).

See § 63*d, e*.

I am glad: ደስ፡ብሎኛል። däss yi̥lʷoññāl.

I am so glad you have come: እንኳ፡መጣህ። ńkwā mḁ́ṭṭāh!, pol. -ጡ። -ṭṭu!, pl. -ጣችሁ። -ṭṭáččyuh!

glass, s. ብርጭቆ bi̥rč̣í̥qʷo.
ብርሌ bi̥rí̥llʸe.
(mirror) መስተዋት mḁstḁ͡uwat.
A glass of water: ብርጭቆ፡ውሃ፡ bi̥rč̣í̥qʷo wúha.
glitter, v.i. አብለጨለጨ abläč̣álläč̣ä (ḁyl-).
glue, s. ማጣበቂያ maṭṭä̃bḁ́qyä̃ (-ä̃yḁ́q-).
glue, v.t. አጣበቀ aṭṭábbḁqḁ.
glued, be, v.p. ተጣበቀ tḁṭábbḁqḁ.
gnat, s. ትንኝ tí̥ni̥ñ (-í̥ññ § 6; §§ 8, 52*a*, δ).
gnaw, v.i. & t. ጋጠ gā́ṭḁ.
go (about, away), v.i. ሔደ hā́dä (hḁ̄́-, hʸḗ-, -dḁ).
Don't go! አትሒድ። attí̥hi̥d!, pl. አትሒዱ። attí̥hi̥du!
Go (away)! ሒድ። hi̥d!, f. ሒጅ። hi̥j!, pl. ሒዱ። hí̥du!
I want to go to Gondar: ጎንደር፡ልሔድ፡እፈልጋለሁ። gʷóndḁr li̥hā́d i̥fḁlli̥gállḁ͡uʰ.
I am going: ልሔድ፡ነኝ። li̥hā́d näñ.
I am not going to ride: አልቀመጥም። ali̥qqḁ́mmḁṭi̥m.
There is nowhere for him (it) to go: መቀመጫ፡ያጣል። mḁqqḁmḁ́č̣ḁ yā́ṭāl.
go away, v.i. ወገደ wώggḁdḁ.
Go away! ወግድ። wώgi̥d!, f. ወግጅ። wώgi̥j!, pl. ወግዱ። wώgi̥du!
go down, v.i. (descend) ወረደ wώrrḁdḁ.
(abate) ጐደለ gwώddḁlḁ.
Go down! ውረድ። wúrḁd!, pl. -ዱ። -du!
When does the water go down? መቼ፡ነው፡እሚጐድል፡ውሃው። mḁčʸé nḁ͡u mmi̥gwώdl úha͡u?
go in, cause or allow to, v.t. አስገባ asgḁ́bbä̃.
go, let, v.i. & t. (release) ለቀቀ lḁ́qqḁqḁ.
ፈታ fḁ́ttä̃.

Let go! ልቀቅ። lįqąq!, pl. -ቁ። -qu!

Let him (it) go: ፍታው። fįtau͡, pl. ፍቱት። fįtut.

go out, v.i. ወጣ wǿṭṭã.

(be extinguished) ጠፋ ṭąffã.

Go out! ውጣ። wŭ́ṭa!, pl. ውጡ። wŭ́ṭu!

We want to go out: ልንወጣ፡እንፈልጋለን። lįnnwǿṭa įnnįfąllįgállän.

The fire has gone out: እሳት፡ጠፍቷል። įsát ṭąftōāl.

go out, cause or allow to, v.t. አስወጣ aswǿṭṭã.

Don't let the fire go out: እሳት፡እንዳይጠፋ። įsát įndai͡ṭáfa.

go round, v.i. ዞረ zʷṓrą.

go up, v.i. ወጣ wǿṭṭã.

v.t. በ-...፡ላይ፡ወጣ bą-... lai͡ (§ 8, § 47*b*) wǿṭṭã.

Go up! ውጣ። wŭ́ṭa!, pl. ውጡ። wŭ́ṭu!

The price will go up: ዋጋ፡ያክላል። wā́ga yákkįlāl.

goat, s. ፍየል fíyyäl.

God, s. እግዚአብሔር įgzįabhʸér (-aẏh-).

goitre, s. እንቅርት (į)ṅqįrt.

gold, s. ወርቅ wǿrq.

Gold braid: ወርቀ፡ዘቦ፡ wǿrqą (§ 9*d*) ząbʷo (-ą́ẏʷo).

goldsmith, s. አንጥረኛ anṭrąññã (-rã́ñ-).

good, adj. ደግ dągg (dägg).

መልካም mąlkám, pl. also መልካክም mąlkákám (§ 8).

ጥሩ ṭįru (ṭŭ́ru).

ድንቅ dįṅq.

It is very good: እጅግ፡ደግ፡ነው። įjjįg dággį (§ 7*d*) nąu͡.

He is a good man: ደግ፡ሰው፡ነው። dägg sąu͡ nąu͡.

A good mule: ጥሩ፡በቅሎ፡ ṭŭ́ru ẏąqlʷo.

What good is this to you? ይህ፡ምንህ፡ነው። yḁhe mḁnḁh (§ 16) nḁu?

good-bye! interj. ደኅና፡ሁን። dähná hun!, pol. ደኅና፡ይሁኑ። dähná yḁhunu!, (to more than one) ደኅና፡ሁኑ። dähná húnu!

good-natured person, s. ገውጋዋ gḁugáwwã (-áuwã).

goodnight! interj. ደኅና፡እደር። dähná ḁdḁr! (-náḁd-), pol. ደኅና፡ይደሩ። dähná yḁdḁru! (-náḁd-), (to more than one) ደኅና፡እደሩ። dähná ḁdḁru! (-náḁd-).

goods, s. እቃ ḁqã.

goose, s. ይብራ yḁbrã (-ḁvr-).

G. ይበር yḁbár (-ḁvá-; § 8).

See § 52*a*, δ.

Gospel, s. ወንጌል wǿńgʸél (§ 8).

Gossypium vitifolium (etc., Broun, Cat. 64), s. ጥጥ tḁt.

got, be, v.p. ተገኘ tḁgáññä (-gáñ-).

Can it be got? ይገኛል። yḁggáññāl?, pl. ይገኛሉ። yiggḁññállu?

gourd (*Cucurbita maxima*, Broun, Cat. 209), s. ቅል qḁl.

gourd-shell, s. ፋጋ fágã.

govern, v.i. ነገሠ nággḁsḁ.

v.t. ገዛ gázzã.

government, s. መንግሥት máńgḁst.

government office, s. ቤተ፡መንግሥት bʸétḁ (§ 9*d*) máńgḁst.

ችሎት čḁlʷot (§ 8).

አደባባይ addḁbábaḁ (-ḁváyaḁ).

governor, s. መኰንን mḁkwǿnnḁn (-nän).

ጋዥ gḁž.

gradually, adv. በጥቂት፡በጥቂት bḁtḁqḁt vḁtḁqḁt.

grain, s. (cereal) እህል ḁhḁl.

ጥሬ tḁrʸe.

gram (*Cicer arietinum*, Broun, Cat. 140), s. ሽምብራ ši̥m-bi̥rã.

granary, s. ጎተራ gʷotḁ́rã (-tắr-; § 8).

grandfather (-mother), s. አያት áyyắt (§ 8).

grant, s. ስጦታ si̥ṭʷṓtã.

grant, v.t. ሰጠ sḁ́ṭṭḁ.

granted, be, v.p. ተሰጠ tḁsḁ́ṭṭḁ́ (täs-).

Gras rifle, s. ኡጅግራ uji̥grã (ű̆ji̥grã § 8).

grass, s. ሣር sār.

Cut (pl.) the grass round the tent: ሣር፡ተድንኳን፡ አጠገብ፡እጨዱት። sār tḁdŭṅkwắn aṭḁ́gḁv i̥čădut.

Short grass: ሰርዶ sḁ́rdʷo (sắr-).

grass-fire, s. ቋያ qwáyyã.

grate, v.i. ስቅቅ፡አለ si̥qi̥qq ắlḁ (impers. § 43*a*; s.v. √በለ, § 44*a*).

It grates on me: ስቅቅ፡ይለኛል። si̥qi̥qq yi̥läññāl.

grateful, be, v.i. ውለታ፡አወቀ wŭlḁtá (-lät-) a͡uwḁqḁ (-wωq-; § 63*d*, *e*), to, ለ- lḁ- (§ 47*a*), or the pers. suff. (§ 12*b*) is added to ውለታ.

I am grateful to you: ውለታህን፡አውቅያለሁ። wŭ-lätắhi̥n a͡uŭqqyállḁu͡ʰ, pol. -ታዎን፡... -tắʷon..., ...you, pl. -ታችሁን፡ -tắčči̥hun (-tắččyuhi̥n § 7*d*)....

gratis, adv. እንዲያው (i̥)ndya͡u (§ 8).

grave, adj. (of persons) [እ]ርጉ ri̥gu (i̥rgu).
ከባድ kḁ́bbắd (§ 8).

grave, s. መቃብር mḁqắbi̥r (-ắvi̥-).

grave, be (become), v.i. (of persons) [እ]ረጋ (i̥)rḁ́ggã.

gravity, s. (of persons) [እ]ርጋት ri̥gắt (i̥rg-; § 8).

graze, v.i. (pasture) G. ተሰማራ tḁsḁmárrã (täsäm-).
Š. ተሰመረ tḁsḁmḁ́rrḁ (täsäm-).

Let the animals go to graze: ከብቱ፡ይሰማራ። kḁ́ftu (§ 52*a*, δ) yi̥ssḁmắra, Š. ...ይሰመር። ...yi̥ssḁ́mär.

graze, v.t. (pasture) G. አሰማሬ assḁmā́rrā̃.
Š. አሰመረ assḁmḁ́rrḁ.
(wound slightly) ጋጠ gā́ṭḁ.

I want a man to graze the mules: ለበቅሎች፡እረኛ፡ እፈልጋለሁ። lḁyḁ́qlʷōčč i̥rrā́ñña i̥fḁlli̥gállḁu͡ʰ.

A stone grazed him (it): ድንጊያ፡ጋጠው። dā́ṅgya gā́ṭa͡u.

grease, s. ሱብ si̥b (si̥v).

Put some grease on it: በሱብ፡ቀበው። bḁsí̥v qí̥va͡u.

grease, v.t. ቀበ qḁ́bbā̃.

greased, be, v.p. ተቀበ tḁqḁ́bbā̃.

great, adj. ትልቅ ti̥lli̥q.

Greece, s. የግሪክ፡አገር yägrík (-rí̥k; s.v. የ-, §§ 47*a*, 70) ā́gḁr (-gär).

greedy, adj. ቀቀታም qi̥qqí̥tám (§ 8).

Greek, adj. & s. ግሪክ grīk (gri̥k).

green, adj. አረንጓዴ arωṅgwā́dʸe.

Dark green is often called ጥቁር ṭǘqur (= black).

greens, s. ጐመን gwώmmḁn (-män).

greeting suitable at any time and for all persons: ጤና፡ይስጥልኝ። ṭʸēna yí̥sṭi̥lli̥ñ, I wish you good health, the reply to which is አብሮ፡ይስጠን። ā́vrʷo yí̥sṭḁn.

grey, adj. አመድማ amḁdí̥mmā̃ (-mäd-).

grey-haired, adj. ሽበታም ši̥bā́tám (-i̥v-, -ā́t-; § 8).

grief, s. አዘን ā́zḁn.

grieve, v.i. አዘነ ázzḁnḁ.

grill, v.t. ጠበሰ ṭḁ́bbḁsḁ.

grind, v.t. ፈጨ fḁ́č̣č̣ä (fā́č̣-).

grindstone, s. መሳል mḁsā́l (§ 8).
መሳያ mḁsā́yā̃ (-ā͡i̥ã).

grip, v.i. & t. ያዘ yā́zḁ (§ 44*c*).

groom, s. ለጓሚ lωggwámi.
ground, s. መሬት mạrʸét (§ 8).
ምድር mịdịr (ḿdịr).
Hard ground: ፎረፎር፡ fʷórạfʷor.
Stony ground: ጭንጫ፡ č̣ịnč̣ā̃.
On the ground: ከምድር፡ kạmdịr.
ground, be, v.p. ተፈጨ tạfạ̈č̣č̣ä (-fáč̣-).
group, s. ስብሳቢ sịbsábi (sịvsávi).
grow, v.t. ዘራ zạrrā̃.
grow (up), v.i. (of persons) አደገ áddạgạ.
(of trees, etc.) በቀለ bạ́qqạlạ (bā́q-).
(become larger) አከለ ákkạlạ.
He has grown up: ትልቅ፡ሁኗል። tịllịq húnŏāl.
Where does it grow? ዬት፡ነው፡እሚበቅል። yēt nạu mmịvạ́qịl?
This child is growing: ይሀ፡ልጅ፡ያከላል። yịhe lịj yákkịlāl.
Gryllus sp., s. ፌንጣ fʸéntạā̃ (§ 52*a*, δ).
guarantor, s. ዋስ wās.
You must get a guarantor: ዋስ፡አምጣ። wās ántạ (§ 7*d*).
Who is your guarantor? ዋስህ፡ማን፡ነው። wásịh mān nạu?
guarantor, be, v.i. (for, v.t.) ተዋሰ tạwásạ (tạuá-).
guarantor, offer as, v.t. አዋሰ awásạ (auá-).
Whom do you offer as guarantor? ማንን፡ታውሳለህ። mánnän tauúsállāh?
guard, s. (individual) ዘበኛ zạbạ́ññā̃ (-ạv-, -áñ-).
ጠባቂ ṭạbbáqi.
ተረኛ tạrạ́ññā̃ (tär-, -ráñ-).
(of one or more) ዘብ zạb (zạv).
Cp. § 52*a*, δ.

Mount a guard over him: ዘበኛ፡አቁምበት። zḁỵáñña ā́qumi̥bbät, pol. ዘበኛ፡ያቁሙበት። zḁỵáñña yā́qumubbḁt, (-በ- to prevent his escape, § 47*a*).

Mount a guard over it: ዘበኛ፡አቁምለት። zḁỵáñña ā́qumi̥llät, pol. ዘበኛ፡ያቁሙለት። zḁỵáñña yā́qumullḁt, (-ለ- to protect it, § 47*a*).

guard, v.t. ጠበቀ ṭḁ́bbḁqḁ.

Guard him (it): ጠብቀው። ṭḁ́bbi̥qḁu͡, pl. -ቁት። -qut.

guard, be on one's, v.i. ተጠነቀቀ tḁṭḁnḁ́qqḁqḁ.

Be on your guard: ተጠንቀቅ። tḁṭḁ́ṅqḁq, pl. -ቁ። -qu.

guarded, be, v.p. ተጠበቀ tḁṭḁ́bbḁqḁ.

guest, s. እንግዳ (i̥)ṅgi̥dā̃ (§ 8).

guide, s. መሪ mḁ́ri (mā́r-).

I want a guide and nothing else: መሪ፡ኢፈልጋለሁ፤ ሌላ፡አልፈልግም። mḁ́ri i̥fḁlli̥gállḁu͡ʰ: lḗla alfḁ́lli̥gi̥m.

They refused to give me a guide: መሪ፡አንሰጥም፡ አሉኝ። mḁ́ri annsḁ́ṭi̥mm (§ 6) ā́luñ.

guide, v.t. መራ mḁ́rrā̃.

Guide him: ምራው። mí̥rau͡.

Guide us: ምራን። mi̥ránnḁ.

guided, be, v.p. ተመራ tḁmḁ́rrā̃.

guinea-fowl (*Numida mitrata*), s. ጅግራ jí̥grā̃ (§ 52*a*, δ).

guitar, s. ክራር kí̥rā́r (§ 8).

Guizotia oleifera (Guidi, Vocab. p. 397), s. ኑግ nū̃g.

gum, s. ሙጫ mū́ččā̃.

(of the teeth) ድድ di̥dd (§ 52*a*, γ).

gun, s. ጠበንጃ ṭḁbḁ́njā̃ (-ḁỵḁ́-).

ብረት bí̥rḁt (-rät).

ነፍጥ nḁfṭ.

(big) መድፍ mḁdf (mḁrf § 7*d*).

gunner, s. መድፈኛ mḁdfḁ́ññā̃ (-ḁrf-, -fā́ñ-, § 7*d*).

gunpowder, s. ባሩድ bárud.
gut, s. አንጀት ánjät.

H

§ refers to the paragraphs of the Grammar (Initia Amharica, Part I).

habit, s. ሥራት sı̥rát (§ 8).
  እድር ı̥́ddı̥r.
  It is my habit: ሥራቴ፡ነው። sı̥rāt^{y}é nḁ͡u.
Hæmatopota sp., s. እውር፡ዝምብ ı̥́wwŭr zı̥mb (§ 52*a*, δ).
hail, s. በረዶ bḁ́rḁdʷŏ.
  በረድ bḁ́rḁd.
hair, s. (esp. of head) ጠጕር ṭḁ́gwŭr.
  (on the face or body) ጭገር č̣ı̥́gḁr (-gär).
  See § 52*a*, γ.
  I want a man to cut my hair: ራሴን፡የሚላጨኝ፡ እፈልጋለሁ። rás^{y}en yämmı̥láč̣č̣äññ ı̥fḁllı̥gállḁ͡u^{h}.
hair-brush, s. ማበጠሪያ mābḁṭṭḁ́ryā̃ (-āy-, -äṭṭár-).
half, adj. & s. እኩል ı̥́kkul (ŭ́kk-).
  s. እኩሌታ ı̥kkul^{y}étā̃ (ŭkk-).
  ገሚስ gḁ́mı̥s.
  Half of it will be enough: እኩሌታው፡ይበቃል። ı̥kkul^{y}éta͡u yı̥yḁ́qāl.
  Half a dollar: የብር፡አላድ፡ yäyı̥́rr alád.
half-caste, adj. ቅልቅል qı̥lı̥́qqı̥l.
halt, v.i. ቆመ qʷŏ́mḁ (§ 42*c*).
  Halt! ቁም። qum!, pl. ቁሙ። qúmu!
  We will halt now: አሁን፡እንቆማለን። áhun ı̥nnı̥qʷomállän.
  Where we halted: የቆምንበት፡ yäqʷomnḁ́bbḁt.

halter, s. ልቡብ lí̥báb (lí̥y̥áy̥; § 8).

Put a halter on it: ለቡበው። lḁ́bbi̥y̥ḁu.

When it has a halter on: ሲለቡብ፡ si̥llḁ́bbḁy̥.

hammer, s. መዶሻ mḁdʷṓšā̃.

hand, s. እጅ i̥jj (§ 52*a*, γ).

With your hand(s): በጅህ፡ bḁ́jji̥h (bā́j-; § 7*a*).

Give it into the Rās's hands: ስጣቸው፡ለራስ፡በጃቸው። si̥ṭā́ččḁu lḁrā́s y̥äjjā́ččḁu.

hand over, v.t. አረከበ arrḁ́kkḁbḁ (-rā́k-, -ḁy̥ḁ).

handkerchief, s. መሐረብ mḁhárrḁb (-ḁy̥).

handle, s. መያዣ mḁyā́žā̃ (mḁi̥á-).

handle, v.t. ዳሰሰ dā́ssḁsḁ.

hang (up), v.t. ሰቀለ sḁ́qqḁlḁ.

አንጠለጠለ anṭḁlḁ́ṭṭḁlḁ.

Hang it up on the wall: ተግድግዳው፡ስቀለው። tḁgi̥rgí̥ddau (§ 7*d*) sí̥qḁlḁu.

hanged, be, v.p. ተሰቀለ tḁsḁ́qqḁlḁ (täs-).

happiness, s. ደስታ dḁ́ss(ĭ̥)tā̃.

happy, be, v.i. ደስ፡አለ dḁss (däss) ā́lḁ (s.v. √ባለ, § 44*a*).

ደስ፡አለው dḁss (-ä-) ā́lḁu (impers. § 43*a*).

See § 63*d*, *e*.

Harar, s. ሐረር (h)árḁr (-rär).

ሐረርጌ (h)árḁrgʸe (-rär-).

Harar, language of, s. ሐረርኛ (h)arḁrí̥ññā̃ (-rär-).

harass, v.t. ነዘነዘ nḁzḁ́nnḁzḁ.

hard, adj. (of materials) ጥኑ ṭí̥nu.

ብርቱ bí̥rtŭ.

ጠንካራ ṭḁṅkárrā̃.

(difficult) ጭንቅ č̣i̥ṅq.

ችጉር čí̥ggur.

Hard wood: ጥኑ፡እንጨት፡ ṭi̥nú (§ 8) nč̣ʸet.

The eggs should be hard: እንቍላል፡ይርጋ። ṅqwŭlál yi̥rga; —should not be hard:—፡አይርጋ። á͡i̥rga.

This book is hard to read: ይህ፡መጣፍ፡ንባቡ፡ጭንቅ፡ነው። yi̥he mḁṭáf (§ 55*b*) ni̥yḁ́yu č̣í̥ṅqi̥ (§ 7*d*) nḁ͡u.

hard-working, adj. ትጉ ti̥gu.

hare (*Lepus abessinicus*), s. ጥንቸል ṭí̥nčäl.

G. ጭንተል č̣í̥ntal (-täl).

ጭንቸል č̣í̥nčäl.

harm, s. (evil) ቢስ bi̥s.

(damage) ጉዳት gwŭdát (§ 8).

There's no harm in him (it): ቢስ፡የለውም። bi̥s yállḁ͡um.

harmful, adj. ቢስ bi̥s (§ 57*b*).

ክፉ ki̥fu (kŭfu, kŭfu, § 7*d*).

harmful, be (become), v.i. ከፋ kḁffā̃.

hartebeest (*Bubalis tora*), s. ቶራ twōrā̃ (§ 52*a*, δ).

harvest, s. አዝመራ azmḁrā̃ (-már-).

haste, s. ችኰላ či̥kkwωlā̃ (čŭkkólā̃ § 7*d*; § 8).

haste, make, v.i. ቻኰለ čḁkkwωlḁ (čώkkolḁ).

ቶሎ፡አለ twólo álḁ (s.v. √ባለ, § 44*a*).

ፈጠነ fḁṭṭḁnḁ (fáṭṭänḁ).

ቀላጠፈ qḁlḁ́ṭṭḁfḁ.

Make haste! ቶሎ፡በል። twólo yḁl!, pl. ቶሎ፡በሉ። twólo vḁlu!

They must make haste: ቶሎ፡ይበሉ። twólo yi̥yḁlu.

Make haste and do it: ቶሎ፡ብለህ፡አድርገው። twólo yi̥läh árgḁ͡u (§ 7*d*).

hasten, (cause to), v.t. አፈጠነ afḁṭṭḁnḁ (afáṭṭänḁ).

አቀላጠፈ aqḁlḁ́ṭṭḁfḁ.

hasty, adj. ችኩል či̥kkul.

hat, s. ባርኔታ barnétā̃.

Have you seen my hat? ባርኔታዬን፡አየሀው። bar-nētáʸen áyyähạ͡u?

Put your hat on: ባርኔታህን፡ልበስ። barnḗtahịn lị́vạs, pol. ባርኔታዎን፡ይልበሱ። barnḗtaʷon yị́lvạsu.

Take your hat off: ባርኔታህን፡አውልቅ። barnḗtahịn á͡ulịq.

We do not consider a man polite that comes in with his hat on: አይመስለንም፡የተቀጣ፡ባርኔታ፡ሳያወልቅ፡የሚገባ። a͡ịmáslännịm yätạqáṭṭa yarnḗta sa͡ịa͡uώlq yämmịgáya.

hate, v.t. ጠላ ṭạllā̃.

hatred, s. ቂያሜ qịyyámʸe.

have, v.t. use አለ állä (§§ 32, 39), ሆነ hʷṓnạ, etc. (s.v. be) with pers. suff. (§ 12*c*).

I have another: ሌላ፡አለኝ። léla állän̈.

Has he a horse? ፈረስ፡አለው። fárạs állä͡u?

I shall have time tomorrow: ነገ፡ጊዜ፡ይኖረኛል። nágạ gị́zʸe yịnʷóräññāl.

(= cause), use causative in አ- a- or አስ- as- (§ 22*a*).

Have it done: አስደርገው። asdárrịgạ͡u.

Have the tree cut down: ዛፉን፡አስቈርጠው። zắfun asqwώrrịṭạ͡u.

hawk, s. ገዴ gáddʸe.

hay, s. ድርቋ dị́rqwā̃.

ድርቆሽ dị́rqʷóš (§ 8).

he, pron. እርሱ ịrsū́ (§ 8), pol. እርሳቸው ịrsáč(č)ạ͡u (§ 12*a*), (usually omitted unless emphatic).

Yes, he is: አወን፡ነው። ắwωn, ná͡u.

It is he: እርሱ፡ነው። ịrsú nạ͡u.

head, s. ራስ rās.

Fore part of head: አናት ánắt (§ 8).

head-man, s. ሹም šum.
ዓይነተኛ a͡i̥nḁtḁ́ññã (-nätáñ-).
(local) ጭቃ፡ሹም č̣i̥qá šum, often abbr. to ጭቃ č̣íqã (§ 8).

head-stall, s. ልባብ li̥báb (lí̥y̥áy̥; § 8).

health, s. (good) ጤና ṭʸénã.
ደኅንነት dähní̥nnḁt (-nät).
How is your health? እንዴት፡ነህ። ndʸét näh? pol. እንዴት፡ነዎ። ndʸét nḁʷo?
Is he in good health? ደኅና፡ነው። dähná nḁ͡u?
Is Rās Gugsa in good health? ራስ፡ጉግሣ፡ደኅና፡ናቸው። rās gúgsa dähná náččḁ͡u?

healthy, adj. (of animate objects) ጤናማ ṭʸẽnámmã.
(of places) ለጤና፡ደግ lḁṭʸéna dḁgg (dägg).
ጤና ṭʸénã (§ 57*b*).
Is he healthy? ጤናማ፡ነው። ṭʸenammá (§ 8) nḁ͡u?
Is it (the place) healthy? ጤና፡ነው። ṭʸẽná nḁ͡u?
Is that country healthy? ያ፡አገር፡ለጤና፡ደግ፡ነው። ya ágḁr lḁṭʸéna dággi̥ (§ 7*d*) nḁ͡u?

heap, s. ክምር kí̥mmi̥r.

heap, v.t. ከመረ kḁ́mmḁrḁ (-mär-).

heaped, be, v.p. ተከመረ tḁkḁ́mmḁrḁ (-mär-).

hear, v.i. & t. ሰማ sḁ́mmã (§ 63*d*, *e*).
Do (did) you hear? ሰማህ። sḁ́mmāh?
I do (did) not hear anything: ምንም፡አልሰማሁ። mí̥ni̥mm alsḁ́mmahŭ (-a͡uʰ § 7*d*).
Can (does § 63*c*) he hear? ይሰማል። yi̥sḁ́māl?
He can't (doesn't) hear: አይሰማም። a͡i̥sḁ́mām.

heard, be, v.p. ተሰማ tḁsḁ́mmã (täs-).
Can it be heard? ይሰማል። yi̥ssḁ́mmāl? (§ 63*c*).
It cannot be heard: አይሰማም። a͡i̥ssḁ́mmām („).

heart, s. ልብ li̥bb.

heat, s. ሙቀት múqḁt.

Damp heat: ላበት lắbḁt (-ắyḁ-, -ät).

heat, v.t. አሞቀ amʷṓqḁ.

heat̠hen, adj. & s. አረመኔ arḁmḁ́nʸe.

heaven, s. ሰማይ sḁ́ma͡i̥ (§ 8).

Good heavens! ወዮ፡ጉድ። wωyyṓ gud!

heavy, adj. ከባድ kḁ́bbắd (-ቢድ -bbī́d, -bbí̥d; § 8).

Are the goods heavy? እቃ፡ ከባድ፡ነው። í̥qa kḁbbắd na͡u̥?

heavy, be, v.i. ከበደ kḁ́bbḁdḁ.

Hebrew, s. & adj. እብራይስጥ i̥brá͡i̥sṭ (i̥ṿr-).

heel, s. ተረከዝ tḁrḁ́k(k)ḁz (§ 52a, γ).

heifer, s. (very young) እምቦሳ (i̥)mbʷóssã.

(during first year) ጥጃ tí̥jjã.

height, s. እርዝመት i̥rzí̥mḁt (-mät).

ቁመት qúmḁt (-mät).

What is his (its) height? ቁመቱ፡ስንት፡ነው። qúmḁtu sí̥ntĭ̥ na͡u̥?

heir, s. ወራሽ wώrắš (§ 8).

Heliotropium sp. (Broun, Cat. 374), s. ጭጎጎት č̣i̥gʷógʷot (§ 8).

helmet, s. ባርኔታ barnétã.

help, s. እርዳታ i̥rdátã.

help, v.i. & t. [እ]ረዳ (i̥)rḁ́ddã.

Help him: እርዳው። í̥rda͡u.

They did not help us: አረዱንም። arrḁ́ddunni̥m.

hen, s. ዶሮ dʷórʷo (§ 54b).

her, pers. pron. (acc.) -āት -āt (§ 12c).

(emph.) እርሷን í̥rsö͡ān (§ 8; § 12a).

her, poss. pron. -ዋ -wã (-ö͡ã; § 12b).

herd, s. መንጋ mḁ́ṅgã.

A herd of cattle: የከብት፡መንጋ፡ yäkḁ́ft mḁ́ṅgã.

herdsman, s. እረኛ i̥rrḁ́ññã (-rā́ñ-).
(nomad) ዘላን zḁ́llā́n (§ 8).

here, adv. እዚህ (i̥)zzíh (-zi̥h; § 8).
ከዚህ kḁ́zzíh (hḁ́-, ተ- tḁ́-, -ā́z-, -zi̥h; § 8).
(= hither) ወዲህ wǿdíh (-di̥h; § 8).

Is it here or there? ከዚህ፡ነው፡ወይ፡ከዚያ። kḁzzíh nḁu wḁ́i̥ kḁ́zzya?

Come here! ና፡ወዲህ። na (pl. ኑ፡ nu) wǿdih!

Is he (it) here (present)? አለ። állä?

Here it is, here: ይህው፡ተዚህ። yi̥hāu tḁ́zzi̥h.

Here you are! (finding something) እነሆ። nnḁhó!
(handing a thing) እንካ። ńka!

Just here: ተዚሁ፡ täzzíhu.

hereabouts, adv. በስተዚህ bḁstḁ́zzíh (-tā́z-, -zi̥h; § 8).
በዚህ፡በኩል bḁzzíh (bäz-, -zi̥h) bḁ́kkul (yḁ́-).

hermaphrodite, s. & adj. ፈናፍንት fḁnā́fi̥nt (ፍና- fi̥ná-).

hers, poss. pron. የርሷ yā́rsǒā́ (§ 8; § 12a).

hew, v.t. ቈረጠ qwǿrrḁtḁ.

hidden, adj. ስዉር si̥wwur (syū́wur).

hide, s. ቆርበት q^{w}órbḁt (-ry̥-, -ät).
(with coat) አጐዛ ag^{w}ózã.

hide, v.i. (oneself, v.r., be hidden, v.p.) ተሰወረ tḁsḁ́uwḁrḁ (täs-).
ተሸሸገ tḁšḁ́ššḁgḁ (täšā́ššägḁ).
ተደበቀ tḁdḁ́bbḁqḁ.

hide, v.t. ሰወረ sḁ́uwḁrḁ.
ሸሸገ šḁ́ššḁgḁ (šā́ššägḁ).
ደበቀ dḁ́bbḁqḁ.

Hide him (it): ሸሽገው። šáššįgḁu, pl. -ጉት። -gut.
hide, cause or allow to (§ 68), v.t. አስደበቀ asdḁ́bbḁqḁ.
hiding-place, s. መሸሸጊያ mḁššḁššḁ́gyā (mäššäššág-).
high, adj. ረጅም rḁ́jjįm (ráj-, -ዠም -žžįm).
This mule is not high (enough): ይህ፡በቅሎ፡ረጅምም፡ አይደል። yi̥he yḁ́qlʷo rájji̥mi̥mm ai̥däl (§ 7*d*).
highland, adj. (highlander, s.) ደገኛ dḁgḁ́ññā (dägáñ-).
highlands, s. ደጋ dágā.
hill, s. ተራራ tḁrárā.
(small) ጎጥ gʷoṭ.
hilt, s. መክድ mḁkd.
him, pers. pron. -u, -ው -u, -ት -t, pol. -ኣቸው -áč(č)ḁu, (§ 12*c*).
emph. እርሱን i̥rsún (§ 8), pol. እርሳቸውን i̥rsáč(č)ḁun, (§ 12*a*).
Have you seen him? አየሀው። áyyähḁu?
I have seen him: አየሁት። áyyähut.
I know Rās Gugsa, I have seen him: ራስ፡ጉግሣ፡ አውቃቸዋለሁ፤አየኋቸው። rās gúgsa auúqāččḁu-állḁu^h, ayyähwáččḁu.
hinder, v.i. & t. ከለከለ kḁlḁ́kkḁlḁ.
Don't hinder him (it): አትከልክለው። atti̥kḁ́lki̥lḁu, pl. -ሉት። -lut.
Don't hinder them: አትከልክላቸው። atti̥kḁlki̥láččḁu, pl. -ሏቸው። -lwáččḁu.
hindered, be, v.p. ተከለከለ tḁkḁlḁ́kkḁlḁ.
hinderer, s. ከልካይ kḁ́lkāi̥ (-áyy § 6, § 8).
hinge, s. ማጠፊያ māṭḁ́fyā.
hip, s. ሟሂት mwāhit (-hi̥t; § 52*a*, γ).
hippopotamus (*H. amphibius*), s. ጉማሬ gumárʸe.
Hippotragus equinus, s. ወንድቤ wωndi̥bbʸe (§ 52*a*, δ).
D. ወደምቢ wωddámbi.

hire (cost of), s. ክራይ kı̥rá͡i̥ (§ 8).
hire, let on, v.t. አከራየ akkḁrā́yyä (-kär-).
hire, (take on), v.t. ተከራየ tḁkḁrā́yyä (-kär-).
ቀጠረ qḁ́ṭṭḁrḁ (-ṭär-).
Hire a mule: በቅሎ፡ተከራይ። bḁ́qlʷo tḁkḁ́ra͡i̥.
I wish to hire a house: ቤት፡ልከራይ፡እፈልጋለሁ። bʸēt li̥kkäráyy i̥fḁlli̥gálla͡u̥ʰ (§ 7*d*).
hired, be, v.p. ተቀጠረ tḁqḁ́ṭṭḁrḁ (-ṭär-).
his, poss. pron. -u, -ው -u, pol. -አቸው -ā́č(č)a͡u̥, (§ 12*b*).
emph. የርሱ yā́rsū́ (§ 8), pol. የርሳቸው yär-sā́č(č)a͡u̥, (§ 12*a*).
hiss, v.i. G. አፏጨ afwā́c̣c̣ä.
Š. አፎኘ afʷṓññä.
hit, v.i. & t. መታ mḁttā̃.
Hit him (it): ምታው። mi̥ta͡u, pl. ምቱት። mi̥tut.
Don't hit him (it): አትምታው። atti̥mta͡u, pl. አት ምቱት። atti̥mtut.
hither, adv. ወዲህ wώdíh (-di̥h; § 8).
hoar-frost, s. አመዳይ amḁdā́͡i̥ (§ 8).
hock, s. (of animal) ቋንጃ qwā́njā̃ (§ 52*a*, γ).
hoe, s. መቆፈሪያ mḁqwωffḁ́ryā̃ (-fā́r-).
hoe, v.i. & t. ቆፈረ qwώffḁrḁ (-fär-).
hoed, be, v.p. ተቆፈረ tḁqwώffḁrḁ (-fär-).
hold, v.i. & t. ያዘ yā́zḁ (§ 44*c*).
(contain) ቻለ čálḁ.
Hold (catch hold of) him (it): ያዘው። yā́za͡u̥, pl. -ዙት። -zut.
(Of a bag, jar, etc.). What does it hold? ስንት፡ ይችላል። si̥nt yi̥či̥lāl?
(Of a nail or peg). Will it hold anything big? ትልቅ፡እቃ፡ይችላል። ti̥lli̥q i̥qa yi̥či̥lāl?

hole, s. (through anything) ቀዳዳ q̥adā́dã.

(cavity) ጉድጓድ gúdgwā́d (-úrgw- § 7*d*; § 8).

There is a hole in the carpet: ተስጋጃ፡ቀዳዳ፡አለ። t̥asi̥gájja q̥adā́da állä (q̥adādállä).

He fell into a hole: ተጉድጓድ፡ወደቀ። t̥agurgwā́d wώddạq̥a.

The steamer had a hole knocked in it: ባቡር፡ተቀደደ። bāy̥úr t̥aq̥ád̥dad̥a.

Sew up the hole(s) in it: ቀዳዳውን፡ስፋ። q̥adā́da͡un (cp. § 52*a*, δ) si̥fa.

He (it) has made a hole in it: ቀዶታል። q̥ádd^{w}otāl.

It has got a hole in it: ተቀዷል። t̥aq̥ádd͡ŏāl.

holiday, s. ባል bāl.

hollow out, v.t. ፈለፈለ f̥al̥áffal̥a.

hollowed out, be, v.p. ተፈለፈለ t̥af̥al̥áffal̥a.

hollowing out, instrument for, s. መፈልፈያ m̥af̥alfáy̥ã (-fäl-, -á͡i̥ã).

holy, adj. ቅዱስ qí̥ddús (§ 8).

home, s. ቤት b^{y}ēt.

Is he at home? ተቤቱ፡ነው። t̥ay^{y}ētu n̥a͡u?, pol. ተቤታቸው፡አሉ። t̥ay^{y}ētā́ččau állu?

honest, adj. ነባይ n̥ábā͡i̥ (nā́-, -y̥ā́-; -áyy § 6; § 8).

እውነተኛ un̥at̥áññã (-nätā́ñ-).

ቅን qi̥n.

(plain) ጭምት či̥mmi̥t.

honey, s. ማር mār.

See whether there are any ants in the honey; if there are, take them out with a spoon, not with your hand: ተማሩ፡እይ፡ቁንጫጭ፡እንዳለበት። እንዳለ፡በማንክ፡አውጣው። በጅህ፡አትንክ። t̥amā́ru i̥y qunčā́č̣ (§ 52*a*, δ) i̥ndállābbat̥; ndállä, y̥amánka á͡uṭa͡u, yájji̥h attí̥nka.

honour, v.t. አከበረ ak̥ábbḁrḁ (-bär-).
honoured, adj. ክቡር kı̥́bur (-ı̥yu-).
honoured, be, v.p. ተከበረ tḁk̥ábbḁrḁ (-bär-).
hoof, s. ኰቴ kwώtt^{y}e.
 ጥፍር ṭı̥́fı̥r.
 See § 52*a*, *γ*.
 Take the dirt out of its hoofs: እድፍ፡ተጥፍሩ፡ አውጣው። ı̥́dı̥f tḁṭı̥́fru áuṭau.
 Pare its hoofs: ጥፍሩን፡ቍረጠው። ṭı̥́frun qwŭ́rḁṭḁu.
hook, s. (for fishing) መቃጥን mḁqáṭı̥n.
 (for fastening) ቍልፍ qwŭlf.
hook, v.t. ቈለፈ qwώllḁfḁ.
 (fish) ያዘ yázḁ (§ 44*c*).
hooked, be, v.p. ተቈለፈ tḁqwώllḁfḁ.
 (fish) ተያዘ tḁyázḁ (tḁi̥á-).
hope, s. ተስፋ t̥ásfā̃ (tā́s-).
hope, v.i. ተስፋ፡አደረገ t̥ásfa (tā́s-) ad̥árrḁgḁ.
 I hope I shall see you again: ደግሞ፡ላይህ፡ተስፋ፡ አደርጋለሁ። dā́gm^{w}o lā́yı̥h tā́sfa adärgállḁu^{h}, pol. ደግሞ፡ላየዎ፡ etc. dā́gm^{w}o lā́yḁ^{w}o etc.
horn, s. ቀንድ qḁnd (§ 52*a*, *γ*).
hornbill, ground (*Bucorax abessinicus*), s. እርኩም ı̥rkúm (§ 8).
horrified, be, v.i. ደነገጠ dḁn̥ággḁṭḁ.
horror, s. ድንጋጤ dı̥ngā́ṭ^{y}e.
horse, s. ፈረስ f̥árḁs.
 What is the price of this horse? ይህ፡ፈረስ፡በስንት፡ ነው። yı̥́he f̥árḁs yḁsı̥́ntı̥ nḁu?
 What is its pace like? ሩጫው፡እንዴት፡ነው። rúč̣ḁu nd^{y}ét nḁu?
 I want a horse with large limbs and a broad chest: ቅልጥማም፡ደረታም፡ፈረስ፡እፈልጋለሁ። qı̥lṭı̥mám dḁrḁtám f̥árḁs ı̥fallı̥gállḁu^{h}.

A horse with long pasterns: ሻሆናው፡የረዘመ፡ፈረስ፡ šḁhʷonáu (§ 52*a*, γ) yärḁzzḁmḁ fḁrḁs.

horse, interj. to urge a, ቼ čʸe!
 to stop it, እሽ i̥šš!

horse-cloth (placed under saddle, namda), s.
 (for riding animals) ምቹ mi̥čču.
 መመቻ mḁmmḁčã.
 (for transport animals) ጤቅ ṭʸēq.
 ዱብዳብ di̥bdáb (di̥y̥-dáy̥; § 8).
 መደላድል mḁdḁládi̥l.

hot, adj. ሙቅ muq.
 Hot water: ሙቅ፡ውሃ፡ muq wŭha.
 Hot weather: ሙቀት፡ múqḁt.

hot, be, v.i. ሞቀ mʷṓqḁ (§ 63*d*, *e*).

hour, s. ሰዓት sḁât (§ 52*a*, δ).
 One hour: አንድ፡ሰዓት፡ and sḁât.
 Two hours: ሁለት፡ሰዓት፡ hulḁtt sḁât.
 How many hours? ስንት፡ሰዓት፡ si̥nt sḁât?
 Bring it in quarter of an hour: በሩብ፡ሰዓት፡ አምጣው። bḁrúy̥ sḁât ámṭḁu (ánṭḁu § 7*d*).
 In half an hour: በኩል፡ሰዓት፡ bḁkkul sḁât.

house, s. ቤት bʸēt.
 (of brick, stone, etc.) ግምብ gi̥mb.

how?, adv. እንዴት (i̥)ndʸét? (-ዲት -dít, -di̥t; § 8).
 እንደምን (i̥)ndámi̥n? (§ 8).
 How do (will) you do it? እንዴት፡ታደርገዋለህ። ndʸét tadärgḁuálläh?
 How are you? እንደምን፡ነህ። ndämi̥n näh? pol. እንዴት፡ሰነበቱ። ndʸét sḁnḁbbḁtu?
 How is it made? እንዴት፡ይበጃል። ndʸét yi̥bbájjāl?

how, adv., (intensive) ምንኛ mịnịññā̃ (§ 15).

How hot it is! (of an object): ምንኛ፡ሙቅ፡ነው። mịnịñña muq nạu! — (of the temperature) ምንኛ፡ሙቀት፡ነው። mịnịñña muqạt (§ 8) nạu!

How it runs! ምንኛ፡ይሮጣል። mịnịñña yịrʷóṭāl!

(intensifying size or quantity) ምን mịn with parts of አክለ q.v.

How large (small) he (it) is! ምን፡ያህላል። mịn yáhlāl!

how, conj. (in indirect questions) እንደ- (ị)ndạ- (-dä-), pref. to simp. perf. (§ 48*a*) or to rel. + cont. (§ 14).

I don't know how he did it: እንዳደረገው፡አላውቅም። ndadárragạu aláuŭqịm.

I don't know how it is made: አላውቅም፡እንደሚበጅ። aláuŭqịmm ịndämmịbbájj.

I will show you how to do it: አሳየሃለኍ፡እንድታደርገው። asāyyähállạuʰ ịndịttādárgạu, (lit. in order that you may do it).

— Except after a negative, the indirect question may be left in its direct form:

Show me how you do it: አሳየኝ፡እንዴት፡ታደርገዋለህ። asáyyäññ ịndʸét tādärgạuállāh.

Show me how it is made: አሳየኝ፡እንዴት፡ይበጃል። asáyyäññ ịndʸét yịbbájjāl.

how much (many)? inter. pron. ስንት sịnt? (indecl., § 15).

How much is there? ስንት፡አለ። sịnt állä?

How many are they? ስንት፡ናቸው። sịntị (§ 7*d*) náččạu?

how much (many)!, (intensive) ምን፡ያህል mịn yáhịl! (yahl, s.v. አክለ).

How many there are! ምን፡ያህል፡አሉ። mịn yahl állu!

howl, v.i. ጮኸ č̣^{w}óhḁ (§ 7*d*).
hull, v.t. ፈለፈለ fḁlḁ́ffḁlḁ.
hulled, be, v.p. ተፈለፈለ tḁfḁlḁ́ffḁlḁ.
hullo!, interj. በስመ፡ አብ። bḁ́smḁ āb ! (āy̥).
  Hullo, you there! አንተ፡ ሰው። antā́ sḁ͡u!
hum, v.i. አንጐራጐረ aṅgwωrággwωrḁ.
humble-bee, s. እንዝዝ (i̥)nzi̥z.
humorous, adj. ቧልተኛ bwāltḁ́ññā̃ (-táñ-).
  ዋዘኛ wāzḁ́ññā̃ (-záñ-).
hundred, card. num. መቶ mḁ́t^{w}ō̃ (§ 20*a*).
hung (up), be, v.p. ተሰቀለ tḁsḁ́qqḁlḁ (täs-).
  ተንጠለጠለ tḁnṭḁlḁ́ṭṭḁlḁ.
  If it is hung up its place is known: ቢሰቀል፡ ስፍራው፡ ይታወቃል። bi̥ssḁ́qqḁl si̥fra͡u yi̥ttá͡uwωqāl.
hunger, s. [እ]ራብ (i̥)rāb (-ā́y̥).
hungry, be, v.i. [እ]ራበው (i̥)rābḁ͡u (-y̥ḁ͡u; impers. § 43*a*).
  ተራበ tḁrābḁ (tär-, -y̥ḁ). See § 63*d*, *e*.
  I am hungry: ራበኝ። rā́y̥ḁñ.
  I am not hungry: አራበኝም። arrā́y̥äññi̥m (§§ 6, 7*c*).
  If he is hungry: ቢርበው፡ bi̥ry̥ḁ͡u.
  They will be hungry: ይርባቸዋል። yi̥ry̥áččḁ͡uāl.
hunt, v.i. & t. አደነ áddḁnḁ.
  I want permission to hunt: ላደን፡ ፍቃድ፡ እፈልጋለሁ። lā́dän fi̥qád i̥fḁlli̥gállḁ͡u^{h}.
hunting, s. አደን ádän.
hurrah!, interj. እሰይ (i̥)ssḁ́͡i̥!
hurricane, s. አውሎ á͡ul^{w}o.
hurried, adj. ችኩል či̥kkul.
hurry, s. ችኰላ či̥kkwωlā̃ (čŭkkólā̃ § 7*d*; § 8).
  I am in a hurry: በችኰላ፡ ነኝ። bḁčŭkkolā́ (§ 8) näñ.
  We were in a hurry: በችኰላ፡ ሆንን። bḁčŭkkolá h^{w}ónnḁ.

hurry, v.i. ቸኰለ čạ̥́kkwωlḁ (čώkkolḁ).
ቶሎ፡አለ t^{w}ólo ā́lḁ (s.v. √በለ, § 44*a*).
ፈጠነ fḁṭṭḁnḁ (fā́ṭṭänḁ).
ቀለጠፈ qḁlạ̥́ṭṭḁfḁ.

Don't hurry: አትቸኵል። attịčạ̥́kkwŭl, pl. -ሉ። -lu.

Hurry up! ቶሎ፡በል። t^{w}ólo ṿḁl!, pl. ቶሎ፡በሉ። t^{w}ólo ṿạ̥́lu!

hurry, be in a great, v.i. ችኩል፡ችኩል፡አለ čị̥́kkul čị̥́k-kull (§ 6) ā́lḁ (s.v. √በለ, § 44*a*).

I am in a great hurry: ችኩል፡ችኩል፡እላለኹ። čị̥́k-kul čị̥́kkull ịlállḁ͡u^{h}.

hurry (cause to), v.t. አፈጠነ afạ̥́ṭṭḁnḁ (afā́ṭṭänḁ).
አቀለጠፈ aqḁlạ̥́ṭṭḁfḁ.

Hurry him: አቀልጥፈው። aqā́lṭịfḁ͡u, pol. ያቀልጥፉት። yāqā́lṭịfut, pl. አቀልጥፉት። aqā́lṭịfut.

Hurry them: አቀልጥፏቸው። aqälṭịfáččḁ͡u, pol. ያቀልጥፏቸው። yāqälṭịfwáččḁ͡u, pl. አቀልጥፏቸው። aqälṭịfwáččḁ͡u.

hurt, v.i. (feel painful) አመመ ámmḁmḁ (§ 63*d*, *e*).

My back hurts: ጀርባዬን፡አመመኝ። järṿā́^{y}en (§ 56*c*) ámmḁmäñ.

hurt, v.t. (cause pain to) አሳመመ asámmḁmḁ.
(injure) ጎዳ gwώddā̃.

Don't hurt him (it): አታሳምመው። attāsámmịmḁ͡u, pl. አታሳምሙት። attāsámmịmut.

The whip hurts him (it): አለንጋ፡ያመዋል። aláṅga yámmḁ͡uāl.

hurt, be, v.p. (feel pain) አመመው ámmḁmḁ͡u (impers. § 43*a*).
(injured) ተጎዳ tḁgwώddā̃.

husband, s. ባል bāl.

husbandman, s. ገበሬ gạ́bạrʸe (-ạ́ỵ-, -är-).
hush!, interj. እሽ ịšš!
ዝም zịmm!
hut, s. ቤት bʸēt.
(rude, temporary) ጎጆ gʷójjʷo.
hyæna (*H. crocuta*), s. ጅብ jịb (jịỵ; § 52*a*, δ).
Hypericum gnidiæfolium (Guidi, Vocab. p. 428), s. አምጃ amịjjā̃.
Hyphaene thebaica (Broun, Cat. 600), s. ጮፋር čịfár (§ 8).

I

§ refers to the paragraphs of the Grammar (*Initia Amharica, Part I*).

I, pers. pron. እኔ ịnʸé (§ 8, § 12*a*), generally omitted unless emphatic.
It is I: እኔ፡ነኝ። ịnʸé näñ.
ibex (*Capra vali* or *walie*), s. ዋልያ wályā̃.
ice, s. በረድ bạ́rạd.
በረዶ bạ́rạdʷo (lit. hail).
ውርጭ wurč̣ (lit. frost).
idea, s. አሳብ ás(s)áb (-ā́ỵ; § 8).
idle, adj. ወስዋሳ wạswā́ssā̃.
አውደልዳይ a͡udạ́ldā́ị (-dál-; -ā́yy § 6; § 8).
idle, be, v.i. አውደለደለ a͡udạlạ́ddạlạ (-däläddäl-).
if, conj. (§ 81) ብ- b(ị)-, (q.v.), pref. to cont. (§ 48*a*).
እንደሆን (ị́)ndạhʷon (-däh-), (q.v.), following cont., rel. + cont., rel. + simp. perf., or gerund.
በ- bạ-, (q.v.), pref. to simp. perf. (§ 48*a*).
If you like: ብትወድ፡ bịttwǿdd (§ 8).

If I am not here (there) wait: እኔ፡ባልኖር፡ቈይ። i̥n^{y}é yáln^{w}or, qwǿi̥, pl. ...ቈዩ። ...qwǿyyu.

If he comes, he buys it: ቢመጣ፡ይገዛዋል። bi̥mḁ́ṭa, yi̥gḁ́za͡uāl.

If he comes, he will buy it: ይመጣ፡እንደሆን፡ይገዛዋል። yi̥mḁṭándḁh^{w}on, yi̥gḁ́za͡uāl, (or እሚመጣ፡ እንደሆን፡ etc. i̥mmi̥mḁṭándḁh^{w}on, etc.).

If they were to bring it, we should buy it: ያመጡት፡ እንደሆን፡እንገዛው፡ነበርን። yāmḁ́ṭṭut (§§ 7*a*, 14) i̥ndḁh^{w}on, i̥nngḁ́za͡u nḁ́bbärn.

If they had brought it, we should have bought it: ባመጡት፡በገዛነው። bāmḁ́ṭṭut, bḁgḁ́zzānḁ͡u.

ill, adj. ታማሚ tãmámi.

ill, be, v.i. ታመመ tấmmamḁ.

አመመው ámmḁmḁ͡u (impers. § 43*a*).

See § 63*d, e.*

Are you ill? ታመሃል። tấmmähāl?, pol. ታመዋል። tấmmḁuāl?; or አሞሃል። ámm^{w}ohāl?, pol. አሞዎአል። ámm^{w}o^{w}ōāl?

He (it) is ill: ታሞአል። tấmmōāl, or አሞታል። ámm^{w}otāl.

He (it) is not ill: አልታመመም። altấmmḁmḁm, or አላመመውም። alámmḁmḁ͡um.

I am ill: ታምምያለሁ። tami̥mmyállḁ͡u^{h}, or አሞኛል። ámm^{w}oññāl.

I am not ill: አልታመምሁም። altámmḁmhum, or አላመመኝም። alámmḁmäññi̥m.

I was ill yesterday: to-day I am better: ትላንት፡ ታምሚ፡ነበር፤ ዛሬ፡በጎ፡ነኝ። ti̥lánt támi̥mm^{y}e nḁ́bbär: zấr^{y}e bḁgg^{w}ó (§ 8) näñ.

He is always ill: በሽተኛ፡ነው። bḁši̥täññá (§ 8) nḁ͡u.

How long have you been ill? ምን፡ ያህል፡ ታመምህ። mi̥n yahl támmḁmh?, pol. ...ታመሙ። ...támmḁmu?

ill, make, v.t. አሳመመ asámmḁmḁ.

It will make you ill: ያሳምመሃል። yāsámmi̥mähāl.

Something I ate to-day has made me ill: ዛሬ፡ መብል፡ በላሁት፡ አሳመመኝ። zárʸe mḁ́ṿi̥l ṿḁ́llahut asámmḁmäñ.

illness, s. በሽታ bḁ́ši̥tã (§ 8).

ill-treat, v.t. በደለ bḁ́ddḁlḁ (bắd-).

ገፋ gḁ́ffã.

Don't ill-treat him (it): አትበድለው። atti̥ṿáddi̥lḁu,
pl. -ሉት። -lut.

Don't ill-treat them: አትበድላቸው። atti̥ṿäddi̥láččḁu,
pl. -ሏቸው። -lwắččḁu.

ill-treated, be, v.p. ተበደለ tḁbḁ́ddḁlḁ (-ḁṿ-, -ắd-).

ተገፋ tḁgḁ́ffã.

illuminate, v.t. አበራ abḁ́rrã (aṿḁ́-).

illustration, s. ምስል mí̥si̥l.

ምሳሌ mi̥ssálʸe.

immediately, adv. ወድያው wǿdyáu (§ 8).

impartial, adj. ትክክል ti̥kí̥kki̥l.

implement, s. ማድረጊያ mādrḁ́gyã (-rắg-).

መሳሪያ mḁssáryã (-yä).

impolite, adj. ባለጌ bálḁgʸe (-läg-).

import, v.t. አስመጣ asmḁ́ṭṭã.

What do they import? ምን፡ ያስመጣሉ። mi̥n yasmḁṭṭállu?

Do they import it? ያስመጡታል። yasmḁ́ṭṭutāl?

important, adj. ቁም qum.

An important matter: ቁም፡ ነገር፡ qum nágär.

importunate, adj. ቸክቻክ čḁkčákkã.

ነዝናዛ nḁznázzã.

importunate, be, v.i. ችክ፡ አለ či̥kk álḁ (s.v. √በለ, § 44*a*).

importune, v.t. ነዘነዘ nḁzḁ́nnḁzḁ.

importunity, s. ንዝንዝ ni̥zí̥nni̥z.

impossible! interj. አይሆንም። a͡i̥hʷóni̥m! [lit. it is not, cannot (§ 63*c*) be].

imprint, v.t. ኀተመ háttḁmḁ.

አተመ áttḁmḁ.

imprison, v.t. አሰረ ássḁrḁ (-sär-).

imprisoned, be, v.p. ታሰረ tássḁrḁ (-sär-).

imprisonment, s. ግዞት gi̥zʷot (§ 8).

impudent, adj. ደፋር dḁ́ffár (§ 8).

impurity, s. እድፍ i̥d(i̥)f.

(moral) ኃጢአት (h)átyát (§ 8).

in, prp. ከ- kḁ- [ተ- tḁ-].

በ- bḁ-.

See § 47*a*.

In the house: ከቤት፡ kḁ́vʸét (§ 8).

In the grass: ተሣር፡ tḁ́sár (§ 8).

In the water: ተውሃው፡ tḁ́u͡ha͡u.

He was killed in battle: በጦርነት፡ሞተ። bḁṭʷori̥n-nät mʷótḁ.

In half an hour: በኩል፡ሰዓት። bḁ́kkul sḁ͡át.

What is there in it? ምን፡አለበት። mi̥n álläbbḁt?

in, come (go), v.i. ገባ gḁ́bbã.

Come (go) in! ግባ። gi̥va!, pol. ይግቡ። yi̥gvu!, pl. ግቡ። gi̥vu!

Don't come (go) in! አትግባ። atti̥gva!, pol. አይግቡ። a͡i̥gvu!, pl. አትግቡ። atti̥gvu!

in, let, v.t. አስገባ asgḁ́bbã.

Don't let him (her, it, them § 61*b*) in: አታስገባ። attasgḁ́bba, pl. -ቡ። -bbu, pol. አያስገቡ። a͡i̥asgḁ́bbu.

in, take (bring, put), v.t. አገባ agḁ́bbã.

Take (bring, put) him (it) in: አግባው። ā́gỵa͡u, pl. -ቡት። -ỵut.

Don't take (etc.) him (it) in: አታግባው። attā́gỵa͡u, pl. -ቡት። -ỵut.

incense, s. እጣን i̥ṭán (§ 8).

incense, v.t. አስቈጣ asqwώṭṭã.

incline, v.i. (slope) ተዘቀዘቀ tḁzḁqḁ́zzḁqḁ.

ዝቅ፡አለ zi̥qq álḁ (s.v. √ባለ, § 44*a*).

incline, v.t. (cause to slope) ዘቀዘቀ zḁqḁ́zzḁqḁ.

include, v.t. ጠቀለለ ṭḁqḁ́llḁlḁ.

አገባ agḁ́bbã.

included, be, v.p. ተጠቀለለ tḁṭḁqḁ́llḁlḁ.

ገባ gḁ́bbã.

including, prp. ከነ- kḁnnḁ- [ተነ- tḁnnḁ-, § 47*a*].

Land including the timber, minerals and water on it: መሬት፡ከነንጨቱ፡ከነደንጊያው፡ከነውኃው። mḁrʸét kḁnnḁ́nč̣ʸetu kḁnnḁdā́ngya͡u kḁnnḁúha͡u.

inclusively, adv. በጥቅሊል bḁṭí̥qli̥l.

increase, s. ጭማሪ č̣i̥mmári.

increase, v.i. (be increased, v.p.) ተጨመረ tḁč̣ḁ́mmḁrḁ (-mär-).

አከለ ákkḁlḁ.

increase, v.t. ጨመረ č̣ḁ́mmḁrḁ (-mär-).

አበለጠ abḁ́llḁṭḁ (aỵḁ́-).

Increase it: ጨምረው። č̣ḁ́mmi̥rḁu, pl. -ሩት። -rut.

incredible, adj. የማይታመን yämma͡i̥ttá̃mmạn (§ 14, s.v. አመነ).

This kind of story is incredible: እንዲህ፡ያለ፡ቃል፡ አይታመንም። ndi̥h yállä qāl a͡i̥ttámmäni̥m.

indeed, adv. እንጂ (i̥)njí.

እንኳን ńkwán (§ 8).

ቢያ bíyyã (§ 8).

It is not white, indeed it is black: ጥቁር፡ነው፡እንጂ፡ ነጭም፡አይደል። ṭŭqúr na͡u̥njí, nắčči̥mm á͡i̥däl (§ 7*d*).

Isn't it disgraceful! ነውር፡አይደለም። ná͡u̥r a͡i̥dälläm? (§ 77). It is indeed: ነው፡እንጂ። ná͡u̥ nji.

indeed?, interj. (= is it so?) እንዲህ፡ነው። ndíhna͡u̥?

indefinite, adj. አጓጉል agwágwŭl.

India, s. ሀንድ hi̥nd.

Indian, adj. የሀንድ yáhi̥nd (§ 8, s.v. የ-, §§ 47*a*, 70).

Indian, s. የሀንድ፡ሰው yähi̥ndi̥ (§ 7*d*) sa͡u̥.

Indian corn (*Zea mays*), s. የባሕር፡ማሽላ yäbáhi̥r (-äyá-) māši̥llã.

indicate, v.t. አመለከተ amạlạ́kkạtạ.

indication, s. (symptom) ማስታወቂያ mãsta͡u̥ώqyã.

industrious, adj. ሰራተኛ sạrrãtạ́ññã (sär-, -táñ-).

ትጉ ti̥gu.

industry, s. (employment) ስራ si̥rã.

(diligence) ትጋት ti̥gát (§ 8).

infant, s. አራስ ắrás (§ 8).

አራስ፡ልጅ arás li̥j.

ጨቅላ čắqlã.

ሕጣን hi̥ṭán (§ 8).

infantry, s. እግረኛ i̥grạ́ññã (-ráñ-).

infect, v.t. ነካ nạ́kkã.

infected, be, v.p. ተነካ tḁnḁ́kkã.

These cattle are infected with plague: ይሀን፡ከብት፡ በሽታ፡ነክቶታል። yi̥háṅ kḁf̣t (§ 52*a*, δ) yḁši̥tá nák-tʷotāl.

infectious, be, v.i. አለፈ állḁfḁ.

It is infectious: ያልፋል። yálfāl.

It is not infectious: አያልፍም። a͡ʸálfi̥m.

inflate, v.t. ነፋ nḁ́ffã.

inform, v.t. አስታወቀ astá͡uwḁqḁ (-wωq-).

አስረዳ asrḁ́ddã.

information, s. (knowledge) እውቀት i̥w(ŭ)qḁt.

(news) ወሬ wώrʸe.

informed, be, v.p. አወቀ á͡uwḁqḁ (-wωq-).

ተረዳ tḁrḁ́ddã.

informer, s. ጠቋሚ ṭḁqqwámi (ṭωq-).

inhabitant, s. ባላገር bālágḁr (-gär; § 52*a*, δ).

inhabited, adj. ለም lḁm (läm).

inherit, v.i. & t. ወረሰ wώrrḁsḁ.

injure, v.t. ጐዳ gwώddã.

Don't injure him (it): አትጕዳው። attí̥gwŭda͡u, pl. -ዱት። -dut.

injured, be, v.p. ተጐዳ tḁgwώddã.

injurious, adj. ክፉ ki̥fu (kúfu, kŭ́fu, § 7*d*).

injurious, be (become), v.i. ከፋ kḁ́ffã.

injury, s. ጕዳት gwŭ́dát (§ 8).

(wrong) በደል bḁ́dḁl (bắdäl).

ink, s. (dark) ጥቁር፡ቀለም ṭŭ́qur qḁ́lḁm.

Red ink: ቀይ፡ቀለም፡ qḁ́͡i̥ qḁ́lḁm.

inn, s. †ሉካንዳ lukándã.

inoffensive, adj. ገር gḁr (gär).

insane, adj. እብድ i̥bd (i̥ỵd).

insanity, s. እብደት í̥bdḁt (í̥ỵd-, -dät).

እብድነት i̥bdí̥nnḁt (i̥ỵd-, -nät).

insect—no general term.

Large buzzing insect: እንዝዝ፡ (í̥)nzi̥z (§ 52*a*, δ).

inside, adv. በውስጥ bḁ́wŭ́sṭ (ከ- kḁ́-, ተ- tḁ́-, -ḁ́u͡ŭ́-; § 8).

inside, prp. በ-...፡ ውስጥ bḁ- (ከ- kḁ-, ተ- tḁ-)... wŭsṭ.

ከ-...፡ በውስጥ kḁ- (ተ- tḁ-)... bḁ́wŭ́sṭ (ỵḁ́-, -ḁ́u͡ŭ́-; § 8).

See § 47*b*.

Inside the house: ከቤት፡ውስጥ፡ kḁỵ^{y}ét wŭsṭ.

inside, s. ውስጥ wŭsṭ.

insincere, adj. (of persons) ለዛዛ lḁzázã.

insolent, be, v.i. ውጥጥ፡ውጥጥ፡አለ wŭ́ṭi̥ṭ wŭ́ṭi̥ṭṭ (§ 6) álḁ (s.v. √በለ, § 44*a*).

Don't be insolent: ውጥጥ፡ውጥጥ፡አትበል። wŭ́ṭi̥ṭ wŭ́ṭi̥ṭṭ áttỵḁl.

inspect, v.t. ጐረጐረ gwωrḁ́ggwωrḁ (-rώgg-).

መረመረ mḁrḁ́mmḁrḁ (märḁ́mmärḁ).

instrument, s. ማድረጊያ mādrḁ́gyã (-rã́g-).

መሣሪያ mḁssáryã (-yä).

intelligent, adj. ጮሌ č̣^{w}óll^{y}e.

ብልሃተኛ bi̥lhātḁ́ññã (-tã́ñ-).

ጥበበኛ ṭi̥bḁbḁ́ññã (-i̥ỵḁỵ-, -ã́ñ-).

አዋቂ ãwáqi (a͡uá-).

ራሳም rásám (§ 8).

interest, s. (on loan) ወለድ wḁ́llḁ́d (wώl-; § 8).

It is not at interest: በወለድም፡አይደል። bḁu͡ωl-lḁ́di̥mm á͡i̥däl (§ 7*d*).

interfere, v.i. ተደበለቀ tadabállaqa (-ayá-).

Š. ተደበለቀ tadabállaqa (-ayá-).

Don't interfere with him in his work: ተስራው፡ አትደብለቅበት። tasira͡u attiddáylaqibbat (§ 47*a*), Š. ...፡ አትደበለቅበት። ...attiddayálaqibbat.

He (it) interferes with him (it): ይደበለቅበታል። yiddayallaqibbatāl, Š. -ደበ- -ddaya- (§ 47*a*).

interior, s. ውስጥ wŭsṭ.

interlace, v.t. ፈተለ fáttala (fáttäla).

interlaced, be, v.p. ተፈተለ tafáttala (-fáttäla).

interpret, v.i. & t. ተረጐመ tarággwωma (tär-).

Interpret for (to) me: ተርጕምልኝ። tárgwŭmilliñ (§ 47*a*).

interpreted, be, v.p. ተተረጐመ tatarággwωma (-tär-).

interpreter, s. አስተርጓሚ astωrgwámi (-tar-).

interrupt, v.t. (a proceeding) አጐለ ággwωla.

Don't interrupt it: አታጕለው። attággʷŭla͡u, pl. -ሉት። -lut.

Don't let him (it) interrupt the work: ስራውን፡ እንዳያጕል። sira͡un inda͡yággwŭl.

interrupted, be, v.p. ታጐለ tággwωla.

intertwine, v.t. ፈተለ fáttala (fáttäla).

intertwined, be, v.p. ተፈተለ tafáttala (-fáttäla).

intestine, s. አንጀት ánjät (§ 52*a*, *γ*).

intestines, (gen.), s. ሆድ፡እቃ hʷŏdiqā.

ፈርስ fars (färs).

into, prp. ከ- ka- (ተ- ta-; § 47*a*).

Put it into a box: ከሳጥን፡አግባው። kasáṭin ágya͡u.

intoxicated, be, v.i. ሰከረ sákkara (-kär-).

introduce, v.t. (bring in) አገባ agḁ́bbã.

(present) አገናኝ aggḁnã́ññä.

Introduce me to the Rās: ተራስ፡አገናኘኝ። tḁrás aggḁnã́ññäñ, pol. ...ያገናኙኝ።...yāggḁnã́ññuñ.

invert, v.t. ገለበጠ gḁlḁ́bbḁṭḁ̣.

Invert it: ገልብጠው። gā́lyi̥ṭḁ͡u, pl. -ጡት። -ṭut.

inverted, adj. ግልብጥ gı̥́lbı̥ṭ (-lyı̥-, gı̥lı̥́bbı̥ṭ).

inverted, be, v.p. ተገለበጠ tḁgḁlḁ́bbḁṭḁ.

invite, v.t. ጠራ ṭḁ́rrã.

invited, be, v.p. ተጠራ tḁṭḁ́rrã.

I have been invited (out): ተጠርቻያለሁ። tḁṭḁri̥č-čyállḁ͡u[h].

irascible, adj. ቍጡ qwǘṭṭu.

iron, s. ብረት bı̥́rḁt (-rät).

(flat-) መተኰሻ mḁtḁkkwṓšã (-tωk-).

iron, v.i. & t. (linen) ተኰሰ tḁ́kkwωsḁ (tώkkosḁ).

ironed, be, v.p. (linen) ተተኰሰ tḁtḁ́kkwωsḁ (-tώkkosḁ).

irrigation channel (جدول), s. መስኖ mḁ́snʷo.

ቦይ bʷṓi̥.

ፈሰስ fḁ́sḁs.

irritable, adj. ቍጡ qwǘṭṭu.

ተናዳጅ tḁnā́ḍáj (§ 8).

አሞታም amʷṓtám (§ 8).

He is irritable: አሞታም፡ነው። amʷōtám nḁ͡u.

irritate, v.t. (provoke) አስቈጣ asqwώṭṭã.

(prickle) ኰሰኰሰ kwωsḁ́kkwωsḁ (-sώkkosḁ).

Don't irritate him (it): አታስቈጣው። attasqwώṭṭa͡u, pl. -ጡት። -ṭṭut.

island, s. ደሴት dḁ́sʸē̃t (§ 8).

it, pers. pron. nom. እሱ ịssū́ / እርሱ ịrsū́ / እርሷ ịrsŏā — §§ 8, 12a; usually omitted unless emphatic.

dat. & acc. -ው -u. / -ት -t after o, u. / -āት āt. — § 12c.

This (that) is it: እሱ ፡ ነው ። ịssū́ nau.

Italian, adj. የጣሊያ yäṭā́lyā.

የጣሊያኒ yäṭalyā́ni.

S.v. የ-, §§ 47a, 70.

Italian, s. ጣሊያኒ ṭalyā́ni, pl. -ኖች -n^{w}ōč (-čč § 6).

Italy, s. እጣሊያ ịṭā́lyā.

ivory, s. ቀንድ qạnd (lit. horn).

የዞሆን ፡ ቀንድ yäzoh^{w}ón qạnd.

J

§ refers to the paragraphs of the Grammar (Initia Amharica, Part I).

jackal, s. ቀበሮ qạ́bạr^{w}o (ቃ- qá-, -ỵạ-, -är-; § 52a, δ).

jacket, s. ግብግብ gịbbịgịbb.

(Eur.) †ኮት k^{w}ōt.

January, s.v. calendar.

jar, s. (large) እንስራ (ị)nsịrā.

(small) ቶፋ t^{w}ōfā.

jasmine (*Jasminum floribundum*, Broun, Cat. 330), s. ጠምበለል ṭạmbạ́lạl (-bā́läl).

jaw, s. መንጋጋ mạṅgā́gā.

Lower jaw of animals: ግንጭል gịnčịl.

jealous, adj. ቀናተኛ qạnnātạ́ññā (-tā́ñ-).

jealous, be (become), v.i. ቀና qḁ́nnã (§ 63*d*, *e*).
He is (will get) jealous: ይቀናል። yi̥qḁ́nāl, pl. ይቀናሉ። yi̥qḁnállu.
jealousy, s. ቅናት qí̥nā́t (§ 8).
jest, s. ቧልታ bwā́ltã.
ዋዛ wā́zã.
Jew, s. አይሁድ a͡i̥húd.
jingle, v.i. ክዩ፡ክዩ፡አለ kyu kyu álḁ (s.v. √በለ, § 44*a*).
ኪች፡ኪች፡አለ ki̥č ki̥čč (§ 6) álḁ („ „).
join, v.i. (meet) ገጠመ gḁ́ṭṭḁmḁ.
join, v.t. (e.g. splice) ቀጠለ qḁ́ṭṭḁlḁ.
(meet) ተገናኘ tḁgḁnã́ññä.
joined, be, v.p. ተቀጠለ tḁqḁ́ṭṭḁlḁ.
joint, s. ማጠፊያ māṭḁ́fyã.
(of the body) ሥር si̥r (§ 52*a*, *γ*).
joke, s. ቧልታ bwā́ltã.
ዋዛ wā́zã.
joy, interj. expressing, እሰይ (i̥)ssḁ͡i̥!
joy, s. ደስታ dḁ́ss(i̥)tã.
judge, s. ወምበር wώmbḁr (-bär).
ዳኛ dā́ññã.
judge, v.i. & t. ፈረደ fḁ́rrḁdḁ ለ- lḁ-, በ- bḁ- (§ 47*a*).
judged, be, v.p. ተፈረደለት tḁfḁ́rrḁdḁllḁt (favourably).
ተፈረደበት tḁfḁ́rrḁdḁbbḁt (unfavourably).
judgment, s. ፍርድ fi̥rd.
jug, s. ማንቈርቈሪያ mañqwωrqwώryã.
juice, s. እዥ i̥ž.
ውሃ (w)ū́hã (úhã).
July, s.v. calendar.
jump, s. ዝላይ zí̥llyã.
jump (over), v.i. & t. ዘለለ zḁ́llḁlḁ.
Jump: ዝለል። zí̥lḁl, pl. ዝለሉ። zí̥lḁlu.

Jump over it: ዝለለው። zi̥lḁla͡u, pl. -ሉት። -lut.
Jump onto it: ዝለሊበት። zi̥lḁli̥bbḁt, pl. -ሉበት። -lubbḁt.

June, s.v. calendar.

juniper (*Juniperus phoenicaea*, Guidi, Vocab. p. 829, Schweinfurth's *J. procera*), s. ጥድ ti̥d (§ 52*a*, δ).

just, adj. ትክክል ti̥ki̥kki̥l.
(of persons) ፍርዱ፡የቀና fi̥rdu yäqḁnnã.
He is just: ፍርዱ፡ትክክል፡ነው። fi̥rdu ti̥ki̥kki̥l (§ 8) nḁ͡u.

just, adv. (only) ብቻ bi̥ččã.
እንደው (i̥)ndḁ͡u (§ 8).
እንዲያው (i̥)ndya͡u (§ 8).
(emphatic) -ው -u (q.v.).
State just what you know: አንተ፡እምታውቀውን፡ብቻ፡ተናገር። ántä mmi̥ttá͡uůqḁ͡un (-tämmttá͡uq-) bi̥ččā tḁnágär.
Just give it me: እንደው፡ስጠኝ። ndḁ́͡u si̥tḁñ.
Just pull it: ሳበው፡እንደው። sāy̥á͡u ndḁ͡u.
Just there: ተዚያው። tḁ́zzyá͡u (§ 8).
All right! I am just coming: እሺ፡መጣኹ። i̥šši̥, mḁ́ṭṭa͡u^{h} (§ 7*d*).

justice, s. ፍርድ fi̥rd.

K

§ *refers to the paragraphs of the Grammar (Initia Amharica, Part I).*

Kanahia laniflora (Broun, Cat. 348), s. የድመት፡ወተት yädi̥mmḁt wώtḁt.

keep, v.i. (remain) ሰነበተ sḁnábbḁtḁ (-bät-).
ቈየ qwώyyä.

Keep here till I come back: ተዚህ፡ቈይ፡እስክመጣ። täzzíh qwωyy i̥ski̥mḁ́ṭa, pl....፡ቈዩ፡እስክ-... qwώy-yu ski̥-.

keep, v.t. ጠበቀ ṭḁ́bbḁqḁ.

Keep it till I come (back): ጠብቀው፡እስክመጣ። ṭḁ́bbi̥qḁ͡u ski̥mḁ́ṭa, pl....-ቁት፡እስክ-... -qut i̥ski̥-.

keepsake, s. ማስታወሻ mãsta͡uḁ́šã (-a͡uώš-).

kept, be, v.p. ተጠበቀ tḁṭḁ́bbḁqḁ.

kerosene, s. †ላምባ lámbã.

kettle, s. መህረጅ mḁ́hrḁj.

key, s. መፍቻ mḁ́fčã.

መክፈቻ mḁkfḁ́čã (-fáč-).

khor (خور), s. ድፋ dí̥ffã.

ፈፋ fḁ́fã.

kick, v.i. & t. መታ mḁ́ttã.

Does it kick? ይመታል። yi̥mḁ́tāl?, f. ትመታለች። ti̥-mḁtálläč?

kid, s. (male) ወጠጤ wώṭḁṭ^{y}e.

(female) ቄብ q^{y}ēb (q^{y}ēy̥).

kidney, s. ኵላሊት kwŭlálit (§ 52*a*, γ).

kill, v.i. & t. ገደለ gḁ́ddḁlḁ (gád-).

Kill him (it): ግደለው። gí̥dḁlḁ͡u, pl. -ሉት። -lut.

Don't kill him (it): አትግደለው። attí̥gdḁlḁ͡u, pl. -ሉት። -lut.

killed, be, v.p. ሞተ m^{w}ótḁ.

He was killed by a lion: በንበሳ፡እጅ፡ሞተ። ban-yḁssájj m^{w}ótḁ.

killed, have, (cause to be), v.t. አስገደለ asgḁ́ddḁlḁ (-gád-).

kind, adj. ቸር čär.

kind, s. ዓይነት a͡ái̥nḁt (-nät).

Of what kind? ምንኛ፡ mi̥ní̥ññã? (§ 15).

የትኛው፡ yĕtí̥ñña͡u? („).

What kind is it? ዓይነቱ፡ምንድር፡ነው። a͡i̥nätu mí̥n-di̥r na͡u̥?

kindness, s. ቸርነት čärí̥nnḁt (-nät).

(kind action) ውለታ wŭlḁ́tã (-lát-).

king, s. ንጉሥ ní̥gũs (§§ 8, 53*b*), pl. ነገሥት nḁ́gḁ́st and ነገሥታት nḁgḁ́stát.

Where is the king? ንጉሥ፡ዬት፡ናቸው። ni̥gús yēt náčča͡u̥?

What did the king say? ንጉሥ፡ምን፡አሉ። ni̥gús mi̥n álu?

kingdom, s. መንግሥት mḁ́ṅgi̥st.

kinship, s. ዝምድና zi̥mdí̥nnã.

kinsman, s. ዘመድ zḁ́mḁd.

ወንድም wǿndi̥m [prop. brother; pl. also ወንድማሞች wω̥ndi̥mámʷōč (-čč § 6)].

kiss, s. መሳም mḁ́sám (§ 8).

(mutual) መሳሳም mḁssássám (§ 8).

kiss, v.t. ሳመ sámḁ.

kissed, be, v.p. ተሳመ tḁsámḁ (täs-).

kitchen, s. [የ]ወጥ፡ቤት (yä)wǿṭ bʸēt (y̥ʸēt).

kite (*Milvus regalis*, Guidi, Vocab. p. 840), s. ጭላት č̣í̥lát (§ 8).

klipspringer (*Oreotragus saltator*), s. ሰሳ sḁ́sã.

knee (-cap), s. ጕልበት gwŭlbḁt (-ly-, -ät; § 52*a*, γ).

kneel (down), v.i. ተምበረከከ tḁmbḁrḁ́kkḁkḁ (-bär-).

(in prayer) ሰገደ sḁ́ggḁdḁ.

kneel (down), cause to, v.t. አምበረከከ ambḁrḁ́kkḁkḁ (-bär-).

Make it kneel down: አምበርክከው። ambárki̥ka͡u̥.

knife, s. (large) ካራ kárrã.

(small) ሰንጢ sḁ́nṭi.

knock, v.i. & t. መታ mạttā̃.
ገጨ gặč̣č̣ä.
Knock before entering: ደጁን፡ምታ፡ሳትገባ። dạ́jjun mịta sāttịgạ́ya.
knock (against), v.i. ተጋጨ tạgắč̣č̣ä.
Don't let them knock against each other: አይጋጩ። a͡iggắc̣u.
knot, s. ቋጥር qwịṭịr (qwŭ́ṭ-).
knot, v.t. ቋጠረ qwắṭṭạrạ (-ṭär-).
know, v.i. & t. አወቀ á͡uwạqạ (-wωq-).
I know: አውቃለሁ። a͡uqálla͡u[h] (§ 7*d*).
I don't know: አላውቅም። alá͡uqịm.
I know him (it): አውቀዋለሁ። a͡uqa͡uálla͡u[h].
I don't know him (it): አላውቀውም። alá͡uqa͡um.
Do you know? ታውቃለህ። ta͡uqálläh?
Do you know him (it)? ታውቀዋለህ። ta͡uqa͡uálläh?
Do you know them? ታውቃቸዋለህ። ta͡uqāčča͡uálläh?
Does he know? ያውቃል። yá͡uqāl?
Do they know? ያውቃሉ። ya͡uqállu?
If you don't know, say so: ባታውቅ፡አላውቅም፡በል። battá͡uq, ala͡uqịm (§ 8) bạl.
knowledge, s. (learning) ትም[ሀ]ርት tịm(h)ịrt (§ 8).
(acquaintance) እውቀት ịw(ŭ)qạt.
known, be, v.p. ታወቀ tá͡uwạqạ (-wωq-).
kopje, s. ጎጥ g[w]oṭ.
(large) አምባ ámbā̃.
kudu (*Strepsiceros kudu*), s. አጋዘን agázạn (-zän).

L

§ *refers to the paragraphs of the Grammar* (*Initia Amharica, Part I*).

labour, s. (work) ሥራ si̥rã.
 (workmen) ሠራተኞች sḁrrãtḁ́ññōč (sär-, -tǟñ-; -ōčč § 6).
labour, v.i. ሠራ sḁ́rrã (sǟr-).
labourer, s. ሠራተኛ sḁrrãtḁ́ññã (sär-, -tǟñ-).
 ባለሟያ bālḁmwā́yã (-á͡i̥ã).
lace, s. (for fastening) ማሰሪያ māsḁ́ryã (-sǟr-, -yä).
lack, v.t. አጣ áṭṭã.
lacking, be, v.i. ታጣ tā́ṭṭã.
 ገደደ gḁ́ddḁdḁ.
 What is lacking? ምን፡ይታጣል። mi̥n yi̥ttáṭṭāl?
ladder, s. መሰላል mḁsḁ́lāl (§ 8).
laden, be, v.p. ተሸከመ tḁšḁ́kkḁmḁ (täšǟk-).
 ተጫነ tḁčā́nḁ.
lady, s. እመቤት (i̥)mmḁ́byét (-ḁ́v̥yét; § 8).
 ወይዘሮ wḁ́i̥zḁrʷo (wω͡i̥-, -zär-), pl. also ወይዛዝር wḁi̥zā́zi̥r [wω͡i̥-, -ዛዝሮች -zā́zi̥rʷōč (-čč § 6)].
 My lady (form of address): እሜት። i̥mmyēt!
 My lady (form of reference): እሜቴ፡ (i̥)mmyétye (§ 12*a*).
 Our Lady: እመቤታችን፡ (i̥)mmḁv̥yētā́čči̥n.
lag behind, v.i. ቀረ qḁ́rrḁ.
 Don't lag behind: አትቅር። attí̥qi̥r, pl. አትቅሩ። attí̥qru.
lake, s. ባሕር bā́hi̥r (-har); s.v. ረጋ.
 (small) ጭምቧት čí̥mbwāt (§ 8).
 Is it a lake or a river? ረግቷል፡ወይ፡ይሔዳል። rḁ́gtω͡āl wω͡i̥ yi̥hā́dāl?

lamb, s. በግ bḁg (§ 52*a*, δ).

lame, adj. አንካሳ aṅkā́ssā̃.

lame, be (become), v.i. አነከሰ ˙anḁ́kkḁsḁ (§ 63*d*, *e*).

He is lame: አንክሷል። áṅki̥so͡āl.

She is lame: አንክሳለች። aṅki̥sálläč.

He will get lame: ያነክሳል። yānḁ́kki̥sāl.

She will get lame: ታነክሳለች። tānḁkki̥sálläč.

lameness, s. እንክስና (i̥)ṅki̥sı́nnā̃.

lamp, s. መብራት mḁ́brā́t (-ḁ́ỵr-; § 8).

ማብሪያ mā́bryā̃ (-ā́ỵr-).

መቅረዝ mḁ́qrḁz.

Lamp oil: †ላምባ፡ lámbā̃.

Light the lamp: መብራቱን፡አብራው። mḁỵrā́tun ā́ỵra͡u.

Put the lamp out: መብራቱን፡አጥፋው። mḁỵrā́tun ā́ṭfa͡u.

The lamp is too high: ማብሪያው፡በርትቷል። mā́ỵrya͡u ỵḁ́rti̥to͡āl (from በረታ).

lamp-shade, s. የመብራት፡መከደኛ yämḁbrā́t (-ḁỵr-) mḁkdḁ́ñā̃ (-dā́ñ-).

lancet, s. መውጊያ mḁ͡úgyā̃.

ወስፌ wώsfʸe.

land, s. ምድር mı̥́di̥r (ḿdi̥r).

(country) አገር ā́gḁr (-gär).

landslip, s. መርግ mḁrg (märg).

language, s. ቋንቋ qwā́ṅqwā̃.

What is your own language? ያንተ፡ራስህ፡ቋንቋህ፡ምንድን፡ነው። yā́ntä rási̥h qwáṅqwāh mi̥ndı̥́n nḁ͡u?

What language does he speak? ምንኛ፡ይናገራል። mi̥nı̥́ñña yi̥nnā́ggḁrāl?

lantern, s. ፋኑስ fā́nus.

large, adj. ትልቅ ti̥lli̥q.

large-boned, adj. ቅልጥማም qi̥lti̥mám (§ 8).

lash, s. (stroke) ግርፋት gi̥rfát (§ 8).

(whip, small) አለንጋ aláṅgã.

(whip, large) ጅራፍ ji̥ráf (§ 8).

If you do that again you will get twenty lashes: ደግሞ ፡ እንዲህ ፡ ያደረግህ ፡ እንደሆን ፡ ሀያ ፡ ትገረፋለህ ። dämm^{w}ó nd^{y}i̥h yādḁ́rrḁgh i̥ndḁh^{w}on hḁã ti̥g-gḁrrḁfálläh.

lashes, give (to), v.t. ገረፈ gḁ́rrḁfḁ (gắr-).

He gave him ten lashes: አሥር ፡ ገረፈው ። ássi̥r gḁ́r-rḁfḁu.

Give him ten lashes: አሥር ፡ ግረፈው ። ássi̥r gi̥rḁfḁu.

lashes, receive, v.i. ተገረፈ tḁgḁ́rrḁfḁ (-gắr-).

How many lashes did you receive? ስንት ፡ ተገረፍህ ። si̥nt tḁgḁ́rrḁfh?

last, adj. ኋለኛ hwālḁ́ññã (-láñ-).

Last month: ያለፈ ፡ ወር ፡ yállḁfḁ wωr.

Last year: አምና ፡ ắmnã.

last, v.i. ኖረ n^{w}ốrḁ.

How long will (does) it last? ምን ፡ ያህል ፡ ይኖራል ። mi̥n yahl yi̥n^{w}órāl?

lasting, adj. ኗሪ nwári.

late, adj.

'Late' is rendered by such verbs as ረፈደ rḁ́ffḁdḁ, to be(come) forenoon, መሸ mḁ́ššä (mắš-), to be(come) evening, according to the time at which one is speaking:

I thought it was too late: (in the morning) ረፍዶብኛል ፡ ብያለሁ ። rḁfd^{w}obbi̥ññāl yi̥yyállḁu^{h}, (in the afternoon) መሽቶብኛል ፡ ብ- mḁ́št^{w}obbi̥ññāl yi̥-.

late, be, v.i. ዘገየ zḁgḁ́yyä.
ቈየ qwώyyä.
See § 63*d*, *e*.
Don't be late: አትዘገይ። atti̥zág̥ga͡i̥, pl. አትዘገዩ። at-ti̥zḁgḁ́yyu (§ 6); or አትቈይ። attíqwω͡i̥, pl. አትቈዩ። atti̥qwώyyu (§ 6).
He (it) is not to be late: አይዘገይ። a͡i̥zág̥ga͡i̥, pl. አይዘገዩ። a͡i̥zḁgḁ́yyu; or አይቈይ። á͡i̥qwω͡i̥, pl. አይቈዩ። a͡i̥qwώyyu.
He will be late: ይዘገያል። yi̥zḁgḁ́yyāl.
He will not be late: አይዘገይም። a͡i̥zḁgḁ́yyi̥m.
He is two hours late: ሁለት፡ሰዓት፡ቈየ። húlḁtt sḁ͡ät qwώyyä.
Why are you late? ስለምን፡ቈየህ። si̥lḁmi̥n qwώyyäh?
It's getting late (in the morning): ሊረፍድ፡ነው። li̥ráfd na͡u̥, (afternoon) ሊመሽ፡ነው። li̥máš na͡u̥.
late, make, v.t. አቈየ aqwώyyä.
What (has) made you (so) late? ምን፡አቈየህ። mi̥n aqwώyyäh?
later (on), adv. በኋላ bḁhwālã (ba͡u̥há- § 7*d*).
latrine, s. ዓይነ፡ምድር a͡i̥nḁ́mdi̥r (-nắm-; § 9*d*).
የሠገራ፡ቤት yäsḁgḁrá b^{y}ēt (-gär-, y̥^{y}ēt).
laugh, v.i. ሣቀ sáqḁ.
What are you laughing at? ለምን፡ትሥቃለህ። lḁmi̥n ti̥si̥qállăh?
Don't laugh at him: አትሣቅበት። attsáqi̥bbät.
lavatory, s. ማጠቢያ māṭḁbyã (-ḁ́y̥yã).
law, s. ትዛዝ ti̥záz (§ 8).
ሥራት si̥rát (§ 8).
(religious) ሕግ hi̥gg, pl. ሕግጋት hi̥ggi̥gát (§ 8).
lead, s. (metal) [እ]ርሳስ (i̥)rsás.

lead, v.t. አስኬደ askḁ̄́dä (-kḁ̄́-, -dḁ).
    (an animal) ሳበ sábḁ (sáy̥ḁ).
    (guide) መራ mḁ́rrā̃.
  Let him put a halter on it and lead it: ለብቦ፡ ይሳበው። lḁ́bbi̥y^{w}o yi̥sáy̥ḁu.
lead to, v.t. ወሰደ wḁ́ssḁdḁ (wώs-).
  Where does this road lead to? ይህ፡መንገድ፡ዬት፡ ይወስዳል። yi̥he mḁ́ṅgḁd yēt yi̥wώsdāl?
leaf, s. (of tree or book) ቅጠል qí̥ṭḁl (§ 52*a*, δ).
leak, v.i. (escape) ፈሰሰ fḁ́ssḁsḁ.
    (allow to escape) አፈሰሰ afḁ́ssḁsḁ.
  The water leaks: ውሃው፡ይፈሳል። wǘhau yi̥fḁ́ssāl.
  The jar leaks: እንስራው፡ያፈሳል። nsi̥rau yafḁ́ssāl.
lean, v.i. ተደገፈ tḁdḁ́ggḁfḁ (tḁgḁ́ddḁfḁ).
    ተጠጋ tḁṭḁ́ggā̃, against, ወደ- wωdḁ- (§ 47*a*).
lean, v.t. አስጠጋ asṭḁ́ggā̃.
  Lean the box against the wall: ሳጥኑን፡ወደግድግዳ፡ አስጠጋው። sāṭi̥nun wωdḁgi̥rgí̥dda (§ 7*d*) asṭḁ́ggau.
  Don't lean it against it: አታስጠጋው። attasṭḁ́ggau.
leap, s. ዝላይ zí̥llyā̃.
leap (over), v.i. & t. ዘለለ zḁ́llḁlḁ.
learn, v.i. & t. ያዘ yázḁ (§ 44*c*).
    ለመደ lḁ́mmḁdḁ.
    ተማረ tḁmárḁ.
  It is hard to learn: አይያዝም። ai̥yyázi̥m (lit. it cannot be learnt, § 63*c*).
  I wish to learn it: ልይዘው፡እፈልጋለሁ። li̥i̥zḁu i̥fḁlli̥gállḁu^{h}.
  I want to learn Amharic: አማርኛ፡ልለምድ፡እፈል ጋለሁ። amārí̥ñña li̥lḁ́md i̥fḁlli̥gállḁu^{h}.
learned, adj. አዋቂ ãwáqi (auá-).

learned man, s. ደብተራ dḁbtḁ́rã (-ḁỵt-, -ḁf̣t-, -tā́r-).

learning, s. ትም[ህ]ርት ti̥m(h)i̥rt (§ 8).

learnt, be, v.p. ተያዘ tḁyā́zḁ (tḁ͡já-).

least, at, ቢያንስ byans (s.v. አነሰ).

There are at least two: ቢያንስ፡ሁለት፡አሉ። byans húlḁtt állu.

leather, s. ቆርበት qʷórbḁt (-rỵ-, -ät).

leave, s. ፍቃድ fi̥qā́d (§ 8).

leave, v.i. & t. [depart (from)] ተነሣ tḁnḁ́ssã ከ- kḁ- (ተ- tḁ-).

When do you leave? መቼ፡ትነሣለህ። mḁ́čʸe ti̥nnḁssálläh? pol. መቼ፡ይነሣሉ። mḁ́čʸe yi̥nnḁssállu? pl. መቼ፡ትነሣላችሁ። mḁ́čʸe ti̥nnḁssallā́ččyuh? (§ 7*d*).

You must leave this place: የግድ፡ተዚህ፡ትነሣለህ። yägi̥ddi̥ tḁzzíh ti̥nnḁssálläh.

leave, v.t. ተወ tḁ́wḁ (tḁ́͡uḁ).

Leave him (it) alone: ተወው። tḁ́͡uḁ͡u.

Leave him (it) here: ከዚህ፡ተወው። kḁzzíh tḁ́͡uḁ͡u.

Leave (pl.) it as it was: እንደነበር፡ተዉት። ndänáb-bḁr tḁ́͡uut.

Leave it open: ተከፍቶ፡ይቀመጥ። tḁkḁ́ftʷo yi̥qqḁ́mḁṭ.

Who left this? የህነን፡ማን፡ተወው። yi̥hánnän mān tḁ́͡uḁ͡u?

Where did you leave him (it)? የት፡ተውሀው። yēt tḁ́͡uhḁ͡u?—you pl.—...ተዋችሁት። ...tḁ͡uáčči̥hut?

You have left this out: ይሀ፡ቀርቷል። yi̥he qā́r-t͡ŏāl.

lectern, s. አትሮንስ ātrʷóni̥s.

led, be, v.p. (guided) ተመራ tḁmḁ́rrã.

(of an animal) ተሳበ tḁsā́bḁ (täs-, -ā́ỵḁ).

left, s. & adj. (left hand) ግራ gi̥rã.

On (to) the left: በግራ፡ bḁgrã.

left, be, v.i. & p. (over) ቀረ qḁ́rrḁ.

(abandoned) ተተወ tḁtḁ́wḁ (-ḁ́u͡ḁ).

There are twenty-one left: ሀያ፡ሐንድ፡ይቀራል። hḁ͡ʸahánd (§ 20*a*) yi̥qḁ́rāl.

leg, s. እግር i̥g(i̥)r (§ 52*a*, γ).

lend, v.i. & t. አበደረ abḁ́ddḁrḁ (aẏ-, -äddärḁ).

Please lend me some ink: እባክህ፡ጥቁር፡ቀለም፡አበድረኝ። i̥ẏákki̥h ṭúqur qḁlḁm aẏáddi̥rāñ.

length, s. እርዝመት i̥rzi̥mḁt (-mät).

ቁመት qúmḁt (-mät).

What is the length of your rope (string)? ገመድህ፡ቁመቱ፡ስንት፡ነው። gḁmḁdi̥h qúmḁtu si̥nti̥ nḁ͡u?

Lent, s. ጦም ṭʷōm.

leopard (*Felis pardus*), s. ነብር nḁbi̥r (ná-, -ẏi̥r).

leprosy, s. ለምጥ lḁmṭ.

Lepus abessinicus (*L. tigrensis*), s. ጥንቻል ṭi̥nčäl.

G. ጭንተል č̣i̥ntḁl (-täl).

ጭንቻል č̣i̥nčäl.

let, v.t. (allow) ተወ tḁ́wḁ (tḁ́͡uḁ).

Use causative in አስ- as- (§ 22*a*); s.v. √ባለ, § 44*a*.

Will he let you go? ልትሔድ፡ይተውሃል። li̥tthä́d yi̥tḁ́͡uhāl?

I will not let him (her, it, them § 61*b*) come: አላስመጣም። alasmḁ́ṭṭām.

Aren't you going to let us pass? አላሳልፋችሁ፡ትላለህ። alasalli̥fáččyuh ti̥lállāh?

The flies wouldn't let me work: ዝምቦች፡አላሰራኝ፡አሉ። zi̥mbʷōčč alassḁ́rrañn álu, or ዝምቦች፡ስራ፡አስፈቱኝ። zi̥mbʷōč si̥ra asfḁ́ttuñ.

She will not let one take it (them): አላስይዝም፡ ትላለች። alasyızım tıláll̈äč.

Directing: use the jussive (§ 34).

Let him (it) come: ይምጣ። yímṭa.

let, v.t. (on hire) አከራየ akkaráyyä (-kär-).

Will you let it (them)? ታከራያለህ። takkarayyálläh?

Will he let it? ያከራየዋል። yakkaráyyauāl?

At how much a month will you let it? በወር፡ስንት፡ ታከራየዋለህ። bauár sınt takkarayyauálläh?

let go, v.i. ለቀቀ láqqaqa.

Let go! ልቀቅ። líqaq!, pl. ልቀቁ። líqaqu!

let go, v.t. ለቀቀ láqqaqa.

ፈታ fátta.

let in, v.t. አስገባ asgábbā.

let out, v.t. አስወጣ aswáṭṭā.

letter, s. ደብዳቤ dabdábbʸe (davd-).

Tell a servant to come to take a letter to the Rās: አሽከር፡ይምጣ፡ደብዳቤ፡ለራስ፡የሚወስድ። áškär yímṭa davdábbʸe larás yämmiwásd.

level, adj. ትክክል tikíkkil.

Level ground: ሜዳ mʸédā.

ሰንጣ sánṭā.

level, v.t. ደለደለ daláddala (däláddäla).

አስተካከለ astakákkala.

Level it: ደልድለው። dáldilau, pl. -ሉት። -lut, or

አስተካክለው። astakáklau, pl. -ሉት። -lut.

level, be, v.i. ተካከለ takákkala.

lever, s. መፈንቀያ mafanqáyā (-áiā).

(of gun) ቃታ qátā.

መከፈቻ makfáčā (-fáč-).

liana, s. አዞ ázzʷo (§ 52*a*, δ).

liar, s. ዋሾ wášʷo.

ውሸታም wŭšátám (§ 8).

አባይ ấbấi̥ (ấy̩ấ-; -áyy § 6; § 8).

liberty, s. አርነት arri̥nnḁt (-nät).

lice, infested with, adj. ቅማላም qi̥málám (§ 8).

lice, ova of, s. ቅጫም qi̥čám (§ 8, § 52*a*, δ).

lick, v.t. ላሰ lásḁ.

licked, be, v.p. ተላሰ tḁlásḁ.

lid, s. መክደኛ mḁkdḁñã (-dáñ-).

ክዳን ki̥dán (§ 8).

lie, s. (untruth) አሰት ássḁt.

ውሸት wi̥šät (wŭš-).

እብለት i̥blḁt (i̥vl-, -lät).

That is a lie: ውሸት፡ነው። wŭšát (§ 8) nḁu.

You had better not tell lies: አትዋሽ፡ይሻልሃል። attuášš yi̥ššálähāl.

lie, v.i. (speak falsely) ዋሸ wáššä.

(recline) ተኛ tḁññã (táñ-, -ñä).

Lie down! ተኛ። táñña! pl. ተኙ። táññu!

lie in wait, v.i. (for, v.t.) አደባ adḁbbã.

life, s. ሕይወት hi̥ywǿt (§ 8).

ነፍስ nḁfs (nä-, -vs).

(mode of) ትዳር ti̥dár (§ 8).

He was sentenced to imprisonment for life: በድሚው፡ሙሉ፡ይታሰር፡ተፈረደበት። bḁdmʸeu múlu yi̥ttásḁr tḁfḁrrḁdḁbbḁt (§ 47*a*).

lift, v.t. አነሣ anḁssã.

Lift him (her, it, them, § 61*b*): አንሣ። ánsa, pl. አንሡ። ánsu.

lifted, be, v.p. ተነሣ tḁnḁssã.

light, adj. (not heavy) ቀላል qḁllál (§ 8).
(not dark) ብርሃን bi̥rhán (§ 8, § 57*b*).
Let it be in a light place: በብርሃን፡ስፍራ፡ይሁን። bḁỵi̥rhán si̥fra yi̥hun.

light, s. (abstract) ብርሃን bi̥rhán (§ 8).
(concrete, e.g. a candle) መብራት mḁbrát (-ḁ́ỵr-; § 8).
ማብሪያ mábryã (-ã́ỵr-).
There is no light: ብርሃን፡የለም። bi̥rhán yálläm.
Bring a light: መብራት፡አምጣ። mḁỵrát ánṭa (§ 7*d*).

light, v.t. (kindle) አነደደ anḁ́ddḁdḁ.
አበራ abḁ́rrã (aỵḁ́-).
Light the fire: እሳቱን፡አንድድ። i̥sátun ándi̥d.
Light a lamp: መብራት፡አብራ። mḁỵrát ã́ỵra.

lighten, v.i. (flash) ብልጭ፡አለ bi̥lli̥č̣č̣ álḁ (s.v. √ብለ, § 44*a*).

lightning, s. ብልጭታ bi̥llí̥č̣tã.
He (it) was struck by lightning: በብራቅ፡ተመታ። bḁỵi̥rā́q tḁmḁ́tta, (s.v. ብራቅ).

like, adj. እንደ- (i̥)ndḁ- (-dä-).
It is like iron: እንደብረት፡ነው። ndäỵi̥rḁt nḁ͡u.
It is very like this: እንደዚህ፡ይሆን፡ይሆናል። i̥ndäz-zíh yi̥h^{w}ón yi̥h^{w}ónāl.
There is nothing like it: አይገኝም። a͡i̥ggḁ́ññi̥m.

like, v.i. & t. ወደደ wώddḁdḁ.
I like him (it): እወደዋለሁ። i̥wωddḁ͡uállḁ͡u^{h}.
I don't like him (it): አልወደውም። alwώddḁ͡um.
Do you like him (it)? ትወደዋለህይ። ti̥wωddḁ͡uál-lähwi̥? (s.v. ወይ), pol. ይወዱታሉይ። yuώddutāllwi̥?, pl. ትወዱታላችሁወይ። ti̥wωddutallā́c̆c̆yuhwḁ͡i̥?

like, be, v.t. መሰለ mḁ́ssḁlḁ (type A § 34).
What is it like? ምን፡ይመስላል። mi̥n yi̥mḁ́si̥lāl?

like each other, v.i. ተዋደዱ tawáddadu (taưá-).

They don't like each other: አይዋደዱም። aiwwáddadum.

liked, be, v.p. ተወደደ tawώddada (tauώ-).

likely, adj.—use ሆነ hʷṓna, to be, become.

Very likely: ይሆናል። yihʷónāl.

It is not at all likely: አይሆንም። aihʷónim.

Is it likely to rain? ይዘንባሉዋይ። yizányāllwi? (s.v. ወይ).

likeness, s. ምስል misil.

ምሳሌ missálʸe.

limb, s. ቅልጥም qiltim (§ 52*a*, γ).

lime, s. (fruit) ሎሚ lʷómī (§ 52*a*, δ).

(mineral) ኖራ nʷórā̃.

limit, s. ዳርቻ dā̃ríččā̃.

limit, v.t. ወሰነ wώssana.

limp, v.i. አነከሰ anákkasa.

line, s. (rank) ሰልፍ salf (sälf).

(on paper etc.) መስመር másmar (-mär; § 52*a*, δ).

lion (*Felis leo*), s. አንበሳ anbássā̃ (ambá-, anyá- § 7*d*).

lip, s. ከንፈር kánfar (-ámf-, -fär, § 7*d*; § 52*a*, γ).

lisping, adj. ዱዳ dúdā̃.

list, s. መዝገብ mázgab (-gay).

Make a list of them: መዝገብ፡አድርግበት። mázgay árgibbat (§ 7*d*).

listen, v.i. (to, v.t.) አደመጠ adámmata.

Listen to me: አድምጠኝ። ádimtañ, pl. -ጡኝ። -tuñ.

little, adj. ትንሽ tínniš.

-ይቱ, -ịቱ -itu (f. art. § 11).

See § 54*c*, *d*.

It got in by a little hole: በቀዳዳይቱ፡ገባ። baqadā̃dáitu gábba.

Use f. dem. pron. (§ 13):

Fetch that little book from the house: ያችን፡ መጣፍ፡ ተቤት፡ ይዘህ፡ ና። yáččịn mḁṭáf tḁy^{y}ét yi̥záh na.

This little one (little thing): ይች፡ yi̥čč (i̥čči̥).

little, a, s. & adv. ጥቂት ṭi̥qi̥t.

Give me a little: ጥቂት፡ ስጠኝ። ṭi̥qi̥t si̥ṭäñ.

Wait a little: ቆይ፡ ጥቂት። qwó͡i̥ ṭi̥qi̥t.

live, v.i. (reside) ኖረ n^{w}őrḁ.

(get a living, exist) አደረ áddḁrḁ (-där-).

Where does he live? መቀመጫው፡ ዬት፡ ነው። mḁq-qḁmḁ́č̣a͡u yēt na͡u?

How does he live? እንዴት፡ ያድራል። nd^{y}ét yádrāl?

liver, s. ጉበት gúbbḁt.

living, s. ትዳር ti̥dár (§ 8).

lizard, s. እንሽላሊት (i̥)nši̥lálit (-li̥t), often f. (§ 54c).

load, s. ሸክም šḁ́ki̥m (šák-).

(animal's) ጭነት č̣i̥nḁt (-nät).

The load is too much for it: ጭነት፡ በዛበት። č̣i̥nät yḁzzábbḁt (§ 47a).

load, v.t. (an animal) ጫነ č̣ánḁ.

Load it (them § 61b): ጫን። č̣ān, pl. ጫኑ። č̣ánu.

I can't load this mule: it is worn out: ይህን፡ በቅሎ፡ እንዴት፡ አድርጌ፡ እጭናለሁ። ደክሞታል። yi̥hán yḁ́ql^{w}o nd^{y}ét ádri̥gg^{y}e i̥č̣i̥nállḁ͡u^{h}? dáki̥m^{w}otāl.

load (be laden), cause or allow to, v.t. አስጫነ asč̣ánḁ.

loaf, s. ዳቦ dább^{w}o.

ቂጣ qi̥ṭṭã.

loaf, v.i. አውደለደለ a͡udḁlḁ́ddalḁ (-däláddäl-).

loafer, s. አውደልዳይ a͡udḁ́ldá͡i̥ (-dál-, -áyy § 6; § 8).

loathe, v.t. ጠላ ṭḁ́llã.

I loathe it: እጠላዋለሁ። i̥ṭḁla͡uállḁ͡u^{h}.

loathsome, adj. ጸያፍ ṣḁ́yyā́f (ጠ- ṭḁ́-; § 8).
lock, s. ቍልፍ qwŭlf.
lock, v.i. (be locked, v.p.) ተቈለፈ tḁqwώllḁfḁ.
  Does it lock? ይቈለፋል። yi̥qqwώllḁfāl? (§ 63c).
  Is it locked? ተቈልፏሎይ። tḁqwώlli̥fo͡āllwi̥? (§ 63d, s.v. ወይ).
lock, v.t. ቈለፈ qwώllḁfḁ.
  በመፍቻ፡ዘጋ bḁmḁ́fča zḁ́ggā̃.
  Shut it, but don't lock it: ዝጋው፡ መች፡ በመፍቻ። zi̥ga͡u, mḁč yḁmḁ́fča.
locust, s. አንበጣ anbḁ́ṭā̃ (amb-, any̥ḁ́- § 7d).
log, s. ግንድ gi̥nd.
  ጠርብ ṭḁrb (ṭä-, -ry̥).
  እንጩት (i̥)nč^{y}et (-ጨት -čḁ̈t).
loin, s. ዳሌ dā́l^{y}e (§ 52a, γ).
  ወገብ wώgḁb (-ḁy̥; § 52a, γ).
long, adj. ረጅም rḁ́jji̥m (rä́j-, -ዥም -žži̥m).
  How long is it? እርዝመቱ፡ስንት፡ነው። i̥rzí̥mḁtu si̥nti̥ nḁ͡u? or ቁመቱ፡ስንት፡ነው። qúmḁtu si̥nti̥ nḁ͡u?
long, adv. ዘመን zḁ́mḁn.
  How long did he stay? ስንት፡ዘመን፡ተቀመጠ። si̥nt zḁ́mḁn tḁqḁ́mmḁṭḁ?
long for, v.t. ተመኘ tḁmḁ́ññä (-mä́ñ-).
  ውልውል፡አለው wŭlli̥wŭll ā́lḁ͡u (§§ 43a, 44a).
longing, s. ናፍቆት nā́fq^{w}ot (ንፍ- ní̥f-).
look, v.i. (at, v.t.) አየ ā́yyä (§ 44b).
  Look! እይ። i̥y! (i̥, ī), pl. እዩ። í̥yu! (í̥u, íu).
  Let me look at him (it): ልየው። líyḁ͡u.
  I want one to look at: አንድ፡ለማየት፡እፈልጋለሁ። and lḁmā́i̥ät i̥fḁlli̥gállḁ͡u^{h}.
  Look out (take care)! ተጠንቀቅ። tḁṭḁ́nqḁq!, pl. -ቀቁ። -qḁqu!

look for, v.t. ፈለገ fḁllḁgḁ.
ጐረጐረ gwωrḁ́ggwωrḁ (-rώgg-).
Look for him (it): ፈልገው። fḁ́lli̥gḁu, pl. -ጉት። -gut.
He has gone to look for one (him, it, them, § 61*b*):
ሊፈልግ፡ሒዷል። li̥fḁ́lli̥g hí̥dŏāl.
look over (through), v.t. ጐረጐረ gwωrḁ́ggwωrḁ (-rώgg-).
Let him look all over the village: መንደሩን፡ይጐርጕር። mḁ́ndḁrun yi̥gwώrgwŭr.
lookout, s. (e.g. customs official's hut) ጎጆ g^{w}ójj^{w}o.
loop, s. (for suspending) ማንጠልጠያ manṭḁlṭḁ́yā̃ (-ṭäl-, -ḁ́i̥ã).
loose, adj. (slack) ልል li̥l.
This parcel is too loosely tied: ይሀ፡እስር፡እሚላላ፡ነው። yi̥he i̥si̥r i̥mmi̥lallá nḁu.
loose(-ned) be (become), v.i. ላላ lállā̃ (§ 63*d*, *e*).
The bandage has got loose: ማሰሪያ፡ላልቷል። mā-sḁ́rya láltŏāl.
His teeth are loose: ጥርሱ፡ተነቃነቀ። ṭi̥rsu (§ 52*a*, γ) tḁnḁqánnḁqḁ.
loose, get, v.i. (of animate objects) ፈታ fḁ́ttā̃.
(cease to fit) ወለቀ wḁ́llḁqḁ (wώl-).
The horse got loose and went off: ፈረስ፡ፈትቶ፡ሔደ። fḁ́rḁs fḁ́tt^{w}o hä́dä.
The nail has got loose: ችንካሩ፡ወልቋል። či̥nkáru wώlqŏāl.
loot, s. እቃ i̥qā̃.
loot, v.i. & t. ዘረፈ zḁ́rrḁfḁ (zä́r-).
ወረረ wώrrḁrḁ.
looted, be, v.p. ተዘረፈ tḁzḁ́rrḁfḁ (täzä́r-).
loquacious, adj. ምላሰኛ mi̥lāsḁ́ññā̃ (-sä́ñ-).
ለፍላፊ lḁfláfi.
ለፍላፋ lḁfláffā̃.

lose, v.t. አጠፋ aṭḁffā̃.

Don't lose him (it): አታጥፋው። attāṭfau, pl. -ፉት። -fut.

Who lost him(it)? ያጠፋው፡ማን፡ነው። yāṭḁffau mán-nḁu?

He has lost my gun: ጠበንጃዬን፡አጠፋብኝ። ṭḁvḁn-jāyen aṭḁffabbi̥ñ (s.v. በ-, § 47*a*).

The watch loses: ሰዓቱ፡ይዘገያል። sḁātu yi̥zḁgḁ́yyāl.

lose a case, game, etc., v.i. ተረታ tḁrḁ́ttā̃ (tär-).

He lost his case in court: በወምበር፡ፊት፡ተረታ። bḁuώmbḁr fi̥t tḁrḁ́tta.

I have lost (the game): ተረታኹኝ። tḁrḁ́ttahwŭñ (§ 61*e*).

loss, s. ጥፋት ṭí̥fát (§ 8).

loss, be at a, v.i. ቸገረው čággа̥rḁu (-gär-; impers. § 43*a*).

lost, be, v.p. ጠፋ ṭḁ́ffā̃.

Is he (it) lost? ጠፍቷል። ṭḁ́ftŏāl? (§ 63*d*).

When was he (it) lost? መቼ፡ነው፡የጠፋ። mḁčā́ nḁu yäṭḁ́ffa?

Where was he (it) lost? የጠፋበት፡ወዴት፡ነው። yä-ṭḁ́ffabbḁt wωdʸét nḁu?

lot, a, s. (many) ብዙ bí̥zu (§ 52*a*, β).

(sors) እጣ í̥ṭā̃.

A lot of people: ብዙ፡ሰው፡ bí̥zu sḁu.

He is a bad lot: ምናምንቴ፡ነው። mi̥nāmi̥ntʸé (§ 8) nḁu.

loud, adj. ትልቅ ti̥lli̥q.

loudly, adv. በትልቅ፡ድምጥ bḁti̥llí̥q (§ 8) di̥mṭ.

louse, s. ቅማል qí̥mál (§ 8, § 52*a*, δ).

Ovum (ova) of louse: ቅጫም qí̥č̣ám (§ 8, § 52*a*, δ).

lousy, adj. ቅማላም qi̥málám (§ 8).

love, s. ውድ wŭdd.

ፍቅር fí̥qi̥r.

love, v.t. ወደደ wώddḁdḁ.
loved, be, v.p. ተወደደ tḁwώddḁdḁ (tḁ͡uώ-).
lover, s. ወዳጅ wώdã́j (§ 8).
low, adj. ጕድጓዳ gwωdgwáddã (-ωrgw- § 7*d*).
This table is too low: ይህ፡ገበታ፡ጕድጓዳ፡ነው። yı̥he gḁṿḁtá gwωrgwaddã́ (§ 8) nḁ͡u.
Low country: ቈላ፡ qwώllã.
አውራጃ፡ a͡urã́jjã.
low, adv. በታች bḁtã́č (§ 8).
ወደታች wωdḁtã́č (§ 8).
low, v.i. አገሣ agḁ́ssã.
low (-er § 58*b*), be, v.i. ዝቅ፡አለ zı̥qq ā́lḁ (s.v. √በለ, § 44*a*).
It is (too) low: ዝቅ፡ይላል። zı̥qq yı̥lāl.
lower, adj. ታችኛ tāččı̥ññã.
lower, v.t. (take down) አወረደ awώrrḁdḁ (a͡uώ-).
(incline) ዘቀዘቀ zḁqḁ́zzḁqḁ.
Lower it: አውርደው። ā́͡uŭrdḁ͡u, pl. -ዱት። -dut.
ዘቅዝቀው። zḁ́qzı̥qḁ͡u, pl. -ቁት። -qut.
lowered, be, v.p. ወረደ wώrrḁdḁ.
(inclined) ተዘቀዘቀ tḁzḁqḁ́zzḁqḁ.
lowland, adj. (lowlander, s.) ቈለኛ qwωllḁ́ñña (-lā́ñ-).
lowlands, s. ቈላ qwώllã.
loyal, adj. አማኝ ā́mā́ñ (-ññ § 6; -mā́͡ı̥ § 7*d*; § 8).
luck, s. (good or bad) እድል ı̥́ddı̥l.
(good) ሀብት habt (haṿt, haf̣t).
He has no luck: ሀብት፡የለውም። haf̣t yállḁ͡um.
lukewarm, adj. ለብ lḁbb.
lunch, s. ምሳ mı̥́sã.
What time will lunch be ready? ምሳ፡በስንት፡ሰዓት፡ ይሰናዳል። mı̥́sā yḁsı̥́nt sḁ͡ā́t yı̥ssḁnáddāl?
lung, s. ሳምባ sā́mbã (§ 52*a*, *γ*).

lupine (*Lupinus Termis*, Broun, Cat. 117), s. ግብጦ gí̥bṭʷo (-í̥ṿṭ-).

lurk, v.i. አደባ adḁ́bbã̄.

Lycaon pictus, s. ተኲላ tḁkwū́lã̄ (§ 8; § 52*a*, δ).

M

§ refers to the paragraphs of the Grammar (Initia Amharica, Part I).

Maba abessinica (Broun, Cat. 328), s. ስርኩኒ sí̥rkuni (Ag.).

machine, s. መኪና mḁkínḁ.

መዘወር mḁzḁ́͡uwḁr.

mad, adj. እብድ i̥bd (i̥ṿd).

Are you mad? አንት፡እብድ፡ነህ። ant í̥ṿdĭ̥ (§ 7*d*) näh?

mad, be (go), v.i. አበደ ábbḁdḁ (§ 63*d*, *e*).

maddening, adj. ማሳበጃ mã̄ssã̄bbā́jã̄.

made, be, v.p. ተበጀ tḁbḁ́jjä (-ḁṿ-, -ā́j-).

What is it made of? ተምን፡ይበጃል። tḁmí̥n yi̥bbā́j-jāl?

madness, s. እብደት í̥bdḁt (í̥ṿd-, -dät).

እብድነት i̥bdí̥nnḁt (i̥ṿd-, -näṭ).

Madoqua Saltiana, s. ምዳቋ mi̥dā́qqwã̄.

Š. የንሹ yánšu.

maggot, s. ትል ti̥l (§ 52*a*, δ).

magic, s. አስማት ásmā́t (§ 8).

magician, s. ቡዳ búdã̄.

አስማተኛ asmātḁ́ññã̄ (-tā́ñ-).

magnificent, adj. ግሩም gí̥rum.

maid, s. ልጃገረድ lịjāgạrạd.

ቈንጆ qwọ́njʷo, pl. also ቈናጅቶች qwọnájịtʷōč (-čč § 6), ቈነጃጅቶች qwọnạjájịtʷōč (-čč § 6).

አሽከር áškạr (-kär).

mail, s. (letters) ደብዳቤ dạbdábbʸe (dạỵd-; § 52*a*).

(service) †ቡስጣ bústā̃.

†ፖስታ pʷóstā̃.

maize (*Zea mays*), s. የባሕር፡ማሽላ yäbáhịr (-äỵá-) māšịllā̃.

make, v.t. አበጀ abạ́jjä (aỵ-, -ā́j-).

ሠራ sạrrā̃ (sā́r-).

I can't make this out: የዚህን፡ፍች፡አላውቅም። yäzíhịn fịčč alá͡uŭqịm.

male, adj. & s. (of persons and animals) ወንድ wọnd.

(of animals) አውራ á͡urā̃ (§ 8).

mallet, s. መምቻ mạmčā̃.

mamma! interj. (cry of child to mother) እማማ ịmámma!

mamma, s. (breast) ጡት ṭut (§ 52*a*, *γ*).

man, s. (human being) ሰው sạ͡u (§ 8), pl. ሰዎች sạ͡uʷōč (-čč § 6).

(not woman) ወንድ wọnd.

Not always expressed:

This man is a liar: ይህ፡ውሸታም፡ነው። yịhe wŭšätā́m nạ͡u.

manage, v.t. ሠራ sạrrā̃ (sā́r-).

Can't you manage it (get it open, shut, in, out, through, etc.)? እምቢ፡አለህ። mbị álāh? (s.v. √በለ).

mane, s. (of horse, mule, donkey) ጋማ gā́mmā̃.

(of lion) አፋሮ affā́rrʷo.

manger, s. መብያ mạbyā̃ (-ạ́ỵy-).

manipulate, v.t. አሸ áššä.

manipulated, be, v.p. ታሸ táššä.

mantis, s. ቀጣኒት qḁṭánit, usually f. (§ 54c).

mantle, s. ከባ kā́bbã.

many, adj. & pron. ብዙ bi̥zu (§ 52a, β, § 53b).

Are there many? ብዝዎች፡ አሉ። bi̥zwōčč állu?

Have many people come? ብዙ፡ ሰው፡ መጣ። bi̥zu sḁ͡u mḁṭṭa?

map, s. ያገር፡ ሥዕል yāgḁr (-gā́r) si̥l.

†ካርታ kártã.

March, s.v. calendar.

march, s. (stage) መናሀሪያ mḁnnaháryã (-ኻ- -χá-, -ká- § 7d).

Forced march: ግስገሳ፡ gi̥sgḁ́sã.

march, v.i. ሔደ hā́dä (hḁ̄́d-, hʸḗd-, -dḁ).

mare, s. ባዝራ bā́zrã.

ሴት፡ ፈረስ sʸēt fḁrḁs.

margin, s. ዳር dār.

ድምበር di̥mbḁr (-bär).

mark, s. (sign) ምልክት mi̥li̥kki̥t.

Make a mark on it: ምልክት፡ አድርግበት። mi̥li̥kki̥t ā́rgi̥bbḁt (§ 7d).

market, s. ገቢያ፡[ገብያ] gḁbyã (-ḁyy-).

Š. ገበያ gḁbḁyã (-ḁyḁ-, -a͡i̥ã).

market fee, s. ድላል di̥lál (§ 8).

marriage, s. ሰርግ sḁrg (särg).

married, be, v.p. ተጋባ tḁgā́bbã.

Is he married? ሴት፡ አለችው። sʸēt álläččyu?

Is she married? ባል፡ አላት። bāl állāt?

marrow, s. ቅልጥም qi̥lṭi̥m.

marry, v.t. አገባ agḁbbã.

He has married her: አግብቷታል። agi̥ytwātāl.

She has married him: አግብታዋለች። agi̥yta͡uálläč.

marsh, s. ረግረግ rḁ́grḁg.

ጨቀጨቅ čáqḁčäq.

martingale, s. እምቢያ፡ጕስም (i̥)mbya gwŭ́si̥m.

marvel, s. (-lous, adj. § 57*b*) ድንቅ di̥ṅq.

mason, s. አናጢ an(n)áṭi.

Mason wasp: ትንዚዛ፡ ti̥nzízā̃ (§ 52*a*, δ).

massacre, v.t. ደበደበ dḁbḁ́ddḁbḁ (däyáddäyḁ).

massacred, be, v.p. ተደበደበ tḁdḁbḁ́ddḁbḁ (-däyáddäyḁ).

massage, v.t. አሻ áššä.

massaged, be, v.p. ታሻ táššä.

Massaua, s. ምጥዋ mi̥ṭi̥wwā̃ (-ṭúww-).

master, s. ጌታ gʸétā̃.

masticate, v.i. & t. ቈረጠመ qwωrḁ́ṭṭḁmḁ.

Masticate it: ቈርጥመው። qwώrṭi̥mḁu, pol. ይቈርጥ ሙት። yi̥qwώrṭi̥mut.

masticated, be, v.p. ተቈረጠመ tḁqwωrḁ́ṭṭḁmḁ.

It should be masticated: ይቈርጠም። yi̥qqwώrṭḁm.

mat, s. ደውጃ dḁ́ujjā̃.

አቴና atʸénā̃.

match, s. ክብሪት ki̥brít (-i̥yr-; § 8; § 52*a*, δ).

material(s), s. (for working or building) መሣሪያ mḁssárуā̃ (-yä).

matter, s. (affair) ነገር nḁ́gḁr (-gär).

ጕዳይ gwi̥ddḁ́i̥ (gwŭ́d-, gúd-; § 8).

(pus) መግል mḁ́gi̥l.

What is the matter with you? ምን፡ሁነሃል። mi̥n húnähāl?

matter, v.i. ቍርጥ፡ሆነ qwŭrṭ hʷŏnḁ.

It doesn't matter: ይቅር። yí̥qi̥r, or ግድ፡የለም። gi̥dd yállām.

What does it matter to me? ምን፡ገደደኝ። mi̥ṅ gḁ́ddḁdäñ?

mattress, s. †ፍራሽ f(i̥)ráš.
mauve, adj. ጫጉማ č̣ãgúmmã.
May, s.v. calendar.
me, pers. pron. -ኝ -ñ (-ññ § 6; § 12*c*).
emph. እኔን i̥nʸén (§ 8; § 12*a*).
meadow, s. መስክ mḁsk.
meal, s. (flour) ዱቄት dŏ̃qʸĕt (§ 8).
(food) መብል mḁ́bi̥l (-ḁ́yi̥-).
(lunch or dinner) ግብር gí̥b(i̥)r (gí̥y-).
mean, adj. (stingy) ሥሡ sí̥ssu.
mean, v.t. አለ álḁ (s.v. √በለ, § 44*a*).
What does it mean? ማለቱ፡ምንድር፡ነው። málḁtu mi̥ndí̥r nḁ͡u?
We didn't mean to do it: አሳስተን፡አደረግነ። assá-si̥tän adḁ́rrḁgnḁ.
meaning, s. ማለት málḁt (-lät).
ፍች fi̥čč.
By all means (= I agree): ምን፡ከፋኝ። mi̥n kḁ́ffañ?, or ምን፡ቸገረኝ። mi̥n čággaräñ?
meanwhile, adv. እያደረ iyyáddarḁ (-ደር -ddḁr, -där-; s.v. አደረ).
measles, s. አንከሊስ ankḁ́lĭs (§ 8).
measure, s. (instrument) መለኪያ mḁlḁ́kkyã (-lák-).
መስፈሪያ mḁsfḁ́ryã (-fár-, -yä; not for liquids).
[s.v. ጣት፡—ስንዝር፡—ክንድ፡ for length,
ቁና፡—ጻውላ፡ for dry measure.]
measure, v.i. (be measured, v.p.) ተለካ tḁlḁ́kkã.
measure, v.t. ለካ lḁ́kkã.
ሰፈረ sḁ́ffḁrḁ (-fär-; not of liquids).
Measure it: ለካው። lḁ́kka͡u, pl. ለኩት። lḁ́kkut.

measurement, s. ልክ li̥kk.
ስፍር si̥fi̥r (not of liquids).
What is its measurement? ልኩ፡ስንት፡ነው። li̥kku si̥nti̥ nḁu?

meat, s. ሥጋ si̥gã.

medicine, s. መድኃኒት mḁdhā́n^{y}it (-dáhnit § 7*d*).

medium, adj. ማሀለኛ mahalḁ́ññã (-láñ-).

meet, v.i. ገጠመ gḁ́ṭṭḁmḁ.

meet, v.t. ተገናኘ tḁgḁnā́ññä.
Where will you meet me? የት፡ተገናኘኛለህ። yēt ti̥ggḁnāññäññálläh? pol. የት፡ይገናኙኛል። yēt yi̥g-gḁnā́ññuññāl? (§§ 12*c*, 32*b*).

Megaloponerus fœtens, s. ግንዳ gi̥ndã (§ 52*a*, δ).

melon, s. ዱባ dúbbã.

melt, v.i. (melted, be, v.p.) ቀለጠ qḁ́llḁṭḁ.
(in a liquid) ሟሟ mwámmwã.

melt, (cause to), v.t. አቀለጠ aqḁ́llḁṭḁ.

menace, v.i. & t. አስፈራራ asfḁrā́rrã (-fär-).

mend, v.t. አበጀ abḁ́jjä (ay-, -ā́j-).
Mend it: አብጀው። ayi̥jjḁu, pl. -ጁት። -jjut.

mended, be, v.p. ተበጀ tḁbḁ́jjä (-ḁy-, -ā́j-).
When it is mended, I will send it to you: ሲበጅ፡ እልክልሃለሁ። si̥bbā́jj, i̥li̥ki̥lli̥hállḁu^{h}, — you pol.: ...፡ እልክለዎአለሁ። ...i̥li̥ki̥llḁ^{w}oállḁu^{h} (§ 7*d*, § 47*a*).

menses, s. ደም däm.
አደፍ ā́däf.
እርግመት i̥rgi̥mḁt.

menstruate, v.i. ደም፡ነበረች däm nḁ́bbḁräč (-äčč § 6).
አደፍ፡ነበረች ā́däf nḁ́bbḁräč („).
For present tense of ነበረች use ናት nāt (§ 13*b*), Š. ነች näč (näčč § 6); for neg. conjug. see §§ 39*c*, 40.

merchant, s. ነጋዴ nḁggád^{y}e.
(European) ኳጃ kwájã.
mercury, s. ባዜቃ bāz^{y}éqã.
mercy, s. ም[ሕ]ረት mį̥(h)rḁt (-rät).
merely, adv. እንዲያው (į̥)ndyau (§ 8).
እንደው (į̥)ndḁu (§ 8).
He merely left it: እንዲያው፡ተወው። ndyáu tḁuḁu.
message, s. ቃል qāl.
(letter) ደብዳቤ dḁbdább^{y}e (-ḁẏd-).
(errand) መላክት mḁ́lákt (§ 8).
I received (heard) the message you (pol.) sent: የላኩትን፡ቃል፡ሰማሁ። yäläkuti̥n (§ 62*c*) qāl sḁ́mmau^{h}.
messenger, s. መላክተኛ mḁlãktḁ́ñña̋ (-ልክ- -li̥k-, -tá̋ñ-).
Messor barbarus, s. ገብረ፡ጕንዳን gḁ́brḁ (-ḁ́ẏr-) gwǘndán (§ 8; § 52*a*, δ).
metal, s. no general term.
metal, worker in, s. (iron) ደበን፡አንሳ dḁbḁnánsã (dḁẏḁ-).
(gold, silver) አንጥረኛ anṭrḁ́ñña̋ (-ráñ-).
mètre, s. †ሜትር m^{y}etr.
metropolitan, s. (of all Abyssinia) አቡን ábun (áẏun, áwun, áuun; before a name -ነ -nḁ).
The Metropolitan Matthew: አቡነ፡ማቴዎስ፡ áẏunḁ māt^{y}e^{w}ós.
mew, v.i. ጮኸ ç̣^{w}óhḁ (§ 7*d*).
micturate, v.i. ሸና šḁ́nnḁ.
(euphem.) ከፈለ kḁ́ffḁlḁ.
middle, adj. ማሀለኛ mahalḁ́ñña̋ (-láñ-).
middle, s. ማሀል máhal.
In the middle: በማሀል። bḁmáhal.
middle-aged, adj. መሉ múlu (ምሉ mi̥lu).
Middle-aged woman: ባልቴት፡ bált^{y}ēt (§ 8).

midnight, s. እኩል፡ሌሊት ŭkkúl l^{y}ēlĭ́t.

እኩለ፡ሌሊት ŭkkū́lḁ (§ 9*d*) l^{y}ēlĭ́t.

ሌት፡እኩል l^{y}ēt ŭ́kkul.

መንፈቀ፡ሌሊት mḁnfḁqḁ l^{y}ēlĭ́t.

At midnight: በኩል፡ሌሊት፡ bḁkkúl l^{y}ēlĭ́t.

midriff, s. እርግብግብት i̥rgi̥bgi̥bā́t (-i̥ỵgi̥ỵā́t; § 8).

midwife, s. አዋላጅ awwā́lā́j (a͡uwā́-; § 8).

midwife, act as, v.i. (to, v.t.) አዋለደች awwā́llḁdäč (a͡uwā́-; -äčč § 6).

migrate, v.i. ተሰደደ tḁsā́ddḁdḁ (täs-).

mild, adj. (of disposition) ገር gḁr (gär).

ልዝብ lí̥zzi̥b (-i̥ỵ).

military, adj. የወታደር yäwωttáddar̥ (-där; s.v. የ-, §§ 47*a*, 70).

milk, s. ወተት wḁ́tḁt (wώt-).

milk, v.i. & t. አለበ állḁbḁ (-ḁỵḁ).

Milk her: እለባት። i̥lḁỵāt.

Have you milked the cow? ላሚቱን፡አለብሃት። lámi̥tun állḁỵhāt? (-ኻት -χāt, -kāt).

milked, be, v.p. ታለበች tā́llḁbäč (-ḁỵä-; -äčč § 6).

Has this cow been milked? ይች፡ላም፡ታለበቾይ። yí̥čči̥ lām tállḁỵäččwi̥? (s.v. ወይ).

mill, s. ወፍጮ wώfč̣^{w}o.

millet, s. ማሽላ māši̥llā̃.

million, card. num. መቶ፡እልፍ mḁ́t^{w}o i̥lf.

†ሚሊዮን mí̥lyṓn (§ 8).

See § 20*a*.

Milvus regalis (Guidi, Vocab. p. 840), s. ጭላት č̣í̥lā́t (§ 8).

mind, s. ልብ li̥bb (nearest term: lit. 'heart').

mind, v.i.

I don't mind: እሺ። í̥šši̥.

Never mind: ይቅር። yi̥qi̥r.
ግድ፡የለም። gi̥dd yā́lläm.

I have lost it: ጠፋብኝ። ṭ̥áffabbi̥ñ. Never mind, it will be found: ግድ፡የለም፤ይገኛል። gi̥dd yā́lläm, yi̥ggḁ́ññāl.

Never mind! (don't be afraid!) አይዞህ። á͡i̥zʷōh!, pol. አይዞዎት። á͡i̥zʷo͡ʷot!, f. አይዞሽ። á͡i̥zʷōš!, pl. አይዟችሁ። a͡i̥zŏ͡ā́ččyuh! (§ 7*d*).

mind, v.t. (keep) ጠበቀ ṭḁ́bbḁqḁ.
  Mind it: ጠብቀው። ṭḁ́bbi̥qḁ͡u, pl. -ቁት። -qut.
  Mind them: ጠብቃቸው። ṭḁbbi̥qáččḁ͡u, pl. -ቋቸው። -qwā́ččḁ͡u.

mine, poss. pron. የኔ yā́nʸé (§ 8, § 12*a*).
  It is mine: የኔ፡ነው። yänʸé nḁ͡u.
  It is not mine: የኔም፡አይደል። yänʸémm (§ 37*b*) á͡i̥däl (§ 40*a*).

mineral, s. ድንጊያ dā́ṅgyā̃, Š. ድንጋይ dā́ṅgá͡i̥ (§ 8), } pl. ድንጎች dā́ṅgʷōč (-čč § 6).

minute, s. ደቂቃ dḁqíqā̃ (§ 52*a*, δ).

mirror, s. መስተዋት mḁstḁ́͡uwā́t (§ 8; -ተወት -tḁ͡uwḁt).

misbehave, v.i. በደለ bḁ́ddḁlḁ (bā́d-).

miscarriage, have a, v.i. አስወረደች aswώrrḁdäč (-äčč § 6).

miscellaneous, adj. ልዩ፡ልዩ líyyu líyyu.

mischievous, adj. ማሽንክ mā́ší̥nk (§ 8).

miser, s. ንፉግ ní̥fug.

miserable, adj. (of persons) ችጋረኛ či̥ggārḁ́ññā̃ (-rā́ñ-).
  (of objects) ግም gi̥m.

misery, s. ችጋር čí̥ggā́r (§ 8).
  መከራ mḁ́kḁ́rā̃ (-kā́r-; § 8).

misery, be in, v.i. ጨነቀው č̣ḁ́nnḁqḁ͡u (impers. § 43*a*; § 63*d*, *e*).

misfortune, s. ችጋር čįggár (§ 8).
misgivings, have, v.i. ቅር፡አለው qįrr ála͡u (impers. § 43*a*; s.v. √በለ, § 44*a*; § 63*d*, *e*), constr. with በ- ba- (§ 47*a*).
I have misgivings about this man: በዚህ፡ሰው፡ቅር፡አለኝ። bäzzįh sa͡u qįrr áläñ.
mislead, v.t. አሳተ assáta.
This is misleading: ይህ፡ያስታል። yįhe yássįtāl.
miss, v.i. & t. (aim) ሳተ sáta.
(way) G. አሰሳተ assasáta.
Š. አሳሳተ assāsáta.
I (have) missed him (it): ሳትሁት። sáthut (-t-h-, not -θ- § 3).
I miss that chair that was lost: ያ፡የጠፋው፡ወምበር፡ትዝ፡ይለኛል። yā yäṭaffa͡u wωmbar tįzz yįläññāl.
miss fire, v.i. እምቢ፡አለ (į)mbį ála (s.v. √በለ, § 44*a*).
አበለ ábbala.
My gun missed fire: ጠበንጃዬ፡አበለብኝ። ṭavanjáye ábbalabbįñ (§ 47*a*).
missed, be, v.p. ተሳተ tasáta (täs-).
mist, s. ጉም gūm.
ጥጋግ ṭįgág (§ 8).
G. ጭጋግ čįgág (§ 8).
mistake, s. ስተት sįtat (-tät).
(inaccuracy) ግድፈት gįdfat.
mistake, v.t. G. አሰሳተ assasáta.
Š. አሳሳተ assāsáta.
mistake, make a, v.i. (act by mistake)
ሳተ sáta.
G. ተሰሳተ tasasáta (täsäs-) } usually impers. (§ 43*a*).
Š. ተሳሳተ tasāsáta (täs-) }
G. አሰሳተ assasáta.
Š. አሳሳተ assāsáta.

(be inaccurate)

ገደፈ gḁ́ddḁfḁ (type A § 34).

ተገደፈው tḁgḁ́ddḁfa͡u (impers. § 43*a*).

I took it by mistake: ተሰስቶኝ፡ [Š. ተሳስቶኝ፡] ወሰድሁት። tḁsḁ́stʷoñ (Š. tḁsástʷoñ) wḁ́ssḁdhut.

They took it by mistake: አሰስተው፡ [Š. አሳስተው፡] ያዙት። assḁ́sta͡u (Š. assásta͡u) yā́zut.

mistress, s. እመቤት (i̥)mmḁ́bʸét (-ḁ́vʸét; § 8).

mistrust, s. ጥርጣሬ ṭi̥ri̥ṭṭári.

mistrust, v.t. ጠረጠረ ṭḁrḁ́ṭṭḁrḁ (ṭärḁ́ṭṭärḁ).

I mistrust him: እጠረጥረዋለሁ። i̥ṭḁrḁṭṭi̥rḁ͡uállḁ͡uʰ.

mistrusted, be, v.p. ተጠረጠረ tḁṭḁrḁ́ṭṭḁrḁ (-ṭärḁ́ṭṭärḁ).

misty, adj. ጉማማ gūmā́mmā̃.

A misty day: ጉማማ፡ ቀን፡ gūmāmmá (§ 8) qḁn.

mix, v.t. ቀላቀለ qḁlā́qqḁlḁ.

ደበለቀ dḁbḁ́llḁqḁ (dḁvḁ́-).

Mix it: ደብልቀው። dḁ́vli̥qa͡u.

Don't mix it: አትደብልቀው። atti̥dḁ́vli̥qa͡u.

mixed, adj. ቅልቅል qi̥lí̥qqi̥l.

mixed, be, v.p. ተቀላቀለ tḁqḁlā́qqḁlḁ.

ተደበለቀ tḁdḁbḁ́llḁqḁ (-ḁvḁ́-).

Š. ተደባለቀ tḁdḁbállḁqḁ (-ḁvá-).

Take care they don't get mixed: እንዳይቀላቀል። nda͡i̥qqḁláqqḁl (sg. for pl. cp. § 52*a*).

moderate, adj. (-ly, adv.) በልክ bḁlí̥kk (§ 8).

He who (one that) drinks moderately: በልክ፡ የሚጠጣ፡ bḁlí̥kk yämmi̥ṭḁ́ṭṭa.

modest, adj. አፋር áffā́r (§ 8).

modest, be, v.i. አፈረ áffḁrḁ (-fär-).

moist, adj. እርጥብ i̥rṭi̥b (-i̥v).

ለዛዛ lḁzā́zā̃.

moist, be (become), v.i. ረጠበ rḁ́ṭṭḁbḁ (-ḁỵḁ; § 63*d*, *e*).
moisten, v.t. ነከረ nḁ́kkḁrḁ (nǟkkärḁ).
  Moisten it: ንከረው። ni̥kḁrḁ͡u, pl. -ሩት። -rut.
moistened, be, v.p. ተነከረ tḁnḁ́kkḁrḁ (-nǟkkärḁ).
  It ought to have been moistened before we started: ሳንነሣ፡ይነከር፡ነበር። sanni̥nnḁ́ssa yi̥nnḁ́kkär nḁ́bbär (§ 63*b*).
mole (*Talpa sp.*), s. ፍልፈል fi̥lfäl.
monastery, s. መነኮሳት mḁnḁkʷósā́t (§ 8).
  ገዳም gḁ́dā́m (gā́d-; § 8).
Monday, s. ሰኞ sḁ́ñño (sā́ñ-).
money, s. ገንዘብ gḁ́nzḁb (-ḁỵ).
  ብር bi̥rr.
monk, s. መለክሴ mḁlώksʸe, pl. also መለኳኵስቶች mḁlḁkwā́kwǖstʷōč (-čč § 6).
monkey, s. ጦጣ ṭʷóṭã.
monkey-bread (*Adansonia digitata*, Broun, Cat. 65), s. ፍርጣጣ fi̥rṭā́ṭã.
month, s. ወር wωr (ʷōr; § 52*a*, δ).
  Six months: መንፈቅ፡ mḁ́nfḁq.
moon, s. ጨረቃ č̣ḁrḁ́qã (§ 8; sometimes f. § 54*e*).
morass, s. ረግረግ rḁ́grḁg.
  ጨቀጨቅ č̣ā́qḁč̣äq.
more, s. adj. & adv. ሌላ lélã (§ 16).
  ደግሞ dḁ́gmʷo (dā́g-).
  ደሞ dḁ́mmʷo (dā́m-).
  የሚበልጥ yämmi̥bḁ́lṭ (-i̥ỵ-, -ā́l-; § 14).
  እሚበልጥ (i̥)mmi̥bḁ́lṭ („ „).
  ይበልጥ yi̥bḁ́lṭ (-i̥ỵ-, -ā́l-; § 58*c*).

The parts of በለጠ above are constructed with ከ- kḁ- [ተ- tḁ, § 47*a*], than (§ 58*a*).

Is there more? ሌላ፡ አለ። léla állä?

I don't want any more: ደግሞ፡ አልፈልግም። dắgmʷo alfḁ́lli̥gi̥m.

That is more than I want: ይህ፡ በዛብኝ። yí̥he bḁ́z-zabbi̥ñ.

Bring (put) some more: ጨምር። čḁ́mmi̥r, pl. -ሩ። -ru.

Bring some more tea: ሻይ፡ ጨምር። šái̥ čḁ́mmi̥r.

More than ten: ታሥር፡ ይበልጥ፡ tắssi̥r yi̥vḁ́lṭ.

I will give you one, but I can't give you more: pol. አንድ፡ እሰጠዎአለሁ፤ ተዚህ፡ ይበልጥ፡ ግን፡ አይቻለኝም። and i̥sḁṭḁʷoállḁuʰ, tḁzzí̥h yi̥vḁ́lṭ gi̥n ai̥ččá-läññi̥m.

moreover, adv. ደግሞ dḁ́gmʷo (dắg-).
ደሞ dḁ́mmʷo (dắm-).
እንግዴህ ṅgdʸéh.
እዛወዲያ (i̥)z(z)áʷωdyã́ (-zắd-; §8), Š. ታዲያ tắdyã (§8).

morning, s. ማለዳ mắlḁ́dã (§8).
ጧት ṭwāt.

In the morning: ጧት፡ ṭwāt.

Good morning! (on meeting) እንዲት፡ አደርህ። ndi̥t (እንዴት፡ ndʸēt) áddärh?, pol. እንዲት፡ አደሩ። ndi̥t áddḁru?, pl. እንዲት፡ አደራችሁ። ndi̥t addḁrắččyuh? (s.v. አደረ). — (=good-bye!) ደኅና፡ ዋል። dähnắ wāl!, pol. ደኅና፡ ይዋሉ። dắhnā yi̥wắlu!, pl. ደኅና፡ ዋሉ። dắhnā wắlu!

Half the morning is gone: ረፍዷል። rḁ́fdōāl.

mortar, s. ቡሆ búhʷo.

Moslem, s. & adj. እስላም í̥slắm (§8).

mosquito, s. ትንኝ tı̥́nı̥ñ (-ı̥́ññ § 6; § 8, § 52*a*, δ).

See that there are no mosquitoes in it: ትንኝ፡እንዳይሆንበት። tı̥́nı̥ññ ı̥ndaı̥hʷónı̥bbḁt (§ 47*a*).

Catch and kill the mosquitoes which are in this room: በዚህ፡ቤት፡ያለውን፡ትንኝ፡ይዘህ፡ግደለው። bḁzzíh yʸēt yállāun tı̥́nı̥ñ yı̥́zäh (§ 74*b*) gı̥́dḁlḁu.

Mosquitoes are a cause of fever: ትንኝ፡የንዳድ፡ምክንያት፡ነው። tı̥nı̥́ñ yänı̥dád mı̥knyát nḁu.

mosquito-net, s. አጎበር agʷóbḁr (-óy̥-, -är).

መጋረጃ mḁggārájā̃.

Lower (close) the mosquito-net: መጋረጃውን፡ጣል። [ዝጋ።] mḁggārájaun ṭāl (zı̥́ga).

See that it is shut everywhere: እየው፡ተሁሉ፡ስፍራ፡እንዲዘጋ። íyḁu tḁhúllu sı̥frá ndı̥zzḁ́gga.

moss, s. ሽበት šı̥́bḁt (-ı̥́y̥-, -ät).

most, adj. ከሁሉ፡የሚበልጥ kḁhúllu (ተሁሉ፡ tḁhúllu) yämmı̥bḁ́lṭ (-ı̥y̥-, -álṭ; § 58).

most, adv. ከሁሉ kḁhúllu (ተሁ- tḁhú-, § 58).

moth, s. የሳትራት yäsátı̥rāt (§ 70*b*).

(in clothes) ብል bı̥l.

See § 52*a*, δ.

mother, s. እናት (ı̥́)nnát (§ 8).

mother-in-law, s. አማት ā́mát (§ 8).

mottled, adj. ዝንጉርጉር zı̥ngúrgur.

mould, s. (earth) አፈር áfḁr (-fär).

mouldy, adj. ሻጋታ šāgátā̃.

mouldy, be (become), v.i. ሸገተ šággа̥tḁ (§ 63*d*, *e*).

It will get mouldy: ይሸግታል። yı̥šággı̥tāl.

mound, s. ጎጥ gʷoṭ.

mount, v.i. & t. (go upwards) ሽቅብ፡ኣለ ši̥qqi̥b (-i̥y) ā́lḁ (s.v. √ባለ, § 44*a*).

(climb) ወጣ wǿṭṭā ከ- kḁ- [ተ- tḁ-, § 47*a*].

(an animal) ተቀመጠ tḁqḁ́mmḁṭḁ.

ተሰቀለ tḁsḁ́qqḁlḁ በ- bḁ- (§ 47*a*).

mountain, s. (large) ኮረብታ kʷorḁ́btā (-ḁ́yt-).

(small) ተራራ tḁrárā.

mountainous, adj. ኮረብታም kʷorḁ́btám (-ḁ́yt-; § 8).

mounted man (mounted troops § 52*a*, δ), s. ፈረሰኛ fḁrḁsḁ́ññā (-sā́ñ-).

mourn, v.i. አዘነ ázzḁnḁ.

(publicly) ተላቀሰ tḁlā́qqḁsḁ.

mourning, s. መርዶ mḁ́rdʷo.

mouse, s. አይጥ áyi̥ṭ (ái̥ṭ), usually f. (§ 54*c*; § 52*a*, δ).

Infested with mice, adj. አይጣም፡ áyi̥ṭám (ái̥ṭ-; § 8).

moustache, s. ጢም ṭim (ṭi̥m).

mouth, s. አፍ āf.

move, v.i. ሔደ hẽ́dä (hā́-, hʸé-, -dḁ, § 7*d*).

ተለወጠ tḁlḁ́uwḁṭḁ.

(without changing gen. position) ተንቀሳቀሰ tḁṅqḁsā́qqḁsḁ.

Don't move: አትንቀሳቀስ። atti̥ṅqḁsā́qḁs, pl. -ቀሱ። -qḁsu.

It has moved from its place: ተስፍሬው፡ተለወጠ። tḁsi̥fráu tḁlḁ́uwḁṭḁ.

He's (it's) not dead, he's (it's) moving: አልሞተም፤ ይንቀሳቀሳል። almʷótḁm, yi̥ṅqḁsáqqḁsāl.

move, v.t. ለወጠ lḁ́uwḁṭḁ.

(heavy objects) ፈነቀለ fḁnḁ́qqḁlḁ.

(without changing gen. position) አንቀሳቀሰ aṅqḁsā́qqḁsḁ.

Don't move it: አትለውጠው። attiláuwŭtau, pl. -ጡት። -ṭut.

move away, v.t. ሳብ፡አደረገ sãbb adárraga.

Move it away a little: ጥቂት፡ሳብ፡አድርገው። ṭíqit sabb ádrigau (árgau § 7*d*), pl. -ጉት። -gut.

mow, v.t. አጨደ áččada (-čädä).

Mrs. ወይዘሮ wáizarʷo (wǽi-, -zär-).

much, s. adj. & adv. ብዙ bízu.

እጅግ íjjig (§ 8).

Is there much? ብዙ፡አለ። bízu állä?

It is too much: ብዙ፡ነው። bízu nau.

It is much too much: እጅግ፡ብዙ፡ነው። ijjíg yízu (§ 7*d*) nau.

mud, s. ጭቃ číqã.

Deep mud: ማጥ፡ mãṭ.

muddle, be in a, v.i. ድብልቅልቅ፡አለ diblíqliqq (diyl-) ála (s.v. √በለ, § 44*a*).

It is in a muddle: ድብልቅልቅ፡ይላል። diyliqlíqq (§ 8) yílãl.

muddled, adj. ድብልቅልቅ diblíqliq (diyl-; § 6).

muddy, adj. (of roads) ጭቃ číqã (cp. § 57*b*).

(of liquids) ድፍርስ dífris.

mule, s. በቅሎ báqlʷo, pl. also አበቁልት abáqwilt (ayá-, -qwŭ-, -ቅ- -qi-, -ሎቶች -ltʷōč; -čč § 6).

Riding mule: የኮርቻ፡በቅሎ፡ yäkʷoríčča yáqlʷo (§ 7*d*).

Baggage mule: አጋስስ፡በቅሎ፡ agássis yáqlʷo.

mule, interj. to urge a, *መጭ* mačč! (mäčč).

to stop it, እሽ išš!

muleteer, s. በቅሎኛ baqlʷóññã.

munch, v.i. & t. ቈረጠመ qwǽráṭṭama.

murder, s. መግደል mágdal (-däl).

murder, v.i. & t. ገደለ gáddala (gád-).

murdered, be, v.p. በ-...፡ እጅ፡ሞተ bḁ-... i̥jj m^{w}ṓtḁ.
He was (has been) murdered: በሰው፡እጅ፡ሞተ። bḁsḁ͡u i̥jj m^{w}ótḁ.

murderer, s. ገዳይ gḁ́dā́i̥ (gā́d-; -ā́yy § 6; § 8).

Musa Ensete (Broun, Cat. 559), s. እንሰት (i̥)nsḁt (-sät).

Musa sapientium (Broun, ib.), s. ሙዝ muz (§ 52*a*, δ).

muscle, s. ሥጋ si̥gã (prop. flesh: s.v. biceps).

muscular, adj. (strong) ጉልበታም gwŭlbḁtā́m (-lỵḁ́-, -ā́t-; § 8).
ጉልበተኛ gwŭlbḁtḁ́ññã (-lỵḁ-, -ätā́ñ-).

mushroom, s. እንጉዳይ (i̥)ṅgúdā͡i̥ (§ 8, § 52*a*, δ).

musk, s. ዝባድ zi̥bā́d (-i̥yā́-; § 8).
ጥርኝ ṭi̥ri̥ñ (-ññ § 6; § 8).

musketry, s. ቱክስ tuks.
ዓላማ፡ቱክስ alāmā́ (§ 8) tuks.

muslin, s. ሻሽ šāš.

must, v.i.—use the juss. (§ 27) and imp. (§ 28):—also:
He must go: የግድ፡ይሔዳል። yägi̥dd yi̥hā́dāl.
It must be taken away: ቍርጥ፡ነው፡እሚወሰድ። qwŭ́rṭi̥ nḁ͡u mmi̥wwώssḁd.
They must have gone: ሔደው፡ይሆናል። hi̥dḁ͡u yi̥h^{w}ónāl (s.v. ሆነ).

mustard, s. ሰናፍጭ sḁnā́fi̥č̣.

mutineer, s. አማጭ ámmā́č̣ (§ 8).

mutiny, s. አመፅ ā́mḁṭ.

mutiny, v.i. አመጠ ámmḁṭḁ.
The troops (have) mutinied: ወታደር፡አመጠ። wωttáddär (§ 52*a*) ámmḁṭḁ.

mutton, s. የበግ፡ሥጋ yäbḁ́g (-äỵḁ́-) si̥gã.

my, poss. pron. -^{y}ĕ, -የ -yä (-^{y}ä), -ዬ -yĕ (-^{y}ĕ), (§ 12*b*).

myrrh, s. ከርቤ kḁ́rb^{y}e (kā́r-, -rỵ^{y}e).

N

§ *refers to the paragraphs of the Grammar* (*Initia Amharica, Part I*).

nail, s. (unguis) ጥፍር ṭi̥fi̥r (§ 52*a*, γ).
(metal) ችንካር či̥ṅkā́r (§ 8, § 52*a*, δ).

naked, adj. ራቁት rā́qut (§ 56*d*) with pers. suff. (§ 12*b*).
I am naked: ራቁቴን፡ ነኝ። rāqutʸén (§ 8) näñ.

namda (Hindustani نمدا), s.
(for riding animals) መረሻት mḁrḁšā́t (mā́räš-; § 8).
ምቹ mi̥ččū.
መመቻ mḁmmḁ̄čā̃.
(for transport animals) ጢቅ ṭʸēq.
ድብዳብ di̥bdā́b (di̥ydā́y § 8).
መደላድል mḁdḁlā́di̥l.

name, s. ስም si̥m.
What is your name? ስምህ፡ ማን፡ ነው። si̥mi̥h mān nḁu?
What is his name? ስሙ፡ ማን፡ ነው። si̥mu mān nḁu?
What is its name? ምን፡ ይባላል። mi̥n yi̥bbā́lāl?

name, v.t. አለ ā́lḁ (s.v. √በለ, § 44*a*).
አሰኘ assā́ññä.

named, be, v.p. ተባለ tḁbā́lḁ (-ḁyā́-).
A man named Warrata: ወረታ፡ እሚባል፡ ሰው፡ wḁrrḁtá mmi̥bbā́l sḁu.

Nanotragus Hemprichianus, s. ምዳቋ mi̥dā́qqwā̃.
Š. የንሹ yā́nšu.

napkin, s. መሐረብ mḁhárrḁb (-ḁy) } (prop. handkerchief).
መሐረሚያ mḁharrḁ̄myā̃ (-rā́m-) }
Š. †መንዲል mḁ̄ndī́l (§ 8).

narrate, v.t. ተረከ tḁ́rrḁkḁ (tắr-).
narrow, adj. ጠባብ ṭḁ́bbắb (-ắỵ; § 8).
narrow, be, v.i. ጠበበ ṭḁ́bbḁbḁ (-ḁỵḁ).
narrow (narrower), make, v.t. አጠበበ aṭḁ́bbḁbḁ (-ḁỵḁ).
The buttonhole is too wide; make it a little narrower: የቍልፍ፡ቀዳዳ፡ሰፊ፡ነው፡፡አጥብበው፡ጥቂት፡፡ yäqwǘlf qḁdắda sḁ́ffi nḁ͡u; ắṭỵi̥ỵḁ͡u ṭí̥qi̥t.
nasty, adj. ጸያፍ ṣḁ́yyắf (ጠ- ṭḁ́-; § 8).
native, s. ባላገር bālắgḁr (-gär; § 52*a*, δ).
Use አገር ágḁr (-gär), country:
The soldiers will not be quartered on the natives: ወታደር፡ባገር፡ተሰሪ፡አይገባም፡፡ wωttáddḁr (§ 52*a*, δ) ỵắgḁr (§§ 7*a*, 47*a*) tḁsắri a͡i̥gắỵām.
natron, s. አምቦ ámbʷo.
nature, s. (character) ባሕሪ báhri (bhắri § 7*d*).
nature, relieve, v.i. እዳሪ፡ወጣ i̥ddắri wώṭṭā̃.
naughty, adj. ማሽንክ mắši̥ṅk (§ 8).
nauseous, adj. ጸያፍ ṣḁ́yyắf (ጠ- ṭḁ́-; § 8).
navel, s. እንብርት (í̥)nbi̥rt (-mb-, -nỵi̥-, § 7*d*).
ጉብር gúbbi̥r.
near, adj. & adv. ቅርብ qi̥rb (-rỵ).
Is he (it) near? ቅርብ፡ነው፡፡ qí̥rỵĭ̥ (§ 7*d*) nḁ͡u?
near, prp. ከ-[ተ-]...፡ ቅርብ kḁ- (tḁ-)... qi̥rb (-rỵ; § 47*b*).
Near me: ተኔ፡ቅርብ፡ tḁnʸḗ qi̥rỵ.
It is not to be near the tent: ተድንኳኑ፡ቅርብ፡አይሁን፡፡ tḁdǘṅkwắnu qi̥rỵ á͡i̥hun.
Hang it near the ground: if it falls it is not far (to fall): ወደመሬት፡አቅርበህ፡ስቀለው፡፤ቢወድቅ፡ይቀርባል፡፡ wωdḁmḁrʸét ắqi̥rỵäh sí̥qḁlḁ͡u: bi̥wώdĭ̥q, yi̥qắrỵāl.
near (nearer), be, v.i. ቀረበ qḁ́rrḁbḁ (-ḁỵḁ).
It ought to have been near(er): ይቀርብ፡ነበር፡፡ yi̥qắrỵ nḁ́bbär.

near (nearer), bring (place, put), v.t. አቀረበ aqḁ́rrḁbḁ (-ḁỵḁ).

Bring it near(er): አቅርበው። á̄qi̥rỵḁu, pl. -ቡት። -ỵut.

nearer, (one), the, dem. pron. [የ]ወዲህኛው yäwωdihí̥ñ-ñáu (-di̥h-; § 8, § 13*a*).

nearly, adv. ያህል yā́hi̥l (yahl).

Nearly 100: መቶ፡ያህል፡ mḁ́t^{w}o yahl.

He nearly died: ሊሞት፡ነበር። li̥m^{w}ót nḁ́bbär.

It is nearly finished: ሊያልቅ፡ነው። li̥álq nḁu.

neat, adj. ጠፍተኛ ṭḁffi̥tḁ́ňñã (-tā́ñ-).

neat, be, v.i. ጠፍ፡አለ ṭḁff ā́lḁ (s.v. √በለ, § 44*a*).

neat, render, v.t. ጠፍ፡አደረገ ṭḁff adḁ́rrḁgḁ.

neatness, s. ጠፍታ ṭḁ́ffi̥tã.

necessary, adj. ቍርጥ qwŭrṭ.

የሚሻ yämmi̥šā́ (§ 14, s.v. ሻ).

Is this necessary? No, we will leave it behind: ይህ፡ቍርጥ፡ነው።—አይዶለም፡ይቀራል። yí̥he qwŭ́rṭĭ̥ (§ 7*d*) nḁu?—ai̥dā́lläm, yi̥qḁ́rāl.

It is necessary: ይሻል። yi̥šál.

It is necessary to life: ለሕይወት፡ቍርጥ፡ነው። lḁhiy̥-wώt qwŭ́rṭĭ̥ nḁu.

necessity, s. ግድ gi̥dd.

neck, s. አንገት áṅgḁt (-gät).

necklace, s. ድሪ dí̥ri.

neck-tie, s. ማተብ mā́tḁb (-ḁỵ).

need, v.t. ፈለገ fḁ́llḁgḁ.

ቸገረው čā́ggḁrḁu (-gär-; impers. § 43*a*).

I need it: እፈልገዋለኍ። i̥fḁlli̥gḁuállḁu^{h}.

I don't need it: አልፈልገውም። alfḁ́lli̥gḁum.

Do you need it? ትፈልገዋለህ። ti̥fḁlli̥gḁuállăh?, pol. ይፈልጉታል። yi̥fḁ́lli̥gutāl?

I was hungry, I needed food: እርቦኝ፡ነበር፤መብል፡ፈለግሁ። i̥rỵ^{w}óñ nḁ́bbḁr, mḁ́ṿi̥l fḁ́llḁghŭ.

needed, be, v.p. ተፈለገ tḁfḁ́llḁgḁ.

It is not needed: ይቅር። yí̥qi̥r (s.v. ቀረ).

needle, s. መርፌ mḁ́rf^{y}e (mā́r-).

neglect, v.t. ቸል፡አለ፡ለ- čäll ā́lḁ lḁ-.

Š. ችላ፡አለ፡ለ- čí̥lla ā́lḁ lḁ-.

S.v. √በለ, § 44*a*; § 47*a*.

Don't neglect your work: ለስራህ፡ቸል፡አትበል። lḁsi̥rā́h čäll attí̥yḁl, pl. ለስራችሁ፡ቸል፡አትበሉ። lḁsi̥rā́č-čyuh (§ 7*d*) čäll atti̥yḁ́lu.

negligence, s. ቸልታ čā́lli̥tā̃.

negligent, adj. ቸልተኛ čälli̥tḁ́ññā̃ (-tā́ñ-).

negro (-gress), s. ጥቁር፡ሰው ṭŭ́qúr (§ 8) sḁu.

ጥቁር ṭŭ́qur.

ሻንቅላ šā̃ṅqi̥llā̃.

neigh, v.i. አስካካ askā́kkā̃.

neighbour, s. ጎረቤት g^{w}órḁb^{y}ét (-ḁy^{y}ét; §§ 8, 52*a*, δ).

nervous, adj. ደንጋጭ dḁ́ṅgā́č̣ (dā́ṅ-; § 8).

ደንጋጣ dḁṅgā́ṭṭā̃ (däṅ-).

(timid) ፈሪ fḁ́ri (fā́ri).

nest, s. ቤት b^{y}ēt.

net, s. (fishing) መረብ mḁ́rḁb (-ḁv).

nettle (*Urtica urens* or *simensis*, Guidi, Vocab. pp. 149, 150), s. ሳማ sā́mmā̃ (§52*a*, δ).

neutral, adj. አጉል ā́gul.

never, adv. ምንም፡ቢሆን፡ mí̥ni̥mm bíh^{w}ón (bí̥h-; § 8) with neg. verb (§ 38).

He will never come: ምንም፡ቢሆን፡አይመጣም። mí̥-ni̥mm bi̥h^{w}ón ai̥mḁ́tām.

new, adj. አዲስ áddi̥s.

news, s. ወሬ wǿr^{y}e.

Good news: ምስራች mi̥ssí̥rā́č (የም- yämi̥-; -čč § 6; § 8).

newspaper, s. ጋዜታ gazʸétã.

next, adj. (coming) ወደኛ wωdḁññã (-dā́ñ-).

የሚመጣ yämmi̥mḁṭa (s.v. የ-, §§ 14, 62).

By next mail: በወደኛ፡ፖስታ፡ bḁ͡uωdā́ñña pʷósta.

Next Tuesday: የሚመጣ፡ማክሰኞ፡ yämmi̥mḁṭa makṣḁñño.

On Tuesday next: በሚመጣ፡ማክሰኞ፡ bḁmmi̥mḁṭa maksḁñño.

nibble, v.i. & t. ጋጠ gā́ṭḁ.

nice, adj. ደግ dḁgg (dägg).

ማለፊያ mālā́fyã.

night, s. ሌሊት lʸēlī́t.

ሌት lʸēt.

Good-night: ደኅና፡እደር። dähná͡i̥dḁr, pol. ደኅና፡ይደሩ። dähná͡i̥dḁru, pl. ደኅና፡እደሩ። dähná͡i̥dḁru.

This night: ዛሬ፡ሌሊት፡ zā́rʸe lʸēlít.

To-morrow night: ነገ፡ሌሊት፡ nḁ́gḁ lʸēlít.

Last night: ትናንትና፡ሌሊት፡ ti̥nánti̥na lʸēlít.

night, pass the, v.i. አደረ áddḁrḁ.

We will pass the night here: ከዚህ፡እናድራለን። käzzi̥h i̥nnadrállän.

The place we passed the night at: ያደርንበት፡ስፍራ፡ yáddärni̥bbḁt (§§ 14, 47*a*) si̥fra.

At (from) the place we passed the night at: ታደርንበት፡ስፍራ፡ táddärni̥bbḁt (§ 62*c*) si̥fra.

Nile, s. (Blue) አባይ ábbá͡i̥ (§ 8).

(White) ነጭ፡አባይ näčč ábbá͡i̥.

nine, card. num. ዘጠኝ zḁ́ṭḁñ (zā́ṭäñ; § 20*a*).

nineteen, card. num. አሥራ፡ዘጠኝ asrāzḁ́ṭḁñ (-zā́ṭäñ; § 20*a*).

ninety, card. num. ዘጠና zḁṭḁ́nã (zäṭ-; § 8, § 20*a*).

nip, v.t. ቈነጠጠ qwωnḁ́ṭṭḁṭḁ.

nipple, s. ጡት ṭut (§ 52*a*, γ).
nit, s. ቅጫም qi̥č̣ám (§ 8, § 52*a*, δ).
Infested with nits, adj. ቅጫማም qi̥č̣ámám (§ 8).
nitre, s. [የ]ጨው፡ባሩድ (yä)č̣a͡u (s.v. የ-, §§ 47*a*, 70) bárud (yá-).
no, adv.
(denying) አይደለም a͡i̥dḁlläm (ad-, -dál-; -mm § 6).
(denying or declining) እንኳን ńkwān (§ 8).
(refusing) እምቢ (i̥)mbi (-bi̥).
(refusing emphatically) አሻፈረኝ ašáffḁrḁñ (-färäñ; -ññ § 6).
No, not yet: አይደለም፤ገና፡ነው። a͡i̥dálläm, gḁ́na na͡u.
I said 'No': አይደለም፡አልሁኝ። a͡i̥dállämm álhuñ (§ 61*e*).
Do you want it?—No, I don't: ትፈልገዋለህ። ti̥fḁlli̥ga͡uálläh?—እንኳን፡አልፈልግም። ńkwān, alfḁ́lli̥gi̥m.
Give it to me.—No, I won't: ስጠኝ። si̥ṭäñ.—እምቢ፡አልሰጥም። ḿbi̥, alsḁ́ṭi̥m.
After a neg. question አወን áwωn (= it is as you say) may be used where we say 'no'.
Has he come?—No: መጣ።—አይደለም። mḁ́ṭṭa?—a͡i̥dálläm.
Hasn't he come?—No: አልመጣም። —አይደለም። almḁ́ṭṭām?—a͡i̥dálläm, or (more commonly) አወን። áwωn.
nobody, indef. pron. ማንም mánni̥m (-mm § 6; § 16) with neg. verb (§ 37*d*).
Nobody is to speak: ማንም፡አይናገር። mánni̥mm a͡i̥nnágḁr.
noise, s. ድምጥ di̥mṭ.
(continuous) ጩኸት č̣úhḁt (-hät § 7*d*).

That noise must stop: ይህ፡ጩኸት፡ዝም፡ይበል። yi̥he č̣úhḁt zi̥mm yi̥vḁl.

It must be fixed (tied) so that it makes no noise: ዝም፡እንዲል፡ይታሰር። zi̥mm i̥ndi̥l yi̥ttásär.

noise, make a, v.i. (of animate objects) እንኳኳ aṅkwák-kwā̃.

(of inanimate objects) ተንኳኳ tḁṅ-kwā́kkwā̃.

Don't make a noise: አታንኳኳ። attaṅkwákwa.

Furniture, etc. that makes a noise (e.g. a creaking table): የሚንኳኳ፡እቃ፡ yämmi̥ṅkwākkwá qa (§ 8).

nomad herdsman, s. ዘላን zḁ́llán (§ 8).

nonsense!, interj. እረግ ḁ́rḁg! (ḁrḁ̄ḁ́g; § 7*d*).

አይሆንም። a͡i̥hʷóni̥m!

nonsense, s. ዋዛ wā́zā̃.

noon, s. ቀትር qáti̥rr.

እኩል፡ቀን i̥kkúl (ŭkk-) qḁn.

እኩለ፡ቀን i̥kkúlḁ (ŭkk-; § 9*d*) qḁn.

At noon: ተኩል፡ቀን፡ tḁkkúl qḁn.

noon, pass (halt for, قيل), v.i. ዋለ wā́lḁ.

We will halt here for noon: ከዚህ፡እንውላለን። käz-zí̥h i̥nni̥wi̥lállän.

The village we halted at for noon: የዋልንበት፡መንደር፡ yäwā́lni̥bbḁt mḁ́ndḁr.

north, s. ስሜን si̥mʸén (§ 8).

ግራ gí̥rā̃.

nose, s. አፍንጫ afí̥nç̣ā̃.

nostril, s. ያፍንጫ፡ቀዳዳ yā̃fí̥nç̣a qḁdā́dā̃ (§ 52*a*, γ).

not, adv. መች mḁč.

See negative conjugation (§ 37, § 38).

Not this: መች፡እሱ። mḁč i̥ssú.

He (it) came: መጣ። mḁ́ṭṭa.

He (it) did not come: አልመጣም። almḁ́ṭṭām.

He (it) is hungry: ራበው። rā́yḁu (§§ 43*a*, 63*d*).

He (it) is not hungry: አራበውም። arrā́yḁum (§ 7*c*).

He is to go: ይሒድ። yí̥hi̥d.

He is not to go: አይሒድ። ái̥hi̥d.

We drink: እንጠጣለን። i̥nnṭḁṭṭállän.

We do not drink: አንጠጣም። annṭḁ́ṭṭām.

If we drink: ብንጠጣ፤ bi̥nnṭḁ́ṭṭa.

If we do not drink: ባንጠጣ፤ bānnṭḁ́ṭṭa.

We shall not drink anything: ምንም፡አንጠጣ። mí̥-ni̥mm annṭḁ́ṭṭa.

One came: አንድ፡መጣ and mḁ́ṭṭa.

One did not come: አንድ፡አልመጣም። and almḁ́ṭ-ṭām.

Not one came: አንድም፡አልመጣ። ándi̥mm almḁ́ṭṭa.

not, he (it) is, v.i. አይደለም ai̥dḁ́lläm (ad-, -dā́l-; § 40).

This is not mine: ይህ፡የኔ፡አይደለም። yí̥he yän^{y}é ai̥dálläm.

It is not bad: ክፉም፡አይደል። kí̥fumm ái̥däl (§ 37*b*).

If it is not right, tell me: ልክ፡እንዳይደል፡ንገረኝ። li̥kk i̥ndái̥däl, ní̥gäräñ.

This is not what I told you: ይህነንም፡አላልሁህ። yi̥hánnäni̥mm alálhuh.

This is not what I want: ይህም፡አይደል፡እምፈልግ። yí̥hi̥mm (yí̥hämm) ái̥däll (§ 6) i̥mmi̥fálli̥g.

notable, s. ዓይነተኛ ai̥nḁṭḁ́ññã (-nätáñ-).

note, s. (letter) ደብዳቤ dḁbdább^{y}e (dḁyd-).

I will make a (mental) note of it: እስተውለዋለሁ። astḁulḁuállḁu^{h}.

note-book, s. ደፍተር dḁ́ftḁr (-tär).

nothing, indef. pron. ምንም mi̥ni̥m (-mm § 6) with neg. verb (§ 16).

It (there) is nothing: ምንም ፡ የለ። mi̥ni̥mm yállä.

I saw nothing: ምንም ፡ አላየሁ። mi̥ni̥mm aláyya͡u^h (§ 7*d*).

They struck him for nothing: እንዲያው ፡ መቱት። ndyá͡u mḁttut.

notice, v.i. & t. አስተዋለ astḁwālḁ (-ta͡uá-).

ተመለከተ tḁmḁlḁ́kkḁtḁ.

I didn't notice (him, her, it, them, § 61*b*): አላስተዋል ሁም። alastḁ͡uālhum, or አልተመለከትሁም። altḁmḁlḁ́kkḁthum (-t-h-, not -*θ*-, § 3).

nourish, v.t. መገበ mḁ́ggḁbḁ (-ḁvḁ).

nourished, be, v.p. ተመገበ tḁmḁ́ggḁbḁ (-ḁvḁ).

November, s.v. calendar.

now, adv. አሁን áhun (-hωn).

(after this) እንግዲህ (i̥)ṅgd^{y}ḗh.

numbed, be, v.p. በደነ bḁ́ddḁnḁ (bắd-; § 63*d, e*).

My hands are numbed: እጄ ፡ በድን ፡ ሆነ። i̥jj^{y}e (§ 52*a*, *γ*) yḁ́di̥nn h^{w}ónḁ.

number, s. ቍጥር qwi̥̊ti̥̊r (-wŭ́ṭ-).

Numida mitrata, s. ጅግራ ji̥grã (§ 52*a*, *δ*).

numnah, s. see namda.

nun, s. መለክሴ mḁlωks^{y}e, pl. also መለኳኵስቶች mḁlḁkwá-kwŭst^{w}ōč (-čč § 6).

nurse, s. ሞግዚት m^{w}ógzit.

O

§ *refers to the paragraphs of the Grammar* (*Initia Amharica, Part I*).

obese, adj. ገፋፋ gạfáfā̃.

obese, be, v.i. ጎፈፍ፡አለ gʷófạff ắlạ (s.v. √በለ, § 44*a*).

obey, v.i. & t. ታዘዘ tā́zzạzạ (with acc. or ለ- lạ- § 47*a*).

ተገዛ tạgạ́zzā̃ (ለ- lạ- § 47*a*).

እሺ፡አለ ịšši (-šị) ắlạ (s.v. √በለ, § 44*a*).

በጄ፡አለ bạ́jjä (bā́j-) ắlạ („ „).

Did he obey you? ታዘዘህ። tázzạzäh?

Does he obey you? ይታዘዝልሃል። yịttázzạzịllịhāl?

He refused to obey: አልሰማማም፡አለ። alsạ́māmm ắlạ.

You must obey him: ታዘዝለት። tā́zạzịllạt, pl. ታዘዙለት። tā́zạzullạt.

observe, v.i. & t. ተመለከተ tạmạlạ́kkạtạ.

አስተዋለ astạwā́lạ (-tạuā́-).

obstinate, adj. ቸክቻክ čạkčā́kkā̃.

obstinate, be, v.i. ችክ፡አለ čịkk ắlạ (s.v. √በለ, § 44*a*; § 63*d*, *e*).

obtain, v.t. አገኘ agạ́ññä (-gā́ñ-).

I want to obtain one (some § 61*b*): ላገኝ፡እፈልጋለሁ። lāgā́ññ ịfạllịgállạuʰ.

obtained, be, v.p. ተገኘ tạgạ́ññä (-gā́ñ-).

Where can it be obtained? የት፡ይገኛል። yēt yịggạ́ññāl? (§ 63*c*).

obvious, adj. እዉቅ ịwuq (ịʷuq).

(to the eye) ትይዩ tị(y)íyyu.

occasion, s. ጊዜ gịzʸe, pl. also ጊዝያት gịzyát (§ 8).

ocean, s. ውቂያኖስ wŭqyánʷos.

Indian Ocean: የህንድ፡ውቂያኖስ፡ yähịnd wŭqyánʷos.

October, s.v. calendar.

Odina fruticosa, (Broun, Cat. 113), s. አምበልታ ambḁltã (-bā́l-).

of, prp. የ- yä-.
  ከ- [ተ-] kḁ- (tḁ-).
  See §§ 47*a*, 70.
  The door of the house: የቤት ፡ ደጅ ፡ yäṿ^{y}ét däjj.
  The depth of the water: የውሃ ፡ ጥልቅ ፡ yä͡uhá ṭi̥lq.
  It is one of these: ተኒህ ፡ አንድ ፡ ነው ፡፡ tḁnníh ándĭ̥ nḁ͡u.
  He died of poison: በመርዝ ፡ ሞተ ፡፡ bḁmḁ́rz m^{w}ótḁ.

off, adv. ከዚህ kḁ́zzíh (hḁ́-, -ā́z-, -zi̥h ; § 8).
  ተዚህ tḁ́zzíh (tā́z-, -zi̥h ; § 8).
  Be off! ና ፡ ሒድ ፡፡ nā́-hi̥d! (§ 8), pl. ኑ ፡ ሒዱ ፡፡ nu hi̥du!
  It's a long way off: ተዚህ ፡ እሩቅ ፡ ነው ፡፡ täzzíh ĭ̥rúq nḁ͡u.

off, prp. ከ- [ተ-] kḁ- (tḁ-; § 47*a*).
  Take it off the mule: ተበቅሎው ፡ አንሣው ፡፡ tḁṿḁ́ql^{w}o͡u ánsa͡u.
  Where are you off to? ዬት ፡ ብለህ ፡፡ yēt ṿi̥läh? (§ 44*a*, § 65*b*).

off, be, v.i. ወገደ wώggḁdḁ.
  Be off! ወግድ ፡፡ wώgi̥d!, f. ወግጅ ፡፡ wώgi̥j! pl. ወግዱ ፡፡ wώgi̥du!

offal, s. ጥምብ ṭi̥mb.

offence, s. ኃጢአት háṭyát (ā́ṭ-; § 8).
  በደል bā́däl.

office, s. (official building) አደባባይ addḁbā́ba͡i̥ (-ḁṿā́ṿa͡i̥).
  ችሎት či̥l^{w}ot (§ 8).

officer, s. ሹም šum, pl. also ሹማምት šumā́mi̥t.
  አምበል ámbḁl (-bäl).

oh!, interj. (of surprise) አረ ḁ́rḁ!
(surprise, admiration) እጡብ i̥ṭū́b! (-y̥, hḁṭūū́y̥!).
(surprise, contempt, disbelief) አረግ ḁ́rḁg! (ḁrḁ̄ā́g!).

oil, s. ዘይት zéi̥t.
ቅበ፡ኑግ qi̥bánug (-i̥yá-).

old, adj. አሮጌ ar^{w}ṓg^{y}e.
(of persons) ሽማግሌ ši̥māgi̥l(l)^{y}e.
ትልቅ tí̥lli̥q.

old, be (become), v.i. አረጀ arájjä (§ 63*d*, *e*).
How old are you? እድሜህ፡ምን፡ታህላለህ። i̥dm^{y}eh mi̥n tahlállāh? (s.v. አከለ).
How old is he (it)? እድሜው፡ምን፡ያህላል። i̥dm^{y}eu mi̥n yáhlāl?

Olea chrysophylla (Guidi, Vocab. p. 587), s. } ወይራ wḁ́i̥rā
olive, s. (wild) } (wώi̥-).

omen, s. ገድ gḁdd.

omoplate, s. መጋፍያ mḁgáfyā.

on, prp. በ-...፡ ላይ bḁ-... lái̥ (§ 8, § 47*b*).
It is on the table: በገበታው፡ላይ፡ነው። bḁgḁvḁtáu lái̥ nḁu.
Give me two dollars if you have them on you: ሁለት፡ብር፡ቅርብ፡እንዳለህ፡ስጠኝ። hulḁ́tti̥ v̥i̥rr qi̥rv̥ i̥ndállāh sí̥tḁñ.

once, adv. (a single time) አንድ፡ግዜ and gí̥z^{y}e (andí̥gz^{y}e).
(formerly) ጥንት ṭi̥nt.
At once (now): ቶሎ፡አሁን፡ t^{w}ólo ā́hun (-hωn).
(immediately): ወድያው፡ wώdyáu (§ 8).

one, card. num. አንድ and, f. አንዲት ándi̥t (§ 20*a*).
Let them come one by one: እንዳንዳቸው፡ይምጡ። andandā́ččḁu (§ 18) yí̥mṭu.

This one: ይሀ፡ yí̥he.

The other one: ሌላው፡ léla͡u (§ 59*c*).

The large one: ትልቁ፡ tí̥lli̥qu („).

The small one: ትንሹ፡ tí̥nni̥šu („).

onion (*Allium cepa*), s. ሹንኵርት šúṅkwŭrt (§ 52*a*, δ).

ቀይ፡ሹንኵርት qḁ́͡i̥ (qḁyy § 6) šúṅkwŭrt.

only, adv. ብቻ bí̥ččã.

Four only: አራት፡ብቻ፡ arắtt ẏí̥čča (§ 7*d*).

If he had only come! ወዮ፡በመጣ። wώyyō ẏḁmḁ́ṭṭa!

open, adj. ክፍት ki̥ft (küft § 7*d*).

(of a garment) ነጠላ nḁṭḁ́lã (§ 8).

Leave it open: ክፍቱን፡ተወው። kí̥ftun (cp. § 56*c*) tḁ́͡uḁ͡u.

Leave the door open: መዝጊያውን፡ክፍት፡ተው። mḁ́zgya͡un ki̥ft tḁ́͡u.

open, v.t. ከፈተ kḁ́ffḁtḁ.

Open it: ክፈተው። kí̥fḁtḁ͡u, pl. -ቱት። -tut.

Do not open it: አትክፈተው። attí̥kfḁtḁ͡u, -pl. -ቱት። -tut.

open, be, v.i. (opened, be, v.p.) ተከፈተ tḁkḁ́ffḁtḁ (§ 63*d*, *e*).

Is it open? ተከፍቷል። tḁkḁ́ftŏ͡āl?

Can it be opened? ይከፈታል። yi̥kkḁ́ffḁtāl? (§ 63*c*).

opinion, s. አሳብ ás(s)ắb (-ắẏ; § 8).

What is your opinion? ምን፡ታስባለህ። mi̥n tāssi̥ẏáläh?

opposite, adv. ትይዩ ti̥(y)íyyu.

opposite, prp. የ-…፡ ትይዩ yä-… ti̥(y)íyyu (§ 47*b*).

Opposite the house: የቤቱ፡ትይዩ፡ yäẏʸétu ti̥íyyu.

oppress, v.t. ገፋ gḁ́ffã.

በደለ bḁ́ddḁlḁ (bắd-).

oppressed, be, v.p. ተገፋ tḁgḁ́ffã.

ተበደለ tḁbḁ́ddalḁ (tḁv-, -ā́d-).

They are oppressed: ይገፋሉ። yi̥ggḁffállu.

oppression, s. ግፍ gi̥f.

or, conj. ወይ wḁ̂i̥ (wǝ́i̥; § 6).

Is it his or yours? የርሱ፡ነው፡ወይ፡ያንተ። yärsú nḁu wǝ́i̥ yántḁ?

—— In questions also with -ስ -ss (q.v.):

Is he coming or not? ይመጣል፡ወይስ፡አይመጣም። yi̥mḁ́ṭāll wǝ́i̥ss ai̥mḁ́ṭām?

—— Commonly omitted:

Is it yours (pl.) or theirs? የናንተ፡ነው፡የርሳቸው። yännánti̥ nḁu yärsā́ččḁu?

orange, s. በክረው፡[በትረው፡] ሎሚ bḁ́krḁu (-ḁ́tr-) l^{w}ṓmī.

order, s. (arrangement) ሥራት si̥rā́t (§ 8).

(command) ትዛዝ ti̥zā́z (§ 8).

Whose order is it? (orders are they? § 52*a*): የማን፡ ትዛዝ፡ነው። yämā́n ti̥zā́z nḁu?

Is the country in good order? አገር፡ቀጥ፡ይላሉይ። ā́gḁr qḁṭṭ yi̥lāllwi̥? (s.v. ወይ).

order, v.i. & t. አዘዘ ázzḁzḁ.

As he ordered: እንዳዘዘ፡ i̥ndázzḁzḁ.

ordered, be, v.p. ታዘዘ tā́zzḁzḁ.

As (he, it) was ordered: እንደታዘዘ። ndḁtázzḁzḁ.

Oreotragus saltator, s. ሰሳ sḁsã.

oribi (*Oribia montana*), s. ፈቆ f^{y}éq^{w}o.

ሜቆ m^{y}éq^{w}o (m^{y}ā́q-).

መወቅ mḁ́^{w}ǝq (mā́^{w}-; § 7*d*).

origin, s. ዘር zḁr (zär).

originally, adv. ጥንት ṭi̥nt.

ornament, s. ጌጥ g^{y}ēṭ.

ornamental, be, v.i. አጌጠ ag^{y}éṭḁ.
ornamented, adj. ሽልም šı̥̆llı̥m.
oryx (*O. beisa*), s. ሳላ sálã.
other, indef. pron. ሌላ lélã (§ 16).

The other: ሌላው፡ lélau͡ (§ 11).
Fetch the other: ሌላውን፡አምጣ። lélau͡n ánṭa (§ 7*d*), pl. -ጡ -ṭu.
Where is the other? ሌላው፡ዬት፡ነው። lélau͡ yēt nḁu͡?
There is no other: ሌላ፡የለም። léla yállām.
Take one and leave the other: አንዱን፡ይዘህ፡አንዱን፡ተው። ándun yı̥̆zäh (§ 74*b*) andún (§ 8) tḁu͡.

otter (*Lutra sp.*), s. አቆስጣ áq^{w}osṭã.
Otus cineraceus (Guidi, Vocab. p. 782), s. ጕጕት gwŭ́g-gwŭt.
ought, v. aux., use past imperf. (§§ 24*b*, 33*a*, 63*b*).

He ought to have gone: ይሔድ፡ነበር። yı̥hád nḁ́b-bär.

See § 67*b*: It ought to be done: ተደራጊ፡ነው። tḁ-dḁrrāgí (§ 8) nḁu͡.

You ought to go: መሔድ፡ይገባሃል። mḁhád yı̥ggḁ́b-bahāl (s.v. ገባ).

'Ought' may be implied by using ቀረ (q.v.) with ስ- and the neg. conjug. (§ 38):

Why didn't you tell me so? (sc. as you ought to have done): ስለምን፡ነው፡እንዲህ፡ያለውን፡ሳትነግረኝ፡ቀረህ። sı̥lḁmı̥́n nḁu͡ ndı̥h yállḁun sāttı̥nágrän qḁ́rräh?, pol. .... ሳይነግሩኝ፡ቀሩ። .... sai͡ı̥nḁ́gruñ qḁ́rru?, pl. .... ሳትነግሩኝ፡ቀራችሁ። .... sāttı̥nḁ́gruñ qḁrráččyuh? (§ 7*d*).

'Ought to have': use past imperf. (§ 24):

It ought to have been done: ይደረግ፡ነበር። yı̥ddḁ́r-rḁg nḁ́bbär.

You ought to have told me: ትለኝ፡ነበርህ። tịlấñ nạbbärh.

ounce, s. ወቄት wóqʸĕt (wώq-; § 8).

our, poss. pron. -ầችን -ấč(č)ịn (§ 12*b*).

ours, poss. pron. የኛ yấññấ (§§ 8, 12*a*, 47*a*).

out, adv. s.v. outside.

Out with you! ና፡ውጣ፡ nau͡ṭa!

out, go, v.i. (issue) ወጣ wώṭṭã.

(be extinguished) ጠፋ ṭạffã.

Has he gone out? ወጥቷል። wώṭịtŏãl? pol. & pl. ወጥተዋል። wώṭịtạuãl?

Go out if you want to: ብትፈልግ፡ውጣ። bịttịfạllịg, wṹṭa, pl. ብትፈልጉ፡ውጡ። bịttịfạllịgu, wṹṭu.

Don't go out: አትውጣ። attịwṹṭa, pl. -ጡ። -ṭu.

When did he go out? መቼ፡ወጣ። mạčä wώṭṭa, pol. & pl. ...፡ወጡ። ...wώṭṭu?

Let it (the fire, etc.) go out: ይጥፋ። yịṭfa.

Don't let it go out: እንዳይጠፋ። ndaịṭạfa.

out, let, v.t. አስወጣ aswώṭṭã (አሶጣ asʷóṭṭã).

Let him (it) out: አስወጣው። aswώṭṭau͡, pol. ያስወጡት። yaswώṭṭut, pl. አስወጡት። aswώṭṭut.

Don't let him (it) out: አታስወጣው። attaswώṭṭau͡, pol. አያስወጡት። a͡ʸaswώṭṭut, pl. አታስወጡት። attaswώṭṭut.

Let them out: አሶጣቸው። asʷoṭṭấččạu͡, pol. ያሶጧቸው። yasʷoṭṭwấččạu͡, pl. አሶጧቸው። asʷoṭṭwấččạu͡.

Don't let them out: አታሶጣቸው። attasʷoṭṭấččạu͡, pol. አያሶጧቸው። a͡ʸasʷoṭṭwấččạu͡, pl. አታሶጧቸው። attasʷoṭṭwấččạu͡.

Who was it that let him (it) out? ያስወጣው፡ማን፡ነው። yāswώṭṭau͡ (§ 14) mấn-nạu͡?

out, put, v.t. አወጣ awώṭṭā̃ (a͡uώ-).
(extinguish) አጠፋ aṭḁ́ffā̃.
Put the bedstead out: አልጋውን፡አውጣው። álga͡un á͡uṭa͡u, pl. -ጡት። -ṭut.
Don't put it out: አታውጣው። attá͡uṭa͡u, pl. -ጡት። -ṭut.
Put the light out: መብራቱን፡አጥፋው። mḁỵrátun áṭfa͡u.
Don't put it out: አታጥፋው። attáṭfa͡u.

outlaw, s. ሽፍታ ší̥ftā̃ (§ 52*a*, δ).

outlawry, s. ሽፍታነት ši̥ftánnḁt (-ፍት- -ftí̥-, -nät).

outside, prp. ከ- ...፡ ውጭ kḁ- (ተ- tḁ-)... wi̥čč̣ (§ 8, § 47*b*).
Outside the house: ከቤት፡ውጭ፡ kḁyʸét wi̥čč̣.

outside, s. & adv. ውጭ wi̥čč̣.
adv. በውጭ bḁ́wí̥čč̣ (bḁ́͡uí̥čč̣; § 8).
እዳሪ i̥ddári.

oven, s. ማብሰያ mābsḁ́yā̃ (-āys-, -ḁ́i̥ā̃).
መጣጃ mḁṭḁ́jā̃.

over, prp. (of position) በ- [ከ-, ተ-]...፡ ላይ bḁ- (kḁ-, tḁ-)... la͡i̥ (§ 8, § 47*b*).
Put this over that: ይህንን፡በዚህ፡ላይ፡አድርገው። yi̥hánnän yḁzzíh la͡i̥ árgḁ͡u (§ 7*d*), pl. -ጉት። -gut.

over, prp. (exceeding) ከ- [ተ-]...፡ የሚበልጥ kḁ- (tḁ-)... yämmi̥bḁ́lṭ (እሚ- (i̥)mmi̥-, -i̥v-, -álṭ; §§ 14, 47*b*, 58*c*).
Over fifty: ታምሳ፡የሚበልጥ፡ támsā yämmi̥válṭ.
They are over fifty: ታምሳ፡ይበልጣሉ። támsā yi̥väl-ṭállu.

over there, adv. ከዚያ kḁ́zzyā̃́ (hḁ́-, -áz-; § 8).
ተዚያ tḁ́zzyā̃́ (táz-; § 8).
በወድያ bḁ͡uώdyā̃́ (§ 8).
Put it over there: ከዚያ፡አኑረው። kḁzzyá ánurḁ͡u, pl. -ሩት። -rut.

overcome, v.t. [እ]ረታ (i̥)rḁ́ttã.

overcome, be, v.p. ተረታ tḁrḁ́ttã.

overfed, adj. ጥጋበኛ ti̥gābḁ́ññã (-āy-, -ā́ñ-).

overrun, v.t. (raid) ወረረ wώrrḁrḁ.

owe, v.t. ነበረ nḁ́bbḁrḁ (-bär-), ነበር nḁ́bbḁr (-bär; § 33), with present ነው nḁ͡u (§ 13b) and አለ állä (§ 32), of which the Eng. object becomes the subject: constr. with በ- bḁ-, ብ- b(i̥)- (§ 47a), or ከ- kḁ- (ተ- tḁ-) of the debtor, and የ- yä- or the pron. pers. suff. (§ 12c) of the creditor:

I owe it: ከኔ፡ነው። kḁnʸé (§ 8) nḁ͡u.

Do you owe it? ካንተ፡ነው። kántḁ nḁ͡u?, pl. ካላንት፡ነው። kḁllánt nḁ͡u?

How much do you owe? ስንት፡እዳ፡አለብህ። si̥nt i̥da álläbbi̥h?

You owed him a dollar: ካንተ፡አንድ፡ብር፡ነበረው። kántä ándi̥ yi̥rr nḁ́bbärḁ͡u, or የርሱ፡አንድ፡ብር፡ነበረብህ። yärsǘ ándi̥ yi̥rr nḁ́bbäräbbi̥h.

You owe me a dollar: የኔ፡አንድ፡ብር፡አለብህ። yänʸé ándi̥ yi̥rr álläbbi̥h, or ታንተ፡አንድ፡ብር፡አለኝ። tántä ándi̥ yi̥rr álläñ.

I owe you a dollar: ያንተ፡አንድ፡ብር፡አለብኝ። yántä ándi̥ yi̥rr álläbbi̥ñ, or በኔ፡አንድ፡ብር፡አለህ። bḁnʸé ándi̥ yi̥rr álläh.

owing to (because of), prp. ስለ- si̥lḁ- (§ 47a).

owl (*Otus sp.*), s. ጉጉት gwǘggwŭt.

own, adj. ገንዘብ- gḁ́nzḁb- (-ḁy-) with pers. suff. (§ 12a).

It is my own: ገንዘቤ፡ነው። gḁnzḁyʸé (§ 8) nḁ͡u.

Is it your own? ገንዘብህ፡ነው። gḁnzḁyi̥h na͡u?, pol. -ብዎ፡ነው። -yʷó nḁ͡u?, pl. -ብችሁ፡ነው። -yäččyuh nḁ͡u?

own, v.t. ገዛ gázzã.

owned, be, v.p. ተገዛ tagázzã.

ox, s. ሰንጋ ፡ በሬ sánga vár^ye.

Oxytenanthera abessinica (Broun, Cat. 677), s. ሽመል šímal (-mäl; § 52*a*, δ).

P

§ *refers to the paragraphs of the Grammar* (*Initia Amharica, Part I*).

pace, s. (running) [እ]ሩጫ (i)rúččã.

pack (up), v.t. ከተተ káttata.

አሰረ ássara (-sär-).

ሰበሰበ sabássaba (savássava).

Pack up this baggage: የህነን ፡ እቃ ፡ ሰብስበህ ፡ እሰረው ። yihánnän iqa sávsiväh isärau.

package, s. እስር isir.

Open those packages that came: ታስሮ ፡ የመጣውን ፡ እቃ ፡ ፍታው ፡ tásr^wo yämáttaun iqā fitau.

packing-needle, s. መስፌ másf^ye.

መሰፈቻ massaffáčã (-fáč-).

pagan, adj. & s. አረመኔ aramán^ye.

paid, be, v.p. ተከፈለ takáffala.

It is to be paid: ይከፈል ። yikkáfal.

It is not to be paid: አይከፈል ። aikkáfal.

Has the money been paid? ገንዘብ ፡ ተከፈለ ። gánzav takáffala?

Has he been paid what was owed him? እዳው ፡ ተከፈለለት ። idau takáffalallat?

pail, s. ጃርዳል jắrdäl.
(metal) ቊርቊሮ qwωrqwώrr^{w}o.
(دلو) መቅጃ mḁ́qjā.

pain, interj. expressing, አ ā!

pain, s. እመም i̥mḁm.
Violent pain: ምጥ mi̥ṭ.
He had a pain in his hand: እጁን፡አመመው። í̥jjun (§ 56c) ámmḁmḁu.

pain, be in, v.i. ጨነቀው č̣ḁ́nnḁqḁu (impers. § 43a).

paint, s. ቀለም qḁ́lḁm.

paint, v.t. (portray) ሣለ sắlḁ (conjug. like ሳለ to cough).
ቀለመ qḁ́llḁmḁ.

painted, be, v.p. ተቀለመ tḁqḁ́llḁmḁ.

painting, s. (picture) ስል si̥l.

palace, s. ግምብ gi̥mb.
አዳራሽ addắrắš (§ 8).
ቤተ፡መንግሥት b^{y}étḁ (§ 9d) mḁ́ngi̥st.
ግቢ gí̥bbi (court).
He is at the palace: ከንጉሥ፡ዘንድ፡ነው። kḁnigū́s zḁ́ndi̥ nḁu.

palate, s. ተናጋ tḁnắgā.

palm, s. (of hand) መዳፍ mḁ́dắf (§§ 8, 52a, γ).
(tree, *Phoenix dactylifera*, Broun, Cat. 595 and *Borassus flabellifer*, ib. 599) ሰሌን sḁ́l^{y}én (§ 8).

pan, s. ፋጋ fắgā (prop. gourd).
ሰሐን sḁ́hắn (§ 8; prop. plate).

pander, s. አቃጣሪ aqqāṭắri.

panther, black, s. ግሥላ gi̥ssí̥llā.

papa!, interj. (cry of child to father) አበባ abábba! (ay̤á-).

paper, s. ወረቀት wạrạqạt.

Ruled paper: መስመር፡ ያለበት፡ ወረቀት፡ mạsmạr yál-läbbạt wạrạqạt.

Blotting-paper: ማምጠጫ፡ mā̃mṭạ́č̣ā̃ (-ṭắč̣-).

paper-knife, s. የወረቀት፡ መቅደጃ yäwạ́rạqạt mạqdạ́jā̃ (-dắj-).

parade, s. (mil.) ሰልፍ sạlf (sälf).

Parade ground, s. መሰለፊያ mạssạllạ́fyā̃ (-sällắf-).

parade, v.i. (be paraded, v.p.) ተሰለፈ tạsạ́llạfạ (täsắl-).

parade, v.t. አሰለፈ assạ́llạfạ (-sắl-).

paralysed, adj. ብዱን bạ́dịn (bắd-; -nn § 6).

paralysed, be, v.i. በደነ bạ́ddạnạ (bắd-).

ሰለለ sạ́llạlạ (sắl-).

See § 63*d*, *e*.

His legs are paralysed: እግሩ፡ ሰሏል። ịgru (§ 52*a*, δ) sắllo͡āl.

parasitic plant, s. ተቀጥላ tạqạṭṭị́llā̃.

parcel, s. እስር ịsịr.

parchment, s. ብራና bịrạ́nnā̃.

pardon, v.t. ማረ mắrạ.

Pardon me (after an inadvertency): pol. ይቅር፡ ይበሉኝ። yịqịr yị́ḅạlullịñ.

pardoned, be, v.p. ተማረ tạmắrạ.

Has he been pardoned? ተምሯል። tạ́mịro͡āl?, pol. and pl. ተምረዋል። tạ́mịrạuāl?

pare, v.t. ቈረጠ qwǿrrạṭạ.

Pare it (them § 52*a*): ቍረጠው። qwǘrạṭa͡u.

pared, be, v.p. ተቈረጠ tạqwǿrrạṭạ.

When the hoofs grow long they should be pared: ጥፍር፡ ሲያድግ፡ ይቈረጥ። ṭịfịr (§ 52*a*, γ) syạ́dịg yịq-qwǿrạṭ.

part, s. (division) ክፍል kị́fịl.

partner, s. ባለኩል bālḁ́kkul.

partridge, s. ሶረን s^{w}ǒrḁn (-rän; § 52*a*, δ).

parturition, s. መውለድ mḁ́wŭlḁd (mḁ́͡ul-).

Pains of parturition: ምጥ mi̥ṭ.

party, s.—s.v. እነ- (i̥)nnḁ-

Tasamma and his party: እነተሰማ፡ nnḁtḁsḁ́mma.

pass, s. (mountain) በር bḁrr.

pass, v.i. & t. አለፈ állḁfḁ.

pass, let, v.t. አሳለፈ asállḁfḁ.

አስኬደ askā̆dä (-kā̆́-, -dḁ).

Let him (it) pass: አሳልፈው። asálli̥fḁ͡u, pol. ያሳልፉት። yāsálli̥fut, pl. አሳልፉት። asálli̥fut.

Don't let him (it) pass: አታሳልፈው። attāsálli̥fḁ͡u, pol. አያሳልፉት። a͡^{y}āsálli̥fut, pl. አታሳልፉት። attāsálli̥fut.

Let them pass: አሳልፏቸው። asalli̥fáččḁ͡u, pol. ያሳልፏቸው። yāsalli̥fwáččḁ͡u, pl. አሳልፏቸው። asalli̥fwáččḁ͡u.

Don't let them pass: አታሳልፏቸው። attāsalli̥fáččḁ͡u, pol. አያሳልፏቸው። a͡^{y}āsalli̥fwáččḁ͡u, pl. አታሳልፏቸው። attāsalli̥fwáččḁ͡u.

pass on a little, to, v.i. እልፍ፡አለ i̥lli̥ff álḁ (s.v. √በለ, § 44*a*).

Pass on a little: እልፍ፡በል። i̥lli̥ffi̥ (§§ 7*d*, 8) ỵḁl, pl. ...፡ በሉ። ... ỵálu.

passage (passing), s. እልፍ i̥lf.

Passover, feast of the, s. ፋሲካ fásikā̃.

pastern, s. ሸሆና šḁh^{w}ónā̃ (šωh-, -ኾ- -χ^{w}ó-, -ኮ- -k^{w}ó-; §§ 8, 7*d*, 52*a*, γ).

ጠናግል ṭḁnági̥l (§ 52*a*, γ).

pasture, s. መስክ mḁsk.

pasture, v.i. G. ተሰማራ tḁsḁmā́rrā̃ (täsäm-).
Š. ተሰመረ tḁsḁmḁ́rrḁ (täsäm-).
v.t. G. አሰማራ assḁmā́rrā̃.
Š. አሰመረ assḁmḁ́rrḁ.

patch, s. መጣፊያ mḁṭā́fyā̃.
Put a patch on it: መጣፊያ፡አድርግበት። mḁṭā́fyā̃ ádri̥gi̥bbḁt (ā́rg-; § 7*d*).

patch, v.t. ጣፈ ṭā́fḁ.
Patch the shirts which have holes in them: የተቀደደውን፡ቀሚስ፡ጣፈው። yätḁqḁ́ddḁdḁun qḁ́mis (§ 52*a*) ṭā́fḁu.

patched, be, v.p. ተጣፈ tḁṭā́fḁ.

path, s. መንገድ mḁ́ṅgḁd.
ጎዳና gwódanā̃.

patience, s. ትግሥት tíǵi̥st (§ 8).
ዝግታ zi̥ggítā̃.

patient, adj. ዝግተኛ zi̥ggi̥tḁ́ññā̃ (-tā́ñ-).
ጭምት čímmi̥t.

patient, be, v.i. ታገሠ tā́ggḁsḁ.

pause, v.i. ቈየት፡አለ qwóyyätt ā́lḁ (s.v. √በለ, § 44*a*).
He (it) has paused: ቈየት፡ብሏል። qwóyyät (§ 6) yílŏāl.

paw, s. መዳፍ mḁ́dā́f (§§ 8, 52*a*, γ).

pay, s. ደሞዝ dḁ́m^{w}óz (§ 8).

pay, v.i. & t. (sum, and to person) ከፈለ kḁ́ffḁlḁ.
Have you paid it (paid him)? ከፈልሀው። kḁ́ffḁlhḁu?
Pay him (pay it): ክፈለው። kífḁlḁu.
Pay them: ክፈላቸው። ki̥fḁláččḁu.
I have paid (it): ከፈልሁ። kḁ́ffḁlhŭ (§ 61*b*).
I have paid him: ከፈልሁት። kḁ́ffḁlhut.
I have paid them: ከፈልኋቸው። kḁffḁlhwáččḁu.

Don't pay it (pay him): አትክፈለው። attịkfạlạu.
I will pay (it): እከፍላለኊ። ịkạflállạuʰ (§ 61*b*).
I will pay him: እከፍለዋለኊ። ịkạflạuállạuʰ.
I will pay them: እከፍላቸዋለኊ። ịkạflāččạuállạuʰ.
I have not paid: አልከፈልሁም። alkạ́ffạlhum (§ 61*b*).
I do (will) not pay: አልከፍልም። alkạ́flịm.
I have to pay for it: ከኔ፡ነው። kạnʸé nạu (s.v. owe).
pay a fine, v.i. (pay as a fine, v.t.) ካሰ kā́sạ.
pay a tax (tribute), v.i. ገበረ gạ́bbạrạ (-bär-).
Do they pay a tax (taxes)? ይገብራሉ። yịgạbbịrállu?
pay, make (cause to), v.t. አስከፈለ askạ́ffạlạ.
He will make them pay: ያስከፍላቸዋል። yaskạffịláččạuāl.
pea, s. አተር ā́tạr (-tär; § 52*a*, δ).
peace, s. እርቅ ị́rq.
peace, make, v.i. ተራረቀ tạrā́rrạqạ (tär-).
ተሰማማ tạsạmā́mmā̃ (täsäm-).
peach, s. ኮክ kʷok.
peasant, s. ባላገር bālā́gạr (-gär; § 52*a*, δ).
pebble, s. ጭንጫ č̣ị́nčā̃ (§ 52*a*, δ).
pedestrian, s. እግረኛ ịgrạ́ññā̃ (-rā́ñ-).
peel, s. ቅርፍት qị́rfịt.
peg, s. (for tethering, suspending etc.) ችካል čịkā́l (§ 8).
(tent-) ካስማ kā́sịmā̃ (-sŭm-; § 52*a*, δ).
Will the peg hold? ችካል፡ይችላል። čịkā́l yịčịlāl?
pelvic bone, s. አኒሳ annísā̃.
pen, s. (enclosure) በረት bạ́rạt (bắrät).
(for writing) ብር bịr.
መጣፊያ mạṭā́fyā̃.
A fountain pen: ቀለም፡ያለበት፡ብር፡ qạ́lạm yálläbbạ́t (§ 8) ṿịr (§ 7*d*).

pencil, s. [እ]ርሳስ (i̥)rsás (§ 8).
    መጣፊያ mḁṭáfyā̃.
penis, s. ቍላ qwū́lā̃.
    ጇላ jállā̃.
    (euphem.) ብልት bi̥lli̥t.
people, s. (persons) ሰው sḁ͡u (§§ 8, 52*a*, δ).
    (tribe) ዘር zḁr (zär; § 8).
  There are many people: ብዙ፡ሰው፡አለ። bi̥zu sḁ͡u állä.
  He incites the people to rebellion: ሰው፡ያሳምጣል። sḁ͡u yāsámmi̥ṭāl.
pepper, s. (black) ቍንዶ፡በርበሬ qúndʷo bḁrbḁrʸe (ya̤r-, -ry̤-, -ā́rʸe).
    (red) በርበሬ bḁrbḁrʸe (bä-, -ry̤-, -ā́rʸe).
per cent., ከመቶ kḁmḁtʷo (ተ- tḁ-; § 47*a*).
  Ten per cent.: ከመቶ፡አሥር፡ kḁmḁtʷo ássi̥r.
Perdrix coturnix (Guidi, Vocab. p. 663), s. ድርጭት di̥r-či̥t (§ 52*a*, δ).
perfect, adj. ሙሉ mū́lu (ምሉ mi̥lu).
perfume, s. ሽታ ší̥ttā̃.
perfume, v.t. አጠነ áṭṭḁnḁ.
perfumed, be, v.p. ታጠነ táṭṭḁnḁ (§ 63*d*, *e*).
perhaps, adv. ወይ wḁ͡i̥ (wǡi̥).
    ቢሆን bíhʷón (bi̥h-; § 8).
    ድንገት dí̥ngḁt.
    ምናልባት mi̥nā̃lbāt (-lyā-, -ባች -yāč).
  Perhaps you will want it: ወይ፡ትፈልገው፡ይሆናል። wḁ͡i̥ ti̥fḁlli̥gḁ͡u yi̥hʷónāl (s.v. √ሀወነ).
peritoneum, s. ሞራ mʷórā̃.
permanence, s. መኖር mḁnʷő̄r (§ 8; inf. of ኖረ q.v.).
permanent, adj. ኗሪ nwā̃ri.
permanent, be, v.i. ኖረ nʷő̄rḁ.

permission, s. ፍቃድ fi̥qád (§ 8).

permit, v.t. ተወ tḁ́wḁ (tḁ́͡uḁ).

I will not permit it: አልተወውም። altḁ́͡uḁ͡um.

If you permit it: ብትተወው፡ bi̥tti̥tḁ́͡uḁ͡u, pol. ቢተ ዉት፡ bitḁ́͡uut.

perseverance, s. ትጋት ti̥gắt (§ 8).

persevere, v.i. ተጋ tḁ́ggā̃.

persevering, adj. ትጉ ti̥gu.

persist (be persistent), v.i. ችክ፡አለ či̥kk álḁ (s.v. √ባለ, § 44*a*; § 63*d, e*).

The rain is persistent: ዝናብ፡ችክ፡ብሏል። zi̥nắy̥ čí̥kkĭ̥ (§ 7*d*) y̥í̥l͡ŏāl.

persistent, adj. ቾክቻክ čḁkčắkkā̃.

person, s. ሰው sḁ́͡u.

(body) ሰውነት sḁ́͡unnḁt (-nät).

Young person: አሽከር፡ áškḁr (-kär).

perspiration, s. ወዝ wḁz (wωz).

ላብ lāb (lāy̥).

perspire, v.i. ወዛ wḁ́zzā̃ (wώz-).

persuade, v.t. አስረዳ asrḁ́ddā̃.

persuaded, be, v.p. ተረዳ tḁrḁ́ddā̃.

pester, v.t. ነዘነዘ nḁzḁ́nnḁzḁ.

He (it) pesters me: ይነዘንዘኛል። yi̥nḁzḁ́nni̥zäññāl.

pestering, adj. ነዝናዛ nḁznắzzā̃.

petroleum, s. †ላምባ lámbā̃.

pewter, s. ቈርቈሮ qwωrqwώrr[w]o.

Phacochoerus æthiopicus, s. እርያ i̥ryā̃.

ከርከሮ kḁrkḁ́rr[w]o (kär-, -kắr-; Gall.).

Phaseolus sp., s. አደንጓሬ adḁṅgwắr[y]e (-dωṅ-).

Phoenix dactylifera (Broun, Cat. 595), s. ሰሌን sḁ́l[y]ḗn (§ 8).

piastre, s. ግርሽ gi̥rš (§ 52*a*, δ).

pick (scrape, off, out), v.t. ሰቀሰቀ sḁqḁ́ssḁqḁ.

Pick it (them § 52*a*, δ) off: ሰቅስቀው። sḁ́qsi̥qḁu͡, pl. -ቁት። -qut.

pick (up), v.t. ለቀመ lḁ́qqḁmḁ.

Pick it (them § 52*a*, δ) (up): ልቀመው። lí̥qḁmḁu͡, pl. -ሙት። -mut.

Where did you pick it up? ተዬት፡ለቀምሀው። tḁyét lḁ́qqḁmhḁu͡?

pick out, v.t. (extract) ነቀሰ nḁ́qqḁsḁ.

Pick it (them § 52*a*, δ) out: ንቀሰው። ní̥qḁsḁu͡, pl. -ሱት። -sut.

Pick out this thorn for me: ይህን፡እሾህ፡ንቀስልኝ። yi̥hánn i̥̥šʷóh ní̥qḁsi̥lli̥ñ.

picking (off, out), instrument for, s. መሰቅሰቂያ mḁsḁq-sḁ́qyã (-sḁ́qyã, -sḁ́čã).

pickaxe, s. መቈፈሪያ mḁqwωffḁ́ryã (-fár-).

picked, be, v.p. ተለቀመ tḁlḁ́qqḁmḁ.

It is (they are § 52*a*, δ) not to be picked: አይለቀም። a͡i̥llḁ́qḁm.

When is the coffee picked? በምን፡ጊዜ፡ነው፡ቡን፡እሚለቀም። bḁmí̥n gi̥zʸé nḁu͡ yunn i̥mmi̥llḁ́qqḁm?

pickles, s. ሆምጣጣ hʷomṭáṭṭã (ኮም- kʷom-, -ጣጤ -ṭáṭʸe).

picture, s. ምስል mí̥si̥l.

ሥ[ዕ]ል si̥l.

ምሳሌ mi̥ssálʸe.

piebald, adj. ሴደርማ sʸedḁrí̥mmã (-där-).

piece, s. ቍራጭ qúrráč̣ (§ 8).

Give me a piece of bread: ጥቂት፡ዳቦ፡ስጠኝ። ṭí̥qi̥t dábbʷo sí̥ṭäñ.

They will work by the piece: በውል፡ይሰራሉ። bḁu͡l yi̥sḁrállu (or በቍርጥ፡...bḁqwúrṭ...).

piecework, do, v.i. በቍርጥ፡ሰራ bḁqwŭ́rṭ sḁ́rrã.
በውል፡ሰራ bḁ͡úl sḁ́rrã.
pierce, v.i. & t. ሰረሰረ sḁrḁ́ssḁrḁ (särḁ́ssärḁ).
ወጋ wώggã (ʷώg-).
pierced, be, v.p. ተሰረሰረ tḁsḁrḁ́ssḁrḁ (-särḁ́ssärḁ).
ተወጋ tḁwώggã (tḁ͡uώ-).
pig, s. አሳማ ãsámã.
pigeon, s. (domestic) [እ]ርግብ rı̥́gı̥b (ı̥́rg-, -ı̥y̥).
(large wild) ቡላል búllál (§ 8).
(small wild) ዋልያ wā̆lyã.
pile, s. ክምር kı̥́mmı̥r.
pile (up), v.t. ከመረ kḁ́mmḁrḁ (-mär-).
Pile it (them § 52*a*, δ) up: ክምረው። kḁ́mmı̥rḁ͡u, pl. -ሩት። -rut.
piled (up), be, v.p. ተከመረ tḁkḁ́mmḁrḁ (-mär-).
pillage, v.i. & t. ዘረፈ zḁ́rrḁfḁ (zā̆r-).
ወረረ wώrrḁrḁ.
Don't pillage it: አትዝረፈው። attı̥́zrḁfḁ͡u, pl. -ፉት። -fut.
pillaged, be, v.p. ተዘረፈ tḁzḁ́rrḁfḁ (täzā̆r-).
It is not to be pillaged: አይዘረፍ። ḁ͡izzḁ́rḁf.
pillow, s. መከዳ mḁk(k)ḁ́ddã.
ትራስ tı̥rā̆s (§ 8).
pimp, s. አቃጣሪ aqqāṭā̆ri.
pin, s. ወረንጦ wḁrḁ́nṭʷo (§ 52*a*, δ).
pincers, s. ጕጠት gwŭ̄ṭḁt (-ṭät).
መቈንጠጫ mḁqwωnṭḁ́č̣ã (-ṭā̆č̣-).
pinch, v.i. & t. ቈነጠጠ qwωnḁ́ṭṭḁṭḁ.
Pinch him (it): ቈንጥጠው። qwώnṭı̥ṭḁ͡u, pl. -ጡት። -ṭut.
pipe, s. (tobacco-) መጠጫ mḁṭḁ́č̣č̣ã.
(water-) ቧምቧ bwā̆mbwã.

Fetch my pipe and tobacco: መጠጫውንም፡ትምበኋንም፡ይዛህ፡ና። mḁṭḁc̣c̣a͡úni̥m ṭi̥mbḁuha͡úni̥m (§ 7*d*) yi̥záh na.

Piper nigrum, s. ቁንዶ፡በርበሬ qúndʷo bḁrbḁrʸe (ṿär-, -rṿ-, -ắrʸe).

Pircunia abessinica (Guidi, Vocab. p. 471), s. እንዶድ (i̥)ndʷod.

pistol, s. ሹጉጥ šŭ́gguṭ.

Pisum sp., s. አተር ắtḁr (-tär; § 52*a*, δ).

pit, s. ጉድጓድ gúdgwắd (gúrg- § 7*d*; § 8).

Pit of the stomach, s. በጃድ bắjäd.

pitch, v.t. (a tent) ተከለ tḁ́kkḁlḁ.

Pitch (pl.) it: ትከሉት። tí̥kḁlut.

Don't (pl.) pitch it: አትትከሉት። attí̥tkḁlut.

Have you (pl.) pitched the tent? ድንኳኑን፡ተክላችኋል። dŭ́ṅkwánun tḁkláčči̥hwāl?

pitched, be, v.p. (of a tent) ተተከለ tḁtḁ́kkḁlḁ.

It is to be pitched here: ከዚህ፡ይተከል። käzzí̥h yi̥ttḁ́kḁl.

It is not to be pitched: አይተከል። a͡i̥ttḁ́kḁl, pl. -ከሉ። -kḁlu.

When it is pitched tell me: ሲተከል፡ንገረኝ። si̥ttḁ́kkḁl ní̥gḁräñ.

pitchfork, s. መንሽ mḁnš (mänš).

pity, s. ም[ሕ]ረት mí̥(h)rḁt (-rät).

አዘን ắzḁn.

pity, v.t. አዘነ ázzḁnḁ ለ- lḁ- (§ 47*a*).

Pity him: እዘንለት። í̥zḁni̥llḁt, pl. -ኑለት። -nullḁt.

place, s. ስፍራ sí̥frā̃.

Š. ስርፋ sí̥rfā̃.

መቀመጫ mḁqqḁmḁ́čā̃.

ቦታ bʷótā̃.

Put it in its place: ከስፍራው፡ አኑረው። kḁsı̥́frau ánurḁu, pl. ...፡ አኑሩት፡። ... ánurut.

Put (pl.) each thing in its place: ሁሉ፡ በየስፍራው፡ አድርጉት። húllu yḁyyási̥frau ádri̥gut (árgut § 7*d*).

Is there no place for it? ስፍራ፡ የለውሞይ። sı̥́fra yállḁummwı̥? (s.v. ወይ).

Who knows the place it came from? የመጣበትን፡ ስፍራ፡ ማን፡ ያውቃል። yämḁṭṭábbḁtun sı̥́fra mān yáuqāl?

place, v.t. አስቀመጠ asqḁ́mmḁṭḁ.
 አደረገ adḁ́rrḁgḁ.
 አኖረ anʷṓrḁ.

placed, be, v.p. ተደረገ tḁdḁ́rrḁgḁ.

plague, s. በሽታ bḁ́ši̥tā.

plain, adj. (obvious) ትይዩ ti̥(y)íyyu.
 (clear) ብሩ bı̥́ru.

plain, s. ሜዳ mʸédā.

Grassy plain: መስክ፡ mḁsk.

plaintiff, s. ከሳሽ kḁ́sā́š (§ 8).

plan, s. (arrangement) ሥራት sı̥rā́t (§ 8).

This plan is not a good one: ይህ፡ ሥራት፡ አይመችም። yı̥he si̥rā́t ai̥mmáčči̥m.

plank, s. ጠርብ ṭḁrb (ṭä-, -ry̥).

plant, s. ትክል tı̥́ki̥l.

plant, v.t. ተከለ tḁ́kkḁlḁ.
 ዘራ zḁ́rrā (zā́r-).

plantain (*Musa sapientium,* Broun, Cat. 559), s. ሙዝ muz (§ 52*a*, δ).

plantain, wild (*Musa Ensete,* Broun, Cat. 559), s.
 እንሰት (ı̥)nsḁt (-sät).
 (inedible) ጉናጉና gunágunā.

planted, be, v.p. ተተከለ tatakkala.
ተዘራ tazárrā (täzär-).
plate, s. ሰሐን sahān (§ 8).
plateau, s. (small) አምባ ámbā.
(large, the high country) ደጋ dágā (däg-).
On the plateau: በደጋ፡ badága.
play, s. ጨወታ čáwatā (čáu-, -ωt-).
play, v.i. ተጫወተ tačáuwata (-wωt-).
playful, adj. ተጫዋች tačáuāč (§ 8).
pleasant, adj. ማለፊያ mālāfyā.
please, v.t. ደስ፡አሰኘ dass (däss) assáññä.
Did he (it) please him? ደስ፡አሰኘው። däss assáññäu?
please (if you), እባክህ ibákkih (ivá-), f. -ክሽ -kkiš, pol. -ክዎ -kkaʷo, pl. -ካችሁ -kkāč(č)yuh (§ 7*d*), according to person or persons addressed.
እስኪ- [-ስቲ-] (i)ski- (-sti-) pref. to imperative.
-ልኝ -lliñ (for me).
-ልን[-ልነ] -llin (-llinna) (for us).
Please give it to me: እባክህ፡ስጠኝ። ivákkih sitañ, pol. እባክዎ፡ይስጡኝ። ivákkaʷo yistuñ.
Please give us some wood: እንጨት፡እስቲስጠን። ńčät istisitan.
Please go away (from us): ሒድልነ፡ተዚህ። hídillinna tazzíh.
pleased, be, v.i. ደስ፡አለ dass (däss) ála.
ደስ፡አለው dass (-ä-) ālau (impers. § 43*a*).
S.v. √በለ, § 44*a*; § 63*d*, *e*.
I am pleased: ደስ፡ይለኛል። däss yilāññāl.

I am pleased with you: ባንተ፡ደስ፡ይሎኛል። bántä (ታንተ፡ tántä) däss y̥ílʷoññāl.

pleasure, interj. expressing, እሰይ (i̥)ssá͡i̥ !

pleasure, s. ደስታ dḁ́ss(ĭ̥)tã.

pledge, s. አደራ ádḁ́rã (-dắr-; § 8).

plentiful, be, v.i. መላ mḁ́llã or ሞላ mʷóllã.

It is plentiful: ሞልቷል። mʷóltŏ͡āl.

plenty, s. ብዙ bí̥zu (§§ 52*a*, 53*b*).

እጅግ í̥jji̥g.

There is plenty: እጅግ፡አለ። í̥jji̥g állä.

This is plenty: ይህ፡እጅግ፡ነው። yi̥he i̥jjíg (§ 8) nḁ͡u.

pliant, adj. (of inanimate objects) ለስላሳ lḁslássã.

pliant, be (become), v.i. ለሰለሰ lḁsḁ́llḁsḁ (§ 63*d*, *e*).

pliant, render, v.t. አለሰለሰ alḁsḁ́llḁsḁ.

It renders it pliant: ያለሰልሰዋል። yālḁsḁ́lli̥sḁ͡uāl.

pliers, s. ጉጠት gwŭ́ṭḁt (-ṭät).

plough, s. ማረሻ mārắšã.

ሞፈር mʷófḁr (-fär).

plough, v.i. & t. አረሰ árrḁsḁ.

(new ground) ገመሰ gḁ́mmḁsḁ.

ploughman, s. አራሽ ắrắš (§ 8).

ploughshare, s. ድግር dí̥gi̥r.

pluck out, v.t. ነጨ nắč̣č̣ä.

ነቀለ nḁ́qqḁlḁ.

plucked out, be, v.p. ተነጨ tḁnắč̣č̣ä.

plum, wild (*Prunus insititia*), s. እንኰይ (í̥)ṅkwḁ͡i̥ (§ 8).

plunder, s. እቃ í̥qã.

plunder, v.i. & t. ዘረፈ zḁ́rrḁfḁ.

ወረረ wώrrḁrḁ.

Anybody that plunders will be punished: የሚዘርፍ፡ይቀጣል። yämmi̥zárf yi̥qqḁ́ṭṭāl.

plundered, be, v.p. ተዘረፈ. tḁzḁ́rrḁfḁ.

It is not to be plundered: አይዘረፍ። a͡izzḁ́rḁf.

Poa abessinica (Guidi, Vocab. p. 836), s. ጤፍ ṭʸēf.

pocket, s. ጂብ jʸēb (jʸēṿ).

ጐስጓስ gwúsgwás (§ 8).

ኪስ kis.

poet, s. አዝማሪ azmári.

point, s. (of a needle, etc.) ሹል šul.

(station) ምዕራፍ mi̥ráf (§ 8).

Up to this point: እስተዚሁ፡ምዕራፍ፡ i̥stäzzi̥h mi̥rāf.

There's no point in it: ፍሬ፡ የለውም። fi̥rʸe yállḁ͡um.

point (out, to), v.i. & t. አመለከተ amḁlḁ́kkḁtḁ.

pointed, adj. ሹል šul (§ 57*b*).

poison, s. መርዝ mḁrz (märz).

He died by poison: በመድኃኒት፡ሞተ። bḁmḁdhánʸi̥t (-dáhnit § 7*d*) mʷótḁ.

poison, v.t. (inanimate object) መርዝ፡አደረገ፡በ- mḁrz adḁ́rrḁgḁ bḁ- (vḁ-; § 47*a*).

(animate object) መርዝ፡አበላ mḁrz abḁ́llã (ayḁ́-).

He poisoned the food: በመብል፡መርዝ፡አደረገበት። bḁmḁ́vi̥l mḁrz adḁ́rrḁgḁbbḁt.

He poisoned him (it): መርዝ፡አበላው። mḁrz ayḁ́lla͡u.

poisonous, adj. መርዛም mḁ́rzám (már-; § 8).

pole, s. መሰሶ mḁsḁ́ssʷo.

polite, adj. የተቀጣ yätḁqḁ́ṭṭã (§ 14; s.v. ቀጣ).

polo, s. እሩር፡ጨዋታ i̥rūr čḁ́͡uωtã.

ገና gḁ́nnã.

polo-stick, s. የሩር፡መምቻ yärūr (§§ 47*a*, 70) mḁ́mčã.

pond, s. ኵሬ kwúrʸe.

pony, s. ፈረስ fḁ́rḁs.

pool, s. ኵሬ kwŭrʸe.
poor, adj. ደኃ dáhã.
(in quality) ምሩጭ mɨ̥rráč̣ (§ 8).
pop, v.i. (produce a slight explosion) ጣጣ፡አለ ṭáṭṭa álḁ (s.v. √ባለ, § 44a).
populous, adj. ለም lḁm (läm).
porcupine (*Hystrix sp.*), s. ጃርት jart.
portfolio, s. ማኅደር máhdḁr (mahád-, -där, § 7d).
Š. †ቦርሳ bʷórsã.
portray, v.t. ሳለ sálḁ (conjug. like ሳለ to cough).
መሰለ mḁssḁlḁ (type B § 35).
position, s. (place) ቦታ bʷótã.
ስፍራ sɨ̥frã.
Š. ስርፋ sɨ̥rfã.
መቀመጫ mḁqqḁmḁč̣ã.
possess, v.t. ገዛ gḁzzã.
possessed, be, v.p. ተገዛ tḁgḁzzã.
possessions, s. ንብረት nɨ̥brḁt (-ɨ̥yr-, -rät).
possible, be, v.i. ተቻለ tḁčálḁ.
post, s. (postal service) †ቡስጣ búsṭã.
†ፖስታ pʷóstã.
(pole) መሰሶ mḁsássʷo.
(station) ፈንታ fḁntã.
post, v.t. (mail) ከቡስጣ፡አገባ kḁyúsṭã agḁbbã (ተቡ- tḁyú-).
ከፖስታ፡አገባ kḁpʷósta agḁbbã (ተፖ- tḁpʷó-).
(station) አቆመ aqʷŏmḁ.
Post this letter: ይህንን፡ደብዳቤ፡ከፖስታ፡አግባው። yɨ̥hánnän dḁydábbʸe kḁpʷósta ágyau.
Post a man there: ሰው፡አቁምበት። sḁu áqumɨ̥bbḁt.
postage-stamp, s. †ቴምብር tämbr (§ 52a, δ).

posted, be, v.p. (mailed) ከቡስጣ፡ገባ kạyústạ gạ́bbā̃ (ተቡ-tạyú-).

ከፖስታ፡ገባ kạpʷósta gạ́bbā̃ (ተፖ-tạpʷó-).

Have all the letters been posted? ደብዳቤ፡ሁሉ፡ተቡስጣ፡ገብቷል። dạydábbʸe (§ 52*a*) húllu tạyúsṭa gạ́ytȭāl?

Stay where you were posted: ከቆምሁበት፡ስፍራ፡ቁይ። kāqʷómhubbạt sịfrá qwǭị, (lit. at the place at which I posted you; s.v. የ-, §§ 14, 62*c*).

postman, s. †ቡስጠኛ busṭạ́ññā̃ (-ṭáñ-).

post-office, s. †የቡስጣ፡ቤት yäyusṭá yʸēt.

†የፖስታ፡ቤት yäpʷostá yʸēt.

See § 8 enclitics; §§ 47*a*, 70.

At the post-office: ከቡስጣ፡ቤት፡ kạyusṭá yʸēt.

pot, s. ቶፋ tʷōfā̃.

ምንቸት mịnčät.

(chamber-) መሸኛ mạšạ́ñā̃ (-šáñ-).

ባሬታ bārʸétā̃.

potato (*Coleus tuberosus,* Guidi, Vocab. p. 676), s. ድንች dịnnịč (-čč § 6; § 52*a*, δ).

potter, s. ሸክላ፡ሰሪ šạ́kla (šák-) sạri (sári).

pottery, s. ሸክላ šạklā̃ (šák-).

pound, s. (weight) ነጥር nạ́ṭịr (náṭ-).

pound, v.t. ወቀጠ wǭqqạṭạ.

pounded, be, v.p. ተወቀጠ tạwǭqqạṭạ (tạuǭ-).

pour (out), v.t. ገለበጠ gạlạ́bbạṭạ.

ቀዳ qạ́ddā̃.

Pour it (e.g. tea) out: ቅዳው። qịdau.

pour away, v.t. አፈሰሰ afạ́ssạsạ.

Pour it away: አፍሰው። afịssạu.

Don't pour it away: አታፍሰው። attafịssạu.

poured (out), be, v.p. ተገለበጠ tḁgḁlḁ́bbḁṭḁ.
ተቀዳ tḁqḁ́ddã.
powder, s. (gen.) ዶቄት d^{w}ṓq^{y}ĕt (§ 8).
(gunpowder) ባሩድ bárud.
power, s. ኃይል hḁ͡il.
(authority) ሹመት šúmḁt (-mät).
ችሎት čí̥l^{w}ot (§ 8).
powerful, adj. (gen.) ኃይለኛ hḁ͡ilḁ́ññã (-lā́ñ-).
(physically) ቀልጥማም qi̥lṭi̥mā́m (§ 8).
ብርቱ bí̥rtŭ.
practice, be (get) out of, v.i.
ተጎዳ tḁgwώddã.
ገደፈ gḁ́ddḁfḁ (type A § 34).
ተገደፈው tḁgḁ́ddḁfḁ͡u (impers. § 43*a*).
See § 63*d*, *e*.

I am out of practice: ተጎድቻለኍ። tḁgwωdi̥ččál-lḁ͡u^{h}, or ተገድፎኛል። tḁgḁ́df^{w}oññāl.

practice, out of, adj. ገዳፋ gḁdā́fã.
praise, s. ምስጋና mi̥sgā́nã.
praise, v.t. አመሰገነ amḁsḁ́ggḁnḁ.
praised, be, v.p. ተመሰገነ tḁmḁsḁ́ggḁnḁ.
prate, v.i. ለፈለፈ lḁfḁ́llḁfḁ.
pray, v.i. ጠለየ ṭḁ́llḁyä (-lḁ͡iä).
prayer, s. ጠሎት ṭḁ́l^{w}ot (§ 8).
precede, v.i. & t. ቀደመ qḁ́ddḁmḁ.
precipice, s. ገደል gḁ́dḁl (gā́däl).
prefer, v.t. ወደደ wώddḁdḁ.
አበለጠ abḁ́llḁṭḁ (ay̥ḁ́-).
(to, ከ- kḁ-, ተ- tḁ-, § 47*a*).

We prefer horses to mules: ተበቅሎ፡ፈረስ፡እንወዳለን። tḁy̥ḁ́ql^{w}o (§ 52*a*) fḁ́rḁs i̥nnwωddállän.

I prefer walking to riding: ከመቀመጥ፡በግሬ፡መሔድ፡ እወዳለሁ። kḁmḁqqḁ́mḁṭ yḁ́grʸe mḁhád i̥wωddállḁ͡uʰ (§ 7*d*).

preferred, be, v.p. ተወደደ tḁwώddḁdḁ (tḁ͡uώ-).

pregnant, adj. ርጉዝ ri̥gúz (§ 8).

እርጉዝ i̥rgúz (§ 8).

prepare, v.i. (oneself, v.r., be prepared, v.p.) ተሰናዳ tḁsḁnắddã (täsän-).

Let him (it) be prepared: ይሰናዳ። yi̥ssḁnáda.

Prepare to go: እንድትሔድ፡ተሰናዳ። ndi̥tthád tḁsḁnáda, pl. እንድትሔዱ፡ተሰናዱ። ndi̥tthádu tḁsḁnádu.

prepare, v.t. አሰናዳ assḁnắddã.

Prepare it: አሰናዳው። assḁnáda͡u, pl. -ዱት። -dut.

Let him prepare it: ያሰናዳው። yassḁnáda͡u, pl. -ዱት። -dut.

prepuce, s. ወሸላ wḁ́šḁlã (wώš-; § 8).

presence, s. መኖር mḁ́nʷőr (§ 8; inf. of ኖረ q.v.).

present, adj.

The present one: ያሁኑ፡ yáhunu (= የ- § 47*a* + አሁን now § 7*a* + art. § 11).

present, s. ስጦታ si̥ṭʷőtã.

መተያያ mḁttḁyắyã (-tḁ͡i̥ắ͡i̥ã).

ጉርሻ gúršã.

It is not our custom to accept presents: በኛ፡ሥራት፡ መተያያ፡አንቀበልም። bḁññá si̥rát mḁttḁ͡i̥á͡i̥a (§ 52*a*) anni̥qqḁ́bbḁli̥m.

present, v.t. (give) ሰጠ sḁ́ṭṭḁ.

(introduce) አገናኘ aggḁnắññä.

present, be, v.i. ኖረ nʷőrḁ.

አለ állä (§§ 32*a*, *d*, 39*a*, *b*).

I wish you to be present: ልትኖር፡እፈልጋለሁ። l̥itti̥-nʷór i̥fḁlli̥gállḁu͡ʰ, ...you (pl.)... -ኖሩ፡ ...-nʷóru....

He is not present: የለም። yállām, pl. የሉም። yállum.

presentiment, have a, v.i. ቅር፡አለው qi̥rr álḁu͡ (impers. § 43*a*; s.v. √በለ, § 44*a*; § 63*d*, *e*), constr. with በ- bḁ- (§ 47*a*).

I have a presentiment about this: በዚህ፡ቅር፡አለኝ። bäzzi̥h qi̥rr áläñ.

press, v.t. (on) ጨቈነ ç̣ḁ́qqwωnḁ (ç̣ώqqonḁ).

(against) ገፋ gḁ́ffā.

pressed, be, v.p. (on) ተጨቈነ tḁç̣ḁ́qqwωnḁ (-ç̣ώqqonḁ).

(against) ተገፋ tḁgḁ́ffā.

pretend, v.i. & t. አደረገ adḁ́rrḁgḁ.

አስመሰለ asmḁ́ssḁlḁ.

He pretends he is ill: ራሱን፡ታማሚ፡ያደርጋል። rásun tāmámi yādárgāl.

He is telling lies and pretending to tell the truth: ውሸት፡ነገር፡አምጥቶ፡እውነት፡አስመስሎ፡ይናገራል። wúšät nágär ámţi̥tʷo únät äsmḁ́ssi̥lʷo yi̥nnággäräl.

He pretended not to know: አላውቅም፡ብሎ፡ዋሸ። aláu͡qi̥m bi̥lʷo wáššä.

pretty, adj. ውብ wŭb (wŭỵ).

prevent, v.t. ከለከለ kḁlḁ́kkḁlḁ.

Neg. conjug. (§ 37) of causative verbs (§ 22*a*) with አለ álḁ (s.v. √በለ, § 44*a*).

Prevent him (it): ከልክለው። kḁ́lki̥lḁu͡, pl. -ሉት። -lut.

Don't prevent him (it): አትከልክለው። atti̥kḁ́lki̥lḁu͡, -ሉት። -lut.

The moon prevented me from sleeping: ጨረቃ፡አላስተኛኝም፡አለች። ç̣ḁrḁqá alastáññāññi̥mm áläč.

prevented, be, v.p. ተከለከለ tḁkḁlḁ́kkḁlḁ.
  He (it) must be prevented: ይከልከል። yi̥kkḁ́lkḁl, pl. -ሉ። -lu.
  He (it) is not to be prevented: አይከልከል። a͡i̥kkḁ́lkḁl, pl. -ሉ። -lu.
previously, adv. አስቀድሞ asqḁ́ddi̥mʷo.
price, s. ዋጋ wágã.
  What is its price? ዋጋው፡ስንት፡ነው። wága͡u si̥nti̥ nḁ͡u?
  It fetched a good price: አኩሎ፡ተሸጠ። ákkŭlʷo tḁšáṭḁ (s.v. አከለ).
prick, v.t. ጠነቈለ ṭḁnḁ́qqwωlḁ.
  ወጋ wώggã (ʷώg-).
  A thorn has pricked me: እሾህ፡ወጋኝ። i̥šʷőh wώggãñ (-őhʷώg-).
pricked, be, v.p. (prick oneself, v.r.) ተወጋ tḁwώggã (tḁ͡uώ-).
  Take care you don't prick yourself: እንዳትወጋ። ndatti̥wwώgga, ...yourselves: -ወጉ። -wwώggu.
prickle, v.t. ኰሰኰሰ kwωsḁ́kkwωsḁ (-sώkkosḁ).
prickly, adj. ኰስኳሳ kwωskwássã.
pride, s. ኩራት kúrát (§ 8).
priest, s. ካህን káhi̥n, pl. also ካህናት káh(i̥)nát (§ 8).
  ቄስ qʸēs, pl. also ቀሳውስት qʸesa͡úst (§ 8), and ቀሳውስቶች qʸesa͡ústʷōč (-čč § 6).
princess, s. ወይዘሮ wḁ͡i̥zḁrʷo (w͡ώi̥-, -zär-), pl. also ወይዛዝር wḁ͡i̥zázi̥r [-ዛዝሮች -zázi̥rʷōč (-čč § 6)].
print, v.t. ኀተመ háttа̥mḁ (አተመ áttа̥mḁ).
printed, be, v.p. ታተመ táttа̥mḁ.
  It is (has been) printed: ታትሟል። tátti̥m͡ōāl.
  It ought to be printed: ይታተም፡ነበር። yi̥ttáttа̥m nḁ́bbär.

printed, cause (allow) to be, v.t. አሳተመ asắttḁmḁ (§ 68).
I will have it printed: አሳትመዋለኍ። asatti̥mḁu͡állạuʰ (§ 7*d*).

prison, s. የግዞት፡ቤት yägi̥zʷót bʸēt (y̥ʸēt).
የስር፡ቤት yäsi̥r bʸēt (y̥-).
የምድር፡ቤት yämdi̥r bʸēt (y̥-).
You must go to prison: ታሰር። tắsḁr, pl. ታሰሩ። tắsḁru.
Take care you don't go to prison: እንዳትታሰር። ndatti̥ttắssḁr, pl. -ሰሩ። -ssḁru.
He must go to prison: ይታሰር። yi̥ttắsḁr, pl. -ሰሩ። -sḁru.
You will go to prison: ትታሰራለህ። ti̥ttāssḁrállāh, pl. -ራላችሁ። -rallắččyuh (§ 7*d*).
If he is found, he will go to prison: ቢገኝ፡ይታሰራል። bi̥ggḁ̆́ñ (§ 6), yi̥ttắssḁrāl, pl. ቢገኙ፡ይታሰራሉ። bi̥g-gḁ̆́ññu yi̥ttāssḁrállu.
He is in prison: ታስሯል። tắsrō͡āl, pol. & pl. ታስረዋል። tắsrḁ͡uāl.
He has come out of prison: ተፈትቷል። tḁfḁ̆́ttō͡āl, pol. & pl. ተፈትተዋል። tḁfḁ̆́ttḁuāl.

prisoner, s. እስረኛ asrḁ̆́ññã (-rắñ-).
(of war) ምርኮኛ mi̥rkʷóññã.
ምርኮ mi̥rkʷo.
See § 52*a*, δ.

prisoner, be taken, v.p. ተማረከ tḁmắrrḁkḁ.

prisoner, take, v.t. ማረከ mắrrḁkḁ.

private, adj. (ground, etc.) ክልክል ki̥li̥kki̥l.

probably, adv. ድንገት di̥ngа̥t (-gät).
(standing alone) ይሆናል። yi̥hʷṓnāl.

proclamation, s. አዋጅ áu͡áj (§ 8).

procreate, v.i. & t. ወለደ wḁ̆́llḁdḁ (wál-, wώl-).

procure, v.t. (for hire) አቃጠረ aqqắṭṭḁrḁ (-ṭär-).

procurer, s. አቃጣሪ aqqāṭári.

profit, s. ትርፍ ti̥rf.

ፍሬ fí̥rʸe, pl. ፍሬዎች fí̥reʷōč (-čč § 6).

What profit did you make? ምን፡ያህል፡አተረፍህ። mi̥n yahl atḁ́rrḁfh?

profit, v.i. አተረፈ atḁ́rrḁfḁ (-tär-).

prohibited, adj. ክልክል ki̥lí̥kki̥l.

promote, v.t. ጨመረ čḁ́mmḁrḁ.

ሾመ šʷṓmḁ.

promoted, be, v.p. ተሾመ tḁšʷōmḁ (täš-).

ተጨመረለት tḁčḁ́mmḁrḁllḁt (impers. § 43*a*; § 47*a*).

When were you promoted? መቼ፡ተሾምህ። mḁ́čʸe tḁšʷómh? (-ምኽ -mk, -ṅk, § 7*d*).

If you act like that you will not get promoted: እንዲህ፡ብታደርግ፡አይጨመርልህም። ndi̥h yi̥ttādárg ai̥čḁ́mmäri̥lli̥hi̥m.

pronunciation, s. አነጋገር annḁgắgḁr (-gär).

ንግግር ni̥gí̥ggi̥r.

proper, adj. (-ly, adv.) በውል bḁ́ul (bḁúl, § 8).

Use the article (§ 11).

Do it properly: በውል፡አድርገው። bḁúl árgḁu (§ 7*d*).

At the proper time: በጊዜው፡ bḁgí̥zʸeu.

This is not the proper place: ይህ፡ስፍራውም፡አይደል። yi̥he si̥fráumm (§ 37*b*) ái̥däl.

property, s. ከብት kḁyt (kḁft § 7*d*).

ገንዘብ gḁ́nzḁb (-ḁy).

ንብረት ní̥brḁt (ní̥yr-, -rät).

proportion, s. ተዋረድ tḁwā́rḁd (tḁ͡uā́-).

Pay them in proportion to their work: እንደስራቸው፡ በተዋረድ፡ክፈላቸው። ndäsi̥rā́ččḁ͡u ṿḁtḁ͡uā́rḁd ki̥fḁ-lā́ččḁ͡u.

proportionally, adv. በተዋረድ bḁtḁwā́rḁd (-ḁ͡uā́-).

prosecute, v.t. ከሰሰ kḁ́ssḁsḁ.

prosecuted, be, v.p. ተከሰሰ tḁkḁ́ssḁsḁ.

prosecutor, s. ከሳሽ kḁ́sā́š (§ 8).

prosperous, adj. ለም lḁm (läm).

prostitute, s. ገለሞታ gḁlḁm^{w}ṓtã.

prostrate oneself (in prayer), v.i. ሰገደ sḁ́ggḁdḁ (sḁ́ggädḁ).

protect, v.t. መከተ mḁ́kkḁtḁ ለ- lḁ- (§ 47*a*).

proud, adj. ኩሩ kúru.

proverb, s. ተረት tḁ́rḁt.

province, s. ግዛት gi̥zā́t (§ 8).

provisions, s. (gen.) መብል mḁ́bi̥l (-ḁ́ṿi̥-).

(for use while travelling) ሥንቅ si̥ṅq.

provoke, v.t. አስቈጣ asqwώṭṭã.

Don't provoke him (it): አታስቈጣው። attasqwώṭṭa͡u, pl. -ጡት። -ṭṭut.

He (it) is provoking: ሰው፡ያስቈጣል። sḁ͡u yasqwώṭ-ṭāl.

He (it) is very provoking (to me): እጅግ፡ያስቈጣኛል። í̥jji̥g yasqwώṭṭaññāl.

prudence, s. ብልሃት bí̥lhā́t (§ 8).

prudent, adj. ብልህ bí̥li̥h.

Is he prudent in business? ለንግድ፡ብልህ፡ነው። lḁ-ní̥gd ṿi̥lí̥h (§ 7*d*, § 8) nḁ͡u?

Prunus insititia, s. እንኰይ (i̥)ṅkwḁ͡i̥ (§ 52*a*, δ).

psalter, s. ዳዊት da͡uít.

Pterolobium abessinicum (Guidi, Vocab. p. 289), s. ቀንጠፋ qḁnṭḁ́ffã.

Ptilonorrhynchus albirostris (Guidi, Vocab. p. 569), s. ዋርዳ wárdā.

pudding, s. ጣፋጭ ṭáfáč̣ (§ 8).

ኣላዋ aláwā (aláuā).

pudenda, s. ብልት bịllịt (§ 52*a*, γ).

puff, v.t. እፍ፡ኣለ ịff ála (s.v. √በለ, § 44*a*).

Pulex irritans, s. ቍንጪ qwŭnịč̣č̣ā (§ 52*a*, δ).

pull, v.i. & t. ሳበ sába (sáya).

Pull: ሳብ። sāy, pl. ሳቡ። sáyu.

Don't pull: ኣትሳብ። attịsáy, pl. -ቡ። -yu.

Pull it: ሳበው። sáyau, pl. -ቡት። -yut.

Don't pull it: ኣትሳበው። attịsáyau, pl. -ቡት። -yut.

pulled, be, v.p. ተሳበ tasába (täs-, -áya).

pumpkin, wild (*Cucurbita maxima*, Broun, Cat. 209), s. ቅል qịl.

punish, v.t. ቀጣ qáṭṭā.

Punish him: ቅጣው። qịṭau, pol. ይቅጡት። yíqṭut.

Punish them: ቅጣቸው። qịṭáččau, pol. ይቅጧቸው። yịqṭwáččau.

Don't punish him: ኣትቅጣው። attíqṭau, pol. ኣይቅጡት። áịqṭut.

Don't punish them: ኣትቅጣቸው። attịqṭáččau, pol. ኣይቅጧቸው። aịqṭwáččau.

Did you punish him? ቀጣሀው። qáṭṭahau?, pol. ቀጡት። qáṭṭut?

punished, be, v.p. ተቀጣ taqáṭṭā.

He will be punished: ይቀጣል። yịqqáṭṭāl, pl. -ጣሉ። -ṭṭállu.

He should be punished: ይቀጣ። yịqqáṭa, pl. -ጡ። -ṭu.

He should not be punished: አይቀጣ። a͡i̥qqḁṭa, pl. -ጡ። -ṭu.

Has he been punished? ተቀጥቷል። tḁqḁṭṭŏāl, pl. -ጥተዋል። -ṭtḁ͡uāl?

punishment, s. ቅጣት qi̥ṭát (§ 8).

pupil, s. (learner) ተማሪ tḁmári.

(of eye) ብረት bi̥rḁt (-rät; § 52*a*, γ).

purchase, s. መግዛት mḁgzát (§ 8).

purchase, v.t. ገዛ gḁzzã.

purchased, be, v.p. ተገዛ tḁgḁzzã.

pure, adj. ጥሩ ṭi̥ru (ṭúru).

pure, be, v.i. ጠራ ṭḁrrã.

purify, v.t. አጠራ aṭḁrrã.

purple, adj. ጫጉማ ç̣ãgúmmã.

purpose, on,—use gerund of አወቀ á͡uwḁqḁ.

I did not do it on purpose: አውቄ፡አላደረግሁም። á͡uŭqq^{y}e aladḁrrḁghum.

I suppose you sent him (it) by mistake.—No, on purpose: አሳስተህ፡ላክሀውወይ።አይዶለም፡አውቄ፡ነው። assási̥täh lákhḁ͡uwwi̥? (lákkḁ͡u- § 7*d*; § 6).—a͡i̥dál-lämm (§§ 6, 7*d*) a͡uŭqq^{y}é (§ 8) nḁ͡u.

purr, v.i. አንኳረፈ aṅkwárrḁfḁ.

purse, s. ከረጢት kḁrḁṭít.

ማፉዳ mãfúdã.

pus, s. መግል mḁgi̥l.

push, v.i. & t. ገፋ gḁffã.

Push: ግፋ። gi̥fa, pl. ግፉ። gi̥fu.

Don't push: አትግፋ። atti̥gfa, pl. -ፉ። -fu.

pushed, be, v.p. ተገፋ tḁgḁffã.

put, v.t. አደረገ adḁrrḁgḁ.

አኖረ an^{w}ŏrḁ.

አስቀመጠ asqḁmmḁṭḁ.

Where did (have) you put it? ዬት፡አደረግሀው። yēt adárraghau?, pl. ዬት፡አደረጋችሁት። yēt adarragáččihut?

Where did (has) he put it? ዬት፡አደረገው። yēt adárragau?, pl. -ጉት። -gut?

I don't know where he (has) put it: ያደረገበትን፡ አላውቅም። yādárragabbatin aláuqim.

Put it here: ከዚህ፡አድርገው። kazzíh ádrigau (árgau § 7d), pl. -ጉት። -gut.

Put it down: አስቀምጠው። asqámmitau, pl. -ጡት። ṭut.

Put it right: በውል፡አድርገው። baúl árgau, pl. -ጉት። -gut.

Put it on the table: በገበታው፡ላይ፡አኑረው። bagayatáu lai ánurau, pl. -ሩት። -rut.

Put it back: መልሰው። mállisau, pl. -ሱት። -sut.

— Use the jussive of other verbs:

Put it near that I may see it: ቅርብ፡ይሁን፡እንዳየው። qiry yíhun (s.v. √ሀወነ) indáiau.

put, be, v.p. ተደረገ tadárraga.

Where was it put? ዬት፡ተደረገ። yēt tadárraga?, pl. -ጉ። -gu?

It is to be put here: ከዚህ፡ይደረግ። käzzíh yiddárag, pl. -ጉ። -gu.

put away, v.t. ወሰደ wássada (wώs-).

Put it away: ውሰደው። wúsadau, pl. -ዱት። -dut.

Put them away: ውሰዳቸው። wusadáččau, pl. -ዷቸው። -dwáččau.

put away, be, v.p. ተወሰደ tawássada (tauá-, -ώs-).

Has it been put away? ተወስዷል። tauώsdōal?, pl. -ደዋል። -daual?

put in (inside, indoors), v.t. አገባ agábbā̃.

Put it in: አግባው። ágyau, pl. አግቡት። ágyut.

Put them in: አግባቸው። āgyáččau, pl. -ቧቸው። -ywáččau.

Don't put it in: አታግባው። attágyau, pl. -ቡት። -yut.

Don't put them in: አታግባቸው። attāgyáččau, pl. -ቧቸው። -ywáččau.

Put the table inside: ገበታውን፡ አግባው። gayatáun ágyau.

put in, (etc.) be, v.p. ገባ gábbā̃.

Has it been put inside? ገብቷልዎይ። gáytōallwį? (s.v. ወይ).

put out, v.t. አወጣ awώṭṭā̃ (auώ-).

(extinguish) አጠፋ aṭáffā̃.

Put the dog out: ውሻውን፡ አውጣው። wúššaun áuṭau.

Put the light out: መብራቱን፡ አጥፋ። mayrātun áṭfa.

Don't put it out: አታጥፋው። attáṭfau.

python, s. ዘንዶ zándʷo.

Q

§ refers to the paragraphs of the Grammar (Initia Amharica, Part I).

quail (*Perdrix coturnix*, Guidi, Vocab., p. 663), s. ድርጭት dįrčįt (§ 52*a*, δ).

quality, s. ዓይነት áinat (-nät).

quantity, s. ልክ likk.

quarrel, s. ክርክር kịrịkkịr.

What is the cause of the quarrel? የክርክር፡ምክንያት፡ ምን፡ነው። yäkịrịkkịr mịknyät mịn-nau?

quarrel, v.i. ተጣላ tạṭällā.

ተከራከረ tạkạrắkkạrạ (-kärắkkär-).

Don't quarrel: አትጣላ። attịṭṭála, pl. -ሉ። -lu.

If you quarrel I shall dismiss you both: ብትጣሉ፡ ሁለታችሁ፡ አሰናብታችኋለሁ። bịttịṭṭállu hulättáč-čyuh assạnabbịtāččyuhállauʰ (§§ 7*d*, 12*c*).

quarrelsome, adj. ጥጋበኛ ṭịgābạ́ññā (-āy-, -áñ-).

quarter, s. (1/4) አራተኛ arāttịññā.

[እ]ሩብ (ị)rúb (-úy).

quarter troops on, v.t. ተሰሪ፡ሰደደ፡በ- tạsári sạ́ddạdạ bạ- (yạ-; § 47*a*).

quartered on, be, v.p. (of troops) ተሰሪ፡ገባ፡በ- tạsári gạ́bbā bạ- (yạ-; § 47*a*).

No troops will be quartered on them: ተሰሪ፡አይገባባቸውም። tạsári (§ 52*a*, δ) aigạyābbáččaum.

queen, s. ንግሥት nịgịst (§ 8).

queer, adj. ጉድ gud.

question, s. ጥያቄ ṭịyyáqʸe.

question, v.t. ጠየቀ ṭạ́yyạqạ (-yäq-).

Question him: ጠይቀው። ṭạ́yyịqạu.

Question them: ጠይቃቸው። ṭạyyịqáččạu.

questioned, be, v.p. ተጠየቀ tạṭạ́yyạqạ (-yäq-).

quick (in action), adj. ቀልጣፋ qạlṭáffā.

ፈጣኝ fạṭáñ (fáṭ-; -áññ § 6; § 8).

quick, be, v.i. ቀለጠፈ qạlạ́ṭṭạfạ.

ቶሎ፡አለ tʷólo álạ (s.v. √ባለ, § 44*a*).

ፈጠነ fạṭṭạnạ (fáṭṭänạ).

Be quick: ቶሎ፡ በል። tʷólo ṿḁl, pl. ቶሎ፡ በሉ። tʷólo ṿḁ́lu.

He is to be quick: ቶሎ፡ ይበል። tʷólo yí̥ṿḁl, pl. -ሉ። -lu.

quick, cause to be, v.t. አቀላጠፈ aqḁlḁ́ṭṭḁfḁ.

quickly, adv. ቶሎ tʷólo, usually with gerund of አለ (§ 44*a*).

Fetch it quickly: ቶሎ፡ ብለህ፡ አምጣው። tʷólo ṿi̥läh ánṭa͡u (§ 7*d*), pl. ቶሎ፡ ብላችሁ፡ አምጡት። tʷólo ṿi̥lḁ́ččyuh (§ 7*d*) ánṭut.

Come back quickly: ቶሎ፡ ብለህ፡ ተመለስ። tʷólo ṿí̥läh tḁmḁ́lḁs, pl. ቶሎ፡ ብላችሁ፡ ተመለሱ። tʷólo ṿi̥lḁ́ččyuh tḁmḁ́lḁsu.

He is to come back quickly: ቶሎ፡ ብሎ፡ ይመለስ። tʷólo ṿí̥lʷo yi̥mmḁ́lḁs, pl. ቶሎ፡ ብለው፡ ይመለሱ። tʷólo ṿí̥lḁ͡u yi̥mmḁ́lḁsu.

quicksilver, s. ባዜቃ bāzʸéqā̃.

quiet, adj. (silent, of animate objects) ዝምተኛ zi̥mmi̥tḁ́ññā̃ (-tā́ñ-).

(silent, of inanimate objects) [እ]ርጉ rí̥gu (í̥rgu).

(tame) ገራም gḁ́rrā́m (§ 8).

(inoffensive) ገር gḁr (gär).

(patient) ጭምት č̣í̥mmi̥t.

Is this mule quiet? ይህ፡ በቅሎ፡ ገራም፡ ነው። yí̥he ṿḁ́qlʷo gḁrrā́m nḁ͡u?

A quiet place: ጭኸት፡ የሌለበት፡ ስፍራ፡ č̣úhḁt yälʸál-läbbḁt (§ 39*b*) sí̥fra.

A quiet person: ጭምት፡ ሰው፡ č̣i̥mmí̥t (§ 8) sḁ͡u.

quiet, v.t. ዝም፡ አሰኘ zi̥mm assḁ́ññä.

quiet, be, v.i. (silent, of animate objects) ዝም፡አለ zi̥mm álḁ.
(silent, of inanimate objects) [እ]ረጋ (i̥)rḁ́g-gã.
(undisturbed) ጸጥ፡አለ ṣḁṭṭ álḁ.
S.v. √በለ, § 44*a*; § 63*d*, *e*.
Be quiet: ዝም፡በል። zi̥mm bäl, pl. ዝም፡በሉ። zi̥mm bḁ́lu.
Tell them to be quiet: ዝም፡ይበሉ። zi̥mm ẏí̥ẏḁlu.
Is the country quiet? አገር፡ጸጥ፡ብኋሎይ። ágḁr ṣḁṭṭ ẏí̥lŏāllwí̥? (s.v. ወይ).
Sit down and be quiet: ዝም፡ብለህ፡ተቀመጥ። zi̥mm bí̥läh tḁqḁ́mḁṭ, pl. ዝም፡ብላችሁ፡ተቀመጡ። zi̥mm bi̥láččyuh tḁqḁ́mḁṭu.
quietly, adv. ዝም zi̥mm or ቀስ qḁss with ger. of አለ álḁ.
quietly, act, v.i. ቀስ፡አለ qḁss álḁ (s.v. √በለ, § 44*a*).
Do it quietly: ቀስ፡ብለህ፡አድርገው። qḁss ẏí̥läh árgḁu (§ 7*d*), pl. ቀስ፡ብላችሁ፡አድርጉት። qḁss ẏi̥láččyuh (§ 7*d*) árgut.
quinine, s. ክኒና ki̥nínã.
quite, adv. በውል bḁ́wű́l (bḁ́uű́l, bḁ́úl; § 8).
በጣም bḁ́ṭám (§ 8).
Wạs it quite boiling? በውል፡ፈልቶ፡ነበር። bḁuű́l fḁ́ltʷo nḁ́bbär?
It has not gone quite in: በጣም፡አልገባም። bḁṭám algḁ́bbām.
Quite hot: ትኩስ፡ tí̥kkús (tű́k-; § 8).

R

§ *refers to the paragraphs of the Grammar* (*Initia Amharica, Part I*).

race, s. (tribe) ዘር zḁr (zär).
radish, s. ሰናፍጭ sḁnáfi̥č̣ (§ 52*a*, δ).
raft, s. ታንኳ táṅkwā.
rag, s. ጨርቅ. č̣ärq.
rage, s. ኵርፊያ kwŭ́rfyā.
 ቍጣ qwŭ́ṭṭā.
rage, get into (be in) a, v.i. (with, v.t.) ተቈጣ tḁqwώṭṭā (§ 63*d*, *e*).
 The chief was in a rage with him: ሹም፡ተቈጥቶት፡ ነበር። šum tḁqwώṭi̥tʷot nḁbbär.
Raḥad (river), s. ሽምፋ ši̥mfā.
raid (raiding party), s. ዘመቻ zḁmḁ́čā (§ 8).
raid, v.i. & t. ወረረ wώrrḁrḁ.
 ወጋ wώggā (ʷώ-).
 They (have) raided our territory: አገራችንን፡ወጉት። agärā́čči̥ni̥n wώggut.
raided, be, v.p. ተወጋ tḁwώggā (ta͡uώ-).
 If our territory is raided, we shall require compensation from you (pol.): አገራችን፡ቢወጋ፡ገንዘባችንን፡ከርስዎ፡እንፈልጋለን። agärā́čči̥n bi̥wwώgga gḁnzḁỵā́čči̥ni̥n kärsḁ́ʷo nni̥fḁlli̥gállän.
railway, s. የባቡር፡መንገድ yäbā́būr (yäỵā́ỵūr; §70) mḁ́ṅgḁd.
 Railway stores: የባቡር፡ሥንቅ፡ yäbābū́r (yäỵāỵū́r; § 8) si̥ṅq.
railway-station, s. መቆሚያ mḁqʷómyā.
 መሐጣ mḁháṭṭā.
railway-train, s. መንኰራኵር mḁṅkwώrā́kwŭr.
 የምድር፡ባቡር yämdi̥r bā́būr (ỵā́ỵūr).

rain, s. ዝናብ zi̥náb (-áy; § 8).
  Heavy rain: ጐርፍ፡ gwωrf.
rain, v.i. ዘነበ zḁnnḁbḁ (zán-, -ḁyḁ).
  If it rains: ቢዘንብ፡ bizáni̥y.
rainbow, s. ቀስተ፡ደመና qástḁ (§ 9d) dḁmmánā̃ (§ 8).
  B. የማርያም፡መቀነት yämáryam (§ 70) mḁqánnḁt (-nät).
rains (rainy season), s. ክረምት ki̥rámt (§ 8).
  Before the rains come on: ክረምት፡ሳይገባ፡ ki̥rámt sa͡igḁya.
raise, v.t. አነሣ anḁssā̃.
  Raise it: አንሣው። ánsa͡u, pl. አንሡት። ánsut.
raise into sight, v.t. ብቅ፡አደረገ bi̥qq adárrḁgḁ.
raised, be, v.p. ተነሣ tḁnássā̃.
  It must be raised: ይነሣ። yi̥nnása, pl. -ሡ። -su.
  If it were raised: የተነሣ፡እንደሆን፡ yätḁnḁssándḁhʷon (§ 81c, ξ), pl. የተነሡ፡እንደሆን፡ yätḁnḁssúndḁhʷon.
raisin, s. ዘቢብ zábīb (záyīy; § 8; § 52a, δ).
ram, s. ወንድ፡በግ wωndi̥ bḁg (yḁg; § 54b).
ramrod, s. የጠበንጃ፡ዘንግ yäṭḁbánja (-ḁyá-; § 70) zḁṅg.
rank, s. (line) ሰልፍ sḁlf (sälf).
  (position) ሹመት šúmḁt (-mät).
Ranunculus sp., s. የውሃ፡በርበሬ yä͡uha bḁrbárʸe (yäryá-).
rapid, adj. ቀልጣፋ qḁlṭáffā̃.
  ፈጣኝ fáṭáñ (fáṭ-; -áññ § 6; § 8).
rapidly, adv. ቶሎ tʷólo.
rapidly, act, v.i. ቶሎ፡አለ tʷólo álḁ (s.v. √በለ, § 44a).
  ቀለጠፈ qḁlḁṭṭḁfḁ.
  ፈጠነ fḁṭṭḁnḁ (fáṭṭänḁ).
  It dries (up) rapidly: ቶሎ፡ብሎ፡ይደርቃል። tʷólo yi̥lʷo yi̥dárqāl.

rapidly, cause to act, v.t. አቀለጠፈ aqḁlḁ́ṭṭḁfḁ.

rapidly, cause to travel, v.t. አገሰገሰ ag(g)ḁsḁ́ggḁsḁ.

Please cause him to travel rapidly: pol. እስቲያገስግሱት። i̥stiyāgḁ́sgi̥sut, ... cause them ... -ገስግሷቸው። -gäsgi̥swḁ́ččḁ͡u.

rapidly, travel, v.i. ገሰገሰ gḁsḁ́ggḁsḁ.

Start now and travel rapidly: አሁን፡ተነሥተህ፡ገስግስ። áhun tḁnḁ́stäh (§ 74*b*) gḁ́sgi̥s, pl. አሁን፡ተነሥታችሁ፡ገስግሱ። áhun tḁnḁstḁ́ččyuh (§ 7*d*) gḁ́s-gi̥su.

rat, s. አይጥ áyi̥ṭ (á͡i̥ṭ), usually f. (§ 54*c*; § 52*a*, δ).

Infested with rats, adj. አይጣም፡ áyi̥ṭám (á͡i̥ṭ-; § 8).

rations, s. ቀለብ qḁ́llḁb (-ḁṿ).

rattle, s. ጸናጽል ṣḁnḁ́ṣi̥l.

rattle, v.i. ኳ፡አለ kwa álḁ (s.v. √በለ, § 44*a*).

See that it doesn't (they don't § 52*a*, δ) rattle: ኳ፡እንዳይል። kwa ndá͡i̥l.

ravage, v.t. ዘረፈ zḁ́rrḁfḁ (zắr-).

ወረረ wώrrḁrḁ.

raw, adj. ጥሬ ṭí̥r^{y}e.

We don't eat it (them § 61*b*) raw: ጥሬ፡አንበላም። ṭí̥r^{y}e anni̥ṿḁ́lām.

ray, s. ጭላንጭል č̣i̥lánč̣i̥l.

razor, s. ምላጭ mí̥lḁ́č̣č̣ (§ 8).

Don't touch my razor(s § 52*a*, δ): ምላጬን፡አትንካው። mi̥láč̣č̣^{y}en attí̥nka͡u.

reach, s.

It is out of reach: እሩቅ፡ነው። ĭ̥rúq nḁ͡u.

reach, v.i. & t. ደረሰ dḁ́rrḁsḁ, constr. with እስከ- i̥skḁ- or በ- bḁ- (ṿḁ-; § 47*a*).

I can't reach it: አልደርስበትም። aldársi̥bbḁti̥m.

He (it) did not reach me before I started: ሳልነሣ፡ አልደረሰኝም። sālịnnássa aldárrasäññim.

You will reach it: ትደርስበታለህ። tidärsibbatálläh, pol. ይደርሱበታል። yidársubbatāl, pl. ትደርሱበታላችሁ። tidärsubbatalláččyuh (§ 7*d*).

Did you reach it? ደረስህበት። dárrashibbat? (-s-h-, not -š-, § 3), pol. ደረሱበት። dárrasubbat?, pl. ደረሳችሁበት። darrasáččihubbat?

reach, cause to, v.t. አደረሰ adárrasa.

read, v.i. & t. አነበበ anábbaba (-aya).

Can you read? ታነባለህ። tānabbálläh? (§ 63*c*).

Read it: አንብበው። ámbiyau (§ 7*d*).

I can (will) read it: አነበዋለሁ። anabbauállau[h] (§ 7*d*).

I can't read it: ማንበቡ፡ አይቻለኝም። mámbayu (§ 30) aiččáläññim.

I will not read it: አላነበውም። alanábbaum.

reading, s. ንባብ níbāb (níyāy; § 8).

ready, be, (get), v.i. ተሰናዳ tasanādda (§ 63*d*, *e*).

Is he (it) ready? ተሰናድቷል። tasanáditōāl? (-nārt- § 7*d*), pl. -ተዋል። -tauāl?

He (it) ought to have been ready: ይሰናዳ፡ ነበር። yissanádda nábbär, pl. -ዱ፡ ነበሩ። -ddu nábbaru.

When will he (it) be ready? መቼ፡ ይሰናዳል። máčä yissanáddāl?, pl. -ናዳሉ። -naddállu?

Get ready: ተሰናዳ። tasanáda, pl. -ዱ። -du.

Be ready before dawn: ሳይጠባ፡ ተሰናዳ። saitáya tasanáda.

I am ready: ተሰናድቻለሁ። tasanādiččállau[h] (§ 7*d*).

I am not ready: አልተሰናዳሁም። altasanáddahum.

I shall be ready before sunrise: ጠሀይ፡ ሳይወጣ፡ እሰናዳለሁ። tahái saiwóta issanaddállau[h].

ready, make (get), v.t. አሰናዳ assḁnā́ddã.

Get it ready: አሰናዳው። assḁnáda͡u, pl. -ዱት። -dut.

Have you got it ready? አሰናዳሀው። assḁnáddahḁ͡u?, pl. አሰናዳችሁት። assḁnaddā́ččı̥hut?

You ought to have got it ready: አንተ፡ታሰናዳው፡ ነበር። ántḁ tassḁnádda͡u nḁ́bbär.

Get lunch ready: ምሳ፡ይቅረብ። mı̥́sā yı̥́qrḁṿ (s.v. ቀረበ).

really, adv. ይሙት yı̥́mut (s.v. ሞተ).

[እ]ኮ (i̥)kk^{w}ó (ŭk-; alone, & suffix).

-ው -u (q.v.).

ቢያ bı́yyā́ (§ 8).

(expressing mild impatience or surprise) አረ ḁ́rḁ!

I really didn't see him (it): ይሙት፡አላየሁትም። yı̥́-mut aláyyähutı̥m.

This is really it: ይሀ፡ነውኮ። yı̥́he nḁ͡ukk^{w}ó.

It is really *you* that (have) killed him (it): አንተው፡ ነሀ፡የገደልሀው። antá͡u näh yägáddälhḁ͡u.

Was this really so? ይሀ፡እንዴሀ፡ሆነ፡ቢያ። yı̥́he nd^{y}éh h^{w}ónḁ bı́yya?

I really don't know: አረ፡አላውቅም። ḁ́rḁ alá͡uqı̥m!

reap, v.i. & t. አጨደ áç̌č̣ḁdḁ (-č̣ädä).

reason, s. (cause) ምክንያት mı̥́knyát (§ 8).

What is the reason? ምክንያቱ፡ምንድር፡ነው። mı̥k-nyátu mı̥́ndı̥r nḁ͡u?

For no reason: ያለምክንያት፡ yālḁmı̥́knyāt, or እን ዲያው፡ (ı̥́)ndya͡u (§ 8).

rebel, s. አመጠኛ ãmḁṭḁ́ññã (-ṭáñ-).

rebel, v.i. ተነሣ tḁnḁ́ssã, against, በ- bḁ- (ṿḁ-; § 47*a*).

አመጠ ámmḁṭḁ ” ” ”

He rebelled against him: ተነሣበት። t̥anás̥sabbat̥, pl. ተነሡበት። t̥anás̥subbat̥; or አመጠበት። ámmat̥̣abbat̥, pl. አመጡበት። ámmat̥̣ubbat̥.

rebellion, s. አመፅ ámat̥̣.

rebellion, incite to, v.t. አሳመጠ asámmat̥̣ḁ.

He incites them to rebellion: ያሳምጣቸዋል። yāsammit̥̣áččḁuāl, pl. ያሳምጧቸዋል። yāsammit̥̣wáččauāl.

rebound, v.i. ነጠረ nát̥t̥̣arḁ (-t̥är-).

receipt, s. (acknowledgment of) ምላሽ mi̥lláš (§ 8).

Wait for the receipt: ምላሹን፡ቈይ። mi̥llášun qwǿi̥.

receive, v.t. ተቀበለ t̥aqábbalḁ.

(take over) ተረከበ t̥arákkabḁ (tärák-, -ḁyḁ).

v.i. (give audience) ተገኘ t̥agáññä.

I received your letter: pol. ደብዳቤዎ፡ደረሰኝ። dḁydábbʸeʷo dárrḁsḁñ.

I did not receive your letter: pol. ደብዳቤዎ፡አልደረሰኝም። dḁydábbʸeʷo aldárrḁsḁññi̥m.

Does the Emperor receive to-day? ንጉሥ፡ዛሬ፡ይገኛሉ። nigús zárʸe yi̥ggḁññállu?

reception-room, s. አዳራሽ addáráš (§ 8).

reckon, v.i. & t. ቈጠረ qwǿt̥t̥̣arḁ (-t̥̣är-).

reckoned, be, v.p. ተቈጠረ t̥aqwǿt̥t̥̣arḁ (-t̥̣är-).

This (that) was not reckoned: ይህ፡አልተቈጠረም። yi̥he altḁqwǿt̥t̥̣arḁm.

recognise, v.t. አወቀ áuwḁqḁ (-wωq-; § 63*d*, *e*).

Do you recognise him (it)? አወቅሀው። áuwωqhḁu?

I should recognise him (it): አውቀው፡ነበር። áuqḁu nḁ́bbär (§§ 26, 81*c*).

recognised, be, v.p. ታወቀ táuwḁqḁ (-wωq-).

reconciled, be, v.i. ተሰማሙ tḁsḁmámmu (täsäm-; § 63*d*,*e*).
They are not reconciled: አልተሰማሙም። altäsä-mámmum.
They will not be reconciled: አይሰማሙም። a͡i̥ssḁ-mámmum.
recount, v.t. ተረከ tḁ́rrḁkḁ (tā́r-).
recover, v.i. (from illness) ዳነ dánḁ.
ተሻለው tḁšálḁ͡u (täš-; impers. § 43*a*).
He (it) will recover: ይድናል። yi̥dí̥nāl, pl. ይድናሉ። yi̥di̥nállu.
He (it) will not recover: አይድንም። a͡i̥dí̥ni̥m, pl. -ኑም። -num.
Have you recovered? ተሻለህ። täšáläh?, pol. -ለዎ። -lḁ͡ʷo?
rectangular, adj. አራት፡ማዘን፡ያለው። arátt mázḁn yállä͡u [lit. four corners (§ 52*a*) which (§ 14) has (s.v. have)].
rectum, s. ቈሽት qwωšt.
red, adj. ቀይ qḁ́͡i̥ (qḁyy § 6).
Red soil: ቦረቦር bʷórḁbʷor (-ḁyʷor).
ቦረንቅ bʷórḁṅq (§ 8).
red, be, v.i. ቀላ qḁ́llā̃.
Red Sea, s. ባሕር፡ኤርትራ báhi̥r (-har) erti̥rā̃.
red-hot, adj. ፍም fi̥m.
reed, s. ሸምበቆ šḁmbḁ́qqʷo.
(large, *Cyperus papyrus*?) ደንገል dáṅgäl. See § 52*a*, δ.
reedbuck (*Cervicapra bohor*), s. ቦሆር bʷóhḁr (-hωr).
reflect, v.i. መከረ mḁ́kkḁrḁ (-kär-).
refusal, s. እምቢታ (i̥)mbitā̃.
refuse, s. እድፍ i̥d(i̥)f.
ጉድፍ gúd(i̥)f.

refuse, v.i. & t. እምቢ፡አለ (i̥)mbi̥ álḁ ((i̥)mbyā́lḁ).
Use the neg. conjug. with አለ ā́lḁ.
S.v. √በለ, § 44*a*.
If you refuse: እምቢ፡ብትል፡ ḿbi̥ y̥i̥tti̥l, pol. እምቢ፡ቢሉ፡ ḿbi̥ y̥ílu, pl. እምቢ፡ብትሉ፡ ḿbi̥ y̥i̥tti̥lu (§ 81*a*, *b*).
If he refuses: እምቢ፡ቢል፡ ḿbi̥ y̥il, pol. and pl. እምቢ፡ቢሉ፡ ḿbi̥ y̥ílu.
Did he refuse? እምቢ፡አለ። ḿbi̥ ā́lḁ?, pol. and pl. እምቢ፡አሉ። ḿbi̥ ā́lu?
He refused to give me the money: ገንዘቡን፡አልሰጥህም፡አለኝ። gḁ́nzḁy̥un alsḁ́ṭi̥hi̥mm ā́läñ, or ገንዘቡን፡አልሰጠኝም፡አለ። gḁ́nzḁy̥un alsḁ́ṭäññi̥mm ā́lḁ.
He refuses to tell us: አልነግራችሁም፡ይለናል። alnḁg-ráččči̥hum yi̥lännāl, or አልነግረንም፡ይለናል። alnḁ́g-ränni̥m yi̥lännāl.

regret, interj. expressing: አይ ā́i!

regret, s. ኀዘን ā́zḁn.

regret, v.t. ኀዘነ ázzḁnḁ ስለ- si̥lḁ- (§ 47*a*).
I regret this: ስለዚህ፡አዝናለሁ። si̥lḁzzí̥h aznállḁu[h] (§§ 7*d*, 26).

reign, s. መንግሥት mḁ́ṅgi̥st.
In King John's reign: ባጤ፡ዮሐንስ፡መንግሥት፡ báṭ[y]e (§§ 7*a*, 47*a*, 70*b*) yohánni̥s mḁ́ṅgi̥st.

reign, v.i. ነገሠ nḁ́ggḁsḁ.

relate, v.t. ተረከ tḁ́rrḁkḁ.

relation, s. (kinsman) ዘመድ zḁ́mḁd.
ወንድም wώndi̥m (prop. brother), pl. also ወንድማሞች wωndi̥mā́-m[w]ōč (-ōčč § 6).
pl. ሥጎች sí̥g[w]ṓč (-ṓčč § 6; § 8).

relationship, s. ዝምድና zi̥mdí̥nnā̃.

release, s. መፍታት mḁ́ftát (§ 8).

To obtain the release of, v.t. አስፈታ asfḁ́ttã.

release, v.t. ፈታ fḁ́ttã.

Release him (it): ፍታው። fi̥tau, pol. ይፍቱት። yi̥ftut.

Release them: ፍታቸው። fi̥táččḁu, pol. ይፍቷቸው። yi̥ftwáččḁu.

I will release him (it): እፈታዋለኍ። i̥fḁtauállḁuʰ.

I will release them: እፈታቸዋለኍ። i̥fḁtāččḁuállḁuʰ.

I will not release him (it): አልፈታውም። alfḁ́taum.

I will not release them: አልፈታቸውም። alfḁtáččḁum.

released, be, v.p. ተፈታ tḁfḁ́ttã.

Has he been released? ተፈትቷል። tḁfḁ́ti̥tŏāl?, pol. & pl. ተፈትተዋል። tḁfḁ́ti̥tḁuāl?

Is he (it) being released? ይፈታል። yi̥ffḁ́ttāl?

Will they be released? ይፈታሉ። yi̥ffḁttállu?

reliable, adj. ታማኝ támáñ (-áññ § 6; § 8).

እሙን i̥mun.

relied on, be, v.p. ታመነ tā̃mmḁnḁ (ger. & part. type A § 34).

He (it) can (§ 63c) be relied on: ይታመናል። yi̥ttámmḁnāl, pl. ይታመናሉ። yi̥ttammḁnállu.

He (it) cannot be relied on: አይታመንም። ai̥ttámmḁni̥m, pl. -ኑም። -num.

relieve nature, v.i. እዳሪ፡ወጣ (i̥)ddári wώṭṭã.

Have you relieved nature? እዳሪ፡ወጥተሃል። i̥ddári wώṭṭähāl?, pol. ...፡ ወጥተዋል። ... wώṭṭḁuāl?

When did you relieve nature? መቼ፡እዳሪ፡ወጣህ። mḁ́čä ddári wώṭṭāh?, pol. ...፡ ወጡ። ... wώṭṭu?

Are you relieving nature every day? በየቀኑ፡እዳሪ፡ትወጣለህ። bḁyyáqḁnu ddári ti̥wωṭállāh?, pol. ...፡ ይወጣሉ። ... yi̥wωṭállu?

religion, s. ሃይማኖት ha͡i̥mán^{w}ot.
rely on, v.t. አመነ ámmḁnḁ.
ታመነ tā́mmḁnḁ (ger. & part. type B § 35).
I rely on him: አምነዋለሁ። amnḁ͡uállḁ͡u^{h} (§ 7*d*).
I do not rely on him: አላምነውም። alámnḁ͡um.
remain, v.i. ቈየ qwώyyä.
ኖረ n^{w}ṓrḁ.
ሰነበተ sḁnḁ́bbḁtḁ (-bät-).
(behind, over) ቀረ qḁ́rrḁ.
ተረፈ tḁ́rrḁfḁ (tā́r-).
I shall remain here ten days: ከዚህ፡አሥር፡ቀን፡እቈያለሁ። käzzíh assi̥r qḁn i̥qwωyyállḁ͡u^{h}, pl. ...፡ እንቈያለን። ... i̥nni̥qwωyyállän.
Remain where you are: በስፍራህ፡ቈይ። bḁsi̥fráh qw͡ώi̥, pl. በስፍራችሁ፡ቈዩ። bḁsi̥frā́ččyuh (§ 7*d*) qwώyyu.
He (it) has remained for a long time: ብዙ፡ጊዜ፡ ኖሯል። bi̥zu gi̥z^{y}e núrō͡āl, pl. ...፡ ኖረዋል። ... núrḁ͡uāl.
He will go on, I shall remain: እርሱ፡ይሔዳል፡እኔ፡ እቀራለሁ። i̥rsú yi̥hádāl, i̥n^{y}é qḁrállḁ͡u^{h} (§ 7*d*), pl. እርሳቸው፡ይሔዳሉ፡እኛ፡እንቀራለን። i̥rsā́ččḁ͡u yi̥hädállu, i̥ññā́ nni̥qḁrállän.
You go on, you remain behind: አንተ፡ሒድ፡አንተ፡ ቅር። antā́ (§ 8) hi̥d, antā́ qi̥r, pl. እላንተ፡ሒዱ፡ እላንተ፡ቅሩ። i̥llántḁ hi̥du, i̥llántḁ qi̥ru.
remainder, s. ቅሬታ qi̥rr^{y}étā.
የተረፈ yätḁ́rrḁfḁ (§§ 14, 62).
የቀረ yäqḁ́rrḁ („).
remember, v.i. & t. አስታወሰ astá͡uwḁsḁ (-wωs-).
አሰበ ássḁbḁ (-ḁyḁ).
See § 63*d, e*.

I don't remember (him, it, etc.): አላስታወስሁም። al-astá͡uwωshum (-s-h-, not -š-, § 3).

I remember him (it): አሰብሁት። ássḁvhut.

remind, v.t. አስታወሰ astá͡uwḁsḁ.

አሳሰበ asa̋ssḁbḁ (-ḁyḁ).

Remind me: አሳስበኝ። asássi̥yäñ.

Remind me to write to him to-morrow: ነገ፡እንድ ጥፍለት፡አስታውሰኝ። nḁ́gḁ ndi̥tí̥fi̥llḁt astá͡uu̇säñ.

You ought to have reminded me: ታሳስበኝ፡ነበር። tāsássi̥yäñ nḁ́bbär (§ 63*b*).

reminder, s. ማስታወሻ mãsta͡uḁ́šã (-a͡uώš-).

Remington rifle, s. ሰናድር sḁnḁ́di̥r (sän-).

remorse, s. አዘን a̋zḁn.

remove, v.t. አነሣ anḁ́ssã.

(some distance) ሳብ፡አደረገ sãbb adḁ́rrḁgḁ.

(entirely) ወሰደ wḁ́ssḁdḁ (wώs-).

Remove this: ይህነን፡አንሣው። yi̥hánnän ánsa͡u, pl. -ሡት። -sut.

Don't remove it: አታንሣው። attánsa͡u, pl. -ሡት። -sut.

removed, be, v.p. ተነሣ tḁnḁ́ssã.

ተወሰደ tḁwḁ́ssḁdḁ (tḁ͡uḁ́-, -ώs-).

Has he (it) been removed? ተነሥቷል። tḁnḁ́stŏ͡āl?, pl. -ተዋል። -tḁ͡uāl? or ተወስዷል። tḁ͡uώsdŏ͡āl?, pl. -ደዋል። -dḁ͡uāl?

This is to be removed: ይህ፡ተወሳጅ፡ነው። yi̥he tḁ͡uωssáj nḁ͡u.

removed, have (allow to be), v.t. አስወሰደ aswḁ́ssḁdḁ (-wώs-).

Please have him (it) removed: pol. እስቲያስወስዱት። i̥stiyaswώssi̥dut.

render, v.t. (cause to be) አሰኘ assáññä.

renew, v.t. አደሰ áddḁsḁ.
rent, s. (hire) ኪራይ kḭrá͡i̥ (§ 8).
rent, v.t. (take on hire) ተከራየ tḁkḁráyyä.
(let on hire) አከራየ akkḁráyyä.
repair, v.t. አበጀ abḁ́jjä (aỵ-, -ā́j-).
Repair it: አብጀው። aỵḭjjḁ͡u.
Repair them: አብጃቸው። aỵḭjjáččḁ͡u.
repaired, be, v.p. ተበጀ tḁbḁ́jjä (tḁỵ-, -ā́j-).
It is to be repaired: ይበጅ። yḭbbäj, pl. ይበጁ። yḭbbā́jju.
The watches have been repaired: ሰዓቶች፡ተበጅተዋል። sḁā́t^{w}ōč tḁỵā́jjḭtḁ͡uāl.
repeat, v.t. ደገመ dḁ́ggḁmḁ (dā́g-).
Repeat it: ድገም። dḭgḁm (§ 61b).
replace, v.t. ተካ tḁ́kkā̃, by, በ- bḁ- (ỵḁ-; § 47a).
He replaced the mule by a donkey: በቅሎውን፡በህያ፡ተካ። bḁ́ql^{w}o͡un yāhíyya tḁ́kka.
replaced, be, v.p. ተተካ tḁtḁ́kkā̃, by, በ- bḁ- (ỵḁ-; § 47a).
repletion, s. ጥጋብ ṭḭgā́b (-ā́ỵ; § 8).
reply, s. ምላሽ mḭllā́š (§ 8).
Wait for a reply: ምላሹን፡ቈይ። mḭllā́šun qw͡ói̥, pl. ...፡ቈዩ። ... qwóyyu.
reply, v.i. & t. መለሰ mḁ́llḁsḁ (mā́l-).
What did he reply? ምን፡መለሰ። mḭn mḁ́llḁsḁ?, pol. & pl. -ሱ። -su?
report, s. (news) ወሬ wór^{y}e.
(of gun) ድምጥ dḭmṭ.
report, v.i. & t. ወሬ፡አመጣ wór^{y}e amḁ́ṭṭā̃.
He reports that they are coming: የመምጣታቸውን፡ወሬ፡አመጣ። yämḁmṭātáččḁ͡un wór^{y}e amḁ́ṭṭa.

reported, be, v.p. ወሬ፡መጣ wώrʸe mḁ́ṭṭā̃ (§ 23*a*).

It is reported that the river is full: ወንዝ፡የሞላ፡ብሎ፡የሚል፡ወሬ፡መጣ። wωnz yämʷólla yı̥lʷo yämmı̥l wώrʸe mḁ́ṭṭḁ (s.v. √ባለ, § 44*a*).

repose, s. እርፈት ı̥rfḁt (-fät).

represent, v.t. (portray) ሳለ sā́lḁ (conjug. like ሳለ to cough).

representative, s. (agent) ሁነኛ hunḁ́ññā̃ (-nā́ñ-).

repulsive, adj. ጸያፍ ṣḁ́yyā́f (ጠ- ṭḁ́-; § 8).

request, v.t. ጠየቀ ṭḁ́yyḁqḁ.

require, v.t. ፈለገ fḁ́llḁgḁ.

I require him (it): እፈልገዋለኍ። ı̥fḁllı̥gḁuállḁuʰ (§ 7*d*), pl. እንፈልገዋለን። ı̥nnı̥fḁllı̥gḁuállän.

I do not require him: አልፈልገውም። alfḁ́llı̥gḁum, pl. አንፈልገውም። annı̥fḁ́llı̥gḁum.

Do you require him? ትፈልገዋለህ። tı̥fḁllı̥gḁuálläh?, pol. ይፈልጉታል። yı̥fḁ́llı̥gutāl?, pl. ትፈልጉታላችሁ። tı̥fḁllı̥gutallā́ččyuh? (§ 7*d*).

required, be, v.p. ተፈለገ tḁfḁ́llḁgḁ.

This (that) is not required: ይሀ፡ይቅር። yı̥he yı̥́qı̥r.

rescue, v.t. አዳነ adā́nḁ.

resemble, v.t. መሰለ mḁ́ssḁlḁ.

It resembles a watch: ሰዓት፡ይመስላል። sḁā́t yı̥mḁ́slāl.

reside, v.i. ኖረ nʷṓrḁ.

ተቀመጠ tḁqḁ́mmḁṭḁ.

Where does he (pol.) reside? ወዴት፡ተቀምጠዋል። wωdʸét tḁqḁ́mṭḁuāl?

residence, s. (place of) መቀመጫ mḁqqḁmḁ́ččā̃.

(fact of) መኖር mḁ́nʷṓr (§ 8).

residency, s. ቤተ፡መንግሥት bʸétḁ (§ 9*d*) mḁ́ngı̥st.

resolute, adj. ጨካኝ čḁ́kkā́ñ (-ññ § 6; § 8).

respect, v.t. አፈረ áffḁrḁ (-fär-).

He doesn't respect him: አያፍረውም። aʸāfrḁ͡um, pl. አያፍሩትም። aʸāfrutı̥m.

He doesn't respect them: አያፍራቸውም። aʸāfráč-čḁ͡um, pl. አያፍሯቸውም። aʸāfrwáččḁ͡um.

respectful, adj. አፋር áffār (§ 8).

rest, s. እርፍት ı̥rfḁt (-fät).

The rest, s. ቅሬታ qı̥rrʸétā̃.

የተረፈ yätḁrrḁfḁ (§§ 14, 62).

የቀረ yäqḁrrḁ („).

Take the rest back: የቀረውን፡መልስ። yäqḁrrḁ͡un mḁ́llı̥s, pl. ...፡ -ሱ። ... -su.

rest, v.i. አረፈ árrḁfḁ.

You are tired: go and rest: ደክሞሃል፤ ሒድህ፡እረፍ። dákmʷohāl (§ 43b): hı̥́däh ı̥rḁf, pl. ደክሟችኋል፤ ሒዳችሁ፡እረፉ። däkmŏ͡áččyuhāl (§ 7d): hı̥dáččyuh ı̥rḁfu.

I can't rest till I have finished it: ሳልጨርሰው፡ አላርፍም። salčḁ́rrı̥sḁ͡u alárfı̥m (§ 63c).

resting-place, s. ማረፊያ mārḁ́fyā̃ (-ráf-).

restore, v.t. (return) መለሰ mḁ́llḁsḁ (mál-).

(repair) አደሰ áddḁsḁ.

restore order, v.i. ዳኘ dáññä.

resurrection, s. ትንሣኤ tı̥nsá͡ı̥.

return, v.i. ተመለሰ tḁmḁ́llḁsḁ (-mál-).

መጣ mḁ́ṭṭā̃.

When I return: ስመለስ፡ sı̥mmállḁs, pl. ስንመለስ፡ sı̥nnı̥mmállḁs (§ 45).

return, v.t. መለሰ mḁ́llḁsḁ (mál-).

When I return him (it): ስመልሰው፡ sı̥mállı̥sḁ͡u, pl. ስንመልሰው፡ sı̥nnı̥mállı̥sḁ͡u.

reveal, v.t. ገለጠ gḁ́llḁṭḁ (gā́l-).
revealed, be, v.p. ተገለጠ tḁgḁ́llḁṭḁ (-gā́l-).
reverse one's position, v.i. ግልብጥ፡አለ gí̥lbi̥ṭṭ (-lyi̥-) ā́lḁ (s.v. √ገለ, § 44*a*).
revolt, s. አመፅ ā́mḁṭ.
revolt, v.i. አመጠ ámmḁṭḁ.
revolt, cause to, v.t. አሳመጠ asámmḁṭḁ.
revolve, v.i. ዞረ z^w ṓrḁ.
ተዟዟረ tḁzḁ́uwḁrḁ.
revolver, s. ሽጉጥ šúgguṭ.
reward, s. ጉርሻ gúršā̃.
rheumatic, adj. ቍርጥማታም qwŭrṭi̥mā́tā́m (§ 8).
rheumatism, s. ቍርጥማት qwŭrṭí̥mā́t (§ 8).
rheumatism, have, v.i. ቈረጠመው qwωrā́ṭṭḁmḁu (impers. § 43*a*; § 63*d*, *e*).
Have you got rheumatism? ቈርጥሞሃል። qwώrṭi̥m^w ohāl?, pol. ቈርጥሞዎታል። qwώrṭi̥m^w o^w otāl?
He has rheumatism: ቈርጥሞታል። qwώrṭi̥m^w otāl.
She has rheumatism: ቈርጥሟታል። qwώrṭi̥mŏātāl.
rhinoceros (*R. bicornis*), s. አውራሪስ aurā́ris (-ri̥s).
rib, s. ጎድን gwώdi̥n.
ጎድን፡አጥንት gwώdi̥n ā́ṭi̥nt.
See § 52*a*, *γ*.
rich, adj. (wealthy) ባለጠጋ bālḁṭḁ́ggā̃.
ሀብታም hábtā́m (háyt-, háft-; § 8).
ቡካሼ bukkā́s^y e.
rich, be, v.i. ከበረ kḁ́bbḁrḁ (-bär-).
Ricinus communis, s. (Broun, Cat. 528) ጕልቋ gwū́lqwā̃.
ride, v.i. & t. ተቀመጠ tḁqḁ́mmḁṭḁ.
ተሳቀለ tḁsḁ́qqḁlḁ (täs-).
I want to ride: ልቀመጥ፡እፈልጋለሁ። li̥qqḁ́mmḁṭ i̥fḁlli̥gállḁu^h.

You (A) ride the pony, you (B) must walk: አንተ፡ ፈረሱን፡ ትቀመጣለህ፤ አንተ፡ በግርህ፡ ትሔዳለህ። ántä fḁ́-rḁsun ti̥qqḁmmḁṭállăh, ántä ẏḁ́gri̥h (§ 52a, γ) ti̥-hädállăh.

Does he ride well? ተቀማጭ፡ ነው። tḁqḁmmáč̣i̥ nḁ͡u?

ridge-pole, s. ጋድም gā́di̥m.

ridiculous, adj. መሣቂያ mḁsā́qyā̃.

right, s. adj. & adv. (-hand) ቀኝ qḁññ.

(correct) [በ]ልክ (bḁ́)lí̥kk (§ 8).

ደኅና dā́hnā (§ 8).

(proper) ደግ dḁgg (dägg).

(adv., quite) በውል bḁ́wū́l (bḁ́͡uū́l, bḁ́͡úl; § 8).

በጣም bḁ́ṭā́m (§ 8).

On your right: ቀኝህን፡ qḁ́ññi̥hi̥n (§ 56d).

When you come to the hill go to the right: ተራራውን፡ ስትደርስ፡ በቀኝ፡ ሒድ። tḁrā́ra͡un si̥tti̥dā́rs (si̥ddā́rs) ẏḁqḁ́ññ hi̥d.

Is this right (correct)? ይህ፡ ልክ፡ ነው። yí̥he lí̥kkĭ̥ nḁ͡u?—(proper): ይህ፡ ደግ፡ ነው። yí̥he dággĭ̥ nḁ͡u?

This is the right way (to do it, for it to be, etc.): እንዲህ፡ ልክ፡ ነው። i̥ndíh lí̥kkĭ̥ (§ 7d) nḁ͡u.

He (it) went right in: በጣም፡ ገባ። bḁṭā́m gḁ́bba.

All right (approving): ይሁን። yí̥hun, or እሺ። í̥šši̥.

They are all right: ደኅና፡ ናቸው። dähnā́ nā́ččḁ͡u.

(= safe: of ground, water, etc.):

It's all right (it will bear, it's not too deep, etc.): ምንም፡ አይል። mí̥ni̥mm á͡i̥l (§§ 37d, 44a, s.v. √በለ).

rigid, adj. ጠንከራ ṭḁnkárrā̃.

rind, s. ቅርፍት qí̥rfi̥t.

ring, s. ቀለበት qḁ́lḁbḁt (-ḁy̥-, -ät).

ring, v.i. & t. ደወለ dḁ́uwḁlḁ (-wωl-).

Ring the bell: ቃጭሉን፡ደውለው። qā́c̣i̥lun dḁ́uwŭlḁ́u.

ripe, adj. ብስል bí̥si̥l.

የበሰለ yäbḁ́ssḁlḁ (yäy̥ḁ́-; §§ 14, 62).

These figs are not ripe: ይህ፡በለስ፡አልበሰለም። yí̥he y̥ḁ́lḁs (§ 52*a*, δ) aly̥ḁ́ssḁlḁm.

Are there any ripe figs? የበሰለ፡በለስ፡አለ። yäy̥ḁ́ssḁlḁ y̥ḁ́lḁs állä?

ripen, v.i. በሰለ bḁ́ssḁlḁ.

It will not ripen here: ከዚህ፡አይበስልም። käzzíh ḁi̥y̥ḁ́sli̥m.

rise, s. (ascent) አቀበት áqḁbḁt (-ḁy̥ḁt; § 8).

rise, v.i. ተነሣ tḁnḁ́ssā̃.

ብድግ፡አለ bí̥di̥gg ā́lḁ (s.v. √በለ, § 44*a*).

Rise: ተነሣ። tḁnḁ́sa, pl. ተነሡ። tḁnḁ́su.

Don't rise: አትነሣ። atti̥nnḁ́sa, pl. -ሡ። -su.

When the river rises: ወንዝ፡ሲሞላ፡ wωnz sim^{w}óla.

rise into sight, v.i. ወጣ wώṭṭā̃.

ብቅ፡አለ bí̥qq ā́lḁ (s.v. √በለ, § 44*a*).

When the sun rises: ጠሀይ፡ሲወጣ፡ ṭḁhái̥ siwώṭa.

When the hippopotamus rises: ጉማሬ፡ብቅ፡ሲል፡ gumár^{y}e bí̥qqi̥ (§ 7*d*) sil.

rising ground, s. ጎራ g^{w}órā̃.

river, s. ወንዝ wωnz.

(Of a river): to rise: መላ mḁ́llā̃ (ሞላ m^{w}óllā̃).

to fall: ጎደለ gwώddḁlḁ.

road, s. መንገድ mḁ́ṅgḁd.

ጎዳና gwώdanā̃.

Do you know the road? መንገዱን፡ታውቃለህ። máṅgadun tau͡qállăh?, pol. ...፡ ያውቃሉ። ... yau͡qállu?, pl. ...፡ ታውቃላችሁ። ... tau͡qallăččyuh? (§ 7*d*).

Which is the road to Gondar? ጎንደርን፡የሚወስድ፡ መንገድ፡ዬቱ፡ነው። gʷóndarin yämmiwásid máṅgad yétu nau͡?

Waggon road: †የሥረገላ፡መንገድ፡ yäsiragálla máṅgad.

Š. †የጋሪ፡መንገድ፡ yägări máṅgad.

See §§ 47*a*, 70.

Is the road fit for waggons? መንገድ፡ሥረገላ፡ (Š. ጋሪ፡) ሊሔድበት፡ይመቻል። máṅgad siragálla (Š. gări) lihădibbat yimmáččāl?

Can laden mules go by that road? የተጫነ፡በቅሎ፡ በዚህ፡መንገድ፡ያስኬዳል። yätačăna yáqlʷo bazzíh máṅgad yaskădāl? (§ 52*a*, δ).

Keep (pl.) together on the road: አብራችሁ፡ቈዩ፡ ተመንገድ። āyrăččyuh (§ 7*d*) qwóyyu tamáṅgad.

We don't want a man that doesn't know the road: መንገዱን፡የማያውቅ፡አንፈልግም። máṅgadun yämmai͡áu͡q annfálligim (§ 37*a*, *b*).

roan antelope (*Hippotragus equinus*), s.

ወንድቤ wωndíbbʸe.

D. ወደምቢ wωddămbi.

See § 52*a*, δ.

roar, v.i. አገሣ agássā.

roast, v.t. ጠበሰ ṭábbasa.

Roast it: ጥበሰው። ṭíyasau͡.

roasted, be, v.p. ተጠበሰ taṭábbasa.

It is to be roasted: ይጠበስ። yiṭṭáyas, pl. -ሱ። -su.

rob, v.t. ቀማ qámmā.

ሰረቀ sárraqa (săr-).

robbed, be, v.p. ተቀማ tḁqḁmmã.

I have been robbed: ተቀማኹ። tḁqḁmmau͡h (§ 7*d*).

robber, s. ወንበዴ wωmbḁdʸe (§ 52*a*, δ).

ቀማኛ qḁmmáññã („).

A robber (Robbers) took it (them § 61*b*) from him: ቀማኛ፡ወሰደበት። qḁmmáñña wώssḁdḁbbḁt (§ 47*a*).

robbery, s. ቅምያ qi̥mmyã.

robust, adj. ብርቱ bi̥rtŭ.

ጕልበታም gwŭlbḁtám (-lẏ-, -át-; § 8).

ጕልበተኛ gwŭlbḁtḁñña̅ (-lẏ-, -ätáñ-).

rock, s. ደንጊያ dáṅgyã, Š. ደንጋይ dáṅga͡i̥ (§ 8), } pl. ደንጎች dáṅgʷōč (-čč § 6).

See § 52*a*, δ.

roll, v.i. (be rolled, v.p.), (move revolving) ተንከባለለ tḁṅkḁbállа̥lḁ (-ḁẏá-).

(curl) ተጠቀለለ tḁṭḁqḁllḁlḁ.

It cannot be lifted, but it will roll: አይነሣም፡ይንከባለላል። a͡i̥nnḁssām (§ 63*c*), yi̥ṅkḁẏállḁlāl.

It is to be rolled, not folded: ይጠቀለል፡አይታጠፍ። yi̥ṭṭḁqlḁl, a͡i̥ttáṭḁf.

It is to be folded, not rolled: ይታጠፍ፡አይጠቀለል። yi̥ttáṭḁf, a͡i̥ṭṭḁqlḁl.

roll, v.t. (move) አንከባለለ aṅkḁbállḁlḁ (-ḁẏá-).

(curl) ጠቀለለ ṭḁqḁllḁlḁ.

Roll it along: አንከባልለው። aṅkḁẏáli̥la͡u̥, pl. አንከባልሉት። aṅkḁẏáli̥lut.

Roll it (e.g. the cloth) up: ጠቅልለው። ṭáqli̥la͡u̥, pl. ጠቅልሉት። ṭáqli̥lut.

rolling stock, s. †የምድር፡ባቡር፡ሥረገላ፡ yämdi̥r ẏáẏūr si̥rḁgḁllã (ሠ- sä-; § 52*a*, δ).

roof, s. ባጥ bāṭ.

room, s. (in a house) ቤት byĕt.

ቅርጥ qi̥rṭ.

(private) እልፍኝ i̥lfi̥ñ (-ññ § 6; § 8).

(space) መቀመጫ mḁqqḁmḁčḁ̃.

When you clean the room: ቤቱን፡ስትጠርግ፡ byétun si̥tti̥ṭárg, pl. -ርጉ፡ -rgu.

There is no room for the chair: ለወምበር፡መቀመጫ፡ የለም። lḁwώmbḁr mḁqqḁmḁ́ča yállām.

root, s. ሥር si̥r (§ 52a, δ).

rope, s. ገመድ gḁ́mḁd.

rose (*Rosa sancta,* Guidi, Vocab. p. 297), s. ቀጋ qḁ́gã (§ 52a, δ).

rough, adj. (violent) ብርቱ bi̥rtŭ.

ኃይለኛ hai̥lḁ́ññã (-láñ-).

(rude) ባለጌ bálḁgye (-läg-).

(of a surface) ሸካራ šḁkárã.

(scabrous) ኰስኳሳ kwωskwássã.

The lake is rough: ባሕር፡ይናወጣል። báhi̥r yi̥nnáu-wωṭāl.

roughly, adv. (violently) በኃይል bḁ́hái̥l (§ 8).

(approximately) ያህል yáhi̥l (yahl; s.v. አከለ).

He seized him roughly: በኃይል፡ያዘው። bḁhái̥l yá-zḁu.

There were roughly 100: መቶ፡ያህል፡ነበር። mḁ́two yahl nḁ́bbär (§ 20a).

round, adj. ክብ ki̥bb.

round, prp. በ-...፡አጠገብ bḁ-... aṭḁ́gḁb (-ḁy; § 47b).

Go right round the hill and come back: ተተራራ፡ ዙርያውን፡ዙረህ፡ና። tḁtḁrára zuryáun (§ 56c) zuráh (§ 8) na.

round, turn, v.i. ዞረ zʷŏrḁ.

Turn round: ዙር። zur, pl. ዙሩ። zúru.

round, turn (cause to), v.t. አዞረ azʷŏrḁ.

Turn him (it) round: አዙረው። ázurḁu͡.

Turn them round: አዙራቸው። azuráččḁu͡.

rouse, v.t. ቀሰቀሰ qḁsḁ́qqḁsḁ.

አስነሣ asnḁ́ssã.

Rouse him: ቀስቅሰው። qḁ́sqi̥sḁu͡.

Rouse them: ቀስቅሳቸው። qḁsqi̥sáččḁu͡.

Rouse me before dawn: ምድር፡ሳይጠባ፡አስነሣኝ። ḿdi̥r sa͡i̥ṭḁya asnḁ́ssāñ.

Don't rouse me: አታስነሣኝ። attasnḁ́ssāñ.

roused, be, v.p. (rouse oneself, v.r.) ተቀሰቀሰ tḁqḁsḁ́qqḁsḁ.

See that I am not roused: እንዳልቀሰቀስ። ndali̥q-qḁsḁ́qqḁs.

rub, v.i. & t. ፈገፈገ fḁgḁ́ffḁgḁ.

አሸ áššä.

(with an unguent) ቀባ qḁ́bbã.

Rub it: ፈግፍገው። fḁ́gfi̥gḁu͡, pl. -ፍጉት። -fi̥gut.

Don't rub it: አትፈግፍገው። atti̥fḁ́gfi̥gḁu͡, pl. -ጉት። -gut.

Don't rub your eyes: ዓይንህን፡አትሸው። á͡i̥ni̥hi̥n (§ 52*a*, *γ*) ãttíšḁu͡.

rub down, v.t. ወለወለ wḁlḁ́uwḁlḁ.

Rub the horse down: ፈረሱን፡ወልውለው። fḁ́rḁsun wḁ́lwi̥lḁu͡ (-lwŭl-).

rubbed, be, v.p. ተፈገፈገ tḁfḁgḁ́ffḁgḁ.

ታሸ táššä.

ተቀባ tḁqḁ́bbã.

It should be rubbed: ይፈግፈግ። yi̥ffḁ́gfḁg, pl. -ፈጉ። -fḁgu.

rubbed down, be, v.p. ተወለወለ tḁwḁlḁ́͡uwḁlḁ (tḁ͡uḁ-).
 Has the horse been rubbed down? ፈረሱ፡ተወል ውሏል። fḁ́rḁsu tḁ͡uḁ́lwŭlö͡āl?, pl. ፈረሶቹ፡ተወልውለዋል። fḁrḁsʷóčču tḁ͡uḁ́lwŭlḁ͡uāl?
rubber (India-), s. ላስቲክ lástík (§ 8).
rubbish, s. ምናምን mi̥námi̥n.
 ጉድፍ gúdi̥f.
 (sweepings, etc.) ጥራጊ ti̥rrági.
 ግብስብስ gi̥bí̥sbi̥s (gi̥ví̥svi̥s).
 ቈሻሻ qwωšášã.
Rubus exsuccus (Guidi, Vocab. p. 533), s. ኰሸሽላ kwωšḁ-ši̥llã (-šωš-; § 52*a*, δ).
rude, adj. (impolite) ባለጌ bálḁgʸe (-läg-).
ruffian, s. ጋዱ gáddu.
rug, s. ምንጣፍ mí̥nṭáf (§ 8).
 (of skin) አጐዛ agʷózã.
 (carpet) ስጋጃ si̥gájjã.
ruin, s. (destruction) ጥፋት tí̥fát (§ 8).
 ፍርስ fi̥rs.
ruin, v.t. አፈረሰ afḁ́rrḁsḁ.
 You have ruined it: አፈረስህው። afḁ́rrḁshḁ͡u (-s-h-, not -š-, § 3), pl. አፈረሳችሁት። afḁrrḁsáčči̥hut.
 He will ruin it: ያፈርሰዋል። yāfársḁ͡uāl, pl. -ሱታል። -sutāl.
ruined, be, v.p. ፈረሰ fḁ́rrḁsḁ (§ 63*d*, *e*).
 It is ruined: ፈርሷል። fársö͡āl, pl. ፈርሰዋል። fár-sḁ͡uāl.
rule, v.i. ነገሠ nággḁsḁ.
 (over, v.t.) ገዛ gḁ́zzã.
ruled (over), be, v.p. ተገዛ tḁgḁ́zzã.
ruler, s. (governor) ገዢ gḁž.
 መኰንን mḁkwώnnḁn (-nän).

rumble, v.i. ግም፡ አለ gi̥mm álḁ (s.v. √በለ, § 44*a*).

Rumex abessinicus (Guidi, Vocab. pp. 80, 81), s. መቅመቆ mḁqmḁ́qqʷo.

rumour, s. ወሬ wǿrʸe.

run, v.i. [እ]ሮጠ (i̥)rʷṓṭḁ.

Run: እሩጥ። i̥ruṭ, pl. ሩጡ። rúṭu.

He is to run: ይሩጥ። yi̥ruṭ, pl. ይሩጡ። yi̥rúṭu.

Don't run: አትሩጥ። atti̥ruṭ, pl. አትሩጡ። atti̥rúṭu.

run away, v.i. ጠፋ ṭḁ́ffã.

(from, v.t.) ሸሸ šḁ́ššä (šáš-).

Take care he (it) doesn't run away: እንዳይጠፋ። nda͡i̥ṭḁ́fa.

(To child):—Run away! ወግድ። wǿgi̥d!, f. ወግጅ። wǿgi̥j!, pl. ወግዱ። wǿgi̥du!

runaway, s. & adj. ካጅ kḁ́ji̥.

Runaway slave: ካጅ kāj.

running, s. [እ]ሩጫ (i̥)rúččḁ̃.

rush (*iuncus sp.*), s. በረቤንዝ bḁrḁbʸénz (-ḁyʸé-; § 52*a*, δ).

Russia, s. የመስቆፍ፡ አገር yämḁ́sqʷof ā̃gḁr.

Russian, adj. የመስቆፍ yämḁ́sqʷof (s.v. የ-, §§ 47*a*, 70).

Russian, s. መስቆፍ mḁ́sqʷof.

rust, s. ዛገና zāgḁ́nnã.

rust (be, become rusty), v.i. ዛገ zágḁ (§ 63*d*, *e*).

Don't let it get rusty: እንዳይዝግ። nda͡i̥zi̥g.

rust (make rusty), v.i. & t. አዛገ azágḁ.

It will make it rusty: ያዝገዋል። yāzi̥ga͡ūāl.

rustic, s. በለጊ bā̃lḁgʸe (-läg-).

በላገር bālā̃gḁr (-gär).

ገበሬ gḁ́bḁrʸe (-ḁ́y-, -är-).

See § 52*a*, δ.

rustle, v.i. ተንኰሸኰሸ tḁṅkwωšákkwωšḁ.

What is that rustling there? ከዚህ፡የሚንኰሸኰሽ፡ምንድር፡ነው። käzzíh yämmi̥ṅkwωšákkwωš mi̥ndí̥r (§ 8) nḁ͡u?

rustle (cause to), v.t. አንኰሸኰሸ aṅkwωšákkwωšḁ.

You (pl.) are making them rustle: ታንኰሻኵሿችኋላችሁ። taṅkwωšakkwŭšwāččạ̊͡uallāččyuh.

S

§ *refers to the paragraphs of the Grammar* (*Initia Amharica, Part I*).

sabbath, s. ሰንበት sḁ́nbḁt (-nỵ-, -ät).

sack, s. ከረጢት kḁrḁṭít.

sacred, adj. ቅዱስ qí̥ddús (§ 8).

sad, be, v.i. አዘነ ázzḁnḁ.

saddle, s. ኰርቻ kʷōrí̥ččā̃.

Put the saddle on: ጫን። čạ̄n.

Let him put the saddle on: ይጫን። yí̥čạ̄n.

Put (pl.) the saddles on: ጫኑ። čạ́nu.

Let them put the saddles on: ይጫኑ። yi̥čạ́nu.

Put the saddle on properly: በውል፡ጫነው። bḁ͡úl čạ́nḁ͡u.

saddle, v.t. ጫነ čạ́nḁ.

Saddle it: ጫነው። čạ́nḁ͡u.

Saddle this horse: ይህን፡ፈረስ፡ጫን። yi̥hắn fḁ́rḁs čạ̄n.

saddle, cause to, (have saddled), v.t. አስጫነ asčạ́nḁ (§ 68).

Have it (them § 61*b*) saddled: አስጪን። ásčị̊n.

Please have it saddled: pol. እስቲያስጪኑት። i̥sti-yásčị̊nut.

saddled, be, v.p. ተጫነ tạčánḁ.

It has not been properly saddled: በውል፡አልተጫነም። bḁúl altḁčánḁm.

saddle-girth, s. መቀነቻ mḁqḁnnḁ́čā.

ቅናት qi̥nát (§ 8).

See § 52*a*, δ.

saddle-pad, s. ዳውላ daúllā.

safe, adj. (-ly, adv.) ደኅና dáhnā (§ 8).

እሙን i̥mun.

Is he (it) safe? ደኅና፡ነው። dähná nḁu?

It is not safe: ደኅናም፡አይደል። dähnámm (§ 37*b*) ái̥däl (§ 40*b*).

Did he arrive safely? ደኅና፡ገባ። dähná gḁ́bba?, pol. & pl. -ቡ። -bbu?

We are safe here: ተዚህ፡እሙን፡ነን። täzzi̥h i̥mún (§ 8) nän.

safety, s. ደኅንነት dähní̥nnḁt (-nät).

አማን ámán (§ 8).

safflower (*Carthamus tinctorius*, Broun, Cat. 316), s. ሱፍ sūf (§ 52*a*, δ).

said, be, v.p. ተባለ tḁbálḁ (-ḁyá-).

Is it said? ይባላል። yi̥bbálāl?

sailor, s. መርከበኛ mḁrkḁbḁ́ññā (mär-, -kḁy-, -áñ-).

saint, s. ቅዱስ qi̥ddús (§ 8).

sake of, for, prp. ስለ- si̥lḁ- (§ 47*a*).

For God's sake: ስለግዚአብሔር፡ si̥lḁgzi̥ḁyhʸér.

salary, s. ደሞዝ dḁ́mʷóz (§ 8).

sale, s. መሸጥ mḁ́šḁṭ (-šäṭ).

For sale: ለመሸጥ፡ lḁmḁ́šäṭ.

It finds a ready sale: ይሸጣል፤እንደውሃ፡ይሔዳል። yi̥ššáṭāl, i̥ndäʷúha yi̥hádāl.

salt, s. ጨው čḁu.

saltpetre, s. [የ]ጨው፡ባሩድ (y̥ä)č̣a͡u (s.v. የ-, §§ 47a, 70) bárud (y̥á-).

salute, v.i. & t. እጅ፡ነሣ i̥jj nḁssã constr. with ለ- lḁ- (§ 47a).

Whom are they saluting? ለማን፡እጅ፡ይነሣሉ። lḁmán i̥jj yi̥nḁsállu?

same, adj. አንድ and.

Use the article (§ 11).

It's all the same: ሁሉ፡አንድ፡ነው። húllu ándi̥ (§ 7d) nḁ͡u.

This is not the same kind: ይህ፡ዓይነቱም፡አይደል። yi̥he a͡i̥nätumm (§ 37b) a͡i̥däl (§ 40b).

Come tomorrow at the same time: ነገ፡በጊዜው፡ና። nḁ́gḁ y̥ḁgi̥zʸe͡u na.

sand, s. አሸዋ ašḁ͡uã.

Š. አሻዋ ašá͡uã.

sandal, s. ነጠላ፡ጫማ nḁṭḁlá č̣ámmã (§ 52a, δ).

Sanseviera agave (cp. Broun, Cat. 560), s. ቃጫ qáč̣ã (§ 52a, δ).

sated, adj. ጥጋበኛ ṭi̥gābḁ́ññã (-āy̥-, -áñ-).

satiety, s. ጥጋብ ṭi̥̥gáb (-áy̥; § 8).

satisfied, be, v.i. (with food etc.) ጠገበ ṭḁ́ggḁbḁ (-ḁy̥ḁ).

(gen.) ደስ፡አለ dḁss (däss) álḁ.

ደስ፡አለው dḁss (-ä-) álḁ͡u (impers. § 43a).

S.v. √በለ, § 44a.

Are you satisfied? ደስ፡ይለሃል። däss yi̥lähāl?

satisfy, v.t. ደስ፡አሰኘ dḁss (-ä-) assáññä.

Saturday, s. & adv. ቅዳሜ qi̥dámʸe.

saucepan, s. ድስት di̥st.

sausage, s. ቋሊማ qwáliṃã.

save, v.i. & t. አዳነ adā́nḁ.

(economise) ቈጠበ qwώṭṭḁbḁ (-ḁyḁ).

He saved his life: ተሞት፡አዳነው። tḁm^{w}ót adā́nḁu͡.

saved, be, v.p. ተቈጠበ tḁqwώṭṭḁbḁ (-ḁyḁ).

With the money that was saved he bought another: በተቈጠበ፡ገንዘብ፡ሌላ፡ገዛ። bḁtḁqwώṭṭḁyḁ (§ 62c) gḁ́nzḁy léla gḁ́zza.

saw, s. መጋዝ mḁ́gázz (§ 8).

say, v.t. አለ ā́lḁ (s.v. √በለ, §§ 44a, 80).

ነገረ nḁ́ggḁrḁ (-gär-).

Say it: በለው። bḁ́lḁu͡.

Don't say it: አትበለው። atti̥yḁ́lḁu͡.

Say it again: ድገም። dí̥gḁm (§ 61b).

Do you hear (understand) what I say? ያልሁትን፡ሰማህ። yā́lhuti̥n (§ 62c) sḁmmāh? (§ 63d), pl. ...፡ ሰማችሁ። ... sḁmmā́ččyuh? (§ 7d).

Did you hear what he said? ያለውን፡ትሰማ፡ነበር። yā́lḁu͡n ti̥sḁ́ma, nḁ́bbär?, pl. ...፡ትሰሙ፡ነበር። ... ti̥sḁ́mu nḁ́bbär?

What did you say? ምን፡አልህ። mi̥n alh? (alk § 7d), pol. ምን፡አሉ። mi̥n ā́lu?, pl. ምን፡አላችሁ። mi̥n ālā́ččyuh?

What does he say? ምን፡ይላል። mi̥n yi̥lāl?, pol. & pl. ...፡ይላሉ። ... yi̥lállu?

I can't say: እንጃ። ńja.

He said nothing: ዝም፡አለ። zi̥mm ā́lḁ, pol. & pl. ዝም፡አሉ። zi̥mm ā́lu.

What is it you said? ምንድር፡ነው፡ያልህ። mí̥ndi̥r nḁu͡ yālh?

I hear (understand) what you say: ያልሀውን፡ሰም ቻለኍ። yā́lhḁu͡n sḁmi̥ččállḁu͡^{h}.

I don't hear (understand) what you say: ያልሀውን፡ አልሰማሁም። yḁ́lhḁ͡un alsḁ́mmahum.

This is what he said: እንዲህ፡ብሎ፡አለ። ndíh yí̥l^{w}o álḁ, pol. & pl. እንዲህ፡ብለው፡አሉ። ndíh yí̥lḁ͡u álu.

How does one say (it) in Amharic? በማርኛ፡እንዴት፡ይባላል። bamāri̥ñña (§§ 7*a*, 47*a*) nd^{y}ét yi̥bbálāl?

saying, s. ቃል qāl.

scabbard, s. ሰገባ sḁgḁ́bā̃ (-ḁ́yā̃; § 8).

scabrous, adj. ኮስኳሳ kwωskwā́ssā̃.

scald, v.i. & t. ተኰሰ tḁ́kkwωsḁ (tώkkosḁ § 7*d*).

scalded, be, v.p. ተተኰሰ tḁtḁ́kkwωsḁ (-tώkkosḁ).

scalding, adj. ፍል fi̥l.

scales, s. (balance) ሚዛን mízán (§ 8).

scandal, talk, v.i. አሾከሾከ ašš^{w}okḁ́šš^{w}okḁ.

scandal-monger, s. አሾክሿኪ ašš^{w}okšwā́ki.

scapula, s. መጋፍያ mḁgáfyā̃.

scatter, v.i. (be scattered, v.p.) ተበተነ tḁbḁ́ttḁnḁ (tḁy-, -áttänḁ).

(spread apart) G. ተረረቁ tḁrḁrḁ́qu (tärär-).

Š. ተራረቁ tḁrāráqu (tär-).

scatter, v.t. በተነ bḁ́ttḁnḁ (báttänḁ).

(drive apart) G. አረረቀ arrḁráqḁ (-rär-).

Š. አራረቀ arrāráqḁ.

Don't scatter it about: አትበትነው። atti̥yátti̥nḁ͡u, pl. -ኑት። -nut.

scent, s. ሽታ ši̥ttā̃.

scent, v.t. (smell) አሸተተ ašḁttḁtḁ (-šát-).

It will scent us: ያሸተናል። yāšáttännāl, pl. ያሸቱ፡ናል። yāšáttunnāl.

It has scented us: አሽቶናል። aši̥tt^{w}onnāl, pl. አሽተውናል። aši̥ttḁ͡unnāl.

scented, be, v.i. (perfumed) ታጠነ táṭṭḁnḁ.
sceptical, adj. ጠርጣሪ ṭḁrṭári (ṭär-).
scholar, s. (learned man) ደብተራ dḁbtḁ́rã (-ḁỵt-, -ḁf̣t-, -tắr-).
(schoolboy) ተማሪ tḁmā́ri (§ 52*a*, δ).
school, s. [የ]ትም[ህ]ርት ፡ ቤት (yä)ti̥m(h)í̥rtĭ̥ (§ 70*b*) bʸēt (ỵʸ-).
Have you been to school? ተትምርት ፡ ቤት ፡ ነበርህ ። tḁti̥mí̥rtĭ ỵʸēt nḁ́bbḁrh?
schoolmaster, s. መም[ህ]ር mḁ́mm(h)i̥r, pl. also መም[ህ]ራን mḁ́mm(h)i̥rā́n (§ 8).
አስተማሪ astḁmā́ri.
scissors, s. መቀስ mḁ́qḁs.
scold, v.i. & t. ተቈጣ tḁqwώṭṭã.
scoop, s. መፈልፈያ mḁfḁlfḁ́yã (-fäl-, -ḁ́͡i̥ã).
scoop, v.t. ፈለፈለ fḁlḁ́ffḁlḁ.
scooped, be, v.p. ተፈለፈለ tḁfḁlḁ́ffḁlḁ.
scorch, v.i. & t. ተኰሰ tḁ́kkwωsḁ (tώkkosḁ § 7*d*).
scorched, be, v.p. ተተኰሰ tḁtḁ́kkwωsḁ (-tώkkosḁ).
Take care it doesn't get scorched: እንዳይተኰስ ። nda͡i̥ttώkkos.
scorching, adj. ትኩስ tí̥kkús (tŭ́k-; § 8).
scorpion, s. ግንጥ gi̥nṭ (usually f. § 54*c*).
Is it a scorpion? ግንጥ ፡ ናት ። gí̥nṭĭ̥ (§ 7*d*) nāt?
scour (scrub), v.t. ሟጨ mwắč̣č̣ä.
Scour (scrub) it: ሟጨው ። mwắč̣č̣ḁ͡u, pl. ሟጩት ። mwắč̣č̣ut.
scoured (scrubbed), be, v.p. ተሟጨ tḁmwắč̣č̣ä.
scouring (scrubbing), instrument for, s. መሟጫ mḁ-mwắč̣ã.
scout, s. ሰላይ sḁ́llắ͡i̥ (sắl-; § 8; § 52*a*, δ).
scout, v.i. ሰለለ sḁ́llḁlḁ (sắl-).
scramble for, v.t. ተሻማ tḁšắmmã (täš-).

scrape, v.i. & t. ፋቀ fā́qḁ.

(off, out v.t.) ሰቀሰቀ sḁqḁ́ssḁqḁ.

Scrape it: ፋቀው። fā́qḁ͡u, pl. ፋቁት። fā́qut.

Don't scrape it: አትፋቀው። atti̥fā́qḁ͡u, pl. -ቁት። -qut.

Scrape it off (out): ሰቅስቀው። sḁ́qsi̥qḁ͡u, pl. -ቁት። -qut.

Don't scrape it off: አትሰቅስቀው። atti̥sḁ́qsi̥qḁ͡u, pl. -ቁት። -qut.

scraped, be, v.p. ተፋቀ tḁfā́qḁ.

scraping (off, out), instrument for, s. መሰቅሰቂያ mḁsḁq-sḁ́qyã (-sā́qyã, -sā́č̣ã).

scratch, v.i. & t. አከከ ákkḁkḁ.

ሟጨረ mŏ͡ā̃č̣č̣ärḁ.

Don't scratch it: አትከከው። attí̥kḁkḁ͡u.

The cat will scratch him: ድመቲቱ፡ትሟጭረዋለች። dí̥mmḁti̥tu ti̥mŏ͡āč̣č̣i̥rḁ͡uállä̌č.

scratch, cause or allow to, v.t. አሳከከ asā́kkḁkḁ (§ 68).

Don't let it scratch it: አታሳክከው። attāsákki̥kḁ͡u.

scratched, be, v.p. (scratch oneself, v.r.) ታከከ tā́kkḁkḁ.

scream (screaming), s. ጩኸት č̣úhḁt (-hät § 7*d*).

scream, v.i. ጮኸ č̣ʷóhḁ.

scrofula, s. ነቀርሳ nḁqḁ́rsã (መቀ- mḁqḁ́-).

scrotum, s. ሰንኰፍ sḁ́ṅkʷof.

የቈለት፡ቆርበት yäqwώlḁt qʷórbḁt (-ry̥-, -ät).

sea, s. ባሕር bā́hi̥r (-har).

የጨው፡ባሕር yäč̣ḁ́͡u (§ 70*b*) bā́hi̥r (y̥á-, -har).

seal, s. (instrument) መኀተሚያ mḁhattḁ́myã (-tā́m-).

(impression) ማኅተም máhtḁm (mḁhā́tḁm § 7*d*).

seal, v.i. & t. ኀተመ háttа̥mḁ.

አተመ áttḁmḁ.

Seal it: ኅትመው። háttịmạ͡u, pol. ይኅትሙት። yịhát-tịmut.

sealed, be, v.p. ታተመ táttạmạ.

It has not been (was not) sealed: አልታተመም። altáttạmạm.

sealed, cause (allow) to be, v.t. አሳተመ asáttạmạ.

Please have it sealed: pol. እስቲያሳትሙት። ịsti-yāsáttịmut.

sealing-wax, s. ማጣበቂያ፡ሰም maṭṭābạqyá (-āy-, -äq-; § 8) sạm.

search, s. ፍለጋ fịllạ́gā (§ 8).

Have a search made for him (it): አስፈልገው። as-fạ́llịgạ͡u, pol. ያስፈልጉት። yasfạ́llịgut.

search, v.i. & t. ጐረጐረ gwωrạ́ggwωrạ (-rώgg-).

(for, v.t.) ፈለገ fạ́llạgạ.

Search him (it): ጐርጕረው። gwώrgwŭrạ͡u, pl. ጐርጕሩት። gwώrgwŭrut.

Search them: ጐርጕራቸው። gwωrgwŭrā́ččạ͡u, pl. -ሯቸው። -rwā́ččạ͡u.

Search for him (it): ፈልገው። fạ́llịgạ͡u, pl. -ጉት። -gut.

Search for them: ፈልጋቸው። fạllịgā́ččạ͡u, pl. -ጓቸው። -gwā́ččạ͡u.

He must search for him (it): ይፈልገው። yịfạ́llịgạ͡u, pl. -ጉት። -gut.

Have you searched for him (it)? ፈለግሀው። fạ́llạg-hạ͡u, pl. ፈለጋችሁት። fạllạgā́ččịhut?

searched, be, v.p. ተጐረጐረ tạgwωrạ́ggwωrạ (-rώgg-).

The house is to be searched: ቤቱ፡ይጐርጐር። bʸétu yịggwώrgwωr.

searched for, be, v.p. ተፈለገ tḁfḁ́llḁgḁ.

He (it) was searched for and found: ተፈልጎ፡ተገኘ። tḁfḁ́lli̥gʷo tḁgḁ́ññä (§ 74*a*).

He (it) was searched for but not found: ተፈልጎ፡ አልተገኘም። tḁfḁ́lli̥gʷo altḁgḁ́ññäm.

seat, s. መቀመጫ mḁqqḁmḁ́č̣ã.

(chair) ወምበር wώmbḁr (-bär).

second, ord. num. ሁለተኛ hulḁttḁ́ññã (-lät-, -tấñ-; § 20*b*).

Menilek II.: ዳግማዊ፡ምኒልክ፡ dāgmấwi mi̥nilí̥k.

secret, adj. ድብቅ dí̥bbi̥q.

s. ምስጢር mí̥sṭir.

secretary, s. ጣፊ ṭấfi.

secretly, adv. Use gerund of ተሰረቀ tḁsḁ́rrḁqḁ (täsấr-).

He went secretly: ተሰርቆ፡ሔደ። täsấrqʷo hấdä.

security, s. (guarantor) ዋስ wās.

(on which a loan is made) መያዣ mḁyấžã (mḁ͡i̥á-).

What is your security: መያዣህ፡ምንድን፡ነው። mḁ-yấžah mi̥ndí̥n (§ 8) nḁ͡u?

You must offer security: መያዣ፡አምጣ። mḁyấža ánṭa (§ 7*d*).

security, stand, v.i. (for, v.t.) ተዋሰ tḁwấsḁ (tḁ͡uá-).

Who will stand security for you? ማን፡ይዋስሃል። mān yuwấsähāl?

sedition, s. አመፅ ấmḁṭ.

seditious, adj. አመጠኛ ãmḁṭḁ́ññã (-ṭấñ-).

seduce, v.t. (corrupt) አሳተ assátḁ.

(a woman) ወሸመ wḁ́ššḁmḁ (wώš-).

see, v.i. & t. አየ ấyyä (§ 44*b*, § 63*d*, *e*).

(examine) መረመረ mḁrḁ́mmḁrḁ (märḁ́mmärḁ).

I will see him (it): አየዋለሁ። ḁ͡i̥ḁ͡uállḁ͡u^{h}.

I see him (it): አይቼዋለሁ። a͡i̥čč^{y}ewállḁ͡u^{h}.

I don't see him (it): አላየውም። alá͡i̥ḁ͡um.

.I have seen (saw) him (it): አየሁት። áyyähut.

I have not seen (did not see) him (it): አላየሁትም። aláyyäḥuti̥m.

Do you see him (it)? አይተሀዋሎይ። á͡i̥tähḁ͡uāllwí̥?, pl. አይታችሁታሎይ። a͡i̥táčči̥hutāllwí̥? (s.v. ወይ).

Do you see them? አይተሃቸዋሎይ። a͡i̥täháččḁ͡uāllwí̥?, pl. አይታችኋቸዋሎይ። a͡i̥tāčči̥hwáččḁ͡uāllwí̥? (-tāč-čyuhá- § 7*d*).

Have you seen (did you see) him (it)? አየሀው። áyyähḁ͡u?, pl. አያችሁት። ayyáčči̥hut?

Have you seen (did you see) them? አየሃቸው። ayyäháččḁ͡u?, pl. አያችኋቸው። ayyāčči̥hwáččḁ͡u? (-ččyuhá- § 7*d*).

Haven't you seen (didn't you see) him (it)? አላየ ሀውም። aláyyähḁ͡um? (-ሀውሞይ። -hḁ͡ummwí̥?), pl. አላያችሁትም። alayyáčči̥huti̥m? (-ትሞይ። -ti̥mmwí̥?).

Go and see: ሒደህ፡እይ። hí̥däh ī, pl. ሒዳችሁ፡እዩ። hi̥dáččyuh íu.

See whether it is broken: መርምረው፡ተሰብሮ፡እንደ ሆን። mármi̥rḁ͡u tḁsḁẏr^{w}óndḁh^{w}on.

We have seen him (it): አይተነዋል። á͡i̥tänḁ͡uāl.

He (it) will see us: ያየናል። yá͡i̥ännāl, pl. ያዩናል። yá͡i̥unnāl.

He (it) sees us: አይቶናል። á͡i̥t^{w}onnāl, pl. አይተውናል። á͡i̥tḁ͡unnāl.

The doctor will see him (it): ሀኪም፡ይመረምሩታል። hákim yi̥mḁrḁ́mmi̥rutāl.

See that it is not left behind: እንዳይቀር። nda͡i̥qḁ́r.

see each other, v. recip. ተያዩ tḁ͡^{y}áyyu.

They do not see each other: አይተያዩም። a͡ḭttḁ͡^{y}áy-yum.

seed, s. ዘር zḁr (zär; § 52*a*, δ).

seek, v.i. & t. ፈለገ fḁ́llḁgḁ.

seem, v.i. መሰለ mḁ́ssḁlḁ (type A § 34).

It seems to me he has lost it: ይመስለኛል፡አጠፋው። yḭmḁ́släññāl aṭḁ́ffa͡u (-ñāll-aṭ- § 6).

seen, be, v.p. ታየ tā́yyä.

(examined) ተመረመረ tḁmḁrḁ́mmḁrḁ (-märḁ́mmärḁ).

He (it) cannot be seen: አይታይም። a͡ḭttáyyḭm, pl. -ዩም። -yyum (§ 63*c*; cp. § 54*c*).

As soon as he (it) is seen: ሲታይ፡ sḭttáyy.

seize, v.t. ያዘ yā́zḁ (§ 44*c*).

Seize him (it): ያዘው። yā́zḁ͡u, pl. ያዙት። yā́zut.

seized, be, v.p. ተያዘ tḁyā́zḁ (tḁ͡ḭá-).

select, v.i. & t. መረጠ mḁ́rrḁṭḁ.

ለቃቀመ lḁqā́qqḁmḁ.

Select one: አንድ፡ምረጥ። and mḭ́rḁṭ, pol. ...፡ይምረጡ። ... yḭ́mrḁṭu.

selected, be, v.p. ተመረጠ tḁmḁ́rrḁṭḁ.

ተለቃቀመ tḁlḁqā́qqḁmḁ.

This is the one that was selected: የተመረጠው፡ይህ፡ነው። yätḁmḁ́rrḁṭḁ͡u (§§ 14, 62) yḭ́he nḁ͡u.

-self, r. pron. ራስ- rās- with pers. suff. (§§ 12*b*, 17).

He himself is here: እርሱ፡ራሱ፡አለ። ḭrsú rā́su állä.

I myself: እኔ፡ራሴ፡ ḭn^{y}é rā́s^{y}e.

You will want it yourself: አንተ፡ራስህ፡ትፈልገዋለህ። ántä rā́sḭh tḭfḁllḭgḁ͡uállāh, pol. እርስዎ፡ራስዎ፡ይፈልጉታል። ḭrsḁ́͡^{w}o rā́sḁ͡^{w}o yḭfḁ́llḭgutāl.

He is by himself: ለብቻው፡ነው። lḁṿi̥ččá͡u nḁ͡u.

Of (by) oneself: እንዲያው (i̥)ndya͡u (§ 8).

እንደው (i̥)ndḁ͡u (§ 8).

They went of themselves: እንዲያው፡ሔዱ። ndyá͡u hắdu.

sell, v.i. & t. ሸጠ šḁ́ṭḁ (šắṭḁ).

Sell it: ሺጠው። ši̥ṭḁ͡u, pl. ሺጡት። ši̥ṭut.

Don't sell it: አትሺጠው። atti̥ši̥ṭḁ͡u, pl. -ጡት። -ṭut.

Sell them: ሺጣቸው። ši̥ṭáččḁ͡u, pl. ሺጧቸው። ši̥ṭwắččḁ͡u.

Don't sell them: አትሺጣቸው። atti̥ši̥ṭáččḁ͡u, pl. -ጧቸው። -ṭwắččḁ͡u.

Will you sell it? ትሸጠዋለህ። ti̥šäṭḁ͡uállăh?

Will he sell it? ይሸጠዋል። yi̥šắṭḁ͡uāl?

What will you sell it for? በስንት፡ትሸጠዋለህ። bḁsi̥nt ti̥šäṭḁ͡uállăh?

What will they sell it for? በስንት፡ይሸጡታል። bḁsi̥nt yi̥šắṭutāl?

Whenever you sell it, divide the proceeds among yourselves: እየሸጣችሁ፡ተካፈሉት። īyyäšäṭáččyuh (§ 61*b*) tḁkáfḁlut.

semen, s. ሽንት ši̥nt (prop. urine).

(euphem.) ኃጢአት (h)áṭyát (§ 8).

send (away), v.i. & t. ላከ lắkḁ.

ሰደደ sḁ́ddḁdḁ.

Send him (it): ላከው። lắkḁ͡u, pol. ይላኩት። yi̥lắkut.

Don't send him (it): አትላከው። atti̥lắkḁ͡u, pol. አይላኩት። a͡i̥lắkut.

Send him the answer: ምላሹን፡ላክለት። mi̥llắšun lắki̥llḁt (§ 47*a*).

Send him with the answer: ተምላሹ፡ጋር፡ላከው። tḁmi̥llắšu gār (§ 47*b*) lắkḁ͡u.

We will send him (it) to you (pl.): እንልክላችኋለን። i̥nni̥li̥ki̥lláččyuhállän (§ 7*d*).

Send me him (it): pol. ይስደዱልኝ። yi̥sdḁdulli̥ñ.

send for, v.t. አስመጣ asmḁ́ṭṭã.

Send for him (it): አስመጣው። asmḁ́ṭṭa͡u, pol. ያስመጡት። yasmḁ́ṭṭut, pl. አስመጡት። asmḁ́ṭṭut.

I will send for him (it): አስመጣዋለኊ። asmḁṭṭa͡u-állḁ͡u^{h}.

I will send for them: አስመጣቸዋለኊ። asmḁṭṭāč-čḁ͡uállḁ͡u^{h}.

I have sent for him (it): አስመጣሁት። asmḁ́ṭṭahut.

I have sent for them: አስመጣኋቸው። asmḁṭṭahwáč-čḁ͡u.

send on (ahead), v.t. አስቀደመ asqḁ́ddḁmḁ.

Send him (it) on ahead: አስቀድመው። asqḁ́ddi̥mḁ͡u, pol. ያስቀድሙት። yasqḁ́ddi̥mut.

Send them on ahead: አስቀድማቸው። asqḁddi̥máč-čḁ͡u, pol. ያስቀድሟቸው። yasqḁddi̥mwáččḁ͡u.

sense, s. (meaning) ማለት málḁt (-lät).

ፍች fi̥čč.

There's no sense in it: ማለት፡የለውም። málät yál-lḁ͡um.

sensitive of, be, v.t. ተሰማው tḁsḁ́mma͡u (impers. § 43*a*; § 63*d*, *e*).

sent (away), be, v.p. ተላከ tḁlákḁ.

Has he (it) been sent (away)? ተልኳል። táli̥kō͡al? (tál-), pol. & pl. ተልከዋል። táli̥kḁ͡uāl?

He (it) has not been sent (away), he (it) is here: አልተላከም፤አለ። altḁlákam, állä, pol. & pl. አልተላኩም፤አሉ። altḁlákum, állu.

Let him (it) be sent: ይላክ። yi̥llāk, pl. ይላኩ። yi̥l-láku.

sentry, s. ዘበኛ zḁbḁ́ññã (zḁỵ-, -áñ-).
ተረኛ tḁrḁ́ññã (tär-, -ráñ-).
ጠባቂ ṭḁbbáqi.
See § 52*a*, *δ*.

separate, adj. (-ly, adv.) s.v. ብቻ bi̥ččã.
Keep it separate: ለብቻው፡ ይሁን። lḁvi̥čča͡u yi̥hun.

separate, v.i. (be separated, v.p.)
(move apart) G. ተረራቁ tḁrḁráqu (tärär-).
Š. ተራራቁ tḁrāráqu (tär-).
Separate more than that: G. ተዚህ፡ ይበልጥ፡ ተረራቁ። täzzi̥h yi̥välṭ tḁrḁráqu, Š. ...፡ ተራራቁ። ... tḁrāráqu.
Don't separate: G. አትረራቁ። atti̥rrḁráqu, Š. አትራራቁ። atti̥rrāráqu.

separate, v.t. (move apart) G. አረራቀ arrḁráqḁ (-rär-).
Š. አራራቀ arrāráqḁ.
(distinguish) ለየ lḁ́yyä (láy-).
Separate them (e.g. combatants): G. አረርቃቸው። arrärqáččḁ͡u, Š. አራር- arrār-: pl. -ቋቸው። -qwáččḁ͡u.
Separate the bad and the good: ክፉንና፡ ደጉን፡ ለየው። ki̥funi̥nna dággun láyyḁ͡u, pl. ...፡ ለዩት። ... láyyut.

separated, be, v.p. (distinguished) ተለየ tḁlḁ́yyä (-láy-).

September, s.v. calendar.

serious, adj. (of persons) [እ]ርጉ ri̥gu (i̥rgu).
ከባድ kḁ́bbád (§ 8).
(of things) ትልቅ ti̥lli̥q.
He is a serious man: ከባድ፡ ሰው፡ ነው። kḁbbád sḁ͡u nḁ͡u, pol. ...፡ ናቸው። ... náččḁ͡u.
This is a serious matter: ይህ፡ ትልቅ፡ ነገር፡ ነው። yi̥he ti̥lli̥q nḁgár (§ 8) nḁ͡u.

servant, s. ኣሽካር áškḁr (-kär).
ሎሌ lʷṓlʸe, pl. also ሎላሊት lʷolā́li̥t.
Table-servant: ኣሳላፊ፡ asallā́fi.
Call a servant: ሎሌ፡ጥራ፡፡ lʷṓlʸe ṭi̥ra.
— To summon a servant whose name one does not know—ኣንት፡ኣሽካር፡፡ ant áškḁr!
servant-girl, s. ገረድ gḁ́rḁd.
serve, v.i. & t. ኣገልገለ agḁlḁ́ggḁlḁ.
How long has he served? ስንት፡ኣገልግሏል፡፡ si̥nt agḁ́lgi̥l͡ŏāl?, pl. -ግለዋል፡፡ -gi̥lḁ͡uāl?
service, s. (mil.) ወታደርነት wωttaddḁrí̥nnḁt (-där-, -nät).
(domestic) ሎልነት lʷolí̥nnḁt (-nät).
sesame (*Sesamum indicum*, Broun, Cat. 429), s. ሰሊጥ sḁ́lī́ṭ (sā́l-; § 8).
set, v.i. (sun, moon & stars) ገባ gḁ́bbā̃.
When the moon sets: ጨረቃ፡ስትገባ፡ çḁrḁqá si̥tti̥gḁ́ya.
set, v.t. (place) ኣደረገ adḁ́rrḁgḁ.
ኣስቀመጠ asqḁ́mmḁṭḁ.
ኣኖረ anʷṓrḁ.
(plant) ተከለ tḁ́kkḁlḁ.
ዘራ zḁ́rrā̃ (zā́r-).
Set it down: ኣኑረው፡፡ ā́nurḁ͡u, pl. -ሩት፡፡ -rut.
set, be, v.p. (placed) ተደረገ tḁdḁ́rrḁgḁ.
(planted) ተተከለ tḁtḁ́kkḁlḁ.
ተዘራ tḁzḁ́rrā̃ (täzā́r-).
Setit (river), s. ተከዜ tḁkkázʸe.
settle, v.i. ተቀመጠ tḁqḁ́mmḁṭḁ.
ሰፈረ sḁ́ffḁrḁ (-fär-).
settle, v.t. (disturbance) ዳኘ dā́ññä.
(define) ወሰነ wώssḁnḁ.
seven, card. num. ሰባት sḁ́bát (-ḁ́yá-; § 8; § 20*a*).

seventeen, card. num. አሥራ፡ሰባት asrāsḁbắt (-ḁỵá-; § 8; § 20*a*).
seventeenth, ord. num. አሥራ፡ሰባተኛ asrāsḁbāttḁ́ññã (-sḁỵā-, -tắñ-; § 20*b*).
seventh, ord. num. ሰባተኛ sḁbāttḁ́ññã (sḁỵā-, -tắñ-; § 20*b*).
seventh (1/7), s. ሰባትያ፡ [ሰባቲያ] sḁbāttíyyã (sḁỵā-; § 20*b*, § 52*a*, δ).
seventieth, ord. num. ሰባኛ sḁbáññã (sḁỵá-; § 20*b*).
seventy, card. num. ሰባ sḁ́bã (sḁ́ỵã; § 20*a*).
severe, adj. ብርቱ bi̥rtŭ.
sew (up, on), v.i. & t. ሰፋ sḁ́ffã.
ጠቀመ ṭḁ́qqḁmḁ (ṭắq-).
Sew it on before it gets lost: ሳይጠፋ፡ስፋው። sai̥-ṭḁfa si̥fa͡u.
Let him sew it up: ይስፋው። yi̥sfa͡u.
sewing, s. ስፌት si̥fʸĕt (§ 8).
sewn (up, on), be, v.p. ተሰፋ tḁsḁ́ffã (täs-).
It is to be sewn (up, on): ይሰፋ። yi̥ssḁ́fa, pl. -ፉ። -fu.
shade, s. ጥላ ṭi̥lã.
Put it in the shade: ተጥላ፡አድርገው። tḁṭi̥la (§ 47*a*) árgḁ͡u (§ 7*d*), pl. -ጉት። -gut.
There is no shade: ጥላ፡የለም። ṭi̥la yálläm.
shadow, s. ጥላ ṭi̥lã.
shake, v.i. (be shaken, v.p.) ተወዘወዘ tḁwḁzḁ́uwḁzḁ (tḁ́͡uḁ-, -ωzḁ́uwωzḁ).
ተነቀነቀ tḁnḁqḁ́nnḁqḁ.
It is not to shake (be shaken): አይወዝወዝ። ai̥w-wώzwωz, pl. -ወዙ። -wωzu.
It shakes when the wind catches it: ንፋስ፡እየነካው፡ይነቀነቃል። ni̥fás īyyänákkḁ͡u yi̥nnḁqánnḁqāl.

shake, v.t. ወዘወዘ wḁzḁ͡uwḁzḁ (wωzḁ͡uwωzḁ).

ነቀነቀ nḁqḁ́nnḁqḁ.

Shake it: ወነዝውዘው። wώzwŭzḁ͡u, pl. -ዙት። -zut, or ነቅንቀው። nḁ́qni̥qḁ͡u, pl. -ቁት። -qut.

Don't shake it: አትወነዝውዘው። atti̥wώzwŭzḁ͡u, pl. -ዙት። -zut, or አትነቅንቀው። ḁtti̥nḁ́qni̥qḁ͡u, pl. -ቁት። -qut.

Shake the bottle: ጠርሙዙን፡ነቅንቀው። ṭḁrmúzun nḁ́qni̥qḁ͡u.

shame, s. (sense of) እፍረት í̥frḁt (-rät).

(matter of) ነውር nḁ͡ur.

shape, s. መልክ mḁlk.

share, s. ክፍል kí̥fi̥l.

Your share: ክፍልህ፡ kí̥fli̥h (§ 12*b*).

This is *your* share: ይህ፡ያንተ፡ክፍል፡ነው። yi̥h yántä (§ 60*b*) ki̥fi̥l (§ 8) nḁ͡u.

share, v.i. & t. ተካፈለ tḁkáffḁlḁ.

Share (pl.) it: ተካፈሉት። tḁkáfḁlut.

sharp, adj. (edged) ስል si̥l.

sharpen, v.t. ሳለ sálḁ (conjug. like ሳለ to cough).

shatter, v.t. ሰባበረ sḁbā́bbḁrḁ (sḁvḁ̄́-, -bärḁ; § 22*b*, *η*).

shattered, be, v.p. ተሰባበረ tḁsḁbā́bbḁrḁ (täsä-, -vḁ̄́-, -bärḁ; § 22*b*, *θ*).

shave, v.i. (oneself, v.r.; be shaved, v.p.) ተላጨ tḁlā́ččḁ̈.

I am going to shave: እላጫለሁ። i̥llāččállḁ͡u[h].

shave, v.i. & t. ላጨ lā́ččä.

This razor won't shave: ይህ፡ምላጭ፡አይላጭም። yi̥he mi̥lā́čč ḁ͡ilā́čči̥m.

shaving-brush, s. †መፋግፋጊያ mḁfḁgfágyā̃.

she, pers. pron. እርሷ i̥rsö͡ā (§ 8, § 12*a*), usually omitted unless emphatic.

shear, v.t. ቀጠጠ qḁ́ṭṭḁṭḁ.

sheared, be, v.p. ተቀጠጠ tḁqḁ́ṭṭḁṭḁ.

shears, s. መቅጠጫ mḁqṭḁ́č̣ã (-ṭắč̣-).

sheath, s. ሰገባ sḁ́gḁ́bã (-ḁ́y̥ã; § 8).

(vet.) ብሌት bí̥lli̥t.

shed, s. ዳስ dās.

Put (pl.) up a shed: ዳስ፡ጣሉ። dās ṭálu.

sheep, s. በግ bḁg (§ 52*a*, δ).

sheep-skin, s. የበግ፡ቆዳ yäbḁ́g (-äy̥ḁ́-; § 47*a*) q^{w}ódã.

(with coat) አጐዛ ag^{w}ózã.

shelf, s. ቆጥ q^{w}oṭ.

On the shelf: ተቆጥ፡ tḁ́q^{w}óṭ (§ 8; § 74*a*).

shelter, s. (straw, temporary) ጐጆ g^{w}ójj^{w}o.

shield, s. ጋሻ gắššã.

shin, s. ማሀል፡አገዳ máhal (māl) ágḁdã (§ 52*a*, γ).

shine, v.i. በራ bḁ́rrã.

What is that shining there? ያ፡እሚበራው፡ምንድር፡ ነው። yā mmi̥y̥ḁ́raû (§ 62*c*) mi̥ndí̥r nḁû?

ship, s. መርከብ mḁ́rkḁb (mắr-, -ḁy̥).

shirt, s. ቀሚስ qḁ́mis (-mi̥s).

እጀ፡ጠባብ í̥jjä (§ 9*d*) ṭḁ́bbáb (-ắy̥; § 8).

(common native) ጨርቅ č̣ärq.

shiver, v.i. ተንቀጠቀጠ tḁṅqḁṭḁ́qqḁṭḁ.

shock, s. (fright) ድንጋጤ di̥ṅgắṭ^{y}e.

He (it) died of (the) shock: በድንጋጤ፡ሞተ። bḁdi̥ṅ-gắṭ^{y}e m^{w}ótḁ.

shocked, be, v.i. ደነገጠ dḁnḁ́ggḁṭḁ.

shoe, s. ጫማ č̣ắmmã (§ 52*a*, δ).

A pair of shoes: ጫማ፡ č̣ámma.

Bring me another pair of shoes: ሌላ፡ጫማ፡አምጣ ልኝ። léla č̣ámma ánṭalli̥ñ (§ 7*d*, § 47*a*).

shoe-horn, s. የጫማ፡ማድረጊያ yäčámma mādrágyã (-rág-) ማግቢያ mágbyã (-gyyã).

shoe-lace, s. የጫማ፡ማሰሪያ yäčámma māsáryã (-sár-, -yä).

shoot, v.i. ተኰሰ tákkwωsa (tώkkosa § 7*d*).

v.t. በጠበንጃ፡መታ baṭabánja (-ayá-) máttã.

Has he learnt to shoot? ቱክስ፡ለምዷል። tuks lámdŏāl?, pl. ...፡ ለምደዋል። ... lámdaūāl?

Did he shoot him (it)? በጠበንጃ፡መታው። baṭayánja máttaū?, pl. ...፡ መቱት። ... máttut?

I am going shooting: አደን፡እሔዳለሁ። ádän ihädállaūʰ, pl. ...፡ እንሔዳለን። ... innihädállän.

He shot himself: ጠበንጃ፡ጠጣ። ṭayánja ṭáṭṭa, or ጠበንጃ፡ጐረሰ። ṭayánja gwώrrasa.

shop, s. እቃ፡ቤት iqá-bʸēt (-yʸ-).

†መጋዘን magázan (-ዚን -zin).

short, adj. አጭር áččir.

short(-er), be, v.i. አጠረ áṭṭara (-ṭära; § 58*b*).

It is (too) short: ያጥራል። yáṭrāl, pl. ያጥራሉ። yāṭrállu.

This is to be shorter than that: ይህ፡ተዚህ፡ይጠር። yihe täzzih yiṭar.

shorten, v.t. አሳጠረ asáṭṭara (-ṭära).

Shorten it: አሳጥረው። asáṭṭiraū, pl. -ሩት። -rut.

shot, be, v.p. በጠበንጃ፡ተመታ baṭabánja (-ayá-) tamáttã.

should, v. aux.—see § 24*b*, note 2; § 81*c*, *d*.

You should have gone: ትሔድ፡ነበር። tihád nábbär, pl. ትሔዱ፡ነበር። tihádu nábbär.

If they brought a good mule I should buy it: ጥሩ፡በቅሎ፡ቢያመጡ፡እገዛው፡ነበር። ṭúru yáqlʷo yyāmáṭu, igázaū nábbär.

shoulder, s. ትከሻ tịkạ́ššā̃.

ጫንቃ č̣áṅqā̃.

(of horse, mule, etc.) እምቢያ (ị)mbyā̃. See § 52*a*, γ.

shoulder-blade, s. መጋፍያ mạgáfyā̃ (§ 52*a*, γ).

shout, v.i. ጮኸ č̣ʷóhạ (§ 7*d*).

Shout: ጩኽ። č̣uh, pl. ጩኹ። č̣úhu.

Don't shout: አትጩኽ። attịč̣uh, pl. -ጩኹ። -č̣úhu.

shout to (at) each other, v.i. ተጯጯኹ tạč̣ŏā́č̣ŏāhu.

Shout to each other: ተጯጯኹ። tạč̣ŏā́č̣ŏahu.

Don't shout at one another: አትጯጯኹ። attịč̣-č̣ŏā́č̣ŏahu.

show, v.i. (appear) ታየ tā́yyä.

v.t. አሳየ asā́yyä.

It doesn't show: አይታይም። aịttáyyịm.

(of a small object) አትታይም። at-tịttáyyịm (§ 54*c*).

Show me (him, it, them, § 61*a*): አሳየኝ። asáyyäñ.

shrink, v.i. (become smaller) ጠበበ ṭạ́bbạbạ (-ạyạ).

It doesn't shrink when washed: ሲታጠብ፡አይጠብም። sịttā́ṭṭạy aịṭạ́bbịm.

shrub, s. ቍጥቋጦ qwŭṭqwā́ṭʷo (§ 52*a*, δ).

shudder, v.i. ስቅቅ፡አለው sịqịqq ā́lạu (impers. § 43*a*; s.v. √በለ, § 44*a*).

It makes me shudder: ስቅቅ፡ይለኛል። sịqịqq yịlā́ñ-ñāl.

shut, adj. ዝግ zịgg.

shut, v.i. (be shut, v.p.) ተዘጋ tạzággā̃.

It is not to be shut: አይዘጋ። aịzzága, pl. -ጉ። -gu.

Is it shut?—Yes, I have shut it: ተዘግቷል። አወን፡ ዘግቼዋለሁ። tạzágtŏāl?—ā́wωn, zạgịččewállạuʰ.

shut, v.t. ዘጋ zḁ́ggā̃.
(a lid) ከደነ kḁ́ddḁnḁ.
Shut it: ዝጋው። zí̥ga͡u, pl. ዝጉት። zí̥gut.
Don't shut it: አትዝጋው። attí̥zga͡u, pl. -ጉት። -gut.
Shut the door: ሳንቃውን፡ዝጋው። sā́ṅqa͡un zí̥ga͡u.
Shut the box and lock it: ሳጥኑን፡ከድነህ፡ቈልፈው። sā́ṭi̥nun kḁ́dnäh qwώlli̥fḁ͡u.

shy, v.i. ደነገጠ dḁnḁ́ggḁṭḁ.
ገረገረ gḁrḁ́ggḁrḁ (gärḁ́ggärḁ).

shy (modest), be, v.i. አፈረ áffḁrḁ (-fär-).
It is shy (wild): ሰው፡አይወድም። sḁ͡u ḁ͡iwώddi̥m.

shying, given to, adj. ደንጋጭ dḁ́ṅgā́č̣ (dǟ́ṅ-; § 8).
ደንጋጣ dḁṅgā́ṭṭā̃ (däṅ-).
ገርጋሪ gḁrgā́ri (gär-).

sick, adj. ታማሚ tā̃mā́mi.

sick, be, v.i. ታመመ tā̃́mmḁmḁ.
አመመው ámmḁmḁ͡u (impers. § 43*a*).
See § 63*d*, *e*; s.v. ill, be.
(vomit) ተፋ tḁ́ffā̃.
You will be sick: ትተፋለህ። ti̥tḁfā́llāh, pl. ትተፋላችሁ። ti̥tḁfallā́ččyuh (§ 7*d*).

sick, make, v.t. አሳመመ asā́mmḁmḁ.
(cause to vomit) አስተፋ astḁ́ffā̃.
It makes (will make) me sick: ያስተፋኛል። yāstḁ́f-faññāl.
It will make you sick: ያስተፋሃል። yāstḁ́ffahāl, … you (pl.) …: ያስተፋችኋል። yāstḁffā́ččyuhāl (§ 7*d*).

sickle, s. ማጭድ mā́č̣i̥d.

sickly, adj. ዷያታም dwayā́tám (-a͡i̥á-; § 8).

sickness, s. በሽታ bḁ́ši̥tā̃.

side, s. ጐድን gwώdi̥n (ጐን gwωnn; § 52*a*, γ).
(part) ወገን wḁ́gḁn (wώg-).

What is the length of the side? ጐኑ፡ስንት፡ነው። gwώnnu sí̥nti̥ nḁ͡u?

Have you a pain in your side? ጐንህን፡አሞሃል። gwώnni̥hi̥n ámmʷohāl?, pol. ጐነዎን፡አሞዎታል። gwώnnḁ͡ʷon ámmʷo͡ʷotāl? (§ 56c).

On this side: (of an object) በዚህ፡ወገን፡ bḁzzíh wώgḁn.

(in regard to an object) በወዲህ፡ bḁ͡uώdíh (-dí̥h; § 8).

On the other side: (=over there) በወዲያ፡ bḁ͡uώ-dyā́ (§ 8).

Go round to the other side: ወዲያ፡ዙር። wωdyā́ zur, pl. ...፡ ዙሩ። ... zúru.

The other side: (of water) ማዶ፡ mā́dʷo.

sieve, s. ወንፊት wḁ́nfit (wώ-, -mf-, -fi̥t).

sift, v.t. ነፋ nḁ́ffā̃.

Sift it: ንፋው። ní̥fa͡u, pl. ንፉት። ní̥fut.

sifted, be, v.p. ተነፋ tḁnáffā̃.

Let it be sifted: ይነፋ። yi̥nnḁ́fa.

sigh, v.i. ተነፈሰ tḁnḁ́ffḁsḁ.

sight, s. (seeing) ማየት mā̃͡i̥ät (mā̃ʸät ; § 44b).

(of gun) መነጣጠሪያ mḁnnḁṭāṭṭḁryā̃ (-ṭā́r-).

He (it) has come into sight: ዘልቋል። zḁ́lq͡ōāl, pl. ዘልቀዋል። zḁ́lqḁ͡uāl (s.v. ዘለቀ).

sight-protector, s. የመነጣጠሪያ፡መከደኛ yämḁnnḁṭāṭṭḁ́rya (§§ 47a, 70a) mḁkdḁ́ñā̃.

sign, s. (signal, gesture) ጥቅሻ ṭí̥q(i̥š)šā̃.

(mark, token) ምልክት mi̥lí̥kki̥t.

(symptom) ማስታወቂያ mā̃sta͡uώqyā̃.

Make a sign (signs) to him: ጥቀሰው። ṭí̥qḁsḁ͡u, pl. -ሱት። -sut.

Make signs to them: ጥቀሱችው። ṭi̥qḁsáččḁu͡, pl. -ሷችው። -swáččḁu͡.

sign, v.i. (beckon) ጠቀሰ ṭḁ́qqḁsḁ.

(write one's name) ስሙን፡ጣፈ si̥mun ṭáfḁ, pol. & pl. ስማችውን፡ጣፉ። si̥máččḁu͡n ṭáfu. (*Note. Abyssinian documents are sealed, not signed.*)

silence!, interj. ዝም፡በል። zi̥mm bḁl!, f. ዝም፡በይ። zi̥mm bḁi̥!, pl. ዝም፡በሉ። zi̥mm bḁlu!

silence, s. (forbearance from causing noise) ዝምታ zí̥m-mi̥tã.

(freedom from noise) [እ]ርጋት rí̥gát (í̥rg-; §8).

silence, v.t. ዝም፡አሰኘ zi̥mm assáññä.

Silence him (it): ዝም፡አሰኘው። zi̥mm assáññäu͡.

silent, adj. (not causing noise) ዝምተኛ zi̥mmi̥tḁ́ññã (-táñ-).

(free from noise) [እ]ርጉ rí̥gu (í̥rgu).

silent, be, v.i. (cause no noise) ዝም፡አለ zi̥mm álḁ (s.v. √ባለ, § 44*a*).

(be free from noise) [እ]ረጋ (i̥)rággã.

Let him be silent: ዝም፡ይበል። zi̥mm yí̥v̥ḁl, pl. ዝም፡ይበሉ። zi̥mm yí̥v̥ḁlu.

silk, s. ሀር harr.

silver, s. ብር bi̥rr.

simpleton, s. ገውጋዋ gḁu͡gáwwã (-áu͡wã).

sin, s. ኃጢአት háṭyát (áṭ-; § 8).

since, conj. ከ- [ተ-] kḁ- (tḁ-) with simple perfect (§ 48*a*).

It is ten days since he started: አሥር፡ቀኑ፡ነው፡ ከተነሣ። ássi̥r qḁ́nu nḁu͡ kḁtḁnḁ́ssa.

Well, go in, then, since you want to: እንኳን፡ግባ፡ ተፈለግህ። ńkwān, gí̥v̥a, tḁfḁ́llḁgi̥h.

sincere, adj. ቁም qum.
ቅን qi̥n.
sinciput, s. አናት ánā́t (§ 8).
sing, v.i. & t. ዘፈነ zḁ́ffḁnḁ (zā́f-).
አቅራራ aqrā́rrā̃.
(chant) ዘመረ zḁ́mmḁrḁ (-mär-).
single, adj. አንድ and, f. አንዲት ándi̥t (§ 20*a*).
አንዲያ andíyyā̃.
sir, interj. አቤት ábʸét (ā́y̧ʸ-; § 8).
sister, s. እኅት í̥hi̥t (hi̥t, i̥t).
sister-in-law, s. ምራት mí̥rā́t (§ 8).
sistrum, s. ጸናጽል ṣḁnā́ṣi̥l.
sit (down), v.i. ተቀመጠ tḁqḁ́mmḁṭḁ.
Sit down: ተቀመጥ። tḁqḁ́mḁṭ, pol. ይቀመጡ። yi̥q-qḁ́mḁṭu, pl. ተቀመጡ። tḁqḁ́mḁṭu.
six, card. num. ስድስት sí̥ddi̥st (§ 20*a*).
sixteen, card. num. አሥራ፡ስድስት asrāsí̥ddi̥st (§ 20*a*).
sixteenth, ord. num. አሥራ፡ስድስተኛ asrā̃si̥ddi̥stḁ́ññā̃ (-tā́ñ-; § 20*b*).
sixth, ord. num. ስድስተኛ si̥ddi̥stḁ́ññā̃ (-tā́ñ-; § 20*b*).
sixth ($^1/_6$), s. ስድስትያ፡[ስድስቲያ] si̥ddi̥stíyyā̃ (§ 20*b*, § 52*a*, δ).
sixtieth, ord. num. ስልሳኛ si̥lsáññā̃ (§ 20*b*).
sixty, card. num. ስልሳ si̥lsā̃ (§ 20*a*).
size, s. ታላቅነት tallāqí̥nnḁt (-nät).
ዓይነት á͡i̥nḁt (-nät).
ቁመት qúmḁt (-mät).
What size is it? ምን፡ያህላል። mi̥n yáhlāl? (s.v. አከለ).
It is about this size: ይህን፡ያህል፡ነው። yi̥hā́nn yahl nḁu͡.
skilful, adj. ብልሃተኛ bi̥lhātḁ́ññā̃ (-tā́ñ-).
ጥበበኛ ṭi̥bḁbḁ́ññā̃ (ṭi̥vḁv-, -ā́ñ-).

skill, s. ብልሃት bi̥lhát (§ 8).
ጥበብ ṭi̥bḁb (ṭi̥y̥ḁy̥).
skin, s. ቆርበት qʷórbḁt (-ry̥-, -ät).
(bag made of) አቁማዳ aqumádã.
Š. ስልቻ si̥lli̥ččã.
(for water) ሩዋት ráuwát (§ 8).
(hide) ቆዳ qʷódã.
(with coat) አጎዛ agʷózã.
skull, s. ቅል qi̥l.
sky, s. ሰማይ sḁ́mái̥ (§ 8).
slack, adj. (loose) ልል li̥l.
slander, v.t. ነገር፡ሰራ nḁ́gḁr (-gär) sḁ́rrã (sár-) በ- bḁ- (yḁ-; § 47*a*).
አማ ámmã.
He slandered him: ነገር፡ሰራበት። nḁ́gḁr sḁ́rrabbḁt.
slanderer, s. ነገረ፡ሰሪ nḁ́gḁrḁ (-gär-; § 9*d*) sḁ́ri (sár-).
አሚ ámi.
slaughter, v.i. & t. አረደ árrḁdḁ.
slave, s. ባርያ bárya͂, pl. ባሮች bárʷōč (-čč § 6).
Runaway slave: ካጅ kāj.
slavery, s. ባርነት bāri̥nnḁt (-nät).
sleep, s. እንቅልፍ (i̥)ṅqi̥lf (§ 7*d*; § 8).
ምኝታ mi̥ññitã (መኚ- mánñi-, -i̥t-).
He needs sleep: መተኛት፡ይሻል። mḁtäññát yi̥šál.
sleep, v.i. ተኛ tḁ́ññã (tán-, -ñä, § 7*d*).
I could not sleep: አልተኛሁም። altáññahum (cp. § 63*c*).
One can't sleep with that noise going on: ይህ፡ጩኸት፡ሰው፡አያስተኛም። yi̥he čúhät sḁ́u aʸastáñ-ñām.
sleep, cause (send) or allow to, v.i. & t. አስተኛ astḁ́ññã (-tán-, -ñä, § 7*d*).

The heat sends me to sleep: ሙቀት፡ያስተኛኛል። múqḁt yastắññāññāl.

sleepy, be, v.i. አንቀላፋ aṅqḁlắffā.

I feel sleepy: አንቀላፋለኍ። aṅqḁlaffállḁu͡^{h} (§ 7*d*).

sleet, s. በረድ bḁ́rḁd.

sleeve, s. እጅጌ ı̥́jjı̥g^{y}e (§ 52*a*, δ).

slender, adj. ቀጭን qḁ́č̣č̣ı̥n, intensive pl. ቀጫጭን qḁč̣ắč̣-č̣ı̥n, ቀጫጭኖች qḁč̣ắč̣č̣ı̥n^{w}ōč (-čč § 6).

slide, v.i. ተንሸተተ tḁnšắttḁtḁ (-tätḁ).

sling, s. የምድር፡ነጕድ yắmdı̥r nḁ́gwωd (§ 8).

(of rifle) ማንገቻ mā̃ṅgḁ́čā̃ (-gắčā̃).

sling over the shoulder, v.t. አነገተ anḁ́ggḁtḁ.

Sling it over your shoulder: በጫንቃህ፡አንግተው። bḁč̣ắṅqāh áṅgı̥tḁu.

slip, v.i. ዳጠ dắṭḁ.

You will slip: ትድጣለህ። tı̥dı̥ṭállăh, pl. ትድጣላችሁ። tı̥dı̥ṭallắččyuh (§ 7*d*).

Take care you don't slip: እንዳትድጥ። ndattı̥dı̥́ṭ, pl. -ድጡ። -dı̥́ṭu.

slip, cause or allow to, v.t. አዳጠ adắṭḁ.

slipper, s. ነጠላ፡ጫማ nḁṭḁlá č̣ắmmā̃.

(with turned-up toe, مركوب) ኩፍ፡ጫማ kuff č̣ắmmā̃.

See § 52*a*, δ.

slippery, adj. (of ground, etc.) ድጥ dı̥ṭ.

Š. ዳጥ dāṭ.

አዳጭ ắdắč̣ (§ 8).

(eluding the grasp) ሙልጭ múllı̥č̣ (-č̣č̣ § 6).

slippery, be (become), v.i. (of ground, etc.) አዳጠ adắṭḁ.

(eluding the grasp) ሙልጭ፡አለ múllı̥č̣č̣ álḁ (s.v. √በለ, § 44*a*; § 63*d*, *e*).

This place is slippery: ይህ፡ስፍራ፡ያድጣል። yi̥he sí̥fra yādí̥ṭāl.

It is very slippery: one can't hold it: እጅግ፡ሙልጭ፡ብሏል፤ አይያዝም። í̥jji̥g múlli̥č̣čĭ̥ yí̥lŏ͡āl: a͡i̥yyázi̥m.

slit, s. ቀዳዳ qḁdáda͂ (§ 52*a*, δ).

There is a slit (are slits) in it: ቀዳዳ፡አለበት። qḁdáda állḁbbḁt.

slit, v.i. (be slit, v.p.) ተቀደደ tḁqḁ́ddadḁ.

It will slit: ይቀደዳል። yi̥qqḁ́ddḁdāl, pl. ይቀደዳሉ። yi̥qqḁddḁdállu.

It has (is) slit: ተቀዷል። tḁqḁ́ddŏ͡āl, pl. -ደዋል። -ddḁ͡ūāl.

Take care it doesn't slit: እንዳይቀደድ። nda͡i̥qqḁ́ddḁd, pl. -ደዱ። -ddḁdu.

slit, v.t. ቀደደ qḁ́ddḁdḁ.

Slit it: ቅደደው። qí̥dḁdḁ͡ū, pl. ቅደዱት። qí̥dḁdut.

Don't slit it: አትቅደደው። attí̥qdḁdḁ͡ū, pl. -ዱት። -dut.

slope, s. ቍልቍለት qwŭlqwŭ́lḁt (-lät; § 8).

When he (it) goes down the slope: ቍልቍለት፡ሲወርድ፡ qwŭlqwŭlḁ́t si̥wǿrd.

slope, v.i. ዝቅ፡አለ zi̥qq álḁ (s.v. √ባለ, § 44*a*; § 63*d*, *e*).

See that it doesn't slope: ዝቅ፡እንዳይል። zi̥qq i̥nda͡i̥l.

sloping, adj. ቍልቍል qwŭ́lqwŭl.

The ground is sloping: ምድር፡ቍልቍል፡ነው። ḿdi̥r qwŭlqwŭ́l (§ 8) nḁ͡ū.

slops, s. እድፍ í̥d(i̥)f.

Pour the slops away and put fresh water in it: እድፉን፡አፍሰህ፡ጥሩ፡ውሃ፡አድርግበት። í̥dfun afí̥ssäh ṭŭ́ru wŭ́ha ádri̥gi̥bbḁt (ṭŭrūhárgi̥bbät).

slow, adj. ዳተኛ dātą̊́ññā̃ (-tą̊́ñ-).
ችልተኛ čį̊llį̊tą̊́ññā̃ (-tą̊́ñ-).

The watch is slow: ሰዓቱ፡ዘግይቷል። są̊ā̂tu zą̊́gyį̊tō̂āl, or ...፣ ቀርቷል። ... qą̊́rtō̂āl.

slowly!, interj. ዝግ zį̊gg!
ቀስ qą̊ss!

slowly, go (act), v.i. ዝግ፡አለ zį̊gg ą̊́lą̊.
ቀስ፡አለ qą̊ss ą̊́lą̊.
S.v. √ባለ, § 44*a*.

Speak slowly: ዝግ፡ብለህ፡ተናገር። zį̊gg yį̊́läh tą̊nā́gär.

Let him speak slowly: ዝግ፡ብሎ፡ይናገር። zį̊́ggį̊̆ (§ 7*d*) yį̊́lʷo yį̊nnā́gą̊r.

small, adj. ትንሽ tį̊́nnį̊š, intensive pls. ትንንሽ tį̊nį̊́nnį̊š, -ንሾች -nnį̊šʷōč (-čč § 6), ትትንሽ tį̊tį̊́nnį̊š, -ንሾች -nnį̊šʷōč (-čč § 6).

They are quite small: ትትንሽ፡ናቸው። tį̊tį̊nnį̊́š (§ 8) nā́čč̌ą̊û.

small-pox, s. ኩፍኝ kúffį̊ñ (-ññ § 6; § 8).

He is pitted by small-pox: ኩፍኝ፡የወጋው፡ነው። kuffį̊ñ yäwωggā́û ną̊û.

Has he had small-pox? ኩፍኝ፡አወጣ። kúffį̊ññ âû-ώtṭa?, pol. & pl. -ጡ። -ṭṭu?

smart, adj. (clever) ጮሌ čʷóllʸe.
(well dressed) ጌጠኛ gʸēṭą̊́ññā̃ (-ṭą̊́ñ-).

smart, be, v.i. (dress well) አጌጠ agʸḗṭą̊.

smash, v.t. ሰባበረ są̊bā́bbą̊rą̊ (są̊yą̊́-, -bärą̊; § 22*b*, η).

smashed, be, v.p. ተሰባበረ tą̊są̊bā́bbą̊rą̊ (täsä-, -yą̊́-, -bärą̊; § 22*b*, θ).

smear, v.t. ቀባ qą̊́bbā̃.
አበሰ ábbą̊są̊.

Smear the boots with grease: ጫማውን፡ስብን፡ቅባው።
č̣ámma͡un (§ 52*a*, δ) sı̥́y̥ı̥n (§ 56*f*) qı̥́y̥a͡u, or ጫማውን፡
በስብ፡ቅባው። č̣ámma͡un bḁsı̥́y̥ qı̥́y̥a͡u.

smeared, be, v.p. (smear oneself, v.r.) ተቀባ tḁqḁ́bbā̃.
ታበሰ tā́bbḁsḁ.

Has it been smeared with grease? ስብን፡ተቀብቷል።
sı̥́y̥ı̥n (§ 56*f*; or በስብ፡ bḁsı̥́y̥) tḁqḁ́y̥tŏ͡al?, pl. ...፡
ተቀብተዋል። ... tḁqḁ́y̥tḁ͡ual?

smell, s. ሽታ šı̥́ttā̃.
(unpleasant) ግማት gı̥mā́t (§ 8).

I can't bear the smell of it: ገማኝ። gḁ́mmañ (§ 61*c*).

smell, v.i. ሸተተ šḁ́ttḁtḁ (šā́t-).
(unpleasantly) ገማ gḁ́mmā̃.
See § 63*d, e*.

He (it) smells: ሸቷል። šā́ttŏ͡al.
(unpleasantly) ገምቷል። gḁ́mtŏ͡al.

smell, v.i. & t. አሸተተ ašḁ́ttḁtḁ (-šā́t-; § 63*d, e*).

I have a cold, I can't smell: ጉንፋን፡ያዘኝ፡አላሸትም።
gumfā́n yázäñ, alašā́ttı̥m (§ 63*c*).

I smell it: አሸቼዋለሁ። ašı̥č̣čʸewállḁ͡uʰ (§ 7*d*), pl. አ
ሸተነዋል። ā́šı̥ttḁnḁ͡ual.

Do you smell it? አሽተሀዋሎይ። ā́šı̥ttähḁ͡uallwı̥́? (s.v.
ወይ), pl. አሽታችሁታሎይ። ašı̥ttā́ččı̥hutāllwı̥́?

smell sweet, v.i. ታጠነ tā́ṭṭḁnḁ (§ 63*d, e*).

It smells sweet: ታጥኗል። tā́ṭı̥̆nŏ͡al, pl. -ነዋል። -nḁ͡ual.

smile, v.i. ፍግግ፡አለ fı̥́gı̥gg ā́lḁ (s.v. √ባለ, § 44*a*).

smith, s. ባለጅ bálā́jj (§ 8).
ቀጥቃጭ qḁ́ṭqā́č̣ (§ 8).

smoke, s. ጢስ ṭīs.
ጭስ č̣īs.

smoke, v.i. ጤሰ ṭʸḗsḁ (§ 42*c*).
(tobacco) v.i. & t. ጠጣ ṭḁ́ṭṭā̃.

Do you smoke? ትምባኋ፡ትጠጣለህ። tı̥mbḁ́uha tı̥ṭḁṭṭálläh?, pol. ...፡ይጠጣሉ።... yı̥ṭḁṭṭállu?
smoked, be, v.p. (of tobacco) ተጠጣ tḁṭḁ́ṭṭā̃.
smoky, adj. ጢሳም ṭī́sám (§ 8).
smooth, adj. ለሽላሳ lḁslássā̃.
ልዝብ lı̥́zzı̥b (-ı̥y̥).
snail, s. ቀሳቦ tḁsā́bbʷo (täs-), usually f. (§ 54c).
snake, s. እባብ ı̥bā́b (ı̥́y̥ā́y̥; § 8).
Is this snake poisonous? ይህ፡እባብ፡መርዛም፡ነው። yı̥h ı̥y̥ā́y̥ mḁrzám nḁu?
snare, s. ማጥመጃ māṭmḁ́jā̃ (-mā́jā̃).
snatch, v.i. & t. ነጠቀ nḁ́ṭṭḁqḁ (nā́ṭ-).
Don't snatch: አትንጠቅ። attı̥́nṭḁq.
sneeze, v.i. አነጠሰ anḁ́ṭṭḁsḁ.
snipe, s. የውሃ፡ድርጭት yäúha dı̥́rčı̥t (§ 52a, δ).
snore, v.i. አንኳረፈ ańkwā́rrḁfḁ.
snow, s. አመዳይ amḁdā́ı̥ (§ 8).
ውርጭ wurč (prop. frost).
snub-nosed, adj. ደፍጣጣ dḁfṭḁ́ṭṭā̃.
snuff, s. ስንቀን sı̥́ńqḁn.
snuff, take, v.i. ስንቀን፡ጠጣ sı̥́ńqḁn ṭḁ́ṭṭā̃.
Do you take snuff? ስንቀን፡ትጠጣለህ። sı̥́ńqḁn tı̥ṭḁṭṭálläh?, pol. ...፡ይጠጣሉ። ... yı̥ṭḁṭṭállu?
so, adv. (consequently) እዛውዲያ (ı̥)z(z)áʷωdyā̃ (-zád-; § 8), Š. ታዲያ tádyā̃.
እንግዴህ (ı̥)ńgdʸḗh.
(thus) እንዲህ (ı̥́)ndíh (-dı̥́h; § 8).
እንደዚህ (ı̥)ndḁ́zzíh (-dā́z-, -zı̥́h; § 8).
(inferential) -አ -ā́? (§§ 6, 8).
I don't wish it so: እንደዚህ፡አልፈልግም። ndḁzzíh alfḁ́llı̥gı̥m.

Quite so: ነው። nḁ͡u, or እውነት፡ነው። unát nḁ͡u.
So you are going? ትሄዳለሃ። ti̥hädállähá?
so-and-so, indef. pron. እገሌ i̥gḁ́lʸe (§ 16).
soap, s. ሳሙና sāmū́nã.
sociable, adj. ተጫዋች tḁčá͡uáč (§ 8).
ጨዋተኛ čḁ͡uatḁ́ññã (-tā́ñ-).
sociable, be, v.i. ተጫወተ tḁčá͡uwḁtḁ (-wωtḁ).
sock, s. ሹራብ šúrráb (-áy̥; § 8, § 52*a*, δ).
soft, adj. ለስላሳ lḁslássã.
It is too soft: ለስላሳ፡ነው። lḁslāssá (§ 8) nḁ͡u.
soft, be (become), v.i. ለሰለሰ lḁsḁ́llḁsḁ.
soften, v.t. አለሰለሰ alḁsḁ́llḁsḁ.
soil, s. መሬት mḁ́rʸḗt (§ 8).
(loose) አፈር ā́fḁr (-fär).
Hard, stony soil: ፎረፎር፡ fʷórḁfʷor.
Red soil: ቦረቦር፡ bʷórḁbʷor (-ḁy̥ʷ-).
ቦረንቅ፡ bʷórḁṅq (§ 8).
soil, v.t. አሳደፈ asáddḁfḁ.
Don't soil it: አታሳድፈው። attāsáddi̥fḁ͡u, pl. -ፉት። -fut.
You will soil it: ታሳድፈዋለህ። tāsaddi̥fḁ͡uállāh, pl. ታሳድፉታላችሁ። tāsaddi̥fútallā́ččyuh (§ 7*d*).
soiled, be (become), v.i. & p. አደፈ áddḁfḁ (§ 23*a*, § 63*d*, *e*).
It is soiled: አድፏል። ádf͡ōāl, pl. አድፈዋል። ádfḁ͡uāl.
It will get soiled: ያድፋል። yā́dfāl, pl. ያድፋሉ። yād-fállu.
See that it doesn't get soiled: እንዳያድፍ። nda͡ʸā́di̥f, ... that they don't ...: እንዳያድፉ። nda͡ʸádfu.
sold, be, v.p. ተሸጠ tḁšḁ́ṭḁ (täšā́ṭḁ).
Let it be sold: ይሸጥ። yi̥ššäṭ, pl. ይሸጡ። yi̥ššā́ṭu.
It is not to be sold: አይሸጥ። á͡i̥ššäṭ, pl. አይሸጡ። a͡i̥ššā́ṭu.

What is it sold at? በስንት፡ይሸጣል። bḁsi̥nt yi̥ššá-
ṭāl?, pl. ...፡ ይሸጣሉ። ... yi̥ššäṭállu?

solder, s. ማጣበቂያ maṭṭãbḁ́qyã (-ãy̥-, -áq-).

solder, v.t. አጣበቀ aṭṭábbḁqḁ.

soldered, be, v.p. ተጣበቀ tḁṭábbḁqḁ.

It must be soldered: ይጣበቅ። yi̥ṭṭấy̥ḁq.

soldier, s. ወታደር wωttáddḁr (-där; § 52*a*, δ).

sole (of foot), s. ጫማ č̣ấmmã (§ 52*a*, γ).

solid, adj. ጥኑ ṭi̥nu.
ብርቱ bi̥rtŭ.
ጠንካራ ṭḁṅkárrã.

solitary, adj. አንዲያ andíyyã.

Somali, s. ሶማሌ sʷomálʸe (-ሊ, -li).

some, indef. pron. (gen.) ያለ yḁ́llä (§§ 7*a*, 14, 32*a*).
(much) አያሌ ayyálʸe (§ 16).
(a few) አንዳንድ ándánd (§ 8), pl. አንዳንዶች andándʷōč (-čč § 6; § 16).

Bring some like the last: እንደኋለኛው፡ያለ፡አምጣ። ndähwāläññáu yállä ámṭa (-llánṭa §§ 7*a*, *d*).

Some are (to be) seen: አንዳንድ፡ይታያል። andánd yi̥ttấyyāl (§ 52*a*, δ).

— often not translated:

Please give me some water: እባክህ፡ውሃ፡ስጠኝ። i̥yákki̥h wúha si̥ṭḁñ.

Is there some? አለ። állä? (§ 32*d*).

Are there some? አሉ። állu?

Was there some? ነበረ። nḁbbḁrḁ? (§ 33*d*).

sometimes, adv. አንዳንድ፡ጊዜ andándi̥ gi̥zʸe.

son, s. ልጅ li̥j.
(as opposed to daughter) ወንድ፡ልጅ wώnd-li̥j (§ 8).

son-in-law, s. አማች ấmáč (§ 8).

song, s. ዘፈን zḁ́fḁn (zắf-).
soon, adv. ቅርብ፡ ጊዜ qi̥rb (-ry̥) gi̥zʸe.
　　በጥቂት፡ በኋላ bḁṭi̥qi̥t bḁhwālā̃ (yḁ-, -ḁ͡uhá-, § 7*d*).
　　(fast) ቶሎ tʷólo.
　I shall start soon: ቅርብ፡ጊዜ፡እንሣለኹ። qi̥ry̥·gi̥zʸe i̥nnḁssállḁ͡uʰ.
　Come as soon as you can: እንደሚቻልህ፡ቶሎ፡ና። ndämmi̥ččāli̥h tʷólo nā.
　He (it) will soon come back now: አሁን፡ቶሎ፡ይመለሳል። áhun tʷólʷo yi̥mmállḁsāl.
soot, s. ጥቀርሻ ṭi̥qḁ́ršā̃ (-qắr-).
sorcerer (-ess), s. ቡዳ búdā̃.
　　አስማተኛ asmātḁ́ññā̃ (-tắñ-).
sorcery, s. አስማት ásmắt (§ 8).
sore, s. ቍስል qwŭ́si̥l.
　To have a sore (sores): ቈሰለ፡ qwώssḁlḁ (§ 63*d*, *e*).
　To cause a sore (sores): አቈሰለ፡ aqwώssḁlḁ.
　He (it) has a sore: ቈስሏል። qwώslŏāl, pl. ቈስለዋል። qwώslḁ͡uāl.
　He (it) will get a sore: ይቈስላል። yi̥qwώslāl, pl. ይቈስላሉ። yi̥qwωslállu.
　It is not to get sores: አይቍሰል። á͡i̥qwŭsäl, pl. አይቍሰሉ። a͡i̥qwŭ́sḁlu.
　It will cause a sore: ያቈስላል። yāqwώslāl.
　If flies settle on a sore it will not get well: ዝንብ፡ ተቍስል፡ቢቀመጥ፡አይሻለውም። zi̥mb (§ 52*a*, δ) tḁqwŭ́si̥l yi̥qqḁ́mmḁṭ a͡i̥ššálḁ͡um.
sorghum (*S. vulgare*, Broun, Cat. 663), s. ማሽላ māši̥llā̃.
sorghum-stalk, s. ትንኪሽ ti̥ṅki̥š (§ 52*a*, δ).
sorrel (*Rumex abessinicus*, Guidi, Vocab. pp. 80, 81), s. መቅመቆ mḁqmḁ́qqʷo.

sorrow, s. ሐዘን ā́zḁn.

sorry, be, v.i. ሐዘነ ázzḁnḁ.

I am very sorry: እጅግ፡ አዝኛለሁ። í̥jji̥g azi̥ññállḁ͡u^{h} (§ 7*d*), pl. ...፡ አዝነናል። ... áznänāl.

sort, s. ዓይነት á͡i̥nḁt (-nät).

What sort of? ዬትኛው yḗtí̥ñña͡u? (§§ 8, 15).

ምንኛ mi̥ní̥ññã? (§ 15).

What sort of houses have they? ቤቶቻቸው፡ ዓይነቱ፡ እንደምንድን፡ ነው። b^{y}ēt^{w}öččáččḁ͡u (§ 55*b*) á͡i̥nätu ndämi̥ndí̥n (§ 8) nḁ͡u?

soul, s. ነፍስ nḁfs (nä-, -vs).

sound, adj. ጥሩ ṭí̥ru (ṭű́ru).

ደኅና dáhnā (§ 8).

sound, s. ድምጥ di̥mṭ.

(continuous) ጩኸት č̣úhḁt (-hät § 7*d*).

sound, v.i. ተሰማ tḁsḁ́mmã (täs-).

sound, v.t. (by blowing) ነፋ nḁ́ffã.

(by percussion) መታ mḁ́ttã.

soup, s. መረቅ mḁ́rḁq.

sour, adj. ሆምጣጣ h^{w}omṭáṭṭã (ኮም- k^{w}om-, -ጣጤ -ṭáṭ^{y}e).

south, s. ደቡብ dḁ́bű́b (dḁ́ṿű́ṿ; § 8).

souvenir, s. ማስታወሻ mãsta͡uḁ́šã (-a͡uώšã).

sow, v.i. & t. (seed, & ground) ዘራ zḁ́rrã.

How do they sow it? እንዴት፡ ይዘሩታል። nd^{y}ét yi̥-zárutāl?

sown, be, v.p. ተዘራ tḁzḁ́rrã (täzár-).

When is it sown? መቼ፡ ይዘራል። mḁ́č^{y}e yi̥zzḁ́rrāl?

space, s. (room) መቀመጫ mḁqqḁmḁ́č̣ã.

spade, s. መቈፈሪያ mḁqwωffḁ́ryã (-fár-).

span, s. (8 inches) ስንዝር sí̥nzi̥r (§ 52*a*, δ).

sparkle, v.i. አብለጨለጨ abläč̣álläč̣ä (ḁṿl-).

speak, v.i. & t. ተናገረ tḁnā́ggḁrḁ (-gärḁ).

Don't speak so fast: ቶሎ፡ቶሎ፡አትናገር። twólo twólo atti̥nnā́gär, pol. ...፡ አይናገሩ። ... a͡i̥nnā́gḁru.

Speak slowly: ዝግ፡ብለህ፡ተናገር። zi̥ggi̥ yi̥läh tḁnā́gär, pol. ዝግ፡ብለው፡ይናገሩ። zi̥ggi̥ yi̥lḁ͡u yi̥nnā́gḁru.

Speak very loudly: ጩኸህ፡ተናገር። čúhäh tḁnā́gär.

I can't speak much Amharic: አማርኛ፡ብዙ፡አልናገርም። amāri̥ñña yi̥zu ali̥nnā́ggäri̥m (§ 63*c*).

Do you speak Arabic? አረብኛ፡ትናገራለህ። arḁyi̥ñña ti̥nnaggḁrállāh?, pol. ...፡ ይናገራሉ። ... yi̥nnaggḁ rállu?

spear, s. ጦር ṭwŏr.

spear-head, s. አፍሬ ā́fr^ye.

spectacles, s. መነጥር mḁnḁ́ṭṭi̥r.

speech, s. ቃል qāl.

spelt, s. አጃ ájjā.

spider, s. ሸረሪት šḁrḁrít (šärär-), usually f. (§ 54*c*).

spill, v.t. አፈሰሰ afḁ́ssḁsḁ.

Don't spill it: አታፍሰው። attāfi̥ssḁ͡u.

You will spill it: ታፈስዋለህ። tāfḁssḁ͡uállāh.

spin, v.i. & t. (thread) አነዘረ anḁ́zzḁrḁ (-zärḁ).

Can she spin? ታነዝራለች። tānḁzrállač? (§ 63*c*).

spindle, s. እንዝርት (i̥)nzi̥rt (§ 8).

spine, s. (vertebræ) አከርካሪ akḁrkā́ri (-kärk-).

spirit, s. (liquor) አረቂ árḁqi (-räq-).

(ghost) ውቃቤ wŭqā́b^ye (-ā́y^ye).

spit, v.i. & t. ትፍ፡አለ ti̥ff ā́lḁ (not Š.).

እንትፍ፡አለ (i̥)nti̥ff (-tŭff) ā́lḁ.

S.v. √ባለ, § 44*a*.

Spit it out: እንትፍ፡በለው። ńti̥ffi̥ yḁ́lḁ͡u.

spleen, s. ጣፍያ ṭáffyā.

splendid, adj. ድንቅ di̥ṅq.

ግሩም gí̥rum.

እጅግ፡መልካም í̥jjig mḁlkám (§ 8).

It is splendid: አይገኝም። a͡i̥ggḁ́ññi̥m.

splice, v.t. ቀጠለ qḁ́ṭṭḁlḁ.

spliced, be, v.p. ተቀጠለ tḁqḁ́ṭṭḁlḁ.

splinter, s. ስንጥር sí̥nṭi̥r.

I have got a splinter in my hand: ስንጥር፡ተጇ፡ገባ። sí̥nṭi̥r tájj^{y}e (§§ 7*a*, 47*a*) gḁ́bba.

split, adj. ሰንጣቃ sḁnṭáqqã.

split, s. ንቅ ni̥q, pl. also ንቃቃት ni̥qáqát (§ 8).

ስንጥቅ sí̥nṭi̥q.

split, v.i. (be, v.p.) ተሰነጠቀ tḁsḁnḁ́ṭṭḁqḁ (täsän-).

ነቃ nḁ́qqã.

It is split: ተሰንጥቋል። täsḁ́nṭi̥q͡ŏāl, pl. -ቀዋል። -qḁ͡ūāl.

It will split: ይሰነጠቃል። yi̥ssḁnḁ́ṭṭḁqāl, pl. ይሰነጠቃሉ። yi̥ssḁnḁṭṭḁqállu.

It won't split: አይሰነጠቅም። a͡i̥ssḁnḁ́ṭṭḁqi̥m, pl. -ጠቁም። -ṭṭḁqum.

Mind it doesn't split: እንዳይሰነጠቅ። nda͡i̥ssḁnḁ́ṭṭḁq.

The wood is going to split: እንጨቱ፡ሊሰነጠቅ፡ነው። nč̣^{y}étu li̥ssḁnḁṭṭáq (§ 8) nḁ͡ū.

This kind is inclined to split: ይህ፡ዓይነት፡ነቂ፡ነው። yi̥he á͡i̥nät nḁqí nḁ͡ū.

split, v.t. ሰነጠቀ sḁnḁ́ṭṭḁqḁ.

Split the wood: እንጨቱን፡ሰንጥቀው። nč̣^{y}étun sḁ́nṭi̥qḁ͡ū, pl. -ቁት። -qut.

spoil, v.i. (be spoiled, v.p.) ተበላሸ tḁbḁlášša (tḁvḁ-).

ፈረሰ fḁ́rrḁsḁ.

It will all be spoiled: ሁሉ፡ይበላሻል። húllu yi̥bbḁláššāl.

spoil, v.t. አበላሸ abbḁlā́ššä.

አፈረሰ afḁ́rrḁsḁ.

If you do that you will spoil it: እንዲህ፡አድርገህ፡ታበላሸዋለህ። ndíh ā́rgäh (§ 7*d*) tabbḁlāššḁ͡uállāh, pol. እንዲህ፡አድርገው፡ያበላሹታል። ndíh ā́rgḁ͡u yabbḁlā́ššutāl, pl. እንዲህ፡አድርጋችሁ፡ታበላሹታላችሁ። ndíh ārgā́ččyuh tabbḁlāššutallā́ččyuh.

You will spoil them: ታበላሻቸዋለህ። tabbḁlāššāččḁ͡uállāh, pl. ታበላሿቸዋላችሁ። tabbḁlāššwāččḁ͡uallā́ččyuh.

spoon, s. ማንካ mã́ṅkã.

spoor, s. ፍለጋ fí̥llḁ́gã (§ 8).

Š. ፈለግ fḁ́lḁg.

ፋራ fā́rã.

See § 52*a*, δ.

spout, s. (of vessel) አፍ āf.

sprain, s. ወለምታ wḁ́lḁmtã.

sprained, be, v.i. ወለም፡አለ wḁ́lḁmm ā́lḁ (s.v. √ባለ, § 44*a*; § 63*d*, *e*).

The joint is sprained: ሥር፡ወለም፡ብሏል። si̥r wḁ́lḁm (§ 6) bí̥lō͡āl.

spread, v.i. ገነነ gḁ́nnḁnḁ.

The fire will spread: እሳት፡ይገናል። i̥sā́t yi̥gḁ́nnāl.

spread (out), v.t. አነጠፈ anḁ́ṭṭḁfḁ.

(to dry) አሰጣ asḁ́ṭṭã.

Spread it out: አንጥፈው። ántḭfḁ͡u, pl. -ፉት። -fut.

አስጣው። ásṭa͡u, pl. -ጡት። -ṭut.

spring, s. (of water) ምንጭ mi̥nč.

(metal) ሽቦ ší̥b^{w}o (ší̥y^{w}o).

(leap) ዝላይ zí̥llyã.

spring, v.i. (over, v.t.) ዘለለ zḁ́llḁlḁ.

He (it) sprang over it: ዘለለው። zḁ́llḁlḁ͡u, pl. ዘለ ሉት። zḁ́llḁlut.

He (it) sprang onto it: ዘለለበት። zḁ́llḁlḁbbḁt (§ 47*a*), pl. ዘለሉበት። zḁ́llḁlubbḁt.

sprinkle, v.t.

(a liquid, or with a liquid) ከፈከፈ kḁfḁ́kkḁfḁ.

ረበረበ rḁbḁ́rrḁbḁ (rḁvḁ́rrḁvḁ).

[እ]ረጨ (i̥)rḁ́č̣č̣ä (-rắč̣-).

(a substance, or with a substance, other than a liquid) ነሰነሰ nḁsḁ́nnḁsḁ.

See § 56*f*.

Sprinkle it with water: ውሃ፡ረብርብበት። wǘha rḁ́vri̥vi̥bbḁt (§ 47̀*a*), or ውሃ፡ረብርበው። wǘha rḁ́vri̥vḁ͡u.

Sprinkle the ground with water: መሬቱን፡ውሃ፡ርጨው። mḁrʸétun úha ri̥č̣ḁ͡u.

Sprinkle the earth over it: አፈሩን፡ነስንስበት። ắfärun nḁ́sni̥si̥bbḁt, pl. ...፡ ነስንሱበት። ... nḁ́sni̥subbḁt.

sprinkled, be, v.p.

(of or with a liquid) ተከፈከፈ tḁkḁfḁ́kkḁfḁ.

ተረበረበ tḁrḁbḁ́rrḁbḁ (tär-, -ḁvḁ́rrḁvḁ).

ተረጨ tḁrḁ́č̣č̣ä (tḁrắč̣-).

(of or with a substance other than a liquid) ተነሰነሰ tḁnḁsḁ́nnḁsḁ.

See § 56*f*.

The ground should be sprinkled with water: መሬት፡ውሃ፡ይከፍከፍ። mḁrʸét úha yi̥kkḁ́fkḁf, or መሬት፡ውሃ፡ይረብረብ። mḁrʸét úha yi̥rrḁ́vrḁv.

Salt should be sprinkled on it: ጨው፡ይነስነስበት። č̣ḁ́u yi̥nnḁ́snḁsi̥bbḁt (§ 47*a*).

sprout, v.i. በቀለ bḁ́qqḁlḁ (bắq-).

spun, be, v.p. (of thread) ተነዘረ tanázzara (-zära).

Show me how it's spun: አሳዩኝ፡እንዴት፡ይነዘራል። asáyyäññ (§ 6) indʸét yinnázzarāl, f. አሳዪኝ፡እን ዴት፡... asáyyiññ indʸét....

spur, s. (calcar) መኰልኰያ makwalkwáyā (-kwωl-, -áiā).

መኰርኰሪያ makwωrkwώryā.

See § 52a, δ.

spur, v.t. ኰረኰረ kwωrákkwωra (-rώk-).

spurge (*Euphorbia sp.*), s. አንተርፋ antárfā (-tár-).

sputum, s. ትፍታ tiffitā.

spy, s. ሰላይ sállāi (sál-; -áyy § 6; § 8).

spy, v.i. & t. (on, v.t.) ሰለለ sállala (sál-).

square, adj.—use rectangular, q.v.

It is in a square tin: ባራት፡ማዘን፡ያለው፡ሳጥን፡አለ። bārátt mázan yállāu sáṭin állä.

square, s. (open space among houses) አደባባይ addabábāi (-ayáyāi; § 8).

squeak, v.i. (of mouse) ሲጥ፡አለች sīṭṭ áläč (-čč § 6; § 54c).

(of inanimate objects) ሲጥጥ፡አለ síṭiṭṭ (siṭiṭṭ) ála.

S.v. √ባለ, § 44a.

squeeze, v.i. & t. አጣበቀ aṭṭábbaqa.

ጨቈነ čáqqwωna (čώqqona § 7d káiy).

Squeeze it: አጣብቀው። aṭṭáyïqāu.

ጨቍነው። čώqqwŭnāu.

Don't squeeze it: አታጣብቀው። attāṭṭáyïqāu.

አትጨቍነው። attičώqqwŭnāu.

squeezed, be, v.p. ተጣበቀ taṭábbaqa.

ተጨቈነ tačáqqwωna (-čώqqona).

If it is squeezed: ቢጣበቅ፡ biṭṭábbaq.

ቢጨቈን፡ biččώqqon.

squeeze out, v.t. ጠመቐ ṭ̥ámmḁqḁ.

Squeeze the' juice out of the lime(s § 52*a*): የሎሚውን፡ውሃ፡ጥመቐው። yälʷōmíun úha ṭ̥ímḁqḁ͡u.

squeezed out, be, v.p. ተጠመቐ tḁṭ̥ámmḁqḁ.

squirrel (*Xerus sp.*, Blandford, Geol. & Zool. pp. 278, 279), s. ሻላ šắlã, often f. (§ 54*c*).

stab, v.i. & t. ወጋ wώggã (ʷώg-).

He stabbed him with a knife: በካራ፡ወጋው። bḁkárra (§ 47*a*) wώgga͡u.

stabbed, be, v.p. ተወጋ tḁwώggã (tḁ͡uώ-).

stable, s. የፈረስ፡ቤት yäfḁrḁ́s (§§ 47*a*, 70; § 8) bʸēt (ṿʸ-).

ጋጥ gāṭ.

Put it in the stable: ከፈረስ፡ቤት፡አድርገው። kḁfḁrḁ́s (ተፈ- tḁfḁ-) ṿʸēṭ ádrḭgḁ͡u (ấrgḁ͡u § 7*d*).

stack, s. ክምር kḭ́mmḭr.

stack, v.t. ከመረ kḁ́mmḁrḁ (-märḁ).

Stack it (them § 52*a*, δ) here: ከዚህ፡ክምረው። käzḭ́h kḁ́mmḭrḁ͡u, pl. -ሩት። -rut.

stacked, be, v.p. ተከመረ tḁkḁ́mmḁrḁ (-märḁ).

Ŝhow him where it is to be stacked: የሚከመርበትን፡ አሳየው። yämmḭkkḁmmärḭ́bbḁtḭn (§ 62*c*) asáyyḁ͡u.

stage (of journey), s. መናሀሬ mḁnnaháryã (-ኻ- -χá-, -ká- § 7*d*; § 52*a*, δ).

stagnant, adj. [እ]ርጉ rḭ́gu (ḭ́rgu).

የማይሔድ yämma͡ḭhád (§§ 14, 37*c*).

stagnant, be, v.i. [እ]ረጋ (ḭ̆)rḁ́ggã (§ 63*d*, *e*).

Use neg. of ሔደ hḁ̃dä (hḁ̃-, hʸḗ-, -dḁ, § 7*d*), to flow.

It is stagnant: አይሔድም። a͡ḭhádḭm.

It is stagnant, it isn't good to drink: ረግቷል፤ለመጠጣት፡ደግም፡አይደል። rḁ́gtŏ͡āl, lḁmḁṭḁ̣ṭṭát dág-gḭmm (§ 37*b*) á͡ḭdäl.

stain, s. ቀለም qḁ́lḁm.
(of dirt) እድፍ i̥d(i̥)f.
stain, v.i. & t. (dye) ቀለመ qḁ́llḁmḁ.
(soil) አሳደፈ asáddḁfḁ.
It will stain it: ያሳድፈዋል። yāsáddi̥fḁ͡ūāl.
stained, be, v.p. (stain oneself, v.r.) ተቀለመ tḁqḁ́llḁmḁ.
(be soiled) አደፈ áddḁfḁ (§ 23*a*).
Mind the cloth doesn't get stained: ጨርቅ፡እንዳያ ድፍ። čärq i̥nda͡^{y}ādǐf.
stale, adj. የኖረ yän^{w}ṓrḁ (§§ 14, 62).
stale, v.i. (vet.) ሸነ šḁ́nnḁ.
stalk, s. አገዳ ágḁdā̃ (§ 52*a*, δ).
stall, s. ጋጥ gāṭ.
stammering, adj. ዱዳ dúdā̃.
stamp, s. (instrument) መኅተሚያ mḁhattḁ́myā̃ (-tā́m-).
(impression) ማኅተም máhtḁm (mḁhā́tḁm § 7*d*).
(postage-) †ቴምብር tā́mbr (§ 52*a*, δ).
stamp, v.t. (imprint) ኅተመ háttḁmḁ (አተመ áttḁmḁ).
stamped, be, v.p. ታተመ tā́ttḁmḁ.
stampede, v.i. ደነበረ dḁnḁ́bbḁrḁ (-bärḁ).
They stampeded and are all lost: ደንብሮ፡ሁሉ፡ጠፉ። dámbi̥r^{w}o húllu ṭḁ́ffa (§ 52*a*).
stand, v.i. ቆመ q^{w}ṓmḁ (§ 42*c*).
Stand here: ከዚህ፡ቁም። käzzi̥h qum, pl. ...፡ቁሙ። ... qúmu.
stand, v.t. አቆመ aq^{w}ṓmḁ.
Stand it here: ከዚህ፡አቁመው። käzzi̥h ā́quma͡u, pl. ...፡አቁሙት። ... ā́qumut.
stand still, v.i. ቀጥ፡አለ፡ qḁṭṭ álḁ (s.v. √በለ, § 44*a*).
Stand still: ቀጥ፡በል። qḁ́ṭṭǐ̥ yḁl, pl. ቀጥ፡በሉ። qḁ́ṭṭǐ̥ yḁ́lu.

stand up, v.i. ተነሣ tḁnḁ́ssã.

ብድግ፡ አለ bi̥di̥gg (§ 6) álḁ (s.v. √በለ, § 44*a*).

Stand up: ብድግ፡ በል። bi̥dí̥g (§ 8) y̥äl.

standard, s. (with flag) ዓላማ፡ ሰንደቅ aláma sḁ́ndḁq.

star, s. ኮከብ k^{w}ókḁb (-ḁy̥), pl. also ከዋክብት kḁu͡ákibt (-i̥yt); see § 52*a*, δ.

starch, s. †አሚዶ ámid^{w}o.

start, v.i. (pro̥ceed) ተነሣ tḁnḁ́ssã.

(begin) ተጀመረ tḁjḁ́mmḁrḁ (-märḁ).

Start: ተነሣ። tḁnḁ́sa, pl. ተነሡ። tḁnḁ́su.

Don't start: አትነሣ። atti̥nnḁ́sa, pl. -ሡ። -su.

Before you start: ሳትነሣ፡ sātti̥nnḁ́ssa, pl. -ሡ፡ -ssu.

When you start: ስትነሣ፡ si̥tti̥nnḁ́ssa, pl. -ሡ፡ -ssu.

Why have you not started? ምን፡ ነው፡ አልተነሣህም። mí̥n-nḁu͡ altḁnḁ́ssahi̥m?, pl. ምን፡ ነው፡ አልተነሣችሁም። mí̥n-nḁu͡ altḁnḁssáčči̥hum?

He is to start: ይነሣ። yi̥nnḁ́sa, pl. -ሡ። -su.

He is not to start, let him wait: አይነሣ፤ ይቈይ። a͡i̥nnḁ́sa, yí̥qwo͡i̥, pl. አይነሡ፤ ይቈዩ። a͡i̥nnḁ́su, yi̥qwóyyu.

Has he started? ተነሥቷል። tḁnḁ́sto͡āl?, pol. & pl. ተነሥተዋል። tḁnḁ́stḁu͡āl?

He is to start at once: ቶሎ፡ አሁን፡ ይነሣ። t^{w}ólo áhun yi̥nnḁ́sa, pl. ...-ሡ። ... -su.

When did he start? መቼ፡ ተነሣ። mḁ́č^{y}e tḁnḁ́ssa?, pol. & pl. መቼ፡ ተነሡ። mḁ́č^{y}e tḁnḁ́ssu?

I am going to start: ልነሣ፡ ነኝ። li̥nnḁssá (§ 8) näñ, pl. ልንነሣ፡ ነን። li̥nni̥nnḁssá nän.

I am not going to start: አልነሣም። ali̥nnḁ́ssām, pl. አንነሣም። anni̥nnḁ́ssām.

Before I start: ሳልነሣ፡ sali̥nnḁ́ssa, pl. ሳንነሣ፡ sanni̥nnḁ́ssa.

When I start: ስነሣ፡ si̥nnḁ́ssa, pl. ስንነሣ፡ si̥nni̥n-nḁ́ssa.

We are not starting yet: አንነሣም፡ገና፡ነው። anni̥n-nḁ́ssām, gḁná (§ 8) nḁ͡u.

I shall start early in the morning: ማለዳ፡እነሣለኊ። māladḁ nnḁssállḁ͡uʰ, pl. ማለዳ፡እንነሣለን። māladḁ nni̥nnḁssállän.

start, v.t. (move) አስነሣ asnḁ́ssã.

(begin) ጀመረ jḁ́mmḁrḁ (-märḁ).

Start the transport: ጓዙን፡አስነሣው። gwázun as-nḁ́ssa͡u, pl. -ሡት። -ssut.

Don't start it: አታስነሣው። attasnḁ́ssa͡u, pl. -ሡት። -ssut.

started, be, v.p. ተጀመረ tḁjḁ́mmḁrḁ (-märḁ).

startle, v.t. አስደነገጠ asdḁnḁ́ggḁṭḁ.

It startled me: አስደነገጠኝ። asdḁnḁ́ggḁṭäñ.

What was it that startled you? ያስደነገጠህ፡ምን፡ነበር። yāsdḁnḁ́ggḁṭäh mi̥n nábbär?

startled, be, v.i. & p. ደነገጠ dḁnḁ́ggḁṭḁ.

starving, adj. [እ]ራብተኛ (i̥)rābtḁ́ññã (-āy̥t-, -táñ-).

state, v.t. አለ álḁ (s.v. √ባለ, § 44*a*).

ነገረ nḁ́ggḁrḁ (-gärḁ).

station, s. (post) ፈንታ fḁ́ntã.

(railway-) መሐጣ mḁháṭ̥ṭ̥ã.

(stopping-place) መቆሚያ mḁqʷṓmyã.

station, v.t. አቆመ aqʷṓmḁ.

Station a man at every fifty yards: አንዳንድ፡ሰው፡በየመቶ፡ክንድ፡አቁም። andánd sḁ͡u yḁyyämḁtʷó (§ 8, § 18) ki̥nd áqum (lit. at every 100 cubits).

stay, s. (residence) መኖር mḁ́nʷṓr (§ 8).

stay, v.i. (remain) ቈየ qwώyyä.

(reside) ተቀመጠ tḁqḁ́mmḁṭḁ.

Stay here: ከዚህ፡ቈይ። käzzi̥h qwω͡i̥, pl. ከዚህ፡ቈዩ። käzzi̥h qwώyyu.

Don't stay (away) long: ብዙ፡አትቈይ። bi̥zu atti̥-qwω͡i̥, pl. ብዙ፡አትቈዩ። atti̥qwώyyu.

I am going to stay here: ከዚህ፡እቀመጣለኍ። käzzi̥h i̥qqḁmmḁṭálla͡u^{h}, pl. ከዚህ፡እንቀመጣለን። käzzi̥h i̥n-ni̥qqḁmmḁṭállän.

I am not going to stay long: ብዙ፡አልቀመጥም። bi̥zu ali̥qqḁ́mmḁṭi̥m, pl. ብዙ፡አንቀመጥም። bi̥zu anni̥q-qḁ́mmḁṭi̥m.

Stay! (where you are) ሁን። hun!, pl. ሁኑ። húnu!

stay behind, v.i. (not proceed) ቀረ qḁ́rrḁ.

Stay behind: ቅር። qi̥r, pl. ቅሩ። qi̥ru.

Don't stay behind: አትቅር። atti̥qi̥r, pl. አትቅሩ። at-ti̥qru.

What did you stay behind for? ለምን፡ቀረህ። lḁmi̥n qḁ́rräh?, pl. ለምን፡ቀራችሁ። lḁmi̥n qḁrráččyuh? (§ 7*d*):—(expressing annoyance) ምን፡ነው፡ቀረ ሀብኝ። mi̥n-na͡u qḁ́rrähi̥bbi̥ñ?, pl. ምን፡ነው፡ቀራ ችሁብኝ። mi̥n-na͡u qḁrráčči̥hubbi̥ñ?

He is to stay behind: ይቅር። yi̥qi̥r, pl. ይቅሩ። yi̥qru.

He is not to stay behind: አይቅር። a͡i̥qi̥r, pl. አይቅሩ። a͡i̥qru.

stay, cause to, v.t. አቈየ aqwώyyä.

steady!, interj. ተው። tá͡u!, f. (e.g. to a mare) ተይ። tá͡i̥!

steady, be, v.i. (of animate objects) [እ]ረጋ (i̥)rággã (§ 63*d*, *e*).

Is this mule steady? ይህ፡በቅሎ፡ረግቷል። yi̥he yḁ́q-l^{w}o rágtō͡al?, f. ይች፡በቅሎ፡ረግታለች። ^{y}i̥čči̥ yḁ́ql^{w}o rḁgtálläč?, pl. እነዚህ፡በቅሎች፡ረግተዋል። nnäzzi̥h yḁ́ql^{w}ōč rḁ́gta͡ual?

steal, v.i. & t. ሰረቀ sḁrrḁqḁ (sắr-).

He will steal it: ይሰርቀዋል። yi̥sắrqḁ͡uāl, pl. ይሰርቁታል። yi̥sắrqutāl.

Mind he doesn't steal it: እንዳይሰርቀው። nda͡ii̥sắr-qḁ͡u, Mind they don't ...: -ርቁት። -rqut.

He has stolen it: ሰርቆታል። sắrqʷotāl, pl. ሰርቀውታል። sắrqḁ͡utāl.

He did not steal it: አልሰረቀውም። alsḁrrḁqḁ͡um, pl. አልሰረቁትም። alsḁ́rrḁquti̥m.

steamer, s. ባቡር bắbũr (bắṿũr; § 8).

የባሕር፡ባቡር yäṿắhi̥r (§§ 47*a*, 70) ṿắṿũr.

steel, s. ብረት bí̥rḁt (-rät).

(for use with flint) ቡላድ búl(l)ắd (§ 8).

stem, s. አገዳ ágḁdã.

stench, s. ግማት gí̥mắt (§ 8).

Stereospermum Kunthianum (Broun, Cat. 426), s. ዛና zắnã.

stew, v.t. ቀቀለ qḁ́qqḁlḁ.

Stew it: ቀቅለው። qḁ́qqi̥lḁ͡u.

steward, s. አዛዥ ázzắž (§ 8).

(of household) አጋፋሪ aggafắri.

stewed, be, v.p. ተቀቀለ tḁqḁ́qqḁlḁ.

It (they § 52*a*, δ) should be stewed: ይቀቀል። yi̥q-qḁ́qḁl.

stick, s. በትር bḁ́tti̥r.

G. & B. also ብትር bí̥tti̥r.

stick, v.i. (adhere) ተጣበቀ tḁṭábbḁqḁ.

It sticks (they stick § 52*a*, δ): ይጣበቃል። yi̥ṭṭábbḁqāl.

It doesn't (they don't) stick: አይጣበቅም። a͡ii̥ṭṭáb-bḁqi̥m.

I found it wouldn't stick: አልጣበቅም፡አለኝ። ali̥ṭ-ṭábbḁqi̥mm (§ 6) ắläñ (s.v. √በለ).

stick, v.i. & t. (cause to adhere) አጣበቀ aṭṭábbḁqḁ.

The gum doesn't stick well: ሙጫ፡ ደኅና፡ አያጣብቅም። múč̣č̣a dáhna a͡ʸaṭṭábbi̥qi̥m.

stiletto, s. መውጊያ mḁ͡úgyã.

ወስፌ wǿsfʸe.

still, adv. (yet) ገና gḁnã.

I still don't understand: ገና፡ አልሰማሁም። gḁ́na alsḁ́mmahum (§§ 37*a*, 63*d*).

still, be, v.i. [እ]ረጋ (i̥)rḁ́ggã (§ 63*d*, *e*).

Keep still: እርጋ። i̥rgā, pl. እርጉ። i̥rgu.

still, stand, v.i. ቆጥ፡ አለ qḁṭṭ ā́lḁ (s.v. √በለ, § 44*a*).

Stand still: ቆጥ፡ በል። qḁ́ṭṭi̥ (§ 7*d*) y̥ḁl, pl. ቆጥ፡ በሉ። qḁ́ṭṭi̥ y̥ḁ́lu.

sting, v.i. & t. ነደፈ nḁ́ddḁfḁ.

It has (they have § 52*a*, δ) stung me: ነደፎኛል። nḁ́dfʷoññāl.

It (they) didn't sting me: አልነደፈኝም። alnḁ́ddḁfḁññi̥m.

It (they) will sting you: ይነድፈሃል። yi̥nḁ́dfḁhāl.

Did it (they) sting you? ነደፈህ። nḁ́ddḁfäh?

sting (habitually), v.i. ተናደፈ tḁnáddḁfḁ.

Does it (do they § 52*a*, δ) sting? ይናደፋሉወይ። yi̥náddḁfāllwi̥? (s.v. ወይ).

It doesn't (they don't) sting: አይናደፍም። a͡i̥nnáddḁfi̥m.

stingy, adj. ሥሡ si̥ssu.

stink, s. ግማት gi̥māt (§ 8).

stink, v.i. ገማ gḁ́mmã (§ 63*d*, *e*).

stinking, adj. ግም gi̥m.

stir, v.i. & t. (a liquid) አማሰለ ammássḁlḁ.

Stir it: አማስለው። ammási̥la͡u.

stirrup, s. [እ]ርካብ i̥rkāb (rí̥k-, -ā́y̥; § 8, § 52*a*, δ).

stirrup-leather, s. ወፍለቅ wώflḁq (-läq; § 52*a*, δ).
stitch, s. ስፌት sı̥fʸḗt (§ 8, § 52*a*, δ).
stockade, s. ገረገራ gḁrḁgḁ́rã.
stocking, s. ረጅም፡ሹራብ rā́jjı̥m šúrrā́b (-ā́y̩; § 8, § 52*a*, δ).
stolen, be, v.p. ተሰረቀ tḁsḁ́rrḁqḁ (täsā́r-).
 It has been stolen: ተሰርቋል። täsā́rqṓāl, pl. -ቀዋል። -qḁ͡uāl.
 Take care it doesn't get stolen: እንዳይሰረቅ። nda͡i̥s-sḁ́rrḁq, ... care they don't...: -ረቁ። -rrḁqu.
stomach, s. ሆድ hʷōd.
 (pit of) በጀድ bā́jäd.
 (of ruminant) ጨጓራ ç̣ḁggwā́rrã (ç̣ωg-).
stone, s. (large) ደንጊያ dā́ṅgyã, Š. ደንጋይ dā́ṅga͡i̥ (§ 8), } pl. ደንጎች dā́ṅ-gʷōč (-čč § 6).
 (small) ጠጠር ṭḁ́ṭḁr (-ṭär).
 See § 52*a*, δ.
stony, adj. ጭንጫማ ç̣ı̥nç̣ā́mmã.
 Stony ground: ጭንጫ፡ ç̣ı̥́nç̣ã.
stool, s. ወምበር wώmbḁr (-bär).
 መቀመጫ mḁqqḁmḁ́ç̣ã.
 ግርምቡድ gı̥rı̥́mbud (gŭrŭ́m-).
stoop, v.i. ተጎነበሰ tḁgwωnḁ́bbḁsḁ.
 Stoop (down): ተጎንበስ። tḁgwώmbḁs (§ 7*d*), pl. -በሱ። -bḁsu.
stop, s. (in writing) ነጥብ nā́ṭı̥b (-ı̥̣y̩; § 52*a*, δ).
 Please put stops in your letters, to make the sense clear: pol. እባክዎ፡ነጥብ፡በደብዳቤ፡ያድርጉበት፡ማለቱ፡እንዲታወቅ። ı̥y̩ákkḁ͡ʷo nā́ṭı̥y̩ y̩ḁdḁy̩dábbʸe yádrı̥gubbḁt, mā́lätu ndı̥ttá͡uwωq.
stop, v.i. (halt) ቆመ qʷṓmḁ.
 ቀጥ፡አለ qḁṭṭ ā́lḁ (s.v. √ባለ, § 44*a*).
 (remain) ቆየ qwώyyä.

Stop: ቁም። qum, pl. ቁሙ። qúmu.

(desist) አታድርግ። attádrig (attárg § 7*d*), pl. -ጉ። -gu.

ተው። tau, f. ተይ። tai, pl. ተዉ። tauu.

stop, v.t. (cause to) አቆመ aqʷṓma.

(prevent) ከለከለ kalákkala.

Use neg. of ተወ taua, to allow, or of causative in አስ- as- (§ 22*a*).

Stop him (it, —from going): አቁመው። áqumau, pl. -ሙት። -mut.

Stop them: አቁማቸው። āqumáččau, pl. አቁሟቸው። āqumwáččau.

Don't stop him: አታቁመው። attáqumau, pl. -ሙት። -mut.

Stop him (it, —from doing a thing): አትተወው። attitáuau, or ከልክለው። kálkilau, pl. አትተዉት። attitáuut, or ከልክሉት። kálkilut.

Stop them: አትተዋቸው። attitauáččau, or ከልክላቸው። kalkiláččau, pl. አትተዉአቸው። attitauŭáččau, or ከልክሏቸው። kalkilwáččau.

Don't stop him: አትከልክለው። attikálkilau, pl. -ሉት። -lut.

The wind stops me from hearing: ንፋስ፡አያሰማኝም። nifás aʸassámmaññim (aas-).

stop a little, v.i. ቈየት፡አለ qwṓyyätt ála (s.v. √በለ, § 44*a*).

Stop a little: ቈየት፡በል። qwωyyát (§§ 6, 8) yal, pl. ቈየት፡በሉ። qwṓyyät yalu.

store, s. እቃ፡ቤት iqá-bʸēt (-yʸ-).

Every day after breakfast tell me what you want from the store: ሀለቀን፡ተበን፡ቁርስ፡በኋላ፡ተቃ፡ቤት፡የምትፈልገውን፡ንገረኝ። hullaqan tayúnn qurs yau-hála ta-qáyʸēt (§§ 7*a*, 47*a*) yämmittfálligaun nígaräñ.

stork, s. (*Ciconia Abdimii*, Blandford, Geol. & Zool. p. 436) ሽመላ šịmálā̃.
(*C. ephippiorrhyncha*, Guidi, Vocab. p. 131) [እ]ራዛ (ị̆)rázā̃.

story, s. (tale) ታሪክ tárik (-rịk).
(of house) ድርብ därb (-rỵ; § 52*a*, δ).
A two-storied house: ሁለት፡ድርብ፡ያለው፡ቤት፡ húlätt därỵ yalláu (§ 8) ỵʸēt.

stout, adj. ወፍራም wώfrám (§ 8), pl. also ወፋፍራም wωfāffị-rám (§ 8).
Very stout: ገፋፋ gạfáfā̃.

stout, be (become), v.i. ወፈረ wώffạrạ (-färạ; § 63*d*, *e*).
He is (too) stout: ወፍሯል። wώffịrŏāl.

stout, be (become) very, v.i. ጎፈፍ፡አለ gʷófạff álạ.
G. ጉፍፍ፡አለ gúfịff (-fŭff) álạ.
S.v. √በለ, § 44*a*; § 63*d*, *e*.
He is very stout: ጎፈፍ፡ብሏል። gʷófạffị̆ (§ 7*d*) ỵị-lŏāl.

straight, adj. (not crooked) ቅን qịn.
ቀና qạ́nnā̃.
ትክክል tịkịkkịl.
Put (make) it straight: ቀጥ፡ይበል። qạṭṭ yịvạl.
Is it a straight road? መንገድ፡ቀና፡ነው። mạńgạd qạnná (§ 8) nạu?

straight, be, v.i. ቀጥ፡አለ qạṭṭ álạ (s.v. √በለ, § 44*a*).
ቀና qạ́nnā̃.
Is it straight? ቀጥ፡ይላሎይ። qạṭṭ yịlāllwị? (s.v. ወይ).
It is not straight: ቀጥ፡አይልም። qạṭṭ áịlịm.
Hold yourself straight: ቀጥ፡ብለህ፡ቁም። qạ́ṭṭị̆ (§ 7*d*) ỵịláh (§ 8) qum, pl. ቀጥ፡ብላችሁ፡ቁሙ። qạ́ṭṭị̆ (§ 7*d*) ỵịláččyuh (§ 7*d*) qúmu.

straighten, v.t. አቀና aqánnã.
Straighten it: አቅናው። áqnau͡, pl. አቅኑት። áqnut.
straightforward, adj. (of persons) ቁም qum.
ቅን qin.
strange, be, v.i. ገረመ gárrama (type A § 34).
stranger, s. እንግዳ (i)ngidã (§ 8).
strangury, s. ሽንት፡ማጥ šint māṭ.
strap, s. ጠፍር ṭáfir.
(for loading animal) መጫኛ mačáñã.
The strap (-s § 52*a*, δ) will break: ጠፍር፡ይበጠሳል። ṭáfir yibbáṭṭasāl.
straw, s. ገለባ gálábã (-áyã; § 8).
Chopped straw (تبن): ደፋጫ dafáčã (-fáčã).
G. ደፋንጫ dafánčã (-fánčã).
(fine) እብቅ ibbiq.
(of *Poa abessinica*) ጭድ čid.
strength, s. ኃይል hai͡l.
ብርታት birtát (§ 8).
ጕልበት gwúlbat (-ly-, -ät).
Strepsiceros kudu (Blandford, Geol. & Zool. pp. 270–272), s. አጋዘን agázan (-zän).
stretch, v.i. (oneself, v.r.) ተጓሰመ tagwássama (-säma).
(be stretched) ተዘረጋ tazarágga (täzär-).
Don't stretch: አትጓሰም። attiggwásam, pl. -ሰሙ። -samu.
It stretches from here to here: ከዚህ፡እስከዚህ፡ድረስ፡ይዘረጋል። kàzzih iskäzzih diras yizzaràggāl.
stretch, v.t. (out) ዘረጋ zarággã (zär-).
(taut) ወጠረ wώṭṭara (-ṭära).
Stretch it: ዘርጋው። zárgau͡, pl. -ጉት። -gut.
ወጥረው። wώṭṭirau͡, pl. -ሩት። -rut.

stretched, be, v.p. ተዘረጋ tḁzḁrḁ́ggã (täzär-).

The rope is to be stretched its whole length: ገመዱ፡እስቲያልቅ፡ድረስ፡ይዘርጋ። gḁ́mḁdu stiyálq dı̥́rḁs yı̥zzä́rga.

strew, v.t. (a substance, or with a substance) ነሰነሰ nḁsḁ́nnḁsḁ (s.v. sprinkle).

strewn, be, v.p. (of or with a substance) ተነሰነሰ tḁnḁsḁ́nnḁsḁ (s.v. sprinkled, be).

strike, v.i. & t. መታ mḁ́ttã.

Strike him (it): ምታው። mı̥́ta͡u, pl. ምቱት። mı̥́tut.

Don't strike him (it): አትምታው። attı̥́mta͡u, pl. -ቱት። -tut.

Who struck you? ማን፡መታህ። mān mḁ́ttāh?

striking-pin, s. (of gun) መትኰሻ mḁtḁkkwώšã (-tωk-).

string, s. ገመድ gḁ́mḁd.

This string is not long enough: ይህ፡ገመድ፡እርዝመቱ፡አይበቃም። yı̥he gḁ́mḁd (§ 55*b*) ı̥rzı̥́mḁtu a͡ı̥yḁ́qām.

stroke, s. ምታት mı̥́tát (§ 8).

(with whip) ግርፋት gı̥́rfát (§ 8).

See § 52*a*, δ.

stroke, v.t. ዳሰሰ dā́ssḁsḁ.

strong, adj. ጠንካራ ṭḁṅkárrã.

ኃይለኛ ha͡ı̥lḁ́ññã (-lä́ñ-).

ብርቱ bı̥́rtŭ.

(muscular) ጕልበታም gwŭlbḁ́tám (-lỵ-, -ä́t-; § 8).

ጕልበተኛ gwŭlbḁtḁ́ññã (-lỵ-, -ät-ä́ñ-).

ቅልጥማም qı̥lṭı̥́mám (§ 8).

strong(-er), be, v.i. በረታ bḁrḁ́ttã (bär-; § 58*b*).

This is the stronger: ይህ፡ይበረታል። yı̥he yı̥yḁrḁ́ttāl.

strop, s. የምላጭ፡ለሁቴ yämi̥láčči̥ (§ 70) lḁhʷótʸe (§ 8).

  መለመጫ mḁlḁmmáčã.

strop, v.t. ለመጠ lḁ́mmḁṭḁ.

  Strop it: ለምጠው። lḁ́mmi̥ṭa͡u.

stropped, be, v.p. ተለመጠ tḁlḁ́mmḁṭḁ.

  It should be stropped: ይለመጥ። yi̥llḁ́mḁṭ, pl. -ጡ። -ṭu.

  It is not to be stropped: አይለመጥ። a͡i̥llḁ́mḁṭ, pl. -ጡ። -ṭu.

struggle, s. ትግል tí̥gi̥l.

struggle, v.i. ታገለ tãggḁlḁ.

Struthio camelus, s. ሰጎን sḁ́gʷon (§ 8).

stubborn, adj. ቸክቻክ čḁkčákkã.

stubborn, be, v.i. ችክ፡አለ či̥kk álḁ (s.v. √በለ, § 44*a*; § 63*d*, *e*).

  He (it) is stubborn: ችክ፡ብሏል። čí̥kki̥ (§ 7*d*) yí̥l͡ŏāl, pl. ችክ፡ብለዋል። čí̥kki̥ yí̥la͡uāl.

stump, s. ግንድ gi̥nd.

stung, be, v.p. ተነደፈ tḁnḁ́ddḁfḁ.

  Have you been stung? ተነድፈሃል። tḁnḁ́dfähāl?, pl. ተነድፋችኋል። tḁnḁdfáččyuhāl? (§ 7*d*).

  You will get stung: ትነደፋለህ። ti̥nnḁddḁfálläh, pl. ትነደፋላችሁ። ti̥nnḁddḁfalláččyuh (§ 7*d*).

  Mind you don't get stung: እንዳትነደፍ። ndatti̥nnḁ́ddḁf, pl. -ደፉ። -ddḁfu, (s.v. እንድ-).

stunted, adj. ልቃም lí̥qqãm (§ 8).

stupid, adj. ሞኝ mʷoññ.

  ደንቆሮ dḁńqwǿrʷo.

stupidity, s. ሞኝነት mʷoññí̥nnḁt (-nät).

  ደንቆሮነት dḁńqwørí̥nnḁt (-nät).

stuttering, adj. ዱዳ dúdã.

subdue, v.t. ገራ gḁ́rrã.

subdued, be, v.p. ተገራ tḁgḁ́rrã.
subject, be, v.i. ገበረ gḁ́bbḁrḁ (-bärḁ), to, ለ- lḁ- (§ 47*a*).
ተገዛ tḁgḁ́zzã, " "
To whom are they subject? ለማን፡ይገብራሉ። lḁmán yi̥gḁbbi̥rállu?
Aren't they subject to Rās Tasamma? ለራስ፡ተሰማ፡አይገዙም። lḁrás täsḁ́mma a͡i̥ggḁ́zzum?
substitute, v.t. ተካ tḁ́kkã, constr. with ለ- lḁ- (§ 47*a*), for, or acc. (cp. § 56*c*) of በታ bʷótã, place.
He substituted a donkey for the mule: አህያ፡ለበቅሎው፡ተካ። ahíyya (§ 56*a*) lḁyḁ́qlʷo͡u tḁ́kka, or የበቅሎውን፡በታ፡አህያ፡ተካ። yäyḁ́qlʷo͡un (§§ 56*b*, 70*b*) bʷóta ahíyya (§ 56*a*) tḁ́kka.
Or use ለወጠ lá͡uwḁṭḁ, to change, to, ለ- lḁ-.
Substitute coffee for tea: ሻይ፡ለቡን፡ለውጠው። šái̥ lḁyúnn lá͡uwüṭa͡u (lit. change the tea to coffee).
substituted, be, v.p. ተተካ tḁtḁ́kkã, constr. as ተካ above.
A donkey has been substituted for the mule: የበቅሎውን፡በታ፡አህያ፡ተተክቷል። yäyḁ́qlʷo͡un bʷóta ahíyya tḁtḁ́kki̥tö͡al.
substitution, s. ምትክ mí̥ti̥kk (§ 8).
succeed, v.i. (prosper) በጀ bḁ́jjä (bä́j-).
The plan has succeeded: ሥራቱ፡በጅቷል። si̥rátu yä́jji̥tö͡al.
It would not succeed: አይበጅም፡ነበር። a͡i̥yä́jji̥m nḁ́bbär (§ 81*c*, λ).
suck, v.i. & t. ጠባ ṭḁ́bbã.
Suck it: ጥባው። ṭí̥ya͡u.
Suck the poison out of it: መርዝ፡እንዲወጣ፡ጥባው። märz i̥ndi̥wóṭa (§ 48*a*) ṭí̥ya͡u.
Don't suck it: አትጥባው። attí̥ṭya͡u.
sucked, be, v.p. ተጠባ tḁṭḁ́bbã.

Sudan, s.—usually called የደርቡሽ፡አገር፡ yädárṿuš å̈gḁr.
suddenly, adv. ድንገት dị́ṅgḁt.
ባድንገት bḁdị́ṅgḁt.
sufficient, be, v.i. በቃ bḁ́qqā̆ (bā̆q-).
That is sufficient: ይህ፡ይበቃል። yị́he yịṿḁ́qāl.
It is not sufficient: አይበቃም። a͡ịṿḁ́qām.
sugar, s. ሱካር súkkā̆r (§ 8).
sugar-cane, s. ሸንኰር šḁ́ṅkwωr (šώṅ-).
suit, v.i. & t. ተመቸ tḁmḁ́ččä (-mā̆č-) ለ- lḁ- (§ 47*a*).
He (it) suits: ይመቻል። yị̥mmḁ́ččāl, pl. ይመቻሉ። yị̥mmḁččállu.
He (it) doesn't suit: አይመችም። a͡ị̥mmā̆ččị̥m, pl. -ቹም። -ččum.
He (it) suits me: ይመቸኛል። yị̥mmā̆ččäññāl, pl. -ቹኛል። -ččuññāl.
He (it) doesn't suit me: አይመቸኝም። a͡ị̥mmā̆ččäñ-ñị̥m, pl. -ቹኝም። -ččuññị̥m.
Does he (it) suit you? ይመቸሃል። yị̥mmā̆ččähāl?, pl. -ቹሃል። -ččuhāl?, ... you (pol.)? ይመቸዎታል። yị̥mmḁččḁ͡ʷotāl?, pl. -ቹዎታል። -ččuʷ͡otāl?
He (it) doesn't suit you: አይመችህም። a͡ị̥mmā̆ččị̥-hị̥m, pl. -ቹህም። -ččuhị̥m, ... you (pol.): አይመቸ ዎም። a͡ị̥mmḁččḁ͡ʷom, pl. -ቹዎም። -ččuʷ͡om.
It wouldn't suit the Rās: ለራስ፡አይመችም፡ነበር። lḁrás a͡ị̥mmā̆ččị̥m nḁ́bbär (§ 81*c*, λ).
suitable, adj. ምቹ mị̥́čču.
sulphur, s. ዲን din (dị̥n).
sum, s. (calculation) ቍጥር qwị̥́ṭị̥r (-wǘṭ-).
(total) ጅምላ jị̥́mlā̆.
summit, s. ጫፍ čạf.
(of ascent) አፋፍ āfā̆f.

summon, v.t. ተጣራ tḁṭárrã.

Please summon him: pol. እስቲይጣሩት። i̥stiyi̥ṭṭárut.

Please summon them: pol. እስቲይጣሯቸው። i̥stiyi̥ṭ-ṭārwáčča͡u.

summoned, be, v.p. ተጠራ tḁṭḁrrã.

Has he been summoned? ተጠርቷል። tḁṭártŏ͡āl?, pl. -ተዋል። -tḁu͡āl?

sun, s. ጠሐይ ṭḁhá͡i̥ (ፀ- ṣḁ́-; ṭhá͡i̥, ṭá͡i̥; sometimes f. § 54*e*).

Take him (it) out of the sun: ተጠሐይ፡አንሣው። tḁ-ṭḁhá͡i̥ ánsa͡u.

When the sun rises: ጠሐይ፡ሲወጣ፡ ṭḁhá͡i̥ si̥wóṭa (ስትወጣ፡ si̥ttwóṭa).

Sunday, s. & adv. እሑድ፡ i̥húd.

support, v.t. ደገፈ dḁ́ggḁfḁ.

ገደፈ gḁ́ddḁfḁ (type B § 35).

Support him (it): ደግፈው። dḁ́ggi̥fa͡u, pl. -ፉት። -fut.

ገድፈው። gḁ́ddi̥fa͡u, pl. -ፉት። -fut.

supported, be, v.p. ተደገፈ tḁdḁ́ggḁfḁ.

ተገደፈ tḁgḁ́ddḁfḁ.

suppose, v.i. & t. አሰበ ássḁbḁ (-ḁyḁ).

መሰለው mḁ́ssḁla͡u (impers. § 43*a*; type A § 34).

What do you suppose? ምን፡ይመስልሃል። mi̥n yi̥mḁ́s-lḁhāl?, pol. ምን፡ይመስልዎታል። mi̥n yi̥mḁ́slḁʷotāl?

I suppose so: ይሆናል። yi̥hʷónāl.

sure, be, v.i. (of something) ተረዳ tḁrḁ́ddã (§ 63*d*, *e*).

I am sure: ተረድቻለሁ። tḁrḁdi̥ččálla͡u^{h} (§ 7*d*).

Are you sure? ተረድተሃል። tḁrḁ́dtḁhāl?, pol. ተረድ-ተዋል። tḁrḁ́dtḁu͡āl?

There is sure to be one (some § 52*a*, δ): አይጠፋም። a͡i̥ṭḁ́fām.

surety, s. ዋስ wās.

surety, be, v.i. (for, v.t.) ተዋሰ tḁwāsḁ (tḁ͡uā́-).

Who will stand surety for you? ማን፡ይዋስሃል። mān yuwā́sḁhāl?

surety, find, v.i. ዋስ፡ጠራ wās ṭḁrrā̃.

ዋስ፡አመጣ wās amḁ́ṭṭā̃.

You must find a surety: ዋስ፡ጥራ። wās ṭí̥ra, or ዋስ፡አምጣ። wās ánṭa (§ 7*d*).

surety, produce as, v.t. አዋሰ awā́sḁ (a͡uā́-).

Whom have you produced as surety? ማንን፡አዋስህ። mā́nnän a͡uā́sh? (-s-h, not -š, § 3).

surpass, v.t. ተሻለ tḁšā́lḁ (täš-) ከ- kḁ- (ተ- tḁ-; § 47*a*).

በለጠ bḁ́llḁṭḁ ከ- kḁ- (ተ- tḁ-; § 47*a*).

surprise, interj. expressing:

(pained) አይ ái! (á͡i̥).

(incredulous) አረግ ḁ́rḁg! (ḁrā̃ḁ́g; § 7*d*).

(admiring) እጡብ í̥ṭúb! (-y̥, § 8, hḁṭūū́y̥).

(horrified) በስመ፡አብ bḁ́smḁ āb! (āy̥).

surprised, be, v.i. ተገረመ tḁgḁ́rrḁmḁ.

ገረመው gḁ́rrḁmḁ͡u (impers. § 43*a*; § 63*d*, *e*).

I am surprised: ገረመኝ። gḁ́rrḁmäñ, pl. -መን። -mḁn.

surrender, v.i. ተማረከ tḁmā́rrḁkḁ.

ተጋዛ tḁgḁ́zzā̃.

survey, v.t. አየ ā́yyä (§ 44*b*).

መረመረ mḁrḁ́mmḁrḁ (märḁ́mmärḁ).

surveyed, be, v.p. ታየ tā́yyä.

ተመረመረ tḁmḁrḁ́mmḁrḁ (-märḁ́mmärḁ).

survive, v.i. ተረፈ tḁ́rrḁfḁ (tā́r-).

v.t. ቻለ čā́lḁ.

A man that survived from the fight: ተውጊ፡የተረፈ፡ሰው። tḁ͡uū́ggi (§ 47*a*) yätḁ́rrḁfḁ́ (§ 8) sḁ͡u.

This child would not survive small-pox: ይህ፡ልጅ፡ ኩፍኝ፡አይችልም። yi̥hé (§ 8) li̥j kuffi̥ññ a͡i̥či̥li̥m.

suspect, v.i. & t. ጠረጠረ ṭḁrḁ́ṭṭḁrḁ (ṭärḁ́ṭṭärḁ), of, በ- bḁ- (yḁ-; § 47*a*).

I suspect him: እጠረጥረዋለኍ። i̥ṭḁrḁṭṭi̥rḁ͡uállḁ͡u^{h} (§ 7*d*), pl. እንጠረጥረዋለን። i̥nni̥ṭḁrḁṭṭi̥rḁ͡uállän.

I don't suspect him: አልጠረጥረውም። alṭḁrḁ́ṭṭi̥rḁ͡um, pl. አንጠረጥረውም። anni̥ṭḁrḁ́ṭṭi̥rḁ͡um.

Whom do you suspect? ማንን፡ትጠረጥራለህ። mánnän ti̥ṭḁrḁṭṭi̥rálläh?, ... you (pol.) ...? ማንን፡ይጠረጥራሉ። mánnän yi̥ṭḁrḁṭṭi̥rállu?

What do you suspect him of? በምን፡ትጠረጥረዋለህ። bḁmi̥n ti̥ṭärḁṭṭi̥rḁ͡uálläh?

suspected, be, v.p. ተጠረጠረ tḁṭḁrḁ́ṭṭḁrḁ (-ṭärḁ́ṭṭärḁ).

suspend, v.t. (hang up) ሰቀለ sḁ́qqḁlḁ.
አንጠለጠለ anṭḁlḁ́ṭṭḁlḁ.
(interrupt) አጐለ ággwωlḁ.

suspended, be, v.p. (hung up) ተሰቀለ tḁsḁ́qqḁlḁ (täs-).
ተንጠለጠለ tḁnṭḁlḁ́ṭṭḁlḁ.
(interrupted) ታጐለ tággwωlḁ.

How is it (are they § 52*a*, δ) suspended? በምን፡ ተሰቅሏል። bḁmi̥n tḁsḁ́ql͡ōāl?

The work has been suspended: ስራ፡ታጕሏል። si̥ra tággwŭl͡ōāl.

suspender, s. መያዣ mḁyážã (mḁi̥á-).

suspicion, s. ጥርጣሬ ṭi̥ri̥ṭṭári.

suspicious, adj. (suspecting) ጠርጣሪ ṭḁrṭári (ṭär-).

swallow, v.i. & t. ዋጠ wáṭḁ.

Swallow it: ዋጠው። wáṭḁ͡u.

Don't swallow it: አትዋጠው። attwáṭḁ͡u.

When you swallow it (them) do so slowly: ስትውጥ፡ እያቈየህ፡ዋጥ። si̥ttwŭ́ṭ īyyāqwώyyäh wāṭ (§ 61*b*).

swamp, s. ረግረግ rḁ́grḁg.
  ጨቀጨቅ č̣ā́qḁč̣äq.
swarm, v.i. ተሰበሰበ tḁsḁbḁ́ssḁbḁ (täs-, -ḁṿḁ́ssḁṿḁ).
  (into, over, v.t.) ወረረ wώrrḁrḁ.
swear, v.i. (at, v.t.) ሰደበ sḁ́ddḁbḁ (-ḁṿḁ).
  Don't swear: አትስደብ። attḭsdḁṿ, pl. -ቡ። -ṿu.
  Don't swear at him (it): አትስደበው። attḭsdḁṿḁ͡u, pl. -ቡት። -ṿut.
swear, v.i. (make oath) ማለ mā́lḁ (§ 80).
  Swear that this is the truth: ማልልኝ፡ ይህ፡ እውነት፡ ነው። mā́lḭllḭñ (§ 47*a*) yḭhe unā́t (§ 8) nḁ͡u.
swearing, s. (abuse) ስድብ sḭ́dḭb (-ḭṿ).
sweat, s. ወዝ wḁz (wωz).
  ላብ lāb (lāṿ).
sweat, v.i. ወዛ wḁ́zzã (wώz-).
sweep, v.i. & t. ጠረገ ṭḁ́rrḁgḁ.
  Sweep it: ጥረገው። ṭḭrḁgḁ͡u, pl. -ጉት። -gut.
sweepings, s. ጉድፍ gúdḭf.
  ጥራጊ ṭḭrrā́gi.
  ግብስብስ gḭbḭ́sbḭs (gḭṿḭ́sṿḭs).
  ቈሻሻ qwωšā́šã.
sweet, adj. ጣፋጭ ṭā́fā́č̣ (§ 8).
sweet, s. †አላዋ alā́wã (alá͡uã).
sweet, be, v.i. ጣፈጠ ṭā́ffḁṭḁ.
swell (be or become swollen), v.i. አበጠ ábbḁṭḁ (§ 63*d, e*).
  It is swollen: አብጧል። áṿṭō̃āl, pl. -ጠዋል። -ṭḁ͡uāl.
  If it swells: ቢያብጥ፡ byaṿṭ, pl. -ጡ፡ -ṭu.
swelling, s. እበጥ ḭbḁṭ (ḭ́ṿ-, -äṭ).
  እብጠት ḭbṭḁt (ḭ́ṿṭ-, -ät).
  እባጭ ḭbbā́č̣ (§ 8).

swept, be, v.p. ተጠረገ tḁṭ̥árrḁgḁ.

Has it been swept? ተጠርጓል። tḁṭárgo͡al?

It has not been swept: አልተጠረገም። altḁṭ̥árrḁgḁm.

It is to be swept: ይጠረግ። yi̥ṭṭ̥árḁg.

swim, v.i. ዋኘ wā́ññä.

I am going for a swim: ልዋኝ፡ነኝ። li̥wā́ññi̥ näñ.

I cannot swim: ዋና፡አላውቅም። wā́na alā́uqi̥m.

Can you swim? ዋና፡ታውቃለህ። wā́na ta͡uqállăh?

Can he (it) swim? ይዋኛል። yuā́ññāl?, pl. ይዋኛሉ። yuāññállu? (§ 63*c*).

swimming, s. ዋና wā́nā̃.

swine, s. አሳማ ā̃sā́mā̃ (§ 52*a*, δ).

switch, s. መንጃ mḁnjā̃.

sword, s. (straight) ሰይፍ sḁ͡i̥f.

(curved) ጐራዴ gwωrā́dʸe.

sycamore, s. (*Ficus sycomorus*, Broun, Cat. 533) ባምባ bā̃mbā̃.

(*Ficus sp.*) ወርካ wḁrkā̃ (wώr-, ዋር- wár-).

(„) ሾላ šʷólā̱.

syce (سائس), s. ለጓሚ lωggwā́mi.

symptom, s. ማስታወቂያ mā̃sta͡uώqyā̃.

syphilis, s. ቂጥኝ qi̥ṭṭi̥ñ (-ññ § 6; § 8).

syphilitic, adj. ቂጥኛም qi̥ṭṭi̥ññā́m (§ 8).

T

§ *refers to the paragraphs of the Grammar* (*Initia Amharica, Part I*).

table, s. Š. ገበታ gḁ́bḁtã (gḁ́ṿḁ-; § 8).
G. ሰደቃ sḁ́dḁ́qã (-dḁ́q-; § 8).
ሰዴቃ sḁdʸéqã.
Put it on the table: ተገበታው፡ላይ፡አድርገው። tḁgḁṿḁtáu (§ 8) lai̥ (§ 47*b*) árgḁu (§ 7*d*).
(Of a meal:) Let it be on the table at eight o'clock: በስምንት፡ሰዓት፡ይቅረብ። bḁsı̥mmı̥nt sḁạt yı̥qrḁṿ.

table-cloth, s. የገበታ፡ልብስ yägḁṿḁtá (§§ 8, 70) li̥bs (li̥ṿs).

table-servant, s. አሳላፊ asalláfi.

taenia, s. ወስፋት wώsfát (§ 8).

tail, s. ጅራት ji̥rát (§ 8).

tailor, s. ሰፊ sḁ́fi, pl. ሰፎች sḁ́fʷōč & (not G.) ሰፊዎች sḁ́fiʷōč (-čč § 6; § 9*b*).

take, v.t. ያዘ yázḁ (§ 44*c*).
(away) ወሰደ wḁ́ssḁdḁ (wώs-).
Take him (it): ያዘው። yázḁu, pl. ያዙት። yázut.
Don't take him (it): አትያዘው። attyázḁu, pl. -ዙት። -zut.
Did you take him (it)? ያዝሀው። yázhḁu?, pl. ያዛችሁት። yāzáčči̥hut?
I have taken him (it): ይዤዋለሁ። yi̥žžʸeuállḁuʰ (§ 7*d*), pl. ይዘነዋል። yı̥zḁnḁuāl.
I have not taken him (it): አልያዝሁትም። alyázhuti̥m, pl. አልያዝነውም። alyáznḁum.
I will take him (it): ኢዘዋለሁ። ı̥zḁuállḁuʰ, pl. እኒዘዋለን። i̥nni̥zḁuállän.

I will not take him (it): አላሊዘውም። alí̥zḁ͡ūm, pl. አኒዘውም። anní̥zḁ͡ūm.

Let us take some water in this: በዚህ፡ውሃ፡እንያዝበት። bḁzzíh wŭhá nnyázi̥bbḁt.

I shall take it to England: ተንግሊዝ፡አገር፡እወስደዋለሁ። tḁṅglíz ágḁr i̥wωsdḁ͡uállḁ͡u^{h} (§ 7*d*).

Who has taken it? ማን፡ወስዶታል። mān wώsd^{w}otāl?

take away, v.t. ወሰደ wḁ́ssḁdḁ (wώs-).

አነሣ anḁ́ssā̃.

Take him (it) away: ውሰደው። úsḁdḁ͡u, pl. -ዱት። -dut, or አንሣው። ánsa͡u, pl. -ሡት። -sut.

Come and take it (him, her, them, § 61*b*) away: ና፡ውሰድ። nā wŭ́sḁd (ná͡usḁd), pl. ኑ፡ውሰዱ። nu wŭ́sḁdu.

Don't take him (it) away: አትውሰደው። attŭ́sḁdḁ͡u, pl. -ዱት። -dut, or አታንሣው። attánsa͡u, pl. -ሡት። -sut.

Don't take the matches away from here: ክብሪት፡ተዚህ፡አታንሣ። ki̥vrít tḁzzíh attánsa.

take hold, v.i. (of, v.t.) ያዘ yā́zḁ (§ 44*c*), s.v. take.

take in (inside, indoors), v.t. አገባ agḁ́bbā̃.

Take him (it) in: አግባው። ágy̥a͡u, pl. -ቡት። -y̥ut.

Don't take him (it) in: አታግባው። attágy̥a͡u, pl. -ቡት። -y̥ut.

take off, v.t. (from the body) አወለቀ awḁ́llḁqḁ (a͡uḁ́-, -ώl-).

Take your boots off: ጫማህን፡አውልቀው። c̣ámmahi̥n á͡uli̥qḁ͡u (§ 52*a*, δ).

Take the bridle off: ልጓም፡አውልቅ። lūgám (§ 7*d*) á͡uli̥q.

take over, v.t. ተረከበ tḁrḁ́kkḁbḁ (tärák-, -ḁyḁ).

taken (away), be, v.p. ተወሰደ tḁwḁ́ssḁdḁ (tḁ͡uḁ́-, -ώs-).

ተነሣ tḁnḁ́ssā̃.

Let it be taken away: ይነሣ። yi̥nnḁ́sa, pl. -ሡ። -su.

It is not to be taken away: አይነሣ። a͡i̥nnḁ́sa, pl. -ሡ። -su.

taken away, have (allow to be), v.t. አስወሰደ aswḁ́ssḁdḁ (-wώs-; § 68).

I will have him (it) taken away: አስወስደዋለሁ። aswωssi̥dḁ͡uállḁ͡uʰ, pl. እናስወስደዋለን። i̥nnaswωssi̥dḁ͡uállän.

Have him (it) taken away: አስወስደው። aswώssi̥dḁ͡u, pol. ያስወስዱት። yaswώssi̥dut, pl. አስወስዱት። aswώssi̥dut.

taken in (inside, indoors), be, v.p. ገባ gḁ́bbã.

Has it been taken indoors? ገብቷል። gḁ́y̥t͡ŏāl?, pl. ገብተዋል። gḁ́y̥tḁ͡uāl?

It must be taken in: ይግባ። yí̥gy̥a, pl. -ቡ። -y̥u.

tale, s. ታሪክ tā́rīk (-ri̥k).

tale-bearer, s. አሾክሿኪ aššʷokšwáki.

tales, carry, v.i. አሾክሾከ aššʷokḁ́ššʷokḁ.

Don't carry tales: አታሾክሹክ። attaššʷokḁ́šŭk, pl. -ሹኩ። -šŭku.

talisman, s. ጠልሰም ṭḁlsḁm.

talk, s. መነጋገር mḁnnḁgā́gḁr (-gär).

ጨዋታ čḁ͡uā́tã.

ወግ wωg.

We will have a talk to-morrow: ነገ፡እንጫወታለን። nḁ́gḁ nni̥ç̌ç̌a͡uwωtállän.

talk, v.i. ተናገረ tḁnā́ggḁrḁ (-gärḁ).

(together) ተነጋገረ tḁnḁgā́ggḁrḁ (-gärḁ).

ተጫወተ tḁč̣áuwḁtḁ (-wωtḁ).

Don't talk: አትናገር። atti̥nnā́gär, pl. (together) አትነጋገሩ። atti̥nnḁgā́gḁru.

It's no use talking: መናገር፡ አይረባም። mḁnnágär a͡i̥rḁ́yām. S.v. speak.

talk too much, v.i. ለፈለፈ lḁfḁ́llḁfḁ.

He talks too much: ይለፈልፋል። yi̥lḁfḁ́lli̥fāl, pl. ይለፈልፋሉ። yi̥lḁfḁlli̥fállu.

Don't talk too much: አትለፍልፍ። atti̥lḁ́fli̥f, pl. -ልፉ። -li̥fu.

talkative, adj. ምላሰኛ mi̥lāsḁññã (-sáñ-).

ለፍላፊ lḁfláfi.

ለፍላፋ lḁfláffã.

talking, s. መናገር mḁnnágḁr (-gär).

tall, adj. ረጅም rḁ́jji̥m (ráj-, ረዥም rḁ́žži̥m, ráž-), intensive pls. ረጃጅም rḁjájji̥m (räj-), ረጃጅሞች rḁjájji̥mʷōč (räj-, -čč § 6).

Talpa sp., s. ፍልፈል fi̥lfäl, usually f. (§ 54*c*).

tamarind (*Tamarindus indica*, Broun, Cat. 171), s. ሆመር hʷṓmḁr (ኮ- kʷṓ-, -mär, § 7*d*).

Š. ሮቃ rʷṓqã.

tame, adj. ገር gḁr (gär).

ገራም gḁ́rrám (§ 8).

ለማዳ lḁmmádã (-máddã).

ልዝብ lí̥zzi̥b (-i̥y).

tame, v.t. ገራ gḁ́rrã.

tame, be (become), v.i. ገረመ gḁ́rrḁmḁ (type B § 35; § 63*d*, *e*).

Is it (are they § 52*a*, δ) tame? ገርሟል። gárri̥mʷāl?

tamed, be, v.p. ተገራ tḁgḁ́rrã.

Can it (they § 52*a*, δ) be tamed? ይገራል። yi̥ggḁ́r-rāl? (§ 63*c*).

tape-worm, s. ወስፋት wósfát (§ 8).

target, s. ዓላማ alámã.

taste, s. መቀመስ mḁqqḁ́mḁs.

(pleasant) ጣም ṭām.

I like the taste of it: ጥምኛል። ṭí̥mʷoññāl.

I don't like the taste of it: አይጥመኝም። a͡i̥ṭí̥mäñ-ñi̥m.

Do you like the taste of it? pol. ይጥመዎታሉይ። yi̥ṭí̥mḁ͡ʷotāllwí̥? (s.v. ወይ).

taste, v.i. (be tasted, v.p.) ተቀመሰ tḁqḁ́mmḁsḁ.

What does it taste like? እንደምን፡ይቀመሳል። ndämí̥n yi̥qqḁ́mmḁsāl?

taste, v.i. & t. ቀመሰ qḁ́mmḁsḁ.

Thank you, I have tasted it (them § 61*b*) before: pol. እግዚአብሔር፡ይስጥልኝ፡ከዚህ፡ፊት፡ቀምሼያለሁ። i̥gzi̥ayḥʸér yí̥sṭi̥lli̥ñ, kḁzzíh fit qḁmi̥ššyállḁ͡uʰ (§ 7*d*).

taste pleasant, v.i. ጣመ ṭā́mḁ (§ 63*d*, *e*).

tasted, be, v.p. ተቀመሰ tḁqḁ́mmḁsḁ.

It cannot be tasted: አይቀመስም። a͡i̥qqḁ́mmḁsi̥m (§ 63*c*).

taught, be, v.p. ተማረ tḁmā́rḁ.

Where were you taught? ወዴት፡ተምረሃል። wωdʸét tḁ́mĭ̥rḁhāl?, pol. ...፡ተምረዋል። ... tḁ́mĭ̥rḁ͡uāl?, pl. ...፡ተምራችኋል። ... tḁmĭ̥rā́ččyuhāl? (§ 7*d*).

Where was he taught? ወዴት፡ተምሯል። wωdʸét tḁ́-mĭ̥r͡ŏāl?, pol. & pl. -ረዋል። -rḁ͡uāl?

tavern, s. መሸታ mḁšḁ́tã (-šä́tã).

tax, s. ግብር gí̥b(ĭ̥)r (gí̥v-).

tax (taxes), pay (a), v.i. ገበረ gḁ́bbḁrḁ (-bärḁ).

Does he pay a tax (taxes)? ይገብራል። yigḁ́bbi̥rāl?, pl. ይገብራሉ። yigḁbbi̥rállu?

tea, s. ሻይ š͡ái̥.

Š. ቻይ č͡ái̥.

After tea: ተሻይ፡በኋላ፡ tḁš͡ái̥ vḁ͡uhā́la (§§ 7*d*, 47*b*).

This tea is too strong—weak: ይህ፡ሻይ፡ወፍራም፡ነው።—ቀጭን፡ነው። y̥he šḁ́i wωfrám (§ 8) nḁu͡—qḁč̣č̣ɪ̥n (§ 8) nḁu͡.

teach, v.i. & t. አስተማረ astḁmárḁ.

Teach him: አስተምረው። astḁ́mɪ̥rḁu͡.

Who taught you? ማን፡አስተማረህ። mānn (§ 6) astḁmárăh?

What does he teach? ምን፡ያስተምራል። mɪ̥n yāstḁ́mɪ̥rāl?, pol. & pl. ምን፡ያስተምራሉ። mɪ̥n yāstḁmɪ̥rállu?

teacher, s. አስተማሪ astḁmári.

teaching, s. ትም[ህ]ርት tɪ̥m(h)ɪ̥rt (§ 8).

tear, s. (in the eye) እንባ (ɪ̥)nbā̃ (-nẏā̃, (ɪ̥)mbā̃; § 52*a*, δ).
(rent) ቀዳዳ qḁdádā̃.

tear, v.i. (be torn, v.p.) ተቀደደ tḁqḁ́ddḁdḁ.
ተበጠሰ tḁbḁ́t̥t̥ḁsḁ (tḁẏḁ́-, -át̥-).

It will tear: ይቀደዳል። yɪ̥qqḁ́ddḁdāl, pl. ይቀደዳሉ። yɪ̥qqḁddḁdállu.
ይበጠሳል። yɪ̥bbḁ́t̥t̥ḁsāl, pl. ይበጠሳሉ። yɪ̥bbḁt̥t̥ḁsállu.

Mind it doesn't tear: እንዳይቀደድ። nda͡ɪ̥qqḁ́ddḁd, pl. -ደዱ። -ddḁdu.
እንዳይበጠስ። nda͡ɪ̥bbḁ́t̥t̥ḁs, pl. -ጠሱ። -t̥t̥ḁsu.

It is torn: ተቀዷል። tḁqḁ́ddō͡āl, pl. -ደዋል። -ddḁu͡āl.
ተበጥሷል። tḁẏát̥t̥ɪ̥sō͡āl, pl. -ሰዋል። -sḁu͡āl.

It is strong, it won't tear: ጠንካራ፡ነው፤አይቀደድም። tḁn̊karrá (§ 8) nḁu͡, a͡ɪ̥qqḁ́ddḁdɪ̥m.

tear, v.t. ቀደደ qḁ́ddḁdḁ.
በጠሰ bḁ́t̥t̥ḁsḁ (bát̥-).

Tear it: ቅደደው። qɪ̥́dḁdḁu͡, pl. ቅደዱት። qɪ̥́dḁdut.
በጥሰው። bát̥t̥ɪ̥sḁu͡, pl. -ሱት። -sut.

Don't tear it: አትቀደደው። attí̥qdḁdḁ͡u, pl. -ዱት። -dut.

አትበጥሰው። atti̥ṿáṭṭi̥sḁ͡u, pl. -ሱት። -sut.

You will tear it: ትቀደዋለህ። ti̥qḁddḁ͡uálläh, pl. ትቀዱታላችሁ። ti̥qḁddutalláččyuh (§ 7*d*).

tease, v.t. (annoy) አስቈጣ asqwώṭṭã.

Don't tease him (it): አታስቈጣው። attāsqwώṭṭa͡u, pl. -ጡት። -ṭṭut.

teat, s. ጡት ṭut (§ 52*a*, γ).

telegram, s. †ቴሌግራም tälägrā́m.

telegraph, s. †ቴሌግራፍ tälägrā́f.

†ስልክ si̥lk.

By telegraph: በቴሌግራፍ፡ bḁtälägrā́f (§ 47*a*).

Telegraph-wire: የቴሌግራፍ፡ሽቦ፡ yätälägrā́f (§§ 47*a*, 70) ší̥ṿ^{w}o.

They erected a telegraph: የቴሌግራፍ፡ሽቦ፡ተከሉ። yätälägrā́f ší̥ṿ^{w}o tḁ́kkḁlu.

He (pol.) had a telegraph erected: የቴሌግራፍ፡ሽቦ፡ አስተከሉ። yätälägrā́f ší̥ṿ^{w}o astḁ́kkḁlu.

telephone, s. †ቴሌፎን täläf^{w}ṓn.

tell, v.i. & t. አለ ā́lḁ (s.v. √ባለ, §§ 44*a*, 80).

ነገረ nḁ́ggḁrḁ (-gärḁ).

(inform) አስታወቀ astá͡uwḁqḁ (-wωqḁ).

(disclose) ገለጠ gḁ́llḁṭḁ (gā́l-).

Use the jussive (§ 27).

I (will) tell you: እላሃለሁ። i̥lḁhállḁ͡u^{h} (§ 7*d*), pl. እንልሃለን። i̥nni̥li̥hállän (App. B § 12*c*).

I can't tell you: እንጃልህ። njálli̥h (s.v. እንጃ, §§ 47*a*, 12*c*).

I told you: ነገርሁህ። nḁ́ggärhuh, pl. ነገርንህ። nḁ́g-gärni̥h.

I told you (pol.): ነገርሁዎ። nḁ́ggḁrhu͡ʷo, pl. ነገርነዎ። nḁ́ggḁrnḁ͡ʷo.

I told you (pl.): ነገርኋችሁ። nḁggḁrhwắččyuh (§ 7*d*), pl. ነገርናችሁ። nḁggḁrnắččyuh.

Did I not tell you? አልነገርሁህም። alnḁ́ggärhuhi̥m?, pl. አልነገርንህም። alnḁ́ggärni̥hi̥m?

Did I not tell you (pl.)? አልነገርኋችሁም። alnḁggḁrhwắčči̥hum?, pl. አልነገርናችሁም። alnḁggḁrnắčči̥hum?

I told him: ነገርሁት። nḁ́ggärhut, pl. ነገርነው። nḁ́ggärnḁ͡u.

I did not tell him: አልነገርሁትም። alnḁ́ggärhuti̥m, pl. አልነገርነውም። alnḁ́ggärnḁ͡um.

I told them (him, pol.): ነገርኋቸው። nḁggärhwắččḁ͡u, pl. ነገርናቸው። nḁggärnắččḁ͡u.

I did not tell them (him, pol.): አልነገርኋቸውም። alnḁggärhwắččḁ͡um, pl. አልነገርናቸውም። alnḁggärnắččḁ͡um.

Tell me: ንገረኝ። ni̥gḁrḁñ (-räñ), pl. ንገሩኝ። ni̥gḁruñ.

Tell him: ንገረው። ni̥gḁrḁ͡u, pl. ንገሩት። ni̥gḁrut.

Don't tell him: አትንገረው። āttí̥ngḁrḁ͡u, pl. አትንገሩት። āttí̥ngḁrut.

Tell them (him, pol.): ንገራቸው። ni̥gḁrắččḁ͡u, pl. ንገሯቸው። ni̥gḁrwắččḁ͡u.

Don't tell them (him, pol.): አትንገራቸው። ātti̥ngḁrắččḁ͡u, pl. አትንገሯቸው። ātti̥ngḁrwắččḁ͡u.

Did you tell him? ነገርሀው። nḁ́ggärhḁ͡u?, pl. ነገራችሁት። nḁggḁrắčči̥hut?

Did you tell them (him, pol.)? ነገርሃቸው። nḁggḁrhắččḁ͡u?, pl. ነገራችኋቸው። nḁggḁrāčči̥hwắččḁ͡u? (-ččyuhắ- §7*d*).

He will tell you: ይለሃል። yı̥lḁhāl, pol. & pl. ይሉሃል። yı̥luhāl.

Won't he tell you? አይነግርህም። a͡i̥nḁ́gri̥hi̥m?, pol. & pl. አይነግሩህም። a͡i̥nḁ́gruhi̥m?

He told me: ነገረኝ። nḁ́ggäräñ, pol. & pl. ነገሩኝ። nḁ́ggḁruñ.

He did not tell me: አልነገረኝም። alnḁ́ggäräññi̥m (§ 6), pol. & pl. አልነገሩኝም። alnḁ́ggḁruññi̥m.

He told us: ነገረን። nḁ́ggärän, pol. & pl. ነገሩን። nḁ́ggḁrun.

He did not tell us: አልነገረንም። alnḁ́ggäränni̥m (§ 6), pol. & pl. አልነገሩንም። alnḁ́ggḁrunni̥m.

Did he tell you? ነገረህ። nḁ́ggäräh?, pol. & pl. ነገሩህ። nḁ́ggḁruh?

Did he tell him? ነገረው። nḁ́ggḁrḁ͡u?, pol. & pl. ነገሩት። nḁ́ggḁrut?

Did he tell them (him, pol.)? ነገራቸው። nḁggḁráč-čḁ͡u?, pol. & pl. ነገሯቸው። nḁggḁrwáččḁ͡u?

Who told you? ማን፡አለህ። mānn (§ 6) ā́läh?

Who told you (pl.)? ማን፡አላችሁ። mānn ālā́ččyuh? (§ 7*d*).

Who told him? ማን፡አለው። ṃānn ā́lḁ͡u?

Who told them (him, pol.)? ማን፡አላቸው። mānn ālā́ččḁ͡u?

Don't tell (disclose it to) anybody: ለማንም፡አትግለጠው። lḁmā́nni̥mm attı̥́glḁṭḁ͡u, pl. -ለጡት። -lḁṭut.

Tell him to come: ና፡በለው። nā ṿḁ́lḁ͡u, or ይምጣ። yı̥́mṭā.

Tell Tḁsḁ́mma to come: ለተሰማ፡ና፡በለው። lḁtḁsḁ́mma nā ṿḁ́lḁ͡u, or ተሰማ፡ይምጣ። tḁsḁ́mma yı̥́mṭa.

Tell him everything: ሁሉንም፡አስታውቀው። húllu-ni̥mm astá͡uqḁ͡u.

Tell him just what I tell you: ንገረው፡እንደምነግርህ፡ብቻ። ní̥gḁrḁ͡u ndämmi̥nḁ́gri̥h ỵí̥čča.

Tell him to give you some money: ገንዘብ፡ስጠኝ፡በለው። gḁ́nzḁỵ sí̥ṭäñ ỵḁ́lḁ͡u, or ገንዘብ፡ይስጥህ። gḁ́nzḁỵ yí̥sṭi̥h.

He told me there wasn't any: የለም፡አለኝ። yállämm áläñ, pol. & pl. የለም፡አሉኝ። yállämm áluñ.

tell a tale, v.i. ተረከ tḁ́rrḁkḁ (tắr-).

See whether you can find me a man that can tell tales: የሚተርክ፡ሰው፡ፈልግልኝ። yämmi̥tärrí̥k (§§ 8, 14, 63*c*) sḁ͡u fḁ́lli̥gi̥lli̥ñ (§ 47*a*), pol. …፡ይፈልጉልኝ። … yi̥fḁ́lli̥gulli̥ñ.

temporary hut or shelter, s. ጎጆ g^{w}ójj^{w}o.

tempt, v.t. ፈተነ fḁ́ttḁnḁ (fắttänḁ).

tempted, be, v.p. ተፈተነ tḁfḁ́ttḁnḁ (-fắttänḁ).

ten, card. num. አሥር ássi̥r (§ 20*a*).

ten thousand, card. num. እልፍ i̥lf (§ 20*a*).

tendon, s. ጅማት jí̥mmát (§ 8; § 52*a*, γ).

tent, s. ድንኳን dí̥ṅkwán (dŭ́ṅ-; §§ 8, 52*a*, δ).

Pitch the tent: ድንኳኑን፡ትከለው። dŭ́ṅkwánun tí̥kḁlḁ͡u, pl. -ሉት። -lut.

Strike the tent: ድንኳኑን፡ንቀለው። dŭ́ṅkwánun ní̥qḁlḁ͡u, pl. -ሉት። -lut.

The tent is to be pitched here: ድንኳኑ፡ከዚህ፡ይተከል። dŭ́ṅkwánu kḁzzíh yi̥ttḁ́kḁl.

tenth, ord. num. አሥረኛ assi̥rḁ́ññã (-rắñ-; § 20*b*).

tenth ($^1/_{10}$), s. አሥርያ፡[አሥሪያ] assi̥ríyyã (§ 20*b*, § 52*a*, δ).

tent-peg, s. ካስማ kási̥mã (-sŭ́mã; § 52*a*, δ).

tent-pole, s. ተራዳ tḁrắdã.

You (A) hold the tent-pole: you (B) pull out the pegs: አንተ፡ተራዳውን፡ያዝ፤ አንተ፡ንቀል። ántä tḁradá͡un (§ 8) yaz: ántä ní̥qḁl.

tepid, adj. ለብ l̥abb.

Terminalia glabra (Broun, Cat. 187), s. ቀይ፡ወምበላ q̥ayy wωmbḁlã.

Terminalia splendida (ib.), s. ጥቁር፡ወምበላ ṭǘqur wωm-bḁlã.

terrified, be, v.i. & p. ፈራ fḁrrã (fā́r-).

(suddenly) ደነገጠ dḁnḁ́ggḁṭḁ.

terrify, v.t. አስፈራ asfḁrrã (-fā́r-).

terror, s. ፍራት fi̥rā́t (§ 8).

(sudden) ድንጋጤ di̥ṅgā́ṭ^{y}e.

test, v.t. ሞከረ m^{w}ókkḁrḁ (-kärḁ).

ፈተነ fḁttḁnḁ (fā́ttänḁ).

I will test him (it): እሞክረዋለሁ። i̥m^{w}okki̥rḁ͡uállḁ͡u^{h} (§ 7*d*), pl. እንሞክረዋለን። i̥nni̥m^{w}okki̥rḁ͡uállän.

tested, be, v.p. ተሞከረ tḁm^{w}ókkḁrḁ (-kärḁ).

ተፈተነ tḁfḁ́ttḁnḁ (-fā́ttänḁ).

It has not been tested: አልተሞከረም። altḁm^{w}ók-kḁrḁm, pl. -ሩም። -rum.

testicle, s. ቈለት qwώlḁt (-lät; § 52*a*, γ).

ብረት bi̥rḁt (-rät; „).

testify, v.t. መሰከረ mḁsḁ́kkḁrḁ (-kärḁ).

testimonial, s. ምስጋና mi̥sgā́nã.

Testudo sp., s. ኤሊ ^{y}éli.

tether, v.t. አሰረ ássḁrḁ (-särḁ).

Tether it to a tree: ተዛፍ፡እሰረው። tḁzā́f i̥sḁrḁ͡u.

tethered, be, v.p. ታሰረ tā́ssḁrḁ (-särḁ).

Has it been tethered? ታስሯል። tā́srṑāl?, pl. ታስረዋል። tā́srḁ͡uāl?

It is to be tethered: ይታሰር። yi̥ttā́sär, pl. -ሰሩ። -sḁru.

than, conj. ከ- kḁ- (ተ- tḁ-; § 58).

Is he older than you? እርሱ፡ታላቅ፡ነው፡ታንተ። i̥rsú tallā́q nḁ͡u tā́ntä? (§ 7*a*).

than that, conj. ከ- k(i̥)- prefixed to contingent (§§ 45 48*a*); tense is not distinguished in the verb it introduces.

I would rather that he should be imprisoned than that he should be put to death: ኪሞት፡ሊታሰር፡እወዳለኍ። kim^{w}ót littássär i̥wωddálla͡u^{h} (§ 7*d*).

It was better that he should be imprisoned than that he should be put to death: ኪሞት፡ቢታሰር፡ተሻለ። kim^{w}ót yittássär täšálḁ.

thanks, s. ምስጋና mi̥sgánã.

thank you, interj. እግዚአብሔር፡ይስጥህ። i̥gzi̥aỵh^{y}ér yí̥sṭi̥h.

ተባረክ። tḁbárak (tḁỵá-).

pol. እግዚአብሔር፡ይስጥልኝ። i̥gzi̥aỵh^{y}ér yí̥sṭi̥lli̥ñ, or … ይስጠዎ። … yí̥sṭḁ͡^{w}o.

Thank you very much, but the doctor has forbidden me this: pol. እግዚአብሔር፡ይስጥልኝ፡በብዙ፡ሀኪም፡ይህነን፡ከልክለውኛል። i̥gzi̥aỵh^{y}ér yí̥sṭi̥lli̥ñ ỵḁỵí̥zu, hakím yi̥hánnän kḁ́lki̥la͡uññāl.

that, conj. (in order that) እንድ- (i̥)nd(i̥)-, prefixed to contingent (§§ 45, 48*a*); tense is not distinguished in the verb it introduces.

I will question him that *I* may hear: እጠይቀዋለኍ፡ራሴ፡እንድሰማ። i̥ṭḁyyi̥qa͡uálla͡u^{h} rás^{y}e ndi̥sáma.

I questioned him that *I* might hear: ጠየቅሁት፡ራሴ፡እንድሰማ። ṭḁ́yyäqhut rás^{y}e ndi̥sḁma.

that, conj. (introducing subst. clause)

s.v. √ባለ.

may be omitted (§ 80).

use infinitive (§ 66).

It is reported that they have crossed the river and are coming here: ወንዙን፡ተሻግረው፡ወዲህ፡ይመጣሉ፡የሚል፡ወሬ፡መጣ። wώnzun tḁšágra͡u wωdíh yi̥mḁṭállu yámmi̥l wώr^{y}e mḁ́ṭṭa.

Does (did) he (A) say that he (B) will come?
ይመጣል፡ አለ። yi̥mą̥ṭāll (§ 6) ā́lḁ?

Does (did) he (A) say that he (A) will come?
እመጣለኹ፡ አለ። i̥mḁṭállau͡ʰ (§ 7*d*) ā́lḁ?

I heard that you had gone: መሔድህን፡ ሰማሁ። mḁ-hā́di̥hi̥n sḁ́mmau͡ʰ (§ 7*d*).

Didn't he know that I was away? አለመኖሬን፡ አላወቀምይ። ālḁmḁnʷṓrʸen aláu͡wωqḁmmwí̥? (s.v. ወይ).

that, dem. pron. (near) ይህ yí̥he (yi̥h, yā́he), f. ይህች yí̥hi̥č (-čč) or ይች yi̥č (ʸi̥-, -čč), pl. እነዚህ (i̥)n-nḁ́zzíh (-nā́z-, እለ- i̥llḁ́-, -lā́z-, -zí̥h) or እኒህ (í̥)nnʸḗh (-ኒህ -nníh, -nní̥h, እሊህ í̥llʸḗh, -ሊህ -llíh, -llí̥h); (§ 8).
(distant) ያ yā̃, also prefix yā̃-, f. ያች yā̃č (-čč), pl. እነዚያ (i̥)nnḁ́zzyā̃́ (-nā́z-, እለ-i̥llḁ́-, -lā́z-) or እኒያ (í̥)nnyā̃́ (እሊያ í̥llyā̃́); (§ 8). See § 13*a*.

That's it: ይህው። yi̥hā́u͡.

This and that: ይህና፡ ይህ፡ yi̥hénna yí̥he.

Give me that (other, over there): ያነን፡ ስጠኝ። yā́n-nän sí̥ṭḁñ.

That man coming: ይህ፡ የሚመጣ፡ ሰው፡ yí̥he yäm-mi̥mḁṭā́ (§ 8) sḁu͡.

That man who was here yesterday: ያሰው፡ ተዚህ፡ ትናንት፡ የነበረው፡ yā́sḁu͡ täzzíh ti̥nánt yänḁ́bbärḁu͡.

Who are those (over there)? እነማን፡ ናቸው፡ እነዚያ። nnḁmán nā́ččḁu͡ nnḁzzyá?

I like these better than those: ተነዚህ፡ እኒህን፡ እወዳለኹ። tännäzzíh (§ 58) i̥nníhi̥n i̥wωddállau͡ʰ (§ 7*d*).

that, rel. pron. s.v. who, which.

thatch, v.t. ከፈከፈ kḁfḁ́kkḁfḁ.

What do they thatch it with? በምን፡ይከፈከፉታል። bḁmɨ̥n (§ 47*a*) yi̥kḁfḁ́kki̥futāl?

thatched, be, v.p. ተከፈከፈ tḁkḁfḁ́kkḁfḁ.

the, art. -u, (-ው -u after a vowel), f. -ቱ -itu (-i̥tu; §§ 11, 59).

theft, s. ስርቆት sɨ̥rqʷot (§ 8).

መስረቅ mḁ́srḁq.

This is called theft: ይህ፡ስርቆት፡ነው፡እሚባል። yɨ̥he si̥rqʷót nḁ͡u mmi̥bbā́l.

Theft is what *we* call it: መስረቅ፡ነው፡እምንለው፡እኛ። mḁsrḁ́q (§ 8) nḁ͡u mmi̥nni̥lḁ͡u (§§ 14, 44*a*) ñña.

their, poss. pron. -ኣቸው -ā́č(č)ḁ͡u (§ 12*b*).

theirs, poss. pron. የርሳቸው yärsā́č(č)ḁ͡u (§§ 12*a*, 47*a*, 70*b*).

them, pers. pron. -ኣቸው -ā́č(č)ḁ͡u (§ 12*c*).

(emph.) እርሳቸውን i̥rsā́č(č)ḁ͡un (§ 12*a*).

(„ , of inanimate objects) እሳቸውን i̥ssā́č(č)ḁ͡un (§ 12*a*).

Often omitted (§ 61*b*):

I don't want them: አልፈልግም። alfḁlli̥gi̥m.

then, adv. (at that time) ያን፡ጊዜ yan gɨ̥zʸe (yáṅgi̥zʸe).

(afterwards) በኋላ bḁhwā́lā̃ (bḁ͡uhā́- § 7*d*).

(after that) እንግዲህ (i̥)ṅgdʸẽ́h.

(donc) -ኣ -ā̃́? (§§ 6, 8).

(consequently) እዝወዲያ (i̥)z(z)ā́ʷωdyā̃́ (-zā̃́d-), Š. ታዲያ tā́dyā̃, (§ 8).

We did not know then that we were coming here: ያን፡ጊዜ፡ወደዚህ፡መምጣታችንን፡አላወቅንም። yáṅgi̥zʸe wωdḁzzíh mḁmṭātā́čči̥ni̥n alā́͡uwωqni̥m.

It should be mended first, then washed: በፊት፡ይበጅ፤በኋላ፡ይታጠብ። bḁfít yi̥bbā́jj, yḁ͡uhā́la yi̥ttā́ṭḁy.

It's downhill as far as the stream: then it's flat: እስከወንዝ፡ድረስ፡ቍልቍለት፡ነው፤እንግዴህ፡ሜዳ፡ነው። i̥skḁ͡uẃnz di̥rḁs qwŭlqwŭlḁ́t (§ 8) nḁ͡u: ṅgdʸéh mʸēdá nḁ͡u.

First I gave him a dollar, then I told him to go: ፊት፡አንድ፡ብር፡ሰጥቼ፡እንግዴህ፡ሂድ፡አልኩት። fit ándi̥ yi̥rr sḁ́ti̥ččʸe ṅgdʸéh hi̥d (§ 80) ắlkut (§ 7*d*).

You don't want him (it), then? አትፈልገውማ። atti̥fḁ́lli̥gḁ͡ummá?

He has understood, then? አውቋላ። áuŭqʷālllá?

thence, adv. ከወዲያ kḁ͡uẃdyắ (ተወ- tḁ͡uẃ-, § 47*a*; § 8).

there, adv. (near) ካዚህ kḁ́zzíh (hḁ́-, ተ- tḁ́-, -ắz-, -zi̥h; § 8).

(distant) ካዚያ kḁ́zzyắ (hḁ́-, ተ- tḁ́-, -ắz-; § 8).

There it is, on the chair: ተዚህ፡ተወምበሩ፡ነው። tḁzzíh tḁ͡uwmbḁ́ru (§ 8) nḁ͡u.

Stay (stop) just there (where you are): ሁን፡ተዚያው። hun tḁzzyá͡u (s.v. -ው; § 73*d*).

— There is (one, some): አለ። állä (q.v.; §§ 32, 39).

There are (some): አሉ። állu.

Is there (some, any) water? ውሃ፡አለ። wúha állä? (uhállä?).

If there is any [if he (it) is there]: እንዳለ፡ ndállä.

If there is not any [if he (it) is not there]: እን ደሌለ፡ ndḁlʸállä.

Isn't he (it) there? ያለ፡አይደለሞይ። yállä a͡i̥dállämmwi̥? (s.v. ወይ), or የለም። yállämˀ?

therefore, adv. ስለዚህ si̥lḁ́zzíh (-lắz-, -zi̥h; § 8).

these, dem. pron. እነዚህ (i̥)nnḁ́zzíh (-nắz-, -zi̥h).

እኒህ (i̥)nnʸḗh (-ኒህ -nníh, -nni̥h).

እላዚህ i̥llḁ́zzíh (-lắz-, -zi̥h).

እሊህ i̥llʸḗh (-ሊህ -llíh, -lli̥h).

See §§ 8, 13*a*.

Bring these: እነዚህን፡አምጣ። nnäzzíhi̥n ánṭa (§ 7*d*), pl. ...፡ አምጡ። ... ánṭu.

I don't like these ponies: እለዚህን፡ፈረሶች፡አል ወድም። i̥lläzzíhi̥n fḁ́rḁsʷōčč alwώddi̥m.

they, pers. pron. እርሳቸው i̥rsáč(č)ḁ͡u (§§ 12*a*, 60*b*), usually omitted unless emphatic.

thick, adj. ወፍራም wώfrā́m (§ 8), intensive pls. ወፋፍራም wωfāffi̥rā́m (§ 8), ወፋፍራሞች wωfāffi̥rā́mʷōč (-ōčč § 6).

ደንዳና dḁndánnā̃.

thick, be (become), v.i. ወፈረ wώffḁrḁ (-färḁ; § 63*d*, *e*).

thief, s. ሌባ lʸébā̃ (lʸéy̥ā̃).

ሰራቂ sḁrā́qi (sär-).

thigh, s. ጭን č̥i̥n (§ 52*a*, γ).

thin, adj. (deficient in one dimension) ሥሥ si̥s.

(deficient in two dimensions) ቀጭን qḁ́č̣č̣i̥n, intensive pls. ቀጫጭን qḁč̣áč̣č̣i̥n, ቀጫጭኖች qḁč̣áč̣č̣i̥nʷōč (-ōčč § 6).

(emaciated, of animate beings) ከሲታ kḁssi̥ttā̃.

(of animals) ጉፋያ gufáyyā̃.

A thin book: ሥሥ፡መጣፍ፡ si̥s mḁ́ṭāf.

Thin cloth: ሥሥ፡ጨርቅ፡ si̥s č̣ärq.

Thin paper: ሥሥ፡ወረቀት፡ si̥s wḁ́rḁqḁt.

A thin (slender) man: ቀጭን፡ሰው፡ qḁ́č̣č̣i̥n sḁ͡u.

A thin stick: ቀጭን፡በትር፡ qḁ́č̣č̣i̥n bḁ́tti̥r.

Thin rope (string): ቀጭን፡ገመድ፡ qḁ́č̣č̣i̥n gḁ́mḁd.

thin, be (become), v.i.

(deficient in one dimension) ሣሣ sā́ssā̃.

(deficient in two dimensions) ቀጠነ qḁ́ṭṭḁnḁ.

(emaciated) ከሳ kḁ́ssā̃.

See § 63*d*, *e*.

This cloth is too thin for me: ይህ፡ጨርቅ፡ሣሣብኝ። y̥ihe čärq sássabbi̥ñ (§ 47*a*).

This rope (string) is too thin for me: ይህ፡ገመድ፡ ቀጠነብኝ። y̥ihe gḁmḁd qḁṭṭḁnḁbbi̥ñ.

He (it) is (has got) thin: ከስቷል። kḁstŏ͡al, f. ከስታለች። kḁstálläč, pl. ከስተዋል። kḁstḁ͡uāl.

thing, s. (matter) ነገር nḁgḁr (-gär).

(object) እቃ i̥qã.

See § 52*a*, δ.

think, v.i. & t. አሰበ ássḁbḁ (-ḁy̥ḁ).

መሰለው mḁssḁlḁ͡u (impers. § 43*a*).

S.v. believe, cp. § 80.

I am thinking: አስባለኍ። assi̥yállḁ͡u^{h} (§ 7*d*), pl. እናስባለን። i̥nnāssi̥yállän.

I think so: ይመስለኛል። yi̥mḁsläññāl.

I should think so: ይሆናል። yi̥h^{w}ṓnāl (s.v. √ሀወነ).

I don't think so: አይመስለኝም። a͡i̥mḁsläññi̥m.

I think it is mine: ይመስለኛል፡የኔ፡ነው። yi̥mḁsläññāl yän^{y}ḗ nḁ͡u.

Do you think it is yours? ይመስልሃል፡ያንተ፡ነው። yi̥mḁsli̥hāl yantá (§ 8) nḁ͡u?

'To think' may be rendered by አለ álḁ (s.v. √ባለ, § 44*a*), esp. when given as a reason for action:

(As) I thought he (it) was (too) near: ቀረበ፡ብዬ። qḁrrḁy̥ḁ y̥íyye (§ 65*b*).

I didn't think we should get here (there): እንደርስም፡ብዬ፡ነበር። anndársi̥m bíyye nḁbbär.

third, ord. num. ሶስተኛ s^{w}ōstḁññā (-täñ-; § 20*b*).

third ($^{1}/_{3}$), s. ሶስትያ፡[ሶስቲያ] s^{w}ōstíyyā (§ 20*b*, § 52*a*, δ).

$^{2}/_{3}$: ሁለት፡ሶስትያ፡ húlätt s^{w}ōstíyyā.

thirst, s. ጥም ṭi̥m.

ውሃ፡ጥም wŭhá (uhá; § 8) ṭi̥m.

thirsty, be, v.i. ጠማው ṭạmmau͡ (impers. § 43*a*; § 63*d*, *e*).

I am thirsty: ጠምቶኛል። ṭạmtʷoññāl, pl. ጠምቶ ናል። ṭạmtʷonnāl.

I am not thirsty: አልጠምቶኝም። alṭạmtʷoññịm, pl. -ቶንም። -tʷonnịm.

Are you thirsty? ጠምቶሃል። ṭạmtʷohāl?

thirteen, card. num. አሥራ፡ሶስት asrásʷŏst (§§ 8, 20*a*).

thirteenth, ord. num. አሥራ፡ሶስተኛ asrāsʷōstạññā̃ (-tā́ñ-; § 20*b*).

thirtieth, ord. num. ሠላሳኛ sạlāsáññā̃ (-sáññā̃; § 20*b*).

thirty, card. num. ሠላሳ sạlásā̃ (§ 20*a*).

this, dem. pron. ይሀ yịhe (yịh, yáhe), f. ይሀች yịhịč (-čč) or ይች yịč (ʸị-, -čč), pl. እነዚሀ (ị)nnạzzíh (-nā́z-, እለ- ịllạ-, -lā́z-, -zịh), እኔሀ (ị)nnʸēh (-ኒሀ -nníh, -nnịh) or እሌሀ ịllʸēh (-ሊሀ -llíh, -llịh); (§§ 8, 13*a*).

I don't want this: ይሀነን፡አልፈልግም። yịhánnän alfạllịgịm.

Like this: እንደዚሀ፡ (ị)ndạzzíh (-dā́z-, -zịh; §§ 8, 47*a*).

Before this: ከዚሀ፡በፊት፡ käzzíh ḅạfít (§§ 8, 47*b*).

Without this: ያለዚሀ፡ yālā́zzíh, G. አለዚሀ፡ ạlā́zzíh, (§§ 8, 47*a*).

Together with this: ተዚሀ፡ጋር፡ täzzíh gār (§ 47*b*).

This is it: ይሀው። yịhau͡.

Take this: ይሀነን፡ያዝ። yịhánnän yaz.

Who is this man? ይሀ፡ሰው፡ማን፡ነው። yịhe sạu͡ mánnạu͡?

Are there more like this? ሌላ፡የዚሀ፡ዓይነት፡አለ። léla yäzzíh ạ͡ịnät állä? (§ 52*a*).

thistle, s. ያሀያ፡እሾሀ yahíyya (§§ 7*a*, 47*a*, 70) šʷōh.

Š. ኰሸሌ kwώšālʸe.

See § 52*a*, δ; s.v. thorn.

thong, s. ጠፍር ṭḁfi̥r.

መጫኛ mḁčáñā.

thorax, s. ደረት dáḁrḁt.

thorn, s. እሾህ í̥šʷṓh (-ṓχ, -ṓk, § 7*d*; §§ 8, 52*a*, δ).

thoroughly, adv. በውል bḁ́wū́l (bḁ͡uū́l, bḁ͡ú̥l; § 8).

በጣም bḁ́ṭám (§ 8).

Let it boil thoroughly: በውል፡ይፍላ። bḁ͡uū́l yí̥flá.

those, dem. pron. እነዚያ (i̥)nnḁ́zzyā́ (-nā́z-).

እኒያ (í̥)nnyā́.

እለዚያ i̥llḁ́zzyā́ (-láz-).

እሊያ í̥llyā́.

See §§ 8, 13*a*.

thou, pers. pron. አንተ ántḁ (-tä, አንት ant, q.v.), f. አንቺ ánči (አንች anč), (§§ 12*a*, 60*b*), usually omitted unless emphatic; s.v. you.

though, conj. ከ- kḁ- (ተ- tḁ-) prefixed to simp. perf. (§ 48*a*).

ብ- bi̥- pref. to cont. (§ 48*a*) which may take the suff. -ም -m (-mm § 6; § 48*b*, § 37*e*).

Though I told him I did not want it he brought it: አልፈልግም፡ታልሁ፡አመጣው። alfḁ́lli̥gi̥m tálhŭ amḁ́ṭṭa͡u, or አልፈልግም፡ብለው፡አመጣው። alfḁ́lli̥gi̥m bí̥lḁ͡u amḁ́ṭṭa͡u. [ብለው = ብ- bi̥- (§ 48*a*) + እል i̥l (§§ 7*a*, 44*a*) + -ḁ- + -ው -u (§ 12*c*)].

Even though it rain I shall go: ቢዘንብም፡እሔዳለሁ። bi̥zā́nyi̥mm i̥hädállḁ͡uʰ (§ 7*d*).

thought, s. አሳብ ás(s)áb (-áv̱; § 8, § 52*a*, δ).

thousand, card. num. ሺህ ši̥h (§ 20*a*).

ሺ ši̥ („).

4000: አራት፡ሺህ፡ aráttĭ̥ ši̥h.

1000 dollars: ሺ፡ብር፡ ší̥vi̥rr (§ 8).

How many thousand? ስንት፡ሺህ፡ sí̥ntĭ̥ ši̥h?

There were about 1000: ሽህ፡ያህል፡ነበር። ši̥h yahl nḁ́bbär.

thousandth, ord. num. ሽህኛ ši̥hi̥ññã (§ 20*b*)

thread, s. ክር ki̥rr.

(warp or woof) ፈትል fḁ́ti̥l (fắt-).

threaten, v.i. & t. አስፈራራ asfḁrắrrã (-fär-).

three, card. num. ሶስት sʷōst (§ 20*a*).

thresh, v.t. ወቃ wώqqã.

threshed, be, v.p. ተወቃ tḁwώqqã (tḁ͡uώ-).

threshold, s. ምድራክ mi̥drák (§ 8).

throat, s. ጉሮሮ guróro.

To clear one's throat: አክ፡አለ፡ akk álḁ (s.v. √በለ, § 44*a*).

throne, s. አልጋ álgã.

ወምበር wώmbḁr (-bär).

through, go, v.i. አለፈ állḁfḁ.

It won't go through: አያልፍም። aʸálfi̥m, pl. -ፉም። -fum.

Has it gone through? አልፏል። álfŏāl?, pl. -ፈዋል። -fḁ͡uāl?

through, put (send, allow to go), v.t. አሳለፈ asállḁfḁ.

I want some drawers that I can put my legs through: እግሬን፡እንደሚያሳልፍ፡ሱሪ፡እፈልጋለሁ። i̥grʸen (§ 52*a*, γ) i̥ndämmyasálli̥f súrri i̥fḁlli̥gállḁ͡uʰ (lit. such that it will allow my leg to pass).

throw, v.t. ወረወረ wḁrḁ͡uwḁrḁ.

(away) ጣለ ṭálḁ.

I have thrown it away: ጥዬዋለሁ። ṭi̥yyewállḁ͡uʰ (§ 43*b*, § 7*d*).

Throw it away: ጣለው። ṭálḁ͡u, pl. ጣሉት። ṭálut.

Don't throw it away: አትጣለው። atti̥ṭálḁ͡u, pl. -ሉት። -lut.

thrown, be, v.p. ተወረወረ tạwạrạ͡uwạrạ (tạ͡uạ-).
(away) ተጣለ tạṭālạ.
It is to be thrown away: ይጣል። yị̣ṭṭāl, pl. ይጣሉ። yịṭṭālu.
It is not to be thrown away: አይጣል። a͡iṭṭāl, pl. አይጣሉ። a͡iṭṭālu.
thumb, s. አውራ፡ጣት a͡ūrā (§ 8) ṭāt (§ 52*a*, γ).
thunder, s. ነጐድጓድ nạgwṓdgwād (-ṓrg- § 7*d*).
G. ንጕድጓድ nịgwŭdgwād (nŭg-).
መብረቅ mạ́brạq (-ạ́yr-; q.v.).
thunder, v.i. መብረቅ፡መታ mạ́brạq (-ạ́yr-) mạ́ttā.
(in the distance) ግም፡አለ gịmm ālạ.
ግም፡ግም፡አለ gịm(mĭ)gịmm ālạ.
S.v. √ባለ, § 44*a*.
Thursday, s. & adv. ሐሙስ ā́mus.
thus, adv. እንዲህ (ị)ndíh (-dịh; § 8).
እንደዚህ (ị)ndạ́zzíh (-dā́z-, -zịh; § 8).
tibia, s. ማህል፡አገዳ máhal (māl) ágạdā (§ 52*a*, γ).
tick, s. (parasite) መዥገር mạ́zgạr (-gär; § 52*a*, δ).
tickle, v.i. & t. ኰረኰረ kwṓrạ́kkwṓrạ (-rṓk-).
ስቅቅ፡አለ sịqịqq ālạ (s.v. √ባለ, § 44*a*).
አሳከከ asā́kkạkạ.
(unpleasantly) ኰሰኰሰ kwṓsạ́kkwṓsạ (-sṓk-kosạ § 7*d*).
See § 63*d*, *e*. These verbs are all commonly used impersonally (§ 43*a*).
It tickles (me): ኰረኰረኝ። kwṓrṓkkwṓrāñ, ስቅቅ፡አለኝ። sịqịqq ā́lāñ, etc.
tidiness, s. ጠፍታ tạffịtā.
tidy, adj. ጠፍተኛ tạffịtạ́ññā (-tāñ-).

tidy, be, v.i. ጠፍ፡አለ ṭḁff álḁ (s.v. √በለ, § 44*a*).

It isn't tidy: ጠፍ፡አይልም። ṭḁff a͡i̥li̥m.

tidy, put (render), v.t. ጠፍ፡አደረገ ṭḁff adḁ́rrḁgḁ.

Put all the things (furniture, baggage) tidy: እቃውን፡ሁሉን፡ጠፍ፡አድርገው። i̥qa͡un húllun ṭḁff árgḁ͡u (§ 7*d*).

tie, s. (neck-tie) ማተብ mátab (-ḁy).

tie (up), v.t. አሰረ ássḁrḁ (-särḁ).

(in something) ቋጠረ qwáṭṭḁrḁ (-ṭärḁ).

Tie it properly: በውል፡እሰረው። bḁúl i̥sḁrḁ͡u, pl. -ሩት። -rut.

Tie the dog up: ውሻውን፡እሰረው። wúšša͡un i̥sḁrḁ͡u.

Tie a little up (in a bag): ጥቂት፡ቋጥር። ti̥qi̥t qwáṭi̥r.

tie into loads, v.t. ቀረቀበ qḁrḁ́qqḁbḁ (-ḁyḁ).

Let them tie (the baggage, goods) into loads: ይቀርቅቡ። yi̥qárqi̥yu.

tied (up), be, v.p. ታሰረ tássḁrḁ (-särḁ).

(in something) ተቋጠረ tḁqwáṭṭḁrḁ (-ṭärḁ).

He (it) is to be tied up: ይታሰር። yi̥ttásär, pl. -ሰሩ። -sḁru.

He (it) is not to be tied up: አይታሰር። a͡i̥ttásär, pl. -ሰሩ። -sḁru.

Has he (it) been tied up? ታስሯል። tásrŏ͡āl?, pl. -ረዋል። -rḁ͡uāl?

It is tied too tight: ጠብቋል። ṭḁyqŏ͡āl.

tied into loads, be, v.p. ተቀረቀበ tḁqḁrḁ́qqḁbḁ (-ḁyḁ).

Has the baggage been tied into loads? እቃ፡ተቀርቅቧል። i̥qa tḁqárqi̥yŏ͡āl?

tight, adj. (compressed) ጥብቅ ṭi̥bq (ṭi̥yq).

(stretched) ውጥር wúṭṭi̥r.

These clothes are too tight: ይህ፡ልብስ፡ውጥር፡ነው። yi̥he li̥ys (§ 52a, δ) wŭṭṭi̥r (§ 8) na͡u.

till, conj. እስከ- (i̥)skḁ- [እስተ- (i̥)stḁ-] prefixed to simp. perf.

እስክ- (i̥)sk(i̥)- [እስት- (i̥)st(i̥)-] prefixed to cont.

See §§ 45, 48a. ድረስ di̥rḁs may follow either tense.

The distinction of tense in the verb introduced by እስከ-, እስክ- is not observed as closely in Amharic as in English, i.e. the present may be used where logically the past is required.

I waited till he arrived: እስተደረሰ፡ቈየኹ። i̥stḁdár-rḁsḁ qwώyyä͡uʰ (§ 7d), or እስቲደርስ፡ቈየኹ። i̥stidárs qwώyyä͡uʰ.

I will wait till you come: እቈያለሁ፡እስትትመጣ። i̥qwωyyálla͡uʰ i̥sti̥tti̥mátḁ.

Till we meet (again): እስትንገናኝ፡ድረስ፡ sti̥nni̥ggḁ-náñ di̥rḁs.

They eat till they are ill: ይበላሉ፡እስኪያማቸው፡ ድረስ። yi̥vḁlállu skyammáčča͡u di̥rḁs.

till. prp. እስከ- (i̥)skḁ- (§ 47a).

እስተ- (i̥)stḁ- („).

እስከ- [እስተ-] ... ፡ ድረስ (i̥)skḁ- [(i̥)stḁ-] .. di̥rḁs (§ 47b).

Wait till Monday: እስከሰኞ፡ቈይ። i̥skḁsḁññó qw͡ώi̥.

Till to-morrow: እስተነገ፡ድረስ፡ i̥stḁnágḁ di̥rḁs.

Up till now: እስታሁን፡ i̥stáhun (§ 7a).

Till then: እስተዚያ፡ድረስ፡ i̥stäzzyá di̥rḁs.

timber, s. እንጨት (i̥)nčʸet [-ጫት -čät].

time, s. ጊዜ፡[ግዜ] gi̥zʸe, pl. also ጊዝያት gi̥zyát (§ 8).

ዘመን zámḁn.

ሰዓት sa͡ät.

See § 52a, δ.

There is still time: ገና፡ጊዜ፡አለ። gḁna gi̥zʸe állä.

How many times? ስንት፡ጊዜ። si̥nti̥ gi̥zʸe?

He struck him three times: ሶስት፡ጊዜ፡መታው። sʷṓsti̥ gi̥zʸe mḁttau͡.

This is not the time for it: አሁን፡ጊዜውም፡አይደል። ā́hun gi̥zʸe͡umm (§ 37*b*) a͡i̥däl (§ 7*d*).

I will see him (it) another time: በሌላ፡ጊዜ፡አየዋለሁ። bḁléla gi̥zʸe a͡i̥ḁ͡uállḁu͡ʰ (§ 7*d*).

In twenty days' time: ተሀያ፡ቀን፡በኋላ፡ tḁhḁā́ qḁn (-hā́qḁn) y̥ḁu͡hā́la (§ 47*b*; § 7*d*).

I haven't time: ጊዜ፡አጠረኝ። gi̥zʸe áṭṭḁräñ (§ 63*d*).

I shall not have time: ጊዜ፡ያጥረኛል። gi̥zʸe yā́ṭräññāl (§ 63*e*).

You will not have time: ጊዜ፡ያጥረሃል። gi̥zʸe yā́ṭrḁhāl.

Let them come one at a time: አንዳንዳቸው፡ይምጡ። andandā́ččḁu͡ (§ 18) yi̥mṭu.

It will not be done in time: አይደርስም። a͡i̥dā́rsi̥m.

Some time or other: መቸም፡ mḁ́čḁm (-čä-; -mm § 6).

In course of time: እያደር፡ iyyáddär (s.v. አደረ).

In course of time it will get wider: እያደረ፡ይሰፋል። īyyáddḁrḁ yi̥sḁ́fāl (s.v. አደረ).

A long time: አያሌ፡ጊዜ፡ ayyālʸe gi̥zʸe.

In Abyssinia the day is reckoned to begin at sunrise, approximately 6 a.m., and the night at sunset, approximately 6 p.m. and each is divided into 12 hours; so that 7 a.m. is called 1 o'clock (of the day), 7 p.m. 1 o'clock (of the night), etc.

What is the time? ስንት፡ሰዓት፡ነው። si̥nt sḁā͡t nḁu͡?

6 o'clock: ስድስት፡ሰዓት፡ si̥ddi̥st sḁā͡t.

At 6 o'clock: በስድስት፡ሰዓት፡ bḁsi̥ddi̥st sḁā͡t.

6.15: ስድስት፡ሰዓት፡ተሩብ፡ si̥ddi̥st sḁā͡t tḁrúy̥.

At 6.15: በስድስት፡ሰዓት፡ተሩብ፡ bḁsí̥ddịst sḁ͡ắt tḁrúỵ.

6.20: ስድስት፡ሰዓት፡ተሶስቲያ፡ sí̥ddịst sḁ͡ắt tḁs^{w}ōstíy-yã.

6.30: ስድስት፡ሰዓት፡ተኩል፡ sí̥ddịst sḁ͡ắt tḁ́kkul.

6.40: ተሰባት፡ሰዓት፡ሶስቲያ፡የጐደለ፡ tḁsḁỵắt sḁ͡ắt s^{w}ōs-tíyya yägwṓddḁlḁ.

At 6.40: በሰባት፡ሰዓት፡ሶስቲያ፡የጐደለ፡ bḁsḁỵắt (cp. § 70*b*) sḁ͡ắt s^{w}ōstíyya yägwṓddḁlḁ.

6.45: ተሰባት፡ሰዓት፡ሩብ፡የጐደለ፡ tḁsḁỵắt sḁ͡ắt ruỵ yä-gwṓddḁlḁ.

If the time is expressed in hours and minutes ተ- tḁ-, and (§ 20), is inserted before the number of minutes.

9.10: ዘጠኝ፡ሰዓት፡ታሥር፡ zắṭäñ sḁ͡ắt tássi̥r (§ 7*a*).

tin, s. (metal and receptacle) ታኒካ tãnikã.
(metal) ቈርቈሮ qwṓrqwṓrr^{w}o.
(receptacle) ሳጥን sắṭi̥n.

tinkle, v.i. ክዩ፡ክዩ፡አለ kyu kyu ắlḁ.
ክች፡ክች፡አለ ki̥č ki̥čč (§ 6) ắlḁ.
S.v. √ባለ, § 44*a*.

tip, s. (gratuity) ጉርሻ gúršã.

tire, v.t. አደከመ adắkkḁmḁ.

tire oneself, v.i. ለፋ lḁ́ffã.

tired, be (become), v.i. ደከመ dắkkḁmḁ.
ደከመው dắkkḁmḁ͡u (impers. § 43*a*).
See § 63*d*, *e*.

I am tired: ደክሞኛል። dắki̥m^{w}oññāl, pl. ደክሞናል። dắki̥m^{w}onnāl.

I am not tired: አልደከምሁም። aldắkkḁmhum, pl. አልደከምነም። aldắkkḁmnḁm; or አልደከመኝም። al-dắkkḁmḁññi̥m, pl. አልደከመንም። aldắkkḁmḁnni̥m.

You will get tired: ትደክማለህ። ti̥däkmállăh, pol. ይደክማሉ። yi̥däkmállu, pl. ትደክማላችሁ። ti̥däkmallắččyuh (§ 7*d*).

Are you tired? ደክሞሃል። dắki̥mʷohāl?, pol. -ሞዎ ታል። -mʷo͡ʷotāl?, pl. -ሟችኋል። -mŏắččyuhāl? (§ 7*d*).

Tell me when you are tired: ሲደክምህ፡ንገረኝ። si̥-dắkmi̥h, nígäräñ.

to, prp. (towards) ወደ- wωdḁ-.

(up to) እስከ- (i̥)skḁ-.

እስተ- (i̥)stḁ-.

እስከ- [እስተ-]...፡ድረስ (i̥)skḁ- [(i̥)stḁ-]... di̥rḁs.

(for) ለ- lḁ-, ሊ- li̥-.

See § 47.

Where has he gone to?—To the river: ወዴት፡ሔደ።—ወደወንዝ። wωdʸét hắdḁ?—wωdḁ͡uώnz.

The water reaches to his neck: ውሃ፡እስታንገቱ፡ደርሷል። wŭhá stángatu dárso͡ăl (§ 63*d*).

Whom is the letter to? ደብዳቤ፡ለማን፡ነው። dḁy-dábbʸe lḁmán nḁ͡u?

Omitted before the names of places:

He has gone to Addis Abeba: አዲስ፡አበባ፡ሒዷል። áddi̥s ayḁyá hídŏ͡ăl.

to, sign of infinitive (§ 30).

See √በለ.

to and fro, be sent, v.p. G. ተለላከ tḁlḁlákḁ.

Š. ተላላከ tḁlālákḁ.

He is sent to and fro: G. ይለላከል። yi̥llḁlákāl, Š. ይላላከል። yi̥llālákāl, pl. G. ይለላከሉ። yi̥llḁlākál-lu, Š. ይላላከሉ። yi̥llālăkállu.

to and fro, carry, v.i. & t. አመላለሰ ammḁlā́llḁsḁ.

Let him carry the plates to and fro: ሰሐን፡ያመላልስ። sḁhā́n (§ 52*a*, δ) yāmmḁlā́ls.

to and fro, come (go, pass), v.i. ተመላለሰ tḁmḁlā́llḁsḁ.

He goes to and fro: ይመላለሳል። yi̥mmḁlā́llḁsāl, pl. ይመላለሳሉ። yi̥mmḁlāllḁsállu.

to and fro, send, v.i. & t. G. አለላከ allḁlákḁ.

Š. አላላከ allālákḁ.

Send them to and fro: G. አለልካቸው። allälḭ̥káččḁ͡u,

Š. አላልካቸው። allālḭ̥káččḁ͡u.

toad, s. እንቁራሪት (i̥)ṅqwŭrárit, usually f. (§ 54*c*).

ጉርጥ gurṭ ” ”

toadstool, s. እንጉዳይ (i̥)ṅgúdá͡i̥ (§ 8).

ቁጫ qwŭ́ččã.

See § 52*a*, δ.

toast, s. (toasted bread) የተጠበሰ፡ዳቦ yätḁṭḁ́bbḁsḁ (§§ 14, 62) dábbʷo.

toast, v.t. ጠበሰ ṭḁ́bbḁsḁ.

Toast it: ጥበሰው። ṭí̥vḁsḁ͡u.

toasted, be, v.p. ተጠበሰ tḁṭḁ́bbḁsḁ.

It should be toasted more than this: ተዚህ፡ይበልጥ፡ይጠበስ። täzzí̥h yi̥vä́lṭ (§ 58*c*) yi̥ṭṭḁ́vḁs.

tobacco, s. ትምባኋ ti̥mbḁ́͡uhã (tŭm-, -bṓhã, § 7*d*).

It may be specified thus:

Cigar: የተጠቀለለ፡ትምባኋ፡ yätḁṭḁqḁ́llḁlḁ (§§ 14, 62) ti̥mbḁ́͡uha.

Cigarette: በወረቀት፡የተጠቀለለ፡ት-፡ bḁ͡uḁ́rḁqḁt yätḁṭḁqḁ́llḁlḁ ti̥-.

Cut tobacco: የተቈረጠ፡ት-፡ yätḁqwώrrḁṭḁ ti̥-.

Pipe tobacco: የመጠጫ፡ት-፡ yämḁṭḁ́č̣č̣a (§§ 47*a*, 70) ti̥-.

to-day, adv. ዛሬ zắrʸe.
What is to-day? ምን፡ቀን፡ነው፡ዛሬ። mi̥n qḁn nḁ͡u zắrʸe?
toe, s. ጣት ṭāt (§ 52*a*, γ).
Big toe: አውራ፡ጣት፡ a͡urắ (§ 8) ṭḁt.
together, adv. አብሮ ábrʷo (ắyr-; gerund § 34).
በንድ band (= በ- bḁ- § 47*a* + አንድ and § 20*a*; § 7*a*).
አንድላይ ánd(i̥)la͡i̥.
Keep (pl.) together: አብራችሁ፡ቈዩ። āyráččyuh (§ 7*d*) qwώyyu.
Are they all together or each by himself (itself)? ሁላቸው፡በንድ፡ናቸው፡ወይ፡በየብቻው። hulláččḁ͡u yándi̥ (§ 7*d*) náččḁ͡u wώ͡i̥ yḁyyäyíčča͡u? (§ 18).
token, s. ምልክት mi̥li̥kki̥t.
told, be, v.p. (be disclosed) ተገለጠ tḁgḁ́llḁṭḁ (-gắl-).
tomato, s. ያቡን፡ወጥ yábun (-ắyu-) wωṭ (§ 52*a*, δ).
to-morrow, adv. ነገ nḁ́gḁ (nắgḁ).
Early to-morrow: ነገ፡ጧት፡ nḁ́gḁ ṭwāt.
The day after to-morrow: ተነገ፡ወድያ፡ tḁnḁ́gḁ wώdyắ (-gḁʷώd-; § 8).
ሠልስት፡ sḁ́li̥st.
tongue, s. ምላስ mi̥lắs (§ 8).
Put out your tongue: ምላስህን፡አውጣው። mi̥láshi̥n (-s-h-, not -š-, § 3) á͡uṭa͡u, pol. መላሰዎን፡ያውጡት። mi̥lắṣḁʷon yá͡uṭut, f. ምላስሽን፡አውጭው። mi̥lắsi̥-ši̥n á͡učyu.
Put it right out: በጣም፡አውጣው። bḁṭắm á͡uṭa͡u.
to-night, adv. ዛሬ፡ሌሊት zắrʸe lʸēlít.
tonsilitis, s. (suppurative) ቁምሆ qi̥mhʷo (qúmho § 7*d*).
tonsure, s. (large) ጋሜ gắmmʸe.
(small) ሳዱላ sādúllā̃.

too, adv. እጅግ i̥jji̥g.
በብዙ bḁbi̥zu (bḁy̱i̥- § 7d).
(also) ደግሞ dḁgmʷo (dǟg-; § 46).
ደሞ dḁmmʷo (dǟm-; § 46).
-ም -m (-mm § 6; § 48b).
This is much too small: ይች፡በብዙ፡ትንሽ፡ናት። ʸi̥čči̥ (§ 54c) y̱ḁy̱i̥zu ti̥nni̥š (§ 8) nāt.
He is to come too: እርሱ፡ደሞ፡ይምጣ። i̥rsǘ (§ 60b) dǟmmʷo yi̥mṭa.
— often omitted:
This is too broad and that too narrow: ይህ፡ወርዱ፡ሰፊ፡ነው፡ያ፡ጠባብ፡ነው። yi̥he wώrdu sḁffí (§ 8) nḁu͡, yā ṭḁbbǟy̱ nḁu͡.
tool, s. ማድረጊያ mādrḁgyā̃ (-rǟg-).
መሣሪያ mḁssáryā̃ (-yä § 7d).
tooth, s. ጥርስ ṭi̥rs (§ 52a, γ).
Bring some water for me to clean my teeth: ጥርሴን፡እምፍቅበት፡ውሃ፡አምጣ። ṭi̥rsʸen i̥mmi̥fi̥qi̥b-bḁt (§ 47a) wǘha ánṭa (§ 7d).
A preparation for the teeth: የጥርስ፡መድኃኒት፡ yäṭi̥rs (§§ 47a, 70) mḁdhánʸit (-dáḥnit § 7d).
toothbrush, s. [የጥርስ፡] መፋቂያ (yäṭi̥rs §§ 47a, 70) mḁ-fǟqyā̃.
መሟጫ mḁmwǟč̣ā̃.
toothpick, s. [የጥርስ፡] መጐርጐሪያ (yäṭi̥rs) mḁgwḁrgwḁryā̃ (-gwωrgwώr-).
መሰቅሰቂያ mḁsḁqsḁqyā̃ (-qsǟq-; -sǟč̣ā̃ App. B § 7d).
መሟጫ mḁmwǟč̣ā̃.
This toothpick has no point: ይህ፡መጐርጐሪያ፡ሹልም፡አይዶል። yi̥he mḁgwωrgwώrya šúli̥mm a͡i̥däl (§ 7d).

tooth-powder, s.—explain thus: የጥርስ፡ እንደዱቄት፡ ያለ፡ መድኀኒት፡ yäṭí̥rs i̥ndädʷōqʸét yállä (§ 7a) mḁdáhnit (§ 7d).

top, s. (summit) ራስ rās.
ጫፍ č̣āf.
(of ascent) አፋፍ āfấf.
(cover) መክደኛ mḁkdḁ́ñā̃ (-dấñā̃).

top, on, adv. ላይ la͡i̥.
በላይ bḁ́la͡i̥ (§ 8).

top of, on, prp. በ- [ከ-, ተ-]...፡ ላይ bḁ- (kḁ-, tḁ-)... lá͡i̥ (§ 8, § 47b).
On top of the house: በቤት፡ላይ፡ bḁyʸét la͡i̥.
On top of each house: በየቤቱ፡ላይ፡ bḁyyäyʸétu (§ 18) la͡i̥.

torch, s. መብራት mḁ́brāt (-ḁ́yr-; § 8).
ማብሪያ mấbryā̃ (-ấyr-).
ፋና fánā̃.

torn, be (get), v.p. ተቀደደ tḁqḁ́ddḁdḁ.
ተበጠሰ tḁbḁ́ṭṭḁsḁ (tḁyḁ́-, -ấṭ-).
It will get torn: ይቀደዳል። yi̥qqḁ́ddḁdāl, pl. ይቀደዳሉ። yi̥qqḁddḁdállu.
ይበጠሳል። yi̥bbḁ́ṭṭḁsāl, pl. ይበጠሳሉ። yi̥bbḁṭṭḁsállu.
Mind it doesn't get torn: እንዳይቀደድ። nda͡i̥qqḁ́ddḁd, pl. -ደዱ። -ddḁdu.
እንዳይበጠስ። nda͡i̥bbḁ́ṭṭḁs, pl. -ጠሱ። -ṭṭḁsu.
It has got torn: ተቀዷል። tḁqḁ́ddŏ͡āl, pl. -ደዋል። -ddḁ͡uāl.
ተበጥሿል። tḁyḁ́ṭṭisŏ͡āl, pl. -ሰዋል። -sḁ͡uāl.

tornado, s. አውሎ a͡ulʷo.
torrent, s. ወንዝ wωnz.
ጕርፍ gwωrf.
tortoise (*Testudo sp.*), s. ኤሊ ʸéli.
total, s. ጅምላ ji̥mlā̆.
ድሙር di̥mmur (ድምር di̥mmi̥r).
touch, v.i. & t. ነካ nḁkkā̆.
Don't touch (him, it, them, § 61*b*): አትንካ። atti̥n̄ka, pl. -ኩ። -ku.
Don't touch it (them) with your fingers, take a cloth: በጣት፡አትንካ፤በጨርቅ። bḁṭát (§ 52*a*, γ) at-ti̥n̄ka, yḁč̣árq.
touched, be, v.p. ተነካ tḁnḁkkā̆.
It is not to be touched: አይነካ። a͡i̥nnḁka, pl. -ኩ። -ku.
towards, prp. ወደ- wωdḁ- (§ 47*a*).
Towards the house: ወደቤት፡ wωdḁvʸét.
Towards me: ወደኔ፡ wωdḁnʸé (§§ 8, 12*a*).
Towards the rains: ወደክረምት፡ wωdḁki̥rḁmt (§ 8).
Towards noon: ወደቀትር፡ wωdḁqḁti̥rr.
towel, s. ማድረቂያ mā̆drḁqyā̆ (-rā̆q-).
ማበሻ mā̆bbḁšā̆ (-bā̆š-).
መጥረጊያ mḁṭrḁgyā̆.
Face-towel: የፊት፡ማድረቂያ፡ yäfi̥t mādrā̆qya.
የፊት፡ማበሻ፡ yäfi̥t mabbḁša.
Bath-towel: የገላ፡ማድረቂያ፡ yägḁla mādrā̆qya.
See §§ 47*a*, 70.
town, s. ከተማ kḁtḁmā̆ (§ 8).
town-crier, s. አዋጅ፡ነጋሪ a͡uā̆j nḁgári.
toy, s. መጫወቻ mḁč̣a͡uáčḁā̆ (-a͡uώčā̆).

track, s. (trace) ፍለጋ fi̥llḁgã (§ 8).
Š. ፈለግ fḁlḁg.
ፋራ fárã.
See § 52*a*, δ.
(path) መንገድ mḁṅgḁd.
ጕዳና gwǿdanã.

track, v.t. ፈለገ fḁllḁgḁ.

tracked, be, v.p. ተፈለገ tḁfḁllḁgḁ.

trade, s. ንግድ ni̥gd.

trade, v.i. ነገደ nḁggḁdḁ.

Does he trade? ይነግዳል። yi̥nḁggi̥dāl?, pl. ይነግዳሉ። yi̥nḁggi̥dállu?

He doesn't trade: አይነግድም። a͡i̥nḁggi̥di̥m, pl. -ዱም። -dum.

What does he trade in? ምን፡ይነግዳል። mi̥n yi̥nḁggi̥dāl?, pl. ምን፡ይነግዳሉ። mi̥n yi̥nḁggi̥dállu?

I have come to trade: ለንግድ፡መጣኹ። lḁni̥gd mḁ́ṭṭa͡u^h (§ 7*d*), pl. ለንግድ፡መጣን። lḁni̥gd mḁ́ṭṭān.

I have not come to trade: ለንግድ፡አልመጣሁም። lḁni̥gd almḁ́ṭṭahum, pl. -ጣንም። -ṭṭāni̥m.

trader, s. ነጋዴ nḁggád^{y}e.
(European) ኳጃ kwájã.
See § 52*a*, δ.

Tragelaphus scriptus decula, s. ዱኵላ dukkwúlã.

train (railway-), s. መ[ን]ኰራኵር mḁ(ṅ)kwørākwür.
[የምድር፡]ባቡር (yämdi̥r §§ 47*a*, 70) bắbūr (y̥áy̥ūr; § 8).

training (condition), be (get) out of, v.i. ተጐዳ tḁgwǿddã.
ከሳ kḁssã.
See § 63*d*, *e*.

He (it) is out of training: ተጐድቷል። tḁgwǿdi̥tŏ͡āl (-ǿrt- § 7*d*), pl. -ተዋል። -tḁ͡uāl.

He (it) will get out of training: ይጐዳል። yi̥ggwǿd-dāl, pl. ይጐዳሉ። yi̥ggwωddállu.

traitor, s. ጠቋሚ ṭḁqqwā́mi (ṭωq-).

translate, v.i. & t. ተረጐመ tḁrḁ́ggwωmḁ (tär-).

Translate (it § 61*b*) for (to) me: ተርጕምልኝ። tā́r-gwŭmi̥lli̥ñ (§ 47*a*).

Translate (it) for (to) him: ተርጕምለት። tā́rgwŭmi̥l-lḁt.

Who will (can § 63*c*) translate it? ማን፡ይተረጕመዋል። mān yi̥tärḁ́ggwŭmḁ͡uāl?

translated, be, v.p. ተተረጐመ tḁtḁrḁ́ggwωmḁ (-tär-).

It has been translated: ተተርጕሟል። tḁtā́rgwŭmō͡al, pl. -ጕመዋል። -gwŭmḁ͡uāl.

It has not been translated: አልተተረጐመም። altḁ-tḁrḁ́ggwωmḁm, pl. -ሙም። -mum.

It must be translated: ይተርጐም። yi̥ttārgwωm, pl. -ሙ። -mu.

translation, s. ትርጉም ti̥rgum.

transport, s. ጓዝ gwāz.

trap, s. ማጥመጃ māṭmḁ́jā (-mā́jā).

ወጥመድ wḁ́ṭmḁd (wǿṭ-, -mäd).

He set a trap: ወጥመድ፡አጠመደ። wḁ́ṭmḁd aṭḁ́m-mḁdḁ.

trash, s. ምናምን mi̥nā́mi̥n.

travel, v.i. ካገር፡ዞረ kā́gḁr (ታ- tá- §§ 7*a*, 47*a*, -gär) zʷṓrḁ.

travel fast, v.i. ገሰገሰ gḁsḁ́ggḁsḁ.

Travel fast: ገስግስ። gḁ́sgi̥s, pl. -ግሱ። -gi̥su.

Don't travel fast: አትገስግስ። atti̥gḁ́sgi̥s, pl. -ሱ። -su.

He is to travel fast: ይገስግስ። yi̥gḁ́sgi̥s, pl. -ሱ። -su.

He is not to travel fast: አይገስግስ። ai̥gḁ́sgi̥s, pl. -ሱ። -su.

Have you travelled fast? ገስግሰሃል። gḁ́sgḭsḁhāl?, pl. ገስግሳችኋል። gḁsgḭsáččyuhāl? (§ 7*d*).

travel fast, cause to, v.t. አገሰገሰ ag(g)ḁsḁ́ggḁsḁ.

Please cause him to travel fast: pol. እስቲያገስግሱት። ḭstiyāgḁ́sgḭsut, ... cause them ... እስቲያገስግሷቸው። ḭstiyāgḁsgḭswā́ččḁ͡u.

traveller, s. መንገደኛ mḁṅgḁdḁ́ññā̃ (-dā́ñ-).

treasure, s. መዝገብ mḁ́zgḁb (-ḁy).

treat badly, v.t. በደለ bḁ́ddḁlḁ (bā́d-).

ገፋ gḁ́ffā̃.

Does he treat him (it) badly? ይበድለዋል። yḭyā́ddḭlḁ͡uāl?, pol. & pl. ይበድሉታል። yḭyā́ddḭlutāl?

Does he treat them badly? ይበድላቸዋል። yḭyäddḭláččḁ͡uāl?, pol. & pl. ይበድሏቸዋል። yḭyäddḭlwā́ččḁ͡uāl?

treated badly, be, v.p. ተበደለ tḁbḁ́ddḁlḁ (tḁy-, -ā́d-).

ተገፋ tḁgḁ́ffā̃.

Is he (it) treated badly? ይበደላል። yḭbbā́ddḁlāl?, pol. & pl. ይበደላሉ። yḭbbäddḁlállu?

ይገፋል። yḭggḁ́ffāl?, pol. & pl. ይገፋሉ። yḭggḁffállu?

treaty, s. ቍርጥ qwŭrṭ.

ውል wŭl.

tree, s. ዛፍ zāf (§ 52*a*, δ).

What is the name of this tree? ይህ፡ዛፍ፡ስሙ፡ማን፡ነው። yḭ́he zāf sḭ́mu mā́n-nḁ͡u?

trefoil, s. ማገጥ mā́gḁṭ.

ዋጅማ wā́jmā̃.

G. ጕርጠብ gwŏ́rṭḁb (-ḁy).

Š. ሲዲሳ sḭddísā̃.

tremble, v.i. ተንቀጠቀጠ ta̦ṅqa̦ṭá̦qqa̦ṭa̦.
He (it) is trembling: ይንቀጠቀጣል። yi̦ṅqa̦ṭá̦qqa̦ṭāl, pl. ይንቀጠቀጣሉ። yi̦ṅqa̦ṭa̦qqa̦ṭállu, (§ 7c, note).
trench, s. ጉድባ gúdbã (-dy̦ã).
G. ጉድብያ gúdbyã (-dy̦yã).
(shallow) ቦይ bʷói̦.
ፈሰስ fá̦sa̦s.
መስኖ má̦snʷo.
tribe, s. ዘር za̦r (zär).
What is this man's tribe? ይህ፡ሰው፡ዘሩ፡ምንድር፡ነው። yi̦he sa̦u za̦ru mi̦ndi̦r na̦u?
tribute, s. ግብር gi̦b(i̦)r (gi̦y̦-).
What is their annual tribute? ግብራቸው፡ባመት፡ስንት፡ነው። gi̦y̦ráčča̦u y̦áma̦t (§§ 7a, 47a) si̦nti̦ na̦u?
tribute, pay, v.i. ገበረ gá̦bba̦ra̦ (-bära̦).
Whom do they pay tribute to? ለማን፡ይገብራሉ። la̦mán yi̦ga̦bbi̦rállu?
trick, s. (artifice) ቅጥፈት qi̦ṭfa̦t (-fät).
ቅጥፍና qi̦ṭfi̦nnã.
እብለት i̦bla̦t (i̦y̦l-, -lät).
trick, v.t. ቀጠፈ qá̦ṭṭa̦fa̦.
አበለ ábba̦la̦ በ- ba̦- (y̦a̦-; § 47a).
አታለለ attállala̦.
አሞኘ amʷóññä.
He tricked them: አበለባቸው። abba̦la̦bbáčča̦u, pl. አበሉባቸው። abba̦lubbáčča̦u.
tried, be, v.p. (tested) ተሞከረ ta̦mʷókka̦ra̦ (-kära̦).
ተፈተነ ta̦fá̦tta̦na̦ (-fáttäna̦).
(judicially) በወምበር፡ፊት፡ተመረመረ ba̦uωmbá̦r (-bär; § 8) fit (fi̦t) ta̦ma̦rá̦mma̦ra̦ (-märá̦mmära̦).

Has he (it) been tried? ተሞክሯል። tḁmʷókki̥ro͡āl?, pl. -ረዋል። -rḁu͡āl?

He will be tried (judicially): በወምበር፡ፊት፡ይመረመራል። bḁ͡uωmbā́r fi̥t yi̥mmḁrḁ́mmḁrāl, pl. ...ይመረመራሉ። ... yi̥mmḁrḁmmḁrállu.

trifling, adj. (frivolous) ቧልተኛ bwāltḁ́ñña͂ (-tā́ñ-).

ዋዘኛ wāzḁ́ñña͂ (-zā́ñ-).

(small) ትንሽ tí̥nni̥š, intensive pls. ትንንሽ ti̥-ní̥nni̥š, -ንሾች -nni̥šʷōč (-čč § 6), ትትንሽ ti̥-tí̥nni̥š, -ንሾች -nni̥šʷōč (-čč § 6).

Trifolium sp., s. ማገጥ mā́gḁṭ.

ዋጅማ wā́jma͂.

G. ጐርጡብ gwώrṭḁb (-ḁv).

Š. ሱዲሳ si̥ddísa͂.

trigger, s. ምላጭ mí̥lā́č̣č̣ (§ 8), often f. (§ 54*c*).

Trinity, s. ሥላሴ si̥llā́sʸe.

Trionyx sp., s. ኤሊ ʸéli.

tripod, s. (on which to hang things)

መስቀያ mḁsqḁ́ya͂ (-ḁ́͡i̥a͂).

ማንጠልጠያ mā͂nṭḁlṭḁ́ya͂ (-ṭäl-, -ḁ́͡i̥a͂).

troop, s. ጦር ṭʷor.

troops, s. ወታደር wωttáddḁr (-där; § 52*a*, δ).

trot, s. ሶምሶማ sʷomsʷóma͂.

trot, v.i. ሶምሶማ፡ሔደ sʷomsʷóma hā́dä (hḁ́-, hʸḗ-, -dḁ).

Can he trot? ሶምሶማ፡ይሔዳል። sʷomsʷóma yi̥hā́-dāl?, f. ... ትሔዳለች። ... ti̥hädállä č?, (§ 63*c*).

trouble, s. መከራ mḁ́kḁ́ra͂ (-kā́ra͂; § 8).

ችጋር čí̥ggā́r (§ 8).

It's no trouble (to me): ምን፡ቸገረኝ። mi̥n čággäräñ?

ምን፡ከፋኝ። mi̥n kḁ́ffāñ?

trouble, v.t. (mentally) አስቸገረ asčággḁrḁ (-gärḁ).
(physically) ቈረቈረ qwωrḁ́qqwωrḁ.

He (it) troubles me: ያስቸግረኛል። yāsčággi̥räññāl, pl. ያስቸግሩኛል። yāsčággi̥ruññāl.

You are troubling me: ታስቸግረኛለህ። tāsčäggi̥räññálläh, pl. ታስቸግሩኛላችሁ። tāsčäggi̥ruññalláččyuh (§ 7*d*).

Don't trouble him: አታስቸግረው። attāsčággi̥rḁ͡u, pl. -ሩት። -rut.

Don't trouble me: አታስቸግረኝ። attāsčággi̥räñ, pl. -ሩኝ። -ruñ.

troubled, be, v.p. (mentally) ቸገረው čággḁrḁ͡u (-gär-; impers. § 43*a*).
(physically) ተቈረቈረ tḁqwωrḁ́qqwωrḁ. See § 63*d*, *e*.

He is troubled: ቸግሮታል። čággi̥r^{w}otāl, pl. ቸግሯቸዋል። čäggi̥rŏ͡áččḁ͡uāl.

I am troubled: ቸግሮኛል። čággi̥r^{w}oññāl, pl. -ሮናል። -r^{w}onnāl.

trousers, s. (Eur.) በንጠሎን bḁnṭḁl^{w}ón.
(native) ሱሪ súrri.

true, adj. እውነት únḁt (únät). ሐቅ hãqq. } See § 57*b*.

It is true: እውነት ፡ ነው። unḁt (§ 8) nḁ͡u.

It is not true: እውነትም ፡ አይዶል። únäti̥mm (§ 37*b*) ḁ́͡idäl (§ 7*d*).

This is a true story: ይህ ፡ ሐቅ ፡ ነገር ፡ ነው። yi̥he háqqi̥ (§ 7*d*) nḁgár (§ 8) nḁ͡u.

true!, interj. እውነት únḁt! (únät).

trumpet, s. መለከት mḁlḁkḁt (§ 8).

trumpeter, s. መለከተኛ mḁlḁkḁtḁññã (-táñ-).

trunk, s. (travelling) ሳጥን sáṭi̥n.
(elephant's) ኩምቢ kúmbi.
(of tree) ግንድ gi̥nd.

trust, s. (belief) እምነት i̥mnḁt (-nät).
(deposit) አደራ ádа̥rã (ádárã; § 8).

trust, v.t. አመነ ámmḁnḁ.
ታመነ tã́mmḁnḁ (ger. & part. type B § 35).

I trust you: አምንሃለሁ። āmni̥hállḁ͡uʰ (አምንሃ- ām-nḁhá- App. B § 12*c*), pl. እናምንሃለን። i̥nnāmni̥hál-län (-ምንሃ- -mnḁhá-).

I don't trust you: አላምንህም። alā́mni̥hi̥m (-mi̥nh-), pl. አናምንህም። annā́mni̥hi̥m (-mi̥nh-).

I trust him: አምነዋለሁ። āmnḁ͡uállḁ͡uʰ, pl. እናምነዋ ለን። i̥nnāmnḁ͡uállän.

I don't trust him: አላምነውም፡ alā́mnḁ͡ūm, pl. አና ምነውም። annā́mnḁ͡ūm.

Do you trust him? ታምነዋለህ። tāmnḁ͡uálläh?, pol. ያምኑታል። yā́mnutāl?

Don't you trust him? አታምነውም። attā́mnḁ͡ūm?, pol. አያምኑትም። a͡i̥ā́mnuti̥m? (aʸ͡ā́-).

Don't trust him: አትመነው። atti̥mḁnḁ͡u, pol. አይ መኑት። á͡i̥mḁnut.

trusted, be, v.p. ታመነ tã́mmḁnḁ (ger. & part. type A § 34).

He (it) cannot be trusted: አይታመንም። a͡i̥ttām-mḁni̥m, pol. & pl. -ኑም። -num, (§ 63*c*).

trustworthy, adj. እሙን i̥mun.
ታማኝ tã́máñ (-ññ § 6; § 8).

truth, s. እውነት únḁt (únät).
ሐቅ hãqq.

This is not the truth: ይህ፡እውነትም፡አይደል። yi̥he únäti̥mm (§ 37*b*) a͡i̥däl (§ 7*d*).

Tell me the truth: ሐቅ፡ንገረኝ። háqqi̥ (§ 7*d*) ni̥gḁräñ.

truthful, adj. ነባይ nạbā͡i̥ (ná-, -yā́-; -áyy § 6; § 8).

እውነተኛ unạtạ́ññã (unätáñ-).

ቁም qum.

ቁም፡ነገረኛ qum nạgạrạ́ññã (-gär-, -áñ-).

ቅን qi̥n.

try, v.i. & t. ሞከረ mʷókkạrạ (-kärạ).

ፈተነ fạttạnạ (fáttänạ).

Try: ሞክር። mʷókki̥r, pol. ይሞክሩ። yi̥mʷókki̥ru, pl. ሞክሩ። mʷókki̥ru.

Don't try: አትሞክር። atti̥mʷókki̥r, pol. አይሞክሩ። a͡i̥mʷókki̥ru, pl. አትሞክሩ። atti̥mʷókki̥ru.

Try it: ሞክረው። mʷókki̥ra͡u̥, pol. ይሞክሩት። yi̥mʷókki̥rut, pl. ሞክሩት። mʷókki̥rut.

You can if you try: ብትሞክረው፡ትችላለህ። bi̥tti̥mʷókki̥ra͡u̥ ti̥či̥lálläh, pol. ቢሞክሩት፡ይችላሉ። bimʷókki̥rut yi̥či̥lállu, pl. ብትሞክሩት፡ትችላላችሁ። bi̥tti̥mʷókki̥rut ti̥či̥lalláččyuh (§ 7*d*).

I will try him (it): እፈትነዋለሁ። i̥fätti̥na͡u̥állạ͡uʰ (§ 7*d*), pl. እንፈትነዋለን። i̥nni̥fätti̥na͡u̥állän.

I will try this horse: ይህን፡ፈረስ፡እሞክረዋለሁ። yi̥hán fạrạs i̥mʷokki̥ra͡u̥állạ͡uʰ.

try a case, v.i. ፈረደ fạrrạdạ.

Who is trying the case? ማን፡ይፈርዳል። mān yi̥fár-dāl?

Tuesday, s. & adv. ማክሰኞ mãksạñño (-sáñ-).

tuft, s. (of hair) ቁንጮ qúnčʷo.

(of grass) ጉችታ gúčči̥tã.

tumble, v.i. ወደቀ wǿddạqạ.

Mind you don't tumble: እንዳትወድቅ። ndatti̥wǿdi̥q, pl. -ቁ። -qu.

tumble off (down), v.i. ዱብ፡አለ dubb álḁ.

(of more than one person or object) ዱብ፡ዱብ፡አለ dubbĭ̥dúbb álḁ.

S.v. √በለ, § 44*a*.

They kept tumbling off (down) and getting broken: ዱብ፡ዱብ፡እያሉ፡ተሰበሩ። dubbĭ̥dúbb īyyálu tḁsḁ́bbḁru, or (§ 52*a*, δ) ... እያለ፡ተሰበረ። ... īyyálḁ tḁsḁ́bbḁrḁ.

tumbler, s. (glass) ብርጭቆ bi̥rč̣í̥qʷo.

tumour, s. እባጥ í̥bḁṭ (í̥y-, -äṭ).

እብጠት í̥bṭḁt (í̥yṭ-, -ṭät).

እባጭ í̥bbáč̣ (§ 8).

turban, s. መጠምጠሚያ mḁṭḁmṭḁ́myā̃.

turbid, adj. ድፍርስ dí̥fri̥s.

turf, s. ሰርዶ sḁ́rdʷo (sā́r-).

turkey, s. ከርከሩሚ kḁrkḁrū́mi (kā́rkär-).

turn, s. (alternate) ፈረቃ fḁrḁ́qā̃ (§ 8).

(in order) ፈንታ fḁntā̃.

ተራ tḁrā̃.

See § 52*a*, δ.

In (alternate) turn: በየፈረቃው። bḁyyäfḁrḁqá͡u (§ 18).

Let them each come in turn: በየተራ፡ይምጡ። bḁyyä́tḁra (§§ 47*a*, 18) yí̥mṭu.

turn (round), v.i. ዞረ zʷṓrḁ.

Turn round: ዙር። zur, f. ዙሪ። zúri, pl. ዙሩ። zúru.

turn (round), v.t. አዞረ azʷṓrḁ.

(a wheel) ዘወረ zḁ́͡uwḁrḁ.

Turn it round: አዙረው። ázurḁ͡u, pl. -ሩት። -rut.

turn, be done in, v.p. (occur, v.i.) **ተፈራረቀ** tḁfḁrắrrḁqḁ.

They are done in turn: **ይፈራረቃሉ።** yi̥ffḁrārrḁqállu.

It is to be done in turn, first like this, then like that: **ፊት፡እንዲህ፡ኋላ፡እንዲህ፡ሁኖ፡ይፈራረቅ።** fit i̥ndíh hwā́la ndíh húnʷo yi̥ffḁrárḁq (§ 52*a*, δ).

turn, do in, v.t. **አፈራረቀ** affḁrắrrḁqḁ.

Do them in turn, this to-day, that to-morrow: **ዛሬ፡ ይህነን፡ነገ፡ይህነን፡ሰርተህ፡አፈራርቅ።** zắrʸe yi̥hắnnän nḁ́gḁ yi̥hắnnän sắrtäh affḁrắri̥q.

turn inside out, v.t. **ገለበጠ** gḁlḁ́bbḁṭḁ.

Turn it inside out: **ገልብጠው።** gắlṿi̥ṭa͡u, pl. -**ጡት።** -ṭut.

Turn them inside out: **ገልብጣቸው።** gälṿi̥ṭắččḁ͡u, pl. -**ጧቸው።** -ṭwắččḁ͡u.

turn out, v.t. (eject) **አወጣ** awώṭṭã (a͡uώ-).

(rouse) **ቀሰቀሰ** qḁsḁ́qqḁsḁ.

Turn him (it) out: **አውጣው።** á͡uṭa͡u, pl. **አውጡት።** á͡uṭut.

Turn them out: **አውጣቸው።** a͡uṭắččḁ͡u, pl. -**ጧቸው።** -ṭwắččḁ͡u.

Turn the men out to work: **ሰዎችን፡እንዲሰሩ፡ቀስቀሳቸው።** sḁ͡uʷṓčči̥n i̥ndi̥sḁ́ru qḁsqi̥sắččḁ͡u.

turn out (to be), v.i. **ሆነ** hʷṓnḁ.

He has turned out (to be) a thief: **ሌባ፡ሁኗል።** lʸéṿa húnṓāl, pl. **ሌቦች፡ሁነዋል።** lʸéṿʷōč húnḁ͡uāl.

turned inside out, be, v.p. **ተገለበጠ** tḁgḁlḁ́bbḁṭḁ.

It has been turned inside out: **ተገልብጧል።** tḁgắlṿi̥ṭṓāl, pl. -**ብጠዋል።** -ṿi̥ṭḁ͡uāl.

It is to be turned inside out: **ይገለበጥ።** yi̥ggắlṿḁṭ, pl. -**በጡ።** -ṿḁṭu.

turned out, be, v.p. (roused) ተቀሰቀሰ tḁqḁsḁ́qqḁsḁ.

They are to be turned out before cock-crow: ዶሮ፡ ሳይጮኽ፡ ይቀስቀሱ። dʷórʷo sa͡i̥č̣ʷóh yi̥qqḁ́sqḁsu.

turtle (*Trionyx sp.*), s. ኤሊ ʸéli.

tweezers, s. መቈንጠጫ mḁqwωnṭḁ́č̣ã (-ṭáč̣ã).

twelfth, ord. num. አሥራ፡ ሁለተኛ asrãhulḁttḁ́ññḁ (-lättáñ-; § 20*b*).

twelfth (1/12), s. አሥራ፡ ሁለትያ፡[-ለቲያ] asrãhulḁttíyyã (-lät-; § 20*b*, § 52*a*, δ).

twelve, card. num. አሥራ፡ ሁለት asrãhúlḁtt (-lätt; § 20*a*).

twentieth, ord. num. ሀያኛ hḁʸáññã (-የኛ -ʸáññã; § 20*b*).

twenty, card. num. ሀያ hḁ́ʸã (hḁ́a͡ã; § 20*a*).

twenty-first, ord. num. ሀያ፡ ሐንደኛ hḁʸahandḁ́ññã (-dáñ-).
ሀያ፡ አንደኛ hḁʸa͡aandḁ́ññã (-ʸānd-, -dáñ-).
See § 20*b*.

twenty-one, card. num. ሀያ፡ ሐንድ hḁʸahánd.
ሀያ፡ አንድ hḁʸa͡aánd (-ʸánd).
See § 20*a*.

twenty-two, card. num. ሀያ፡ ሁለት hḁʸahúlḁtt (-lätt; § 20*a*).

twice, adv. ሁለት፡ ጊዜ húlḁtti̥ (-lätti̥) gí̥zʸe (-tti̥zgʸe)

twin, s. መንታ mḁ́ntã (§ 52*a*, δ).

She (has) had twins: መንታ፡ ወለደች። mḁ́nta wωllḁdäč.

They are twins: መንቶች፡ ናቸው። mḁ́ntʷōč náččḁu͡.

twine, s. ፈትል fḁ́ti̥l.

twine, v.i. (be twined, v.p.) ተጠመጠመ tḁṭḁmḁ́ṭṭḁmḁ, round, በ- bḁ- (ẏḁ-; § 47*a*).

It twines round it: ይጠመጠምበታል። yi̥ṭṭḁmḁṭṭḁmí̥bbḁtāl, pl. ይጠመጠሙበታል። yi̥ṭṭḁmḁṭṭḁmúbbḁtāl.

twine, v.t. ጠመጠመ ṭḁmḁ́ṭṭḁmḁ, round, በ- bḁ- (ẏḁ-; § 47*a*).

Twine it round it (them § 52*a*, δ): ጠምጥምበት ። ṭạ́mṭịmịbbạt, pl. ጠምጥሙበት ። ṭạ́mṭịmubbạt.

twist, v.t. ጠመዘዘ ṭạmạ́zzạzạ.

Twist it: ጠምዝዘው ። ṭạ́mzịzạ͡u, pl. -ዝዙት ። -zịzut.

Don't twist it: አትጠምዝዘው ። attịṭạ́mzịzạ͡u, pl. -ዝዙት ። -zịzut.

twisted, be, v.i. & p. ተጠመዘዘ tạṭạmạ́zzạzạ.

It is (has got) twisted: ተጠምዝዟል ። tạṭạ́mzịzo͡āl, pl. -ዝዘዋል ። -zịzạ͡uāl.

It must be twisted: ይጠምዘዝ ። yịṭṭạ́mzạz, pl. -ዘዙ ። -zạzu.

It must not be twisted: አይጠምዘዝ ። a͡iṭṭạ́mzạz, pl. -ዘዙ ። -zạzu.

He (it) has got a twisted gut: አንጀቱ ፡ ታጥፏል ። ánjätu tạ́ṭfo͡āl.

twitter, v.i. ጫ ፡ ጫ ፡ አለ çạ̈-çạ̈́ ạ́lạ (s.v. √በለ, § 44*a*).

two, card. num. ሁለት húlạtt (-lätt; § 20*a*).

U

§ *refers to the paragraphs of the Grammar* (*Initia Amharica, Part I*).

udder, s. ጡት ṭut (§ 52*a*, γ).

ugly, adj. ጅል jịl.

(of persons) ገጠ ፡ ቢስ gạ́ṭṭạ bịs (vịs).

Ugly person: ሺል ፡ šil (šịl).

ugly, be, v.i. ጀለ jạ́lạ (§ 63*d*, *e*).

We think she is ugly because we are not accustomed to her: እኛ ፡ ታልለመድናት ፡ ጅላለች ፡ እንላለን ። ịññá tāllạ́mmạdnāt (= ተ- tạ- § 48*a* + አል- al- §§ 37*c*, 7*a* + ለመድን lạ́mmạdnạ + -ãት -āt § 12*c*) jịlállăčč (§ 6) innịlállän (s.v. √በለ, § 44*a*).

umbrella, s. ጥላ ṭịlã.

unadulterated, adj. ጥሩ ṭi̥ru (ṭŭ́ru).

unarmed, adj. ያለመሣሪያ yālḁmḁssā́ryā̃ (-yä; §§ 47*a*, 52*a*, δ).

Are they unarmed? ያለመሣሪያ፡ናቸው። yālḁmḁssár-ya nā́ččau̥͡?, or መሣሪያ፡የላቸውም። mḁssárya yäl-lā́ččau͡m?

unbending, adj. (rigid) ጠንካራ ṭḁṅkárrā̃.

uncertain, adj. (insincere) ለዛዛ lḁzázā̃.

uncivil, adj. ባለጌ bā́lḁgʸe (-läg-).

uncle, s. አጐት ággwωt.

uncomfortable, be, v.i. ተቈረቈረ tḁqwωrḁ́qqwωrḁ.

ስቅቅ፡አለው si̥qi̥qq ā́lḁu͡ (impers. § 43*a*; s.v. √ባለ, § 44*a*).

See § 63*d*, *e*.

Are you uncomfortable? ተቈርቍረሃል። tḁqwώrqwŭ-rähāl?, pol. ተቈርቍረዋል። tḁqwώrqwŭrḁ͡ūāl?, pl. ተቈርቍራችኋል። tḁqwωrqwŭrā́ččyuhāl? (§ 7*d*).

I am uncomfortable: ተቈርቍርያለሁ። tḁqwωrqwŭr-ryállḁ͡uʰ (§ 7*d*), or ስቅቅ፡አለኝ። si̥qi̥qq ā́läñ.

uncomfortable, render (make), v.t. ቈረቈረ qwωrḁ́qqwωrḁ.

It makes me uncomfortable: ይቈረቍረኛል። yi̥qwω-rḁ́qqwŭräññāl.

uncouth, adj. ባለጌ bā́lḁgʸe (-läg-).

uncover, v.t. ገለጠ gḁ́llḁṭḁ (gā́l-).

Uncover it: ግለጠው። gi̥lḁṭḁ͡u, pl. -ጡት። -ṭut.

Don't uncover it: አትግለጠው። atti̥glḁṭḁ͡u, pl. -ጡት። -ṭut.

Uncover them: ግለጣቸው። gi̥lḁṭáččau̥͡, pl. -ጧቸው። -ṭwā́ččau̥͡.

Don't uncover them: አትግለጣቸው። atti̥glḁṭáččau̥͡, pl. -ጧቸው። -ṭwā́ččau̥͡.

uncovered, be, v.p. ተገለጠ tag̥állat̥ḁ (-gál-).

If it is uncovered: ቢገለጥ፡ biggállat̥, pl. -ጡ፡ -t̥u (§ 48*a*).

It is not to be uncovered: አይገለጥ። a͡iggálat̥, pl. -ጡ። -t̥u.

undecided, adj. (in attitude or intention) አጉል águl.

(indefinite) አጓጒል agwágwŭl.

under (-neath), prp. በ-...፡ ታች bḁ-... tāč (-čč § 6).

ከ-[ተ-]...፡ ሥር kḁ- (tḁ-)... si̥r.

See §§ 8, 47*b*.

Under the table: በገበታው፡ታች፡ bḁgḁvḁtáu tāč.

Under the big tree: ከትልቁ፡ዛፍ፡ሥር፡ kḁti̥lli̥qu zāf si̥r.

What is it under? ተምን፡ሥር፡ነው። tḁmi̥n si̥r na͡u?

underdrawers, s. ሱሪ súrri.

underneath, adv. በታች bátáč (-čč § 6; § 8).

understand, v.i. & t. ሰማ sámmã (§ 42*a*).

አወቀ a͡uwḁqḁ (-wωqḁ).

See § 63*d*, *e*.

I understand: ሰምቻለሁ። sḁmi̥ččálla͡uʰ (§ 7*d*), pl. ሰምተናል። sámtḁnāl.

(generally) እሰማለሁ። i̥sḁmálla͡uʰ (§ 7*d*), pl. እንሰማለን። i̥nnisḁmállän.

I understand it: አወቅሁት። a͡uwωqhut.

I don't understand: አልሰማሁም። alsámmahum, pl. -ማንም። -mmāni̥m.

(gen.) አልሰማም። alsámām, pl. አንሰማም። annsámām.

Do you understand? ሰማህ። sạ́mmāh?, pol. ሰሙ። sạ́mmu?, pl. ሰማችሁ። sạmmáččyuh? (§ 7*d*).
(gen.) ትሰማለህ። tịsạmállāh?, pol. ይሰማሉ። yịsạmállu?, pl. ትሰማላችሁ። tịsạmalláččyuh? (§ 7*d*).

Don't you understand? አልሰማህም። alsạ́mmahịm?, pol. አልሰሙም። alsạ́mmum?, pl. አልሰማችሁም። alsạmmáččịhum?
(gen.) አትሰማም። attsạ́mām? pol. አይሰሙም። a͡isạ́mum?, pl. አትሰሙም። attsạ́mum?

Have you understood? ሰምተሃል። sạ́mtạhāl?, pol. ሰምተዋል። sạ́mtạ͡uāl?, pl. ሰምታችኋል። sạmtáččyuhāl? (§ 7*d*): or
አውቅህ። á͡uwωqh? (-ωqq § 7*d*), pol. አውቁ። á͡uwωqu?, pl. አውቃችሁ። a͡uwωqáččyuh? (§ 7*d*).

Do you understand what he says? ያለውን፡ሰማህ። yálạ͡un sạ́mmāh?, Do you (pol.)...? ... ሰሙ። ... sạ́mmu?

Do you understand what they say? ያሉትን፡ሰማህ። yálutịn sạ́mmāh?

Do you understand Galla? ጋልኛ፡ትሰማለህ። gallị́ñña tịsạmállāh?

Does he understand Arabic? አረብኛ፡ይሰማል። arạyị́ñña yịsạ́māl?

undervest, s. ሹራብ šúrrāb (-áy; § 8).

undo, v.t. (unfasten) ፈታ fḁttā.

Undo it: ፍታው። fi̥ta͡u, pl. ፍቱት። fi̥tut.

Don't undo it: አትፍታው። atti̥ftau͡, pl. -ፍቱት። -ftut.

Undo them: ፍታቸው። fi̥táččḁ͡u, pl. ፍቷቸው። fi̥-twáččḁ͡u.

Don't undo them: አትፍታቸው። atti̥ftáččḁ͡u, pl. -ፍቷ ቸው። -ftwáččḁ͡u.

I can't undo it: እምቢ፡አለኝ። ḿbi̥ ā́läñ.

Can't you undo it? እምቢ፡አለህ። ḿbi̥ ā́läh?, pl. ... አላችሁ። ... ālā́ččyuh? (§ 7*d*).

undone, be, v.p. (come, v.i.) ተፈታ tḁfḁ́ttā.

It comes (will come) undone: ይፈታል። yi̥ffḁ́ttāl, pl. ይፈታሉ። yi̥ffḁttállu.

It does (will) not come undone: አይፈታም። a͡i̥ffḁ́t-tām, pl. -ቱም። -ttum.

It is to be undone: ይፈታ። yi̥ffḁ́ta, pl. -ቱ። -tu.

It is not to be undone: አይፈታ። a͡i̥ffḁ́ta, pl. -ቱ። -tu.

It has come undone: ተፈትቷል። tḁfḁ́ttŏ͡āl, pl. ተፈት ተዋል። tḁfḁ́ttḁ͡uāl.

undress, v.i. ልብሱን፡አወለቀ li̥bsun (li̥vs-) awḁ́llḁqḁ (a͡uḁ́-, -ώl-).

I am going to undress: ልብሴን፡ላወልቅ፡ነኝ። li̥v-s^y^en lā͡uωlqi̥ (§§ 7*d*, 48*a*) näñ.

I am undressed: ራቁቴን፡ነኝ። rāqut^y^én (§§ 8, 56*d*) näñ.

uneasy, be (feel), v.i. ስቅቅ፡አለው si̥qi̥qq ā́lḁ͡u (impers. § 43*a*; § 63*d*, *e*).

unemployed, adj. ፈት fḁtt.

ስራ፡ፈት si̥ra fḁtt.

uneven, adj. ጐርባጣ gwωrbā́ṭṭā (-ryā́-).

On uneven ground: በጐርባጣ፡ምድር፡ bḁgwωryaṭṭá (§ 8) mdi̥r.

unexpectedly, adv. ድንገት dí̥ṅgḁt.

በድንገት bḁdí̥ṅgḁt.

unexpectedly, enter, v.i. ዘው ፡ አለ zḁ͡uw (§ 6) ā́lḁ (s.v. √በለ, § 44*a*).

Don't come in unexpectedly: ዘው ፡ ብለህ ፡ አትግባ ። zḁ͡uwi̥ yí̥läh attí̥gya.

unfasten, v.t. ፈታ fḁttã (s.v. undo).

unfastened, be, v.p. (come, v.i.) ተፈታ tḁfḁ́ttã (s.v. undone, be).

ungrateful, be, v.i. ውለታ ፡ አጠፋ wŭlḁtá (-lät-) aṭḁ́ffã, to, የ- yä- (§ 47*a*), or pers. suff. (§ 12*b*).

He was not ungrateful to me: ውለታዬን ፡ አላጠፋም ። wŭlätá͡ʸen alaṭḁ́ffām (§ 37*a*).

uniform, adj. ትክክል ti̥kí̥kki̥l.

uniform, s. የሰልፍ ፡ ልብስ yäsḁ́lf (-sálf; § 70) li̥bs (li̥vs).

መሰለፊያ mḁssḁllḁ́fyã (-sälláf-).

uniform, be, v.i. ተካከለ tḁkā́kkḁlḁ.

They are uniform: ይተካከላሉ ። yi̥ttḁkākkḁlállu.

uniform, render, v.t. አስተካከለ astḁkā́kkḁlḁ.

unimpaired, adj. ጥሩ ṭi̥ru (ṭŭru).

ደኅና dáhnā (§ 8).

unlawful, be declared, v.p. ተገዘተ tḁgḁ́zzḁtḁ.

Has it been declared unlawful? ተገዝቷል ። tḁgḁ́zzi̥t͡ōāl?

unlawful, declare, v.t. ገዘተ gḁ́zzḁtḁ.

unless, conj. (= if not), use neg. verb (§ 37*c*) in conditional constr. (§ 81); s.v. if.

He is not to come unless he wishes: ባይወድ ፡ አይምጣ ። ba͡iwɔ́dd, a͡i̥mṭa.

Don't take it unless you want it: ባትፈልገው ፡ አትውሰደው ። bātti̥fḁ́lli̥gḁ͡u attŭ́sḁdḁ͡u.

He won't come unless you fetch him: ባታመጣው፡ አይመጣም። bāttāmạ́ṭạ͡au a͡imạ́ṭām.

I should not pay him unless he brought it: አላምጥቶት፡ ቢሆን፡ አልከፍለውም፡ ነበር። alā́mtịtʷot yí-hʷon, alkạ́flạ͡um nạ́bbạr.

Unless he had come, I should have sold it: ያልመጣ፡ እንደሆን፡ እሸጠው፡ ነበር። yalmạṭṭándạhʷon, ịšạ́ṭạ͡u nạ́bbạr.

unload, v.t. አወረደ awώrrạdạ (a͡uώ-).

Unload the baggage: እቃውን፡ አውርደው። ịqa͡un ā́wŭrdạ͡u, pl. -ዱት። -dut.

Unload the mule: ተበቅሎ፡ አውርድለት። tạyạ́qlʷo ā́wụ̈rdịllạt, pl. -ዱለት። -dullạt, (§ 47*a*).

unlucky, adj. (ill-omened) ጉደሎ gwώdạlʷo.

It is unlucky: ጉደሎ፡ እድል፡ ነው። gwωdạlʷó (§ 8) ddịl nạ͡u.

He is unlucky: ሀብት፡ የለውም። haḟt yā́llạ͡um.

unripe, adj. ያልበሰለ yālbạ́ssạlạ (-lyạ́-; §§ 14, 7*a*, 37*c*).

unripe, be, v.i.—use neg. of በሰለ bạ́ssạlạ, to ripen.

It is unripe: አልበሰለም። alyạ́ssạlạm, pl. -ሉም። -lum, (§ 63*d*).

unsaddle, v.i. & t. አራገፈ arrā́ggạfạ.

Unsaddle: አራግፍ። arrā́gịf, pl. -ግፉ። -gịfu.

Don't unsaddle: አታራግፍ። attarrā́gịf, pl. -ፉ። -fu.

Unsaddle the pony: ፈረሱን፡ አራግፍ። fạ́rạsun arrā́-gịf.

Unsaddle him: አራግፈው። arrā́gịfạ͡u, ... her: -ፋት። -fāt.

Don't unsaddle him: አታራግፈው። attarrā́gịfạ͡u, ... her: -ፋት። -fāt.

unsteady, be, v.i. ተነቀነቀ tạnạqạ́nnạqạ.

This table is unsteady: ይህ፡ገበታ፡ይነቀነቃል። yḫe gạvạtá yịnnạqạ́nnạqāl.

untie, v.t. ፈታ fạ́ttā̃ (s.v. undo).

Untie the knot: ቍጥሩን፡ፍታው። qwṹṭịrun fịtâu.

untied, be, v.p. (come, v.i.) ተፈታ tạfạ́ttā̃ (s.v. undone, be).

until, conj. እስከ- (ị)skạ- [እስተ- (ị)stạ-] prefixed to simple perfect.

እስክ- (ị)sk(ị)- [እስት- (ị)st(ị)-] pref. to contingent (§ 45).

See § 48*a*; ድረስ dịrạs may follow either tense; s.v. till.

until, prp. እስከ- (ị)skạ- (§ 47*a*).

እስተ- (ị)stạ- („).

እስከ-[እስተ-]...፡ድረስ (ị)skạ- [(ị)stạ-]... dịrạs (§ 47*b*). S.v. till.

untrue, adj. ውሸት wịšät (wṹš-; § 57*b*).

untrustworthy, adj. የማይታመን yämmai̯ttā̃mmạn (s.v. አመነ, §§ 14, 37*c*).

untrustworthy, be, v.i.—use neg. of ታመነ tā̃mmạnạ (ger. & part. type A § 34).

He is untrustworthy: አይታመንም። ai̯ttā́mmạnịm, pl. -ኑም ። -num.

untruth, s. ውሸት wịšät (wṹš-).

እሰት ássạt.

እብለት ịblạt (ịvl-, -lät).

See § 52*a*, δ.

untruthful, adj. ዋሾ wā́šʷo.

ውሸታም wŭšātám (§ 8).

አባይ ā̃bâi̯ (ā̃y-; -áyy § 6; § 8).

up, adv. (above) ላይ lá͡i̥.
 በላይ bḁlá͡i̥ (§ 8).
 (upwards) ወደላይ wωdḁlá͡i̥ (§ 8).
 ሽቅብ šíqqi̥b (-i̥v).
up, prp. ከ- kḁ- (§ 47*a*).
 ተ- tḁ- („).
 He (it) is up the tree: ተዛፍ፡ነው። tḁzáf nḁ͡u.
up, go (come), v.i. ወጣ wώṭṭã.
 v.t. በ-....፡ላይ፡ወጣ bḁ-.... la͡i̥ (§ 8, § 47*b*) wώṭṭã.
 Go up: ውጣ። wǘṭa, pl. ውጡ። wǘṭu.
 Don't go up: አትውጣ። attǘṭa, pl. -ጡ። -ṭu.
 Has he (it) gone up? ወጥቷል። wώṭtŏ͡al?, pol. & pl. ወጥተዋል። wώṭtḁ͡uāl?
 Go up the hill: በተራራ፡ላይ፡ውጣ። bḁtḁrārá la͡i̥ wǘṭa.
 The price went up: ዋጋ፡አከለ። wága ákkḁlḁ.
up to, prp. እስከ- (i̥)skḁ- (§ 47*a*).
 እስተ- (i̥)stḁ- („).
 እስከ-[እስተ-]...፡ድረስ (i̥)skḁ-[(i̥)stḁ-]... di̥rḁs (§ 47*b*).
 Up to now: እስካሁን፡ i̥skáhun.
 Up to here: እስተዚህ፡ድረስ፡ i̥stäzzi̥h di̥rḁs.
uphill, adv. አቀበት áqḁbḁt (-ḁvḁt; § 8).
 When he (it) goes uphill: አቀበት፡ሲወጣ፡ áqḁvḁt si̥wώṭa.
upon, prp. በ-[ከ-, ተ-]...፡ላይ bḁ- (kḁ-, tḁ-)... la͡i̥ (§ 8, § 47*b*).
 Upon the chair: ተወምበሩ፡ላይ፡ tḁ͡uωmbḁ́ru la͡i̥.
uproot, v.t. ነቀለ nḁ́qqḁlḁ.
uprooted, be, v.p. ተነቀለ tḁnḁ́qqḁlḁ.
upside down, adv. በግልብጥ bḁgi̥lbi̥ṭ (-lvi̥ṭ, -gi̥líbbi̥ṭ).
 It is upside down: በግልብጥ፡ነው። bḁgi̥li̥bbíṭ (§ 8) nḁ͡u.

upwards (upstream), adv. ሽቅብ šịqqịb (-ịv).

upwards (upstream), go, v.i. አሻቀበ ašā́qqạbạ (-ạvạ).
ሽቅብ ፡ አለ šịqqịb (-ịv) ā́lạ (s.v. √በለ, § 44*a*).

He (it) has gone upwards: አሻቅቧል ። ašā́qqịvŏāl, pl. -በዋል ። -vạūāl, or ሽቅብ ፡ ብሏል ። šịqqịv yị-lŏāl, pl. ... ብለዋል ። ... yịlạūāl.

urethra, s. የሽንት ፡ ሥር yäšịnt sịr.
(male) የቊላ ፡ ሥር yäqwŭlā́ sịr.
See §§ 8, 70.

urinal, s. መሽኛ mạšạ́ñā̃ (-šā́ñā̃).
በሬታ bārʸétā̃.

urinate, v.i. ሸና šạ́nnạ.
(euphem.) ከፈለ kạ́ffạlạ.

urine, s. ሽንት šịnt.

Urtica urens (or *simensis*, Guidi, Vocab. pp. 149, 150), s. ሳማ sā́mmā̃ (§ 52*a*, δ).

us, pers. pron. -ን -n (-nn § 6, -ኖ -nnạ, § 12*c*).
emphatic እኛን ịññā́n (§ 8, § 12*a*).

Don't bring it near *us*: ወደኛ ፡ አታምጣው ። wωdạññā́ (§ 47*a*) attā́ntạū (§ 7*d*), pl. ... -ጡት ። -ṭut.

usage, s. ወግ wωg.
ሥራት sịrā́t (§ 8).
እድር ịddịr.

use, s. (utility) ጥቅም ṭịqịm.

What is the use of it? ለምን ፡ ይረባል ። lạmịn yịrā́-vāl?

It's no use: (of a course of action) ፍሬ፡የለውም። fi̥r^{y}e yállḁ͡um.
(of an object) አይረባም። a͡i̥rḁ́yām, pl. -ቡም። -yum.
አይጠቅምም። a͡i̥ṭáqmi̥m, pl. -ሙም። -mum.

I have no use for it: ለኔ፡አይጠቅመኝም። lḁn^{y}é a͡i̥ṭá-qi̥mäññi̥m.

It's no use his shouting: ዝም፡ቢሎ፡ነው፡እሚጮኽ። zi̥mm bi̥l^{w}ó (§ 8) nḁ͡u mmi̥č̣^{w}óh (§§ 7*d*, 14).

use, v.t. ሰራ፡በ- sḁrrā̃ (sár-) bḁ- (yḁ-; § 47*a*).

What do you use it for? ምን፡ትሰራበታለህ። mi̥n ti̥-sḁrabbḁtálläh?

How does one use it? እንዴት፡ይመቻል። nd^{y}ét yi̥m-máččāl?

We used to go every month: በየወሩ፡እንሔድ፡ነበርን። bḁyyäwώru (§ 18) nni̥hád nábbḁrn (§ 24*b*, § 33*a*).

used, be, v.p. (in use, be, v.i.) ተለመደ tḁlámmḁdḁ.

Is this word used? ይህ፡ቃል፡ይለመዳሎይ። yi̥he qāl yi̥llámmḁdāllwi̥? (s.v. ወይ).

used to, be (become), v.t. ለመደ lámmḁdḁ (§ 63*d*, *e*).

He (it) is used to it (them § 61*b*): ለምዷል። lám-dŏāl, pl. ለምደዋል። lḁmdḁ͡uāl.

You will get used to it (them): ትለምዳለህ። ti̥lḁm-dálläh, pol. ይለምዳሉ። yi̥lḁmdállu, pl. ትለምዳላችሁ። ti̥lḁmdalláččyuh (§ 7*d*).

useful, adj. የሚረባ yämmi̥rḁ́bā̃ (-ḁ́yā̃; § 14).

useful, be, v.i. ረባ rḁ́bbā̃.
ጠቀመ ṭḁ́qqḁmḁ (ṭáq-).

He (it) is useful: ይረባል። yi̥rḁ́yāl, pl. ይረባሉ። yi̥rḁ-yállu.

useless, adj. የማይረባ yämmai̥rḁbā̃ (-ḁ́yā̃; §§ 14, 37c).
ምናምን mi̥nā́mi̥n.
uterus, s. ማሕጠን máh(i̥)ṭḁn.
ማጠን mā́ṭḁn.
uvula, s. አንቃር áṅqār (§ 8).

V

§ *refers to the paragraphs of the Grammar* (*Initia Amharica, Part I*).

vagabond, s. አውደልዳይ a͡udḁldā́i̥ (-dā́l-; -ā́yy § 6; § 8).
vagina, s. እምስ i̥ms.
(euphem.) ብልት bi̥lli̥t.
vain, in, adv.—use gerund of ዝም፡አለ zi̥mm ālḁ (s.v. √በለ, § 44*a*).
He begged in vain: ዝም፡ብሎ፡ለመነ። zi̥mm bi̥lʷo lḁ́mmḁnḁ, pl. ዝም፡ብለው፡ለመኑ። zi̥mm bi̥lḁ͡u lḁ́mmḁnu.
valley, s. ሸለቆ šḁ́lḁqʷo (šώlωqʷo).
vanguard, s. አውራሪ a͡urā́ri.
Commander of vanguard: ፊታውራሪ fita͡urā́ri (fi̥t-).
various, adj. ልዩ፡ልዩ líyyu líyyu.
vegetable, s. ትክል ti̥ki̥l, pl. also አታክልት atáki̥lt.
(green) ጎመን gwώmmḁn (-män; § 52*a*, δ).
vegetable marrow, s. ዱባ dúbbā̃.
veil, s. መሸፈኛ mḁšḁffḁ́ñā̃ (-šäffā́ñā̃).
veil, v.t. ሸፈነ šḁ́ffḁnḁ (šā́f-).
veiled, be, v.p. (veil oneself, v.r.) ተሸፈነ tḁšḁ́ffḁnḁ (täšā́f-).
Is she veiled? (now) ተሸፍናለች። täšäffi̥nállač?, pl. ተሸፍነዋል። täšā́ffi̥nḁ͡uāl?
(generally) ትሸፈናለች። ti̥ššḁffḁnállač?, pl. ይሸፈናሉ። yi̥ššḁffḁnállu?

vein, s. ሥር si̥r (§ 52*a*, γ).

velvet, s. ከፈይ kḁ́fḁi̥.

venereal disease, s. (gonorrhœa) ጨብጥ čḁṿṭ.

(syphilis) ቂጥኝ qi̥ṭṭi̥ñ (-ññ § 6; § 8).

veranda, s. ሰብሳብ si̥bsáb (si̥ṿsáṿ; § 8).

G. አይጠየፍ ai̥ṭṭḁyäf (-ḁ́i̥äf).

B. ደጃፍ dájjáf (§ 8; in G. & Š. doorway).

(of church) ደጀ፡ሰላም dájjä (§ 9*d*) sḁlám (§ 8).

On the veranda: ተሰብሳብ፡ tḁsi̥ṿsāṿ (§ 47*a*).

G. ሃይጠየፍ፡ hai̥ṭṭḁi̥äf („).

vermifuge, s. ኮሶ k^{w}ós^{w}o.

versatile, adj. ብልሃተኛ bi̥lhātḁññã (-táñ-).

ጥበበኛ ṭi̥bḁbḁ́ññã (ṭi̥ṿḁṿ-, -áñ-).

versatility, s. ብልሃት bi̥lhát (§ 8).

ጥበብ ṭi̥bḁb (ṭi̥ṿḁṿ).

very, adv. እጅግ i̥jji̥g.

በብዙ bḁbi̥zu (bḁṿi̥-).

Very nice: እጅግ፡ማለፊያ፡ i̥jji̥g mālāfyã.

He (it) is very tall: እጅግ፡ረጅም፡ነው። i̥jji̥g räjji̥m nḁu.

vest, s. (under-) ሹራብ šúrrāb (-āṿ; § 8).

Vetterli rifle, s. ወጨፎ wḁčḁf^{w}o.

vice, s. ክፋት ki̥fát (kúf-, kŭf-, § 7*d*; § 8).

Vicia faba (Broun, Cat. 141), s. ባቄላ bāq^{y}élã (§ 52*a*, δ).

vicious, adj. ክፉ ki̥fu (kúfu, kŭfu, § 7*d*).

(of animals) ቍጡ qwŭṭṭu.

vicious, be (become), v.i. ከፋ kḁffã (§ 63*d*, *e*).

This mule is (has got) vicious: ይህ፡በቅሎ፡ከፍቷል። yi̥he ṿḁql^{w}o kḁftōāl.

victory, s. ድል dḭl.

They (he, pol.) fought and gained a victory: ተዋግተው፡ ድል፡ አደረጉ። ta͡uágta͡u dḭl adárragu, or ... ድል፡ ነሡ። ... dḭl nássu.

vigilance, s. ንቅነት nḭqḭnnat (-nät).

vigilant, adj. ንቁ nḭqu.

vigorous, adj. ጕልበታም gwŭlbatám (-ly-, -ắt- ; § 8).

ጕልበተኛ gwŭlbatáññã (-ly-, -ätắñ-).

vigour, s. ጕልበት gwŭlbat (-ly-, -ät).

village, s. መንደር mándar (-där).

አገር ắgar (-gär).

See § 52*a*, δ.

In the village: ተመንደር፡ tamándar (§ 47*a*).

Are there many villages on the road? ብዙ፡ መንደር፡ አለ፡ ተመንገዱ፡ላይ። bḭzu mándär állä tamangádu (§ 8) la͡i? (§ 47*b*).

vinegar, s. ጉምጥጥ gúmtḭt.

ሆምጣጣ hʷomtáttã (ኮም- kʷom-, -ጣጤ -tátʸe).

violence, s. ኃይል ha͡il.

violent, adj. ኃይለኛ ha͡iláññã (-lắñ-).

violet, adj. ጨጉማ çăgúmmã.

violin, s. ማሽንቆ mãšḭnqʷo.

viper, s. ፉኝት fŭññit, often f. (§ 54*c*).

virgin, adj. ድንግላይ dḭngḭla͡i (§ 8).

virgin, s. ድንግል dḭngil, pl. also ደናግል danágil.

viscera, s. ሆድ፡ እቃ hʷŏdiqã.

ፈርስ fars (färs).

Viverra civetta, s. ዝባድ zḭbád (-ḭyá-; § 8).

ጥርኝ tḭrḭñ (-ññ § 6; § 8).

Usually f. (§ 54*c*).

voice, s. ድምጥ dḭmt.

voluntarily, adv. በገዛ፡እጅ- bḁgḁzzájj- (§ 8) with personal suffixes (§ 12*b*); (s.v. ገዛ).

He did it voluntarily: በገዛ፡እጁ፡አደረገው። bḁgḁzzájju adárrḁgḁu͡.

She came voluntarily: በገዛ፡እጇ፡መጣች። bḁgḁzzájjwa mḁ́ṭṭāč.

vomit, v.i. & t. ተፋ tḁ́ffã.

Have you vomited? ተፋህ። tḁ́ffāh?, pol. ተፉ። tḁ́ffu?

vomit, cause to, v.i. & t. አስተፋ astḁ́ffã.

It will cause you to vomit: ያስተፋሃል። yāstḁ́ffahāl, ... you (pol.) ...: ያስተፋዎታል። yāstḁ́ffaʷotāl.

vomited, be, v.p. ተተፋ tḁtḁ́ffã.

vulture, s. የጥምብ፡አሞራ yätí̥mb (§ 70) amʷő̃rã.

አሞራ amʷő̃rã.

vulva, s. እምስ i̥ms.

(euphem.) ብልት bí̥lli̥t.

W

§ *refers to the paragraphs of the Grammar* (*Initia Amharica, Part I*).

wager, s. ውርርድ wŭrí̥rri̥d.

wages, s. ደሞዝ dḁ́mʷóz (§ 8).

waggon, s. †ሥረገላ si̥rḁgḁ́llã (ሠ- sä-).

Š. †ጋሪ gāri.

Waggon road: †የሥረገላ፡መንገድ፡ yäsi̥rḁgḁ́lla mḁ́ṅgḁd.

Š. †የጋሪ፡መንገድ፡ yägāri mḁ́ṅgḁd.

See §§ 47*a*, 70; s.v. road.

waist, s. ወገብ wṓgḁb (-ḁy̥).

waistband, s. መቀነቻ mḁqḁnnḁ́čã.

ድግ di̥g.

waistcoat, s. ግብግብ gí̥bbi̥gi̥bb.

wait, v.i. (for, v.t.) ቈየ qwώyyä.

ጠበቀ ṭḁ́bbḁqḁ.

Wait: ቈይ። qwώ͡i̥, pl. ቈዩ። qwώyyu.

Don't wait: አትቈይ። attí̥qwω͡i̥, pl. አትቈዩ። atti̥qwώyyu.

He (it) is to wait: ይቈይ። yí̥qwω͡i̥, pl. ይቈዩ። yi̥qwώyyu.

He (it) needn't wait: አይቈይ። á͡i̥qwω͡i̥, pl. አይቈዩ። a͡i̥qwώyyu.

I cannot wait: መቈየት፡አይቻለኝም። mḁqwώyyät a͡i̥ččáläññi̥m, pl. -ለንም። -lḁnni̥m.

Wait for him (it): ቈየው። qwώyya͡u, pl. ቈዩት። qwώyyut.

ጠብቀው። ṭḁ́bbi̥qḁ͡u, pl. -ቁት። -qut.

Wait for them: ቈያቸው። qwωyyáččḁ͡u, pl. ቈይዋቸው። qwωyyuáččḁ͡u.

ጠብቃቸው። ṭḁbbi̥qáččḁ͡u, pl. -ቋቸው። -qwáččḁ͡u.

wait a little, v.i. ቈየት፡አለ qwώyyätt álḁ (s.v. √በለ, § 44*a*).

Wait a little: ቈየት፡በል። qwωyyát (§§ 6, 8) yḁl, pl. ቈየት፡በሉ። qwώyyät yḁ́lu.

wait, cause or allow to, v.t. አቈየ aqwώyyä.

አስቈየ asqwώyyä.

Make him wait: አቈየው። aqwώyya͡u, pl. አቈዩት። aqwώyyut.

Make them wait: አቈያቸው። aqwωyyáččḁ͡u, pl. አቈዩአቸው። aqwωyyuáččḁ͡u.

wait for each other, v. recip. ተቈያዩ tḁqwω͡i̥áyyu.

Don't wait for each other: አትቈያዩ። atti̥qqwω͡i̥á͡i̥u.

They are not to wait for each other: እንዳይቈያዩ። nda͡i̥qqwω͡i̥áyyu.

We will wait for each other: እንቈያያለን። i̥nni̥q-qwω͡i̥ayyállän.

waiting, keep, v.t. አስቈየ asqwώyyä.

Don't keep him (it) waiting: አታስቈየው። attās-qwώyyä͡u, pol. አያስቈዩት። a͡^{y}āsqwώyyut, pl. አታስ ቈዩት። attāsqwώyyut.

Don't keep them waiting: አታስቈያቸው። attās-qwωyyắččą͡u, pol. አያስቈዩአቸው። a͡^{y}āsqwωyyuắč-čą͡u, pl. አታስቈዩአቸው። attāsqwωyyuắččą͡u.

wake, v.i. ነቃ ną́qqã.

I shall wake anyhow: እንዲያው፡እነቃለኍ። ndyá͡u nąqállą͡u^{h} (§ 7*d*).

I shall not wake unless you call me: ባታስነሣኝ፡ አልነቃም። bāttāsną́ssaññ (§§ 6, 37*c*) alną́qām.

wake, v.t. አነቃ aną́qqã.

አስነሣ asną́ssã.

Wake me: አንቃኝ። áṅqāñ.

አስነሣኝ። asną́ssāñ.

Don't wake me: አታንቃኝ። attắṅqāñ.

አታስነሣኝ። attāsną́ssāñ.

Wake me before dawn: ተንጋት፡በፊት፡አንቃኝ። tą-ni̥gắt y̥ąfít ắṅqāñ.

walk, s. (gait) አካሔድ akkắhäd.

walk (about, off), v.i. ሔደ hắdä (hą́-, h^{y}ḗ-, -dą, § 7*d*).

Can he (it) walk? ይሔዳል። yi̥hắdāl?, pol. & pl. ይ ሔዳሉ። yi̥hädállu? (§ 63*c*).

He (it) can't walk: አይሔድም። a͡i̥hắdi̥m, pol. & pl. -ዱም። -dum (§ 63*c*).

walk, v.t. (about) አስኬደ askä́dä (-kḁ̈́-, -dḁ).
(along) ሳበ sábḁ (sáỵḁ).

Walk the horse (about): ፈረሱን፡አስኪደው። fḁ́rḁsun áski̥dḁ͡u.

Walk it about until it is dry: አስኪደው፡እስቲደርቅ። áski̥dḁ͡u sti̥dárq.

Walk the horse along: ፈረሱን፡ሳበው። fḁ́rḁsun sáỵḁ͡u.

walk, go for a, v.i. ተናፈሰ tḁnä́ffḁsḁ.

I am going out for a walk: እናፈሳለኹ፡ወጥቼ። i̥nnaffḁsállḁ͡u[h] wώṭi̥čč[y]e.

wall, s. (high) ግድግዳ gi̥dgí̥ddā̃ (gi̥rg- § 7*d*).
(low) ንድቅ ní̥ddi̥q.
እድሞ í̥dm[w]o.

wallet, s. ከረጢት kḁrḁṭít.
(wicker-work) አኮፋዳ ak[w]ofádā̃.

wallow, v.i. ተንከባለለ tḁṅkḁbállḁlḁ (-ḁỵá-).

He (it) wallows in the mud: ከጭቃ፡ይንከባለላል። kḁčí̥qa yi̥ṅkḁỵállḁlāl, pl. -ባለሉ። -ỵallḁlállu, (§ 7*c*, note 1).

want, v.t. ፈለገ fḁ́llḁgḁ.

Do you want him (it)? ትፈልገዋለህ። ti̥fḁlli̥gḁ͡uálläh?, pol. ይፈልጉታል። yi̥fḁ́lli̥gutāl?, pl. ትፈልጉታላችሁ። ti̥fḁlli̥gutallä́ččyuh? (§ 7*d*).

Don't you want him (it)? አትፈልገውም። atti̥fḁ́lli̥gḁ͡um?, pol. አይፈልጉትም። a͡i̥fḁ́lli̥guti̥m?, pl. አትፈልጉትም። atti̥fḁ́lli̥guti̥m?

What do you want? ምን፡ትፈልጋለህ። mi̥n ti̥fḁlli̥gálläh?, pol. ምን፡ይፈልጋሉ። mi̥n yi̥fḁlli̥gállu?, pl. ምን፡ትፈልጋላችሁ። mi̥n ti̥fḁlli̥gallä́ččyuh?

I want him (it): እፈልገዋለኹ። i̥fḁlli̥gḁ͡uállḁ͡u[h] (§ 7*d*), pl. እንፈልገዋለን። i̥nni̥fḁlli̥gḁ͡uállän.

I don't want him (it): አልፈልገውም። alfḁ́lli̥gḁ͡um, pl. አንፈልገውም። anni̥fḁ́lli̥gḁ͡um.

I want to go: ልሔድ፡እፈልጋለኍ። li̥hā́d i̥fḁlli̥gál-lḁ͡u^{h}, pl. ልንሔድ፡እንፈልጋለን። li̥nnhā́d i̥nni̥fḁlli̥gál-län.

I don't want to go: ልሔድ፡አልፈልግም። li̥hā́d alfḁ́l-li̥gi̥m, pl. ልንሔድ፡አንፈልግም። li̥nnhā́d anni̥fḁ́lli̥-gi̥m.

Do you want to go? ልትሔድ፡ትፈልጋለህ። li̥tthā́d ti̥fḁlli̥gálläh?, pol. ሊሔዱ፡ይፈልጋሉ። lihā́du yi̥fḁl-li̥gállu?, pl. ልትሔዱ፡ትፈልጋላችሁ። li̥tthā́du ti̥fḁlli̥-gallā́ččyuh?

Don't you want to go? ልትሔድ፡አትፈልግም። li̥tthā́d atti̥fḁ́lli̥gi̥m?, pol. ሊሔዱ፡አይፈልጉም። lihā́du a͡i̥fḁ́l-li̥gum?, pl. ልትሔዱ፡አትፈልጉም። li̥tthā́du atti̥fḁ́l-li̥gum?

Ḥe has sold the mule I wanted: በቅሎውን፡ሸጠብኝ። bḁ́qlʷo͡un šḁ́ṭḁbbi̥ñ (s.v. በ-, §§ 47*a*, 71).

want of, be in, v.t. ገደደው gḁ́ddḁdḁ͡u (cp. § 43*a*).

አጣ áṭṭā̃.

See § 63*d*, *e*.

What are you in want of? ምን፡ገዶሃል። mi̥n gḁ́d-dʷohāl?, pol. ምን፡ገዶዎታል። mi̥n gḁ́ddʷo͡ʷotāl? (-dʷōt-), pl. ምን፡ገዷችኋል። mi̥n gḁddŏ͡āččyuhāl? (§ 7*d*).

wanted, be, v.p. ተፈለገ tḁfḁ́llḁgḁ.

He (it) is not wanted: ይቅር። yí̥qi̥r, pl. ይቅሩ። yí̥qru.

wanting, be, v.i. ገደደ gḁ́ddḁdḁ.

ታጣ tā́ṭṭā̃.

See § 63*d*, *e*.

There is nothing wanting: ምንም፡አይገድ። mi̥ni̥mm (§ 6) a͡igadd (§ 37*d*), or ምንም፡የገደደ፡የለ። mi̥ni̥m (§ 6) yägḁ́ddḁdḁ (§ 14) yállä (§ 39*b*).

war, s. ጦርነት ṭʷori̥nnḁt (-nät).
ጦር ṭʷŏr.
In time of war: የጦር፡ጊዜ፡ yäṭʷór (§§ 56*c*, 70) gi̥zʸe.
War material: የጦር፡መሳሪያ፡ yäṭʷór mḁssárya.

war, go to, v.i. ዘመተ zḁ́mmḁtḁ.
If he goes to war: ቢዘምት፡ bizḁ́mt, pol. & pl. ቢዘምቱ፡ bizḁ́mtu.

war, send to, v.t. አዘመተ azzḁ́mmḁtḁ.
Does he send him to war? ያዘምተዋል። yazzḁ́mmi̥tḁ͡uāl?, pol. & pl. ያዘምቱታል። yazzḁ́mmi̥tutāl?

war, take to, v.t. አዘመተ azḁ́mmḁtḁ.
Does he take him to war? ያዘምተዋል። yāzḁ́mtḁ͡uāl?, pol. & pl. ያዘምቱታል። yāzḁ́mtutāl?

warm, adj. ሙቅ muq.
Very warm: ትኩስ፡ ti̥kkús (tŭ́k-; § 8).

warm, v.t. አሞቀ amʷŏ́qḁ.
Warm it: አሙቀው። ámuqḁ͡u.
Don't warm it: አታሙቀው። attámuqḁ͡u.
Warm it up a little: ለብ፡አድርገህ፡አሙቀው። lḁbb árgäh (§ 7*d*) ámuqḁ͡u.

warm, be, v.i. ሞቀ mʷŏ́qḁ (§ 63*d*, *e*).
It is (too) warm: ሙቋል። múqŏ͡āl.
Š. ሞቋል። mʷóqŏ͡āl.
It isn't warm (enough): አልሞቀም። almʷóqḁm.

warmth, s. ሙቀት múqḁt.

warp, s. (in weaving) ፈትል fḁti̥l (fát-).

warp, v.i. ዘበ zḁbbã.

It will warp: ይዘባል። yi̥zḁ́ỵāl, pl. ይዘባሉ። yi̥zḁỵállu.

It will not warp: አይዘባም። a͡i̥zḁ́ỵām, pl. -ቡም። -ỵum.

It is warped: ዘብቷል። zḁ́ỵtŏ͡āl, pl. -ተዋል። -tḁ͡uāl.

wart, s. ክንታሮት ki̥ntā́r^{w}ot, usually f. (§ 54*c*).

wart-hog (*Phacochœrus æthiopicus*), s. እርያ i̥ryã.

ከርካሮ kḁrkḁ́rr^{w}o (kär-, -kā́r-; Galla).

wash, v.i. (wash oneself, v.r.) ታጠበ tā́ṭṭḁbḁ (-ḁỵḁ).

I am going to wash: ልታጠብ፡ነኝ። li̥ttāṭṭḁ́ỵ (§ 8) näñ, pl. ልንታጠብ፡ነን። li̥nni̥ttāṭṭḁ́ỵ (§ 8) nän.

I am washing: እታጠባለሁ። i̥ttāṭṭḁỵállḁ͡u^{h}, pl. እንታጠባለን። i̥nni̥ttāṭṭḁỵállän.

I haven't washed yet: አልታጠብሁም፡ገና፡ነኝ። altā́ṭṭḁỵhum, gḁnā́ näñ, pl. አልታጠብንም፡ገና፡ነን። altā́ṭṭḁỵnḁm, gḁnā́ nän.

I shan't wash now: አሁን፡አልታጠብም። ā́hun ali̥ttā́ṭṭḁỵi̥m, pl. አሁን፡አንታጠብም። ā́hun anni̥ttā́ṭṭḁỵi̥m.

Before I wash: ሳልታጠብ፡ sali̥ttā́ṭṭḁỵ, pl. ሳንታጠብ፡ sanni̥ttā́ṭṭḁỵ.

When I wash: ስታጠብ፡ si̥ttā́ṭṭḁỵ, pl. ስንታጠብ፡ si̥nni̥ttā́ṭṭḁỵ.

When I have washed: ታጥቤ፡ tā́ṭi̥bb^{y}e (§ 29), pl. ታጥበን፡ tā́ṭỵḁn.

Wash yourself: ታጠብ። tā́ṭḁỵ, pl. ታጠቡ። tā́ṭḁỵu.

Aren't you going to wash? አትታጠብም። atti̥ttā́ṭṭḁỵi̥m?, pl. -ቡም። -ỵum?

wash, v.t. አጠበ ḁ́ṭṭḁbḁ (-ḁỵḁ).

Wash him (it): እጠበው። i̥ṭḁỵḁ͡u, pl. -ቡት። -ỵut.

Don't wash him (it): አትጠበው። attḭṭḁvḁ͡u, pl. -ቡት። -vut.

Have you washed him (it)? አጠብሀው። áṭṭḁvhḁ͡u?, pl. አጠባችሁት። aṭṭḁváččḭhut?

I want to wash my hands: እጄን፡ ልታጠብ፡ እፈል ጋለኍ። ḭjjʸen (§§ 52*a*,*γ*, 56*c*) lḭttáṭṭḁv ḭfḁllḭgállḁ͡uʰ.

Wash your hands: እጅህን፡ ታጠብ። ḭjjḭhḭn táṭḁv, pl. እጃችሁን፡ ታጠቡ። ḭjjáččḭhun táṭḁvu.

washed, be, v.p. ታጠበ táṭṭḁbḁ (-ḁvḁ).

Has he (it) been washed? ታጥቧሎይ። táṭḭvō͡allwḭ? (s.v. ወይ), pl. ታጥበዋሎይ። táṭḭvḁ͡uāllwḭ?

It is to be washed: ይታጠብ። yḭttáṭḁv, pl. -ቡ። -vu.

It is not to be washed: አይታጠብ። a͡ḭttáṭḁv, pl. -ቡ። -vu.

It must be washed in hot water: በሙቅ፡ ውሃ፡ ይታ ጠብ። bḁmúq wúha yḭttáṭḁv.

washing, s. (process) እጥበት ḭṭbḁt (ḭṭv-, -ät).

These clothes want washing: ይህ፡ ልብስ፡ እጥበት፡ ይ ፈልጋል። yḭhe lḭvs (§ 52*a*, *δ*) ḭṭvḁt yḭfḁllḭgāl.

washing-place, s. ማጠቢያ māṭḁbyā̃ (-ḁvyā̃).

wasp, s. የውሻ፡ ንብ yā͡ušša̋-nḭb (-nḭv; §§ 47*a*, 70).

Mason (solitary) wasp: ትንዚዛ፡ tḭnzízā̃.

See § 52*a*, *δ*.

waste, v.t. አጠፋ aṭḁffā̃.

Don't waste it: አታጥፋው። attáṭfa͡u, pl. -ፉት። -fut.

watch, s. ሰዓት sḁ͡ät, sometimes f. (§ 54*c*), see Addenda.

Is it going? ይዞራል። yḭzʷórāl?

Has it stopped? ቁሟል። qúmō͡al?

Š. ቆሟል። qʷómō͡al?

Wind it up: ሙላው። múla͡u.

It loses: ይቀራል። yḭqḁrāl.

It is slow: ቀርቷል። qártŏ͡āl.

ዘግይቷል። zḁ́gyi̥tŏ͡āl.

It gains: ይቀድማል። yi̥qḁ́dmāl.

It is fast: ቀድሟል። qḁ́dmŏ͡āl.

Put it on (forward): አስቀድመው። asqḁ́ddi̥mḁ͡ū.

Put it back: አስቀረው። asqḁ́rrḁ͡ū.

It is right: ትክክል፡ነው። ti̥ki̥kki̥l (§ 8) nḁ͡ū.

ልክ፡ነው። lí̥kki̥ (§ 7*d*) nḁ͡ū.

It is not right: ልክ፡አይደለም። li̥kk a͡i̥dḁ́llām (§ 7*d*).

Put it right: አስተካክለው። astḁkákki̥lḁ͡ū.

How much has it lost (is it slow)? ምን፡ያህል፡ቀረ። mi̥n yahl qḁ́rrḁ?

How much has it gained (is it fast)? ምን፡ያህል፡ቀደመ። mi̥n yahl qḁ́ddḁmḁ?

It is wound up: ሞላ። mʷólla.

It is not wound up: አልሞላም። almʷóllām.

watch, v.i. & t. ተመለከተ tḁmḁlḁ́kkḁtḁ.

Watch him (it): ተመልከተው። tḁmálkḁtḁ͡ū, pl. -ቱት። -tut.

watchman, s. ተረኛ tḁrḁ́ññã (tär-, -áñ-).

ዘበኛ zḁbḁ́ññã (zḁv-, -áñ-).

ጠባቂ ṭḁbbáqi.

See § 52*a*, δ.

watch-tower, s. ሰገነት sḁgḁ́nnät.

water, s. ውሃ wúhã (úhã).

Š. also ወሃ wḁhã.

Warm (hot) water: ሙቅ፡ውሃ፡ muq wúha.

Boiling water: ፍል፡ውሃ፡ fi̥l wúha.

Cold water: ቀዝቃዛ፡ውሃ፡ qḁzqázza wúha.

Clear (pure) water: ጥሩ፡ውሃ፡ ṭi̥ru wúha.

Clean water: ንጡሕ፡ውሃ፡ ni̥ṭúh wúha.

Fresh water: አዲስ፡ውሃ፡ áddi̥s wúha.

Bring some water: ውሃ፡አምጣ። wúha ámṭā (uhán-ṭā § 7*d*).

Tie up a little water in a skin: ጥቂት፡ውሃ፡ተሩዋት፡ቋጥረው። ṭiqiṭ wúha taraûwát qwáṭirau.

Where did you get this water from? ይህን፡ውሃ፡ተዬት፡አመጣህው። yihán wúha tayét amáṭṭahau?

water, v.t. አጠጣ aṭáṭṭã.

Have you watered him? አጠጣህው። aṭáṭṭahau?

Have you watered her? አጠጣሃት። aṭáṭṭahāt?

Have you watered them? አጠጣሃቸው። aṭaṭṭaháč-čau?

Water (pl.) the animals: ከብቶችን፡አጠጧቸው። kaf-tʷóččin aṭaṭṭwáččau.

Don't water the pony yet: ፈረሱን፡አታጠጣው፤ገና፡ነው። fárasun attāṭáṭṭau, ganá (§ 8) nau.

water, pass, v.i. ሸና šánna.

When you pass water: ስትሸን፡ sittišán, pol. ሲሸኑ፡ sišánu.

Are you passing water without difficulty? በጤናህ፡ትሸናለህ። baṭʸénāh tišanállāh?, pol. በጤናዎ፡ይሸናሉ። baṭʸēnáʷo yišanállu?

water-bottle, s. (travelling) ሩዋት ráuwát (§ 8).

ረዋት rawát (rauát; § 8).

ሩውሃት ráuhát (§ 8).

ዘምዘሚያ zamzamíyã.

(pottery, glass) ማብረጃ mãbrájã (mãyr-, -áj-).

The water-bottle is (-tles are § 52*a*, δ) to be wetted and kept wet: ሩዋት፡ይነከር፤ሁለግዜ፡እርጥብ፡ይሁን። rauwát yinnákar; húllagzʸé rṭiy (§ 7*d*) yíhun.

waterbuck (*Cobus defassa*), s. ድፋሳ difásã.

water-cooler, s. ማብረጃ mãbrájã (mãyr-, -áj-).

water-course, s. ወንዝ wωnz.

(small) ዲፋ dı̥ffã.

ፈፋ fḁfã.

watered, be, v.p. (drink) ጠጣ ṭḁ́ṭṭã.

Has he (it) been watered? ጠጥቷል። ṭḁ́ṭṭı̥tŏ͡āl?, f. ጠጥታለች። ṭḁṭṭı̥tállăč?, pl. ጠጥተዋል። ṭḁ́ṭṭı̥tḁ͡uāl?

He (it) is to be watered: ይጠጣ። yı̥ṭḁ́ṭṭa, f. ትጠጣ። tı̥ṭḁ́ṭṭa, pl. ይጠጡ። yı̥ṭḁ́ṭṭu.

He (it) is not to be watered: አይጠጣ። a͡i̥ṭḁ́ṭṭa, f. አትጠጣ። attı̥ṭḁ́ṭṭa, pl. አይጠጡ። a͡i̥ṭḁ́ṭṭu.

water-hole, s. አዘቅት ā̃zḁqt (§ 8).

ጉድጓድ gúdgwā̃d (gúrgw- § 7*d*; § 8).

watering-place, s. (place for drawing water) መቅጃ mḁ́q-jã.

(place for drinking) መጠጫ mḁṭḁ́č̣č̣ã.

water-jar, s. እንስራ (i̥)nsı̥rã.

water-pipe, s. (conduit) ቡምባ búmbã.

ቧምቧ bwámbwã.

wave, s. ሞገድ mʷŏgḁd (§ 52*a*, δ).

wave, v.i. (be waved, v.p.) ተርገበገበ tḁrgḁbḁ́ggḁbḁ (tär-, -ḁṿḁ́ggḁṿḁ, § 7*c*, note 1).

wave, v.t. አራገበ arrã́ggḁbḁ (-ḁṿḁ).

አርገበገበ argḁbḁ́ggḁbḁ (-ḁṿḁ́ggḁṿḁ).

wax, s. ሰም sḁm.

way, s. (road) መንገድ mḁ́ṅgḁd.

ጐዳና gwώdanã.

Way down: መውረጃ፡ mḁ͡urḁ́jã.

Way out or up: ማውጫ፡ máu͡č̣ã.

Way in: መግቢያ፡ mḁ́gbyã (-gṿyã).

Which is the way? መንገዱ፡ወዴት፡ነው። mḁ́ṅgḁdu wωdʸét nḁ͡u?

Which is the way to Addis Abeba? በዬት፡ነው፡ ያዲስ፡አበባ፡መንገድ። bḁʸét nḁ͡u yáddi̥s ayḁyá mḁ́ṅgḁd?

Which way did he go? በወዴት፡እኩል፡ሔደ። bḁ͡uω-dʸét ǘkkul hǻdä?

Come this way: በዚህ፡ና። bäzzíh nā.

Go out that way: በዚያ፡ውጣ። bḁzzyá wǘṭa (-yá͡uṭa).

In this (that) way: እንዲህ፡ (i̥)ndíh (-di̥h; § 8).

እንደዚህ፡ (i̥)ndḁ́zzíh (-dǻz-, -zi̥h; § 8).

Don't do it that way: እንዲህ፡አታድርገው። ndíh attádri̥gḁ͡u (attárgḁ͡u § 7*d*).

To be some way off: ሳብ፡አለ፡ sãbb álḁ (s.v. √ሳበ, § 44*a*).

It is some way off: ሳብ፡ይላል። sabb yi̥lāl.

A long way: እሩቅ፡ i̥rúq.

He (it) has gone a long way: እሩቅ፡ሒዷል። i̥rúq hi̥dő͡āl.

One can see him (her, it, them, § 61*b*) a long way off: በሩቅ፡ያያል፡ሰው። bḁrúq (§ 7*a*) ya͡i̥ál (§ 8) sḁ͡u.

Make way! ጕድን። gwǿdi̥n!

Get out of the way! ወግድ። wǿgi̥d!, f. ወግጅ። wǿgi̥j!, pl. ወግዱ። wǿgi̥du!

Get out of his (its) way! ወግድለት። wǿgi̥di̥llḁt!, f. -ጅለት። -ji̥llḁt!, pl. -ዱለት። -dullḁt!

wayfarer, s. መንገደኛ mḁṅgḁdḁ́ññã (-dǻñ-).

we, pers. pron. እኛ i̥ññá (§§ 8, 12*a*, 60*b*), usually omitted unless emphatic.

weak, adj. (of animate objects) ደካማ däkkámã.

(gen.) ሰነፍ sḁnḁf.

This rope is too weak: ይሀ፡ገመድ፡ሰነፍ፡ነው። yı̥he gḁ́mḁd sḁnḁ́f (§ 8) nḁ͡u.

This coffee is too weak: ይሀ፡ቡን፡ቀጭን፡ነው። yı̥he ỵunn qḁč̣č̣ı̥n (§ 8) nḁ͡u.

weak, be (become), v.i.

(of animate objects) ደከመ dắkkḁmḁ.

ደከመው dắkkḁmḁ͡ū (impers. § 43*a*).

See § 63*d*, *e*.

He (it) is (too) weak: ደክሞታል። dắkĭ̥m^{w}otāl, f. ደክሚታል። dắkĭ̥moͣātāl, pl. ደክሚቸዋል። däkĭ̥moͣáč-čḁ͡uāl.

weaken, v.t. (exhaust) አደከመ adắkkḁmḁ.

It weakens one: ሰው፡ያደክማል። sḁ́͡u yādákĭ̥māl.

weakness, s. (of animate objects) ድካም dı̥kám (§ 8).

(gen.) ስንፍና sı̥nfı̥nnã.

wealth, s. ባለጠግነት bālḁṭḁggı̥nnḁt (-nät).

wealthy, adj. ባለጠጋ bālḁṭḁ́ggã.

ሀብታም hábtām (háỵt-, háf̣t-; § 8).

ቡካሴ bukkás^{y}e.

weapon, s. መሳሪያ mḁssáryã (-yä § 7*d*).

ብረት bı̥rḁt (-rät).

wear, v.t. (put on) ለበሰ lḁ́bbḁsḁ (§ 56*c*).

አደረገ adḁ́rrḁgḁ.

Wear it: ልበሰው። lı̥ỵḁsḁ͡u, f. ልበሺው። lı̥ỵḁšyu.

Don't wear it: አትልበሰው። attı̥lỵḁsḁ͡u, f. -በሺው። -ỵḁšyu.

I shall wear it: እለብሰዋለኍ። ı̥lḁỵsḁ͡uállḁ͡u^{h}.

I shall not wear it: አልለብሰውም። allḁ́ỵsḁ͡um.

To-morrow I shall wear these boots: ነገ፡ይሀንን፡ጫማ፡አደርገዋለኍ። nḁ́gḁ yı̥hánnän č̣ámma (§ 52*a*, δ) adärgḁ͡uállḁ͡u^{h}.

wear (out), v.t. (consume) በላ bḁllã.

The stones will wear it out: ድንጊያ፡ይበላዋል። dấn-gya (§ 52*a*, δ) yi̥vḁla͡uāl.

weary, v.t. አደከመ adákkḁmḁ.

weather, s.

Fair weather: ብራ፡ bi̥rrã.

weave, v.i. & t. ፈተለ fḁttḁlḁ (fáttälḁ).

Do they weave it here? ከዚህ፡ይፈትሉታል። käzzi̥h yi̥fáti̥lutāl?

weaver, s. ፈታይ fḁta͡i̥ (fát-; -áyy § 6; § 8).

ሸማኔ šḁmmán^{y}e (šäm-).

Wednesday, s. & adv. ሮብ r^{w}õb (r^{w}õy̥).

weed, s. አረም árḁm (አረሞ árḁm^{w}o; § 52*a*, δ).

weed (out), v.t. አረመ árrḁmḁ.

Weed the corn: እህሉን፡አርመው። i̥hi̥lun árri̥ma͡u̥, pl. -ሙት። -mut.

Weed out the grass from the corn: ሣሩን፡ተህሉ፡አርመው። sárun táhi̥lu árri̥ma͡u̥.

weeded (out), be, v.p. ታረመ tárrḁmḁ.

This hasn't been weeded: ይህ፡አልታረመም። yi̥he altárrḁmḁm.

week, s. ሳምንት sámmi̥nt (§ 52*a*, δ).

weep, v.i. አለቀሰ alḁqqḁsḁ.

weigh, v.i. (be weighed, v.p.) ተመዘነ tḁmḁzzḁnḁ.

መዘነ mḁzzḁnḁ (q.v.).

How much does it weigh? ስንት፡ይመዝናል። si̥nt yi̥mmḁzzḁnāl?

It must be weighed: ይመዘን። yi̥mmḁzḁn.

Which weighs the more (most)? ማናቸው፡ይመዝናል። mānnáčča͡u̥ yi̥mḁzzi̥nāl?

This weighs more than that: ይህ፡ተዚህ፡ይመዝናል። yi̥he tḁzzíh yi̥mḁzzi̥nāl (§ 58*b*).

He (it) weighs a lot: ከብዷል። kạ́ydŏ͡āl, pl. ከብደዋል። kạ́ydạ͡ūāl, (§ 63*d*).

He (it) doesn't weigh much: አልከበደም። alkạ́bbạdạm, pl. -በዱም። -bbạdum, (§ 63*d*).

weigh, v.t. መዘነ mạ́zzạnạ.

Weigh it: መዝነው። mạ́zzịnạ͡ū.

weighing-machine, s. ሚዛን mízán (§ 8).

weight, s. ሚዛን mízán (§ 8).

By weight: በሚዛን፡ bạmízān (§ 47*a*).

What is its weight? ሚዛኑ፡ስንት፡ነው። mīzánu sịntị nạ͡ū?

[S. vv. ፈረሱላ፡ — ነጥር፡ — ወቄት፡].

weighty (important), adj. ቁም qum.

welfare, s. ደኅንነት dähnịnnạt (-nät).

well, adj. ደኅና dáhnā (§ 8).

(after illness) በኀ bạ́ggʷo.

Are you well? ደኅና፡ነህ። dähná näh?, f. ደኅና፡ነሽ። dähná näš?, pol. ደኅና፡ነዎ። dähná nạ͡ʷo?, (§ 13*b*).

Aren't you well? ደኅና፡አይደለህምይ። dähná a͡ịdállähịmmwị?, f. -ደለሽምይ። -dállāšịmmwị?, pol. -ደሉምይ። -dállummwị?, (§§ 7*d*, 40*a*, s.v. ወይ).

I am not well: አሞኛል። ámmʷoññāl.

Are you well again? እግዚአብሔር፡ይማርህ፡በኀ፡ነህ። ịgzịayhʸér yịmárịh, yạggʷó (§§ 7*d*, 8) näh?, f. ... ይማርሽ፡በኀ፡ነሽ። ... yịmárịš, yạggʷó näš?, pol. ... ይማረዎ፡በኀ፡ነዎ። ... yịmárạ͡ʷo, yạggʷó nạ͡ʷo? (lit. God have mercy on you, are you well?).

well, adv. ደኅና dáhnā (§ 8).

(thoroughly) በጣም bạ́ṭám (§ 8).

(adversative) እንኳን (ị)ṅkwán (§ 8).

(expletive) እንግዲህ (ị)ṅgdʸéh.

(resumptive) -ማ -mmā̃.

He cooks well: ደኅና፡ወጥ፡ይሰራል። dáhnā wωṭ yi̥-sárāl.

He speaks Amharic well: አማርኛ፡መልከም፡አድርጎ፡ይናገራል። amāri̥ñña mḁlkám ádri̥g^{w}o (árg^{w}o § 7*d*) yi̥nnággạrāl.

You write very well indeed: ድንቅ፡አድርገህ፡ትጥፋለህ። di̥ñq ádri̥gäh (árgäh) ti̥ṭi̥fálläh, pol. ድንቅ፡አድርገው፡ይጥፋሉ። di̥ñq ádri̥gḁu͡ (árgḁu͡) yi̥ṭi̥fállu.

Do you know him (it) well? በጣም፡ታውቀዋለህ። bḁṭám tau͡qḁu͡álläh?

Well, we will go: እንኳን፡እንሔዳለን። ńkwān (§ 7*d*), i̥nnhädállän.

Well, we won't go: እንኳን፡አንሔድም። ńkwān, annhádi̥m.

Well, I must be going: እንግዴህ፡ሔድሁኝ። ṅgd^{y}éh hádhuñ (ሔድኩኝ hádkuñ, hárk-, § 7*d*; § 61*e*), pl. እንግዴህ፡ሔድን። ṅgd^{y}éh hádnḁ (Part I, p. xxiii).

Well, I hope he won't throw you off: እንግዴህ፡እንዳይጥልህ። ṅgd^{y}éh i̥ndai͡ṭi̥li̥h.

And afterwards? ኋላስ። hwálāss?—Well, afterwards we came back: ኋላማ፡ተመለስን። hwālámmā tḁmállạsnạ.

Very well! (all right!) እሺ። i̥šši! (-ši̥).
በጄ። bạjjä! (báj-).

Well off (well provided for), adj. ዓለመኛ፡ ālạmáññã (ālämáñ-).

well, s. ጉድጓድ gúdgwád (gúrgw- § 7*d*; § 8).
አዘቅት ázạqt (§ 8).

How deep is the well? ጉድጓድ፡እርዝመቱ፡ስንት፡ነው። gurgwád (§ 55*b*) i̥rzi̥mḁtu si̥nti̥ nḁu͡?

well, get, v.i. ዳነ dánḁ.
ተሻለው tḁšálạu͡ (täš-; impers. § 43*a*).

He (it) will get well: ይድናል። yidinal, f. ትድናለች። tidinálläč, pol. ይድናሉ። yidinállu.

He (it) will not get well: አይድንም። aidinim, f. አትድንም። attidinim, pol. አይድኑም። aidinum.

He (it) has got well: ድኗል። dinóal, f. ድናለች። dinálläč, pol. ድነዋል። dinaual.

well-behaved, adj. የተቀጣ yätaqáttã (§ 14, s.v. ቀጣ).

well-born, adj. ባላባት bālábbát (§ 8).

well-fed, adj. ጥጋበኛ tigābáññã (-āy-, -áñ-).

west, s. ምዕራብ mirāb (-áy; § 8).

wet, adj. እርጥብ írtib (-iy).

ርጥብ rítib (-iy).

wet, v.t. ነከረ nákkara (nákkära).

Wet it: ንከረው። nikarau.

Don't wet it: አትንከረው። attínkarau.

wet, be or become, v.i. ረጠበ ráttaba (-aya; § 63*d*, *e*).

[እ]ራሰ (i)rása (§ 63*d*, *e*).

(weather) ዘነበ zánnaba (-aya).

The ground is wet: መሬት፡ ረጥቧል። maryét ratyóal.

When the cloth is wet: ጨርቁ፡ ሲርስ፡ čárqu siris.

If it is wet (weather): ቢዘንብ፡ bizány (-ámb).

wet season, s. ክረምት kirámt (§ 8).

wether, s. ሙክት፡ በግ múkkit bag (yag).

ሙክት múkkit.

wetted, be, v.p. (get wet, v.i.) ተነከረ tanákkara (-nákkära).

He (it) has got wet: ተነክሯል። tanákróal, pl. ተነከረዋል። tanákraual.

He (it) has not got wet: አልተነከረም። altanákkaram, pl. -ከሩም። -karum.

It is to be wetted: ይነከር። yinnákar, pl. -ሩ። -ru.

It is not to be wetted: አይነከር። ainnákar, pl. -ሩ። -ru.

Mind it doesn't get wet: እንዳይነከር። ndainnákkar, pl. -ሩ። -ru.

Wetterly rifle, s. ወጫፎ wḁč̣ḁfʷo.

what?, inter. pron. ምን mi̥n?

ምንድር mi̥ndi̥r?

ምንድን mi̥ndi̥n (-nn § 6).

See § 15.

What (do you say)? ምን፡ አልህ። mi̥n ālh?, f. ምን፡ አልሽ። mi̥n ālš?, pol. ምን፡ አሉ። mi̥n ālu?

What is it? ምኑ። mi̥nu?

ምንድር፡ ነው። mi̥ndi̥r nḁū?

What is the name of this place? ይህ፡ ስፍራ፡ ስሙ፡ ማን፡ ነው። yi̥he si̥fra si̥mu mā́n-nḁū?

And what about this? ይህሳ። yi̥hässá? (s.v. -ስ, -ሳ).

— intensive, ምን mi̥n with parts of አከለ q.v.

What a lot! ምን፡ ያህል፡ ነው። mi̥n yahl nḁū!

What a (large, small) horse! ይህ፡ ፈረስ፡ ምን፡ ያህላል። yi̥he fḁ́rḁs mi̥n yáhlāl!

what, rel. pron. የ- yä- (q.v.) pref. to simple perfect.

የም- yämm(i̥)- [እም- (i̥)mm(i̥)-] pref. to contingent.

The above are nom. & acc., sg. & pl.; see §§ 14, 62.

Tell me what he said: ያለውን፡ ንገረኝ። yálḁūn (§ 7*a*) ni̥gäräñ.

Do you know what they eat? የሚበሉትን፡ ታውቀዋለህ። yämmiy̥ḁ́luti̥n (-mi̥y̥- § 7*d*) tau̯ŭqḁu̯állāh?

I forget what he (it) does: የሚያደርገውን፡ እረሳሁት። yämmyādā́rgḁūn i̥rḁ́ssahut (§ 63*d*).

That is not what I asked: ይህንን፡ አልጠየቅሁም። yi̥hánnän alṭḁ́yyäqhum.

What kind of? የትኛው yĕti̥ññau? (§§ 8, 15).

ምንኛ mi̥ni̥ññā? (§ 15).

what's-his-name, indef. pron. እንቶ[ን] (i̥)ntʷō(n) (§ 16).

Call what's-his-name: እንቶን፡ጥራው። ńtʷōn ti̥rau͡.

what's-its-name, indef. pron. እንትን (i̥)nti̥n (§ 16).

wheel, s. መንኰራኵር mḁṅkwωrákwŭr (መኰ- mḁkwω-; § 52*a*, δ).

wheel-handle, s. መዘወሪያ mḁzzḁu͡wḁryā̆ (-wár-).

when?, adv. መቼ mḁ́čʸe?

መቸ mḁ́čä?

When does (will) he (it) come? መቼ፡ይመጣል። mḁ́čʸe yi̥mḁ́ṭāl?

When did he (it) come? መቼ፡መጣ። mḁ́čʸe mḁ́ṭṭa?

when, conj. ስ- s(i̥)- (q.v.) pref. to contingent (§ 45); tense is not distinguished.

በ- bḁ-, pref. to simple perfect followed by ጊዜ gí̥zʸe.

See § 48*a*.

When he comes: ሲመጣ፡ simḁ́ṭa (si̥m- § 7*d*).

When he came: በመጣ፡ጊዜ፡ bḁmḁ́ṭṭa gí̥zʸe.

When you clear the things away, leave this: እቃ፡ ስታነሣ፡ይህንን፡ተወው። i̥qa (§ 52*a*, δ) si̥ttānḁ́sa, yi̥hánnän tḁ́u͡ḁu͡.

Didn't you see it when you cleared the things away? እቃ፡ስታነሣ፡አላየሀውሞይ። i̥qa si̥ttānḁ́sa aláyyähḁu͡mmwi̥? (s.v. ወይ).

— before a negative verb use ብ- b(i̥)- pref. to cont. (§§ 37*c*, 45); tense is not distinguished.

When I am (was) not here: ተዚህ፡ያልኖር፡ tḁzzíh yālnʷór (§ 7*a*); [ሳልኖር፡ sālnʷór = before I am (was)].

— may be rendered by putting the verb of either the subordinate or the principal English clause into the gerund (cp. §§ 65*a*, 74) in Amharic.

When I have seen them I will come (back): ኣይ ቻቸው፡እመጣለሁ። a͡i̥ččáččḁ͡u i̥mḁṭállḁ͡u^{h}.

When cattle drink they walk into the water: ከብት፡ተውሃ፡ገብቶ፡ይጠጣል። kḁḟt (§ 52*a*, δ) tḁ͡uhá gḁ́ẏt^{w}o yi̥ṭḁ́ṭṭāl.

whence?, adv. ከዬት kḁyét?
ተዬት tḁyét?
See § 47*a*.

where (to)?, adv. ወዴት wωd^{y}ét?
ዬት yēt?

Where is he (it)? ዬት፡ነው። yēt nḁ͡u?

Where is he (it) to be found? ወዴት፡አለ። wωd^{y}ét állä?

Where has he (it) gone to? ዬት፡ሔደ። yēt hā́dä?

Where do you come from? ተዬት፡ትመጣለህ። tḁyét ti̥mḁṭálläh?

where, conj.—expressed by the relative (§§ 14, 62) and -ባት -bbḁt (= in it, § 47*a*); but, except after a negative, indirect questions may retain their direct form (§ 78).

Ask him where he (it) is: ያለባትን፡ጠይቀው። yallā́bbḁti̥n ṭḁ́yyi̥qḁ͡u, or ጠይቀው፡ዬት፡ነው። ṭḁ́yyi̥qḁ͡u yēt nḁ͡u.

Ask them where he (it) has gone to:
የሔደበትን፡ጠይቃቸው። yähädā́bbḁti̥n ṭḁyyi̥qáččḁ͡u, or
ጠይቃቸው፡ወዴት፡ሔደ። ṭḁyyi̥qáččḁ͡u wωd^{y}ét hā́dä.

Ask him where he (it) comes from:
እሚመጣበትን፡ጠይቀው። i̥mmimḁṭábbḁti̥n (i̥m-mi̥m- § 7*d*) ṭḁ́yyi̥qḁ͡u, or
ጠይቀው፡ተዬት፡ይመጣል። ṭḁ́yyi̥qḁ͡u tḁyét yi̥mḁ́ṭāl.

I don't know where he (it) is: ያለበትን፡አላውቅም። yallábbḁti̥n alá͡uqi̥m.

They don't know where he (it) has gone to: የሔደበትን፡አያውቁም። yähädábbḁti̥n a͡i̥á͡uqum.

He refused to say where he came from: የመጣበትን፡ አልናገርም፡አለ። yämḁṭṭábbḁti̥n ali̥nnággäri̥mm álḁ.

whether, conj. ብ- b(i̥)-, pref. to contingent (§ 45).

እንደሆን (i̥)ndḁhʷon (-däh-; § 8) q.v., following contingent or gerund.

I don't know whether you will return: ብትመለስ፡ አላውቅም። bi̥tti̥mmállḁs alá͡uqi̥m.

I must see whether I can find some: ባገኝ፡ልፈልግ። bāgắññ li̥fḁ́lli̥g.

I don't know whether I shall go: እሔድ፡እንደሆን፡ አላውቅም። i̥hắd í̥ndḁhʷon alá͡uqi̥m.

I don't know whether he went: ሔዶ፡እንደሆን፡አላውቅም። hi̥dʷóndḁhʷon alá͡uqi̥m.

Go and see whether dinner is ready: ሔድ፡እይ፡ እራት፡ተሰናድቶ፡እንደሆን። hi̥d īʿi̥rắt täsänādi̥tʷón-dḁhʷon (täsänārtʷóndḁhʷon § 7*d*).

See whether there is a hole (are any holes § 52*a*, δ) in it: መርምረው፡ቀዳዳ፡እንዳለበት። mắrmi̥ra͡u qḁ-dắda ndálläbbḁt.

Whether he comes or not, I shall go: የሚመጣ፡ ቢሆን፡የማይመጣ፡ቢሆን፡እሔዳለሁ። yämmi̥mḁ́ta yí̥-hʷon yämma͡i̥mḁ́ta yí̥hʷon, i̥hädálla͡uʰ.

See whether there is water or not: ውሃ፡መኖሩንና፡ ያለመኖሩን፡መርምር። wŭ́ha mḁnʷóruni̥nna (§§ 30, 72*a*) yālḁmḁnʷórun (§ 37*a*) mắrmi̥r.

whet-stone, s. መሳል mḁ́sāl (§ 8).

መሳያ mḁsā́yã (-ā́͡i̥ã).

ለሆቴ lḁ́hʷótʸe (§ 8).

which ?, inter. pron. ዬቱ፡ yḗtu ?, acc. ዬቱን yḗtun ?, f. ዬቷ፡ yḗtwā̃ ?, acc. ዬቷን yḗtwā̃n ?, pl. እኔቱ፡ (i̥)nnʸḗtu ?, acc. -ቱን -tun ?

ዬትኛው yḗti̥ññā̂u ?, acc. -ኛውን -ññā̂un ?, (§ 8), f. ዬትኛይቱ፡ yḗti̥ññā̂i̥tu ?, acc. -ቱን -tun ?, pl. ዬትኞቹ፡ yḗti̥ññṓčču ?, acc. -ቹን -ččun ?, or ዬትኞች yḗti̥ññōč ? (§ 8; -čč § 6), acc. ዬትኞችን yḗti̥ññṓčči̥n ?

(of two or more) ማናቸው mānnáč(č)ḁ̂u ?, acc. -ቸውን -č(č)ḁ̂un ?, f. ማናቿይቱ፡ mānnáč(č)ʷô̥i̥tu ?, acc. -ቱን -tun ?, pl. ማናቸዎች mānnáč(č)ḁ̂uʷōč (-ቿዎች -č(č)ʷoʷōč ?, -čč § 6), acc. -ችን -čči̥n ?

See § 15.

Which horse has he saddled ? ዬቱን፡ፈረስ፡ጫነ። yḗtun fḁ́rḁs ç̌ánḁ ?

In indirect questions the relative (§§ 14, 62) may be used (§ 78*a*, *b*):

Go and see which horse he has saddled: ዬቱን፡ ፈረስ፡ጫነው፡ሒድ፡እይ። yḗtun fḁ́rḁs ç̌ánḁ̂u hi̥d ī, or የጫነውን፡ፈረስ፡ሒደህ፡እይ። yäç̌ánḁ̂un fḁ́rḁs hí̥däh ī, (§§ 65*a*, 74*c*).

which, rel. pron. የ- yä- (q.v.) pref. to simple perfect.

የም- yämm(i̥)- [እም- (i̥)mm(i̥)-] pref. to contingent.

The above are nom. & acc., sg. & pl.; see §§ 14, 62.

The horse which was (has been) saddled is to come: የተጫነው፡ፈረስ፡ይምጣ። yätḁç̌ánḁ̂u fḁ́rḁs yí̥mṭa.

Let him bring the horse which was (has been) saddled: የተጫነውን፡ፈረስ፡ይዞ፡ይምጣ። yätḁč̣á-nḁ͡un fḁ́rḁs yı̥́zʷo yı̥́mṭa (s.v. ያዘ).

The horse which he (has) saddled is to come: የጫነው፡ፈረስ፡ይምጣ። yäč̣ánḁ͡u fḁ́rḁs yı̥́mṭa.

Let him bring the horse which he (has) saddled: የጫነውን፡ፈረስ፡ይዞ፡ይምጣ። yäč̣ánḁ͡un fḁ́rḁs yı̥́zʷo yı̥́mṭa (s.v. ያዘ).

Let the horse which is being saddled come: የሚጫነው፡ፈረስ፡ይምጣ። yämmič̣č̣ánḁ͡u (እሚጫነው፡ ı̥mmič̣č̣ánḁ͡u; -mı̥č̣- § 7*d*) fḁ́rḁs yı̥́mṭa.

I don't want the horse which he is saddling: የሚጭነውን፡ፈረስ፡አልፈልግም። yämmič̣ı̥́nḁ͡un (እሚጭነውን፡ ı̥mmič̣ı̥́nḁ͡un; -mı̥č̣- § 7*d*) fḁ́rḁs alfḁ́llı̥gı̥m.

Let the mules which I don't want go away: የማልፈልጋቸው፡በቅሎች፡ይሒዱ። yämmalfḁllı̥gáččḁ͡u bḁ́qlʷōč yı̥́hı̥du.

Take (pl.) away the mules which I do not want: እኔ፡እማልፈልጋቸውን፡በቅሎች፡ውሰዷቸው። ı̥nʸé mmal-fḁllı̥gáččḁ͡un bḁ́qlʷōč wŭsḁdwáččḁ͡u.

Where are the boxes which arrived yesterday? ትላንት፡የደረሱቱ፡ሳጥኖች፡ወዴት፡ናቸው። tı̥lánt yä-dḁ́rrḁsutu sáṭı̥nʷōč wωdʸét náččḁ͡u?

while, conj. ሲ- sı̥-, pref. to contingent (§ 45, § 48*a*).

ኢየ-[እየ-] ĭyyä- (q.v.), pref. to simple perfect.

Let them sit down while they wait: ሲቈዩ፡ይቀመጡ። siqwώyyu (sı̥q- § 7*d*) yı̥qqḁ́mḁṭu.

Let them sing while they work: ኢየሰሩ፡ይዝፈኑ። iyyäsḁ́rru yı̥́zfḁnu.

whip, s. (small) አለንጋ aláṅgā̃.

(large) ጅራፍ jı̥́ráf (§ 8).

(driving) መንጃ mḁ́njā̃.

whip, v.t. ገረፈ gḁ́rrḁfḁ (găr-).
Whip him (it): ግረፈው። gí̥rḁfa͡u.
Don't whip him (it): አትግረፈው። attí̥grḁfa͡u.
Did you whip him (it)? ገረፍሀው። gḁ́rrḁfha͡u?
whipped, be, v.p. ተገረፈ tḁgḁ́rrḁfḁ (-găr-).
He (it) has been whipped: ተገርፏል። tḁgắrfŏ͡āl, pl. ተገርፈዋል። tḁgắrfa͡uāl.
He (it) will be whipped: ይገረፋል። yi̥ggḁ́rrḁfāl, pl. ይገረፋሉ። yi̥ggḁrrḁfállu.
He (it) is to be whipped: ይገረፍ። yi̥ggḁ́rḁf, pl. -ፉ። -fu.
He (it) is not to be whipped: አይገረፍ። a͡i̥ggḁ́rḁf, pl. -ፉ። -fu.
whisper, v.i. & t. G. አንኰሻኰሽ ańkwωšákkwωšḁ.
Š. አንሾካሾከ anšʷokáššʷokḁ.
Whisper: G. አንኰሻኩሽ። ańkwωšăkwŭš.
Š. አንሾካሹክ። anšʷokăšŭk.
Don't whisper: G. አታንኰሻኩሽ። attańkwωšăkwŭš.
Š. አታንሾካሹክ። attanšʷokăšŭk.
He whispered this to me: ይህንን፡አንኰሻኩሾ፡[G.; አንሾካሽኮ፡ Š.] ነገረኝ። yi̥hắnnän ańkwωšăkwŭšʷo (G.; anšʷokăškʷo Š.) nḁggäräñ.
whistle, s. (sound) ፉጨት fúčät.
(instrument) መጥሪያ mḁ́ṭryã.
whistle, v.i. አፏጨ afwắččä.
Š. አፎጨ afŏččḁ.
G. አንፏጨ anfwắččä.
ፍዩ፡አለ fyū (fyūū) álḁ (s.v. √ባለ, § 44*a*).
Whistle: Š. አፎጭ። ắfočč, pl. አፎጩ። afóčču.
G. አንፏጭ። ắnfwāč, pl. አንፏጩ። anfwắču.

Don't whistle: Š. አታፎጭ። attáfoč̣č̣, pl. አታፎጩ። attāfóč̣č̣u.
G. አታንፏጭ። attáṅfwāč̣, pl. አታን ፏጩ። attānfwáč̣u.

white, adj. ነጭ nḁč̣č̣ (näč̣č̣).

White Nile, s. ነጭ፡አባይ፡ näč̣č̣ ábba͡i̥ (§ 8).

white, be (become), v.i. ነጣ nḁ́ṭṭã.

Whatever a black man may do he will never become white: ጥቁር፡አሥር፡ቢበላ፡አይነጣም። ṭṹqur ássi̥r yi̥yḁ́la a͡i̥náṭām [lit. if he should eat ten (men's food)].

white of eye, s. ዓይን፡ሞራ፡ á͡i̥nḁ (-nä; § 9) mʷórã (§ 52a, δ).

white-haired, adj. ሽበታም ši̥bḁ́tám (ši̥y-, -át-; § 8).

who?, inter. pron. sg. & pl. nom. ማን mān? (-nn § 6), acc. ማንን mánnän?, pl. also እነማን (i̥)nnḁ́mán? (እለማን i̥llḁ́mán?, § 8; -nn § 6), acc. እነማንን (i̥)nnḁmánnän? (እለማ- i̥llḁmá-).

Who came? ማን፡መጣ። mān mḁ́ṭṭa?, pl. እነማን፡መጡ። i̥nnḁmán mḁ́ṭṭu?

In indirect questions the relative (§§ 14, 62) may be used:

Did you see who came? የመጣን፡አየህ። yämḁ́ṭṭān áyyäh?, ... who (pl.) came? የመጡን፡... yämḁ́ṭṭun ...?

who, rel. pron. የ- yä- (q.v.) prefixed to simple perfect.
የም- yämm(i̥)- [እም- (i̥)mm(i̥)-] pref. to contingent.

The above are all numbers, genders, cases and persons; see §§ 14, 62.

The man who killed the soldier: ወታደሩን፡የገደለው፡ሰው፡ wωttáddarun yägḁ́ddalḁ͡u (§ 8) sḁ͡u.

The soldier who killed the man: ሰዉን፡የገደለው፡ ወታደር፡ sḁ́uun yägḁ́ddḁlḁ͡u wωttáddḁr.

The man whom the soldier killed: ወታደር፡የገደለው፡ ሰው፡ wωttáddḁr yägáddḁlḁ́u (§ 8) sḁ͡u.

The soldier whom the man killed: ሰው፡የገደለው፡ ወታደር፡ sḁ́͡u yägáddḁlḁ͡u wωttáddḁr.

Do you know the man who killed the soldier? ወታደሩን፡የገደለውን፡ሰው፡ታውቀዋለህ፡፡ wωttáddḁ-run yägáddḁlḁ́un (§ 8) sḁ͡u tá͡uŭqḁ͡uállăh?

Did you know the man whom the soldier killed? ወታደር፡የገደለውን፡ሰው፡ታውቀው፡ነበር፡፡ wωttáddḁr yägáddḁlḁ́un (§ 8) sḁ͡u tá͡uŭqḁ͡u nḁ́bbḁr? (§ 33*a*, *β*).

I who went did not see him (it): እኔ፡የሔድሁ፡አላየሁትም፡፡ ịnʸé yähádhwŭ aláyyähutịm, pl. እኛ፡ የሔድን፡አላየነውም፡፡ ịññá yähádnḁ aláyyänḁ͡um.

Sit down you who have come: አንተ፡የመጣህ፡ሰው፡ ተቀመጥ፡፡ ántḁ yämḁṭṭáh (§ 8) sḁ͡u tḁqḁ́mḁṭ, pl. እላ ንት፡የመጣችሁ፡ሰዎች፡ተቀመጡ፡፡ ịllánt yämḁṭṭáč-čyuh (§ 7*d*) sḁ͡uʷōč tḁqḁ́mḁṭu.

Come on, you who are coming! እምትመጣ፡ናኮ፡፡ ịmmịttịmḁ́ta nákkʷó! (s.v. እኮ), pl. እምትመጡ፡ ኑኮ፡፡ ịmmịttịmḁ́tu nŭkkʷó!

whole, s. ድሙር dịmmur (ድምር dịmmịr).
ጅምላ jịmlã.

why?, adv. (asking cause) ስለምን sịlḁ́mịn? (§ 8).
(asking object) ለምን lḁ́mịn? (§ 8).
(expressing surprise or annoyance) ምን፡ ነው፡፡ [ምነው፡፡] mịnnḁ͡u?
See §§ 15, 47*a*, 78*a*.

Why did you do it? ለምን፡አደረግሀው፡፡ lḁmịn adḁ́r-rḁghḁ͡u? (-ግኸው፡፡ -gχḁ͡u, -kkḁ͡u § 7*d*).

Ask him why he did it: ጠይቀው፡ለምን፡አደረገው። ṭḁ́yyi̥qḁ͡u lḁmí̥n adḁ́rrḁgḁ͡u.

I don't know why he did it: አላውቅም፡ለምን፡አደ ረገው። alá͡uŭqi̥m lḁmí̥n adḁ́rrḁgḁ͡u.

Or ምን mi̥n may be the object of the gerund of አለ ā́lḁ (s.v. √በለ, § 44*a*):

Why should I do it? ምን፡ብዬ፡ላድርገው። mi̥n bíyye ládri̥gḁ͡u?, pl. ምን፡ብለን፡እናድርገው። mi̥n bí̥lḁn i̥nnádri̥gḁ͡u?, (§ 27).

Why should he go? ምን፡ብሎ፡ይሒድ። mi̥n bí̥lʷo yí̥hi̥d?, pol. & pl. ምን፡ብለው፡ይሒዱ። mi̥n bí̥lḁ͡u yí̥hi̥du?

why!, interj. (advancing reason) -ማ -mmā̃ (§ 8).

(expressing surprise) አረ ḁ́rḁ!

A child couldn't do it: but he, why, he's a man! ልጅ፡አይችለውም፤እርሱማ፡ትልቅ፡ነው። li̥j a͡i̥čí̥lḁ͡um: i̥rsúmmā ti̥llí̥q (§ 8) nḁ͡u!

Why, I never saw him (it)! አረ፡አላየሁትም። ḁ́rḁ, aláyyähuti̥m!

Why, you've had a wash! አረ፡ታጥበሃል። ḁ́rḁ, tā́ṭyḁhāl!

wick, s. ክር ki̥rr.

wicked, adj. ክፉ kí̥fu (kúfu, kŭ́fu, § 7*d*).

wicked, be (become), v.i. ከፋ kḁ́ffā̃ (§ 63*d, e*).

wickedness, s. ክፋት kí̥fā́t (kúf-, kŭ́f- § 7*d*; § 8).

wicker-work bag, s. አኰፋዳ akʷofā́dā̃.

wide, adj. ሰፊ sḁ́ffi.

ወርዳም wḁ́rdā́m (wώr- § 7*d*; § 8).

wide, be (become), v.i. ሰፋ sḁ́ffā̃.

It is (too) wide: ይሰፋል። yi̥sḁ́fāl, pl. ይሰፋሉ። yi̥sḁfállu.

It is not wide (enough): አይሰፋም። ḁisḁfām, pl. -ፉም። -fúm.

widen, v.t. አሰፋ asḁffā.

Widen it: አስፋው። ásfa͡u, pl. አስፉት። ásfut.

Don't widen it: አታስፋው። attásfa͡u, pl. -ፉት። -fut.

width, s. ወርድ wḁrd (wωrd § 7*d*).

ስፋት si̥fát (§ 8).

What is its width? ወርዱ፡ስንት፡ነው። wωrdu si̥ntı̥ nḁ͡u?

What is, roughly, the width of the river? ወንዝ፡ ስፋቱ፡ምን፡ያህል፡ነው። wωnz si̥fátu mi̥n yahl nḁ͡u?

wife, s. G. ምሽት mi̥št.

Š. ምስት mi̥st.

Is it his wife? G. ምሽቱ፡ናት። mi̥štu nāt?

Š. ምስቱ፡ነች። mi̥stu näč?

wild, adj. የበረሃ yäbḁrḁhā (yäyḁ-; § 47*a*; = of the country).

Wild beast: አርዌ á͡urʸe (§ 7*d*), pl. አራዊት aráwít (§ 8), see § 52*a*, δ.

wild dog, s. ተኩላ tḁkwúlā (§§ 8, 52*a*, δ).

wild fig, s. (*Ficus sycomorus*, Broun, Cat. 533) ባምባ bámbā.

(*Ficus vasta*) ወርካ wḁrkā (wωr-, ዋር- wár-).

(*Ficus sp.*) ሾላ šʷólā.

win, v.i. & t. (game, case) [እ]ረታ (i̥)rḁttā.

(battle) ድል፡አደረገ di̥l adárrḁgḁ.

ድል፡ነሣ di̥l nḁssā.

I won two dollars from him over a bet: በሁለት፡ብር፡ ተወራርጄ፡ረታሁት። bḁhulátti̥ yi̥rr tḁ͡uωrári̥jjʸe rḁttahut.

He won his case in court: በወምበር፡ፊት፡ረታ። bḁ͡uωmbḁr (§ 8) fi̥t rḁtta.

Winchester rifle, s. ወሻሽተር wḁšáštär.

wind, s. ንፋስ n̥fás (§ 8).

Violent wind: አውሎ፡ a͡ulʷo.

wind, v.i. (wind oneself, v.r.) ተጠመጠመ ṭḁṭḁmḁ́ṭṭḁmḁ, round, በ- bḁ- (ṿḁ-; § 47*a*).

It winds round it: ይጠመጠምበታል። yi̥ṭṭḁmḁṭṭḁmí̥bbḁtāl, pl. ይጠመጠሙበታል። yi̥ṭṭḁmḁṭṭḁmúbbḁtāl.

wind, v.t. ጠመጠመ ṭḁmḁ́ṭṭḁmḁ, round, በ- bḁ- (ṿḁ-; § 47*a*).

Wind it (them § 61*a*) round him (it; them § 52*a*, δ): ጠምጥምበት። ṭḁ́mṭi̥mi̥bbḁt, pl. ጠምጥሙበት። ṭḁmṭi̥mubbḁt.

Wind it round your arm: በክንድህ፡ ጠምጥመው። bḁkí̥ndi̥h ṭḁ́mṭi̥ma͡u.

wind, break, v.i. (of persons) ቁቅ፡ አለ quqq álḁ.
(of animals) ጣጣ፡ አለ ṭáṭṭa álḁ.
S.v. √ባለ, § 44*a*.

wind (up), v.t. (clock, etc.) መላ mḁ́llã.
ሞላ mʷóllã.

Wind it up: ምላው። mi̥la͡u.
ሙላው። mŭla͡u.

Don't wind it up: አትምላው። atti̥mla͡u.
አትሙላው። atti̥mŭla͡u.

Wind up the clock (watch): ሰዓቱን፡ ምላው። sḁa͡tun mi̥la͡u.

Don't you wind it up, bring it to me: አንተ፡ አት ምላው፤ ለኔ፡ አምጣ። ántä atti̥mla͡u, lḁnʸé ánṭa (§ 7*d*).

window, s. መስኮት mḁ́skʷot (§ 52*a*, δ).

wine, s. ጠጅ ṭḁjj (ṭäjj).

wink, s. ጥቅሻ ṭí̥q(i̥š)šã.

wink, v.i. ጠቀሰ ṭḁ́qqḁsḁ.

wipe, v.t. አበሰ ábbḁsḁ.
ወለወለ wḁlá͡uwḁlḁ.

Wipe it: እበሰው። i̥y̥ḁsḁ͡u.
አብሰው። ábbi̥sḁ͡u.
ወልውለው። wḁlwŭlḁ͡u.

Don't wipe it with this (that): በዚህ፡ አትበሰው። bäz-zi̥h atti̥y̥ḁsḁ͡u (… አታብሰው። … attábbi̥sḁ͡u, … አትወልውለው። … atti̥wḁlwŭlḁ͡u).

wiped, be, v.p. ታበሰ tā́bbḁsḁ.
ተወለወለ tḁwḁlḁ͡uwḁlḁ (tḁ͡uḁ-).

It must be wiped: ይታበስ። yi̥ttáy̥ḁs, pl. -በሱ። -y̥ḁsu.
ይወልወል። yi̥wwḁ́lwḁl, pl. -ወሉ። -wḁlu.

wire, s. ሽቦ ší̥bʷo (ší̥y̥ʷo).
†ሲልክ si̥lk.
†ሲልኪ si̥lkī (Tña.).

wisdom, s. ጥበብ ṭí̥bḁb (ṭí̥y̥ḁy̥).

wise, adj. ጥበበኛ ṭi̥bḁbḁ́ññã (ṭi̥y̥ḁy̥-, -áñ-).
አዋቂ ãwáqi (a͡uá-).

wise, be, v.i. ተጠበበ tḁṭḁ́bbḁbḁ (-ḁy̥ḁ).

wish, s. ምኞት mí̥ññot (§ 8).
ፍቃድ fí̥qād („).

wish, v.i. & t. ፈለገ fḁ́llḁgḁ.
ፈቀደ fḁ́qqḁdḁ.

Do you wish to? ትፈልጋለህ። ti̥fḁlli̥gállah?, pol. ይፈልጋሉ። yi̥fḁlli̥gállu?, pl. ትፈልጋላችሁ። ti̥fḁlli̥gal-lā́ččyuh? (§ 7*d*).

Don't you wish to? አትፈልግም። atti̥fḁ́lli̥gi̥m?, pol. አይፈልጉም። a͡i̥fḁ́lli̥gum?, pl. አትፈልጉም። atti̥fḁ́l-li̥gum?

As you wish: እንደፍቃድህ። ndäfi̥qādi̥h, pol. እንደፍቃደዎ። ndäfi̥qādḁ͡ʷo (§ 12*b*).

If you wish (it): ብትፈልግ፡ bi̥tti̥fḁ́lli̥g, pol. ቢፈልጉ፡ bifḁ́lli̥gu (bi̥f- § 7*d*).

I wish to see him (it): ላየው፡እፈልጋለኹ። lá͡i̥ḁ͡u i̥fḁl-li̥gállḁ͡u[h] (§ 7*d*), pl. ልናየው፡እንፈልጋለን። li̥nná͡i̥ḁ͡u nni̥fḁlli̥gállän.

I wish to go: ልሔድ፡እፈልጋለኹ። li̥hā́d i̥fḁlli̥gállḁu[h], pl. ልንሔድ፡እንፈልጋለን። li̥nnhā́d i̥nni̥fḁlli̥gállän.

I do wish we had gone! ወዮ፡በሔድን። wωyyṓ ṿḁ-hā́dnḁ!

witch, s. ቡዳ búdā̃.

አስማተኛ asmātḁñña̋ (-tā́ñ-).

with, prp. (accompanying) ከ-[ተ-]...፡ ጋር kḁ-(tḁ-)...gār (ጋራ gárā̃; § 8; § 47*b*).

ከ-[ተ-]...፡ ዘንድ kḁ- (tḁ-) ... zḁnd (§ 47*b*).

አብሮ ā́br[w]o (ā́ṿr-; ger. § 34) with pers. suff. § 12*c*.

He is to go with me: ተኔ፡ጋር፡ይሔድ። tḁn[y]é gār yi̥hi̥d, pl. ... ይሔዱ። ... yi̥hi̥du.

Did he come with him? አብሮት፡መጣ። ā́ṿr[w]ot mḁ́ṭ-ṭā?, f. አብራው፡መጣች። ā́ṿra͡u mḁ́ṭṭāč?, pol. & pl. አብረውት፡መጡ። ā́ṿrḁ͡ut mḁ́ṭṭu?

Did he come with her? አብሯት፡መጣ። ā́ṿrŏ͡āt mḁ́ṭṭa?, f. አብራት፡መጣች። ā́ṿrāt mḁ́ṭṭāč?, pol. & pl. አብረዋት፡መጡ። ā́ṿrḁ͡uāt mḁ́ṭṭu?

Did he come with them (him, pol.)? አብሯቸው፡መጣ። āṿrŏ͡áččḁ͡u mḁ́ṭṭa?, f. አብራቸው፡መጣች። āṿráččḁ͡u mḁ́ṭṭāč?, pol. & pl. አብረዋቸው፡መጡ። āṿrḁ͡uáččḁ͡u mḁ́ṭṭu?

Did he come with you? አብሮህ፡መጣ። ā́ṿr[w]oh mḁ́ṭṭa?, f. አብራህ፡መጣች። ā́ṿrāh mḁ́ṭṭāč?, pol. & pl. አብረውህ፡መጡ። ā́ṿrḁ͡uh mḁ́ṭṭu?

Did he come with you (f.)? አብሮሽ፡መጣ። ā́ṿrʷoš mḁ́ṭṭa?, f. አብራሽ፡መጣች። ā́ṿrāš mḁ́ṭṭāč?, pol. & pl. አብረውሽ፡መጡ። ā́ṿrḁ͡uš mḁ́ṭṭu?

Did he come with you (pol.)? አብሮዎት፡መጣ። ā́ṿ-rʷo͡ʷot mḁ́ṭṭa?, f. አብራዎ፡መጣች። ā́ṿra͡ʷo mḁ́ṭṭāč?, pol. & pl. አብረውዎት፡መጡ። ā́ṿrḁ͡uʷot mḁ́ṭṭu?

Did he come with you (pl.)? አብሯችሁ፡መጣ። āṿ-r͡ŏā́ččyuh (§ 7*d*) mḁ́ṭṭa?, f. አብራችሁ፡መጣች። āṿrā́č-čyuh mḁ́ṭṭāč?, pol. & pl. አብረዋችሁ፡መጡ። āṿrḁ͡u-ā́ččyuh mḁ́ṭṭu?

He came with me: አብሮኝ፡መጣ። ā́ṿrʷoñ mḁ́ṭṭa, f. አብራኝ፡መጣች። ā́ṿrāñ mḁ́ṭṭāč, pol. & pl. አብረውኝ፡መጡ። ā́ṿrḁ͡uñ mḁ́ṭṭu.

He came with us: አብሮን፡መጣ። ā́ṿrʷon mḁ́ṭṭa, f. አብራን፡መጣች። ā́ṿrān mḁ́ṭṭāč, pol. & pl. አብረውን፡መጡ። ā́ṿrḁ͡un mḁ́ṭṭu.

Did you come with him? አብረሀው፡መጣህ። ā́ṿrḁhḁ͡u mḁ́ṭṭāh?, f. አብረሽው፡መጣሽ። ā́ṿräšyu mḁ́ṭṭāš?, pol. አብረውት፡መጡ። ā́ṿrḁ͡ut mḁ́ṭṭu?, pl. አብራችሁት፡መጣችሁ። āṿrā́ččᵢ̥hut mḁṭṭā́ččyuh? (§ 7*d*).

Did you come with her? አብረሃት፡መጣህ። ā́ṿrḁhāt mḁ́ṭṭāh?, f. አብረሻት፡መጣሽ። ā́ṿräšāt mḁ́ṭṭāš?, pol. አብረዋት፡መጡ። ā́ṿrḁ͡uāt mḁ́ṭṭu?, pl. አብራችኋት፡መጣችሁ። āṿrā́ččyuhāt (§ 7*d*) mḁṭṭā́ččyuh?

Did you come with them (him, pol.)? አብረሃቸው፡መጣህ። āṿrḁhā́ččḁ͡u mḁ́ṭṭāh?, f. አብረሻቸው፡መጣሽ። āṿräšā́ččḁ͡u mḁ́ṭṭāš?, pol. አብረዋቸው፡መጡ። āṿrḁ͡u-ā́ččḁ͡u mḁ́ṭṭu?, pl. አብራችኋቸው፡መጣችሁ። āṿrāč-čyuhā́ččḁ͡u (§ 7*d*) mḁṭṭā́ččyuh?

If you come with me: አብረሀኝ፡ብትመጣ፡ ā́ṿrḁhäñ bi̥tti̥mḁ́ṭa, f. አብረሽኝ፡ብትመጪ፡ ā́ṿräši̥ñ bi̥tti̥mḁ́č̣, pol. አብረውኝ፡ቢመጡ፡ ā́ṿrḁ͡uñ bimḁ́ṭu, pl. አብራችሁኝ፡ብትመጡ፡ āṿrā́ččᵢ̥huñ bi̥tti̥mḁ́ṭu.

If you come with us: አብረሀን፡ብትመጣ፡ áỵrḁhän bi̥tti̥mḁ́ṭa, f. አብረሽን፡ብትመጪ፡ áỵräši̥n bi̥tti̥mḁ́č̣, pol. አብረውን፡ቢመጡ፡ áỵrḁ͡un bimḁ́ṭu, pl. አብራችሁን፡ብትመጡ፡ āỵráčči̥hun bi̥tti̥mḁ́ṭu.

I will go with him: አብሬው፡እሔዳለኍ። āỵí̥rrʸe͡u i̥hädállḁ͡uʰ (§ 7*d*), pl. አብረነው፡እንሔዳለን። áỵrḁnḁ͡u nni̥hädállän.

I will go with her: አብሯት፡እሔዳለኍ። āỵí̥rryāt i̥hädállḁ͡uʰ, pl. አብረናት፡እንሔዳለን። áỵrḁnāt i̥nni̥hädállän.

I will go with them (him, pol.): አብሯቸው፡እሔዳለኍ። āỵi̥rryáččḁ͡u i̥hädállḁ͡uʰ, pl. አብረናቸው፡እንሔዳለን። āỵrḁnáččḁ͡u nni̥hädállän.

I will go with you: አብሬህ፡እሔዳለኍ። áỵi̥rrʸeh i̥hädállḁ͡uʰ, pl. አብረንህ፡እንሔዳለን። áỵräni̥h i̥nni̥hädállän.

I will go with you (f.): አብሬሽ፡እሔዳለኍ። áỵi̥rrʸeš i̥hädállḁ͡uʰ, pl. አብረንሽ፡እንሔዳለን። áỵräni̥š i̥nni̥hädállän.

I will go with you (pol.): አብሬዎ፡እሔዳለኍ። āỵí̥rrʸe͡ʷo i̥hädállḁ͡uʰ, pl. አብረነዎ፡እንሔዳለን። áỵrḁnḁ͡ʷo nni̥hädállän.

I will go with you (pl.): አብሯችሁ፡እሔዳለኍ። āỵi̥rryáččyuh (§ 7*d*) i̥hädállḁ͡uʰ, pl. አብረናችሁ፡እንሔዳለን። āỵrḁnáččyuh i̥nni̥hädállän.

(possessing) ባለ- bālḁ- (§ 9*d*).

The man with the tent: ባለድንኳን፡ bālḁdű́nkwān.

The woman with the sunshade: ባለጥላ፡ሴት፡ bālḁṭi̥lá (§ 8) sʸēt.

(by means of) በ- bḁ- (ỵḁ-; § 47*a*).

gerund of ያዘ yázḁ (§ 44*c*).

What does he sew it with? በምን፡ይሰፋዋል። bḁmí̥n yi̥sḁ́fa͡uāl?

What does he sew with it? ምን፡ይሰፋበታል። mi̥n yi̥sḁfábbḁtāl?

Cut it with a knife: ካራ፡ይዘህ፡ቍረጠው። kárra yí̥zäh (λαβών) qwŭ́rḁṭḁ͡u.

(manner) gerund, especially of compounds of አለ (s.v. √በለ, § 44*a*).

The gun burst with a bang: ጠበንጃ፡ጓ፡ብሎ፡ፈነዳ። ṭḁyḁ́nja gwā yi̥l^{w}o fḁnḁ́dda.

Do it with great care: በጣም፡ዝግ፡ብለህ፡አድርገው። bḁṭḁ́m zí̥ggi̥ yi̥läh ádri̥gḁ͡u (ắrgḁ͡u § 7*d*).

withdraw, v.i. (oneself, v.r.) ሔደ hắdä.

ወጣ wώṭṭā̃.

ወገደ wώggḁdḁ.

He refused to withdraw: አልሔድም፡አለ። alhắdi̥mm ắlḁ, pl. አንሔድም፡አሉ። annhắdi̥mm ắlu, (s.v. √በለ).

withdraw, v.t. ወሰደ wḁ́ssḁdḁ (wώs-).

አነሣ anḁ́ssā̃.

withdrawn, be, v.p. ተወሰደ tḁwḁ́ssḁdḁ (tḁ͡uḁ́-, -ώs-).

ተነሣ tḁnḁ́ssā̃.

wither, v.i. ደረቀ dḁ́rrḁqḁ.

withered, adj. ደረቅ dḁ́rḁq.

(paralysed) በድን bḁ́di̥n (bắd-; -nn § 6).

withers, s. መጋፍያ mḁgắfyā̃ (§ 52*a*, γ).

within, prp. (of space) በ-...፡ውስጥ bḁ- (yḁ-, ከ- kḁ-, ተ- tḁ-) ... wŭ́sṭ.

ከ-...፡በውስጥ kḁ-(ተ-tḁ-)... bḁ́wŭ́sṭ (yḁ́-, -ḁ́͡uŭ́-; § 8).

በ-...፡ግቢ bḁ-(yḁ-) ... gí̥bbi.

(of time and distance) ከ-[ተ-]...፡ወዲህ kḁ-(tḁ-)... wώdíh (-dí̥h; § 8).

See § 47*b*.

Within the house: ተቤት፡ውስጥ፡ tḁy̥ʸét wŭsṭ.

Within half an hour: ተኩል፡ሰዓት፡ወዲህ፡ tḁ́kkul sḁ͡āt wώdih.

without, prp. ያለ- yālḁ-.

G. አለ- ālḁ-.

የሌለበት yälʸálläbbḁt (§§ 39, 62).

See § 47*a*.

Don't go without him: ያለርሱ፡አትሒድ። yālärsú attḭhḭd, pl. -ዱ። -du.

I am not going without you: ያላንተ፡አልሔድም። yālā́ntä alhā́di̥m, pl. ... አንሔድም። ... annhā́di̥m.

A house without windows: መስኮት፡የሌለበት፡ቤት፡ mḁskʷót (§ 52*a*, δ) yälʸálläbbḁ́t (§ 8) y̥ʸēt.

In a house without windows: መስኮት፡በሌለበት፡ቤት፡ mḁskʷót y̥ḁlʸálläbbḁ́t y̥ʸēt.

witness, s. ምስክር mi̥sí̥kki̥r.

Have you got witnesses? ምስክሮች፡አሉህ። mi̥sí̥kki̥rʷōčč álluh?

witness, bear, v.i. መሰከረ mḁsḁ́kkḁrḁ (-kärḁ),

for: ለ- lḁ-.

against: በ- bḁ- (y̥ḁ-).

See §§ 47*a*, 71.

witty, adj. ቧልተኛ bwāltḁ́ññā̃ (-tā́ñ-).

wizard, s. ቡዳ búdā̃.

አስማተኛ asmātḁ́ññā̃ (-tā́ñ-).

woman, s. ሴት sʸēt.

— may be expressed by using the feminine:

That is a pretty woman: ያች፡ውብ፡ናት። yāč wŭy̥ nāt.

Young woman: ቈንጆ qwώnjʷo, pl. also ቈናጅቶች qwωnā́ji̥tʷōč (-čč § 6), ቈነጃጅቶች qwωnḁjā́ji̥tʷōč (-čč § 6).

Middle-aged or oldish woman: ባልቴት báltʸét (§ 8).

womb, s. ማሕጠን máh(ᵢ̥)ṭḁn.
ማጠን mắṭḁn.
wonder, s. (-ful, adj.) ድንቅ di̥ṅq.
ታሪክ tắrīk (-ri̥k).
I think it wonderful: ደነቀኝ። dḁ́nnḁqäñ.
wonder, v.i. ደነቀው dḁ́nnḁqa͡u (impers. § 43*a*; § 63*d*, *e*).
wonderful, adj. ግሩም gi̥rum.
It is wonderful: ግሩም፡ነው። gi̥rúm (§ 8) na͡u.
wonderful, be, v.i. ደነቀ dḁ́nnḁqḁ.
wood, s. (substance) እንጨት (i̥)nč̣ʸet [-ጨት -č̣ät].
(forest) ውድማ wŭ́dmā̃.
ዱር dūr.
It is made of wood: የንጨት፡ነው። yänč̣ʸét (§§ 47*a*, 7*a*, 8) na͡u.
woof, s. ፈትል fḁti̥l (fắt-).
wool, s. የበግ፡ጠጕር yäbḁ́g (-äyḁ́-; §§ 47*a*, 70) ṭḁgwŭr.
woollen cloth, s. ማቅ māq.
word, s. ነገር nḁ́gḁr (-gär).
ቃል qāl.
See § 52*a*, δ.
work, s. ሥራ si̥rā̃.
(employment) ተግባር tḁ́gbắr (-gyắr; § 8).
The work is not finished: ሥራ፡አልፈታም። si̥ra alfḁ́ttām, or ሥራ፡አልተፈታም። si̥ra altḁfḁ́ttām.
Has he got work? ተግባር፡አለው። tḁgyắr álla͡u?
Hard work: ትግልት፡ ti̥gi̥lt (§ 8).
It needs hard work: በትግልት፡ነው። bḁti̥gi̥lti̥ (§ 7*d*) na͡u.
work, v.i. & t. ሰራ sḁ́rrā̃ (sắr-).
He works: ይሰራል። yi̥sḁ́rāl, f. ትሰራለች። ti̥sḁrálläč, pol. & pl. ይሰራሉ። yi̥sḁrállu.

He doesn't work: አይሰራም። ḁ͡isḁ́rām, f. አትሰራም። atti̥sḁ́rām, pol. & pl. አይሰሩም። ḁ͡isḁ́rum.

He has worked well: መልከም፡ሰርቷል። mḁlkám sắr-tŏ͡āl, f. ... ሰርታለች። ... särtálläč, pl. ... ሰርተዋል። ...sắrtḁ͡uāl.

He has not worked well: መልከም፡አልሰራም። mḁl-kắm alsḁ́rrām, f. ... አልሰራችም። ... alsḁ́rrāčči̥m, pl. ... አልሰሩም። ... alsḁ́rrum.

They will not work by the day but by the piece: በቀን፡አይሰሩም፤በውል፡ነው፡እንጂ። bḁqḁ́n ḁ͡isắrum, bḁ͡úl nḁ͡unjí.

I can't work until (unless) that noise stops: ይህ፡ጩኸት፡ዝም፡እስቲል፡ስራ፡አይቻለኝም። yi̥he čúhḁt zi̥mm i̥sti̥l sɨ́ra ḁ͡iččáläññi̥m.

work for, v.t. አገለገለ agḁlḁ́ggḁlḁ.

How many years have you worked for him? ስንት፡ዓመት፡አገለገልሀው። si̥nt ắmḁt agḁlḁ́ggḁlhḁ͡u?, ... him (pol.)? ... አገለገልሃቸው። agḁlḁggḁlháččḁ͡u?

work hard, v.i. ታገለ tắggḁlḁ.

He works hard: ይታገላል። yi̥ttággḁlāl, pl. ይታገላሉ። yi̥ttaggḁlállu.

He doesn't work hard: አይታገልም። ḁ͡ittággḁli̥m, pl. -ሉም። -lum.

workman, s. ሰራተኛ sḁrrātḁ́ññā̃ (sär-, -tắñ-).

world, s. ዓለም ắlḁm.

worm, s. ትል ti̥l (§ 52*a*, δ), usually f. (§ 54*c*).

worn, be, v.p. ተለበሰ tḁlḁ́bbḁsḁ.

How is it (are they § 52*a*, δ) worn? እንዴት፡ይለበሳል። ndʸét yi̥llḁ́bbḁsāl?

It is (they are § 52*a*, δ) not worn: አይለበስም። ḁ͡illḁ́b-bḁsi̥m.

worn out, adj. (of inanimate objects) ውራጅ wǘrrắj (§ 8).

These clothes are worn out: ይህ፡ልብስ፡ውራጅ፡ነው። yi̥he li̥ys (§ 52a, δ) wǘrrắj na͡u̥.

worn out, be (become), v.i.

(of animate objects) ደከመ dắkkḁmḁ.

ደከመው dắkkḁma͡u̥ (impers. § 43a).

(of inanimate objects) አለቀ állа̥qḁ.

See § 63d, e.

It is worn out: አልቋል። álqŏāl, pl. አልቀዋል። álqa͡ūāl.

He (it) is worn (tired) out: ደክሞታል። dắki̥mʷotāl, f. ደክሟታል። dắki̥mŏātāl, pol. & pl. ደክሟቸዋል። dăki̥mŏắčča͡ūāl.

He (it) is old and worn out: አረጀ፡አበቃ። arắjjä, ayа̥́qqa (§ 74c).

I am worn out: ደክሞኛል። dắki̥mʷoññāl, pl. ደክሞናል። dắki̥mʷonnāl.

worried, be, v.i. & p. (troubled) ቸገረው čắggḁra͡u̥ (-gär-; impers. § 43a; § 63d, e).

I am worried: ቸገረኝ። čắggäräñ, pl. -ረን። -rän.

worry, s. ችጋር či̥ggắr (§ 8).

worry, v.t. (trouble) አስቸገረ asčắggḁrḁ (-gärḁ).

(pester) ነዘነዘ nḁzа̥́nnḁzḁ.

Don't worry me: አታስቸግረኝ። attāsčắggi̥räñ, pl. -ሩኝ። -ruñ.

አትነዝንዘኝ። atti̥nḁ́zni̥zäñ, pl. -ዙኝ። -zuñ.

Don't worry us: አታስቸግረን። attāsčắggi̥rän, pl. -ሩን። -run.

አትነዝንዘን። atti̥nḁ́zni̥zän, pl. -ዙን። -zun.

He (it) worries me: ያስቸግረኛል። yāsčággi̥räññāl,
pl. -ሩኛል። -ruññāl.
ይነዘንዘኛል። yi̥nḁzḁ́nni̥zäññāl,
pl. -ዙኛል። -zuññāl.

He (it) worries us: ያስቸግረናል። yāsčággi̥rännāl,
pl. -ሩናል። -runnāl.
ይነዘንዘናል። yi̥nḁzḁ́nni̥zännāl,
pl. -ዙናል። -zunnāl.

worse, be, v.i. ከፋ kḁ́ffã (§ 63*d, e*), than, ከ- kḁ-, ተ- tḁ- (§ 58*b*).

He (it) is worse: ከፍቷል። kḁ́fto͡āl, pl. -ተዋል። -tḁu͡āl.

worship, v.i. & t. ሰገደ sḁ́ggḁdḁ (sḁ́ggädḁ).

worth, be, v.i. አከለ ákkḁlḁ (q.v.).

What is this worth? ይህ፡ምን፡ያህላል። yi̥he mi̥n yáhlāl? (Š. ያክላል። yákki̥lāl), pl. እነዚህ፡ምን፡ያህላሉ። nnäzzíh mi̥n yahlállu? (Š. ያክላሉ። yakki̥lállu).

It isn't worth that: ይህንን፡አያህልም። yi̥hánnän a͡yáhli̥m (Š. አያክልም። a͡yákki̥li̥m), pl. -ሉም። -lum.

It is worth half a dollar: የቡር፡እኩል፡ያህላል። yäṿi̥rr ŭ́kkul yáhlāl (Š. ያክላል። yákki̥lāl).

would, v.aux. see § 81*c, d*.

It would be splendid: ድንቅ፡ነበር። di̥nq nḁ́bbär.

wound, s. ቍስል qwúsi̥l.

wound, v.t. (tearing) አቈሰለ aqwώssḁlḁ.
(penetrating) ወጋ wώggã (wώg-).

Did you wound him (it)? አቈሰልሀው። aqwώssḁlhḁ͡u?
ወጋሀው። wώggahḁ͡u?

He (it) wounded me: አቈሰለኝ። aqwώssḁlḁñ.
ወጋኝ። wώggāñ.

He (it) didn't wound me: አላቈሰለኝም። alaqwώssḁläññi̥m.
አልወጋኝም። alwώggaññi̥m.

wound, be, v.p. ተጠመጠመ tḁṭḁmḁ́ṭṭḁmḁ, round, በ- bḁ-(yḁ-; § 47*a*).

It is (has been) wound round it: ተጠምጥሞበታል። tḁṭḁmṭi̥mʷóbbḁtāl, pl. ተጠምጥመውበታል። tḁṭḁmṭi̥mḁ͡úbbḁtāl.

wound (up), be, v.i. & p. (of clock, etc.) መላ mḁllā̃.
ሞላ mʷóllā̃.

Is it (has it been) wound up? መልቷል። mḁltŏ͡āl?
ሞልቷል። mʷóltŏ͡āl?

wounded, adj. ቊስለኛ qwŭslḁ́ñña̋ (-láñ-).

wounded, be, v.i. & p. (torn) ቈሰለ qwώssḁlḁ.
(penetrated) ተወጋ tḁwώggā̃ (tḁ͡ŭώ-).
See § 63*d*, *e*.

Are you wounded? ተወግተሃል። tḁ͡ŭώgtähāl?

Where are you wounded? ተምንህ፡ቈሰልህ። tḁmí̥ni̥h (§§ 47*a*, 15) qwώssḁlh?

woven, be, v.p. ተፈተለ tḁfḁ́ttḁlḁ (-fättälḁ).

wrap, v.t. (roll up) ጠቀለለ ṭḁqḁ́llḁlḁ.
(cover) ሸፈነ šḁ́ffḁnḁ (šäf-).

Wrap it up in a cloth: በጨርቅ፡ጠቅልለው። bḁčärq ṭáqli̥lḁ͡ŭ.
በጨርቅ፡ሽፍነው። bḁčärq šäffi̥nḁ͡ŭ.

wrapped, be, v.p. (rolled up) ተጠቀለለ tḁṭḁqḁ́llḁlḁ.
(wrap oneself, v.r.) ተሸፈነ tḁšḁ́ffḁnḁ (täšäf-).

It is to be wrapped in a cloth:
በጨርቅ፡ይጠቀለል። bḁčärq yi̥ṭṭḁ́qlḁl.
በጨርቅ፡ይሸፈን። bḁčärq yi̥ššáfḁn.

wrapping-cloth, s. መጠቅለያ mḁṭḁqlḁ́yā̃ (-ṭäq-, -ḁ͡i̥ā̃).

wrestle, v.i. ታገለ tággalḁ.

wrestling, s. ትግል tí̥gi̥l.

wretched, adj. (of persons) ችጋረኛ či̥ggārḁ́ñña͂ (-ra͂́ñ-).
(of animals and inanimate objects) ግም gi̥m.

wring (out), v.t. ጠመቀ ṭḁ́mmḁqḁ.

Wring it out: ጥመቀው። ṭi̥mḁqḁ͡u.

wrist, s. መለያ mḁllḁ́yyā.
የጅ፡አንገት yäjj (§ 70) áṅgḁt (-gät).
See § 52*a*, *γ*.

On his wrist(s): በጁ፡አንገት፡ báj̲ju áṅgät.

write, v.i. & t. ጣፈ ṭā́fḁ.
G. ጸፈ ṣā́fḁ.

I will write: እጥፋለኍ። i̥ṭi̥fállḁ͡u^{h} (§ 7*d*).
G. እጽፋለኍ። i̥ṣi̥fállḁ͡u^{h}.

I will write it: እጥፈዋለኍ። i̥ṭi̥fḁ͡uállḁ͡u^{h}.

I will write to him: እጥፍለታለኍ። i̥ṭi̥fi̥llḁtállḁ͡u^{h} (§ 47*a*).

I will write to them (him, pol.): እጥፍላቸዋለኍ። i̥ṭi̥fi̥llāččḁ͡uállḁ͡u^{h}.

I will write to you: እጥፍልሃለኍ። i̥ṭi̥fi̥lli̥hállḁ͡u^{h}.

I will write to you (pol.): እጥፍለዎታለኍ። i̥ṭi̥fi̥llḁ͡^{w}o-tállḁ͡u^{h}.

I want to write: ልጥፍ፡እፈልጋለኍ። li̥ṭí̥f i̥fḁlli̥gállḁ͡u^{h}.

I will not write: አልጥፍም። alṭí̥fi̥m.

I wrote: ጣፍሁ። ṭā́fhu.

I did not write: አልጣፍሁም። alṭā́fhum.

Write: ጣፍ። ṭāf.

Don't write: አትጣፍ። attí̥ṭāf.

Have you written? ጥፈሃል። ṭí̥fḁhāl?

Did you write? ጣፍህ። ṭāfh?

Can (§ 63*c*) you write? ትጥፋለህ። ti̥ṭi̥fálläh?

Can he write? ይጥፋል። yi̥ṭí̥fāl?

writer, s. ጣፊ ṭáfi.
G. ጻፊ ṣáfi.

writing, s. ጥፈት ṭi̥fḁt (G. ጽ- ṣí̥-; -fät).
Writing materials: መጣፊያ mḁṭáfyã (G. መጻ- mḁṣá-).

written, be, v.p. ተጣፈ tḁṭáfḁ (G. ተጻ- tḁṣá-).

wrong, adj. & adv. (incorrect) ገዳፋ gḁdáfã.
That's wrong (not correct): ይሀ፡በሥራትም፡አይደል። yí̥he ẏḁsi̥ráti̥mm a͡íi̥däl, or ይሀ፡በውልም፡አይደል። yí̥he ẏḁ͡úli̥mm a͡íi̥däl, (§ 7*d*).
Or use parts of ሳተ sátḁ (q.v.), to miss:
You have counted wrong: ቈጥረሀ፡ሳትሀ። qwώṭräh sáth (-t-h, not -θ, § 3).

wrong, s. (injury) በደል bḁ́dḁl (bǻdäl).

wrong (incorrect), be, v.i. ገደፈ gḁ́ddḁfḁ (type A § 34).
ተገደፈው tḁgḁ́ddḁf͡ḁu (impers. § 43*a*).
See § 63*d*, *e*.
He is wrong: ገድፏል። gǻdf͡ŏāl.
ተገድፎታል። tḁgǻdfʷotāl.

wrong, do, v.i. በደለ bḁ́ddḁlḁ (bǻd-).
He has done wrong: በድሏል። bǻddi̥l͡ŏāl, pol. & pl. በድለዋል። bǻddi̥l͡ḁuāl.
You have done wrong: በድለሃል። bǻddi̥lḁhāl, pl. በድላችኋል። bäddi̥láččyuhāl (§ 7*d*).

wrung (out), be, v.p. ተጠመቀ tḁṭḁ́mmḁqḁ.

X

Xerus sp. (Blandford, Geol. & Zool. pp. 278, 279), s. ሸላ šálã, usually f. (§ 54*c*).

Y

§ *refers to the paragraphs of the Grammar (Initia Amharica, Part I).*

yawn, v.i. አዛጋ azzággā.

Don't yawn: አታዛጋ። attazzága.

year, s. ዓመት ā́mạt (ā́mät; § 52*a*, δ).

This year (adv.): ዘንድሮ፡ zạnd(ỵ)rʷo (zắn-).

Last year (adv.): አምና፡ ā́mnā.

Next year (adv.): በሚመጣ፡ዓመት፡ bạmmịmạ́ṭa (§ 62*c*) ā́mät.

Five years: አምስት፡ዓመት፡ ámmịst ámät.

Five years ago: ታምስት፡ዓመት፡በፊት፡ támmịst (§ 7*a*) ā́mạt yạ́fit (§ 8; § 47*b*).

አምስት፡ዓመት፡አደረገ፡ ámmịst ámạt adạ́rrạgạ.

In five years' time: ባምስት፡ዓመት፡ bámmịst ámät.

Every year: ባመት፡ባመት፡ bā́mät yā́mät (§ 7*d*).

How many years? ስንት፡ዓመት፡ sịnt ámät?

yell, s. ጩኸት çúhạt (-hät § 7*d*).

yell, v.i. ጮኸ çʷóhạ (§ 7*d*).

yellow, adj. ብጫ bịçā.

yes, adv. አወን ā́wωn (ā́uωn, ā́uω);—after a negative question አወን means no (q.v.), and yes is expressed by repeating the verb in the positive.

Don't you like it?—Yes: አትወደውም።—እወደዋለሁ። attịwώddạūm?—ịwωddạuállạuʰ.

Yes indeed! እውነት፡ነው። unát (§ 8) nạu!

yesterday, adv. ትላንት tịlánt (§ 8).

ትላንትና tịlántịnā.

Š. ትናንት tịnánt (§.8).

ትናንትና tịnántịnā.

The day before yesterday: ተትናንት፡ወድያ፡ tḁti̥-nánt wώdya, or ሠልስትና፡ sḁlí̥st(ĭ̥)nã.

yet, adv. ገና gḁ́nã.

Haven't they gone yet? ገና፡አልሔዱሞይ። gḁ́na al-hã́dummwí̥? (s.v. ወዬ).

Not yet: ገና፡ነው። gḁná (§ 8) nḁ͡u.

yield, v.i. (in war) ተማረከ tḁmã́rrḁkḁ.

(to persuasion) እሺ፡አለ (í̥)šši (-ši̥, -šʸ) ã́lḁ.

(to pressure) ለበጥ፡አለ lḁ́bḁṭṭ (-ḁ́yḁ-) ã́lḁ.

G. ለጥ፡አለ lḁṭṭ (läṭṭ) ã́lḁ.

S.v. √ባለ, § 44*a*.

yoke, s. ቀምበር qḁ́mbḁr (-bär).

ወስኮ wώskʷo.

yoke, v.t. ጠመደ ṭḁ́mmḁdḁ.

yoked, be, v.p. ተጠመደ tḁṭḁ́mmḁdḁ.

yolk, s. አስኳል áskwã́l (§ 8).

yonder, adj. ያ yã, also prefix yã-, f. ያች yãč (-čč), pl. እነዚያ (i̥)nnḁ́zzyã́ (-nã́z-, እለ- i̥llḁ́-, -lã́z-) or እኒያ (í̥)n-nyã́ (እሊያ í̥llyã́).

See §§ 8, 13*a*; s.v. that, dem. pron.

yonder, adv. ካዚያ kḁ́zzyã́ (hḁ́-, -ã́z-; § 8).

ተዚያ tḁ́zzyã́ (tã́z-; § 8).

you, pers. pron.—see § 12*a*: the disjunctive forms are usually omitted unless they are emphatic (§ 60*b*).

አንተ ántḁ (-tä).

አንት ant (q.v.)

f. አንቺ ánči.

አንች anč (q.v.).

pol. እርስዎ í̥rsḁ́͡ʷo (እሰ- í̥ssḁ́-, -ስዎ -sʷṓ, እርሶ í̥rsʷṓ, እስዎ, እሶ í̥ssʷṓ; § 8).

pol., but less so than እርስዎ, አንቱ ántu (see Appendix B § 12*a*).

pl. እላንት i̥llánt (እና- (i̥)nná-; § 8; -ንተ -ntḁ, -ntä).
(acc. & dat.) -ህ -h, f. -ሽ -š, pol. -(ḁ)ዎ -(ḁ)^{w}o, -(ḁ)ዎት -(ḁ)^{w}ot, pl. -ắችሁ -ắč(č)i̥hu (-ắč(č)yuh § 7*d*); see § 12*c*.
The suffix corresponding to አንቱ is -ኍ -hwŭ or -ሁ -hu (-uh, after a vowel -u^{h}, § 7*d*), see App. B § 12*c*.
(acc. emph.) አንተን ántḁn (-tän), f. አንቺን ánčin, pol. እርስዎን i̥rsḁ͡^{w}on (እሰ- i̥ssḁ́-, etc.; § 8), አንቱን ántun, pl. እላንትን i̥llánti̥n (እና- (i̥)nná-, -ንተን -ntḁn, -ntän).

You there! አንተ፡ሰው። antắ (§ 8) sḁ͡u!

He saw you: አየህ። áyyäh.

„ you (f.): አየሽ። áyyäš.

„ you (pol.): አየዎ። áyyä͡^{w}o (አየዎት። áyyä͡^{w}ot).
አየኍ። áyyä͡u^{h}.

„ you (pl.): አያችሁ። ayyắččihu (-ắččyuh).

We saw you: አየንህ። áyyäni̥h.

„ you (f.): አየንሽ። áyyäni̥š.

„ you (pol.): አየነዎ። áyyänḁ͡^{w}o (-ነዎት። -nḁ͡^{w}ot).
አየንዎ። áyyän^{w}o (-ንዎት። -n^{w}ot).
አየንኍ። áyyänhwŭ (-nuh).

„ you (pl.): አየናችሁ። ayyänắčči̥hu (-náč-čyuh).

I will give you it (them § 61*a*):
እሰጠሃለኍ። i̥sḁṭḁhállḁ͡u^{h}.
እሰጥሃለኍ። i̥sḁṭi̥hállḁ͡u^{h} (App. B § 12*c*).

I will give you (f.) it (them § 61*a*):
እሰጥሻለኍ። i̥sḁṭi̥šállḁ͡u^{h}.

I will give you (pol.) it (them § 61*a*):

እሰጠዎአለኍ። i̥sḁṭḁʷoállu̥ūʰ.

እሰጠዎታለኍ። i̥sḁṭḁʷotállu̥ūʰ.

እሰጥዎአለኍ። i̥sḁṭʷoállu̥ūʰ.

እሰጥዎታለኍ። i̥sḁṭʷotállu̥ūʰ.

እሰጠኋለኍ። i̥sḁṭḁhwállu̥ūʰ (i̥sḁṭḁūhállu̥ūʰ).

I will give you (pl.) it (them § 61*a*):

እሰጣችኋለኍ። i̥sḁṭāčči̥hwállu̥ūʰ (i̥sḁṭāččyu-hállu̥ūʰ).

They will give you it (them § 61*a*): ይሰጡሃል። yi̥sḁ́ṭuhāl.

young, adj. ትንሽ tí̥nni̥š, intensive pls. ትንንሽ ti̥nínni̥š, -ንሾች -nni̥šʷōč (-čč § 6), ትትንሽ ti̥tí̥nni̥š, -ንሾች -nni̥šʷōč (-čč § 6), very young.

ሶታ sʷṓtã.

Young man: አሽከር፡ áškḁr (-kär).

ጐበዝ፡ gwώbḁz (gwώẏḁz), pl. also ጐበዛዝት gwωbḁzázi̥st (gwωẏḁ-; § 8).

your, poss. pron. (addressing one) -ህ -h, f. -ሽ -š, pol. -ዎ -ḁʷo (-ዎ -ʷo), -ኍ -hwŭ (-ሁ -hu, -uh, -uʰ, App. B § 12*b*).

(addressing more than one) -ᾶችሁ -ā́č(č)i̥hu (-ā́č(č)yuh § 7*d*), (§ 12*b*).

yours, poss. pron. (addressing one) ያንተ yántä, f. ያንቺ yánči, pol. የርሰዎ yā́rsḁʷo (§ 8), ያንቱ yántu (App. B § 12*a*).

(addressing more than one) የላንት yā́llánt or የናንት yā́nnánt (§ 8).

See §§ 7*a*, 12*a*, 47*a*, 70.

youth, s. (abstract) አሽከርነት aškḁrí̥nnḁt (-kär-, -nät).

ጕብዝና gwŭbzí̥nnã (gwŭẏz-).

Z

§ *refers to the paragraphs of the Grammar* (*Initia Amharica, Part I*).

Zea mays, s. የባሕር፡ማሽላ yäbáhịr (yäỵá-) māšịllā̃.

zebra, s. የሜዳ፡አህያ yämʸéda ahíy(y)ā̃ (-dāh-), (§ 52*a*, δ).

Zizyphus mucronata and *Z. spina-Christi* (Broun, Cat. 105), s. ገባ gḁ́bā̃ (gḁ́ỵā̃).

Z. spina-Christi: አበተሬ abḁttḁ́rʸe (aỵ-, -ättár-).

Š. ቁርቁሬ qurqúr(r)ā̃.

ADDENDA.

§ *refers to the paragraphs of the Grammar* (*Initia Amharica, Part I*).

abolish, v.t. ሻረ šárḁ.

abolished, be, v.p. ተሻረ tḁšárḁ (täš-).

It ought to be abolished: ይሻር፡ነበር። yi̥ššár nḁ́bbḁr.

It ought not to be abolished: አይሻርም፡ነበር። a͡i̥ššári̥m nḁ́bbḁr.

abolition, s. ሽረት ší̥rḁt (-rät).

abortion, s. ሺል šil (ši̥l).

acquiesce, v.i. እሺ፡አለ (í̥)šši (-ši̥, -š^{y}) álḁ.

ብጅ፡አለ bḁ́jjä (báj-) álḁ.

G. ልጥ፡አለ lḁṭṭ (läṭṭ) álḁ.

Š. ለበጥ፡አለ lḁ́bḁṭṭ (-ḁ́yḁ-) álḁ.

S.v. √በለ, § 44*a*.

adhere, v.i. ተጣበቀ tḁṭábbḁqḁ.

It adheres: ይጣበቃል። yi̥ṭṭábbḁqāl, pl. ይጣበቃሉ። yi̥ṭṭabbḁqállu.

It does not adhere: አይጣበቅም። a͡i̥ṭṭábbḁqi̥m, pl. -ቁም። -qum.

advantage, s. ፍሬ fí̥r^{y}e, pl. ፍሬዎች fí̥re^{w}ōč (-čč § 6).

affection, s. ፍቅር fí̥qi̥r.

affectionate, adj. ፍቅረኛ fi̥q(i̥)rḁ́ññã (-rãñ-).

aged, adj. (elderly) ሽማግሌ ši̥māgí̥ll^{y}e (-gí̥l^{y}e).

aim, v.i. & t. ደገነ dḁ́ggḁnḁ (dǟ́g-), at, በ- bḁ- (ṿḁ-; § 47*a*).

Aim at him (it): ደግንበት። dǟ́ggi̥ni̥bbḁt, pl. ደግኑበት። dǟ́ggi̥nubbḁt.

Don't aim at him (it): አትደግንበት። atti̥dǟ́ggi̥ni̥bbḁt, pl. -ግኑበት። -ggi̥nubbḁt.

I aimed at him (it): ደገንሁበት። dǟ́ggḁnhubbḁt.

I didn't aim at him (it): አልደገንሁበትም። aldäggḁnhúbbḁti̥m.

aimed, be, v.p. ተደገነ tḁdḁ́ggḁnḁ (-dǟ́g-), at, በ- bḁ- (ṿḁ-; § 47*a*).

alternately, adv. በየፈረቃው bḁyyäfḁrḁqa͡u (§ 18).

alternately, be done, v.p. (occur, v.i.) ተፈራረቀ tḁfḁrǟ́rrḁqḁ.

alternately, do, v.t. አፈራረቀ affḁrǟ́rrḁqḁ.

alternation, s. ፈረቃ fḁ́rḁqā̃ (§ 8).

always, adv. ወትሮ wώtrʷo.

ant-hill, s. Š. ኩይሳ kúyyi̥sā̃ (§ 52*a*, δ).

anus, s. (not Š.) ሙርጥ murṭ.

ascend, v.i. ሽቅብ፡አለ ší̥qqi̥b (-i̥ṿ) ā́lḁ (s.v. √በለ, § 44*a*).

Does the road ascend? መንገዱ፡ሽቅብ፡ይላል። mḁ́ṅgḁdu ší̥qqi̥ṿ yí̥lāl?

Ascension, s. ዕርገት í̥rgḁt.

aside, ạdv.

Move aside! ጐድን። gwώdi̥n!

assist, v.i. & t. አገዘ ággḁzḁ (G. type A § 34, Š. type B § 35).

Please assist us: pol. G. እስቲይገዙን። i̥stiyí̥gḁzun.

Š. እስቲያግዙን። i̥stiyággi̥zun.

Please assist them: pol. G. እስቲይገዟቸው። i̥stiyi̥gḁzwǟ́ččḁ͡u.

Š. እስቲያግዟቸው። i̥stiyaggi̥zwǟ́ččḁ͡u.

assisted, be, v.p. ታገዘ tággḁzḁ.
He will be assisted: ይታገዛል። yi̥ttággḁzāl, pol. & pl. ይታገዛሉ። yi̥ttaggḁzállu.

Assumption, s. ፍልሰታ fi̥lsḁtā̃ (16th to 21st ነሐሴ, s.v. calendar), sometimes f. (§ 54*e*).

asthma, s. ስምቡብ si̥mbḁb (-ḁv).
He has asthma: ስምቡብ፡ይዘታል። si̥mbḁv yí̥zʷotāl.

asthmatic, adj. ስምበብም si̥mbḁbám (-ḁvám; § 8).

attend, v.i. (to, v.t.) ልብ፡አደረገ li̥bb adḁrrḁgḁ, constr. with acc. or ለ- lḁ- (§ 47*a*).
Attend to it: ልብ፡አድርግለት። li̥bb ádri̥gi̥llḁt (ár-gi̥llḁt § 7*d*).
Attend to this: ይህንን፡ልብ፡አድርገው። yi̥hánnän li̥bb ádri̥gḁ͡u (árgḁ͡u § 7*d*).

back, be put, v.p. ተመለሰ tḁmállа̥sḁ (-mál-).

back, put, v.t. መለሰ mḁllḁsḁ (mál-).
Put it back into its place: ተስፍራው፡መልሰው። tḁ-si̥fra͡u mállі̥sḁ͡u, pl. -ሱት። -sut.

Balanites ægyptiaca (Broun, Cat. 88), s. ሙጫ mṹč̣č̣ā̃.
Š. ጀሞ jámmʷo.

bank, s. (commercial) ግምጃ፡ቤት gi̥mjá-bʸēt (-v̥ʸēt; § 8).
†ባንክ bańk.

basket, s. (bowl-shaped) ቅምብጫ qi̥mbíččā̃.
ጮጮ č̣ʷóč̣ʷo.

bath, s.
I am going to have a bath: ገላዬን፡እታጠባለሁ። gḁla͡i̥en (§ 56*c*) i̥ttāṭṭḁvállа̥͡uʰ.

bed, s. (-clothes) †ፍራሽ f(i̥)ráš.

before, adv. (time and place) በፊት bḁfít (-fi̥t; § 8).
ፊት fīt (fi̥t).
(time) ቀደም qḁ́d(d)ḁm (-mm § 6).
በቀደም bḁqḁ́d(d)ḁm (-mm § 6).

belt, s. Š. ቀበቶ q̥abåttʷo (q̥aṿå-).

bend down, v.i. (bend oneself down, v.r.) ተደፋ t̥adåffã.

Bend down: ተደፋ። t̥adåfa, pl. ተደፉ። t̥adåfu.

If you bend down: ብትደፋ፡ bi̥tti̥ddåffa, pl. -ፉ፡ -ffu.

bend down, v.t. ደፋ dåffã.

Bend it down: ድፋው። di̥fau͡, pl. ድፉት። di̥fut.

bent, adj. ጐበጣ gwωbắṭã (-ωṿå-).

bent down, be, v.p. ተደፋ t̥adåffã.

bicycle, s. †የሰይጣን፡ፈረስ yäsḁi̥ṭắn (s.v. የ-, §§ 47, 70) fḁ̊rḁs.

big, adj. ትልቅ ti̥lli̥q, intensive pls. ትልልቅ ti̥li̥lli̥q, -ልቆች -lli̥qʷõč (-čč § 6), ትትልቅ ti̥ti̥lli̥q, -ልቆች -lli̥qʷõč (-čč § 6), very big.

blossom, s. ... usually f. (§ 54*c*).

blotting-paper, s. †ማምጠጫ mãmṭåčã̱ (-ṭåčã).

bother, s. ችጋር či̥ggắr (§ 8).

bother, v.i. & t. አስቸገረ asčåggarḁ (-gärḁ).

ነዘነዘ nḁzḁ̊nnḁzḁ.

S.v. worry.

Don't bother: ዝም፡በል። zi̥mm bḁl, pl. ዝም፡በሉ። zi̥mm bḁ̊lu.

bothered, be, v.i. ቸገረው čåggarḁu͡ (-gär-; impers. § 43*a*; § 63*d*, *e*).

bung, s. መድፈኛ mḁdfåñã (-fắñã), usually f. (§ 54*c*).

bung (up), v.t. ደፈነ dåffḁnḁ (dắffänḁ).

Bung it up: ድፈነው። di̥fḁnḁu͡, pl. -ኑት። -nut.

bunged up, adj. ድፍን di̥fi̥n.

bunged (up), be, v.p. ተደፈነ t̥adåffḁnḁ (-dắffänḁ).

It is to be bunged up: ይደፈን። yi̥ddåfḁn, pl. -ኑ። -nu.

busy, be, v.i. ስራ፡ያዘ si̥ra yắzḁ (§ 44*c*, § 63*d*, *e*).

I am busy: ስራ፡ይዣለኝ። si̥ra yi̥žžållḁu͡ʰ (App. B § 44*c*), pl. ስራ፡ይዞናል። si̥ra yi̥zḁnãl.

buy, v.i. & t.

I should have bought it: (as rendered on p. 43, and, perhaps more commonly) ገዝቼ ፡ ነበር ። gḁ́zi̥č-čye nḁ́bbḁr (§§ 61*b*, 81*d*).

called, cause to be, v.t. አስጠራ asṭḁ́rrā (§ 68).
Calotropis procera (Broun, Cat. 347), s. ጦብያ ṭwóbbyā.
cancel, v.t. ሻረ šárḁ.
cancelled, be, v.p. ተሻረ tḁšárḁ (täš-).
It is (has been) cancelled: ተሽሯል ። tášịrōal.
cancellation, s. ሽረት ši̥rḁt (-rät).
captive, adj. & s. አስረኛ asrḁ́ññā (-ráñ-).
(taken in war) adj. ምርክ mi̥rk.
s. ምርኮ mi̥rkwo.
adj. & s. ምርኮኛ mi̥r-kwóññā.
See § 52*a*, δ.
Carduus sp., s. Š. ኰሻሌ kwǫ́šälye (§ 52*a*, δ), usually f. (§ 54*c*).
careless, adj. ቸልተኛ čälli̥tḁ́ññā (-táñ-).
careless, be (become), v.i. ቸል ፡ አለ čäll álḁ.
G. & B. ቸላ ፡ አለ čála álḁ.
Š. ችላ ፡ አለ či̥lla álḁ.
S.v. √በለ, § 44*a*; § 63*d*, *e*.
carelessness, s. ቸልታ čálli̥tā.
cart (carriage), s. Š. †ጋሪ gári.
Carthamus tinctorius (Broun, Cat. 316), s. ሱፍ sūf.
Cassia goratensis (Broun, Cat. 166), s. ዝግጣ zigi̥ṭṭā.
G. ድግጣ digi̥ṭṭā.
castrate, v.t. ሰለበ sḁ́llḁbḁ (-ḁyḁ).
castrated, adj. ስልብ si̥lb (-ly̥).
ጎማዳ gwomádā.
castrated, be, v.p. ተሰለበ tḁsḁ́llḁbḁ (täs-, -ḁyḁ).

caterpillar, s. ተምች tḁmč (tämč; § 52*a*, δ), usually f. (§ 54*c*).

certain, be, v.i. (of something) ተረዳ tḁrḁ́ddā̃ (§ 63*d*, *e*).

I am certain: ተረድቻለሁ። tḁrḁdi̥ččálla͡u̥ʰ, pl. ተረድተናል። tḁrḁ́dtḁnāl.

Are you certain? ተረድተሃል። tḁrḁ́dtḁhāl?, pol. ተረድተዋል። tḁrḁ́dta͡u̥āl?, pl. ተረድታችኋል። tḁrḁdtắč-čyuhāl? (§ 7*d*).

chant, v.i. & t. ዘመረ zḁ́mmḁrḁ (-märḁ).

chatter, v.i. ለፈለፈ lḁfḁ́llḁfḁ.

He chatters: ይለፈልፋል። yi̥lḁfḁ́lli̥fāl, pl. ይለፈልፋሉ። yi̥lḁfḁlli̥fállu.

Don't chatter: አትለፍልፍ። atti̥lḁ́fli̥f, pl. -ልፉ። -li̥fu.

chatterbox, s. ምላሰኛ mi̥lāsḁ́ññā̃ (-sắñ-).

ለፍላፊ lḁflắfi.

ለፍላፋ lḁflắffā̃.

cheese, s. መጣጣ፡አይብ mḁṭắṭa á͡i̥b (á͡i̥ṿ, mḁṭāṭá͡i̥ṿ).

chew, v.i. & t. ቈረጠመ qwωrḁ́ṭṭḁmḁ.

Chew it: ቈርጥመው። qwώrṭi̥ma͡u̥, pol. ይቈርጥሙት። yi̥qwώrṭi̥mut.

Don't chew it: አትቈርጥመው። atti̥qwώrṭi̥ma͡u̥, pol. አይቈርጥሙት። a͡i̥qwώrṭi̥mut.

chewed, be, v.p. ተቈረጠመ tḁqwωrḁ́ṭṭḁmḁ.

civet cat, s. … usually f. (§ 54*c*).

clap, s. (gonorrhœa) ጨብጥ čḁṿṭ.

close together, adj. ግጥም gí̥ṭṭi̥m (-i̥mm § 6).

close(r § 58*b*) together, be, v.i. ግጥም፡አለ gí̥ṭṭi̥mm (§ 6) ắlḁ (s.v. √በለ, § 44*a*; § 63*d*, *e*).

The things are to be close(r) together: እቃው፡ግጥም፡ይበል። í̥qa͡u (§ 52*a*) gí̥ṭṭi̥m yí̥ṿḁl.

The things are not to be (so) close together: እቃው፡ግጥም፡አይበል። í̥qa͡u gí̥ṭṭi̥mm á͡i̥ṿḁl.

The things are (too) close together: እቃው፡ግጥም፡ብሏል። i̥qa͡u gi̥tti̥m bi̥lo͡al.

close(r § 58*b*) together, stand, v.i. ተነባበሩ tḁnḁbábbḁru (-ḁyá-, -bäru).

Stand close(r) together: ተነባበሩ። tḁnḁyā́yḁru.

close (up), v.t. (an aperture) ደፈነ dḁ́ffḁnḁ (dā́ffänḁ).

Close it up: ድፈነው። di̥fḁna͡u, pl. -ኑት። -nut.

Don't close it up: አትድፈነው። atti̥dfḁna͡u, pl. -ኑት። -nut.

closed (up), adj. ድፍን di̥fi̥n.

closed (up), be, v.p. (of an aperture) ተደፈነ tḁdḁ́ffḁnḁ (-dā́ffänḁ).

Let it be closed up: ይደፈን። yi̥ddḁ́fḁn, pl. -ኑ። -nu.

clover (*Trifolium sp.*), s. ማገጥ mā́gḁt, usually f. (§ 54*c*).

Coleus gomphophyllus (H. M. Broun), s. ጒደራ gwū́dḁ́rā̃ (-dā́rā̃; § 8), usually f. (§ 54*c*).

colic, s.

He (it) has colic: አንጀቱን፡ታማል። ánjätun (§ 56*c*) támmo͡al (§ 63*d*).

Colobus guereza (Guidi, Vocab. p. 728), s. ጉሬዛ gurḗzā̃ (§ 52*a*, δ), sometimes f. (§ 54*c*).

colon, s. (med.) ደንዳኔ dḁndā́nnʸe.

commission, s. (commercial) ጉርሻ gúršā̃.

(errand) መልክት mḁ́lákt (§ 8).

The commission is 1%: ጉርሻ፡ከመቶ፡አንድ፡ነው። gúrša kḁmḁ́two ándi̥ na͡u.

conduit, s. ቡምባ búmbā̃.

ቧምቧ bwā́mbwā̃.

conquer, v.i. & t. ድል፡አደረገ di̥l adḁ́rrḁgḁ.

ድል፡ነሣ di̥l nḁ́ssā̃.

conquered, be, v.p. ድል፡ሆነ di̥l hwṓnḁ.

ድል፡ተነሣ di̥l tḁnḁ́ssā̃.

control, v.t. G. ለጥ፡አደረገ lḁṭṭ (läṭṭ) adḁrrḁgḁ.
  Š. ለበጥ፡አደረገ lạbḁṭṭ (lḁvḁṭṭ) adḁrrḁgḁ.
  He (pol.) controls them: G. ለጥ፡ያደርጓቸዋል። lḁṭṭ yādärgwáččḁūāl.
  Š. ለበጥ፡ያደርጓቸዋል። lḁvḁṭṭ yādärgwáččḁūāl.

convince, v.t. አስረዳ asrḁddā.

convinced, be, v.i. & p. ተረዳ tḁrḁddā (tär-; § 63*d*, *e*).
  Are you convinced? ተረድተሃሉይ። tḁrḁdtḁhāllwi̥? (s.v. ወይ), pol. ተረድተዋሉይ። tḁrḁdtḁūāllwi̥?
  I am convinced: ተረድቻለሁ። tḁrḁdịččállḁūʰ (§ 7*d*), pl. ተረድተናል። tḁrḁdtḁnāl.
  I am not convinced: አልተረዳሁም። altḁrḁddahum, pl. አልተረዳንም። altḁrḁddani̥m.

Coreopsis macrantha (H. M. Broun), s. አዳበባ adábḁbā (-ávḁvā; § 52*a*, δ), usually f. (§ 54*c*).

cork, s. (stopper) መድፈኛ mḁdfḁñā (-fáñā), usually f. (§ 54*c*).

cotton soil, s. Š. መረሬ mḁrḁrʸe (-rär-).

cranium, s. ጭንቅላት č̣i̥nqi̥llát (č̣i̥nq-; § 8).

creak, v.i.
  I don't like things that creak: የሚንኳኳ፡አልወድም። yämmi̥nkwákkwa alwǿddi̥m.

crooked, adj. ጉባጣ gwωbáṭā (-ωvá-).

crowd (together), v.i. ተነባበሩ tḁnḁbábbḁru (-ḁvá-, -bäru).
  Don't crowd: አትነበበሩ። atti̥nnḁvávḁru.

Crucifixion, s. ስቅለት si̥qlḁt (-lät).
  ስቅለተ፡ክርስቶስ si̥qlḁtḁ (-lätḁ; § 9*d*) kri̥stʷós.

custom house, s. †ጉምሩክ gúmruk.
  †ጁምሩክ júmruk.

Cynoglossum cœruleum (H. M. Broun), s. ጭጎጎት č̣ig^w^ó-g^w^ot (§ 8).
ፍርሽጥኑ fịrịšṭịnu.
Usually f. (§ 54*c*).

dark(er § 58*b*), be, v.i. ጠቈር፡አለ ṭạqwωrr (ṭώqωrr) ála (s.v. √በለ, § 44*a*).
It is darker than this: ተዚሂ፡ጠቈር፡ይላል። täzzịh ṭώqωrr yịlāl.
Datura stramonium, s. Š. አጠፋሪስ aṭạfáris.
day, s.
A few days: ሰሞን፡ sạm^w^on.
In a few days: ቅርብ፡ቀን፡ qịrỵị qạn.
በዚሂ፡ሰሞን፡ bäzzịh sạm^w^on.
deafness, s. ደንቈርነት dạṅqwωrịnnạt (-nät).
decrease, v.t. አሳነሰ asánnạsạ.
defend, v.t. መከተ፡ለ- mạkkạtạ lạ- (§ 47*a*).
Delphinium dasycaulon (H. M. Broun), s. የመስቀል፡አበባ yämạsqạl (§§ 47*a*, 70) ábạbā̃ (áỵạỵā̃; § 52*a*, δ), usually f. (§ 54*c*).
depose (dismiss from office), v.t. ሻረ šārạ.
deposed, be, v.p. ተሻረ tạšārạ (täš-).
Has he (pol.) been deposed? ተሽረዋል። täšịrạ͡ūāl?
deposition, s. ሽረት šịrạt (-rät).
deride, v.t. ሣቀ፡በ- sáqạ bạ- (ỵạ-; § 47*a*).
derision, s. ሣቅ sāq.
descend, cause or allow to, v.t. አስወረደ aswώrrạdạ.
desert, s. በዳ bạdā̃ (bắdā̃).
ምድረ፡በዳ mịdrạ́ (§ 9*d*) bạdā̃ (bắdā̃, ỵạ́-, ỵắ-, § 7*d*).
dik-dik, s. Š. የንሹ yắnšu, usually f. (§ 54*c*).
diminish, v.t. አሳነሰ asánnạsạ.

dirty (make), v.t. አሰደፈ asáddḁfḁ.

Don't make it dirty: አታሰድፊው። attāsáddi̥fḁ͡u, pl. -ፉት። -fut.

disgrace, s. (shameful matter) ነውር nḁ͡ur.

distressed, be, v.i. ጨነቀው č̣ḁ́nnḁqḁ͡u (impers. § 43*a*).

ተጨነቀ tḁč̣ḁ́nnḁqḁ.

See § 63*d*, *e*.

ditch, s. ጉድብ gúdbã (-dṿã).

G. ጉድብያ gúdbyã (-dṿyã).

docile, adj. ለማዳ lḁmmā́dã (-mā́ddã).

Dorylus (*Anomma*) *nigricans*, s. ጕንዳን gwū́ndā́n (§ 8; § 52*a*, δ), sometimes f. (§ 54*c*).

double, v.t. (consonant in pronunciation) አጠበቀ aṭḁ́b-bḁqḁ.

double(d), be, v.i. (consonant in pronunciation) ጠበቀ ṭḁ́bbḁqḁ (type A § 34; § 63*d*, *e*).

It is doubled: ጡብቋል። ṭḁ́ṿqŏ͡āl.

Is it double? ጡብቋሎዪ። ṭḁ́ṿqŏ͡āllwí̥? (s.v. ወዪ).

It isn't doubled: አልጠበቀም። alṭḁ́bbḁqḁm.

doubt, s. ጥርጣሬ ṭi̥ri̥ṭṭári.

dream, v.i. & t. (dream of, v.t.) አለመ állḁmḁ.

dreamed (of), be, v.p. ታለመ tā́llḁmḁ.

dried meat, s. ቋንጣ qwā́nṭã.

duiker, s. Š. የንሹ yā́nšu, usually f. (§ 54*c*).

early (earlier § 58), adv. (previously) ቀደም qḁ́d(d)ḁm (-mm § 6).

በቀደም bḁqḁ́d(d)ḁm (-mm § 6).

early (earlier § 58*b*), be, v.i. ቀደም፡አለ qḁ́d(d)ḁmm (§ 6) ā́lḁ (s.v. √ባለ, § 44*a*).

Let him come early this afternoon: ተኩለቀን፡ወዲያ፡ ቀደም፡ብሎ፡ይምጣ። tḁkkúlḁqḁn wωdyá̃ qḁ́d(d)ḁm bı̥lʷo (qḁ́d(d)ḁmmı̥̆ y̤ı̥lʷo § 7*d*) yı̥́mṭa, pl. ... ቀደም፡ ብለው፡ይምጡ። ... qḁ́d(d)ḁm bı̥́lḁu͡u (qḁ́d(d)ḁmmı̥̆ y̤ı̥́lḁu͡u) yı̥́mṭu.

eighteenth, ord. num. አሥራ፡ስምንተኛ asrā̃sı̥mmı̥ntḁ́ññā̃ (-tá̃ñ-; § 20*b*).

eighth, ord. num. ስምንተኛ sı̥mmı̥ntḁ́ññā̃ (-tá̃ñ-; § 20*b*).

eighth (1/8), s. ስምንትያ፡[-ንቲያ] sı̥mmı̥ntı́̃yyā̃ (§ 20*c*, § 52*a*, δ).

eightieth, ord. num. ሰማንያኛ sḁmā̃nyáññā̃ (§ 20*b*).

eleventh, ord. num. አሥራ፡ሐንደኛ asrā̃handḁ́ññā̃ (-dá̃ñ-; § 20*b*).

eleventh (1/11), s. አሥራ፡ሐንድያ፡[ሐንዲያ] asrā̤̃handı́̃yyā̃ (§ 20*c*, § 52*a*, δ).

enceinte, be (become), v.i. አረገዘች arḁ́ggḁzäč (-čč § 6; § 63*d*, *e*).

endure, v.i. (last) ጠና ṭḁ́nnā̃ (§ 63*d*, *e*).

engine, s. ባቡር bábū̃r (bá̃y̤ū̃r § 7*d*; § 8).

epiglottis, enlargement (hypertrophy) of, s. እንጥል (ı̥)nṭı̥l.

errand, s. መላክት mḁ́lákt (§ 8).

error, s. (inaccuracy) ግድፈት gı̥́dfḁt.

eunuch, s. ስልብ sı̥lb (-ly̤).
ጎማዳ gʷomá̃dā̃.

Euphorbia sp. (spurge), s. አንተርፋ antḁ́rfā̃ (-tá̃r-), usually f. (§ 54*c*).

examine, v.t. ጐረጐረ gwωrḁ́ggwωrḁ (-rώgg-).

Examine it: ጐርጕረው። gwώrgwū̃rḁu͡u, pl. -ሩት። -rut.

examined, be, v.p. ተጐረጐረ tḁgwωrḁ́ggwωrḁ (-rώgg-).

Has the baggage been examined? እቃ፡ተጐርጕሯል። ı̥qa tḁgwώrgwū̃rŏ͡āl?

exceedingly, adv. አጥብቆ áṭbı̥qʷo (áṭy̤ı̥-, áṭı̥bqʷo, -ı̥y̤q-).

expectorate, v.i. & t. ትፍ፡አለ ti̥ff álḁ (not Š.).
እንትፍ፡አለ (i̥)nti̥ff (-tŭff) álḁ.
S.v. √በለ, § 44*a*.

extend, v.i. ተዘረጋ tḁzḁrḁ́ggã (täzär-).
Where does it extend to? እስተወዴት፡ድረስ፡ይዘረጋል። i̥stḁ͡ūωdʸét dír̥ḁs yi̥zzḁrḁ́ggāl?

fat, be (become) very, v.i. ጎፈፍ፡አለ gʷófḁff álḁ.
G. ጉፍፍ፡አለ gúfi̥ff (-fŭff) álḁ.
S.v. √በለ, § 44*a*; § 63*d, e*.
He is very fat: ጎፈፍ፡ብሏል። gʷófḁffi̥ (§ 7*d*, G. ጉፍፍ፡ gúfi̥ffi̥) y̥íl͡ōāl̥.

father, s.
The question ዮት፡አባት- yēt abbát- with personal suffixes (§ 12*b*) *is, like* ምን፡አባት- mi̥n abbát- etc., *a term of abuse.*

Felis caracal, s. ጫኺ፡አንበሳ č̣͡ōáhi anbḁ́ssã (ambḁ́-, any̥ḁ́- § 7*d*), usually f. (§ 54*c*).

fever, s. Š. ዎባ wóbã (wóy̥ã).

fibre, s. ቃጫ qáč̣ã.

Ficus vasta (Broun, Cat. 533), s. ወርካ wḁ́rkã (wώr-, ዋር- wár-).

fifteenth, ord. num. አሥራ፡አምስተኛ asrammi̥stḁ́ññã (-táñ-; § 20*b*).

fifth, ord. num. አምስተኛ ammi̥stḁ́ññã (-táñ-; § 20*b*).

fifth (1/5), s. አምስትያ፡[አምስቲያ] ammi̥stíyyḁ̃ (§ 20*c*, § 52*a*, δ).

fiftieth, ord. num. አምሳኛ amsáññã (§ 20*b*).

fine, be paid as, v.p. ተካሰ tḁkásḁ.

fine, pay a, v.i. (pay as, v.t.) ካሰ kásḁ.

firm, be, v.i. ጠና ṭḁ́nnã (§ 63*d, e*).

first (at), adv. በፊት bḁ́fī́t (-fi̥t; § 8).
ፊት fīt (fi̥t).
fist, s. Š. ጡጫ ṭúč̣č̣ā̃ (§ 52*a*, *γ*).
flax (*Linum usitatissimum*), s. ተልባ tḁ́lbā̃ (tā́l-, -lỵā̃).
flower, s. … usually f. (§ 54*c*).
fœtus, s. ሺል šil (ši̥l).
footprint, s. ፍለጋ fi̥llḁ́gā̃ (§ 8).
Š. ፈለግ fḁ́lḁg.
ፋራ fárā̃.
See § 52*a*, *δ*.
forbidden, adj. ክልክል ki̥lí̥kki̥l.
foreskin, s. ወሸላ wḁ́šḁlā̃ (wώš-; § 8).
forest, s. ደን dḁn (-nn § 6).
Is there forest there? ደን፡አለበት። dḁnn állābbḁt?
foretell, v.t. ተነበ tḁnḁ́bbā̃.
formerly, adv. ፊት fīt (fi̥t).
fortieth, ord. num. አርበኛ arbáññā̃ (arỵá-; § 20*b*).
fourteenth, ord. num. አሥራ፡አራተኛ asrārāttḁ́ññā̃ (-tā́ñ-; § 20*b*).
fourth, ord. num. አራተኛ arāttḁ́ññā̃ (-tā́ñ-; § 20*b*).
fourth (1/4), s. አራትኛ arātti̥ññā̃ (-ትያ, -ቲያ -tī́yyā̃).
[እ]ሩብ (i̥)rúb (-úỵ).
See § 20*c*, § 52*a*, *δ*.
3/4: ሶስት፡አራትኛ፡ sʷōst arātti̥ñña.
Friday, s.
On Friday: አርብ፡ arỵ.
Good Friday: ስቅለት፡ si̥qlḁt (-lät).
ስቅለተ፡ክርስቶስ፡ si̥qlḁtḁ (-lätḁ; § 9*d*) kri̥stʷós.
friendly, adj. ፍቅረኛ fi̥q(i̥)rḁ́ññā̃ (-ráñ-).
fruit, s.—no general term; s.v. ፍሬ fi̥rʸe.
fungus, s. (inedible) ቍቻ qwŭ́ččā̃ (§ 52*a*, *δ*).

genet cat (*Genetta abessinica*), s. አነር ā́nḁr (ā́när).
German, adj. የጀርመን yäjā́rmḁn (s.v. የ-, §§ 47*a*, 70).
German, s. ጀርመን jā́rmḁn.
Germany, s. የጀርመን፡ አገር yäjā́rmḁn (§ 70) ā́gḁr (-gär).
  [ነምሳ (نمسا) more properly = Austria].
get, v.i.
  I can't get at it now: አሁን፡ እሩቅ፡ ነው። áhun i̥rúq nḁ͡u.
gift, s. ጉርሻ gúršã.
give, v.i. (yield to pressure) ለበጥ፡ አለ lḁ́bḁṭṭ (-ḁ́vḁ-) ā́lḁ.
  G. ለጥ፡ አለ lḁṭṭ (läṭṭ) álḁ.
  It doesn't give: ለበጥ፡ አይለም። lḁ́vḁṭṭ a͡i̥li̥m, pl. ...፡ አይሉም። ... a͡i̥lum.
gonorrhœa, s. ጨብጥ č̣ḁvṭ.
  Have you got gonorrhœa? ጨብጥ፡ ይዞሃል። č̣ḁvṭ yí̥zʷohāl?
good, s.
  For good (always): ወትሮ፡ wátrʷo.
govern, v.t. G. ለጥ፡ አደረገ lḁṭṭ (läṭṭ) adḁ́rrḁgḁ.
  Š. ለበጥ፡ አደረገ lḁ́bḁṭṭ (-ḁ́vḁ-) adḁ́rrḁgḁ.
grammar, s. †ሰዋሰው sḁwásu (sḁ͡uá-).
gratuity, s. ጉርሻ gúršã.
great, adj. ትልቅ tí̥lli̥q, intensive pls. ትልልቅ ti̥lí̥lli̥q, -ልቆች -lli̥qʷōč (-čč § 6), ትትልቅ ti̥tí̥lli̥q, -ልቆች -lli̥qʷōč (-čč § 6) very great.
ground, s.
  Hard ground: Š. ኰረኰንች kwárḁkwánč.
ground-squirrel (*Xerus rutilus*, Blandford, Geol. & Zool. pp. 278, 279), s. ሻላ šálã, usually f. (§ 54*c*).

hairpin, s. ወለበ wálḁ́bã (-ḁ́vã; § 8).
hand over, v.i. & t. አስረከበ asrḁ́kkḁbḁ (-rák-, -ḁvḁ).

Hand the things over: እቃውን፡አስረክበው። i̥qa͡un (§ 52*a*, δ) asrä́kki̥yḁ͡u.

hard, be, v.i. ጠና ṭḁ́nnã (§ 63*d*, *e*).

It is hard and strong: ጠንቷል፤ጠንካሩ፡ነው። ṭḁ́nto͡ʊāl, ṭḁṅkarrä́ (§ 8) nḁ͡u.

Hawä́sh, s. አዋሽ a͡uä́š.

heal, v.i. (of a wound) ሻረ šä́rḁ.

It will heal: ይሽራል። yi̥ši̥rāl.

It won't heal: አይሽርም። a͡i̥ši̥ri̥m.

It has healed: ሽሯል። ši̥ro͡ʊāl.

It has not healed: አልሻረም። alšä́rḁm.

help, v.i. & t. አገዘ ággа̥zḁ (G. type A § 34, Š. type B § 35).

Help him: G. እገዘው። i̥gḁzḁ͡u, pl. -ዙት። -zut.

Š. አግዘው። ággi̥zḁ͡u, pl. -ዙት። -zut.

Help them: G. እገዛቸው። i̥gḁzä́ččḁ͡u, pl. -ዟቸው። -zwä́ččḁ͡u.

Š. አግዛቸው። aggi̥zä́ččḁ͡u, pl. -ዟቸው። -zwä́ččḁ͡u.

helped, be, v.p. ታገዘ tä́ggḁzḁ.

He has not been helped: አልታገዘም። altággа̥zḁm, pol. & pl. -ዙም። -zum.

We have not been helped: አልታገዝነም። altággḁznḁm.

Herpestes gracilis (*H. mutgigella*, Blandford, Geol. & Zool. pp. 43, 234, 235), s. ሙጭጭላ muči̥č̣i̥llã.

Š. ምጥማጥ mi̥ṭmä́ṭ (§ 8).

Usually f. (§ 54*c*).

hide, s. ቆዳ qʷódã.

hidden, adj. ደበቅ dḁ́bḁq (-ḁ́yḁ-).

history, s. ታሪክ tárīk (-ri̥k).

hive, s. ቀፎ qḁ́fʷo.

hold up, v.t. ደገፈ dḁ́ggḁfḁ.

ገደፈ gḁ́ddḁfḁ (type B § 35).

Hold him (it) up so that he (it) doesn't fall: በጅህ፡ ገድፈው፡እንዳይወድቅ። bájjịh (= በ- bạ-, with § 47*a* + እጅህ ịjjịh, your hands § 52*a*, γ) gáddịfạu ndaị-wǿdịq, pl. በጆችሁ፡ ገድፉት፡... bäjjáččyuh (§ 7*d*) gáddịfut....

hoof, s.

Long hoofs: ያደገ፡ጥፍር፡ yáddạgạ (s.v. አደገ) tịfịr.

horrify, v.t. አስደነገጠ asdạnággạṭạ.

hot, adj.

Very hot: (of objects) ትኩስ፡ tịkkús (túk-; § 8).
(of weather, places) እሳት፡ ịsát.

hotel, s. †ዎቴል ʷőtʸél (§ 8).
†ሉካንዳ lukándã.

hunchback, s. ጐበጣ gwωbáṭã (-ωyá-).

hundredth, ord. num. መቶኛ mạtʷóññã (§ 20*b*).

Two hundredth: ሁለት፡መቶኛ፡ húlätt mạtʷóñña.

hut, s. ዳስ dās.

Hystrix sp., s. ጃርት jart, sometimes f. (§ 54*c*).

ichneumon (*Herpestes sp.*, Blandford, Geol. & Zool. pp. 43, 234, 235), s. ሙጭጭላ mučịčịllã.
Š. ምጥማጥ mịṭmáṭ (§ 8).
Usually f. (§ 54*c*).

identification, means of, s. ምልክት mịlịkkịt.

iliac bone, s. አኒሳ annísã.

Impatiens Irvingii (H. M. Broun), s. ግሽርጥ gịšrịṭ.
G. ጉሽርጥ gúšrịṭ.
Š. ግርሽጥ gịršịṭ.

inaccuracy, s. ግድፈት gịdfạt.

inaccurate (incorrect), adj. ገዳፋ gạdáfã.

inaccurate (incorrect), be, v.i. ገደፈ gḁ́ddḁfḁ (type A § 34).
ተገደፈው tḁgḁ́ddḁfḁ͡u (impers. § 43*a*).
See § 63*d*, *e*.

increase, v.i. በዛ bḁ́zzã (báz-).

increase, v.t. አበዛ abḁ́zzã (ay̥ḁ́-, -áz-).
Increase it: አብዛው። áy̥za͡u, pl. አብዙት። áy̥zut.

Indian, s. ሀንዲ hḭndi, pl. -ዶች -dʷōč (-ōčč § 6).

India-rubber, s. ላስቲክ lástík (§ 8).

inn, s. ማረፊያ mārḁ́fyã (-ráf-).
(European) †ዎቴል ʷṓtʸél (§ 8).

inspected, be, v.p. ተመረመረ tḁmḁrḁ́mmḁrḁ (-märḁ́m-märḁ).
ተጐረጐረ tḁgwωrḁ́ggwωrḁ (-rώgg-).
That house is to be inspected: ይህ፡ቤት፡ተጐርጓሪ፡ ነው። yḭhe yʸēt tḁgwωrgwārí (§ 8) nḁ͡u.

instead of, prp. በ-...፡ ምትክ bḁ-... mḭtḭkk (§ 8, § 47*b*).
Instead of this: በዚህ፡ምትክ፡ bäzzḭh mḭtḭkk.
Let another man come instead of you: በንተ፡ምትክ፡ ሌላ፡ሰው፡ይምጣ። bántḁ mḭtḭ́kkḭ̆ (§ 7*d*) lēlá (§ 8) sḁ͡u yḭ́mṭa.

intercourse, s. ጨዋታ č̣ḁ́wḁtã (č̣ḁ́͡u-, -ωtã).
ወግ wωg.
Sexual intercourse: ብዳት፡ bḭdát (§ 8).

intestine, s.
Large intestine: ደንዳኔ፡ dḁndánnʸe.

iron, s.
Galvanised iron: ቆርቆሮ qwωrqwώrrʷo.
ታኒካ tánikã.

irrigation channel, s. Š. ማገት mágḁt.

itch (-ing), s. እከክ ḭkḁk.
Affected with itch: እከካም፡ ḭkḁ́kám (§ 8).

itch, v.i. አሳከከ asā́kkḁkḁ.

አሳከከው asā́kkḁkḁ͡u (impers. § 43*a*).

See § 63*d*, *e*.

My back itches: ጀርባዬን፡አሳከከኝ። járỵa͡i̥en (§ 56*c*) asákkḁkäñ.

knotted, be, v.p. ተቋጠረ tḁqwā́ṭṭḁrḁ (-ṭärḁ).

knowledge, s.

Without the knowledge of, prp. ድፍን- dí̥fi̥nn- (§ 6), with personal suffixes (§ 12*b*).

ከ-[ተ-, ለ-]...፡ድፍን kḁ- (tḁ-, lḁ-)... dí̥fi̥n (§ 47*b*).

Without my knowledge: ድፍኔ፡ dí̥fi̥nn^{y}e.

ተኔ፡ድፍን፡ tän^{y}é dí̥fi̥n.

Without his knowledge: ድፍኑ፡ dí̥fi̥nnu.

ለርሱ፡ድፍን፡ lärsú dí̥fi̥n.

Without their knowledge: ድፍናቸው፡ di̥fi̥nnáč̣-čḁ͡u.

ተርሳቸው፡ድፍን፡ tär-sáččḁ͡u dí̥fi̥n.

This was done without our knowledge: ይህ፡ለኛ፡ድፍን፡ተደረገ። yi̥he läññá dí̥fi̥n tḁdḁ́rrḁgḁ.

knuckle, s. ኩርኩም kúrkum (§ 8, § 52*a*, γ).

labourer, s. Š. ጉራጌ gurág^{y}e, pl. ጉራግዮች gurágyōč (-ōčč § 6).

large,| adj. ትልቅ ti̥lli̥q, intensive pls. ትልልቅ ti̥lí̥lli̥q, -ልቆች -lli̥q^{w}ōč (-čč § 6), ትትልቅ ti̥tí̥lli̥q, -ልቆች -lli̥q^{w}ōč (-čč § 6), very large.

larva, s. ትል ti̥l.
(of lepidoptera) ተምች tḁmč (tämč).
(hirsute) አባ፡ጨጓሬ ábba č̣ḁg-gwā́r^{y}e.
(of bee) እጭ i̥č̣.
Š. ህጭ hi̥č̣.
See § 52*a*, δ; usually f. (§ 54*c*).

last, v.i. ጠና ṭḁnnā (§ 63*d*, *e*).

laughter, s. ሣቅ sāq.

lean, adj. (of persons) መጣጣ mḁṭā́ṭā.

lean (over), v.i. ተጐነበሰ tḁgwωnḁ́bbḁsḁ.
Lean over: ተጐንበስ። tḁgwώmbḁs (§ 7*d*), pl. -በሱ። -bḁsu.
Don't lean over: አትጐንበስ። atti̥ggwώmbḁs, pl. -በሱ። -bḁsu.

leper, s.
leprous, adj. } ለምጣም lḁ́mṭām (§ 8).

lessen, v.t. አሳነሰ asánnḁsḁ.

like, adj.
What is it like? እንደምንድር፡ነው። ndämi̥ndí̥r (§ 8) nḁ͡u?, pl. እንደምንድር፡ናቸው። ndämí̥ndi̥r náččḁ͡u?

Linum usitatissimum, s. ተልባ tḁ́lbā (tál-, -lỵā).

litter, s. (sweepings, etc.) ጥራጊ ti̥rrági.
ግብስብስ gi̥bí̥sbi̥s (gi̥v̥í̥sv̥i̥s).
ቈሻሻ qwωšā́šā.

little, adj. ትንሽ tí̥nni̥š, intensive pls. ትንንሽ ti̥ní̥nni̥š, -ንሾች -nni̥š^{w}ōč (-čč § 6), ትትንሽ ti̥tí̥nni̥š, -ንሾች -nni̥š^{w}ōč (-čč § 6), very little.

long, adj. ረጅም rḁ́jji̥m (ráj-, ረዠም rḁ́žži̥m, ráž-), intensive pls. ረጃጅም rḁjájji̥m (räj-), -ጅሞች -jji̥m^{w}ōč (-čč § 6).

loosen, v.t. አረገበ arḁ́ggḁbḁ (-ḁyḁ; § 41*d*).
አረገበ arrḁ́ggḁbḁ (-ḁyḁ; § 41*f*).
Loosen it: አርግበው። ắrgi̥yḁ͡u, pl. -ግቡት። -gi̥yut.
አረግበው። arrḁ́ggi̥yḁ͡u, pl. -ግቡት። -gi̥yut.
lose, v.i. (battle) ድል፡ሆነ di̥l hʷṓnḁ.
ድል፡ተነሣ di̥l tḁnḁ́ssã.
love, v.t. አፈቀረ afḁ́qqḁrḁ.
love each other, v.i. ተፈቃቀሩ tḁfḁqắqqḁru.
They don't love each other: አይፈቃቀሩም። a͡i̥ffḁqắqqḁrum.
loving, adj. ፍቀረኛ fi̥q(ĭ)rḁ́ññã (-rắñ-).
lynx (*Felis caracal*), s. ጨኺ፡አንበሳ č̣ŏắhi anbḁ́ssã (ambḁ́-, anyḁ́-, § 7*d*), usually f. (§ 54*c*).

mail-carrier, s. †ቡስጠኛ bust̤ḁ́ññã (-t̤ắñ-).
moist, adj. ርጥብ ri̥t̤i̥b (-i̥y).
Monday, s.
On Monday: ሰኞ፡ sḁ́ñño.
mongoose (*Herpestes gracilis*, *H. mutgigella*, Blandford, Geol. & Zool. pp. 43, 234, 235), s. ሙጪጪላ muč̣i̥č̣i̥llã.
Š. ምጥማጥ mí̥tmắt̤ (§ 8).
Usually f. (§ 54*c*).
monkey, s. (*Colobus guereza*, Guidi, Vocab. p. 728) ጉሬዛ gurḗzã (§ 52*a*, δ), sometimes f. (§ 54*c*).
multiply, v.i. (be multiplied, v.p.) በዛ bḁ́zzã (bắz-).
ተጨመረ tḁč̣ḁ́mmḁrḁ (-märḁ).
multiply, v.t. አበዛ abḁ́zzã (ayḁ́-, -ắz-).
ጨመረ č̣ḁ́mmḁrḁ (-märḁ).
አበለጠ abḁ́llḁt̤ḁ (ayḁ́-).

nature, s. (temperament) አመል ámḁl (ámäl).

neglect, v.t. G. & B. ቸላ፡አለ፡ለ- čála ā́lḁ lḁ- (s.v. √በለ, §§ 44*a*, 47*a*, 63*d*, *e*).

nineteenth, ord. num. አሥራ፡ዘጠነኛ asrā̃zḁṭḁnḁ́ññā̃ (-zäṭänā́ñ-; § 20*b*).

ninetieth, ord. num. ዘጠናኛ zḁṭḁnáññā̃ (zäṭ-; § 20*b*).

ninth, ord. num. ዘጠነኛ zḁṭḁnḁ́ññā̃ (zäṭänā́ñ-; § 20*b*).

ninth (1/9), s. ዘጠንያ፡[ዘጠኒያ] zḁṭḁníyyā̃ (zäṭän-; § 20*c*, § 52*a*, δ).

notice, v.i. & t. ልብ፡አደረገ li̥bb adḁ́rrḁgḁ, constr. with acc. or ለ- lḁ- (§ 47*a*).

Notice him (it): ልብ፡አድርገው፡ li̥bb ádrigḁ͡u (ā́rgḁ͡u § 7*d*), or ልብ፡አድርግለት። li̥bb ádri̥gi̥llḁt (ā́rg-).

I didn't notice: ልብ፡አላደረግሁም። li̥bb aladḁ́rrḁghum.

I didn't notice him (it): ልብ፡አላደረግሁለትም። li̥bb aladḁrrḁghúllḁti̥m.

I didn't notice this: ይህንን፡ልብ፡አላደረግሁትም። yi̥hā́nnän li̥bb aladḁ́rrḁghuti̥m.

Numida ptilorrhynca (Blandford, Geol. & Zool. pp. 421–423: *N. meleagris*, Guidi, Vocab. p. 638), s. ጅግራ ji̥grā̃ (§ 52*a*, δ), sometimes f. (§ 54*c*).

on, prp. በ- bḁ- (y̥ḁ-; § 47*a*).

Put it (them § 61*b*) on it: አስቀምጥበት። asqḁ́mmi̥ṭi̥bbḁt.

ostrich (*Struthio camelus*), s. ሰጎን sḁ́gʷon (§ 8).

paid as fine, be, v.p. ተከሰ tḁkásḁ.

pass, v.i. አለፈ állḁfḁ.

v.t. አለፈ፡ከ- állḁfḁ kḁ- (ተ- tḁ-, § 47*a*).

He (it) has passed the house: ተቤቱ፡አልፏል። tḁ-y̥ʸétu álfo͡āl, pl. ...፡አልፈዋል።... álfḁ͡uāl.

pass through (an aperture), v.i. ሾለከ šʷóllaka (šól-, šál-).
v.t. ሾለከ፡በ- šʷóllaka (etc.) ba- (ya-; § 47a).

He (it) has passed through here: በዚህ፡ሾልኳል። bazzih šólkʷāl.

penis, s. Š. ሙርጥ murt.

Pentanisia Schweinfurthii (H. M. Broun), s. G. ጥንጁት tínjut. Š. መራርጬ mararíččā. Usually f. (§ 54c).

perpetually, adv. ወትሮ wótrʷo.

persist, v.i. ጠና tánnā (§ 63d, e).

picking out (extracting), instrument for, s.
መቈንጠጫ maqwontáčā (-táčā).
መንቃሻ manqášā.

piled (up), be, v.i. ተነበበረ tanabábbara (-ayá-, -bära; § 63d, e).

pip, s. ፍሬ fírʸe, pl. ፍሬዎች fírewōč (-čč § 6; § 52a, δ).

pipe, s. (to carry water) ቡምባ búmbā.

plucked (pulled) out, be, v.p. ተነቀለ tanáqqala.

It must be pulled out: ይነቀል። yinnáqal, pl. -ሉ። -lu.

plug, s. መድፈኛ madfáñā (-fáñā), usually f. (§ 54c).

plug, v.t. ደፈነ dáffana (dáffäna).

plugged, adj. ድፍን dífin.

plugged, be, v.p. ተደፈነ tadáffana (-dáffäna).

pocket, s.

It fell out of my pocket: ተለብሴ፡ውስጥ፡ወደቀብኝ። talívsʸe wüst (§ 47b) wóddaqabbiñ (§ 47a).

point, v.i. & t.

Point him (her, it, them, § 61*a*) out to me: አመልክትልኝ። amálki̥ti̥lli̥ñ, pl. -ቱልኝ። -tulli̥ñ.

point, v.t. (a weapon) ደገነ dḁ́ggḁnḁ (dág-), at, በ- bḁ- (yḁ-; § 47*a*).

He pointed his gun at him (it): ጠበንጃውን፡ደገነበት። ṭḁyḁ́nja͡ūn dággḁnḁbbḁt.

pointed, be, v.i. & p. (of a weapon) ተደገነ tḁdḁ́ggḁnḁ (-dág-), at, በ- bḁ- (yḁ-; § 47*a*).

The (his) gun was pointed at me: ጠበንጃው፡ተደገነብኝ። ṭḁyḁ́nja͡ū tḁdággḁnḁbbi̥ñ.

pollute, v.t. አሳደፈ asáddḁfḁ.

He (it) pollutes it: ያሳድፈዋል። yāsáddi̥fḁ͡ūāl, pl. -ፉታል። -futāl.

polluted, be, v.p. አደፈ áddḁfḁ (§ 23*a*, § 63*d*, *e*).

pomegranate (*Punica granatum*), s. ሮማን r^{w}ommán.

possible, be, v.i.

It is possible: ይቻላል። yi̥ččálāl; or (§ 63*c*) ይሆናል። yi̥h^{w}ónāl, or ይደረጋል። yi̥ddḁ́rrḁgāl.

It is not possible: አይቻልም። a͡i̥ččáli̥m; or አይሆንም። a͡i̥h^{w}óni̥m, or አይደረግም። a͡i̥ddḁ́rrḁgi̥m.

preaching, s. ትንግርት tíngi̥rt (§ 8).

pregnant, be (become), v.i. (woman) አረገዘች arḁ́ggḁzäč (-čč § 6).

(animal) ከበደች kḁ́bbḁdäč (-čč § 6).

See § 63*d*, *e*.

previously, adv. ፊት fīt (fi̥t).

በፊት bḁ́fīt (-fi̥t; § 8).

ቀደም qḁ́d(d)ḁm (-mm § 6).

በቀደም bḁqḁ́d(d)ḁm (-mm § 6).

prisoner, s. እስር i̥si̥r.

prophecy, s. ትንቢት ti̥nbĭ́t (tí̥mbĭ́t, tí̥nṿĭ́t, § 7*d*; § 8).
prophesy, v.i. & t. ተነበ tḁnḁ́bbã.
prophet, s. ነቢይ nḁ́bi (nắ-, -ṿi), pl. also ነቢያት nḁ́biát (nắ-, -ṿi-; § 8).
prurigo, s. እከክ i̥kḁk.
pubes, s. የብልት፡ጠጕር yäbí̥llịt (yäṿí̥-; §§ 47*a*, 70) ṭḁ́gwŭr.
pudding, s. †አላዋ alắwã (aláuã).
Punica granatum, s. ሮማን r^w^ommán.
pursue, v.i. & t. ፈለገ fḁ́llḁgḁ with gerund of ተከተለ tḁkắttḁlḁ (§ 65*a*).
Pursue him: ተከትለህ፡ፈልገው። tḁkḁ́tti̥läh fḁ́lli̥gḁu, pl. ተከትላችሁ፡ፈልጉት። tḁkḁtti̥lắččyuh (§ 7*d*) fḁ́lli̥gut.
Pursue them: ተከትለህ፡ፈልጋቸው። tḁkḁ́tti̥läh fḁlli̥gắččḁu, pl. ተከትላችሁ፡ፈልጓቸው። tḁkḁtti̥lắččyuh fḁlli̥gwắččḁu.
In the negative use ተከተለ alone:
Don't pursue him: አትከተለው። atti̥kkḁ́tḁlḁu, pl. -ተሉት። -tḁlut.

quarter (1/4), s. አራትያ፡[አራቲያ] arāttíyyã (§§ 20*c*, 52*a*, δ).
3/4: ሶስት፡አራትያ፡ s^w^ōst arāttíyya.
quinsy, s. ቅምሆ qí̥mh^w^o (qúmho).

regret, interj. expressing, አይ ắi! (ắi̥).
resin, s. ሙጫ mṹč̣č̣ã.
rigid, be, v.i. ጠና ṭḁ́nnã (§ 63*d*, *e*).

sack, s. ከሻ kḁ́šã (kắšã).
ዱኒያ duníyã.
saliva, s. ትፍታ tí̥ffi̥tã.
school, s. የተማሪ፡ቤት yätḁmắri (§ 70*b*) b^y^ēt (ṿ^y^ēt).

scissors, s. መቍረጪት mạqwŭrạ́čịt (-ráč̣-).

scorn, s. ሣቅ sāq.

scorn, v.t. ሣቀ፡በ- sā́qạ bạ- (yạ-; § 47*a*).

He would scorn it: ይሥቅበት፡ነበር። yịsị́qịbbạt nạ́bbär, pol. & pl. ይሥቁበት፡ነበር። yịsị́qubbạt nạ́bbär, (§§ 81*c*, λ, 33*a*, *β*).

scraggy, adj. (of persons) መጣጣ mạṭā́ṭā̃.

scrotum, s. አቁማዳ aqumā́dā̃.

Š. ስልቻ sịllị́ččā̃.

secret, adj. ደበቅ dạ́bạq (-ạ́yạ-).

send for, v.t. አስጠራ asṭạ́rrā̃ (§ 68).

Please send for him: pol. እስቲያስጠሩት። ịstiyasṭạ́rrut.

Please send for them: pol. እስቲያስጠሯቸው። ịstiyasṭạrrwā́ččạ͡u.

serious, be, v.i. (of illness) ጠና ṭạ́nnā̃ (§ 63*d*, *e*).

It is serious: ጠንቷል። ṭạ́ntŏ͡āl.

It is not serious: አልጠናም። alṭạ́nnām.

sew, v.i. & t.

Sew it (the hole) up before it gets big: ሳይሰፋ፡ስፋው። sai̯sạ́fa sị́fa͡u.

sexual intercourse, s. ብዳት bị́dā́t (§ 8).

Shoa, s. ሸዋ šạ́͡uā̃.

Shoan, adj. የሸዋ yäšạ́͡uā̃ (§§ 47*a*, 70).

Shoan, s. ሸዋ šạ́͡uā̃, pl. ሸዎች šạ́͡uōč (-čč § 6).

shock, v.t. አስደነገጠ asdạnạ́ggạṭạ.

skin, s. (for water) ረዋት rạ́wā́t (rạ́͡uā́t; § 8).

ራውሃት rā́͡uhā́t (§ 8).

slandered, be, v.p. ታማ tā́mmā̃.

sneezing, remark to a person on their:

እግዚአብሔር፡ይማርህ። i̥gzi̥ay̥hʸér yi̥mári̥h!, f. -ርሽ። -ri̥š!, pol. -ሬዎ። -rḁʷo!, may God have mercy on you!

The reply is:

አብሮ፡ይማረን። áy̥rʷo yi̥márḁn!, may He abide with us and have mercy on us!

solid, be, v.i. ጠና ṭḁnnā̃ (§ 63*d*, *e*).

It is solid: ጠንቷል። ṭḁntōāl.

It is not solid: አልጠናም። alṭḁnnām.

solitary, adj. ገላላ gḁlálā̃ (B. ግላ- gi̥lá-).

A solitary place: ገላላ፡ስፍራ፡ gḁlálḁ si̥fra.

Solitary wasp: ትንዚዛ፡ ti̥nzízā̃ (§ 52*a*, δ), usually f. (§ 54*c*).

sooner, adv. ቀደም qḁ́d(d)ḁm (-mm § 6).

በቀደም bḁqḁ́d(d)ḁm (-mm § 6).

spill, v.i. (be spilt, v.p.) ተደፋ tḁdḁ́ffā̃.

It will spill: ይደፋል። yi̥ddḁ́ffāl.

spill, v.t. ደፋ dḁ́ffā̃.

Don't spill it: አትድፋው። attí̥dfau̯, pl. -ፉት። -fut.

You will spill it: ትደፋዋለህ። ti̥dḁfau̯állăh, pl. ትደፉታላችሁ። ti̥dḁfutalláččyuh (§ 7*d*).

stand close(r) together, v.i. ተነበበሩ tḁnḁbábbḁru (-ḁy̥á-, -bäru).

Let them stand close(r) together: ይነበበሩ። yi̥nnḁy̥áy̥ḁru.

They are not to stand (so) close together: አይነበበሩ። ai̥nnḁy̥áy̥ḁru.

stand up, v.i.

Stand (pl.) up: ብድግ፡በሉ። bí̥di̥g y̥ḁlu.

starve, v.i. በራብ፡ሞተ bḁráb (-áy̥) mʷṓtḁ.

starve, v.t. በራብ፡ገደለ bḁráb (-ā́y̥) gḁ́ddḁlḁ (gā́d-).
stop (up), v.t. (an aperture) ደፈነ dḁ́ffḁnḁ (dā́ffänḁ).
  Stop it up: ድፈነው። dı̥fḁnḁ͡u, pl. -ኑት። -nut.
  Don't stop it up: አትድፈነው። attı̥dfḁnḁ͡u, pl. -ኑት። -nut.
stopped (up), adj. ድፍን dı̥fı̥n.
stopped (up), be, v.p. (of an aperture) ተደፈነ tḁdḁ́ffḁnḁ (-dā́ffänḁ).
  It has been (is § 63*d*) stopped up: ተደፍኗል። tḁ-dā́fnŏ͡āl, pl. -ነዋል። -nḁ͡ūāl.
stopper, s. መድፈኛ mḁdfḁ́ñā (-fā́ñā), usually f. (§ 54*c*).
stretch, v.i. (oneself, v.r.) ተንጠራራ tḁnṭḁrā́rrā (-ṭär-).
stretch, v.t. (one's limbs) አንጠራራ anṭḁrā́rrā (-ṭär-).
strong, be, v.i. ጠና ṭḁ́nnā (§ 63*d*, *e*).
subdue, v.t. G. ለጥ፡አደረገ lḁṭṭ (läṭṭ) adḁ́rrḁgḁ.
  Š. ለበጥ፡አደረገ lḁ́bḁṭṭ (-ḁ́y̥ḁ-) adḁ́rrḁgḁ.
  He (pol.) subdued them: G. ለጥ፡አደረጓቸው። lḁṭṭ adarrḁgwā́ččḁ͡u.
  Š. ለበጥ፡አደረጓቸው። lḁ́-y̥ḁṭṭ adḁrrḁgwā́ččḁ͡u.
submit, v.i. G. ለጥ፡አለ lḁṭṭ (läṭṭ) álḁ.
  Š. ለበጥ፡አለ lḁ́bḁṭṭ (-ḁ́y̥ḁ-) álḁ.
  S.v. √ባለ, § 44*a*.
summon (have summoned), v.t. አስጠራ asṭḁ́rrā.
  The Rās summoned him: ራስ፡አስጠሩት። rās asṭḁ́r-rut (cp. § 52*b*).
  The Emperor will summon them: ጃንሆይ፡ያስጠሯቸዋል። jánhʷoi̥ yāsṭḁrrwā́ččḁ͡ūāl.
sunshade, s. ጥላ ṭı̥lā.

taken (hold of), be, v.p. ተያዘ tḁyázḁ (tḁ͡iá-).
telegraph, s. †ስልኪ sı̥lkī (Tña.).

temper (temperament), s. አመል ámḁl (-mäl).

He (it) has a good temper: አመሉ፡ደግ፡ነው። ámḁlu dǻggi̥ nḁ͡u.

testicle, s. Š. ቍላ qwú̃lā̃ (§ 52a, γ).

they, pers. pron. እነርሱ (i̥)nnḁ́rsū̃ (-nā́r-; § 8).

(of inanimate objects) እሳቸው i̥ssā́č-(č)ḁ͡u.

እነሱ (i̥)nnḁ́ssū̃ (-nā́s-; § 8).

See § 12a, s.v. እነ-.

though, conj.—may be rendered by the gerund:

She went in though she knew he was not there: ባይኖር፡አውቃ፡ነው፡የገባች። ba͡i̥nʷór (§ 37c) a͡uqā́ (§ 8) nḁ͡u yägḁ́bbāč, or አለመኖሩን፡አውቃ፡... ālḁ-mḁnʷőrun (§ 37a) a͡uqā́… .

through, prp. በ- bḁ- (yḁ-; § 47a).

I came through Harar: በሐረርጌ፡መጣኍ። bḁhárar̥-gʸe mḁ́ṭṭa͡uʰ, (§ 7d).

through, pass, (an aperture) v.i. ሾለከ šʷóllḁkḁ (šól-, šḁ́l-).

v.t. ሾለከ፡በ- šʷóllḁkḁ (etc.) bḁ- (yḁ-; § 47a).

He (it) passed through the hole and has got away: በቀዳዳው፡ሾልኮ፡ሒዷል። bḁqḁdā́da͡u šólkʷo hí̥dő͡āl.

tick, s. Š. መሽገር mḁ́šgḁr (-gär); usually f. (§ 54c).

Take the ticks off it: መዝገር፡አንሣለት። mḁ́zgḁr ánsāllḁt (§§ 47a, 71).

tight, be (tied), v.i. ጠበቀ ṭḁ́bbḁqḁ (type A § 34).

ጠበቅ፡አለ ṭḁ́bḁqq (-ḁ́yḁ-) álḁ (s.v. √ባለ, § 44a).

See § 63d, e.

It is (too) tight: ጡብቋል። ṭḁ́yqő͡āl, pl. ጡብቀዋል። ṭḁ́yqḁ͡uāl.

See that it is not too tight: እንዳይጠብቅ። nda͡i̥ṭḁ́yq, pl. -ቁ። -qu.

tighten, v.t. አጠበቀ aṭḁ́bbḁqḁ.

ጠበቅ፡አደረገ ṭḁ́bḁqq (-ḁ́yḁ-) adḁ́rrḁgḁ.

Tighten it: አጥብቀው። ā́ṭyi̥qḁ͡u, pl. -ቁት። -qut.

አጠብቀው። aṭḁ́bbi̥qḁ͡u, pl. -ቁት። -qut.

Don't tighten it: አታጥብቀው። attā́ṭyi̥qḁ͡u, pl. -ቁት። -qut.

አታጠብቀው። attāṭḁ́bbi̥qḁ͡u, pl. -ቁት። -qut.

Tighten the girths: ጠበቅ፡አድርገህ፡ጫነው። ṭḁ́yḁqq ádri̥gäh (ā́rgäh § 7*d*) č̣ā́nḁ͡u.

time, s.

In (good) time: በጊዜ፡ bḁgí̥z^{y}e.

tomato, s. የፈረንጅ፡እንኰይ yäfḁrḁ́nj (-färā́nj; § 70) í̥n-kwa͡i̥ (§ 52*a*, δ).

tournament, s. ጉክስ guks.

train, v.t. (a gun) ደገነ dḁ́ggḁnḁ (dā́g-), on, በ- bḁ- (yḁ-; § 47*a*).

trained, be, v.p. (of a gun) ተደገነ tḁdḁ́ggḁnḁ (-dā́g-), on, በ- bḁ- (yḁ-; § 47*a*).

treaty, s.

He made a treaty: ውል፡አደረገ። wŭl adḁ́rrḁgḁ, pol. & pl. -ረጉ። -rrḁgu.

Tuesday, s. B. ማስክኞ mā̃skḁ́ñño.

turn down, v.t. ደፋ dḁ́ffā̃.

turned down, be, v.p. (turn down, v.i.) ተደፋ tḁdḁ́ffā̃.

twenty, card. num. Š. ሀያ há^{y}a (há͡ā̃, ሃ hā, ኻያ χá^{y}a, ká^{y}a, χá͡ā̃, ká͡ā̃, ኻ χā, kā; § 20*a*).

unfrequented, adj. ገላላ gḁlálā̃ (B. ግላ- gi̥lá-).

uninhabited country, s. ባዳ bḁ́dã (bádã).

ምድረ፡ባዳ mi̥drḁ́ (§ 9*d*) bádã (bá-dã, ỵḁ́-, ỵá-, § 7*d*).

upset, v.t. ደፋ dḁffã.

Don't upset it: አትድፋው። attí̥dfa͡u, pl. -ፉት። -fut.

upset, be, v.p. (upset, v.i.) ተደፋ tḁdḁffã.

Mind it doesn't upset: እንዳይደፋ። nda͡i̥ddḁffã.

very, adv. አጥብቆ áṭbi̥q^{w}o (áṭỵi̥-, áṭi̥bq^{w}o, -i̥ỵq-).

watch, s.—phrases, making ሰዓት f. (§ 54*c*):—

Is it going? ትዞራለች። ti̥z^{w}orálläč?

Has it stopped? ቁማለች። qumálläč?

Š. ቆማለች። q^{w}omálläč?

Wind it up: ሙላት። múlāt.

It loses: ትቀራለች። ti̥qḁrálläč.

It is slow: ቀርታለች። qärtálläč.

ዘግይታለች። zḁgyi̥tálläč.

It gains: ትቀድማለች። ti̥qḁdmálläč.

It is fast: ቀድማለች። qḁdmálläč.

Put it on (forward): አስቀድማት። asqḁ́ddi̥māt.

Put it back: አስቀራት። asqḁrrāt.

It is right: ትክክል፡ናት። ti̥ki̥kki̥l (§ 8) nāt, Š. ...፡ነች። ... näč.

ልክ፡ናት። lí̥kki̥ (§ 7*d*) nāt, Š....፡ነች። ... näč.

It is not right: ልክ፡አይደለችም። li̥kk a͡i̥dálläčči̥m (§ 7*d*).

Put it right: አስተካክላት። astḁkáki̥lāt.

How much has it lost (is it slow)? ምን፡ያህል፡ቀረች። mi̥n yahl qḁ́rräč?

How much has it gained (is it fast)? ምን፡ያህል፡ቀደመች። mi̥n yahl qḁ́ddḁmäč?

It is wound up: ሞላች ። mʷóllāč.

It is not wound up: አልሞላችም ። almʷóllāččḭm.

It won't go: አልሰራም ፡ አለች ። alsḁ́rāmm ā́läč (s.v. √ባለ).

watch, v.i. & t. (guard) ጠበቀ ṭḁ́bbḁqḁ (type B § 35).

አጠበቀ aṭḁ́bbḁqḁ.

Watch him (it): ጠብቀው ። ṭḁ́bbḭqḁ͡u, pl. -ቁት ። -qut.

አጥብቀው ። ā́ṭyḭqḁ͡u, pl. -ቁት ። -qut.

አጠብቀው ። aṭḁ́bbḭqḁ͡u, pl. -ቁት ። -qut.

week, s. ሰሞን sḁ́mʷon.

what's-his-name, indef. pron. እንተን (ḭ)ntḁn (-tän), acc. እንተንን (ḭ)ntḁnḭn (-tän-), (§ 16).

where?, adv. G. ወት wωt?

window, s.

A house without windows: ድፍን ፡ ቤት ፡ dḭfḭ́n (§ 8) bʸēt.

wood, s. (forest) ዷን dḁn (-nn § 6).

wrong, adv.

There's nothing wrong with him (it): አልከፋውም ። alkḁ́ffa͡um, ...with them: አልከፋቸውም ። alkḁffáč-čḁ͡um, (§ 63*d*).

APPENDIX A

PRINCIPAL PARTS OF VERBS

[ADDITIONS to Appendix to Part I]

Part I. p. 280, l. 27, *omit* (= ተገደሬ).

p. 286, l. 14, *add* (= ተደገሬ).

p. 306, l. 14, yḁ́mrāl, *add* (yāmı̥́rāl).

p. 310, l. 4, *for* arrḁ́ggḁbḁ, yā̆rrḁ́g(ı̥̆)b, yā̆rrḁ́g(ı̥̆)bāl,
read arḁ́ggḁbḁ, yā̆rḁ́g(ı̥̆)b, yā̆rḁ́g(ı̥̆)bāl.

p. 314, l. 14, yā̆́ssı̥qāl, *add* (yā̆ssı̥́qāl).

p. 316, l. 20, *for* yā̆ssı̥tāl, *read* yā̆́ssı̥tāl (yā̆ssı̥́tāl).

p. 341, ll. 26, 27, *for* አዝማች ázmáč *read* አዘማች az-zḁ́mmā̆́č.

p. 344, l. 10, yā́dı̥nāl, *add* (yādı̥́nāl).

p. 345, l. 13, *for* ádı̥n^{w}o *read* ā̆́dı̥n^{w}o.

p. 374, l. 21, *add* (= ደገሬ).

p. 388, l. 18, *for* ሬጅ *read* ሬጀ.

NOTE.—In causatives in አ- (regular triliteral type አለቀመ alə̥qqə̥mə̥ § 41*d*), in the parts in which two adjacent radicals become sắdi̥s (§ 4*a*), i.e. in the gerund, compound perfect, jussive and imperative, the usual pronunciation, so far as I have observed, is for the first radical to receive no vowel while the second receives i̥: thus አለቀመ ger. አልቅሞ ắlqi̥mʷo, juss. ያልቅም yắlqi̥m, etc.; the less common variation of pronunciation (§ 7*d*) being for the first radical to receive i̥ and the second no vowel: ger. áli̥qmʷo, juss. yáli̥qm, etc., (with long á-, yá-, since they now form open accented syllables). In some verbs, however, the reverse is the case, áli̥qmʷo etc. being the usual pronunciation, and ắlqi̥mʷo etc. the less common variation. Generally speaking ắlqi̥mʷo is commoner in G. and áli̥qmʷo in Š.: but occasionally both forms are to be heard in the same verb both in G. and in Š.[1]

[1] Guidi (Gram. p. 34) gives as paradigm አነገረ anággara, ger. አንግሮ anᵉgrố, but juss. ያንግር yāngĕr.

Since writing the appendix to Part I. I have heard the following variations in addition to the pronunciation given there:—

አለቀመ ger. ā́li̥qm^{w}o, comp. perf. ā́li̥qmŏ͡āl, juss. yā́li̥q(ĭ̥)m, imp. ā́li̥q(ĭ̥)m.

አለቀሰ ger. ā́li̥qs^{w}o, etc.

አለበሰ „ ā́li̥bs^{w}o (-i̥ṿs^{w}o).

አመጣ „ G. ãmí̥ṭt^{w}o.

አሰጣ „ ãsí̥ṭt^{w}o.

አሰፋ „ ā́sfi̥t^{w}o.

አቀና „ ā́qni̥t^{w}o.

አበራ „ ā́bri̥t^{w}o (ā́ṿr-).

አበሰለ „ ā́bi̥sl^{w}o (ā́ṿi̥-).

አበቃ „ ā́bi̥qt^{w}o (ā́ṿi̥-).

አተረፈ „ ā́tri̥f^{w}o.

አነሣ „ ā́ni̥st^{w}o.

አነቃ „ ā́ni̥qt^{w}o.

አነጠሰ „ ā́ni̥ṭs^{w}o.

አነጠፈ „ ā́ni̥ṭf^{w}o.

አወለቀ „ á͡uŭlq^{w}o.

አወረደ „ á͡uri̥d^{w}o (-rŭd-).

አወጣ „ á͡uṭi̥t^{w}o.

አደላ „ ā́dli̥t^{w}o.

አደመጠ „ ā́dmi̥ṭ^{w}o.

አደረገ „ ā́di̥rg^{w}o.

አገሣ „ ā́gsi̥t^{w}o.

አገባ „ ā́gbi̥t^{w}o (ā́gṿi̥-).

አገደደ „ **አግድ·ዶ** ā́gdi̥d^{w}o

አፈላ „ ā́fli̥t^{w}o.

አፈረሰ „ ā́fri̥s^{w}o.

Simp. perf. (§ 25)		Comp. perf. (§ 32)	Contingent (§ 26)	Comp. imperf. (§ 32)
ለፈለፈ l̥af̥ál̥l̥af̥ḁ	chatter, i.	ለፍልፏል lḁ́fli̥fŏ͡āl	ይለፈልፍ yi̥l̥af̥ál̥li̥f	ይለፈልፋል yi̥l̥af̥ál̥li̥fāl
ሟሟ mwấmmwā̃	dissolve, i.	ሟምቷል mwámtŏ͡āl	ይሟሟ yi̥mwấm- mwā̃	ይሟሟል yi̥mwấm- mwāl
መከተ mḁ́kkḁtḁ	defend, i.	መክቷል mḁ́kki̥tŏ͡āl	ይመክት yi̥mḁ́kki̥t	ይመክታል yi̥mḁ́kki̥tāl
ሟጨ mwấč̣č̣ä 2nd ሟጨሀ mwấč̣č̣äh, etc.	scour, t.	ሟጭቷል mwấč̣(ĭ̥)tŏ͡āl	ይሟጭ yi̥mwấč̣č̣	ይሟጫል yi̥mwấč̣č̣āl
ረበረበ r̥ab̥ár̥rḁbḁ (r̥aṿár̥rḁṿḁ)	sprinkle, t.	ረብርቧል rḁ́bri̥bŏ͡āl (rắ-, -ṿri̥ṿŏ-)	ይረበርብ yi̥r̥ab̥ár̥ri̥b (yi̥rä-, -ṿắrri̥ṿ)	ይረበርባል yi̥r̥ab̥árri̥- bāl (yi̥rä-, -ṿắrri̥ṿāl)
[እ]ረጨ (ĭ̥)rḁ́č̣č̣ä (-rắč̣-) 2nd -ጨሀ -č̣č̣äh, etc.	sprinkle, t.	[እ]ረጭቷል (ĭ̥)rḁ́č̣(ĭ̥)tŏ͡āl (-rắč̣-)	ይረጭ yi̥rḁ́č̣ (-rắč̣)	ይረጫል yi̥rḁ́č̣āl (-rắč̣-)
ሰለበ sḁ́ll̥ab̥ḁ (-ḁṿḁ)	castrate, t.	ሰልቧል sḁ́lbŏ͡āl (sắl-; -lṿŏ-)	ይሰልብ yi̥sḁ́lb (-sắl-, -lṿ)	ይሰልባል yi̥sḁ́lbāl (-sắl-, -lṿāl)
ሰቀሰቀ s̥aqás̥sḁqḁ	pick, t.	ሰቅስቋል sḁ́qsi̥qŏ͡āl	ይሰቀስቅ yi̥s̥aqás̥si̥q	ይሰቀስቃል yi̥s̥aqás̥si̥- qāl

Jussive (§ 27)	Imperative (§ 28)	Gerund (§ 29)	Infinitive (§ 30)	Participle (§ 31)
ይለፍልፍ yi̥lḁ́fli̥f	ለፍልፍ lḁ́fli̥f	ለፍልፎ lḁ́fli̥fʷo	መለፍለፍ mḁlḁ́flḁf	ለፍላፊ lḁflā́fi
ይሟሟ yi̥mwā́mwã		ሟምቶ mwā́mtʷo	መሟሟት mḁmwā́m-wā́t (§ 8)	ሟሚ mwā́mi
ይመክት yi̥mḁ́kki̥t	መክት mḁ́kki̥t	መክቶ mḁ́kki̥tʷo	መመከት mḁmḁ́kkḁt	መካች mḁ́kkā́č(§ 8)
ይሟጭ yí̥mwā́č̣ (-ā̃́č̣č̣ § 6; § 8)	ሟጭ mwāč̣ (mwã̄č̣č̣ § 6)	ሟጭቶ mwā́č̣(ĭ̥)tʷo	መሟጨት mḁmwā́č̣ät (-ā̃́č̣č̣ät)	
ይረብርብ yi̥rḁ́bri̥b (yi̥rā̃-, -ỵri̥ỵ)	ረብርብ rḁ́bri̥b (rā̃́-, -ỵri̥ỵ)	ረብርቦ rḁ́bri̥bʷo (rā̃́-, -ỵri̥ỵʷo)	መረብረብ mḁrḁ́brḁb (märā̃́-, -ỵrḁỵ)	ረብራቢ rḁbrā́bi (rḁỵrā́ỵi)
ይርጭ yí̥r(ĭ̥)č̣	[እ]ርጭ (ĭ̥)rí̥č̣	[እ]ረጭቶ (ĭ̥)rḁ́č̣(ĭ̥)tʷo (-rā̃́č̣-)	መርጨት mḁ́rč̣ät (mā̃́r-)	[እ]ረጭ (ĭ̥)rḁ́č̣ (-rā̃́-, -ጪ.-č̣i)
ይስለብ yí̥slḁb (-ḁỵ)	ስለብ sí̥lḁb (-ḁỵ)	ሰልቦ sḁ́lbʷo (sā̃́l-, -lỵʷo)	መስለብ mḁ́slḁb (-ḁỵ)	ሰላቢ sḁlā́bi (-ā̃́ỵi)
ይሰቅስቅ yi̥sḁ́qsi̥q	ሰቅስቅ sḁ́qsi̥q	ሰቅስቆ sḁ́qsi̥qʷo	መሰቅሰቅ mḁsḁ́qsḁq	ሰቅሳቂ sḁqsā́qi

Simp. perf. (§ 25)		Comp. perf. (§ 32)	Contingent (§ 26)	Comp. imperf. (§ 32)
ሾለከ šʷóllḁkḁ (šól-, šḁ́l-)	pass through, i.	ሾልኳል šʷólkŏ͡āl (šól-, šḁ́l-)	ይሾልክ yi̥šʷólk (-šólk, -šḁ́lk)	ይሾልካል yi̥šʷólkāl (-šól-, -šḁ́l-)
ሽረ šắrḁ	heal, i. abolish, t.	ሽሯል ší̥rŏ͡āl	ይሽር yi̥ší̥r	ይሽራል yi̥ší̥rāl
ቀለጠፈ qḁlḁ́ṭṭḁfḁ	hasten, i.	ቀልጥፏል qḁ́lṭi̥fŏ͡āl (qḁ̆́l-)	ይቀለጥፍ yi̥qḁlḁ́ṭṭi̥f	ይቀለጥፋል yi̥qḁlḁ́ṭṭi̥fāl
ቈረቈረ qwωrḁ́q- qwωrḁ	trouble, t.	ቈርቍሯል qwώrqwŭ- rŏ͡āl	ይቈረቍር yi̥qwωrḁ́q- qwŭr	ይቈረቍራል yi̥qwωrḁ́q- qwŭrāl
ቀረቀበ qḁrḁ́qqḁbḁ (-ḁṿḁ)	tie into loads, t.	ቀርቅቧል qḁ́rqi̥bŏ͡āl (qḁ̆́r-, -i̥ṿŏ-)	ይቀረቅብ yi̥qḁrḁ́qqi̥b (-i̥ṿ)	ይቀረቅባል yi̥qḁrḁ́qqi̥- bāl (-i̥ṿāl)
ቈረበ qwώrrḁbḁ (-ḁṿḁ)	communicate, i.	ቈርቧል qwώrbŏ͡āl (-rṿŏ-)	ይቈርብ yi̥qwώrb (-rṿ)	ይቈርባል yi̥qwώrbāl (-rṿāl)
ቈረጠመ qwωrḁ́ṭṭḁ- mḁ	chew, t.	ቈርጥሟል qwώrṭi̥mŏ͡āl	ይቈረጥም yi̥qwωrḁ́ṭ- ṭi̥m	ይቈረጥማል yi̥qwωrḁ́ṭṭi̥- ʽmāl
ቀጠጠ qḁ́ṭṭḁṭḁ	clip, t.	ቀጧል qḁ́ṭṭŏ͡āl	ይቀጥ yi̥qḁ́ṭṭ	ይቀጣል yi̥qḁ́ṭṭāl
ቦከ bʷókkā̆	ferment, i.	ቦክቷል bʷóktŏ͡āl	ይቦክ yi̥bʷókā̆ (yi̥ṿʷó-)	ይቦካል yi̥bʷókāl (yi̥ṿʷó-)

Jussive (§ 27)	Imperative (§ 28)	Gerund (§ 29)	Infinitive (§ 30)	Participle (§ 31)
ይሹለክ yí̥šulḁk	ሹለክ šúlḁk	ሾልኮ šʷólkʷo (šól-, šḁ́l-)	መሹለክ mḁ́šulḁk	ሾላኪ šʷolā́ki (šol-, šḁl-)
ይሻር yi̥šā́r (§ 8)	ሻር šār	ሽሮ ši̥rʷo	መሻር mḁ́šā́r (§ 8)	ሻሪ šā́ri
ይቀልጥፍ yi̥qḁ́lṭi̥f (-qā́l-)	ቀልጥፍ qḁ́lṭi̥f (qā́l-)	ቀልጥፎ qḁ́lṭi̥fʷo (qā́l-)	መቀልጠፍ mḁqḁ́lṭḁf	ቀልጣፊ qḁlṭā́fi
		ቈርቍሮ qwώrqwŭ-rʷo	መቈርቈር mḁqwώr-qwωr	ቈርቋሪ qwωrqwā́ri
ይቀርቅብ yi̥qḁ́rqi̥b (-qā́r-, -i̥ṿ)	ቀርቅብ qḁ́rqi̥b (qā́r-, -i̥ṿ)	ቀርቅቦ qḁ́rqi̥bʷo (qā́r-, -i̥ṿʷo)	መቀርቀብ mḁqḁ́rqḁb (-qā́r-, -ḁṿ)	
ይቍረብ yi̥qwŭ́rḁb (-ḁṿ)	ቍረብ qwŭ́rḁb (-ḁṿ)	ቈርቦ qwώrbʷo (-rṿʷo)	መቍረብ mḁ́qwŭrḁb (-ḁṿ)	ቈራቢ qwωrā́bi (-ā́ṿi)
ይቈርጥም yi̥qwώrṭi̥m	ቈርጥም qwώrṭi̥m	ቈርጥሞ qwώrṭi̥mʷo	መቈርጠም mḁqwώr-ṭḁm	ቈርጣሚ qwωrṭā́mi
ይቅጠጥ yí̥qṭḁṭ	ቅጠጥ qí̥ṭḁṭ	ቀጦ qḁ́ṭṭʷo	መቅጠጥ mḁ́qṭḁṭ	ቀጣጭ qḁṭā́č̣ (§ 8)
ይቡካ yí̥bŭkā̃ (yí̥ṿŭ-, yŭ́ṿkā̃)		ቦክቶ bʷóktʷo	መቡካት mḁ́bŭkā́t (mḁ́ṿŭ-; § 8)	ቦኪ bʷóki

Simp. perf. (§ 25)		Comp. perf. (§ 32)	Contingent (§ 26)	Comp. imperf. (§ 32)
በዳ bḁ́ddã (bắḍ-)	copulate (of the male), t.	በድ·ቷል bḁ́d(ĭ̥)tŏ͡āl (bắd-, bḁ́rt-, bắrt-, § 7*d*)	ይበዳ yi̥bḁ́dã (yi̥ṿ-, -ắdã)	ይበዳል yi̥bḁ́dāl (yi̥ṿ-, -ắd-)
በጠሰ bḁ́ṭṭḁsḁ (bắṭ-)	tear, t.	በጥሷል bḁ́ṭṭi̥sŏ͡āl (bắṭ-)	ይበጥስ yi̥bḁ́ṭṭi̥s (yi̥ṿḁ́-, -ắṭ-)	ይበጥሳል yi̥bḁ́ṭṭi̥sāl (yi̥ṿḁ́-, -ắṭ-)
ታለመ tắllḁmḁ	dreamed, be, p.	ታልሟል tắlmŏ͡āl	ይታለም yi̥ttắllḁm	ይታለማል yi̥ttắllḁmāl
ተለመጠ tḁlḁ́mmḁṭḁ	be stropped, p.	ተለምጧል tḁlḁ́mmi̥-ṭŏ͡āl	ይለመጥ yi̥llḁ́mmḁṭ	ይለመጣል yi̥llḁ́mmḁ-ṭāl
ተለበሰ tḁlḁ́bbḁsḁ	be worn, p.	ተለብሷል tḁlḁ́bsŏ͡āl (-ḁ́ṿs-)	ይለበስ yi̥llḁ́bbḁs	ይለበሳል yi̥llḁ́bbḁsāl
ታማ tắmmã	be slandered, p.	ታምቷል tắmtŏ͡āl	ይታማ yi̥ttắmmã	ይታማል yi̥ttắmmāl
ተሟጨ tḁmwắč̣č̣ä 2nd -ጨህ -č̣č̣äh, etc.	be scoured, p.	ተሟጭቷል tḁmwắč̣(ĭ̥)-tŏ͡āl	ይሟጭ yi̥mmwắč̣č̣	ይሟጫል yi̥mmwắč̣-č̣āl
ተረበረበ tḁrḁbḁ́rrḁ-bḁ (tär-, -ḁṿḁ́rrḁṿḁ)	be sprinkled, p.	ተረብርቧል tḁrḁ́bri̥bŏ͡āl (tärắ-, -ṿri̥ṿŏ-)	ይረበረብ yi̥rrḁbḁ́rrḁb (-ḁṿḁ́rrḁṿ)	ይረበረባል yi̥rrḁbḁ́rrḁ-bāl (-ḁṿḁ́rrḁṿāl)

Jussive (§ 27)	Imperative (§ 28)	Gerund (§ 29)	Infinitive (§ 30)	Participle (§ 31)
ይብዳ yí̥bdã (yí̥ṿdã)	ብዳ bí̥dã	በድቶ bḁ́d(ĭ̥)t^{w}o (bắd-, bḁ́rt-, bắrt-, § 7*d*)	መብዳት mḁ́bdắt (mḁ́ṿd-; § 8)	በጅ bḁj (bäj, -ጂ -ji)
ይበጥስ yi̥bḁ́ṭṭi̥s (yi̥ṿḁ́-, -ắṭ-)	በጥስ bḁ́ṭṭi̥s (bắṭ-)	በጥሶ bḁ́ṭṭi̥s^{w}o (bắṭ-)	መበጠስ mḁbḁ́ṭṭḁs (mḁṿḁ́-, -ắṭ-)	በጣሽ bḁ́ṭṭắš (bắṭ-; § 8)
		ታልሞ tắlm^{w}o	መታለም mḁttắlḁm	
ይለመጥ yi̥llḁ́mḁṭ		ተለምጦ tḁlḁ́mmi̥ṭ^{w}o	መለመጥ mḁllḁ́mḁṭ	ተለማጭ tḁlḁ́mmắč̣ (§ 8)
ይለበስ yi̥llḁ́bḁs (-ḁ́ṿḁs)		ተለብሶ tḁlḁ́bs^{w}o (-ḁ́ṿs^{w}o)	መለበስ mḁllḁ́bḁs (-ḁ́ṿḁs)	ተለባሽ tḁlḁ́bbắš (§ 8)
ይታማ yi̥ttắmã		ታምቶ tắmt^{w}o	መታማት mḁttắmắt (§ 8)	ታሚ tắmi
ይሟጭ yí̥mmwắč̣ (§ 8)		ተሟጭቶ tḁmwắč̣- (ĭ̥)t^{w}o	መሟጨት mḁmmwắ- č̣ät	ተሟጪ tḁmwắč̣i (-ắč̣č̣i)
ይረብረብ yi̥rrḁ́brḁb (-ḁ́ṿrḁṿ)		ተረብርቦ tḁrḁ́bri̥b^{w}o (tärắ-, -ṿrí̥ṿ^{w}o)	መረብረብ mḁrrḁ́brḁb (-ḁ́ṿrḁṿ)	

Simp. perf. (§ 25)		Comp. perf. (§ 32)	Contingent (§ 26)	Comp. imperf. (§ 32)
ተረከበ tạrákkạbạ (tär-, -rák-, -ạyạ)	take over, t.	ተረክቧል tạrák(ị)-bŏ͡āl [tär-, -rák-, -(ị)yŏ-]	ይረከብ yịrrákkạb (-rák-, -kạy)	ይረከባል yịrrákkạ-bāl (-rák-,-ạyāl)
ተረዳ tạráddā̃ (tär-)	be persuaded, p.	ተረድቷል tạrádtŏ͡āl (tär-,-rárt-, -rárt-, § 7*d*)	ይረዳ yịrráddā̃	ይረዳል yịrráddāl
ተረጨ tạráččä (täráč-) 2nd -ጨህ -ččäh, etc.	be sprinkled, p.	ተረጭቷል tạráč(ị)tŏ͡āl (täráč-)	ይረጭ yịrráčč (-ráčč)	ይረጫል yịrráččāl (-ráč-)
ተሰለበ tạsállạbạ (täs-, -ạyạ)	be castrated, p.	ተሰልቧል tạsálbŏ͡āl (täsál-, -lyŏ-)	ይሰለብ yịssállạb (-ạy)	ይሰለባል yịssállạbāl (-ạyāl)
ተሳመ tạsámạ (täs-)	be kissed, p.	ተስሟል tásịmŏ͡āl (tás-)	ይሳም yịssám	ይሳማል yịssámāl
ተሰጣጡ tạsạṭáṭṭu (täsäṭ-)	give each other, t.	ተሰጣጥተዋል tạsạṭáṭ-tạ͡uāl (täsäṭ-)	ይሰጣጡ yịssạṭáṭṭu	ይሰጣጣሉ yịssạṭáṭ-ṭállu
ተሻረ tạšárạ (täš-)	be abolished, p.	ተሽሯል tášịrŏ͡āl (táš-)	ይሻር yịššár	ይሻራል yịššárāl

Jussive (§ 27)	Imperative (§ 28)	Gerund (§ 29)	Infinitive (§ 30)	Participle (§ 31)
ይረክብ yi̥rrḁ́kḁb (-rǻk-, -ḁẏ)	ተረክብ tḁrḁ́kḁb (tär-, -rǻk-, -ḁẏ)	ተረክቦ tḁrḁ́k(ĭ̥)bʷo [tär-, -rǻk-, -(ĭ̥)ẏʷo]	መረክብ mḁrrḁ́kḁb (-rǻk-, -ḁẏ)	ተረካቢ tḁrḁkkǻbi (tär-, -räk-, -ǻẏi)
ይረዳ yi̥rrḁ́dã		ተረድቶ tḁrḁ́dtʷo (tär-, -rḁ́rt-, -rǻrt-, § 7*d*)	መረዳት mḁrrḁ́dǻt (§ 8)	ተረጂ tḁ́rḁ́j (tǻrǻj; § 8; -ጂ -ji)
ይረጭ yí̥rrḁ́č̣ (-rǻč̣; § 8)	ተረጭ tḁ́rḁ́č̣ (tǻrǻč̣; § 8)	ተረጭቶ tḁrḁ́č̣(ĭ̥)tʷo (tärǻč̣-)	መረጫት mḁrrḁ́č̣ät (-rǻč̣-)	
ይሰልብ yi̥ssḁ́lḁb (-ḁẏ)		ተሰልቦ tḁsḁ́lbʷo (täsǻl-, -lẏʷo)	መሰልብ mḁssḁ́lḁb (-ḁẏ)	ተሳላቢ tḁsḁlǻbi (täs-, -ǻẏi)
ይሳም yí̥ssǻm (§ 8)		ተስሞ tḁ́si̥mʷo (tǻs-)	መሳም mḁ́ssǻm (§ 8)	
ይሰጣጡ yi̥ssḁṭǻṭu	ተሰጣጡ tḁsḁṭǻṭu (täsäṭ-)	ተሰጣጥተው tḁsḁṭǻṭtḁ͡u (täsäṭ-)	መሰጣጠት mḁssḁṭǻṭḁt	
ይሻር yí̥ššǻr (§ 8)		ተሽሮ tḁ́ši̥rʷo (tǻš-)	መሻር mḁ́ššǻr (§ 8)	

Simp. perf. (§ 25)		Comp. perf. (§ 32)	Contingent (§ 26)	Comp. imperf (§ 32)
ተቈረቈረ tḁqwωrḁ́q- qwωrḁ	be troubled, p.	ተቈርቍሯል tḁqwώrqwŭ- rŏ͡āl	ይቈረቈር yi̥qqwωrḁ́q- qwωr	ይቈረቈራል yi̥qqwωrḁ́q- qwωrāl
ተቀረቀበ tḁqḁrḁ́qqḁ- bḁ (-ḁṿḁ)	be tied into loads, p.	ተቀርቅቧል tḁqḁ́rqi̥- bŏ͡āl (-qā́r-, -i̥ṿŏ-)	ይቀረቀብ yi̥qqḁrḁ́q- qḁb (-ḁṿ)	ይቀረቀባል yi̥qqḁrḁ́q- qḁbāl (-ḁṿāl)
ተቈረጠመ tḁqwωrḁ́ṭ- ṭḁmḁ	be chewed, p.	ተቈርጥሟል tḁqwώrṭi̥- mŏ͡āl	ይቈረጠም yi̥qqwωrḁ́ṭ- ṭḁm	ይቈረጠማል yi̥qqwωrḁ́ṭ- ṭḁmāl
ተቀባበሉ tḁqḁbáb- bḁlu (-ḁṿá-)	receive from each other, t.	ተቀባብለዋል tḁqḁbā́b(ĭ̥)- lḁ͡uāl [-ḁṿā́ṿ(ĭ̥)l-]	ይቀባበሉ yi̥qqḁbáb- bḁlu (-qḁṿá-)	ይቀባበላሉ yi̥qqḁbab- bḁlā́llu (-qḁṿa-)
ተቈያዩ tḁqwω͡i̥áyyu	await each other, recip.	ተቈያይተዋል tḁqwω͡i̥á͡i̥- tḁ͡uāl	ይቈያዩ yi̥qqwω͡i̥- áyyu	ይቈያያሉ yi̥qqwω͡i̥- ayyā́llu
ተቋጠረ tḁqwā́ṭṭḁrḁ (-ṭärḁ)	be knotted, p.	ተቋጥሯል tḁqwā́ṭrŏ͡āl	ይቋጠር yi̥qqwā́ṭṭḁr (-ṭär)	ይቋጠራል yi̥qqwā́ṭṭḁ- rāl (-ṭär-)
ተቀጠጠ tḁqḁ́ṭṭḁṭḁ	be clipped, p.	ተቀጧል tḁqḁ́ṭṭŏ͡āl	ይቀጠጥ yi̥qqḁ́ṭṭḁṭ	ይቀጠጣል yi̥qqḁ́ṭṭḁṭāl
ተባባሉ tḁbābā́lu (tḁṿāṿā́-)	say to each other, t.	ተባብለዋል tḁbā́b(ĭ̥)lḁ͡u- āl [tḁṿā́ṿ(ĭ̥)l-]	ይባባሉ yi̥bbābā́lu (-āṿā́-)	ይባባላሉ yi̥bbābā- lā́llu (-āṿā-)

Jussive (§ 27)	Imperative (§ 28)	Gerund (§ 29)	Infinitive (§ 30)	Participle (§ 31)
		ተቈርቍሮ tḁqwŕ̥rqwŭ- rʷo	መቈርቈር mḁqqwώr- qwωr	ተቈርቋሪ tḁqwωr- qwā́ri
ይቀርቀብ yi̥qqḁ́rqḁb (-qā́r-, -ḁỵ)		ተቀርቅቦ tḁqḁ́rqi̥bʷo (-qā́r-,-i̥ỵʷo)	መቀርቀብ mḁqqḁ́rqḁb (-qā́r-, -ḁỵ)	
ይቈርጠም yi̥qqwώr- ṭḁm		ተቈርጥሞ tḁqwώr- ṭi̥mʷo	መቈርጠም mḁqqwώr- ṭḁm	ተቈርጣሚ tḁqwωrṭā́mi
ይቀባበሉ yi̥qqḁbā́- bḁlu (-ḁỵā́ỵḁ-)	ተቀባበሉ tḁqḁbā́bḁlu (-ḁỵā́ỵḁ-)	ተቀባብለው tḁqḁbā́b(ĭ̥)- lḁ͡u [-ḁỵā́ỵ(ĭ̥)l-]	መቀባበል mḁqqḁbā́- bḁl (-ḁỵā́ỵḁl, -ỵäl)	ተቀባባይ tḁqḁbā́- bā́͡i̥ (-ḁỵā́ỵā́͡i̥; § 8; -ā́yy § 6)
ይቈያዩ yi̥qqwω͡i̥á͡i̥u	ተቈያዩ tḁqwω͡i̥á͡i̥u	ተቈያይተው tḁqwωi̥á͡i̥- tḁ͡u	መቈያየት mḁqqwω͡i̥- á͡i̥ät	
ይቋጠር yi̥qqwā́ṭḁr (-ṭär)		ተቋጥሮ tḁqwā́ṭrʷo	መቋጠር mḁqqwā́ṭḁr (-ṭär)	ተቋጣሪ tḁqwāṭā́ri
ይቀጠጥ yi̥qqḁ́ṭḁṭ		ተቀጦ tḁqḁ́ṭṭʷo	መቀጠጥ mḁqqḁ́ṭḁṭ	ተቀጣጭ tḁqḁ́ṭā́č̣ (§ 8)
ይባባሉ yi̥bbābā́lu (-āỵā́-)	ተባባሉ tḁbābā́lu (tḁỵāỵā́-)	ተባብለው tḁbā́b(ĭ̥)lḁ͡u [tḁỵā́ỵ(ĭ̥)l-]	መባባል mḁbbā́bā́l (-ā́ỵā́l; § 8)	ተባባይ tḁbā́bā́͡i̥ (tḁỵā́ỵā́͡i̥; § 8; -ā́yy § 6)

Simp. perf. (§ 25)		Comp. perf. (§ 32)	Contingent (§ 26)	Comp. imperf. (§ 32)
ተበዳች tḁbḁ́ddāč (täbá̄d-, täyá̄-; -āčč § 6)	copulate (of the female), p.	ተበድታለች tḁbḁd(ï̥)- tá̄lläč (täbä-, täyäd-, -ärt- § 7*d*; -äčč § 6)	ትበዳ ti̥bbḁ́ddā̃ (-bá̄d-)	ትበዳለች ti̥bbḁddá̄l- läč (-bäd-; -äčč § 6)
ተበጠሰ tḁbḁ́ṭṭḁsḁ (tḁyḁ́-, -á̄ṭ-)	be torn, p.	ተበጥሷል tḁbḁ́ṭṭi̥sð͡āl (tḁyḁ́-, -á̄ṭ-)	ይበጠስ yi̥bbḁ́ṭṭḁs (-bá̄ṭ-)	ይበጠሳል yi̥bbḁ́ṭṭḁsāl (-bá̄ṭ-)
ተተካ tḁtḁ́kkā̃	be substituted, p.	ተተክቷል tḁtḁ́kki̥tð͡āl (-tá̄k-)	ይተካ yi̥ttḁ́kkā̃	ይተካል yi̥ttḁ́kkāl
ተተፋ tḁtḁ́ffā̃	be vomited, p.	ተተፍቷል tḁtḁ́ftð͡āl	ይተፋ yi̥ttḁ́ffā̃	ይተፋል yi̥ttḁ́ffāl
ተነሰነሰ tḁnḁsḁ́n- nḁsḁ	be sprinkled, p.	ተነስንሷል tḁnḁ́sni̥sð͡āl (täná̄s-)	ይነሰነስ yi̥nnḁsḁ́n- nḁs	ይነሰነሳል yi̥nnḁsḁ́n- nḁsāl
ተነቀለ tḁnḁ́qqḁlḁ	be uprooted, p.	ተነቅሏል tḁnḁ́qlð͡āl	ይነቀል yi̥nnḁ́qqḁl	ይነቀላል yi̥nnḁ́qqḁlāl
ተነባ tḁnḁ́bbā̃	prophecy, t.	ተነብቷል tḁnḁ́btð͡āl (-ḁ́yt-)	ይነባ yi̥nnḁ́bbā̃	ይነባል yi̥nnḁ́bbāl
ተነባበረ tḁnḁbábbḁ- rḁ (-nḁyá-, -bärḁ).	be piled up, i. stand close together, i.	ተነባብሯል tḁnḁbá̄b- rð͡āl (-ḁyá̄yr-)	ይነባበር yi̥nnḁbáb- bḁr (-ḁyá-, -bär)	ይነባበራል yi̥nnḁbáb- bḁrāl (-ḁyá-, -bär-)

Jussive (§ 27)	Imperative (§ 28)	Gerund (§ 29)	Infinitive (§ 30)	Participle (§ 31)
ትበዳ ti̥bbḁ́dã (-bắd-)		ተበድታ tḁbḁ́d(ĭ̥)tã (täbắ-, täṿắd-, -ắrt- § 7*d*)	መበዳት mḁbbḁ́dắt (-bắd-; § 8)	
ይበጠስ yi̥bbḁ́ṭḁs (-bắṭ-)		ተበጥሶ tḁbḁ́ṭṭi̥sʷo (tḁṿḁ́-, -ắṭ-)	መበጠስ mḁbbḁ́ṭḁs (-bắṭ-)	ተበጣሽ tḁbḁ́ṭṭắš (tḁṿḁ́-; § 8)
ይተካ yi̥ttḁ́kã		ተተክቶ tḁtḁ́kki̥tʷo (-tắk-)	መተካት mḁttḁ́kắt (§ 8)	
ይተፋ yi̥ttḁ́fã		ተተፍቶ tḁtḁ́ftʷo	መተፋት mḁttḁ́fắt (§ 8)	
ይነስነስ yi̥nnḁ́snḁs		ተነስንሶ tḁnḁ́sni̥sʷo (tänắs-)	መነስነስ mḁnnḁ́snḁs	
ይነቀል yi̥nnḁ́qḁl		ተነቅሎ tḁnḁ́qlʷo	መነቀል mḁnnḁ́qḁl	ተነቃይ tḁnḁ́qqá͡i̥ (§ 8; -ắyy § 6)
ይነባ yi̥nnḁ́bã (-ḁ́ṿã)	ተነባ tḁnḁ́bã (-ḁ́ṿã)	ተነብቶ tḁnḁ́btʷo (-ḁ́ṿtʷo)	መነባት mḁnnḁ́bắt (-ḁ́ṿắt; § 8)	
ይነባበር yi̥nnḁbắbḁr (-ḁṿắṿ-, -är)	pl. ተነባበሩ tḁnḁbắbḁru (-ḁṿắṿ-, -äru)	ተነባብሮ tḁnḁbắbrʷo (-ḁṿắṿrʷo)	መነባበር mḁnnḁbắ-bḁr (-ḁṿắṿ-, -är)	ተነባባሪ tḁnḁbābári (-ḁṿāṿá-)

Simp. perf. (§ 25)		Comp. perf. (§ 32)	Contingent (§ 26)	Comp. imperf. (§ 32)
ተነዘረ tḁnḁ́zzḁrḁ (-zärḁ)	be spun, p.	ተነዝሯል tḁnḁ́zrŏ͡āl	ይነዝር yi̥nnḁ́zzḁr (-zär)	ይነዝራል yi̥nnḁ́zzḁrāl (-zär-)
ተንጠራራ tḁnṭḁrā́rrā̃ (-ṭär-)	stretch oneself, r.	ተንጠራርቷል tḁnṭḁrā́r- tŏ͡āl (-ṭär-)	ይንጠራራ yi̥nṭḁrā́rrā̃ (§ 7*c note*; -ṭär-)	ይንጠራራል yi̥nṭḁrā́rrāl (§ 7*c note*; -ṭär-)
ተካ tḁ́kkā̃	substitute, t.	ተክቷል tḁ́kki̥tŏ͡āl (tä́k-)	ይተካ yi̥tḁ́kkā̃	ይተካል yi̥tḁ́kkāl
ተከሰ tḁkā́sḁ	be paid (as fine), p.	ተክሷል tḁ́ki̥sŏ͡āl (tä́k-)	ይከስ yi̥kkā́s	ይከሳል yi̥kkā́sāl
ተኳተ tḁkwā́tḁ	be dug, p.	ተኰቷል tḁ́kwŭtŏ͡āl (tä́k-)	ይኳት yi̥kkwā́t	ይኳታል yi̥kkwā́tāl
ተከፈከፈ tḁkḁfḁ́k- kḁfḁ	be sprinkled, p.	ተከፍክፏል tḁkḁ́fki̥fŏ͡āl	ይከፈክፍ yi̥kkḁfḁ́k- kḁf	ይከፈክፋል yi̥kkḁfḁ́k- kḁfāl
ተወቃ tḁwώqqā̃ (tḁ͡ūώ-)	be threshed, p.	ተወቅቷል tḁwώqtŏ͡āl (tḁ͡ūώ-)	ይወቃ yi̥wwώqqā̃ (yuwώ-)	ይወቃል yi̥wwώqqāl (yuwώ-)
ተዘረጋ tḁzḁrḁ́ggā̃ (täzär-)	be stretched, p.	ተዘርግቷል tḁzḁ́rgi̥tŏ͡āl (täzä́r-)	ይዘረጋ yi̥zzḁrḁ́ggā̃ (-zär-)	ይዘረጋል yi̥zzḁrḁ́ggāl (-zär-)
ተያዩ tḁ͡ʸá͡yyu	see each other, recip.	ተያይተዋል tḁ͡ʸái̥tḁ͡ūāl	ይተያዩ yi̥ttḁ͡ʸáyyu	ይተያያሉ yi̥ttḁ͡ʸayyā́l- lu

Jussive (§ 27)	Imperative (§ 28)	Gerund (§ 29)	Infinitive (§ 30)	Participle (§ 31)
ይነዘር yi̥nnḁ́zḁr (-zär)		ተነዝሮ tḁnḁ́zr^{w}o	መነዘር mḁnnḁ́zḁr (-zär)	
ይንጠራራ yi̥nṭḁrā́rã (§ 7*c note*; -ṭär-)	ተንጠራራ tḁnṭḁrā́rã (-ṭär-)	ተንጠራርቶ tḁnṭḁrā́rt^{w}o (-ṭär-)	መንጠራራት mḁnṭḁrā́rā́t (§ 7*c note*; -ṭär-; § 8)	
ይተካ yi̥tḁ́kkã	ተካ tḁ́kkã	ተክቶ tḁ́kki̥t^{w}o (tắk-)	መተካት mḁtḁ́kkā́t (§ 8)	
ይካስ yí̥kkā́s (§ 8)		ተክሶ tḁ́ki̥s^{w}o (tắk-)	መካስ mḁ́kkā́s (§ 8)	ተካሽ tḁ́kā́š (§ 8)
ይኳት yí̥kkwā́t (§ 8)		ተኩቶ tḁ́kwŭ́t^{w}o (tắk-)	መኳት mḁ́kkwā́t (§ 8)	
ይከፍክፍ yi̥kkḁ́fkḁf		ተከፍክፎ tḁkḁ́fki̥f^{w}o	መከፍከፍ mḁkkḁ́fkḁf	ተከፍካፊ tḁkḁfkā́fi
ይወቃ yi̥wwώqã (yuwώ-)		ተወቅቶ tḁwώqt^{w}o (tḁ͡uώ-)	መወቃት mḁwwώqā́t (mḁ͡uwώ-; § 8)	ተወቂ tḁwḁ́qi (tḁ͡uḁ́-, -ώqi)
ይዘርጋ yi̥zzḁ́rgã (-zắr-)		ተዘርግቶ tḁzḁ́rgi̥t^{w}o (-zắr-)	መዘርጋት mḁzzḁ́rgā́t (-zắr-; § 8)	ተዘርጊ tḁzḁ́rgi (täzắr-)
ይተያዩ yi̥ttḁ^{y}ái̥u	ተያዩ tḁ^{y}ái̥u	ተያይተው tḁ^{y}ái̥tḁ͡u	መተያየት mḁttḁ^{y}ái̥ät	

Simp. perf. (§ 25)		Comp. perf. (§ 32)	Contingent (§ 26)	Comp. imperf. (§ 32)
ተደበቀ tḁdḁ́bbḁqḁ	be hidden, p.	ተደብቋል tḁdḁ́bbi̥-qŏ͡āl	ይደበቅ yi̥ddḁ́bbḁq	ይደበቃል yi̥ddḁ́bbḁ-qāl
ተደበደበ tḁdḁbḁ́d-dḁbḁ (-dä-ỵá̈ddäỵḁ)	be massacred, p.	ተደብድቧል tḁdḁ́bdi̥-bŏ͡āl (-dá̈ỵdi̥ỵŏ-)	ይደበደብ yi̥ddḁbḁ́d-dḁb (-däỵá̈ddäỵ)	ይደበደባል yi̥ddḁbḁ́d-dḁbāl (-dä-ỵá̈ddäỵāl)
ተደገነ tḁdḁ́ggḁnḁ (-dá̈g-)	be aimed, p.	ተደግኗል tḁdḁ́ggi̥-nŏ͡āl (-dá̈g-)	ይደገን yi̥ddḁ́ggḁn (-dá̈g-)	ይደገናል yi̥ddḁ́ggḁ-nāl (-dá̈g-)
ተደፋ tḁdḁ́ffā̃	be turned down, p.	ተደፍቷል tḁdḁ́ftŏ͡āl	ይደፋ yi̥ddḁ́ffā̃	ይደፋል yi̥ddḁ́ffāl
ተደፈነ tḁdḁ́ffḁnḁ (-dá̈ffänḁ)	be closed up, p.	ተደፍኗል tḁdḁ́f(ĭ̥)nŏ͡āl (-dá̈f-)	ይደፈን yi̥ddḁ́ffḁn (-dá̈ffän)	ይደፈናል yi̥ddḁ́ffḁnāl (-dá̈ffän-)
ታጐለ tá̈ggwωlḁ	be inter-rupted, p.	ታጕሏል tá̈ggwŭlŏ͡āl	ይታጐል yi̥ttá̈ggwωl	ይታጐላል yi̥ttá̈ggwω-lāl
ተገለጠ tḁgḁ́llḁṭḁ (-gá̈l-)	be disclosed, p.	ተገልጧል tḁgḁ́lṭŏ͡āl (-gá̈l-)	ይገለጥ yi̥ggḁ́llḁṭ (-gá̈lläṭ)	ይገለጣል yi̥ggḁ́llḁṭāl (-gá̈l-)
ታገመ tá̈ggḁmḁ	be cupped, p.	ታግሟል tá̈gmŏ͡āl	ይታገም yi̥ttá̈ggḁm	ይታገማል yi̥ttá̈ggḁ-māl
ተገረዘ tḁgḁ́rrḁzḁ	be circum-cised, p.	ተገርዟል tḁgḁ́rri̥zŏ͡āl (-gá̈r-)	ይገረዝ yi̥ggḁ́rrḁz	ይገረዛል yi̥ggḁ́rrḁ-zāl

Jussive (§ 27)	Imperative (§ 28)	Gerund (§ 29)	Infinitive (§ 30)	Participle (§ 31)
ይደበቅ yi̥ddḁ́bḁq (-ḁ́ỵḁq)	**ተደበቅ** tḁdḁ́bḁq (-ḁ́ỵḁq)	**ተደብቆ** tḁdḁ́bbi̥q^{w}o	**መደበቅ** mḁddḁ́bḁq (-ḁ́ỵḁq)	**ተደባቂ** tḁdḁbbắqi
ይድብድብ yi̥ddḁ́bdḁb (-dắỵdäỵ)		**ተድብድቦ** tḁdḁ́bdi̥b^{w}o (-dắỵdi̥ỵ^{w}o)	**መድብድብ** mḁddḁ́b- dḁb (-dắỵdäỵ)	
ይደገን yi̥ddḁ́gḁn (-dắg-)		**ተደግኖ** tḁdḁ́ggi̥n^{w}o (-dắg-)	**መደገን** mḁddḁ́gḁn (-dắg-)	
ይደፋ yi̥ddḁ́fã	**ተደፋ** tḁdḁ́fã	**ተደፍቶ** tḁdḁ́ft^{w}o	**መደፋት** mḁddḁ́fắt (§ 8)	**ተደፊ** tḁdḁ́fi
ይደፈን yi̥ddḁ́fḁn (-dắfän)		**ተደፍኖ** tḁdḁ́f(i̥)n^{w}o (-dắf-)	**መደፈን** mḁddḁ́fḁn (-dắfän)	**ተደፋኝ** tḁdḁ́ffắñ (-dắf-; § 8; -ññ § 6)
ይታጐል yi̥ttắgwωl		**ታጕሎ** tắggwŭl^{w}o	**መታጐል** mḁttắgwωl	
ይገለጥ yi̥ggḁ́lḁṭ (-gắläṭ)		**ተገልጦ** tḁgḁ́lṭ^{w}o (-gắl-)	**መገለጥ** mḁggḁ́lḁṭ (-gắläṭ)	**ተገላጭ** tḁgḁ́llắč̣ (-gắl- ; § 8)
ይታገም yi̥ttắgḁm	**ታገም** tắgḁm	**ታግሞ** tắgm^{w}o	**መታገም** mḁttắgḁm	
ይገረዝ yi̥ggḁ́rḁz		**ተገርዞ** tḁgḁ́rri̥z^{w}o (-gắr-)	**መገረዝ** mḁggḁ́rḁz	**ተገራዥ** tḁgḁ́rrắž (§ 8)

Simp. perf. (§ 25)		Comp. perf. (§ 32)	Contingent (§ 26)	Comp. imperf. (§ 32)
ተጐረጐረ tḁgwωrḁ́g- gwωrḁ (-rώgg-)	be inspected, p.	ተጐርጕሯል tḁgwώrgwi̥- rŏ͡āl (-gwŭrŏ-)	ይጐረጐር yi̥ggwωrḁ́g- gwωr (-rώgg-)	ይጐረጐራል yi̥ggwωrḁ́g- gwωrāl (-rώgg-)
ተኳሰመ tḁgwā́ssḁ- mḁ (-sämḁ)	stretch oneself, r.	ተኳስሟል tḁgwā́s(ĭ̥)- mŏ͡āl	ይኳሰም yi̥ggwā́s- sḁm (-säm)	ይኳሰማል yi̥ggwā́ssḁ- māl (-säm-)
ተጐተተ tḁgwώttḁtḁ	be dragged, p.	ተጐትቷል tḁgwώt- (ti̥)tŏ͡āl	ይጐተት yi̥ggwώttḁt (-tät)	ይጐተታል yi̥ggwώttḁ- tāl
ታገዘ tā́ggḁzḁ	be helped, p.	ታግዟል G. tā́gzŏ͡āl Š. tā́ggi̥zŏ͡āl	ይታገዝ yi̥ttā́ggḁz	ይታገዛል yi̥ttā́ggḁzāl
ተገዘተ tḁgḁ́zzḁtḁ	be excom- municated, p.	ተገዝቷል tḁgḁ́zzi̥tŏ͡āl	ይገዘት yi̥ggḁ́zzḁt (-zät)	ይገዘታል yi̥ggḁ́zzḁtāl
ተገደፈ tḁgḁ́ddḁfḁ	end (of a fast), i.—impers. (§ 43*a*); be inaccu- rate, i.	ተገድፏል tḁgḁ́dfŏ͡āl (-gā́d-)	ይገደፍ yi̥ggḁ́ddḁf	ይገደፋል yi̥ggḁ́ddḁ- fāl
ተጠለፈ tḁṭḁ́llḁfḁ	be embroi- dered, p.	ተጠልፏል tḁṭḁ́lfŏ͡āl (-ṭā́l-)	ይጠለፍ yi̥ṭṭḁ́llḁf	ይጠለፋል yi̥ṭṭḁ́llḁfāl
ተጠባ tḁṭḁ́bbā̃	be sucked, p.	ተጠብቷል tḁṭḁ́btŏ͡āl (-ḁ́y̥t-)	ይጠባ yi̥ṭṭḁ́bbā̃	ይጠባል yi̥ṭṭḁ́bbāl

Jussive (§ 27)	Imperative (§ 28)	Gerund (§ 29)	Infinitive (§ 30)	Participle (§ 31)
ይጕርጕር yi̥ggwώr-gwωr		ተጕርጕሮ tḁgwώr-gwi̥r^{w}o (-gwŭr^{w}o)	መጕርጕር mḁggwώr-gwωr	ተጕርጓሪ tḁgwωr-gwấri
ይጓሰሟ yi̥ggwấsḁm (-säm)	ተጓሰም tḁgwấsḁm (-säm)	ተጓስሞ tḁgwấs(ĭ̥)-m^{w}o	መጓሰም mḁggwấ-sḁm (-säm)	ተጓሳሚ tḁgwāsấmi
ይጕተት yi̥ggwώtḁt (-ṭät)	ተጕተት tḁgwώtḁt (-tät)	ተጕትቶ tḁgwώt-(ti̥)t^{w}o	መጕተት mḁggwώtḁt (-tät)	ተጕታች tḁgwώt(t)ấč (§ 8)
ይታገዝ yi̥ttấgḁz		ታግዞ G. tấgz^{w}o Š. tấggi̥z^{w}o	መታገዝ mḁttấgḁz	ታጋዥ G. tấgấž (§ 8) Š. tấggấž (§ 8)
ይገዘት yi̥ggḁ́zḁt (-zät)	ተገዘት tḁgḁ́zḁt (-zät)	ተገዝቶ tḁgḁ́zzi̥t^{w}o	መገዘት mḁggḁ́zḁt (-zät)	ተገዛች tḁgḁ́zzấč (§ 8)
ይገደፍ yi̥ggḁ́dḁf		ተገድፎ tḁgḁ́df^{w}o (-gấd-)	መገደፍ mḁggḁ́dḁf	
ይጠለፍ yi̥ṭṭḁ́lḁf		ተጠልፎ tḁṭḁ́lf^{w}o (-ṭấl-)	መጠለፍ mḁṭṭḁ́lḁf	
ይጠባ yi̥ṭṭḁ́bã (-ḁ́ẏã)		ተጠብቶ tḁṭḁ́bt^{w}o (-ḁ́ẏt-)	መጠባት mḁṭṭḁ́bất (-ḁ́ẏất; § 8)	

Simp. perf. (§ 25)		Comp. perf. (§ 32)	Contingent (§ 26)	Comp. imperf. (§ 32)
ተጨነቀ tḁč̣ḁ́nnḁqḁ	be distressed, i.	ተጨንቋል tḁč̣ḁ́nqŏ͡āl (-ḁ́ṅq-)	ይጨነቅ yi̥č̣č̣ḁ́nnḁq	ይጨነቃል yi̥č̣č̣ḁ́nnḁ- qāl
ተጯጯኹ tḁč̣ŏ͡ā́č̣ŏ͡ãhu (§ 7*d*)	cry to each other, recip.	ተጯጩኸዋል tḁč̣ŏ͡ā́č̣ŭ- hḁ͡uāl	ይጯጯኹ yi̥č̣č̣ŏ͡ā́č̣ŏ͡ã- hu	ይጯጯኻሉ yi̥č̣č̣ŏ͡ãč̣ŏ͡ã- hã́llu
ተፋ tḁ́ffã	vomit, t.	ተፍቷል tḁ́ftŏ͡āl	ይተፋ yi̥tḁ́fã	ይተፋል yi̥tḁ́fāl
ተፈለፈለ tḁfḁlḁ́ffḁlḁ	be scooped, p.	ተፈልፍሏል tḁfḁ́lfi̥lŏ͡āl (-fä́l-)	ይፈለፈል yi̥ffḁlḁ́ffḁl (-fäl)	ይፈለፈላል yi̥ffḁlḁ́ffḁlāl
ተፈራረቀ tḁfḁrä́rrḁqḁ	alternate, i.	ተፈራርቋል tḁfḁrä́r(ĭ̥)- qŏ͡āl	ይፈራረቅ yi̥ffḁrä́rrḁq	ይፈራረቃል yi̥ffḁrä́rrḁ- qāl
ተፈቃቀሩ tḁfḁqā́q- qḁru	love each other, recip.	ተፈቃቅረዋል tḁfḁqā́q(ĭ̥)- rḁ͡uāl	ይፈቃቀሩ yi̥ffḁqā́q- qḁru	ይፈቃቀራሉ yi̥ffḁqāqqḁ- rã́llu
ተፈተለ tḁfḁ́ttḁlḁ (-fä́ttälḁ)	be woven, p.	ተፈትሏል tḁfḁ́t(ĭ̥)lŏ͡āl (-fä́t-)	ይፈተል yi̥ffḁ́ttḁl (-fä́ttäl)	ይፈተላል yi̥ffḁ́ttḁlāl (-fä́ttäl-)
ነሰነሰ nḁsḁ́nnḁsḁ	sprinkle, t.	ነስንሷል nḁ́sni̥sŏ͡āl (nä́s-)	ይነሰንስ yi̥nḁsḁ́nni̥s	ይነሰንሳል yi̥nḁsḁ́nni̥- sāl

Jussive (§ 27)	Imperative (§ 28)	Gerund (§ 29)	Infinitive (§ 30)	Participle (§ 31)
		ተጨንቆ tḁč̣ḁ́nqʷo (-ḁ́ṅq-)	መጨነቅ mḁč̣č̣ḁ́nḁq	
ይጯጯኹ yi̥č̣č̣ŏ͡ā́č̣ŏ͡ã- hu	ተጯጯኹ tḁč̣ŏ͡ā́č̣ŏ͡ãhu	ተጯጩኸው tḁč̣ŏ͡ā́č̣ŭhḁ͡u	መጯጯኽ mḁč̣č̣ŏ͡ā́č̣ŏ͡áh (§ 8)	ተጯጯኺ tḁč̣ŏ͡ãč̣ŏ͡áhi
ይትፋ yí̥tfã	ትፋ tí̥fã	ተፍቶ tḁ́ftʷo	መትፋት mḁ́tfā́t (§ 8)	ተፊ tḁ́fi
ይፈልፈል yi̥ffḁ́lfḁl (-fā́lfäl)		ተፈልፍሎ tḁfḁ́lfi̥lʷo (-fā́l-)	መፈልፈል mḁffḁ́lfḁl (-fā́lfäl)	ተፈልፋይ tḁfḁ́lfā͡í̥ (-fā́l-; § 8; -ā́yy § 6)
ይፈራረቅ yi̥ffḁrā́rḁq		ተፈራርቆ tḁfḁrā́r(ĭ̥)- qʷo	መፈራረቅ mḁffḁrā́rḁq	ተፈራራቂ tḁfḁrārā́qi
ይፈቃቀሩ yi̥ffḁqā́qḁru	ተፈቃቀሩ tḁfḁqā́qḁru	ተፈቃቅረው tḁfḁqā́q(ĭ̥)- rḁ͡u	መፈቃቀር mḁffḁqā́qḁr	ተፈቃቃሮች tḁfḁqāqā́- rʷōč (-ōčč § 6)
ይፈተል yi̥ffḁ́tḁl (-fā́täl)		ተፈትሎ tḁfḁ́t(ĭ̥)lʷo (-fā́t-)	መፈተል mḁffḁ́tḁl (-fā́täl)	ተፈታይ tḁfḁ́tā͡í̥ (-fā́t-; § 8; -ā́yy § 6)
ይነስንስ yi̥nḁ́sni̥s (-nā́s-)	ነስንስ nḁ́sni̥s (nā́s-)	ነስንሶ nḁ́sni̥sʷo (nā́s-)	መነስነስ mḁnḁ́snḁs	ነስናሽ nḁ́snā́š (§ 8)

Simp. perf. (§ 25)		Comp. perf. (§ 32)	Contingent (§ 26)	Comp. imperf. (§ 32)
ነዘነዘ nḁzḁ́nnḁzḁ	pester, t.	ነዝንዟል nḁ́zni̥zŏ͡āl	ይነዘንዝ yi̥nḁzḁ́nni̥z	ይነዘንዛል yi̥nḁzḁ́nni̥- zāl
አለመ állḁmḁ	dream, t.	አልሟል ā́lmŏ͡āl	ያልም yā́l(ĭ̥)m	ያልማል yā́l(ĭ̥)māl
አረከበ arrḁ́kkḁbḁ (-rā́k-, -ḁṿḁ)	hand over, t.	አረክቧል arrḁ́kki̥- bŏ͡āl (-rā́k-, -i̥ṿŏ-)	ያረክብ yā̆rrḁ́kki̥b (-rā́k-, -i̥ṿ)	ያረክባል yā̆rrḁ́kki̥- bāl (-rā́k-, -i̥ṿāl)
አረገበ arḁ́ggḁbḁ (-ḁṿḁ)	loosen, t.	አርግቧል ā́rgi̥bŏ͡āl (-i̥ṿŏ-)	ያረግብ yā̆rḁ́g(ĭ̥)b [-(ĭ̥)ṿ]	ያረግባል yā̆rḁ́g(ĭ̥)bāl [-(ĭ̥)ṿāl]
አረገበ arrḁ́ggḁbḁ (-ḁṿḁ)	loosen, t.	አረግቧል arrḁ́ggi̥bŏ͡āl (-i̥ṿŏ-)	ያረግብ yā̆rrḁ́ggi̥b (-i̥ṿ)	ያረግባል yā̆rrḁ́ggi̥bāl (-i̥ṿāl)
አረገዘች arḁ́ggḁzäč (-čč § 6)	be pregnant, i.	አርግዛለች ā̆rgi̥zā́lläč (-čč § 6)	ታረግዝ tā̆rḁ́gz	ታረግዛለች tā̆rḁgzā́lläč (-čč § 6)
አስለቀቀ aslḁ́qqḁqḁ	cause to give up, t.	አስለቅቋል aslḁ́qqi̥qŏ͡āl	ያስለቅቅ yā̆slḁ́qqi̥q (-lā́q-)	ያስለቅቃል yā̆slḁ́qqi̥qāl (-lā́q-)
አስረከበ asrḁ́kkḁbḁ (-rā́k-, -ḁṿḁ)	hand over, t.	አስረክቧል asrḁ́kki̥bŏ͡āl (-rā́k-, -i̥ṿŏ-)	ያስረክብ yā̆srḁ́kki̥b (-rā́k-, -i̥ṿ)	ያስረክባል yā̆srḁ́kki̥bāl (-rā́k-, -i̥ṿāl)
አስረዳ asrḁ́ddā̆	persuade, t.	አስረድቷል asrḁ́ddi̥tŏ͡āl	ያስረዳ yā̆srḁ́ddā̆	ያስረዳል yā̆srḁ́ddāl

Jussive (§ 27)	Imperative (§ 28)	Gerund (§ 29)	Infinitive (§ 30)	Participle (§ 31)
ይነዝንዝ yi̥nḁzni̥z	ነዝንዝ nḁzni̥z	ነዝንዞ nḁzni̥zʷo	መነዝነዝ mḁnḁznḁz	ነዝናዥ nḁznā́ž (§ 8)
		አልሞ ā́lmʷo	ማለም mā́lḁm	አላሚ ālā́mi
ያረክብ yārrḁ́kki̥b (-rā́k-, -i̥ỵ)	አረክብ arrḁ́kki̥b (-rā́k-, -i̥ỵ)	አረክቦ arrḁ́kki̥-bʷo (-rā́k-, -i̥ỵʷo)	ማረክብ mārrḁ́kkḁb (-rā́k-, -ḁỵ)	አረካቢ arrḁkkā́bi (-räk-, -ā́ỵi)
ያርግብ yā́rgi̥b (-i̥ỵ)	አርግብ ā́rgi̥b (-i̥ỵ)	አርግቦ ā́rgi̥bʷo (-i̥ỵʷo)	ማርገብ mā́rgḁb (-ḁỵ)	አርጋቢ argā́bi (-ā́ỵi)
ያረግብ yārrḁ́ggi̥b (-i̥ỵ)	አረግብ arrḁ́ggi̥b (-i̥ỵ)	አረግቦ arrḁ́ggi̥bʷo (-i̥ỵʷo)	ማረገብ mārrḁ́ggḁb (-ḁỵ)	አረጋቢ arrḁggā́bi (-ā́ỵi)
ታርግዝ tā́rgi̥z	አርግዥ ā́rgi̥ž	አርግዛ ā́rgi̥zā	ማርገዝ mā́rgḁz	አርጋዥ ā́rgā́ž (§ 8)
ያስለቅቅ yāslḁ́qqi̥q (-lā́q-)	አስለቅቅ aslḁ́qqi̥q (-lā́q-)	አስለቅቆ aslḁ́qqi̥qʷo (-lā́q-)	ማስለቀቅ māslḁ́qqḁq	አስለቃቂ aslḁqqā́qi
ያስረክብ yāsrḁ́kki̥b (-rā́k-, -i̥ỵ)	አስረክብ asrḁ́kki̥b (-rā́k-, -i̥ỵ)	አስረክቦ asrḁ́kki̥bʷo (-rā́k-, -i̥ỵʷo)	ማስረከብ māsrḁ́kkḁb (-rā́k-, -ḁỵ)	አስረካቢ asrḁkkā́bi (-räk-, -ā́ỵi)
ያስረዳ yāsrḁ́ddā	አስረዳ asrḁ́ddā	አስረድቶ asrḁ́ddi̥tʷo	ማስረዳት māsrḁ́ddā́t (§ 8)	አስረጅ ā́srḁ́jj (-rā́jj; § 8; -ጂ. -jji)

Simp. perf. (§ 25)		Comp. perf. (§ 32)	Contingent (§ 26)	Comp. imperf. (§ 32)
አስቈየ asqwώyyä 2nd -የህ -yyäh, etc.	cause to wait, t.	አስቈይቷል asqwώyyi̥-to͡āl	ያስቈይ yä̃sqwώyy	ያስቈያል yä̃sqwώyyāl
አስቈጣ asqwώṭṭã	annoy, t.	አስቈጥቷል asqwώṭṭi̥-to͡āl	ያስቈጣ yä̃sqwώṭṭã	ያስቈጣል yä̃sqwώṭṭāl
አሳተመ asắttḁmḁ	cause to seal, t.	አሳትሟል asắtti̥mo͡āl	ያሳትም yä̃sắtti̥m	ያሳትማል yä̃sắtti̥māl
አስተፋ astḁ́ffã	cause to vomit, t.	አስተፍቷል astḁ́ffi̥to͡āl	ያስተፋ yä̃stḁ́ffã	ያስተፋል yä̃stḁ́ffāl
አሳነሰ asánnḁsḁ	lessen, t.	አሳንሷል asánni̥so͡āl	ያሳንስ yä̃sánni̥s	ያሳንሳል yä̃sánni̥sāl
አሳከከ asắkkḁkḁ	cause to scratch, t.	አሳክኳል asắkki̥ko͡āl	ያሳክክ yä̃sắkki̥k	ያሳክካል yä̃sắkki̥kāl
አስወረደ aswώrrḁdḁ	cause to descend, t.	አስወርዷል aswώrri̥do͡āl	ያስወርድ yä̃swώrri̥d	ያስወርዳል yä̃swώrri̥-dāl
አስወጣ aswώṭṭã	cause to come out, t.	አስወጥቷል aswώṭṭi̥to͡āl	ያስወጣ yä̃swώṭṭã	ያስወጣል yä̃swώṭṭāl
አስደበቀ asdḁ́bbḁqḁ	cause to hide, t.	አስደብቋል asdḁ́bbi̥-qo͡āl	ያስደብቅ yä̃sdḁ́bbi̥q	ያስደብቃል yä̃sdḁ́bbi̥-qāl

Jussive (§ 27)	Imperative (§ 28)	Gerund (§ 29)	Infinitive (§ 30)	Participle (§ 31)
ያስቈይ yã́sqwώyy (§ 8)	አስቈይ ã́sqwώyy (§ 8)	አስቈይቶ asqẉώy- yi̥two	ማስቈየት mãsqwώy- yät	
ያስቈጣ yãsqwώṭṭã	አስቈጣ asqwώṭṭã	አስቈጥቶ asqwώṭṭi̥two	ማስቈጣት mãsqwώṭṭát (§ 8)	አስቈጭ asqwώč̣č̣ (-ጪ. -č̣č̣i)
ያሳትም yãsã́tti̥m	አሳትም asã́tti̥m	አሳትሞ asã́tti̥mwo	ማሳተም mãsã́ttḁm	አሳታሚ asãttã́mi
ያስተፉ yãstḁ́ffã	አስተፉ astḁ́ffã	አስተፍቶ astḁ́ffi̥two	ማስተፉት mãstḁ́ffát (§ 8)	አስተፌ astḁ́ffi
ያሳንስ yãsánni̥s	አሳንስ asánni̥s	አሳንሶ asánni̥swo	ማሳነስ mãsánnḁs	አሳናሽ asánnã́š (§ 8)
ያሳክክ yãsã́kki̥k	አሳክክ asã́kki̥k	አሳክኮ asã́kki̥kwo	ማሳከክ mãsã́kkḁk	አሳካኪ asãkkã́ki
ያስወርድ yãswώrri̥d	አስወርድ aswώrri̥d	አስወርዶ aswώrri̥dwo	ማስወረድ mãswώrrḁd	አስወራጅ aswώrrã́j (§ 8)
ያስወጣ yãswώṭṭã	አስወጣ aswώṭṭã	አስወጥቶ aswώṭṭi̥two	ማስወጣት mãswώṭṭát (§ 8)	አስወጭ aswḁ́č̣č̣ (-wώč̣č̣, -ጪ. -č̣č̣i)
ያስደብቅ yãsdḁ́bbi̥q	አስደብቅ asdḁ́bbi̥q	አስደብቆ asdḁ́bbi̥qwo	ማስደበቅ mãsdḁ́bbḁq	አስደባቂ asdḁbbã́qi

Simp. perf. (§ 25)		Comp. perf. (§ 32)	Contingent (§ 26)	Comp. imperf. (§ 32)
አስደበደበ asdḁbḁ́d- dḁbḁ (-däẏá̧ddä- ẏḁ)	cause to kill, t.	አስደብድቧል asdḁ́bdi̥- bŏ͡āl (-dā́ẏdi̥ẏŏ-)	ያስደበድብ yā̃sdḁbḁ́d- di̥b (-däẏá̧ddi̥ẏ)	ያስደበድባል yā̃sdḁbḁ́d- di̥bāl (-däẏá̧ddi̥- ẏāl)
አስደነገጠ asdḁnḁ́g- gḁṭḁ	startle, t.	አስደንግጧል asdḁ́ṅgi̥ṭŏ͡āl (-dā́ṅ-)	ያስደነግጥ yā̃sdḁnḁ́g- gi̥ṭ	ያስደነግጣል yā̃sdḁnḁ́g- gi̥ṭāl
አሳደፈ asáddḁfḁ	soil, t.	አሳድፏል asáddi̥fŏ͡āl	ያሳድፍ yā̃sáddi̥f	ያሳድፋል yā̃sáddi̥fāl
አስገባ asgḁ́bbā̃	cause to enter, t.	አስገብቷል asgḁ́bbi̥tŏ͡āl	ያስገባ yā̃sgḁ́bbā̃	ያስገባል yā̃sgḁ́bbāl
[አሶጣ as^w óṭṭā̃ = አስወጣ asw ώṭṭā̃	etc., -ሶ- for -ስወ- -s^w ó-for-sw ώ- throughout conjug.]			
አሳጠረ asáṭṭḁrḁ (-ṭärḁ)	shorten, t.	አሳጥሯል asáṭṭi̥rŏ͡āl	ያሳጥር yā̃sáṭṭi̥r	ያሳጥራል yā̃sáṭṭi̥rāl
አስጠራ asṭḁ́rrā̃	cause to call, t.	አስጠርቷል asṭḁ́rri̥tŏ͡āl (-ṭā́r-)	ያስጠራ yā̃sṭḁ́rrā̃	ያስጠራል yā̃sṭḁ́rrāl
አስጫነ asčá̧nḁ	cause to saddle, t.	አስጭኗል ā̃́sči̥nŏ͡āl	ያስጭን yā̃́sčí̥n (§ 8)	ያስጭናል yā̃sčí̥nāl

Jussive (§ 27)	Imperative (§ 28)	Gerund (§ 29)	Infinitive (§ 30)	Participle (§ 31)
ያስደብድብ yãsdḁ́bdi̥b (-dã́ỵdi̥ỵ)	አስደብድብ asdḁ́bdi̥b (-dã́ỵdi̥ỵ)	አስደብድቦ asdḁ́bdi̥bʷo (-dã́ỵdi̥ỵʷo)	ማስደብደብ mãsdḁ́b- dḁb (-dã́ỵdäỵ)	አስደብዳቢ asdḁbdã́bi (-däỵdã́ỵi)
ያስደንግጥ yãsdḁ́ṅgi̥ṭ (-dã́ṅ-)	አስደንግጥ asdḁ́ṅgi̥ṭ (-dã́ṅ-)	አስደንግጦ asdḁ́ṅgi̥ṭʷo (-dã́ṅ-)	ማስደንገጥ mãsdḁ́ṅgḁṭ (-dã́ṅgäṭ)	አስደንጋጭ asdḁ́ṅgã́č̣ (-dã́ṅ- ; § 8)
ያሳድፍ yãṣáddi̥f.	አሳድፍ asáddi̥f	አሳድፎ asáddi̥fʷo	ማሳደፍ mãsáddḁf	አሳዳፊ asaddã́fi
ያስገባ yãsgḁ́bbã	አስገባ asgḁ́bbã	አስገብቶ asgḁ́bbi̥tʷo	ማስገባት mãsgḁ́bbã́t (§ 8)	አስገቢ asgḁ́bbi
ያሳጥር yãsáṭṭi̥r	አሳጥር asáṭṭi̥r	አሳጥሮ asáṭṭi̥rʷo	ማሳጠር mãsáṭṭḁr (-ṭär)	አሳጣሪ asaṭṭã́ri
ያስጠራ yãsṭḁ́rrã	አስጠራ asṭḁ́rrã	አስጠርቶ asṭḁ́rri̥tʷo (-ṭã́r-)	ማስጠራት mãsṭḁ́rrã́t (§ 8)	አስጠሪ asṭḁ́rri (-ṭä́r-)
ያስጭን yã́sč̣i̥n Š. ያስጫን yã́sč̣ã́n (§ 8)	አስጭን ã́sč̣i̥n Š. አስጫን ã́sč̣ã́n (§ 8)	አስጭኖ ã́sč̣i̥nʷo	ማስጫን mã́sč̣ã́n (§ 8)	አስጫኝ ã́sč̣ã́ñ (§ 8; -ññ § 6; -ኚ -ññi)

Simp. perf. (§ 25)		Comp. perf. (§ 32)	Contingent (§ 26)	Comp. imperf. (§ 32)
አቀለጠፈ aqḁlḁ́ṭṭḁfḁ	cause to hasten, t.	አቀልጥፏል aqḁ́lṭi̥f͡ŏāl (-qā́l-)	ያቀለጥፍ yā̃qḁlḁ́ṭṭi̥f	ያቀለጥፋል yā̃qḁlḁ́ṭṭi̥fāl
አቃጠረ aqqā́ṭṭḁrḁ (-ṭärḁ)	procure for hire, t.	አቃጥሯል aqqáṭ(ĭ̥)- r͡ŏāl	ያቃጥር yā̃qqā́ṭṭi̥r	ያቃጥራል yā̃qqā́ṭṭi̥rāl
አበዛ abḁ́zzā̃ (aṿḁ́-, -ā́z-)	increase, t.	አብዝቷል ábzi̥t͡ŏāl (ā́ṿz-, ábi̥zt-, ā́ṿi̥-)	ያበዛ yḁbḁ́zā̃ (yā̃ṿḁ́-, -ā́zā̃)	ያበዛል yā̃bḁ́zāl (yā̃ṿḁ́-, -ā́zāl)
አነዘረ anḁ́zzḁrḁ (-zärḁ)	spin, t.	አንዝሯል ā́nzi̥r͡ŏāl (ā́ni̥zr-)	ያነዝር yā̃nḁ́z(ĭ̥)r	ያነዝራል yā̃nḁ́z(ĭ̥)rāl
አንጠራራ anṭḁrā́rrā̃ (-ṭär-)	stretch, t.	አንጠራርቷል anṭḁrárt͡ŏāl (-ṭär-)	ያንጠራራ yā̃nṭḁrā́rrā̃ (-ṭär-)	ያንጠራራል yā̃nṭḁrā́rrāl (-ṭär-)
G. አንፏጨ anfwā́ç̌ç̌ä 2nd -ጨሀ -ç̌ç̌äh, etc.	whistle, i.	አንፏጭቷል anfwā́ç̌t͡ŏāl (-fwáyyt- § 7*d*)	ያንፏጭ yā̃nfwā́ç̌ç̌	ያንፏጫል yā̃nfwā́ç̌ç̌āl
አዋለደች awwā́llḁdäč (a͡ūw-; -äčč § 6)	act as midwife to, t.	አዋልዳለች awwāl(ĭ̥)- dā́lläč (a͡ūw-; -äčč § 6)	ታዋልድ tā̃wwā́lli̥d (ta͡ūw-)	ታዋልዳለች tā̃wwā̃lli̥- dā́lläč (ta͡ūw-; -äčč § 6)
አወረረ awώrrḁrḁ (a͡ūώ-)	start on a raid, i.	አውሯል ā́wŭrr͡ŏāl (á͡uŭ-)	ያወር yā̃wώrr (ya͡ūώ-)	ያወራል yā̃wώrrāl (ya͡ūώ-)

Jussive (§ 27)	Imperative (§ 28)	Gerund (§ 29)	Infinitive (§ 30)	Participle (§ 31)
ያቀልጥፍ yãqḁ́lṭi̥f (-qã́l-)	አቀልጥፍ aqḁ́lṭi̥f (-qã́l-)	አቀልጥፎ aqḁ́lṭi̥fʷo (-qã́l-)	ማቀልጠፍ mãqḁ́lṭḁf	አቀልጣፊ aqḁlṭáfi
ያቃጥር yãqqã́ṭi̥r	አቃጥር aqqã́ṭi̥r	አቃጥሮ aqqã́ṭ(ĭ̥)rʷo	ማቃጠር mãqqã́ṭḁr (-ṭär)	አቃጣሪ aqqāṭári
ያብዛ yábzã (yã́ṿzã)	አብዛ ã́bzã (ã́ṿzã)	አብዝቶ ã́bzi̥tʷo (ã́ṿz-, ábi̥ztʷo, ã́ṿi̥-)	ማብዛት mã́bzã́t (mã́ṿzã́t; § 8)	አብዢ ã́bži (ã́ṿži)
ያንዝር yã́nzi̥r [yã́ni̥z(ĭ̥)r]	አንዝር ã́nzi̥r [ã́ni̥z(ĭ̥)r]	አንዝሮ ã́nzi̥rʷo (ã́ni̥zrʷo)	ማንዘር mã́nzḁr (-zär)	አንዛሪ anzã́ri
ያንጠራራ yãnṭḁrã́rã (-ṭär-)	አንጠራራ anṭḁrã́rã (-ṭär-)	አንጠራርቶ anṭḁrã́rtʷo (-ṭär-)	ማንጠራራት mãnṭḁrã́rãt (-ṭär-; § 8)	
ያንፏጭ yã́nfwã́č̣ (§ 8)	አንፏጭ ã́nfwã́č̣ (§ 8)	አንፏጭቶ anfwã́č̣tʷo (-fwáyyt- § 7*d*)	ማንፏጨት mãnfwã́č̣ät	አንፏጪ anfwã́č̣č̣i
ታዋልድ tãwwã́l(ĭ̥)d (tá͡uw-)	አዋልጅ awwã́l(ĭ̥)j (â͡uw-)	አዋልዳ awwã́l(ĭ̥)dã (â͡uw-)	ማዋለድ mãwwã́lḁd (mâ͡uw-)	አዋላጅ awwã́láj (â͡uw-; § 8)
ያውር yáwŭr (yá͡uŭr)	አውር ã́wŭr (á͡uŭr)	አውሮ ã́wŭrrʷo (á͡uŭ-)	ማውረር mã́wŭrḁr [má͡u(ŭ)r-, -rär]	አውራሪ awŭrã́ri [â͡u(ŭ)r-]

Simp. perf. (§ 25)		Comp. perf. (§ 32)	Contingent (§ 26)	Comp. imperf. (§ 32)
አዘመተ azḁ́mmḁtḁ	take to war, t.	**አዝምቷል** ázi̥mtŏ͡āl	**ያዘምት** yā̃zḁ́mt	**ያዘምታል** yā̃zḁ́mtāl
አዘመተ azzḁ́mmḁtḁ	send to war, t.	**አዘምቷል** azzḁ́mmi̥-tŏ͡āl	**ያዘምት** yā̃zzḁ́mmi̥t	**ያዘምታል** yā̃zzḁ́mmi̥-tāl
አዛገ azā́gḁ	rust, t.	**አዝጓል** ázi̥gŏ͡āl	**ያዝግ** yā́zi̥g	**ያዝጋል** yā́zi̥gāl (yāzí̥gāl)
አደረሰ adḁ́rrḁsḁ	cause to arrive, t.	**አድርሷል** ā́di̥rsŏ͡āl	**ያደርስ** yā̃dḁ́rs (-dā́rs)	**ያደርሳል** yā̃dḁ́rsāl (-dā́r-)
አደረቀ adḁ́rrḁqḁ	dry, t.	**አድርቋል** ā́di̥rqŏ͡āl (ā́dri̥q-)	**ያደርቅ** yā̃dḁ́rq (-dā́rq)	**ያደርቃል** yā̃dḁ́rqāl (-dā́r-)
አዳጠ adā́ṭḁ	cause to slip, t.	**አድጧል** ā́di̥ṭŏ͡āl	**ያድጥ** yā́di̥ṭ	**ያድጣል** yā́di̥ṭāl (yādí̥ṭāl)
አጐለ ággwωlḁ	interrupt, t.	**አጕሏል** ággwŭlŏ͡āl	**ያጕል** yā́ggwŭl	**ያጕላል** yā́ggwŭlāl
አገመ ággḁmḁ	cup, t.	**አግሟል** ā́gmŏ͡āl	**ያግም** yā́g(ĭ̥)m	**ያግማል** yā́gmāl
አገሰገሰ ag(g)ḁsḁ́g-gḁsḁ	cause to travel fast, t.	**አገስግሷል** ag(g)ḁ́sgi̥-sŏ͡āl [-(g)ā́sg-]	**ያገሰግስ** yā̃g(g)ḁsḁ́g-gi̥s (-sā́g-)	**ያገሰግሳል** yā̃g(g)ḁsḁ́g-gi̥sāl (-sā́g-)

Jussive (§ 27)	Imperative (§ 28)	Gerund (§ 29)	Infinitive (§ 30)	Participle (§ 31)
ያዝምት yắzi̥mt	አዝምት ắzi̥mt	አዝምቶ ắzi̥mt^{w}o	ማዝመት mắzmḁt (-mät)	አዝማች ắzmắč (§ 8)
ያዘምት yãzzḁ́mmi̥t	አዘምት azzḁ́mmi̥t	አዘምቶ azzḁ́mmi̥- t^{w}o	ማዘመት mãzzḁ́m- mḁt (-mät)	አዘማች[1] azzḁ́mmắč (§ 8)
ያዝግ yắzi̥g		አዝጎ ắzi̥g^{w}o	ማዛግ mázắg (§ 8)	አዛጊ ắzági (§ 8)
ያድርስ yắdi̥rs	አድርስ ắdi̥rs	አድርሶ ắdi̥rs^{w}o	ማድረስ mắdrḁs	አድራሽ ắdrắš (§ 8)
ያድርቅ yắdi̥rq (yắdri̥q)	አድርቅ ắdi̥rq (ắdri̥q)	አድርቆ ắdi̥rq^{w}o (ắdri̥q-)	ማድረቅ mắdrḁq	አድራቂ adrắqi
		አድጦ ắdi̥ṭ^{w}o	ማዳጥ mắdắṭ (§ 8)	አዳጭ ắdắč̣ (§ 8)
ያጕል yắggwŭl	አጕል ággwŭl	አጕሎ ággwŭl^{w}o	ማጐል mắggwωl	
ይገም yí̥gḁm	እገም í̥gḁm	አግሞ ắgm^{w}o	ማገም mắgḁm	አጋሚ agắmi
ያገስግስ yãg(g)ḁ́sgi̥s [-(g)ǻsg-]	አገስግስ ag(g)ḁ́sgi̥s [-(g)ǻsg-]	አገስግሶ ag(g)ḁ́s- gi̥s^{w}o [-(g)ắsg-]	ማገስገስ mãg(g)ḁ́s- gḁs	አገስጋሽ ag(g)ḁ́sgắš (§ 8)

[1] Not **አዝማች**, as given in Part I, p. 341.

Simp. perf. (§ 25)		Comp. perf. (§ 32)	Contingent (§ 26)	Comp. imperf. (§ 32)
አገዘ ággḁzḁ	help, t.	አግዟል G. ā́gzŏ͡āl Š. ággḭzŏ͡āl	ያግዝ G. yā́g(ḭ̆)z Š. yā́ggḭz	ያግዛል G. yā́gzāl Š. yā́ggḭzāl
አጠበቀ aṭḁ́bbḁqḁ	tie tight, t. guard, t.	አጥብቋል ā́ṭbḭqŏ͡āl (ā́ṭṿḭ-, ā́ṭḭbq-, -ḭṿq-) አጠብቋል aṭḁ́bbḭqŏ͡āl	ያጠብቅ yāṭḁ́bq (-ḁ́ṿq, -ḁ́bbḭq)	ያጠብቃል yāṭḁ́bqāl (-ḁ́ṿq-, -ḁ́bbḭq-)
አፈራረቀ affḁrā́rrḁqḁ	alternate, t.	አፈራርቋል affḁrā́r(ḭ̆)- qŏ͡āl	ያፈራርቅ yāffḁrā́rrḭq	ያፈራርቃል yāffḁrā́rrḭ- qāl
አፈቀረ afḁ́qqḁrḁ	love, t.	አፍቅሯል ā́fqḭrŏ͡āl (ā́fḭqr-)	ያፈቅር yāfḁ́q(ḭ̆)r	ያፈቅራል yāfḁ́qrāl
አፎጨ Š. afṓč̣č̣ḁ 2nd -ጨህ -č̣č̣ḁh, etc.	whistle, i.	አፎጭቷል afṓč̣č̣ḭtŏ͡āl	ያፎጭ yāfṓč̣č̣	ያፎጫል yāfṓč̣č̣āl
ካሰ kā́sḁ	pay (as fine), t.	ክሷል kḭ́sŏ͡āl	ይከስ yḭkḭ́s	ይከሳል yḭkḭ́sāl
ኰሰኰሰ kwωsḁ́k- kwωsḁ (-sώkkosḁ)	prickle, t.	ኰስኵሷል kwώskwŭ- sŏ͡āl	ይኰሰኵስ yḭkwωsḁ́k- kwŭs (-sώk-)	ይኰሰኵሳል yḭkwωsḁ́k- kwŭsāl (-sώk-)

Jussive (§ 27)	Imperative (§ 28)	Gerund (§ 29)	Infinitive (§ 30)	Participle (§ 31)
G. ይገዝ yi̥gḁz Š. ያግዝ yā́ggi̥z	G. እገዝ i̥gḁz Š. አግዝ ággi̥z	አግዞ G. ā́gz^{w}o Š. ággi̥z^{w}o	ማገዝ G. mā́gḁz Š. mā́ggḁz	አጋዥ G. ā́gā́ž (§ 8) Š. ággā́ž (§ 8)
ያጥብቅ yā́ṭbi̥q (-ṭv̇i̥q, yā́ṭi̥bq, -i̥v̇q)	አጥብቅ ā́ṭbi̥q (ā́ṭv̇i̥q, ā́ṭi̥bq, -i̥v̇q)	አጥብቆ ā́ṭbi̥q^{w}o (ā́ṭv̇i̥-, ā́ṭi̥bq^{w}o, -i̥v̇q-)	ማጥበቅ mā́ṭbḁq (-ṭv̇ḁq)	አጥባቂ aṭbā́qi (-ṭv̇ā́-)
ያጠብቅ yā̃ṭḁ́bbi̥q	አጠብቅ aṭḁ́bbi̥q	አጠብቆ aṭḁ́bbi̥q^{w}o	ማጠበቅ mā̃ṭḁ́bbḁq	አጠባቂ aṭḁbbā́qi
ያፈራርቅ yā̃ffḁrári̥q	አፈራርቅ affḁrári̥q	አፈራርቆ affḁrā́r(i̥)-q^{w}o	ማፈራረቅ mā̃ffḁrárḁq	አፈራራቂ affḁrārā́qi
ያፍቅር yḁ̄́fqi̥r [yā́fi̥q(ĭ̥)r]	አፍቅር ā́fqi̥r [ā́fi̥q(ĭ̥)r]	አፍቅሮ ā́fqi̥r^{w}o (ā́fi̥qr^{w}o)	ማፍቀር mā́fqḁr	አፍቃሪ afqā́ri
ያፎጭ yā́fṓč̣č̣ (§ 8)	አፎጭ ā́fṓč̣č̣ (§ 8)	አፎጭቶ afṓč̣č̣i̥t^{w}o	ማፎጨት mā̃fṓč̣č̣ät	አፏጪ af^{w}ā́č̣i
ይካስ yi̥kā́s (§ 8)	ካስ kās	ክሶ kí̥s^{w}o	መካስ mḁkā́s (§ 8)	ካሽ kāš
		ኮስኩሶ kwώskwŭ-s^{w}o	መኮስኮስ mḁkwώs-kwωs	ኮስኳሽ kwώskwā́š (§ 8)

Simp. perf. (§ 25)		Comp. perf. (§ 32)	Contingent (§ 26)	Comp. imperf. (§ 32)
ኳተ kwátḁ	dig, t.	ኵቷል kwŭ́tŏ͡āl	ይኵት yi̥kwŭ́t	ይኵታል yi̥kwŭ́tāl
ወረረ wώrrḁrḁ	loot, t.	ወሯል wώrrŏ͡āl	ይወር yi̥wώrr (yuώ-)	ይወራል yi̥wώrrāl (yuώ-)
ወቃ wώqqā̃	thresh, t.	ወቅቷል wώqtŏ͡āl	ይወቃ yi̥wώqā̃ (yuώ-)	ይወቃል yi̥wώqāl (yuώ-)
ወገደ wώggḁdḁ	withdraw, i.	ወግዷል wώg(gi̥)dŏ͡āl	ይወግድ yi̥wώg(gi̥)d (yuώ-)	ይወግዳል yi̥wώg(gi̥)-dāl (yuώ-)
ዘለቀ zḁ́llḁqḁ	come into (pass out of) sight, i.	ዘልቋል zḁ́lqŏ͡āl	ይዘልቅ yi̥zḁ́lq	ይዘልቃል yi̥zḁ́lqāl
ዛገ zágḁ	rust, i.	ዝጓል zí̥gŏ͡āl	ይዝግ yi̥zí̥g	ይዝጋል yi̥zí̥gāl
ደበቀ dḁ́bbḁqḁ	hide, t.	ደብቋል dḁ́bbi̥qŏ͡āl	ይደብቅ yi̥dḁ́bbi̥q	ይደብቃል yi̥dḁ́bbi̥qāl
ደበደበ dḁbḁ́ddḁbḁ (däỵáddä-ỵḁ)	massacre, t.	ደብድቧል dḁ́bdi̥bŏ͡āl (dáỵdi̥ỵŏ-)	ይደበድብ yi̥dḁbḁ́ddi̥b (-däỵáddi̥ỵ)	ይደበድባል yi̥dḁbḁ́ddi̥-bāl (-dä-ỵáddi̥ỵāl)
ደገነ dḁ́ggḁnḁ (dág-)	aim, t.	ደግኗል dḁ́ggi̥nŏ͡āl (dág-)	ይደግን yi̥dḁ́ggi̥n (-dág-)	ይደግናል yi̥dḁ́ggi̥nāl (-dág-)

Jussive (§ 27)	Imperative (§ 28)	Gerund (§ 29)	Infinitive (§ 30)	Participle (§ 31)
ይኳት yi̥kwā́t (§ 8)	ኳት kwāt	ኵቶ kwŭ́tʷo	መኳት mḁ́kwā́t (§ 8)	ኳች kwāč
ይውረር yí̥wŭrḁr (yŭ́r-, -rär)	ውረር wŭ́rḁr (-rär)	ወሮ wώrrʷo	መውረር mḁ́wŭrḁr (mḁ́͡ur-, -rär)	ወራሪ wωrā́ri
ይውቃ yí̥wŭqā̆ (yύqā̆)	ውቃ wŭ́qā̆	ወቅቶ wώqtʷo	መውቃት mḁ́wŭqā́t (mḁ́͡uq-; § 8)	ወቂ wḁ́qi (wώqi)
ይውገድ yí̥wŭgḁd (yŭ́g-)	ውገድ wŭ́gḁd	ወግዶ wώg(gi̥)dʷo	መውገድ mḁ́͡ugḁd	
ይወግድ yi̥wώg(g)i̥d (yuώ-)	ወግድ wώg(g)i̥d		መወገድ mḁwώggḁd (mḁ͡uώ-)	
ይዝለቅ yí̥zlḁq	ዝለቅ zí̥lḁq	ዘልቆ zḁ́lqʷo	መዝለቅ mḁ́zlḁq	ዘላቂ zḁlā́qi
ይዛግ yí̥zā́g (§ 8)		ዝጎ zí̥gʷo	መዛግ mḁ́zā́g (§ 8)	ዛጊ zā́gi
ይድብቅ yi̥dḁ́bbi̥q	ድብቅ dḁ́bbi̥q	ድብቆ dḁ́bbi̥qʷo	መደበቅ mḁdḁ́bbḁq	ደባቂ dḁbbā́qi
ይድብድብ yi̥dḁ́bdi̥b (-dā́ṿdi̥ṿ)	ድብድብ dḁ́bdi̥b (dā́ṿdi̥ṿ)	ድብድቦ dḁ́bdi̥bʷo (dā́ṿdi̥ṿʷo)	መድብድብ mḁdḁ́bdḁb (-dā́ṿdäṿ)	ድብዳቢ dḁbdā́bi (däṿdā́ṿi)
ይደግን yi̥dḁ́ggi̥n (-dā́g-)	ደግን dḁ́ggi̥n (dā́g-)	ደግኖ dḁ́ggi̥nʷo (dā́g-)	መደገን mḁdḁ́ggḁn (-dā́g-)	ደጋኝ dḁ́ggā́ñ (dā́g-; § 8)

Simp. perf. (§ 25)		Comp. perf. (§ 32)	Contingent (§ 26)	Comp. imperf. (§ 32)
ደፋ dḁ́ffã	turn down, t.	ደፍቷል dḁ́ftŏ͡āl	ይደፋ yi̥dḁ́fã	ይደፋል yi̥dḁ́fāl
ደፈነ dḁ́ffḁnḁ (dắffänḁ)	close up, t.	ደፍኗል dḁ́f(ĭ̥)nŏ͡āl (dắf-)	ይደፍን yi̥dḁ́f(ĭ̥)n (-dắf-)	ይደፍናል yi̥dḁ́f(ĭ̥)nāl (-dắf-)
ገለጠ gḁ́llḁṭḁ (gắl-)	disclose, t.	ገልጧል gḁ́lṭŏ͡āl (gắl-)	ይገልጥ yi̥gḁ́lṭ (-gắlṭ)	ይገልጣል yi̥gḁ́lṭāl (-gắl-)
ገማ gḁ́mmã	stink, i.	ገምቷል gḁ́mtŏ͡āl	ይገማ yi̥gḁ́mã	ይገማል yi̥gḁ́māl
ጐረሰ gwώrrḁsḁ	devour, t.	ጐርሷል gwώrsŏ͡āl	ይጐርስ yi̥gwώrs	ይጐርሳል yi̥gwώrsāl
ገረዘ gḁ́rrḁzḁ	circumcise, t.	ገርዟል gḁ́rri̥zŏ͡āl (gắr-)	ይገርዝ yi̥gḁ́rri̥z (-gắr-)	ይገርዛል yi̥gḁ́rri̥zāl (-gắr-)
ገበረ gḁ́bbḁrḁ (-bärḁ)	pay a tax, i. improve, i.	ገብሯል gḁ́bbi̥rŏ͡āl	ይገብር yi̥gḁ́bbi̥r	ይገብራል yi̥gḁ́bbi̥rāl
ጐተተ gwώttḁtḁ	drag, t.	ጐትቷል gwώt(ti̥)tŏ͡āl	ይጐትት yi̥gwώt(ti̥)t	ይጐትታል yi̥gwώt-(ti̥)tāl
ገዘተ gḁ́zzḁtḁ	excommunicate, t.	ገዝቷል gḁ́zzi̥tŏ͡āl	ይገዝት yi̥gḁ́zzi̥t	ይገዝታል yi̥gḁ́zzi̥tāl

Jussive (§ 27)	Imperative (§ 28)	Gerund (§ 29)	Infinitive (§ 30)	Participle (§ 31)
ይድፉ yí̥dfä̃	ድፉ dí̥fä̃	ደፍቶ dḁ́ftʷo	መድፉት mḁ́dfä́t (§ 8)	ደፊ dḁ́fi
ይድፈን yí̥dfḁn (-fän)	ድፈን dí̥fḁn (-fän)	ደፍኖ dḁ́f(ĭ̥)nʷo (dä́f-)	መድፈን mḁ́dfḁn (-fän)	ደፋኝ dḁ́fä́ñ (dä́f-; § 8; -ññ § 6)
ይግለጥ yí̥glḁṭ (-läṭ)	ግለጥ gí̥lḁṭ (-läṭ)	ገልጦ gḁ́lṭʷo (gä́l-)	መግለጥ mḁ́glḁṭ (-läṭ)	ገላጭ gḁ́lä́č̣ (gä́l-; § 8)
		ገምቶ gḁ́mtʷo	መግማት mḁ́gmä́t (§ 8)	
ይጕረስ yí̥gwŭrḁs	ጕረስ gwŭ́rḁs	ጐርሶ gwώrsʷo	መጕረስ mḁ́gwŭrḁs	ጐራሽ gwώrä́š (§ 8)
ይገርዝ yi̥gḁ́rri̥z (-gä́r-)	ገርዝ gḁ́rri̥z (gä́r-)	ገርዞ gḁ́rri̥zʷo (gä́r-)	መገረዝ mḁgḁ́rrḁz	ገራዥ gḁ́rrä́ž (§ 8)
ይገብር yi̥gḁ́bbi̥r	ገብር gḁ́bbi̥r	ገብሮ gḁ́bbi̥rʷo	መገበር mḁgḁ́bbḁr (-bär)	ገባሪ gḁbbä́ri
ይጎትት yi̥gwώt(ti̥)t	ጎትት gwώt(ti̥)t	ጎትቶ gwώt(ti̥)tʷo	መጎተት mḁgwώttḁt (-tät)	ጎታች gwώttä́č (§ 8)
ይገዝት yi̥gḁ́zzi̥t	ገዝት gḁ́zzi̥t	ገዝቶ gḁ́zzi̥tʷo	መገዘት mḁgḁ́zzḁt (-zät)	ገዛች gḁ́zzä́č (§ 8)

Simp. perf. (§ 25)		Comp. perf. (§ 32)	Contingent (§ 26)	Comp. imperf. (§ 32)
ጠለፈ ṭḁ́llḁfḁ	embroider, t.	ጠልፏል ṭḁ́lfo͡āl (ṭā́l-)	ይጠልፍ yi̥ṭḁ́lf (-ṭā́l-)	ይጠልፋል yi̥ṭḁ́lfāl (-ṭā́l-)
ጠና ṭḁ́nnā̃	be strong, i.	ጠንቷል ṭḁ́nto͡āl	ይጠና yi̥ṭḁ́nā̃	ይጠናል yi̥ṭḁ́nāl
ጨነቀው č̣ḁ́nnḁqḁ͡ū (§ 43*a*)	be distressed, i.	ጨንቆታል č̣ḁ́nqʷotāl (č̣ḁ́ṅq-)	ይጨንቀው yi̥č̣ḁ́nqḁ͡ū (-ḁ́ṅq-)	ይጨንቀዋል yi̥č̣ḁ́nqḁ͡ūāl (-ḁ́ṅq-)
ፈለፈለ fḁlḁ́ffḁlḁ	scoop, t.	ፈልፍሏል fḁ́lfi̥lo͡āl (fā́l-)	ይፈለፍል yi̥fḁlḁ́ffi̥l	ይፈለፍላል yi̥fḁlḁ́ffi̥lāl
ፈተለ fḁ́ttḁlḁ (fā́ttälḁ)	weave, t.	ፈትሏል fḁ́t(ĭ̥)lo͡āl (fā́t-)	ይፈትል yi̥fḁ́t(ĭ̥)l (-fā́t-)	ይፈትላል yi̥fḁ́t(ĭ̥)lāl (-fā́t-)

Jussive (§ 27)	Imperative (§ 28)	Gerund (§ 29)	Infinitive (§ 30)	Participle (§ 31)
ይጥለፍ yí̥ṭlḁf	ጥለፍ ṭí̥lḁf	ጠልፎ ṭḁ́lfʷo (ṭä́l-)	መጥለፍ mḁ́ṭlḁf	ጠላፊ ṭḁláfi
ይጥና yí̥ṭnã	ጥና ṭí̥nã	ጠንቶ ṭḁ́ntʷo	መጥናት mḁ́ṭnát (§ 8)	ጠኝ ṭḁñ (ṭäñ)
		ጨንቆት č̣ḁ́nqʷṓt (č̣ḁ́ṅq- ; § 8)	መጭነቅ mḁ́č̣nḁq (mä́č̣-)	
ይፈልፍል yi̥fḁ́lfi̥l (-fä́l-)	ፈልፍል fḁ́lfi̥l (fä́l-)	ፈልፍሎ fḁ́lfi̥lʷo (fä́l-)	መፈልፈል mḁfḁ́lfḁl (-fä́lfäl)	ፈልፋይ fḁlfá͡i̥ (fä́l-; § 8; -äyy § 6)
ይፍተል yí̥ftḁl (-täl)	ፍተል fí̥tḁl (-täl)	ፈትሎ fḁ́t(ĭ̥)lʷo (fä́t-)	መፍተል mḁ́ftḁl (-täl)	ፈታይ fḁtá͡i̥ (fä́t-; § 8; -äyy § 6)

APPENDIX. B

GRAMMATICAL NOTE

§ refers to the paragraphs of the Grammar (Initia Amharica, Part I).

§ 7*d*, p. 26, l. 4: (*add*) g͡ịẓ in ሀ, ሐ, ኀ, ኸ, ዐ is usually a (§ 4*b*): but it is ḁ in

ár̥ḁ! ኧረ why!,

and ḁ, ä in ሀ interchanging with ኸ, ከ, e.g. in the simple perfect and gerund sg. 2nd m. (§§ 25, 29) on their receiving the suffixes (§ 12*c*) which have ḁ (ä) as connecting vowel:

álhäñ አልሀኝ (álχäñ አልኸኝ, álkäñ አልከኝ) you told me;

qwώṭrḁh͡ḁu ቈጥረሀው you counting it;

and in the preposition

hḁ- ሀ- G.=kḁ- ከ- (§ 47*a*) at, in, from.

§ 7*d*, p. 28: ráyị, ã: (*add*) Pronunciations such as wḁ́rka (wώr-) ወርካ for wárka ዋርካ sycamore, gḁmbịllʷo ገምቢሎ for gambịllʷo ጋምቢሎ gardenia, zḁṅgḁ́da (-gā́da) for zḁṅgā́da ዘንጋዳ *Eleusine multiflora*, heard in Dámbya and Dāmʷót, are probably due to the influence of Áuṅi (Agḁ͡úñña)[1].

---

[1] Cp. Reinisch, Quara., § 7 :... vermengt das Quaresa häufig gedehntes *ā* mit hellem *a*. Cp. Reinisch, Chamir., § 11.

§ 7*d*, p. 32, l. 4: (*add*) ቀ with following i, y, or ʸ is sometimes pronounced ç̣ (cp. ምንጭ and Eth. መንቅዒ):

ç̣ēs for qʸēs ቄስ, priest,

mąsąqsáç̣ā for mąsąqsáqyā መሰቅሰቂያ tooth-pick.

§ 7*d*, p. 35, l. 10: (*add*) and ž arising from zi, zʸe (§ 7*b*) does not interchange with j, but I have heard occasionally in Dámbya and Gʷojjám

yįjjʸe for yįžžʸe ይገዥ (§ 44*c*), I seizing.

§ 9*b*, p. 51, l. 10: (*read*) The pl. is formed by adding -ʷõች -ʷõč (ʷ-õčč before a vowel § 6) to the last consonant of the sg.

§ 12*a*, p. 56, l. 6: (*add*) sg. 2nd, pol., but less so than እርስዎ, nom. አንቱ ántu[1], you, acc. አንቱን ántun, pl. እላንት.

— with article and preposition:

ያንቱውን፡አመጣ። yántuun (-twun) amą̊ṭṭa, he brought yours (m., e.g. bull), ያንቱይቱን፡አመጣ። yántuitun (-twįt-) amą̊ṭṭa, he brought yours (f., e.g. cow);

---

[1] Declared by some to be obsolescent; e.g. Guidi, Vocab. p. 466, 'አንቱ፡ non è più in uso nelle città,' and Guidi, Prov. p. 82 '... ora l'አንቱ፡ e specialmente il -ኍ non si usano quasi più.' I accordingly omitted this pronoun and the suffixes and verbal forms corresponding to it in compiling Part I, such experience as I had at the time (1905) agreeing with Guidi's remarks. Since then, however, I have heard them fairly frequently in Wɷlqait, Ṣą̊gądʸe, Wɷ́gąra, Sįmʸēn, Ṭāqwɷ́ssa, Dámbya, Bʸé-gämdįr, Gʷojjám, Dāmʷɷ́t and Šą̊ua (Shoa), both in town and country, and therefore append them here.

— conjunctive with nouns (§ 12*b*), the suffix:
-ኍ -hwŭ or -ሁ -hu (usually -uh § 7*d* pp. 26, 27, after a vowel -uʰ § 7*d* p. 30):
(*α*) ቤትኍ bʸéthwŭ[1] (-tuh), your house, acc. ቤትኍን bʸéthwŭn[1];
(*β*) ጌታኍ gʸétahwŭ (-a͡uʰ), your master,
(*γ*) በቅሎኍ bḁ́qlʷohwŭ (-o͡uʰ), your mule;
— conjunctive with verbs (§ 12*c*), the suffix (infix):
-ኍ -hwŭ or -ሁ -hu (with displacement of u as above): connecting vowel, ḁ (ä) and none:
(*α*) ይንገርኍ yí̥ṅgḁrhwŭ (-ruh), let him tell you,
ይነግረኋል yi̥nḁ́grḁhwāl (-rähwāl, -rḁ͡uhāl), he tells you;
አይነግረሁም a͡i̥nḁ́grḁhum (-räh-), he will not tell you;
(*β*) ሰጠችኍ sḁ́ṭṭäčči̥hwŭ (-ččuh), she gave you;
(*γ*) ነገረኍ nḁ́ggḁrḁ͡uʰ, he told you;
አልነገረሁም alnḁ́ggḁrḁhum, he did not tell you;
(*δ*) ነገሩኍ nḁ́ggḁruhwŭ (-ru͡uh, -rwuh), they told you;
(*ζ*) ሰማኍ sḁ́mmahu (-ma͡uʰ), he heard you;
(*η*) ሰጥቼኋለሁ sḁṭi̥̥ččʸehwállḁ͡uʰ (-čyuhál-), I have given to you;
(*θ*) ነግሮኋል nḁ́grʷohwāl (-rʷo͡uhāl), he has told you.
(§ 13*b*) ነሁ nḁ́hu (náhu, nḁ́͡uʰ), you are.
(§ 17) ራስኍ ráshwŭ[2] (-suh), ነፍስኍ nḁ́fshwŭ[2] (ná-, -vs-, -suh), በገዛ፡እጅኍ፡ bḁgḁzzáj-jhwŭ (-juh), etc., yourself.

---

[1] -t-h-, not -θ-, (§ 3). [2] -s-h-, not -š-, (§ 3).

Indicative simp. perf. (§ 25)

sg. 2nd pol. suffix -ኈ -hwŭ or -ሁ -hu (-hŭ, or with displacement of u as above, also -ku, -kŭ after a consonant § 7*d* p. 31): last radical sắdi̥s;

Contingent (§ 26)

Prefix ት- ti̥-, suffix -u;

Gerund (§ 29)

suffix -ạኈ, -ạhwŭ (-ähwŭ, -ạ͡uʰ).

(§ 32*a*) አለኈ állạhwu (-läh-, -lạ͡uʰ), you are;

(§ 32*b*) ትለቅሙታለኈ ti̥lạqmutállạ͡uʰ, you are picking it.

(§ 34) Ind. simp. perf. ለቀምኈ lạ́qqạmhwŭ (-ạmuh, -mhŭ, -mku, -mkŭ), you picked,

Comp. perf. ለቅመኋል lạ́qmạhwāl (-mäh-, -mạ͡uhāl), G. also ለቀምሁናል lạ́qqạmhunnāl,

Comp. imperf. ትለቅማለኈ ti̥lạqmállạ͡uʰ,

Cont. ትለቅሙ ti̥lạ́qmu,

Imp. ልቀሙ lí̥qạmu,

Ger. ለቅመኈ lạ́qmạhwŭ (-mäh-, -mạ͡uʰ).

(§ 43*a*) ራበኈ rắbạhwŭ (rắy̥-, -äh-, -y̥ạ͡uʰ), you were or (§ 63*d*) are hungry.

(§ 47*a*) ላከልኈ lắkạlli̥hwŭ (lākạ́-, -lluh), he sent to or for[1] you.

ይልክልኋል yi̥lí̥ki̥lli̥hwāl (-li̥kí̥-, -lluhāl), he will send to or for[1] you.

§ 12*a*, p. 56, l. 7: *for* እርሳችው *read* እርሳቸው.

---

[1] Sent for = misit, not arcessivit.

§ 12*a*, p. 56, l. 8: (*add*) The polite forms of address and reference include both genders.

§ 12*c*, p. 61, l. 24: ይነግረሃል yi̥nắgrḁhāl (-äh-): (*add*) occasionally ይነግርሃል yi̥nắgri̥hāl.

§ 12*c*, p. 61, note 1: (*add*) or ይንገርዎ yí̥ṅgḁrʷo (-gär-), or ይንገሯዎት yí̥ṅgḁrḁ͡ʷot (-gär-).

§ 13*b*, p. 69, ነው

(*add*) sg. 2nd pol. also ናችው nắč(č)ḁ͡ū.

„ 3rd f. Š. ነች näč (-čč § 6).

§ 44*c*, p. 138, l. 11: *for* yi̥žắllḁ͡ūʰ *read* yi̥žžắllḁ͡ūʰ.

APPENDIX C

NOTE ON PROF. GUIDI'S REVIEW OF PART I.

in the Göttingische gelehrte Anzeigen, Nov. 1909, pp. 933–7.

p. 934, ll. 21–28. For the accentuation of ቍሬ, ቡሉ, ቡላ see that of the type ጓሩ (§ 8, p. 43).

„ ll. 29–32. "le questioni glottologiche o comparative;" these are touched on in Part III.

p. 936, ll. 8–21. It was not until I had heard the compound perfect in -ናል repeatedly used (by Amhāras of G^{w}ojjā́m) that I proceeded to describe it in § 32*c*. On enquiry I was told that it was የደገኛ፡ንግግር፡. It is used much less commonly than the form ለቅሟል, but I have heard it fairly often in G^{w}ojjā́m and Dām^{w}ṓt from M^{w}óta to Búr^{y}e, and was told there that it was especially in use in Dárḁy^{y}e[1].

[1] Guidi is of course not responsible for a remark of Afevork which he quotes: "Egli così mi scrive: ለቀመናል፡.... እንኳን፡ በጎጃም፡በሽንቅላም፡አገር፡እንዲህ፡የተበላሸ፡አማረኛ፡አለ፡አይመ ስለኝም።" (lḁ́qqḁmḁnnāl.... I don't believe there is such bad Amharic even in the country of the blacks, much less in G^{w}ojjā́m). I am inclined to question whether an expression of disbelief in and abuse of a form with which one is not familiar has much scientific value, not to mention good taste.

p. 937, l. 9. "...non si vede chiara l'utilità di questa lunga appendice, in luogo della quale sarebbe stato più opportuno porre dei dialoghi ovvero dei brevi e facili testi." This refers to the long list of principal parts of verbs. I considered it necessary in view of the incomplete treatment of the verb in the body of the grammar, and because a list of this kind is what I myself should most have liked to have in my hands when first I began to try to speak Amharic. Phrases and dialogues will be found in Parts II. and III.

CAMBRIDGE UNIVERSITY PRESS
ORIENTAL LANGUAGES, ETC.

Initia Amharica, an Introduction to Spoken Amharic. By C. H. ARMBRUSTER, M.A., Sudan Civil Service. Demy 8vo. Part I. Grammar, 12*s. net.*

"...Il libro dell'Armbruster, originale e ben ordinato, è scritto con molta conoscenza della materia e con accuratezza straordinaria. I numerosi esempi, tratti dal parlar familiare, sono in amarico genuino ed accompagnati da trascrizione esattissima ...La correzione tipografica è straordinariamente esatta...L'edizione è bellissima."—Prof. I. GUIDI in the Göttingische gelehrte Anzeigen, Nov. 1909.

A Grammar of the Arabic Language, translated from the German of Caspari, and edited, with numerous additions and corrections, by W. WRIGHT, LL.D. Third Edition. Revised by W. ROBERTSON SMITH and M. J. DE GOEJE. Demy 8vo. Vol. I. 12*s.* 6*d.* Vol. II. 15*s.*

Elementary Arabic. A Grammar. By FREDERIC DU PRE THORNTON, being an abridgement of Wright's Arabic Grammar. Edited by REYNOLD A. NICHOLSON, M.A., Lecturer in Persian in the University of Cambridge. Crown 8vo. 6*s. net.*

Elementary Arabic. First Reading-Book. By FREDERIC DU PRE THORNTON and REYNOLD A. NICHOLSON, M.A. Crown 8vo. 6*s. net.*

Elementary Arabic. Second Reading-Book. By REYNOLD A. NICHOLSON, Litt.D. Crown 8vo. 6*s. net.*

The Modern Egyptian Dialect of Arabic. A Grammar, with Exercises, Reading Lessons and Glossaries, from the German of Dr K. VOLLERS. With numerous additions by the Author. Translated by F. C. BURKITT, M.A. Crown 8vo. 10*s.* 6*d.*

Poems of Beha ed din Zoheir of Egypt. With a Metrical Translation, Notes and Introduction, by E. H. PALMER, M.A. 2 vols. Crown 4to. Vol. I. The Arabic Text. 10*s.* 6*d.* Vol. II. English Translation. 10*s.* 6*d.*

Vocabularies of the Kamba and Kikuyu Languages of East Africa. By HILDEGARDE HINDE (Mrs SIDNEY L. HINDE). Crown 8vo. 3*s. net.*

The Masai Language. Grammatical Notes, together with a Vocabulary. Compiled by HILDEGARDE HINDE. Crown 8vo. 3*s.* 6*d.*

A Grammar of the Somali Language with Examples in Prose and Verse. And an account of the Yibir and Midgan Dialects. By J. W. C. KIRK, B.A., King's College, Cambridge, Lieutenant, Duke of Cornwall's Light Infantry and 6th (Somaliland) Battalion, King's African Rifles. Demy 8vo. 7*s.* 6*d. net.*

Dictionary of the Hausa Language. By the Rev. CHARLES HENRY ROBINSON, M.A., Lecturer in Hausa in the University of Cambridge, assisted by W. H. BROOKS, B.A., Christ's College. Demy 8vo.

Vol. I. Hausa-English. *Second edition, revised and enlarged.* 12*s. net.*
Vol. II. English-Hausa. 9*s. net.*

Specimens of Hausa Literature. By the Rev. CHARLES HENRY ROBINSON, M.A. Small 4to. 10*s.* Translation, Transliteration and Notes, without Facsimiles, 5*s.*

Lectures on the Comparative Grammar of the Semitic Languages from the papers of WILLIAM WRIGHT, LL.D. Demy 8vo. 14*s.*